THE SCIENCE OF EXPERTISE

Offering the broadest review of psychological perspectives on human expertise to date, this volume covers behavioral, computational, neural, and genetic approaches to understanding complex skill. The chapters show how performance in music, the arts, sports, games, medicine, and other domains reflects basic traits such as personality and intelligence, as well as knowledge and skills acquired through training. In doing so, this book moves the field of expertise beyond the duality of "nature vs. nurture" toward an integrative understanding of complex skill. This book is an invaluable resource for researchers and students interested in expertise, and for professionals seeking current reviews of psychological research on expertise.

David Z. Hambrick is Professor in the Department of Psychology, Michigan State University, USA. His research on expertise has been widely published in scholarly journals and featured in the mainstream media, including *The New York Times*, *The Boston Globe*, and *The New Yorker*. He received his PhD in Experimental Psychology from the Georgia Institute of Technology in 2000, and is a Fellow of the Association for Psychological Science.

Guillermo Campitelli is Senior Lecturer in Psychology at Edith Cowan University, Perth, Australia. His research aims to understand individual differences in performance, judgment and decision making, with a particular interest in the cognitive processes underlying expertise. He received his PhD in Psychology from the University of Nottingham, UK, in 2003.

Brooke N. Macnamara is Assistant Professor in the Department of Psychological Sciences at Case Western Reserve University, Cleveland, Ohio, USA. Her diverse research interests include the acquisition of expertise, working memory, and bilin- ·r PhD in Psychology from Princeton University in 2014.

FRONTIERS OF COGNITIVE PSYCHOLOGY
Series Editors

Nelson Cowan, *University of Missouri-Columbia*
David A. Balota, *Washington University in St. Louis*

Frontiers of Cognitive Psychology is a new series of cognitive psychology books, which aims to bring together the very latest research in the discipline, providing a comprehensive and up-to-date review of the latest empirical, theoretical and practical issues in the field. Each volume will concentrate on a traditional core area of cognitive psychology, or an area which is emerging as a new core area for the future, and may include interdisciplinary perspectives from areas such as developmental psychology, neuroscience, evolutionary psychology, forensic psychology, social psychology, and the health sciences.

Published

Working Memory: The Connected Intelligence
Tracy Packiam Alloway & Ross G. Alloway

Neuroeconomics and Decision Making
Valerie F. Reyna & Evan Wilhelms

Motivation and Cognitive Control
Todd S. Braver

Big Data in Cognitive Science
Michael N. Jones

Forthcoming

New Methods in Cognitive Psychology
Daniel H. Spieler & Eric Schumacher

THE SCIENCE OF EXPERTISE

Behavioral, Neural, and Genetic Approaches to Complex Skill

Edited by David Z. Hambrick, Guillermo Campitelli, and Brooke N. Macnamara

With a foreword by Robert Plomin

Routledge
Taylor & Francis Group

NEW YORK AND LONDON

First published 2018
by Routledge
711 Third Avenue, New York, NY 10017

and by Routledge
2 Park Square, Milton Park, Abingdon, Oxon, OX14 4RN

Routledge is an imprint of the Taylor & Francis Group, an informa business

Library of Congress Cataloging-in-Publication Data
Names: Hambrick, David Z., author. | Campitelli, Guillermo, author. |
    Macnamara, Brooke N., author.
Title: The science of expertise : toward an integrated understanding of
    human excellence / David Z. Hambrick, Guillermo Campitelli, and
    Brooke N. Macnamara ; with a foreword by Robert J. Plomin.
Description: New York, NY : Routledge, 2017. | Series: Frontiers of
    cognitive psychology
Identifiers: LCCN 2017014237 | ISBN 9781138204379 (hard back : alk.
    paper) | ISBN 9781138204386 (paper back : alk. paper) |
    ISBN 9781315113371 (ebook)
Subjects: LCSH: Expertise.
Classification: LCC BF378.E94 H36 2017 | DDC 153.9—dc23
LC record available at https://lccn.loc.gov/2017014237

ISBN: 978-1-138-20437-9 (hbk)
ISBN: 978-1-138-20438-6 (pbk)
ISBN: 978-1-315-11337-1 (ebk)

Typeset in Bembo
by Swales & Willis Ltd, Exeter, Devon, UK

CONTENTS

Contributors   *ix*
Foreword   *xiv*
    Robert Plomin
Acknowledgements   *xviii*

1 Introduction: A Brief History of the Science of Expertise
    and Overview of the Book   1
    David Z. Hambrick, Guillermo Campitelli, and
    Brooke N. Macnamara

PART I
Behavioral Approach   **11**

2 *Primer* – Statistical Methods in the Study of Expertise   13
    Samuel T. McAbee and Frederick L. Oswald

3 Cognitive Processes in Chess   31
    Guillermo Campitelli

4 An Investigation of Problem-Solving Expertise   47
    James J. Staszewski

5 How Important Is Intelligence in the Development of Professional Expertise? Combining Prospective and Retrospective Longitudinal Data Provides an Answer   73
Jonathan Wai and Harrison J. Kell

6 The Link Between Child Prodigies and Autism   87
Joanne Ruthsatz, Kimberly Stephens, and Mark Matthews

7 Why Deliberate Practice Is Not Enough: Evidence of Talent in Drawing   101
Jennifer E. Drake and Ellen Winner

8 The Development of Expertise in the Visual Arts   129
Rebecca Chamberlain

9 The Deliberate Practice View: An Evaluation of Definitions, Claims, and Empirical Evidence   151
Brooke N. Macnamara, David Z. Hambrick, David J. Frank, Michael J. King, Alexander P. Burgoyne, and Elizabeth J. Meinz

PART II
Neural Approach   **169**

10 *Primer* – Neural Approaches in Research on Expertise   171
Alessandro Guida, Audrey Noël, and Pierre-Yves Jonin

11 The Neural Underpinnings of Expertise in Games   182
Merim Bilalić, Anna Conci, Mario Graf, and Nemanja Vaci

12 The Neural Underpinnings of Perceptual Expertise   200
Mackenzie Sunday and Isabel Gauthier

13 The Neuroscience of Motor Expertise in Real-World Tasks   218
Ellen M. Kok and Anique B. H. de Bruin

PART III
Genetic Approach   **239**

14 *Primer* – Theoretical Concepts in the Genetics of Expertise   241
Elliot M. Tucker-Drob

15 The Etiology of Reading and Math Expertise: The
    Western Reserve Reading and Math Project   253
    Lee A. Thompson, Carol A. Gross, Susan I. Gross,
    Sarah Lukowski, and Stephen A. Petrill

16 Genetic Influences on Music Expertise   272
    Miriam A. Mosing, Isabelle Peretz, and Fredrik Ullén

17 The Molecular Genetic Basis of Music Ability and
    Music-Related Phenotypes   283
    Yi Ting Tan, Gary E. McPherson, and Sarah J. Wilson

PART IV
Integrative Models   **305**

18 Expertise Development from an IMTD Perspective   307
    Françoys Gagné

19 Creativity and Expertise: Creators Are Not Equivalent
    to Domain-Specific Experts!   328
    Dean Keith Simonton

20 Computational Models of Expertise   347
    Fernand Gobet, Martyn Lloyd-Kelly, and
    Peter C. R. Lane

21 The Multifactorial Gene-Environment Interaction
    Model (MGIM) of Expert Performance   365
    Fredrik Ullén, Miriam A. Mosing, and
    David Z. Hambrick

22 The Role of Passion in the Development of Expertise:
    A Conceptual Model   376
    Arielle Bonneville-Roussy and Robert J. Vallerand

23 Play During Childhood and the Development of
    Expertise in Sport   398
    Karl Erickson, Jean Côté, Jennifer Turnnidge, Veronica Allan,
    and Matthew Vierimaa

PART V
Perspectives 417

24 Four Kinds of Expertise 419
Robert J. Sternberg

25 The Relationship Between Expertise and Giftedness:
A Talent Development Perspective 427
*Rena F. Subotnik, Paula Olszewski-Kubilius, and
Frank C. Worrell*

26 Experience, Skill Acquisition, and Deliberate Practice 435
Robert W. Proctor and Aiping Xiong

27 Scientific Methodology and Expertise Studies:
Massaging the Scar Tissue 444
Robert R. Hoffman

Index *453*

CONTRIBUTORS

Veronica Allan
School of Kinesiology and Health Studies, Queen's University, Kingston, ON, Canada

Merim Bilalić
Institute of Psychology, University of Klagenfurt, Klagenfurt, Austria
Department of Psychology, University of Northumbria at Newcastle, UK

Arielle Bonneville-Roussy
Department of Education, Roehampton University, London, UK

Alexander P. Burgoyne
Department of Psychology, Michigan State University, East Lansing, MI, USA

Guillermo Campitelli
School of Arts and Humanities, Edith Cowan University, Joondalup WA, Australia

Rebecca Chamberlain
Department of Psychology, Goldsmiths, University of London

Anna Conci
Institute of Psychology, University of Klagenfurt, Austria

Jean Côté
School of Kinesiology and Health Studies, Queen's University, Kingston, ON, Canada

Anique B. H. de Bruin
School of Health Professions Education, Maastricht University, The Netherlands

Jennifer E. Drake
Department of Psychology, Brooklyn College, and the Graduate Center, City University of New York, Brooklyn, NY, USA

Karl Erickson
Department of Kinesiology, Michigan State University, East Lansing, MI, USA

David J. Frank
Department of Psychological Sciences, Case Western Reserve University, Cleveland, OH, USA

Françoys Gagné
Professor of Psychology (retired), University of Quebec, Montreal, Canada

Isabel Gauthier
Department of Psychology, Vanderbilt University, Nashville, TN, USA

Fernand Gobet
Department of Psychological Sciences, University of Liverpool, England, UK

Mario Graf
Institute of Psychology, University of Klagenfurt, Austria

Carol A. Gross
Department of Psychological Sciences, Case Western Reserve University, Cleveland, OH, USA

Susan I. Gross
Department of Psychological Sciences, Case Western Reserve University, Cleveland, OH, USA

Alessandro Guida
Department of Psychology, University of Rennes 2, France

David Z. Hambrick
Department of Psychology, Michigan State University, East Lansing, MI, USA

Robert R. Hoffman
Institute for Human and Machine Cognition, Pensacola, FL, USA

Pierre-Yves Jonin
Department of Neurology, Central Hospital of the University of Rennes, France

Harrison J. Kell
Educational Testing Service, Princeton, NJ, USA

Michael J. King
Department of Psychological Sciences, Case Western Reserve University, Cleveland, OH, USA

Ellen M. Kok
School of Health Professions Education, Maastricht University, The Netherlands

Peter C. R. Lane
School of Computer Science, University of Hertfordshire, Hatfield, England, UK

Martyn Lloyd-Kelly
Department of Psychological Sciences, University of Liverpool, England, UK

Sarah Lukowski
Department of Psychology, The Ohio State University, Columbus, OH, USA

Brooke N. Macnamara
Department of Psychological Sciences, Case Western Reserve University, Cleveland, OH, USA

Mark Matthews
Department of Psychology, The Ohio State University at Mansfield, OH, USA

Samuel T. McAbee
Department of Psychology, Illinois Institute of Technology, Chicago, IL, USA

Gary E. McPherson
Melbourne Conservatorium of Music, The University of Melbourne, Australia

Elizabeth J. Meinz
Department of Psychology, Southern Illinois University, Carbondale, IL, USA

Miriam A. Mosing
Department of Neuroscience and Department of Medical Epidemiology and Biostatistics, Karolinska Institutet, Stockholm, Sweden

Audrey Noël
Department of Psychology, University of Rennes 2, France

Paula Olszewski-Kubilius
School of Education and Social Policy, Northwestern University, Evanston, IL, USA

Frederick L. Oswald
Department of Psychology, Rice University, Houston, TX, USA

Isabelle Peretz
International Laboratory for Brain, Music and Sound Research, Department of Psychology, Université de Montréal, Montréal, QC, Canada

Stephen A. Petrill
Department of Psychology, The Ohio State University, Columbus, OH, USA

Robert Plomin
Social, Genetic and Developmental Psychiatry Centre, King's College, London, UK

Robert W. Proctor
Department of Psychological Sciences, Purdue University, West Lafayette, IN, USA

Joanne Ruthsatz
Department of Psychology, The Ohio State University at Mansfield, OH, USA

Dean Keith Simonton
Department of Psychology, University of California, Davis, CA, USA

James J. Staszewski
Department of Psychology, Carnegie Mellon University, Pittsburgh, PA, USA

Kimberly Stephens
Department of Psychology, The Ohio State University at Mansfield, OH, USA

Robert J. Sternberg
Department of Human Development, College of Human Ecology, Cornell University, Ithaca, NY, USA

Rena F. Subotnik
Center for Psychology in the Schools and Education, American Psychological Association, Washington, DC, USA

Mackenzie Sunday
Department of Psychology, Vanderbilt University, Nashville, TN, USA

Yi Ting Tan
Melbourne Conservatorium of Music, The University of Melbourne, Australia

Lee A. Thompson
Department of Psychological Sciences, Case Western Reserve University, Cleveland, OH, USA

Elliot M. Tucker-Drob
Department of Psychology, The University of Texas at Austin, TX, USA

Jennifer Turnnidge
School of Kinesiology and Health Studies, Queen's University, Kingston, ON, Canada

Fredrik Ullén
Department of Neuroscience, Karolinska Institutet, Stockholm, Sweden

Nemanja Vaci
Institute of Psychology, University of Klagenfurt, Austria

Robert J. Vallerand
Department of Psychology, University of Quebec, Montreal, Canada
School of Psychology, Australian Catholic University, Banyo, Australia

Matthew Vierimaa
Department of Kinesiology and Health Science, Utah State University, Logan, UT, USA

Jonathan Wai
Autism and Developmental Medicine Institute, Geisinger Health System, Lewisburg, PA, USA
Department of Psychology, Case Western Reserve University, Cleveland, OH, USA

Sarah J. Wilson
Melbourne School of Psychological Sciences, The University of Melbourne, Victoria, Australia

Ellen Winner
Department of Psychology, Boston College, Chestnut Hill, MA, USA
Graduate School of Education, Project Zero, Harvard University, Cambridge, MA, USA

Frank C. Worrell
Graduate School of Education, University of California, Berkeley, CA, USA

Aiping Xiong
Department of Psychological Sciences, Purdue University, West Lafayette, IN, USA

FOREWORD

Robert Plomin

SOCIAL, GENETIC AND DEVELOPMENTAL PSYCHIATRY CENTRE,
KING'S COLLEGE, LONDON, UK

H. L. Mencken's famous dictum is particularly apt for the science of expertise: "For every complex problem there is an answer that is clear, simple, and wrong." Expertise is an area where the talent versus training argument has rumbled on for decades long after most fields of behavioral sciences have left such nature–nurture issues for dead.

The Science of Expertise will be a watershed for understanding that there is no simple answer to the question of what it takes to become an expert. It's not just training, and it's not just talent. Training without talent will not take you to the top tiers of expertise, nor will talent without training. It's not just nature, and it's not just nurture; experts are born *and* made. The complexity and multivariate nature of the phenomenon means that it takes a community of scientists to understand expertise—behavioral scientists, neuroscientists, and geneticists. This book will help to create that interdisciplinary community and will, I hope, attract future researchers to this important area.

The primers on behavioral, neural, and genetic approaches at the beginning of each section help to make the chapters in each section understandable, even to people naïve to these approaches. The behavioral primer introduces statistical issues critical to all research on expertise. The neural primer succinctly summarizes the major functional and structural approaches to studying the brain. This is followed by discussions on how to use these techniques specifically to study expertise and how to interpret neural changes with acquisition of expertise. The genetic primer outlines genetic techniques and focuses on the interface between genes and environment, which is particularly relevant to the interface between genes and expert training.

The authors of the chapters in the three sections on behavioral, neural, and genetic approaches include leaders in each field. Their chapters cover the basic behavioral, neural, and genetic research on the science of expertise. They also touch on the intrinsically interesting topics of expertise such as chess, music, drawing, visual arts, Rubik's Cube, child prodigies, and sport, as well as the roles of deliberate practice, intelligence, and perceptual and motor expertise.

Part IV presents models and processes that begin to integrate behavioral, neural, and genetic approaches to the science of expertise. Three of the chapters in this section consider crosscutting processes that are intrinsically integrative: passion, creativity, and play. Three chapters present integrative models. What they have in common is the theme of this book: Expertise is a highly multifactorial phenomenon that cannot be explained by a single-factor model such as deliberate practice. The first model highlights integration of behavioral processes. The second model focuses on the precision and specification offered by computational models, which are most compatible with sensory, perceptual, and neural approaches. The third model is the Multifactorial Gene-Environment Interaction Model (MGIM) of expert performance. The model is called multifactorial because it considers the impact of psychological traits, physical traits, and neural mechanisms as they affect and are affected by deliberate practice. MGIM assumes that the variance of all of these traits and the covariance between them can be affected by both genetic and environmental factors as well as by the correlation and interaction between genetic and environmental factors.

As a behavioral geneticist, I think genetics has a lot to offer towards the integration of behavioral, neural, and genetic approaches. The first law of behavioral genetics is that all traits show significant and substantial genetic influence. A related finding is that phenotypic correlations between traits show significant and substantial genetic mediation. For expert performance, these widely replicated findings make it safe to predict that genetic influence is significant and substantial for all components of the MGIM and for the links between them.

Another genetic finding especially relevant to the science of expertise is known by the rubric: *abnormal is normal*. Research consistently finds that genetic and environmental effects operate continuously throughout the distribution, as discussed in the chapter on genetics of reading and mathematics expertise. In other words, the extremes of performance are merely the quantitative extremes of the same genetic and environmental factors that affect the rest of the distribution. Stated more provocatively, this means there is nothing special etiologically about expert performance. However, this research has been limited to the top 1 percent of performance, which is a long way from the handful of elite performers, so it remains to be seen how far the abnormal-is-normal hypothesis extends.

Behavioral genetics has revealed almost as much about the environment as it has about genetics because it takes both genetics and environment into account. Behavioral genetic research provides the best available evidence for the importance of environmental influences: The second law of behavioral genetics is that no traits are 100 percent heritable.

Two specific findings about the environment are especially relevant to the science of expert performance. The first is that most environmental effects are not shared by children growing up in the same family. This finding is relevant for understanding the origins of expertise because it means that the salient environmental influences do not make children growing up in the same family similar. Second, most measures of the "environment" widely used in the behavioral sciences show significant genetic influence. This finding has already been reflected in research on expertise in that individual differences in music practice show genetic influence, as indicated in the chapter on genetics and music expertise. These findings are an example of gene–environment correlation. The importance of gene–environment correlation suggests a new way of thinking about the interface between nature and nurture that moves beyond a passive model, which assumes one-size-fits-all training regimes that are imposed on individuals, to an active model in which people select, modify, and create their own environments that foster the acquisition of expertise, in part on the basis of their genetic propensities.

These research findings emerged primarily from research using the twin method that compares resemblance for monozygotic and dizygotic twins. The future of genetic research lies with the DNA revolution. In the section on genetics, two of the chapters review attempts to find specific DNA differences responsible for the heritability of various aspects of music-related traits. Although not much progress has been made with candidate gene or genome-wide linkage studies, I predict that genome-wide association studies will revolutionize the science of expertise.

Genome-wide association studies throughout the life sciences have shown that heritability of complex traits is caused by thousands of DNA differences, each of very small effect. Massive genome-wide association studies with samples in the hundreds of thousands are needed to detect these minuscule effects. Such studies are underway, such as UK Biobank with 500,000 participants and national biobanks in many other countries.

What good are such tiny effects? Not much by themselves, but these effects can be aggregated to create a polygenic score for a trait, like constructing a composite scale from many items. Polygenic scores will make it possible to predict genetic strengths and weaknesses for individuals.

For example, it is now possible, using polygenic scores derived solely from DNA, to predict about 20 percent of the variance in height, 10 percent of the variance in weight, 5 percent of the variance in intelligence, and 10 percent of the variance in educational achievement. Although huge samples are needed to power genome-wide association studies, polygenic scores can be used in reasonably sized samples. The need for large and special samples—for example, twins—has been a major impediment for integrating genetics and neuroimaging research and other types of intensive research related to expertise such as training. In contrast, a polygenic score that predicts 10 percent of the variance of a trait only needs a sample size of 60 unrelated individuals to detect the effect (one-tailed P = 0.05, power = 80%).

Polygenic scores will revolutionize research by bringing individual-level genetic prediction to bear on issues that are central to research on expertise, such as development (how early can expert performance be predicted), multivariate issues (links between psychological, neural and physical traits in the MGIM), and the interface between genes and environment (especially gene-environment interaction and correlation). Importantly, polygenic score predictions of adult traits are just as strong at birth as they are in adulthood because inherited DNA sequence differences do not change during development. Polygenic scores can provide a direct test of the abnormal-is-normal hypothesis: the extent to which genetic influences are the same qualitatively and quantitatively for the expert extreme of a distribution and the rest of the distribution.

I believe that the DNA revolution will be a major force for integrating behavioral, neural, and genetic approaches to expertise. More than that, it will also integrate the science of expertise with all the life sciences. *The Science of Expertise* is an important step towards integrating the multifactorial influences on expert performance.

ACKNOWLEDGEMENTS

We are grateful to Nelson Cowan and David Balota for inviting us to edit this volume, and to the 62 contributors who have shared their research so generously. For assistance and encouragement along the way, we thank Paul Dukes, Talia Graf, Xian Gu, Katharine Bartlett, and Tamsin Ballard of the publisher. And we are especially grateful to Genie Hambrick for her copy-editing work.

1

INTRODUCTION

A Brief History of the Science of Expertise and Overview of the Book

David Z. Hambrick, Guillermo Campitelli, and Brooke N. Macnamara

The Science of Expertise: A Brief History

Nearly everyone has witnessed a display of complex skill that is so extraordinary—so far outside the normal range of human capabilities—that it defies belief. The 1968 Olympics in Mexico City were witness to arguably the greatest athletic feat of all time, when Bob Beamon won the gold medal in the long jump with a leap of 29 feet 2¼ inches. In an event usually won by a few inches, Beamon bettered silver medalist Klaus Beer by a bewildering 28 inches. Nearly a half-century later, his Olympic record still stands. More recently, the world watched as 60-year old Diana Nyad swam the 110 miles between Havana, Cuba, and Key West, Florida. Performances of prodigies are especially memorable for their seeming otherworldliness, as when the pianist Evgeny Kissin made his debut with the Moscow Philharmonic Orchestra at the age of 12, and when 13-year-old Magnus Carlsen famously played chess World No. 1 Garry Kasparov to a draw. We also admire extraordinary skill in everyday life—the master mechanic for uncanny ability to diagnose and fix what ails our automobiles, the surgeon for acumen in removing disease with surgical instruments without harming the patient, the potter who transforms lumps of clay into elegant bowls, the pilot who deftly lands a jumbo jet in bad weather, and so on.

What is the origin of individual differences in expertise? This is a central question for the science of expertise, and the major focus of this book. Given that individual differences in skill are so obvious through casual observation, it may also be one of humankind's earliest existential questions. Consider that in prehistoric art we see what may well have been celebration of exceptional performance: Paintings up to 20,000 years old in the Lascaux cave in France include images of wrestlers and sprinters, and in the Cave of Swimmers in present-day Egypt, depictions of archers and swimmers date to 6000 B.C.E. Several thousand

FIGURE 1.1 Raphael. The School of Athens. Detail from 1873 illustration of the fresco (1510–1512), which is in the Vatican. Image credit: bauhaus1000.

years later, the Ancient Greeks laid the foundation for the contemporary debate over the origins of expertise. In *The Republic* (ca. 380 B.C.E.), Plato made the innatist argument that "no two persons are born alike but each differs from the other in individual endowments." Aristotle, Plato's student who is often regarded as the "first empiricist," countered that experience is the ultimate source of knowledge. These differing philosophies are symbolized in the fresco *School of Athens* (1509–1511) by the Italian Renaissance artist Raphael (Figure 1.1). Plato and Aristotle are pictured in the center of the fresco; each holds a book in his left hand and gestures with his right—Plato upward to the heavens and Aristotle outward to the concrete world.

What might be considered the first scientific study of expertise was published in 1835 by the Ghent-born statistician and sociologist Adolphe Quetelet (see Simonton, 2016), who introduced the normal curve to describe individual differences. Using archival data, Quetelet documented that output in famous French and English dramatists peaked at about age 50. Some 35 years later, making use of Quetelet's statistical work, Francis Galton (1869) published his groundbreaking volume *Hereditary Genius*. Galton's major question was whether intellectual ability is heritable in the same way that his half-cousin Charles Darwin had argued that physical characteristics of creatures such as the size and length of birds' beaks are heritable. There were no standardized tests of intelligence in the mid-1800s, so Galton scoured *Who's Who*-type biographical dictionaries and used reputation as a proxy for ability. Galton discovered that, within a given field, eminent individuals tended to be biologically related more than would be expected by chance. For example, he noted that there were more than 20 eminent musicians in the Bach family—Johann Sebastian being just the most famous—and he observed that the Bernoulli family "comprised an extraordinary number of eminent mathematicians and men of science." Galton concluded that genius arises almost inevitably from "natural ability."

Galton's (1869) book created a stir. The Swiss botanist Alphonse Pyrame de Candolle (1873) conducted his own biographical study and found that some countries produced more scientists than others, taking population into account. For example, his native Switzerland produced over 10 percent of the scientists in his sample, but accounted for less than 1 percent of the European population. De Candolle concluded that environmental factors—or what he called "causes favorables"—were the primary antecedents of eminence (Fancher, 1983). In a similar vein, Edward Thorndike (1912), the father of educational psychology, claimed that "when one sets oneself zealously to improve any ability, the amount gained is astonishing" and added that "we stay far below our own possibilities in almost everything we do . . . not because proper practice would not improve us further, but because we do not take the training or because we take it with too little zeal" (p. 108). John Watson (1930) added that "practicing more intensively than others . . . is probably the most reasonable explanation we have today not only for success in any line, but even for genius" (p. 212).

Thus, from antiquity on, the pendulum has swung between the view that experts are "born" and the view that they are "made." In psychology, the experts-are-made view has dominated the scientific study of expertise for the better part of 50 years. Building on earlier work by de Groot (1946/1978), Chase and Simon (1973) had participants representing three levels of chess skill (novice, intermediate, and master) view and attempt to recreate arrangements of chess positions that were either plausible game positions or random. The major finding was that chess skill facilitated recall of the game positions, but not the random positions. Thus, Chase and Simon concluded that the primary factor underlying chess skill is not superior short-term memory capacity, but a large "vocabulary" of game positions. More generally, they argued that although "there clearly must be a set of specific aptitudes . . . that together comprise a talent for chess, individual differences in such aptitudes are largely overshadowed by immense differences in chess experience. Hence, the overriding factor in chess skill is practice" (Chase & Simon, 1973, p. 279).

Subsequent research showed just how powerful the effects of training on performance can be. As a particularly striking example, Ericsson, Chase, and Faloon (1980) reported a case study of a college student (S.F.), who through more than 230 hours of practice, increased the number of random digits he could recall from a typical 7 to a world record 79 digits. (Today, the world record for random digit memorization is an astounding 456 digits.) Verbal reports revealed that S.F., a collegiate track runner, accomplished this feat by recoding sequences of digits as running times, ages, or dates, and encoding the groupings into long-term memory *retrieval structures*. For example, he remembered 3596 as "3 minutes, 59.6 seconds, fast 1-mile time." Ericsson *et al.* concluded that there is "seemingly no limit to improvement in memory skill with practice" (1980, p. 1182).

The consensus that emerged from all this research was that expertise reflects acquired characteristics (nurture), with essentially no important role for genetic factors (nature). This environmentalist view reached its apogee in the early 1990s, with publication of Ericsson, Krampe, and Tesch-Römer's (1993) seminal article on "deliberate practice." In a pair of studies, Ericsson *et al.* found positive correlations between estimated amount of deliberate practice (practice alone) and skill level in music. The most skilled musicians had accumulated thousands of hours more deliberate practice than their less accomplished counterparts. In the spirit of Watson (1930), Ericsson *et al.* concluded that "high levels of deliberate practice are necessary to attain expert level performance" (Ericsson *et al.*, p. 392) and explained that their "account does not depend on scarcity of innate ability (talent)" (Ericsson *et al.*, p. 392). Another important event was the publication of the field's first handbook—the 900-page *Cambridge Handbook on Expertise and Expert Performance* (Ericsson, Charness, Feltovich, & Hoffman, 2006). Though this volume was a valuable resource for the field, it seems fair to say that the focus was overwhelmingly on experiential determinants of expertise (i.e. practice/ training). There are, for example, 102 index entries for "deliberate practice" and "training," compared to 12 for "talent" and "genetics."

There was, however, growing dissent in the literature. Simonton (1999), one of the most eloquent commentators, acknowledged that "it is extremely likely that environmental factors, including deliberate practice, account for far more variance in performance than does innate capacity in every salient talent domain" (p. 454), but continued: "Even so, psychology must endeavor to identify all of the significant causal factors behind exceptional performance rather than merely rest content with whatever factor happens to account for the most variance" (p. 454). In a similar vein, Gagné (1999) argued that there is "[n]o doubt that the single most important source of individual differences in the case of SYSDEV [systematically developed] abilities is the amount of LTP [learning, training, and practice]. But . . . genetic endowment is also a significant, albeit indirect, cause of individual differences in these abilities."

Dissent grew into empirical challenge in the mid-2000s—which, coincidentally or not, was around the time the environmentalist view was popularized in books such as Malcolm Gladwell's (2008) bestseller *Outliers: The Story of Success* and Geoff Colvin's (2010) *Talent is Overrated: What Really Separates World-Class Performers from Everybody Else*. In one of the first direct tests of the deliberate practice view, Gobet and Campitelli (2007) found that there was massive variability in the amount of deliberate practice required for chess players to reach "master" status—from about 3,000 hours to over 23,000 hours. The implication of this finding was that factors other than deliberate practice must also play an important role in becoming highly skilled in chess.

Subsequently, the three of us (with numerous colleagues around the world) published a series of papers demonstrating that deliberate practice is an important piece of the expertise puzzle, just not the only important piece. As one example, Meinz and Hambrick (2010) found that *working memory capacity*, which is known to be substantially heritable, added to the prediction of individual differences in piano sight-reading skill, above and beyond deliberate practice. (To be sure, in terms of variance explained, the effect of deliberate practice was larger than the effect of working memory capacity—45 percent vs. 7 percent. However, the latter effect size is not trivial from either a statistical or theoretical perspective.) A few years later, a special issue of the journal *Intelligence* brought together a collection of articles on the acquisition of expertise—nearly all of which challenged the environmentalist stance on expertise. We and our colleagues (Hambrick *et al.*, 2014) reported that deliberate practice accounted for no more than about a third of the variance in expertise in chess and music, leaving the rest unexplained and potentially explainable by other factors. Plomin and colleagues showed that genetic factors accounted for over half of the variance between expert and non-expert readers (Plomin, Shakeshaft, McMillan, & Trzaskowski, 2014), and Ruthsatz and colleagues (Ruthsatz, Ruthsatz-Stephens, & Ruthsatz, 2014) summarized evidence showing that prodigies are extremely high in working memory.

What all this evidence indicated to us is that expertise can never be adequately understood by focusing on only environmental factors (or, of course, only genetic factors). Rather, what is needed to advance scientific understanding of expertise are *multifactorial models* that take into account *all* relevant factors. Figure 1.2 displays a general framework for thinking about expertise from this perspective (theoretical models presented later in the book give more specific guidance). There are seven major categories of predictor constructs: (1) *developmental factors*, including age and starting age; (2) *background factors*, such as socioeconomic status, country of origin, and parental involvement; (3) *ability factors*, including basic cognitive, perceptual, and physiological traits; (4) *non-ability factors*, such as personality, motivation, and temperament; (5) *domain-specific knowledge*, including

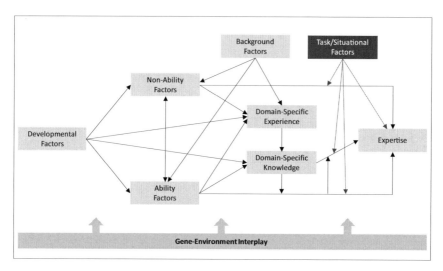

FIGURE 1.2 General framework for multifactorial perspective on expertise. See Hambrick *et al.* (2016) for an expanded version of this model.

specialized knowledge, skills, and strategies; (6) *domain-specific experience*, including training and other forms of experience; and (7) *task/situational factors*, such as task complexity, time pressure, the presence of external evaluation, and the predictability of the task environment. These factors can have both direct and indirect effects of the predictor constructs on expertise; also, genetic and environmental influences are assumed to operate throughout the model, leaving open the possibility that even factors such as training that are assumed to be purely "environmental" may have some genetic basis.

Overview of this Book

For us, the big picture created from all this recent research is that the "nature vs. nurture" debate in scientific research on expertise is over—or it certainly should be. We agree with Wai (2014) that "if we wish to appropriately represent the full network of evidence surrounding the acquisition of expertise, the phrase 'made, not born' really should be changed to 'born, then made'" (p. 74). With this overarching theme, this volume is the first attempt to bring together a collection of papers exploring the multifactorial nature of expertise; the contributors include 62 scientists, representing 39 institutions/organizations in 9 countries. What is particularly exciting is that much of the work discussed in the chapters is the contributors' own original research.

The book is organized into five parts. The first three parts cover the major approaches to research on expertise. Part I covers the *behavioral approach*. A primer chapter by Samuel McAbee and Frederick Oswald (Chapter 2) explains methodological and statistical issues and pitfalls in expertise research (e.g., sample size, restriction of range, reliability). The following chapters discuss the role of various ability and non-ability factors in expertise. Guillermo Campitelli (Chapter 3) covers processes underlying chess expertise, while James Staszewski analyzes expertise in Rubik's Cube solving (Chapter 4). Jonathan Wai and Harrison Kell (Chapter 5) discuss the role of intelligence for developing professional expertise. Joanne Ruthsatz and colleagues summarize findings from the largest-ever study of prodigies (Chapter 6). Jennifer Drake and Ellen Winner (Chapter 7) give an update on the role of talent in drawing, and Rebecca Chamberlain (Chapter 8) presents evidence from her multifactorial study of drawing expertise. Brooke Macnamara and colleagues (Chapter 9) end the section with a critique of the deliberate practice view of expertise.

Part II covers the *neural approach*. A primer chapter by Alessandro Guida and colleagues (Chapter 10) provides an overview of neuroimaging techniques, particularly as applied to expertise research. The next three chapters cover neural underpinnings of expertise in three domains. Merim Bilalić and colleagues (Chapter 11) discuss neural underpinnings of expertise in games such as Go and chess. Mackenzie Sunday and Isabel Gauthier (Chapter 12) cover perceptual expertise—more specifically, expertise in object recognition in activities such as identifying cars and birds. Ellen Kok and Anique de Bruin (Chapter 13) identify neural correlates of motor expertise in real-world domains such as surgery.

Part III covers the *genetic approach*. In the primer chapter, Elliot Tucker-Drob (Chapter 14) presents a framework for understanding the acquisition of expertise in terms of gene-environment interplay that draws on pioneering work by Robert Plomin, the author of the Foreword. The next three chapters examine the role of genetic factors to expertise in specific domains. Lee Thompson and colleagues (Chapter 15) review evidence for genetic and environmental contributions to reading and math expertise. Miriam Mosing, Isabelle Peretz, and Fredrik Ullén (Chapter 16) review evidence from twin studies for genetic influences on music expertise, while Yi Ting Tan, Gary McPherson, and Sarah Wilson (Chapter 17) identify specific genes that may underlie music expertise.

Six theoretical models of expertise are presented in Part IV. The models address expertise from different perspectives, but all are multifactorial in flavor. Expanding his influential Differentiated Model of Giftedness and Talent (DMGT), François Gagné (Chapter 18) introduces the Integrative Model of Talent Development (IMTD). Dean Simonton (Chapter 19) offers a philosophical analysis of the distinction between creativity and expertise. Fernand Gobet, Martyn Lloyd-Kelly, and Peter Lane (Chapter 20) explain the benefits of a computational approach to research on expertise. Fredrik Ullén, Miriam Mosing, and Zach Hambrick (Chapter 21) describe the Multifactorial Gene-Environment Interaction model of expertise. Arielle Bonneville-Roussy and Robert Vallerand (Chapter 22) present a conceptual model of the role of passion in expertise. Karl Erickson, Jean Côté, and colleagues (Chapter 23) discuss the role of "deliberate play" in the context of their Developmental Model of Sport Participation (DMSP).

Part V, the final section, presents commentaries on the other chapters, each by a scientist who has made an eminent contribution to the science of expertise. Robert Sternberg (Chapter 24) discusses the history of expertise research and distinguishes among four types of expertise—*analytical, creative, practical,* and *wisdom-based.* Reba Subotnick, Paula Olszewski-Kubilius, and Frank Worrell (Chapter 25) comment on giftedness and talent, offering their mega-model for talent development. Robert Proctor and Aiping Xiong (Chapter 26) link findings and ideas discussed in the chapters to the broader literature on skill acquisition. Finally, Robert Hoffmann (Chapter 27) discusses issues surrounding the definition and measurement of expertise, warning against "methodolatry"— growing too attached to a particular methodological approach.

Moving Ahead

Over the past decade, scientific interest in expertise has exploded. Empirical research generated by this interest has identified numerous factors that may contribute to variation in expertise, but little effort has been made to integrate these findings. Consequently, while it is obvious now that expertise is a puzzle with many pieces, it is not clear how these pieces fit together. We hope that this volume will encourage integrative thinking about expertise, and in so doing increase scientific collaboration toward understanding this topic that fascinates scientists and non-scientists alike.

References

Chase, W. G., & Simon, H. A. (1973). The mind's eye in chess. In W. G. Chase (Ed.), *Visual information processing* (pp. 215–281). New York: Academic Press.

Colvin, G. (2010). *Talent is overrated. What really separates world-class performers from everybody else.* New York: Penguin.

de Candolle, A. (1873). *Histoire des sciences et des savants depuis deux siècles: suivie d'autres études sur des sujets scientifiques.* Geneva: Fayard.

de Groot, A. D. (1946/1978). *Thought and choice in chess.* The Hague: Mouton.

Ericsson, K. A., Charness, N., Feltovich, P. J., & Hoffman, R. R., (Eds.). *The Cambridge handbook of expertise and expert performance* (pp. 683–703). New York: Cambridge University Press.

Ericsson, K. A., Chase, W. G., & Faloon, S. (1980). Acquisition of a memory skill. *Science, 208,* 1181–1182. doi: 10.1126/science.7375930

Ericsson, K. A., Krampe, R. Th., & Tesch-Römer, C. (1993). The role of deliberate practice in the acquisition of expert performance. *Psychological Review, 100,* 363–406. doi:10.1037/0033-295X.100.3.363

Fancher, R. E. (1983). Alphonse de Candolle, Francis Galton, and the early history of the nature-nurture controversy. *Journal of the History of the Behavioral Sciences, 19,* 341–352. doi:10.1002/1520-6696

Gagné, F. (1999). My convictions about the nature of abilities, gifts, and talents. *Journal for the Education of the Gifted, 22,* 109–36.

Galton, F. (1869). *Hereditary genius*. London: Macmillan.

Gladwell, M. (2008). *Outliers: The story of success*. New York: Little, Brown, and Co.

Gobet, F., & Campitelli, G. (2007). The role of domain-specific practice, handedness, and starting age in chess. *Developmental Psychology, 43*, 159–172. doi:10.1037/0012-1649.43.1.159

Hambrick, D. Z., Macnamara, B. N., Campitelli, G., Ullen, F., & Mosing, M. (2016). A new look at expertise: Beyond the experts are born vs. made debate. *Psychology of Learning and Motivation, 64*, 1–55.

Hambrick, D. Z., Oswald, F. L., Altmann, E. M., Meinz, E. J., Gobet, F., & Campitelli, G. (2014). Deliberate practice: Is that all it takes to become an expert? *Intelligence, 45*, 34–45. doi:10.1016/j.intell.2013.04.001

Meinz, E. J., & Hambrick, D. Z. (2010). Deliberate practice is necessary but not sufficient to explain individual differences in piano sight-reading skill: The role of working memory capacity. *Psychological Science, 21*, 914–919. doi:10.1177/0956797610373933

Plomin, R., Shakeshaft, N. G., McMillan, A., & Trzaskowski, M. (2014). Nature, nurture, and expertise. *Intelligence, 45*, 46–59. doi: 10.1016/j.intell.2013.06.008

Ruthsatz, J., Ruthsatz-Stephens, K., & Ruthsatz, K. (2014). The cognitive bases of exceptional abilities in child prodigies by domain: Similarities and differences. *Intelligence, 44*, 11–14.

Simonton, D. K. (1999). Talent and its development: An emergenic and epigenetic model. *Psychological Review, 106*, 435-457. doi: 10.1037/0033-295X.106.3.435

Simonton, D. K. (2016). Quetelet, Adolphe. In S. K. Whitbourne (Ed.), *The Encyclopedia of Adulthood and Aging*. John Wiley & Sons. *The Republic*. Retrieved from: http://classics.mit.edu/Plato/republic.html

Thorndike, E. L. (1912). *Education: A first book*. Charleston, SC: BiblioBazaar.

Wai, J. (2014). What does it mean to be an expert? *Intelligence, 45*, 122–123.

Watson, J. B. (1930). *Behaviorism*. Chicago, IL: The University of Chicago Press.

PART I
Behavioral Approach

2

Primer

STATISTICAL METHODS IN THE STUDY OF EXPERTISE

Samuel T. McAbee and Frederick L. Oswald

Introduction

Experts are those rare people with high levels of skill who collectively contribute to the prosperity of nations, the competitive advantage of organizations, and the well-being of families and communities. They are often revered by society—think of Albert Einstein in physics, Bill Gates in business, Yo-Yo Ma in music, and Annie Duke in poker. Books whose subjects feature experts like these are often popular, not only because these people are inherently fascinating, but also because readers believe they might learn ways to become better themselves (if not experts).

Whether, and how, one might act on insights might be best informed not by biographies, but by addressing a variety of scientific research questions, such as these: What are the abilities, personality traits, interests, and other psychological characteristics of experts? How can experts in the same domain sometimes be so radically different? What motivates experts to maintain deep interest in a topic, sometimes uninterrupted for years, to become so prodigious? How do people overcome failure, discouragement, and other setbacks on the road to expertise?

Scientific research on expertise seeks to answer questions like these. To do so effectively, research needs to be founded on a bedrock of good study design, representative sample sizes, and appropriate statistical analyses and statistical power. This chapter provides practical guidance on these foundational issues for scientific research on expertise, while realizing that other issues are equally important (e.g., developing psychometrically sound measures of expertise, having good theories guide the research design and associated sampling and measurement).

Statistical Concerns for Research on Expertise

Sample Size

One ubiquitous concern in research on expertise is the overreliance on relatively small sample sizes (Howard, 2012). Concerns over statistical power in small samples have been well documented over several decades of psychological research (e.g., Cohen, 1988, 1992) and have been raised more specifically in research on expertise (e.g., Ackerman, 2014). Even a cursory review of highly cited expertise research will reveal typical sample sizes of 30 or fewer (e.g., Ericsson, Krampe, & Tesch-Römer, 1993; Jabusch, Alpers, Kopiez, Vauth, & Altenmüller, 2009) to slightly over 100 participants (e.g., Campitelli & Gobet, 2008; Halpern & Wai, 2007), though notable large-sample exceptions exist (e.g., Charness, Tuffiash, Krampe, Reingold, & Vasyukova, 2005; Howard, 2012). Of course, many domains of research on expertise are substantially limited by the fact that there are very few experts to study (Ackerman, 2014), which can place limitations on statistical precision and/or the generalizability of inferences made. These issues can be successfully addressed to some extent by studying individual experts qualitatively and/or through intensive repeated measurement designs (Walls & Schafer, 2006); one then can maximize the amount of reliable information coming from limited samples of experts. Yet an alternative approach that would yield larger sample sizes, higher statistical power, and potentially greater generalizability is to study ability and skill acquisition in broad samples, such as large representative national or community samples.

Power and Precision

Generally speaking, correlations and mean differences based on small sample sizes will be associated with large amounts of sampling error variance (random error), and this reduces statistical power and precision. Having low statistical power means that the chance of detecting a specified effect in the population is disappointing (usually operationalized as less than an 80 percent chance). To address this problem, *a priori* power analysis helps provide researchers with specific information on required sample sizes in order to detect a given effect size as statistically significant. Even though a researcher will not know what the effect size in the population actually is (because if one did, then why conduct the research?), it is still worth determining the sample size required to detect the smallest effect size that one deems as practically significant in one's data.

Statistical precision applies to how well the degree of practical significance can be determined. For instance, take the correlation between log hours of serious study and current skill rating in chess of $r = .54$ reported by Charness *et al.* (2005, sample 1). Figure 2.1 illustrates the effects of sampling error variance on 95 percent confidence intervals at three levels of sample size,[1] using results reported in

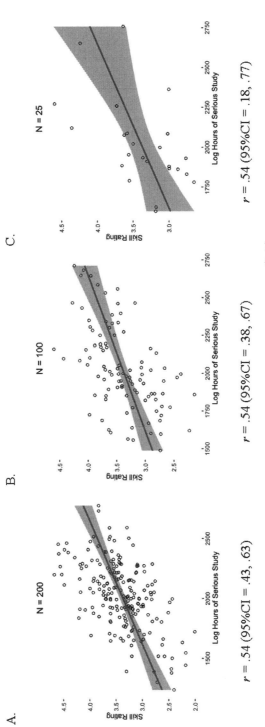

FIGURE 2.1 Influence of sample size (sampling error variance) on confidence intervals for correlation coefficients. Illustrative data sampled from a bivariate normal distribution.

Charness *et al.* (2005). Charness *et al.* used 200 participants in their study, where the 95 percent confidence interval ranges from $r = .43$ to $r = .63$ (see Figure 2.1A). Most, if not all, researchers would therefore conclude from this finding that there is a strong relationship between hours of serious study and skill. However, if this effect were obtained in a sample of 100 participants (often viewed as a large sample size in the expertise literature), then the 95 percent confidence interval around this effect would range from $r = .38$ to $r = .67$ (see Figure 2.1B). And if this same effect were obtained in a sample of experts that even the expertise literature would tend to consider small, say 25 participants, then the 95 percent confidence interval around a correlation of .54 is very wide, ranging from $r = .18$ to $r = .77$ (see Figure 2.1C). In these cases, researchers should be cautious in interpreting whether the population effect for the relationship between hours of serious study and skill is small-to-moderate or quite strong. Regrettably, even with lack of precision, researchers often conclude that effects are strong in the population of study, so long as the effect is statistically significant.

Consistent with one's intuition, estimated correlations are more precise in larger samples and less precise in smaller samples; the real question comes in determining just *how* precise correlations are for a given sample size. Note that an investment in larger sample sizes has a greater precision payoff when the sample size is small to begin with (e.g., when increasing a sample by 30 people, moving from $N = 20$ to 50 results in a much larger precision increase than moving from $N = 500$ to 530).

Statistical versus Practical Significance

The aforementioned concerns regarding power and precision lead directly to another general need for advancing the literature on expertise: Moving forward, the literature on expertise should not rely too heavily on *p*-values alone, or even other inferential indices such as Bayes Factors, which are often highly related (Wetzels *et al.* 2011). Instead, expertise researchers and related expertise journals should increasingly incorporate more direct indices of the precision of sample estimates as established through confidence intervals (or the probability of population estimates through credibility intervals in the Bayesian framework). Historically, heavy reliance on *p*-values has encouraged *dichotomous thinking* (Cumming & Fidler, 2009; Nickerson, 2000), where results are interpreted as being either statistically significant or not (below a $p = .05$ or .01 hurdle), rather than focusing on the effect size and its associated precision as indicators of practical significance. By focusing on effect sizes (e.g., standardized mean differences indexed by *d*-values, standardized relationships indexed by correlations), meta-analysis has helped to emphasize practical significance (Schmidt & Hunter, 2015), although there is no reason why individual studies cannot increase their focus on effect sizes as well, as has been encouraged in the editorial policies of journals (Eich, 2014). Expertise researchers should not only increase their habit of reporting effect sizes; they should also report the descriptive statistics (means and standard deviations) that are required to calculate those effect sizes and to put them in context. With this information, for example, a reader can verify that a *d*-value was calculated correctly (e.g., that the means between groups are in fact in the direction implied) and, importantly, the *d*-value can be supplemented with knowledge of where the raw means lie along the measurement scale. Researchers should also report reliability coefficients when available (e.g., alpha, test-retest reliability), because the less psychometrically reliable a measure is, the more attenuated the observed effect will be. Although there are psychometric disattenuation formulas that attempt to correct for unreliability (measurement error variance; see Schmidt & Hunter, 1996), the remainder of this chapter will focus on sampling issues, starting with range restriction.

Range Restriction

Another frequent concern in studies of expertise is the phenomenon of range restriction (e.g., Ackerman, 2014). Almost by definition, experts are those people who reside within a restricted range of performance in a given domain, but to be more specific, the question is this: How restricted is the range of performance in a researcher's particular sample relative to (a) the population of experts in which one is interested (e.g., elite violinists) or (b) the general population of people who perform in that given domain (e.g., all violinists)? Range restriction occurs when variance in the sample in hand is smaller than corresponding variance in the population of interest. This in turn leads to observed sample means, variances, correlations, and *d*-values that are biased estimates of their population counterparts (e.g., sample means are more extreme, variances are reduced, and correlations are less extreme than those for the population of interest). We provide examples below that illustrate how range restriction affects correlation coefficients (for thorough details, see Sackett & Yang, 2000), but similar examples could just as well pertain to *d*-values (see Bobko, Roth, & Bobko, 2001)

Direct Range Restriction

Direct range restriction happens when subjects are selected (or excluded) directly on the basis of their standing on a measured variable of interest. As an example of direct range restriction, selecting the top 10 percent of SAT scorers will reduce the variance of SAT, and it will also reduce the variance of any outcomes with which SAT is correlated, such as high-school grades and graduation. Although students' standing on the SAT and these outcomes will be high as a function of selection on the SAT, the correlation between these variables will be lower as a result.

In the context of expertise, researchers might encounter direct range restriction on outcome variables (i.e., expert performance measures), where data are often restricted to the upper end of the distribution. For example, one of the most frequently used archival databases for research on expert performance in chess is the World Chess Federation (FIDE) database (Howard, 2006; Vaci, Gula, & Bilalić, 2014). Although this database is an invaluable asset to researchers interested in studying historical trends in chess expert performance, the FIDE data are limited to individuals with Elo (1978) ratings of 2000 or higher (Vaci *et al.*, 2014). As such, this database is affected by direct range restriction on FIDE ratings, which in turn attenuates correlations between these FIDE ratings and any related variables.

Equation 2.1 presents the formula for the impact of attenuation due to range restriction on the magnitude of correlation coefficients when the standard deviation on outcome measure, *Y*, is restricted in the sample compared to the standard deviation in the population:

$$r'_{XY} = \frac{r_{XY}\left(\frac{s'_Y}{s_Y}\right)}{\sqrt{1 - r_{XY}^2 + r_{XY}^2 \left(\frac{s'_Y}{s_Y}\right)^2}} \, , \tag{2.1}$$

where r'_{XY} the observed (restricted) correlation between *X* and *Y* in the sample, r_{XY} is the unrestricted correlation in the population, s'_Y is the restricted estimate of the standard deviation of *Y* in the population, and s_Y is the unrestricted estimate of the standard deviation of *Y* in the sample. (This formula is nearly identical when correcting for direct range restriction on *X*, such that the restricted and unrestricted standard deviations for *X* replace those for *Y* in Equation 2.1.)

Equation 2.1 can be rearranged into Equation 2.2 in order to estimate the magnitude of the population correlation in the restricted sample, known as the correction for attenuation due to range restriction formula:

$$r_c = \frac{r'_{XY}\left(\frac{s_Y}{s'_Y}\right)}{\sqrt{1 - r_{XY}^{'2} + r_{XY}^{'2} \left(\frac{s_Y}{s'_Y}\right)^2}} \, , \tag{2.2}$$

where r_c is the estimate of the correlation corrected for attenuation due to range restriction (notation otherwise matches that for Equation 2.1). Note that in order to correct for attenuation due to range restriction, an estimate of the variability in the unrestricted measure (here, s_Y) in the population must also be obtained.

Recently, Vaci *et al.* (2014) examined the effects of range restriction on relations between years of experience and performance in chess. These authors demonstrated substantial range restriction on Elo ratings in the FIDE database (M = 2,122, SD = 182) by comparing it with the German Chess Federation national database (M = 1,387, SD = 389). Moreover, Vaci *et al.* (2014) compared trajectories of skill acquisition and decline across ages in the German national database with those reported by past research (e.g., Howard, 2005; Roring & Charness, 2007) using the FIDE. Results indicated a steeper rate of skill acquisition and a slower rate of decline among participants from the more heterogeneous German sample than those observed for the range-restricted FIDE expert sample.

In research on expert performance in chess, researchers often classify those with Elo ratings at or above 2000 as "experts" and those with ratings at or above 2200 as "masters" (e.g., Gobet & Campitelli, 2007; Hambrick *et al.*, 2014), with increasing prestige designated at higher ratings (e.g., Campitelli & Gobet, 2011). To demonstrate the impact of direct range restriction on expert performance measures, we created a small-scale simulation examining relations between (1) general mental ability, (2) log hours of deliberate practice, and (3) Elo ratings, given the prominence of these individual difference characteristics in the expert performance literature (e.g., Burgoyne *et al.*, 2016; Hambrick *et al.*, 2014). For this demonstration, we obtained estimates for the relationship between general mental ability and Elo ratings from Grabner, Stern, and Neubauer (2007), who observed a correlation of r = .35 between scores on a general mental ability measure (M = 13.53, SD = 14.05) and Elo ratings (M = 1869, SD = 247) in a sample of 90 Austrian tournament chess players. We next obtained estimates of the relationship between deliberate practice in chess and Elo ratings from Gobet and Campitelli (2007), who observed a correlation of r = .57 between log hours of (total) practice (M = 3.9, SD = .40) and national ratings in chess (M = 1991, SD = 221) in a sample of Argentinian chess players.

To illustrate, we simulated a multivariate normal distribution[2] with a sample size of 1000, and we used the sample size weighted mean and standard deviations of the Elo ratings (M = 1934.40, SD = 233.06) from Grabner *et al.* (2007) and Gobet and Campitelli (2007) as the basis for the distribution of performance ratings in the data. The correlation between general mental ability and hours of practice was set at r = .00, given findings indicating near-zero estimates for correlations between ability and deliberate practice in the broader expertise literature (e.g., Meinz & Hambrick, 2010). The top row of Figure 2.2 presents the results of this simulation for the full range of data.

To demonstrate the impact of direct range restriction on performance measures on correlation coefficients in expertise research, we classified simulated participants with Elo ratings at or above 2000 as experts, consistent with common practice in research on chess expertise (e.g., Gobet & Campitelli, 2007; Hambrick *et al.*, 2014; Vaci *et al.*, 2014). All simulated participants with Elo ratings below 2000 were therefore excluded from the sample (restricted Elo M = 2172.63, SD = 131.73). The bottom row of Figure 2.2 demonstrates the

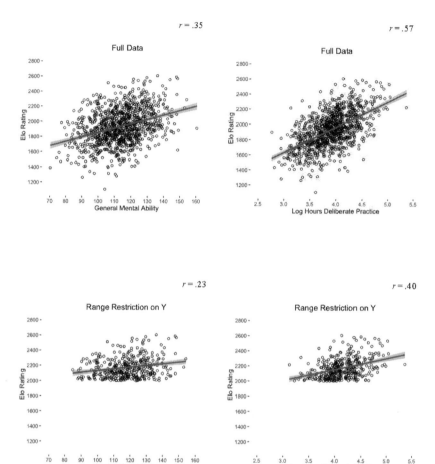

FIGURE 2.2   Illustrations of the impact of direct range restriction on correlations between ability and Elo ratings (left column) and deliberate practice and Elo ratings (right column). Full data (top row) versus direct range restriction on Elo ratings (bottom row).

pattern of finding for this restricted sample. Note that the correlation between general mental ability and performance was reduced from $r = .35$ to $r = .23$ after restricting the range of the data. Similarly, the correlation between log hours of deliberate practice dropped from $r = .57$ in the full sample to $r = .40$ in the restricted sample. As evidenced by this simulated example, relationships between predictors and performance in a domain of expertise can be *substantially* underestimated to the extent that participants are sampled from one extreme (typically the upper portion) of the distribution with respect to the population of interest.

Range restriction can also occur directly on the predictors of expert performance in several ways. Take for example one of the most hotly debated predictors of expert performance across domains: general mental ability (Campitelli & Gobet, 2011; Ericsson, 2014; Ericsson & Charness, 1994; Hambrick, Macnamara, Campitelli, Ullén, & Mosing, 2016). Specifically, research on expert performance is often limited to those who are already classified as proficient in a domain of interest (see our previous discussion). Note, however, that when researchers *do* include participants from a wider range of performance (e.g., novices and those at intermediate levels of expertise), they are often college students (e.g., Halpern & Wai, 2007), who themselves are range-restricted with respect to the general population in terms of general mental ability (i.e., they are admitted to universities in part based on ability as reflected in their standardized test scores, such as the SAT and ACT in the US; Kuncel, Hezlett, & Ones, 2004). Again, how range restricted the sample is depends on the population of interest. A sample of expert chess players is not restricted if this sample reflects the expert population of interest; it is restricted, however, if the desired population is tournament chess players instead; and it is even more restricted if the desired population is all chess players at large.

Incidental Range Restriction

A more complex picture regarding range restriction is evident when we consider how selection on correlated variables that *are not* of primary interest to a study might still result in range restriction on the variables that are of primary interest. This phenomenon is known as *incidental* range restriction. The formula that corrects an observed correlation between X and Y for incidental range restriction effects, based on selection on a third variable Z, is as follows:

$$r_c = \frac{r'_{XY} + r'_{XZ} r'_{ZY} \left(\frac{s^2_{ZY}}{s^{2'}_Z} - 1 \right)}{\sqrt{1 + r^{2'}_{XZ} \left(\frac{s^2_{XZ}}{s^{2'}_Z} - 1 \right)} \sqrt{1 + r^{2'}_{ZY} \left(\frac{s^2_Z}{s^{2'}_Z} - 1 \right)}}, \tag{2.3}$$

where notation is analogous to that for the direct range restriction formula explained previously (also see Sackett & Yang, 2000, for an excellent exposition on the different forms of range restriction that might arise in a sample).

An example situation in which expertise researchers might encounter incidental range restriction is in research on deliberate practice and performance in sports (e.g., Macnamara, Hambrick, & Oswald, 2014; Macnamara, Moreau, & Hambrick, 2016). Ericsson and his colleagues (e.g., Ericsson et al., 1993) have long suggested that physical characteristics, such as height, might account for incremental variance in performance outcomes over and above amount of deliberate practice. For example, one might intuitively suspect that height influences the amount of deliberate practice accrued among basketball players: Young basketball players who are taller are likely to receive positive outcomes from their activities, as well as additional encouragement, in their continued pursuit and practice of basketball. Conversely, young basketball players who are shorter might begin to limit and discontinue their engagement in the sport, ultimately restricting the range of height among basketball players over time, relative to when they began to engage in the sport.

To demonstrate the effect of incidental range restriction in height on the relationship between deliberate practice and performance, we simulated 1,000 participants with varying levels of height, log hours of deliberate practice, and performance in sports. Heights were randomly distributed around the average height for males in the United States ($M = 69.5$ inches, $SD = 3$ inches; see e.g., Ogden, Fryar, Carroll, & Flegal, 2004), and estimates of the mean and standard deviation for log hours of deliberate practice ($M = 8.28$, $SD = 7.99$) were obtained from the sample size weighted meta-analytic average reported in Macnamara *et al.* (2016). Performance in sports was estimated using a standard normal distribution ($M = 0$, $SD = 1$). In addition, we obtained the sample size weighted meta-analytic correlation of $\bar{r} = .43$ between deliberate practice and performance reported in Macnamara *et al.* (2016). For this demonstration, we simulated both the correlation between height and deliberate practice, and that between height and performance at $r = .30$ (a medium effect size, Cohen, 1988). All variables were simulated to be distributed as multivariate normal.

Figure 2.3 compares the correlation observed in the full sample, versus the correlation in the sample of those who exceeded 72.5 inches in height (i.e., players

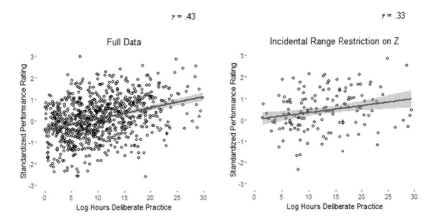

FIGURE 2.3 Illustrations of the impact of incidental range restriction in height (Z) on the correlation between deliberate practice (X) and performance in sports (Y): Full data (left) versus incidental range restriction in height (right). Restricted correlations of $r = -.03$ vs. $r = .30$ (unrestricted) between height and deliberate practice, and $r = .16$ vs. $r = .30$ (unrestricted) between height and performance (top 15.7% of simulated participants were selected on height).

who are one standard deviation above the average height in the population simulated). Note that this scenario is for illustrative purposes, as nature will not generally be so precise (i.e., the height cut-off would be more fuzzy and implicit, based on basketball players who naturally drop out of the sport). As shown in Figure 2.3, the correlation between deliberate practice and performance is noticeably reduced as a function of this incidental range restriction on height, from the original $r = .43$ to $r = .33$. Thus, researchers should be aware of potential incidental range restriction effects that might weaken the strength of observed relationships.

The direct and incidental range restriction effects just described deal with top-down selection (on Y or on a third variable Z, respectively). The next section discusses extreme groups designs, which reflect selection on both end points of a continuum and a "missing middle" (Taylor & Greiss, 1976), rather than top-down selection.

Extreme Groups Designs

One particular sampling concern that often arises in research on expertise warrants further discussion: research designs that exclusively sample from the extremes of a distribution (e.g., only from the upper and lower quartiles), known as the *extreme groups design* (Preacher, 2015; Preacher, Rucker, MacCallum, & Nicewander, 2005). There are a number of benefits to the use of extreme groups designs, most notably in terms of cost-efficiency (McClelland & Judd, 1993; Preacher *et al.*, 2005). That is, given limitations to the number of participants available for a study, sampling participants exclusively from the upper and lower regions (e.g., quartiles) of a distribution will increase statistical power when compared to a sample of equal size that is drawn from the full range of possible scores. As such, the use of extreme groups designs is useful for having the data support (1) whether an effect exists (i.e., is statistically significant suggestive of a non-zero effect), and (2) the direction of the effect (i.e., a positive or negative trend).

Note, however, that the magnitude of an effect in standardized units, such as the correlation coefficient or Cohen's d, is overestimated with respect to effects in the population of interest—sometimes substantially so—when an extreme groups design is used (Cortina & DeShon, 1998; Preacher *et al.*, 2005). This upward bias in the magnitude of the observed relationship happens because the variance in extreme groups design is *larger* than that in the full range of the distribution. The result is a condition known as *range enhancement* (Cortina & DeShon, 1998; Preacher *et al.*, 2005). Just as effects can be corrected for direct range restriction, they can be corrected for direct range enhancement using the same formula (Equation 2.2).

Returning to our example for direct range restriction in chess performance, Figure 2.4 presents an example for the effects of range enhancement on the correlations between participants' standing on either general mental ability or log hours of deliberate practice and Elo ratings. To demonstrate the impact on selecting participants using an extreme groups design, we excluded those simulated participants with Elo ratings between 1700 (representing those with "above average" Elo ratings, but who do not meet the "expert" cut-off of Elo ratings greater than 2000) and 2200 (representing those who are often classified as "masters") from the data. Note that the standard deviation for Elo ratings increased from 233.06 in the full sample to 381.54 in this restricted sample. As shown in the bottom row of Figure 2.4, the correlation between general mental ability and Elo ratings increased from $r = .35$ in the population to $r = .53$ in the extreme groups sample. Similarly, the correlation between log hours of deliberate practice and

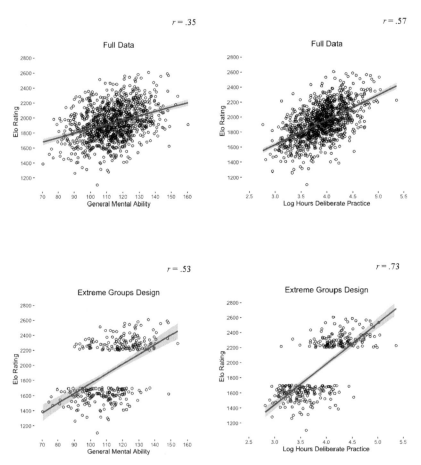

FIGURE 2.4   Illustrations of the impact of range enhancement on correlations for ability with Elo ratings (left column) and deliberate practice with Elo ratings (right column). Full data (top row) versus extreme groups design (bottom row).

Elo ratings increased from the population correlation of $r = .57$ to a correlation of $r = .73$ in the extreme groups sample. Importantly, the magnitude of these relations under the extreme groups design is likely an underestimate of the impact of range enhancement in the literature, as researchers tend to recruit novices for such studies (i.e., participants who would obtain substantially lower Elo ratings than those simulated in our example).

There are several other potential concerns with the use of extreme groups designs for the study of expertise. First, as noted, standardized effect size measures (e.g., r, d) are biased when participants are sampled exclusively from the extremes of a distribution, given the potentially marked increase in the standard deviation of the variable on which selections were made. As such, relative comparisons of standardized effects are largely rendered useless (Cortina & DeShon, 1998). This is of particular concern for research on expertise, where researchers are often interested in comparing the relative contributions of various predictors (e.g., general mental ability, deliberate practice) to the prediction of expert performance.

A second concern with extreme groups designs is the questionable generalizability of the findings due to non-representative samples. Specifically, extreme groups designs implicitly assume that the form of the relationship between X (e.g., log hours of deliberate practice, general mental ability) and Y (e.g., Elo ratings) in the extreme groups is consistent across the full range of the distribution of scores (Preacher *et al.*, 2005). To the extent that the form of the relationship differs across the range of scores (e.g., the X-Y relationship is moderated by third variables or is otherwise nonlinear), then conclusions drawn from the observed effect under the extreme groups design may inadequately represent the underlying relationship between the variables of interest.

Given these potential limitations, the use of extreme groups designs is likely most beneficial in the initial stages of determining whether a statistically significant relationship exists between two (or more) variables of interest—such as during pilot testing. Once such an effect is detected, however, researchers should avoid the use of extreme groups designs in order to assess the magnitude of an effect in the population more accurately, as concerns about the practical significance of an effect are likely to be of greater import for theory development and practice.

Classifying Levels of Expertise

Beyond the use of extreme groups designs, a related area of concern is how, in the literature on expertise, participants are classified as experts/non-experts and on other potential variables of interest. The primary concern regarding group assignment is whether participants are assigned to groups using seemingly arbitrary or non-arbitrary cut-offs. In some situations, group assignment might be based on objective (or, at minimum, measured and widely accepted) distinctions in skilled performance. For example, as previously noted, chess players with Elo ratings greater than 2000 are often classified as "expert," whereas those with Elo ratings greater than 2200 are often classified as "master" (e.g., Gobet & Campitelli, 2007; Hambrick *et al.*, 2014). Note, however, that even in such cases, experts with ratings at or around specific cut-off scores (e.g., 2000 or 2200, respectively) will demonstrate minimal differences in their actual (true) levels of performance.

Outside of a few well-researched domains (e.g., chess, sports), objective standards by which to classify levels of expertise are less apparent. More commonly, researchers elect to categorize participants using assumed distinctions in their data. For example, researchers might classify levels of expertise by function of known group membership (e.g., academic major or year in major, Kauffman & Carlsen, 1989; professional vs. amateur sports players, Duffy, Baluch, & Ericsson, 2004), which serves as a proxy for individual differences in motivation, experience, or other potential characteristics of interest (of course, teams of experts may also have their own motivating characteristics, above and beyond individual differences). Note that in addition to variation in deliberate practice *between* putative or assigned groups based on skill level, there is often substantial variation in deliberate practice *within* groups; in other words, not all participants who are classified at similar levels of expertise have reached the same number of hours of deliberate practice (see e.g., Campitelli & Gobet, 2011, who note considerable variation in the number of hours of deliberate practice among experts in chess).

The primary issue here is that groupings are almost always artificial (e.g., expert vs. intermediate vs. novice) yet can be useful in practice, such as when assigning people to classes with limited resources (e.g., chess training or gifted and talented courses), or when some cut-off indicates the accomplishment of an educational or professional skill by most reasonable standards (e.g., graduation, licensure, or certification). Nonetheless, the underlying reality is that individual differences in skill, expertise, and their indicators (e.g., starting age) actually fall along a continuum of scores. Researchers may elect to discretize the data for convenience of illustrating the comparison between groups, or because researchers have "ANOVA mindset syndrome" (MacCallum, 1998) and do not appreciate the underlying statistical problem as a regression problem. Problems with artificial discretization of continuous data are well known in the statistical and psychological literatures (e.g., MacCallum, Zhang, Preacher, & Rucker, 2002). Apart from conceptual concerns (i.e., the fact that expert vs. novice are not naturally occurring groups), discretizing data (e.g., a median split) can result in a substantial loss of statistical power for detecting effects, attenuate the magnitude of observed relations, and in some cases may produce interaction effects that are spurious (see e.g., Maxwell & Delaney, 1993; McClelland & Judd, 1993).

Conclusion

Experts are those rare people who demonstrate exceptional performance in a given domain, whether, for example, as an astronomer, violinist, triathlete, or SCRABBLE® player. Sometimes the metrics for identifying levels of expertise are relatively constrained and well defined (e.g., winning games of tournament chess against other expert players); yet many other times, metrics for expertise are broad and somewhat ambiguous (e.g., metrics for being a world-class architect or inventor). In future research, all forms of expertise should be investigated further in ways that go beyond traditional metrics (e.g., longitudinal intensive sampling of behavior to understand styles of expert performance). In addition, researchers must continue their investigation of skill acquisition broadly, going beyond the experts themselves in order to identify characteristics of individuals (e.g., ability, motivation), groups (e.g., teamwork, peer pressure), and environments (e.g., training), all of which contribute to the development of individual expertise. Broad theoretical and empirical frameworks of skill acquisition serve this end. Such frameworks have been targeted within domains, such as employment (e.g., Kanfer & Ackerman, 2005; Judge, Higgins, Thoresen, & Barrick, 1999), education (e.g., Dweck, 1986; Kell, Lubinski, & Benbow, 2013), and general life activities (Gottfredson, 1997; Gow, Pattie, & Deary, 2017); but these and other frameworks could be usefully interwoven and applied across domains to understand expertise and skill acquisition in a more integrated manner. We hope that this chapter highlighting fundamental methodological issues in the study of expertise is useful to this end.

Notes

1 Confidence intervals are based on the standard error of the correlation coefficient, estimated as $\frac{1}{\sqrt{N-3}}$, once the correlation has been Fisher's r-to-Z transformed. The confidence limits are then back-transformed to the correlation metric.

2 Our demonstration assumed multivariate normality of all variables. We note, however, that the distribution of hours of deliberate practice is often moderately to substantially skewed in studies of expertise (see e.g., Charness *et al.*, 2005). One typical strategy to mitigate the effects of skew that is often adopted in the literature is to take the log of the number of hours of practice. As such, we selected estimates from the literature based on log-transformed hours of practice.

References

Ackerman, P. L. (2014). Nonsense, common sense, and science of expert performance: Talent and individual differences. *Intelligence, 45*, 6–17. doi:10.1016/j.intell.2013.04.009

Bobko, P., Roth, P. L., & Bobko, C. (2001). Correcting the effect size of *d* for range restriction and unreliability. *Organizational Research Methods, 4*, 46–61. doi:10.1177/109442810141003

Burgoyne, A. P., Sala, G., Gobet, F., Macnamara, B. N., Campitelli, G., & Hambrick, D. Z. (2016). The relationship between cognitive ability and chess skill: A comprehensive meta-analysis. *Intelligence, 59*, 72–83. doi:10.1016/j.intell.2016.08.002

Campitelli, G., & Gobet, F. (2008). The role of practice in chess: A longitudinal study. *Learning and Individual Differences, 18*, 446–458. doi:10.1016/j.lindif.2007.11.006

Campitelli, G., & Gobet, F. (2011). Deliberate practice: Necessary but not sufficient. *Current Directions in Psychological Science, 20*, 280–285. doi:10.1177/0963721411421922

Charness, N., Tuffiash, M., Krampe, R., Reingold, E., & Vasyukova, E. (2005). The role of deliberate practice in chess expertise. *Applied Cognitive Psychology, 19*, 151–165. doi:10.1002/acp.1106

Cohen, J. (1988). *Statistical power analysis for the behavioral sciences* (2nd ed.). Hillsdale, NJ: Erlbaum.

Cohen J. (1992). A power primer. *Psychological Bulletin, 112*, 155–159. doi:10.1037/0033-2909.112.1.155

Cortina, J. M., & DeShon, R. P. (1998). Determining relative importance of predictors with the observational design. *Journal of Applied Psychology, 83*, 798–804. doi:0021-90IO/98/S3.00

Cumming, G., & Fidler, F. (2009). Confidence intervals: Better answers to better questions. *Zeitschrift für Psychologie/Journal of Psychology, 217*, 15–26. doi:10.1027/0044-3409.217.1.15

Duffy, L. J., Baluch, B., & Ericsson, K. A. (2004). Dart performance as a function of facets of practice amongst professional and amateur men and women players. *International Journal of Sport Psychology, 35*, 232–245.

Dweck, C. S. (1986). Motivational processes affecting learning. *American Psychologist, 41*, 1040–1048. doi:10.1037/0003-066X.41.10.1040

Eich, E. (2014). Business not as usual [Editorial]. *Psychological Science, 25*, 3–6.

Elo, A. E. (1978). *The rating of chessplayers, past and present.* New York: Arco.

Ericsson K. A. (2014). Why expert performance is special and cannot be extrapolated from studies of performance in the general population: A response to criticisms. *Intelligence, 45*, 81–103. doi:0.1016/j.intell.2013.12.001

Ericsson, K. A., & Charness, N. (1994). Expert performance: Its structure and acquisition. *American Psychologist, 69*, 725–747. doi:10.1037/0003-066X.49.8.725

Ericsson, K. A., Krampe, R. Th., & Tesch-Römer, C. (1993). The role of deliberate practice in the acquisition of expert performance. *Psychological Review, 100*, 363–406. doi:10.1037/0033-295X.100.3.363

Gobet, F., & Campitelli, G. (2007). The role of domain-specific practice, handedness, and starting age in chess. *Developmental Psychology, 43*, 159–172. doi:10.1037/0012-1649.43.1.159

Gottfredson, L. S. (1997). Why *g* matters: The complexity of everyday life. *Intelligence, 24*, 79–132. doi:10.1016/S0160-2896(97)90014-3

Gow, A. J., Pattie, A., & Deary, I. J. (2017). Lifecourse activity participation from early, mid, and later adulthood as determinants of cognitive aging: The Lothian Birth Cohort 1921. *The Journals of Gerontology: Psychological Sciences & Social Sciences, 72*, 25–37. doi:10.1093/geronb/gbw124

Grabner, R. H., Stern, E., & Neubauer, A. C. (2007). Individual differences in chess expertise: A psychometric investigation. *Acta Psychologica, 124*, 398–420. doi:10.1016/j.actpsy.2006.07.008

Halpern, D. F., & Wai, J. (2007). The world of competitive Scrabble: Novice and expert differences in visuospatial and verbal abilities. *Journal of Experimental Psychology: Applied, 13*, 79–94. doi:10.1037/1076-898X.13.2.79

Hambrick, D. Z., Oswald, F. L., Altmann, E. M., Meinz, E. J., Gobet, F., & Campitelli, G. (2014). Deliberate practice: Is that all it takes to become an expert? *Intelligence, 45,* 34–45. doi:10.1016/j.intell.2013.04.001

Hambrick, D. Z., Macnamara, B. N., Campitelli, G., Ullén, F., & Mosing, M. A. (2016). Beyond born versus made: A new look at expertise. *Psychology of Learning and Motivation, 64,* 1–55. doi:10.1016/bs.plm.2015.09.001

Howard, R. W. (2005). Objective evidence of rising population ability: A detailed examination of longitudinal chess data. *Personality and Individual Differences, 38,* 347–363. doi:10.1016/j.paid.2004.04.013

Howard, R. W. (2006). A complete database of international chess players and chess performance ratings for varied longitudinal studies. *Behavior Research Methods, 38,* 698–703. doi:10.3758/BF03193903

Howard, R. W. (2012). Longitudinal effects of different types of practice on the development of chess expertise. *Applied Cognitive Psychology, 26,* 359–369. doi:10.1002/acp.1834

Jabusch, H.-C., Alpers, H., Kopiez, R., Vauth, H., & Altenmüller, E. (2009). The influence of practice on the development of motor skills in pianists: A longitudinal study in a selected motor task. *Human Movement Science, 28,* 74–84. doi:10.1016/j.humov.2008.08.001

Judge, T. A., Higgins, C. A., Thoresen, C. J., & Barrick, M. R. (1999). The Big Five personality traits, general mental ability, and career success across the life span. *Personnel Psychology, 52,* 621–652. doi:10.1111/j.1744-6570.1999.tb00174.x

Kanfer, R., & Ackerman, P. L. (2005). Work competence: A person-oriented perspective. In A. J. Elliot & C. S. Dweck (Eds.), *Handbook of competence and motivation* (pp. 336–353). New York: Guilford Press.

Kauffman, W. H., & Carlsen, J. C. (1989). Memory for intact music works: The importance of music expertise and retention interval. *Psychomusicology, 8,* 3–20. doi:10.1037/h0094235

Kell, H. J., Lubinski, D., & Benbow, C. P. (2013). Who rises to the top? Early indicators. *Psychological Science, 24,* 648–659. doi:10.1177/0956797612457784

Kuncel, N. R., Hezlett, S. A., & Ones, D. S. (2004). Academic performance, career potential, creativity, and job performance: Can one construct predict them all? *Journal of Personality and Social Psychology, 86,* 148–161. doi:10.1037/0022-3514.86.1.148

MacCallum, R. C. (1998). Commentary on quantitative methods in I-O research. *Industrial-Organizational Psychologist, 35,* 19–30. doi:10.1037/e577062011-002

MacCallum, R. C., Zhang, S., Preacher, K. J., & Rucker, D. D. (2002). On the practice of dichotomization of quantitative variables. *Psychological Methods, 7,* 19–40. doi:10.1037//1082-989X.7.1.19

Macnamara, B. N., Hambrick, D. Z., & Oswald, F. L. (2014). Deliberate practice and performance in music, games, sports, education, and professions: A meta-analysis. *Psychological Science, 25,* 1608–1618. doi:10.1177/0956797614535810

Macnamara, B. N., Moreau, D., & Hambrick, D. Z. (2016). The relationship between deliberate practice and performance in sports: A meta-analysis. *Perspectives on Psychological Science, 11,* 333–350. doi:10.1177/1745691616635591

Maxwell, S. E., & Delaney, H. D. (1993). Bivariate median splits and spurious statistical significance. *Psychological Bulletin, 113,* 181–190. doi:10.1037/0033-2909.113.1.181

McClelland, G. H., & Judd, C. M. (1993). Statistical difficulties of detecting interactions and moderator effects. *Psychological Bulletin, 114,* 376–390. doi:10.1037/0033-2909.114.2.376

Meinz, E. J., & Hambrick, D. Z. (2010). Deliberate practice is necessary but not sufficient to explain individual differences in piano sight-reading skill: The role of working memory capacity. *Psychological Science, 21*, 914–919. doi:10.1177/0956797610373933

Nickerson, R. S. (2000). Null hypothesis significance testing: A review of an old and continuing controversy. *Psychological Methods, 5*, 241–301. doi:10.1037/1082-989X.5.2.241

Ogden, C. L., Fryar, C. D., Carroll, M. D., Flegal, K. M. (2004). *Mean body weight, height, and body mass index, United States 1960-2002* (pp. 1–17). Department of Health and Human Services, Centers for Disease Control and Prevention, National Center for Health Statistics.

Preacher, K. J. (2015). Extreme groups designs. In R. L. Cautin & S. O. Lilienfeld (Eds.), *The encyclopedia of clinical psychology* (Vol. 2, pp. 1189–1192). Hoboken, NJ: John Wiley & Sons, Inc.

Preacher, K. J., Rucker, D. D., MacCallum, R. C., & Nicewander, W. A. (2005). Use of the extreme groups approach: A critical reexamination and new recommendations. *Psychological Methods, 10*, 178–192. doi:10.1037/1082-989X.10.2.178

Roring, R. W., & Charness, N. (2007). A multilevel model analysis of expertise in chess across the life span. *Psychology and Aging, 22*, 291–299. doi:10.1037/0882-7974.22.2.291

Sackett, P. R., & Yang, H. (2000). Correction for range restriction: An expanded typology. *Journal of Applied Psychology, 85*, 112–118. doi:10.1037//0021-9010.85.1.112

Schmidt, F. L., & Hunter, J. E. (1996). Measurement error in psychological research: Lessons from 26 research scenarios. *Psychological Methods, 1*, 199–223.

Schmidt, F. L., & Hunter, J. E. (2015). *Methods of meta-analysis: Correcting error and bias in research findings* (4th ed.). Thousand Oaks, CA: SAGE.

Taylor, E. K., & Greiss, T. (1976). The missing middle in validation research. *Personnel Psychology, 29*, 5–11. doi:10.1111/j.1744-6570.1976.tb00397.x

Vaci, N., Gula, B., & Bilalić, M. (2014). Restricting range restricts conclusions. *Frontiers in Psychology, 5* (569). doi:10.3389/fpsyg.2014.00569

Walls, T. A., & Schafer, J. L. (Eds.). (2006). *Models for intensive longitudinal data*. New York: Oxford University Press.

Wetzels, R., Matzke, D., Lee, M. D., Rouder, J. N., Iverson, G. J., & Wagenmakers, E. -J. (2011). Statistical evidence in experimental psychology: An empirical comparison using 855 *t*-tests. *Perspectives on Psychological Science, 6*, 291–298. doi:10.1177/17456916 11406923

3

COGNITIVE PROCESSES IN CHESS

Guillermo Campitelli

Introduction

In November 2016, two chess prodigies played the World Chess Championship match in New York. The world champion Magnus Carlsen (Norwegian, 25 years old) faced the challenger Sergey Karjakin (Ukraine-born Russian, 26 years old). Carlsen obtained the international grandmaster (GM) title[1] at the age of 13. He was the youngest player to reach the Number 1 in the world ranking at the age of 19, obtained the highest chess rating[2] in the history of chess at the age of 22, and became world champion in the same year. Karjakin was the youngest player to obtain the international master (IM) title just before turning 12, and the GM title at the age of 12 years and 7 months. (He still holds both records.)

Chess is a discipline with all the ideal ingredients to study cognitive processes and expertise:

- There are a number of prodigies;
- Unlike in sports, there are a number of older adults maintaining high levels of performance; hence, development of expertise could be studied along the whole lifespan;
- There is an objective measure of chess expertise: The Elo (1978) system (and related systems) used by the world chess federation, national federations, local districts, and chess clubs;
- There are massive archives of ranking lists and chess games;
- Chess playing involves several cognitive processes such as pattern recognition, attention, memory, imagery, thinking, and decision making;
- Chess is played at different time rhythms (from 2 minute games up to 5 to 6 hour games), allowing to study the interaction between cognitive process and time.

Three main lines of research have been developed in the psychology of chess expertise: (1) development of chess expertise (e.g., Bilalić, McLeod, & Gobet, 2007; Charness, Tuffiash, Krampe, Reingold, & Vasyukova, 2005; Gobet & Campitelli, 2007); (2) cognitive processes in chess expertise (e.g., Bilalić, McLeod, & Gobet, 2008; Campitelli & Gobet, 2004, 2005, 2011; Chase & Simon, 1973a & b; de Groot, 1946/1978; Gobet & Simon, 1996, 1998; Saariluoma, 1991; Saariluoma & Kalakowski, 1997); and (3) neural implementations of chess expertise (e.g., Bilalić, Langner, Erb, & Grodd, 2010; Bilalić, Langner, Ulrich, & Grodd, 2011; Bilalić, Turella, Campitelli, Erb, & Grodd, 2012; Campitelli, Gobet, Head, Buckley, & Parker, 2007; Campitelli, Gobet, & Parker, 2005).

In this chapter, I will touch very briefly on the first area of research, development of chess expertise, and focus on the second area, cognitive processes in chess expertise. The third area of research, neural implementation of chess expertise, is beyond the scope of this chapter (see Chapter 11, The Neural Underpinnings of Expertise in Games).

Development of Chess Expertise

Studies on the development of chess expertise have been strongly influenced by the deliberate practice framework (Ericsson, Krampe, & Tesch-Römer, 1993). Details of this framework are explained in Chapter 9, The Deliberate Practice View. Here I mention only that this framework implies that expertise is acquired as a function of the number of hours of deliberate practice and that no other factors are important (see Campitelli & Gobet, 2011, and Hambrick, Oswald, Altmann, Meinz, Gobet, & Campitelli, 2014 for this interpretation of the deliberate practice framework).

In a review of studies on the role of deliberate practice in chess performance, Campitelli and Gobet (2011) found that the correlation of chess performance with individual practice varied from .45 to .54, with group practice varying from .26 to .54, and total practice from .57 to .90. In a meta-analysis, Hambrick *et al.* (2014) estimated that deliberate practice explained 34 percent of the variance of chess performance, leaving 66 percent of the variance unexplained. These results indicate that deliberate practice is at this time the most important factor identified for explaining chess expertise, but it is not the *only* factor. Researchers have identified other factors (e.g., starting age, Campitelli & Gobet, 2008; handedness, Gobet & Campitelli, 2007; season of birth, Gobet & Chassy, 2008; cognitive abilities, see Burgoyne, Sala, Gobet, Macnamara, Campitelli, & Hambrick, 2016, for a meta-analysis). I will discuss the role of individual differences in cognitive abilities later in this chapter.

Cognitive Processes in Chess Expertise

Although there were previous studies, scientific research on cognitive processes in chess players started with de Groot's (1946/1978) seminal work on chess players' problem solving and memory (see Bilalić *et al.*, 2008, for an overview of the impact of this study in cognitive psychology). De Groot carried out a problem-solving study and a memory study. In the former, he presented chess players of different skill levels with a position taken from an actual chess game unknown to the players. He asked them to pretend they were playing a chess game from that position and to consider what they would move in that position. Also, the players had to say out loud what they were thinking. The surprising finding was that the strongest players did not think further ahead than weaker players. GMs considered better options and chose better moves than expert players of a lower level, but they did not search deeper or consider more options. In the memory study, the chess players were shown a chess position for a brief period of time (2–15 seconds), and immediately after that presentation, they were asked to reconstruct that position on an empty board. GMs proved to have a much greater recall of chess positions than that of the chess experts.

Herbert Simon, who aimed to test his economic theory of *bounded rationality*, was impressed by de Groot's work and used chess to investigate cognitive processes underlying humans' decision making. Chase and Simon (1973a) replicated de Groot's results in the memory task, and then added a condition in which the players performed the same task but the positions, instead of being taken from an actual game, were constructed by randomly placing chess pieces on the chess board. The results showed that the difference in performance between GMs and expert players almost disappeared (see Gobet & Simon, 1998, for a meta-analysis of memory for random chess positions).

These two seminal studies inspired many cognitive scientists to investigate cognitive processes in chess players, not only to understand chess expertise per se but also as a model to study the cognitive processes that underlie decision making in general. In the remainder of this section, I will discuss three cognitive processes that were investigated in chess players: *pattern recognition, search*, and *imagery*.

Pattern Recognition

Based on the findings discussed above, Chase and Simon (1973a, 1973b) developed the *chunking* theory. This theory postulates that, as a function of their training and participation in tournaments, chess players store chunks (typical configurations of 3 or 4 chess pieces) in their long-term memory (LTM). They estimated that skilled players accumulate roughly 50,000 chunks in LTM. In their chunking theory, Chase and Simon indicated that pattern recognition guides the search of possible moves and potential consequences in a selective way, as well as evaluations of positions. The recognition of familiar chunks allows chess players to reduce the amount of time spent searching because only the most relevant possibilities are considered. This theory explained performance in de Groot's memory task by assuming that chess players recognize familiar patterns of chess pieces presented in the chess board by activating the chunks stored in LTM, and that pointers to those chunks are placed in short-term memory (STM). Stronger players perform better than weaker players because they possess more and larger chunks in LTM; hence, they can remember more chess pieces than novices. However, when random positions are presented the advantage of stronger players almost vanishes because random positions do not contain familiar patterns, or only one or two patterns appear by chance. Therefore, the activation of chunks stored in LTM rarely occurs.

The chunking theory had the advantage of explaining the results described above, proposing (and implementing) computational mechanisms, as well as being consistent with the general theories of cognition that postulate that the STM store has limited capacity. However, a number of findings put the theory into question. Gobet and Simon (1996) used de Groot's memory task, but they presented players with more than one position. Although the percentage of pieces recalled decreased as a function of the number of positions presented, the total number of pieces recalled increased up to 60 pieces in masters, and to about 80 in an international master who was trained in this task. This finding cannot be accounted for by the chunking theory. Therefore, in order to address some shortcomings of the chunking theory, but maintain the core processes and structures of that theory, Gobet and Simon (1996) developed the *template* theory and then Gobet (see Gobet, Lane, Croker, Cheng, Jones, Oliver, & Pine, 2001 for an overview) implemented the theory into the *CHREST computational model* (see Chapter 20, Computational Models of Expertise, for more details on the computational approach to expertise).

In the template theory, some chunks stored in LTM evolve into more complex structures called templates. Templates are patterns of around 12 chess pieces typically found in openings or well-known pawn structures in the middle game. Moreover, templates contain slots in which additional information could be located, such as chunks, possible moves, and concepts (e.g., typical plans in the position contained in the template). Holding (1992) criticized the chunking theory and indicated that pattern recognition alone could not explain how chess players actually play chess. Rather, high-level conceptual knowledge and search mechanisms are important. However, the template theory not only accounts for the results in the multiple board memory experiments, but also takes into account the calls for inclusion of high-level knowledge and search in theories of chess expertise. Gobet and Simon (1996) indicated that high-level knowledge information such as typical plans, name of the opening, players who frequently play that opening, etc., could be part of the information added to the templates' slots. The issue of search mechanisms will be explained in the next section.

Search

De Groot's (1946/1978) finding that GMs do not search deeper than expert chess players inspired *pattern recognition* theories. This gave the wrong impression that pattern recognition theories did not take into account search. In fact, Gobet and Simon (1998) published an article with the title "Pattern recognition makes search possible" in response to the criticisms that Holding (1992) raised against the chunking theory. Gobet and Simon indicated that, for the chunking theory, search is recursive pattern recognition in the "mind's eye" (see Chase & Simon, 1973b). When players are playing a chess game and considering which move to play they recognize patterns in the current position in the chess board, which "suggests" a move to play. Instead of actually playing that move, they generate that move in the "mind's eye." Now the mind's eye holds a slightly different position than that of the actual chess board, and players apply pattern recognition over the position in the mind's eye. This idea was implemented in SEARCH (Gobet, 1997), a mathematical model that combines pattern recognition, search, and mental imagery. Simulations have shown that depth of search increases as a function of skill.

Given that SEARCH predicts that depth of search is a function of chess skill, it was surprising that the data did not support this prediction. Thus, Campitelli and Gobet (2004) suspected that the positions used by de Groot did not actually require very deep search to find the best move. Hence, GMs did not search deeper because they did not need to do so. Campitelli and Gobet used three positions that required deep search to find the best move, and they found a very strong correlation between chess rating and depth of search, number of moves considered, and speed of search.

Van Harreveld, Wagenmakers, and van der Maas (2007) proposed that the reason for the lack of skill differences in depth of search in de Groot's (1948/1978) study is that the style of chess has changed over time, with current chess requiring more and deeper search than in the first part of the 20th century. This claim is consistent with Gobet, Campitelli and Waters's (2002) description of the changes in the chess competitive environment over time, which includes changes in the speed of games, introduction of chess software for playing, and databases for training. For example, in the 1986 world championship match, players had to play their first 40 moves in 150 minutes, whereas in the 2004 world championship match, players had 90 minutes for their first 40 moves. Other changes over this period include the launch of the first digital chess database, ChessBase (in 1987), which professional chess players started using to study openings and their opponents' games.

Connors, Burns and Campitelli (2011) tested that claim by replicating de Groot's study and comparing their results to those of de Groot (1946/1978)—carried out in the 1930s and 1940s—and those of Gobet (1998)—conducted in 1986. The results support van Harreveld *et al.*'s claim. The speed of search and number of nodes searched were much higher in Connors *et al.* than in previous studies, irrespective of skill level. Their study showed that players were capable of searching more than 10 nodes per minute, which is faster than in de Groot and in Gobet's studies, but consistent with the speed of the search of masters in

Campitelli and Gobet (2004). Moreover, Connors *et al.* (2011), in an analysis that combined the three studies, found differences between masters and intermediate players in speed and depth of search. This does not reflect a change over time because those differences were present in de Groot's study; however, they were not reported or did not have enough statistical power. Thus, although there is a change in the way chess players analyze chess positions, the skill differences in pattern recognition remain unchanged.

Imagery

The previous section mostly tackled the outcomes of the search process (e.g., how deep and fast the search is). In this section we pay more attention to the nature of the search process. This process involves generating possible moves and evaluating the consequences of those moves. That is, search in chess involves *imagery*. The investigation of imagery in chess started at the end of the 19th century. Binet (1893/1966) asked renowned chess players of his time to fill in a questionnaire about the characteristics of their images while playing blindfold chess.[3] Most players reported that their images are not a replica of an actual chess board. For example, they do not include physical properties of the pieces and board such as the color and style of pieces. Fine (1965), a GM who played blindfold chess, among other insights indicated that using a blank chess board to potentially help the imagery process was more of a hindrance than a help for him. On the other hand, Koltanowski—who held the record of playing 34 simultaneous blindfold chess games—indicated that using an empty board was useful.

The study of imagery in chess with objective measures was promoted by Saariluoma in a number of ingenious experiments. Using chess notation in the absence of a chessboard, Saariluoma (1991) aurally presented to participants a chess game at a rate of one move per second. When the game reached move 15, and again at move 25, the participants were asked to indicate orally the location of all the pieces. While they were performing that primary task the chess players had to perform one of three interference tasks: (1) control (no interference task), (2) imagery interference (the participants had to imagine the Finnish syllable "TAK" and mentally walk along the side of the letters and indicate if they had to turn right or left when they reached the corners of the letters), and (3) verbal interference (participants had to continuously repeat the syllable "TIK"). As expected, masters performed better than intermediates, and, relative to the control condition, the imagery interference condition, but not the verbal interference condition, showed a decrease in performance. This suggests that imagery is important to follow a game without looking at the pieces. In another experiment, Saariluoma presented games, as in the previous experiment, and random games. In the latter, the moves were randomly generated. The performance of players decreased in the random games condition. These results resemble those of Chase and Simon (1973a), indicating that the typical chunks stored in LTM greatly influence the imagery of chess moves.

In a similar study, Saariluoma and Kalakoski (1997) presented the games as follows. An empty chess board was presented on a computer screen. The piece that moved was presented for 1 second in its original square, and after 1 second, it was presented again in its destination square for 2 seconds. The same procedure was followed for each move. The participants had to reconstruct the current position at moves 15 and 25 seconds. This was the control condition; in an experimental condition the presentation of the moves was the same, except that a black dot was presented instead of the actual moving piece. The players were able to know which piece was moving because of their knowledge of the original position in chess games (e.g., if a black dot was presented in the square b1, players knew that the moving piece was a knight because in the original position there is a knight in that square). The most important result was that there were no differences in performance between the black dot condition and the control condition. This provides some support to the anecdotal evidence provided by Binet (1893/1966) that players do not represent the physical characteristics of the pieces. In another study, the control condition was the same. In the experimental condition, the presentation was the same as the control condition, but the players had to assume that the chess board was cut into halves and the right half was transposed into the left half. Performance dramatically decreased in the transposed board condition. This result also gives support to the existence of location-specific chunks stored in LTM. That is, both the configuration of pawns in the squares f2-g3-h2 and that of the pawns in squares b2-c3-d2 are stored in LTM, even when those configurations are identical when the location of the board is not taken into account (see Gobet & Simon, 1998, and Holding, 1992 for a discussion on location specificity of chunks).

Campitelli and Gobet (2005) were interested in whether players use an actual chess board to guide their imagery of movement of pieces. This issue is not only important to understand the nature of imagery in chess, but also has broader theoretical implications. Proponents of the *extended cognition approach* (e.g., Clark & Chalmers, 1998) propose that cognitive processes do not occur only in the brain, but they are extended in the environment. A quintessential example is widespread use of mobile phones to communicate, memorize, and make calculations. Following Saariluoma's approach of interfering with the imagery of moving pieces, the authors developed a different type of interference. Instead of the participants being asked to perform a secondary task, the interference occurred in the location where the information of the moving piece had to be picked up. In their first experiment, the games were presented as in Saariluoma and Kalakoski's (1997) first experiment; hence, the control condition was almost identical. There were two interference conditions: In one of them, instead of moves presented on an empty chess board, the board contained the 32 pieces located in their original positions, but these pieces remained in the board for the whole trial. In the other interference condition, the initial position was presented in the middle of the board (i.e., instead of the white pieces being located in the first two rows and the black pieces in the last two rows, the former were located in the third and fourth rows and the latter in the fifth and sixth rows). Because of the overlap between the moving piece and the interference pieces, the moving piece was surrounded by a green circle in all the conditions. The results showed no differences between conditions.

Campitelli and Gobet (2005) hypothesized that players either did not need to use the chess board to help them hold the current position of the game, or the players used the external chess board but were able to filter the irrelevant information. In order to tease apart those alternatives, Campitelli and Gobet designed a similar experiment. The control condition was identical, and in both interference conditions the initial position of a chess game was used in its original location. In both interference conditions, the pieces of the interference position changed, instead of being static. The researchers use this manipulation based on one of the mechanisms of the computational implementation of the template theory—CHREST. In this model, the attention focus changes location due to novelty or change. Campitelli and Gobet hypothesized therefore that the movement of the interfering pieces was likely to interfere with the imagery process. The difference between the interference conditions was that in one of them there was one move per move of the target game, and in the other condition there was a change on the interfering position every five moves of the target game. The results showed that the performance was better in the control condition than in both interference conditions. The results provide some evidence in favor of the second alternative, but it may be that the interference occurred when players were trying to look at the moving piece, not when they were mentally holding its new location.

Campitelli, Gobet, Williams, and Parker (2007) used a different methodology to disentangle these possibilities. Unlike in Campitelli and Gobet's experiments, in which the information of the moving pieces was presented in the chess board, in this experiment the information of the moving pieces was presented in a grid under the chess board, using chess notation. The chessboard presented a middlegame position of a tournament game, which remained static for the whole trial. Participants had to mentally "make" the moves presented in the grid to follow a chess game that continued from the presented position in the chess board. At several times, the participants were prompted to indicate which piece was located in a square shown in a blue box beside the chess board (i.e., the name of a square, say "e4," was presented in that box). Eye-movements between the chess board and the grid were recorded. On average, there was approximately one eye shift from the grid to the chessboard and back for every move presented in the grid. In suggesting that players use the chessboard (i.e., part of the environment) to aid their imagination of chess moves, this result supports extended cognition approaches.

Transfer and Individual Differences

The previous sections, among other issues, illustrated the richness of the game of chess in terms of underlying cognitive processes. Moreover, the examined studies have shown how chess players are capable of feats that are mindboggling for the general population (e.g., simultaneous blindfold chess). Based on this, researchers have been interested in two issues. First, given that practicing chess is cognitively demanding, does practicing chess improve performance in cognitive disciplines not related to chess (e.g., academic performance, particularly mathematics)? This topic is called *transfer*. Second, again given the cognitive demands of competitive chess, do those who have higher cognitive abilities perform better at chess than those with lower cognitive abilities? This is the topic of *individual differences*.

Transfer

The issue of transfer from chess to other disciplines is of particular interest to chess coaches and educators, especially those advocating the importance of compulsory chess classes at schools. Gobet and Campitelli (2006) conducted a critical review of transfer studies available at that time and found that none of the studies claiming transfer was properly conducted. They provided methodological suggestions on how to conduct appropriate studies, and, while their study was not well received in the chess environment, it inspired new research, with better designs which found effects of chess training on cognitive abilities and mathematics (e.g., Aciego, Garcia, & Betancort, 2012).

Sala and Gobet (2016) conducted a meta-analysis of studies of transfer from chess to cognitive abilities, mathematics, and reading abilities. They included 24 studies conducted from 1976 to 2015. They found an overall effect size $g = .338$, with duration of training and publication status as moderators. The effect size for studies with 25 hours or more of training was $g = .427$ and that of those with less than 25 hours of training was $g = .303$. Published studies had a higher effect size ($g = .540$) than that of unpublished studies ($g = .230$). The overall effect size for studies of transfer from chess to cognitive abilities was $g = .330$, to mathematics $g = .382$, and to reading ability $g = .248$. Although these results look promising most of the effects are not in the "zone of desired effects" (Hattie, 2009), which is $g > .4$.

Individual Differences

As indicated in this chapter's section on the development of chess expertise, deliberate practice is, at this time, the most important factor for the acquisition of chess expertise, but it is not the only factor. Hambrick *et al.*'s (2014) review estimated that deliberate practice accounts for only 34 percent of the variance of chess skill. Therefore, researchers were interested in finding other factors. In this section we focus on cognitive abilities. Campitelli and Gobet (2011) reviewed the evidence on the relationship between chess skill and cognitive abilities. They indicated that in all the studies with children there was a positive relationship between chess skill and cognitive abilities. Moreover, these studies found that children who practiced chess scored higher in cognitive abilities than the general population. On the other hand, studies with adult chess players showed mixed results: Most studies found no relationship between cognitive abilities and chess skill, with the most recent study—Grabner, Stern and Neubauer (2007)—finding a positive relationship. Likewise, some studies found no differences in cognitive abilities between chess players and the general population, and others (Grabner et al., 2007, and Doll & Mayr, 1987) found differences in favor of chess players. Based on these results they proposed three hypotheses. First, individuals with higher cognitive abilities are more attracted to chess than those with lower cognitive abilities. Second, differences in cognitive abilities among children are related to differences in chess performance. Third, at more advanced levels differences in cognitive abilities are less important and differences in amount of deliberate practice become more important.

Burgoyne et al. (2016) conducted a more comprehensive meta-analysis of studies relating chess skill to cognitive abilities in which they classified cognitive abilities following the Cattell-Horn-Carroll model of intelligence (see McGrew, 2009) as an organizing framework. They found an average correlation of .24 for fluid intelligence, .15 for comprehension-knowledge, .25 for short-term memory and .24 for speed of processing. In fluid intelligence, the correlation was higher in low skill level samples ($r = .32$) than in high skill samples ($r = .14$), and higher in youth samples ($r = .32$) than in adult samples ($r = .11$). These results provide evidence in favor of Campitelli and Gobet's (2011) second and third hypotheses.

Regarding the first hypothesis, Sala, Burgoyne, Macnamara, Hambrick, Campitelli and Gobet (in press) conducted a meta-analysis of studies comparing cognitive abilities in chess players with that of non-chess players. They found an average effect size of Cohen's $d = .44$, which is compatible with the first hypothesis.

A New Model of Chess Expertise

Campitelli, Gobet, and Bilalić (2014) presented the Practice, Plasticity, and Processes (PPP) mathematical model of the development of chess expertise. This model was developed with the aim of accounting for a number of phenomena uncovered in research into chess expertise:

1. Existence of remarkable achievements of young chess players (see the examples of Magnus Carlsen and Sergey Karjakin at the beginning of this chapter);

2. Correlation between hours of practice and chess skill (Hambrick *et al.*, 2014, found an average correlation of .49 in a meta-analysis);

3. Existence of a critical or sensitive period (Gobet & Campitelli, 2007, found a negative correlation between the age at starting to play chess and current chess rating after controlling for the number of hours of practice; moreover, they found that children who started playing at the age of 12 or earlier had a much greater chance of becoming a master than those who started after that age);

4. Correlation between chess skill and cognitive abilities is stronger in children than in adults (see this chapter, Individual Differences);

5. Decline in chess skill in older adults (Charness *et al.*, 2005, showed that players reached peak performance at about the age of 35, where a decline begins, with the rating at age 65 being similar to that at age 20).

As shown in Figure 3.1, the Practice, Plasticity, Processes (PPP) model includes 12 variables, which belong to 6 levels of explanation: (1) The variable chess rating belongs to the performance level; (2) chess skill is a domain-specific trait; (3) practicing and playing chess are domain-specific behaviors; (4) pattern recognition and heuristics are domain-specific processes; (5) motivation and intelligence are general traits; and (6) neural plasticity and two forgetting functions, *ploss* and *hloss,* are brain processes. In the PPP model, chess rating (which is based on results of chess tournaments) is a function of chess skill. Following the template theory, chess skill is a function of the number of useful chess chunks

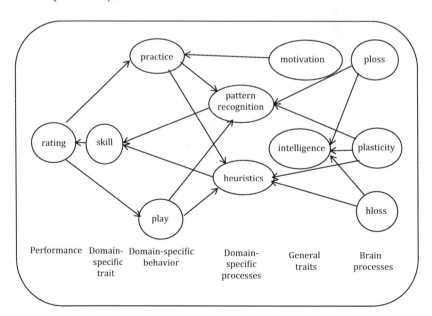

FIGURE 3.1 The Practice, Plasticity, Processes (PPP) model.

and templates that allow efficient pattern recognition, and as suggested by the SEARCH model (Gobet, 1997), of the number of useful heuristics. Chess rating influences the amount of practice and playing. That is, players who increase their rating are more likely to play and practice more. Both practice (as suggested by Ericsson *et al.*, 1993) and playing (as suggested by Gobet & Campitelli, 2007) increase the number of chunks, templates, and heuristics. Regarding the general traits, individual differences in motivation level affect the number of hours of practice; however, intelligence does not directly influence chess skill.

The amount of learning of chunks, templates, and heuristics per hour of practice and playing chess is influenced by individual differences in brain plasticity and forgetting rates (i.e., ploss and hloss). Moreover, individual differences in brain plasticity and forgetting rates influence intelligence. This assumption follows Garlick's (2002) model of intelligence, in which individual differences in intelligence are the consequence of individual differences in brain plasticity and in environmental stimulation. The implication of this assumption is that the correlation between chess rating and intelligence (or cognitive abilities) observed in the literature is due to the fact that brain plasticity and forgetting rates affect both the acquisition of cognitive abilities and the acquisition of chess skill.

Note that the incorporation of forgetting rates was necessary in the model because of the following: The model assumes that neural plasticity is high at early ages and reduces dramatically until the age of 12, and after this age it remains low (this assumption follows Gobet and Campitelli's (2007) finding of a sensitive period until the age of 12). The problem of this explanation is that a 2-year-old would learn chess chunks, templates, and heuristics at a higher rate than an adult, and, in reality, children of that age cannot learn chess. Therefore, two forgetting functions were added to the model. The forgetting rate is higher at early ages and reduces over time, to remain stable in adulthood, and then it increases again in older adults.

Campitelli *et al.* (2014) ran a mathematical simulation to determine the feasibility of the model against the five criteria mentioned above. The mathematical simulation had 10,000 chess players with an age range from 6 to 45. It simulated these players' participation in chess tournaments for 30 years, with a group of 250 6-year-old children entering the sample every year. Therefore, at the end of the simulation there were 17,250 chess players differing in their brain plasticity, forgetting rates, and motivation. This, in turn, influenced the number of hours of practice and the number of chunks, templates and heuristics the players learned per hour, and consequently, their chess skill. At the end of each year the mathematical simulation assigned values for all the variables to all the chess players. Thus, at each simulated year it was possible to run analyses and test how well the model fit the five phenomena explained above. The PPP model was compared to two other models. One was the implementation of Ericsson *et al.*'s (1993) deliberate practice framework, in which the only variable influencing acquisition of chunks, templates, and heuristics was the amount of practice.

The other model is inspired in Howard's (2005) emphasis on the role of individual differences in intelligence on the acquisition of chess skill. In this model, intelligence not only influenced the acquisition of chunks, templates, and heuristics, but also influenced the acquisition of chess skill directly.

The results of the simulation showed that PPP captured very well four of the five phenomena, whereas the other models captured fewer phenomena. The criterion that PPP did not capture well was the stronger correlation between chess and cognitive abilities in children than in adults. One possible explanation for this is that the simulation did not include attrition. Although there are no data to support this, it may be the case that more intelligent people tend to give up playing chess because they are successful in other disciplines.

Conclusions and Future Directions

This chapter reviewed the topic of cognitive processes in chess showing that pattern recognition is an essential cognitive process for chess playing. Pattern recognition is not only useful for recognizing positions and generating possible moves in the current position, but it is also an integral part of the search process. Instead of moving pieces in the actual chess board, chess players simulate their movement in the mind's eye, and they recursively apply pattern recognition over the positions held in the mind's eye. Research into imagery in chess showed that chess players use the external board to guide their imagery process, and that when they imagine pieces moving on the board, the physical characteristics of the pieces are not present.

Research into the transfer of cognitive abilities from chess to other disciplines has improved in quality over time. Older studies were poorly conducted, and claims of transfer were unjustified. However, new research is showing small effects of transfer. It is to be hoped that future research will keep increasing in quality (e.g., using appropriate control groups and extended periods of practice) and be able to capture stronger effects. Previous research into individual differences in cognitive abilities provided mixed results. However, recent meta-analytic studies have shown that individual differences in cognitive ability account for up to 6 percent of the variance in chess rating.

The integrative approach developed by Campitelli *et al.* (2014) combines, in a mathematical model, research into cognitive processes in chess and research into the development of chess expertise. This model follows the healthy tradition in the field initiated by Simon, and continued by Gobet, of developing formal models to reduce vagueness in theories.

In terms of future directions, Campitelli (2015) proposed that the fact that experts overcome the limits of short-term memory capacity calls into question traditional models of the cognitive architecture. Unlike previous theories of expertise (e.g., template theory, Gobet & Simon, 1996; long-term working memory theory, Ericsson & Kintsch, 1995) which maintain the differentiation between STM and LTM, Campitelli proposed that the STM store should be eliminated.

In fact, the whole idea of the existence of stores should be abandoned for a model that incorporates multiple knowledge structures (e.g., templates, retrieval structures, schemata, scripts, chunks, slotted structure, etc.). This proposal is parsimonious because it eliminates structures; and it is capable of accounting for the same or higher number of phenomena than the traditional models. Campitelli's (2015) proposal targets memory phenomena, touching on the pattern recognition processes mentioned in this chapter. A challenge for this proposal would be extension of the explanation to search and imagery. At the moment, the best explanation of imagery and search involves the use of the mind's eye to perform movement of pieces. Campitelli's parsimonious approach would also likely remove the mind's eye structure from the cognitive architecture. Future theoretical work would determine whether this is possible or not.

Notes

1 The World Chess Federation (also known as FIDE, for its initials in French) awards outstanding chess players with three titles according to their tournament results. In descending order: International Grand Master (GM), International Master (IM), FIDE Master (FM).
2 The FIDE ranking orders chess players (248,859 players in the July 2016 ranking) according to their chess rating, which is calculated based on official tournament games using the Elo (1978) system. The highest ever rating was 2,882 points. Roughly, players with 2,500+ are GMs, 2,400+ IMs, 2,300+ FMs, 2,200+ national masters, 2,000+ candidate masters (sometimes confusingly called "experts" in the literature), 1,800+ club class A players, 1,600+ club class B players, 1,400+ club class C players, and below 800 points are considered beginners. Note that all the players with more than 2,000 points are considered expert chess players.
3 Blindfold chess is a modality of playing chess in which at least one of the participants plays without looking at the board. The player indicates to his/her opponent the move he/she intends to play using chess notation (e.g., Bishop to f4) and the opponent replies in the same way. In simultaneous blindfold chess one player plays against multiple opponents without looking at the board. The current record is 46 simultaneous blindfold games played by German master Marc Lang in 2011.

References

Aciego, R., Garcia, L., & Betancort, M. (2012). The benefits of chess for the intellectual and socio-emotional enrichment in schoolchildren. *Spanish Journal of Psychology, 15*, 551–559.
Bilalić, M., Langner, R., Erb, M., & Grodd, W. (2010). Mechanisms and neural basis of object and pattern recognition: A study with chess experts. *Journal of Experimental Psychology: General, 139*(4), 728.
Bilalić, M., Langner, R., Ulrich, R., & Grodd, W. (2011). Many faces of expertise: Fusiform face area in chess experts and novices. *The Journal of Neuroscience, 31*(28), 10206–10214.
Bilalić, M., McLeod, P., & Gobet, F. (2007). Does chess need intelligence?—A study with young chess players. *Intelligence, 35*, 457–470.
Bilalić, M., McLeod, P., & Gobet, F. (2008). Why good thoughts block better ones: The mechanism of the pernicious Einstellung (set) effect. *Cognition, 108*, 652–661.

Bilalić, M., Turella, L., Campitelli, G., Erb, M., & Grodd, W. (2012). Expertise modulates the neural basis of context dependent recognition of objects and their relations. *Human Brain Mapping, 33*, 2728–2740.

Binet, A. (1893/1966). Mnemonic virtuosity: A study of chess players. *Genetic Psychology Monographs, 74*, 127–164. (Original work published in 1893 in French)

Burgoyne, A. P., Sala, G., Gobet, F., Macnamara, B. N., Campitelli, G., & Hambrick, D. Z. (2016). The relationship between cognitive ability and chess skill: A comprehensive meta-analysis. *Intelligence, 59*, 72–83.

Campitelli, G. (2015). Memory behavior requires knowledge structures, not memory stores. *Frontiers in Psychology, 6*, 1696.

Campitelli, G., & Gobet, F. (2004). Adaptive expert decision making: Skilled chess players search more and deeper. *International Computer Games Association Journal, 27*, 209–216.

Campitelli, G., & Gobet, F. (2005). The mind's eye in blindfold chess. *European Journal of Cognitive Psychology, 17*, 23–45.

Campitelli, G., & Gobet, F. (2008). The role of practice in chess: A longitudinal study. *Learning and Individual Differences, 18*, 446–458.

Campitelli, G., & Gobet, F. (2011). Deliberate practice: Necessary but not sufficient. *Current Directions in Psychological Science, 20*, 280–285.

Campitelli, G., Gobet, F., & Bilalić, M. (2014). Cognitive processes and development of chess genius: An integrative approach. In D. K. Simonton (Ed.), *The Wiley Handbook of Genius* (pp. 350–374). Chichester, UK: John Wiley & Sons.

Campitelli, G., Gobet, F., Head, K., Buckley, M., & Parker, A. (2007). Brain localisation of memory chunks in chessplayers. *International Journal of Neuroscience, 117*, 1641–1659.

Campitelli, G., Gobet, F. & Parker, A. (2005). Structure and stimulus familiarity: An fMRI study of memory in chess players. *Spanish Journal of Psychology, 8*, 238–245.

Campitelli, G., Gobet, F., Williams, G., & Parker, A. (2007). Integration of perceptual input and visual imagery in chess players: Evidence from eye movements. *Swiss Journal of Psychology, 66*, 201–213.

Charness, N., Tuffiash, M., Krampe, R., Reingold, E., & Vasyukova, E. (2005). The role of deliberate practice in chess expertise. *Applied Cognitive Psychology, 19*, 151–165.

Chase, W. G., & Simon, H. A. (1973a). Perception in chess. *Cognitive Psychology, 4*, 55–81.

Chase, W. G., & Simon, H. A. (1973b). The mind's eye in chess. In W. G. Chase (Ed.), *Visual information processing*. New York: Academic Press.

Clark, A., & Chalmers, D. (1998). The extended mind. *Analysis, 58*, 7–19.

Connors, M., Burns, B., & Campitelli, G. (2011). Expertise in complex decision making: The role of search in chess 70 years after de Groot. *Cognitive Science, 35*, 1567–1579.

de Groot, A. D. (1946/1978). *Thought and choice in chess*. The Hague: Mouton. (Original work published in 1946 in Dutch).

Doll, J., & Mayr, U. (1987). Intelligenz und Schachleistung – eine Untersuchung an Schachexperten. *Psychologische Beiträge, 29*, 270–289.

Elo, A. (1978). *The rating of chess players, past and present*. New York, NY: Arco.

Ericsson, K. A., & Kintsch, W. (1995). Long-term working memory. *Psychological Review, 102*, 211–245.

Ericsson, K. A., Krampe, R. T., & Tesch-Römer, C. (1993). The role of deliberate practice in the acquisition of expert performance. *Psychological Review, 100*, 363–406.

Fine, R. (1965). The psychology of blindfold chess: An introspective account. *Acta Psychologica, 24*, 352–370.

Garlick, D. (2002). Understanding the nature of the general factor of intelligence: The role of individual differences in neural plasticity as an explanatory mechanism. *Psychological Review, 109*, 116–136.

Gobet, F. (1997). A pattern-recognition theory of search in expert problem solving. *Thinking and Reasoning, 3*, 291–313.

Gobet, F. (1998). Chess players' thinking revisited. *Swiss Journal of Psychology, 57*, 18–32.

Gobet, F., & Campitelli, G. (2006). Educational benefits of chess instruction: A critical review. In T. Redman (Ed.), *Chess and education: Selected essays from the Koltanowski conference* (pp. 124–143). Dallas, TX: Chess Program at the University of Texas at Dallas.

Gobet, F., & Campitelli, G. (2007). The role of domain-specific practice, handedness and starting age in chess. *Developmental Psychology, 43*, 159–172.

Gobet, F., Campitelli, G., & Waters, A. J. (2002). Rise of human intelligence. Comments on Howard (1999). *Intelligence, 30*, 303–311.

Gobet, F., & Chassy, P. (2008). Season of birth and chess expertise. *Journal of Biosocial Science, 40*, 313–316.

Gobet, F., Lane, P. C., Croker, S., Cheng, P. C., Jones, G., Oliver, I., & Pine, J. M. (2001). Chunking mechanisms in human learning. *Trends in Cognitive Sciences, 5*, 236–243.

Gobet, F., & Simon, H. A. (1996). Templates in chess memory: A mechanism for recalling several boards. *Cognitive Psychology, 31*, 1–40.

Gobet, F., & Simon, H. A. (1998). Pattern recognition makes search possible: Comments on Holding (1992). *Psychological Research, 61*, 204–208.

Grabner, R. H., Stern, E., & Neubauer, A. C. (2007). Individual differences in chess expertise: A psychometric investigation. *Acta Psychologica, 124*, 398–420.

Hambrick, D. Z., Oswald, F. L., Altmann, E. M., Meinz, E. J., Gobet, F., & Campitelli, G. (2014). Deliberate practice: Is that all it takes to become an expert? *Intelligence, 45*, 34–45.

Hattie, J. (2009). *Visible learning: A synthesis of over 800 meta-analyses relating to achievement.* New York: Routledge.

Holding, D. H. (1992). Theories of chess skill. *Psychological Research, 54*, 10–16.

Howard, R. W. (2005). Objective evidence of rising population ability: A detailed examination of longitudinal chess data. *Personality and Individual Differences, 38*, 347–363.

McGrew, K. S. (2009). CHC theory and the human cognitive abilities project: Standing on the shoulders of the giants of psychometric intelligence research. *Intelligence, 37*, 1–10.

Saariluoma, P. (1991). Aspects of skilled imagery in blindfold chess. *Acta Psychologica, 77*, 65–89.

Saariluoma, P., & Kalakoski, V. (1997). Skilled imagery and long-term working memory. *American Journal of Psychology, 110*, 177–201.

Sala, G., & Gobet, F. (2016). Do the benefits of chess instruction transfer to academic and cognitive skills? A meta-analysis. *Educational Research Review, 18*, 46–57.

Sala, G., Burgoyne, A. P., Macnamara, B. N., Hambrick, D. Z., Campitelli, G., & Gobet, F. (in press). Checkmate to the "academic selection" argument: Chess players outperform non-chess players in cognitive skills related to intelligence: A meta-analysis. *Intelligence*.

van Harreveld, F., Wagenmakers, E.-J., & van der Maas, H. L. J. (2007). The effects of time pressure on chess skill: An investigation into fast and slow processes underlying expert performance. *Psychological Research, 71*, 591–597.

4

AN INVESTIGATION OF PROBLEM-SOLVING EXPERTISE

James J. Staszewski

Introduction

Exceptional performance on an undeniably difficult task—the seemingly magical doing of what most people can't do and sometimes believe can't be done—rivets attention, provokes wonder, and inflames curiosity. For the scientists, it begs for explanation. So it goes with high levels of human expertise.

This chapter reports findings from an investigation of the capabilities of an expert problem solver who not only solves different randomly generated instantiations of the notoriously difficult Rubik's Cube puzzle with invariant success, but also does so with striking speed and surprising flexibility. This inquiry starts by describing this expert's performance, followed by the results of efforts to identify the cognitive structures and processes that produce the performance, and findings from explorations of the flexibility of his skill. This inquiry closes by relating the findings to theoretical mechanisms prior research has identified as pillars of exceptional performance, particularly tenets of Skilled Memory Theory (Chase and Ericsson, 1982; Ericsson & Staszewski, 1989), as well as problem-solving expertise (Anzai & Simon, 1979; Chi, Feltovich, & Glaser, 1981; Larkin, McDermott, Simon, & Simon, 1980) and flexibility issues related to automaticity and transfer (Kimball & Holyoak, 2000; Lewandowsky & Thomas, 2009).

The Problem: Rubik's Cube

In its standard, original form Rubik's Cube (See Color Plate 1) consists of a cube composed of 26 subcubes, referred to as cubies, arranged in a 3x3x3 matrix. In its un-permuted state, which is the problem's goal state, the nine cubie faces on each of the cube's six sides are the same color: white, red, blue, orange, green, and yellow. For the version used in this study, white is opposite blue, yellow is opposite green, and orange is opposite red, and the blue, red, white, and orange are arranged clockwise in that order. On each face are three types of cubies. *Center cubies* have a single colored face; *edge* cubies have two colors, and corner cubies have three. A few random rotations to the puzzle's outside faces and/or its vertical and horizontal middle slices quickly scrambles the cube into a mosaic.

Figure 4.1 shows the structure-transforming operations the cube permits. The solver's task is to restore the cube to its original state. The problem can take 43 quintillion (4.3252×10^{19}) states, contributing to its difficulty; learning and retaining specific sequences of operators is obviously an intractable solution strategy, assuming that the solver can find solutions.

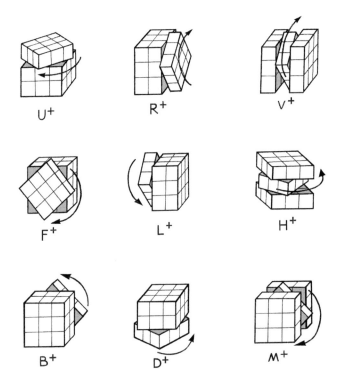

FIGURE 4.1 Primitive structure–transforming operations shown with the notation (Singmaster, 1980) that represents each operation symbolically. Each letter identifies the slice manipulated from the solver's viewing perspective. The superscript + signifies 90° clockwise rotation of a "slice" of cubies, as shown here. Figures 4.2 and 4.3, Table 4.1, and Color Plate 4 include this symbol, along with superscript − signifying 90° counter clockwise rotation, and 2 signifying a 180° rotation of the slice in question. The expert's solution paths on individual trials can be described by sequences of these symbols interspersed with symbols for structure-preserving reorientations of the cube (see lower portion of Figure 4.5).

Background and Motivation

Still interesting the general public since its invention in 1974 and commercial distribution in the early 1980s, the puzzle has served as a vehicle for inquiry by computer scientists (Korf, 1985, 1997; Kunkle & Cooperman, 2007, 2008) and mathematicians (Larsen, 1985; Palmer, 2008; Turner & Gold, 1985). Group theorists in mathematics have sought to discover optimal solutions to the problem. This is because the cube's elements move in groups when structure-transforming operations are applied; operators applied to position a particular cubie also move the 7 or 8 other cubies in the slice being manipulated.

Computer science research has also pursued effective solution methods and optimization; however, early artificial intelligence (AI) research with the puzzle focused initially on the challenge it posed to the general theory of problem solving (GPS) proposed by Newell and Simon (1972). A consequence of the cube's group structure is that subgoals solved with primitive operators (face or slice rotations) are non-serializable (Banerji, 1983; Korf, 1982). In other words, once cubies have been placed in their proper locations (e.g., one face is completed) subsequent operations intended to advance the solution move the positions of cubies in the solved portion of the puzzle, frustrating incremental step-by-step progress. This undermined the generality of subgoaling and means-ends analysis—core heuristics of GPS—using primitive operators. Cube solutions required application of sequences of primitive operators whose execution temporarily displaced previously solved portions of the puzzle, but upon completion restored the previously solved portions and produced further progress. The construct of integrated or chunked sequences are called macro-operators, or macros for short (Banerji, 1983; Korf, 1982, 1985). Korf (1982)'s computer simulation showed that macros could solve the problem and, moreover, further work showed that macros could be learned (Korf, 1985). These results, at least within the context of AI, resolved the theoretical challenge to GPS and expanded its generality. This body of work served to guide analysis of this expert problem solver's performance, begging "what," "where," "when," and "how" questions about macros and their application. See Color Plates 2 and 3.

Theoretical guidance came from two additional sources. First, the influential investigations by Chi, Feltovich, and Glaser (1981) and Larkin *et al.* (1980) of expert–novice differences in physics problem-solving directed investigation to search for abstract pattern recognition processes that triggered actions and hierarchical knowledge structures. With hopes for theoretical integration in mind, this largely exploratory investigation examined the generality of the physics expertise research.

The body of work investigating Skilled Memory (Chase & Ericsson, 1981, 1982; Ericsson & Polson, 1988; Ericsson & Staszewski, 1989; Richman, Staszewski, & Simon, 1995; Staszewski, 1988; Wenger & Payne, 1995) also contributed mechanisms for which to search prospectively. Skilled Memory Theory

(SMT) postulated that experts in task domains that imposed high working memory demands (digit-span, immediate chessboard retention, table waiting, and mental calculation) develop and use memory mechanisms that effectively expand their working memory capacity. The resulting increased information processing efficiency (relative to novices) supports experts' superior performance. Two mechanisms that work in concert to support experts' skilled memory according to SMT are (a) meaningful chunks of information and (b) retrieval structures; that is, stable hierarchical knowledge structures used to encode, store, and retrieve sequential information. Whether one or both of these mechanisms supported extraordinary performance of the expert at hand was a question prospectively guiding this investigation of problem-solving expertise.

Expert Performance

The expert of interest in this chapter, referred to as AP, was an undergraduate at Carnegie Mellon University whom the author encountered when teaching a cognitive psychology survey course. AP's claim of Rubik's Cube proficiency prompted an informal demonstration of his skill that quickly led to systematic study of his capabilities and thought processes. Like many others in the early 1980s, he discovered Rubik's Cube and learned how to solve it initially from published instructions. He reported refining his knowledge of the puzzle and improving his performance through practice and discovery of new solution procedures via his own experimentation.

In a series of trials administered in testing sessions dispersed over several months, AP was presented with cubes permuted by applying sequences of twelve randomly selected (with replacement) primitive operations. Instructions directed him to solve these problems as quickly as possible. His manipulations of the cube were videotaped for analysis of his solution processes. See examples at scienceofexpertise.com/ch4_soe_videos.

AP succeeded in solving the cube in 100 percent of the 83 trials he received. His mean solution time was 42.4 seconds (SD = 12.8). The mean number of structure-deforming operations per trial was 70.1 (SD = 21.6). When these data were collected in the late 1980s, individuals with mean solution times in the 3–5 minute range were rated Rubik's Cube experts; those with times below 3 minutes were considered masters. Hofstadter (1985) reported only two individuals with mean solution times faster than AP. Differences in testing procedures between those used here and in contemporary Rubik's competitions confound direct comparison of current solution times, but AP's fastest recorded time of 3.2 seconds beats the fastest recorded single trial time (4.90 seconds). His mean solution time is, however, well above the fastest contemporary average time (Mean = 6.54, SD = 0.45, N = 5). Although no clear performance standard defines expertise in this domain, AP's invariant success and a mean of 606 milliseconds per solution operation suggest extraordinary proficiency.

Process Analysis

Analysis began with documenting AP's solution processes step-by-step and describing regularities found in the resulting solution sequences. The speed of his manipulations combined with the portions of the cube being obscured from camera view by his hands made even frame-by-frame video analysis challenging. This analysis yielded a corpus of 42 confirmed exhaustive and replicable solution sequences. (A single error in recording these sequences renders a trial protocol unreplicable.) Fortunately, the other 41 solution sequences were largely complete and revealed the same patterns observed in the exhaustive (i.e., complete) sequences.

Three striking regularities emerged from detailed comparison of solution paths. First, focusing on the states of the cube, on 79 of the 83 trials AP received, his solutions followed the same general set of milestones. Initial operations would position and orient single cubies of the blue face[1] of the cube (functional completion involved his leaving one blue edge cubie out of position and/or orientation, as this location served as a workspace whose occupant cubies were displaced by each sequence of moves later used to position and orient the white face's edge cubies). He then reoriented the cube to show the white face and procedures would position the corner cubies of the white face (relative to one another) first. The next sequence of operators properly oriented the white corner cubies. The sequences used to achieve these two intermediate states moved multiple white corner cubies to the desired positions or orientations simultaneously. The next sequence of operations iteratively positioned and oriented each of any out-of-place white edge cubies. Completion of this stage also positioned and oriented the edge cubie on the blue face that was left out of place. The final major phase of the solution strategy manipulated the edge cubies of the middle slice which remained either out of position (relative to the other three remaining middle slide edge cubies), out of proper orientation (if they were in the right position), or both. Most often, like white face corners, AP consistently first positioned the middle slice edges and then oriented them—unless he recognized a particular arrangement (i.e., local subpatterns of the middle slice cubies) that could be positioned and oriented by a single sequence of operations to solve the problem. Having completed this stage, which now left the elements of the blue face, white face, and middle slices all in proper position and orientation relative to each other, all that remained was to align the intact slices of the cube to return the puzzle to its starting state, thus completing the solution process. The structure of this general solution strategy is illustrated in Figure 4.2. The stability with which most of AP's solutions show the same sequence of problem states leads to inferring that his solutions were mediated by a durable memory representation that functioned as his goal structure.

The solutions for four trials that did not conform to this scheme differed in distinct ways. First, they stood out for the speed with which they were solved, 3.2, 5.2, 6.7 (Example 1 at scienceofexpertise.com/ch4_soe_videos),

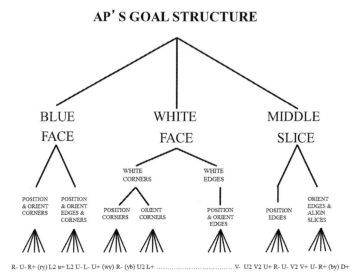

FIGURE 4.2   Goal structure inferred from 95% of the solutions the expert produced
on trials testing solution speed. Note the ordering of subgoals for the
blue face solutions is highly variable and assumed to be opportunistic.
Elsewhere, the ordering of subgoals is invariant. This structure was
inferred from the regularities in the sequence of problem states
produced from solution paths of 79 of 83 speeded test trials.

and 15.3 seconds and the paucity of operations (Mean = 4.75, SD = 1.5).
Second, they occurred on trials in which the initial state of the cube was considerably less scrambled than the other 79; multiple pairs and triplets of cubies
from the solved configuration remained clumped together. Close examination
of the random perturbation sequences used to generate starting states showed
that for these four trials multiple perturbing moves were reversed or functionally "canceled" by subsequent operations with unusually high frequency. AP's
solution behavior also differed qualitatively on these trials. He took noticeably
more time (although not much—obviously, with a three-second solution) to
examine the starting states before initiating any moves than he did on "regular"
trials. Individual solution operations were interleaved with pauses resembling
those found at the junctures of his typical algorithmic solution strategy. This
behavior contrasts sharply with the fluent, ballistic execution of moves in his
macros. In response to post-trial questioning about these striking solutions,
AP reported that he was "just trying to figure out how to reverse the scrambling" as opposed to executing his usual solution strategy. In theoretical terms,
his solutions for these outlying trials more closely resembled problem solving

using a working-backwards strategy, than application of a largely automatized skill, with search preceding solution operations. After observing the extreme strategic consistency that AP's speeded trial solutions showed, the flexibility he demonstrated on the four outlying trials was striking.

Macros

A search for identical sequences of operations, i.e., macros, within the corpus of confirmed solution protocols on which AP used his standard strategy confirmed his use of macros. Initial macro operations moved the positions of previously "solved" cubies, thus temporarily reversing the progress that had been achieved by previous operations, making the cube more scrambled that it just had been. Completion of macros, however, restored the positions of the moved cubies and added one or more cubies to their appropriate final positions. Plates 2 and 3 illustrate these sequences of initial disruption followed by restoration with progress for two macros found in the expert's solutions.

Examination of these sequences yielded several findings. First, the identical sequences that appeared across trials were segregated within the units of the goal structure described above. That is, specific sequences were used only to achieve ends delimited by his goal structure. Second, two categories of macros were used. An example of each is shown in Plate 4. One operated on only one cubie at a time. These functioned to position and orient either blue face cubies or white edge cubies. The other type of macro either positioned or oriented multiple cubies as a group. Third, sequence lengths varied from 2 to 13 primitive operations. Although the two kinds of macros overlapped in length, those that manipulated single cubies tended to be shorter than their counterparts. The longer, more efficient macros were used to either restore white corners as a group to their proper locations or complete solutions by moving a group of edge cubies on the middle slice. Fourth, the content of most macros showed redundancies consistent with internal hierarchical organization. Figure 4.3 illustrates this feature. Fifth, AP's operator library contained different goal-specific sequences of differing lengths that were functionally equivalent. Finally, the speed and fluency with which AP's executed macro gave them a ballistic character: their performance was a blur of continuous movement, absent any distinct pauses until their completion. In general, the compatibility of these observations with Korf's (1985) characterization of macro-operators and Anzai & Simon's (1979) identification of operator chunks in skilled problem-solving invited interpreting macros as chunks, more specifically, *procedural* chunks.

How did AP choose which of several macros to apply to achieve a specific goal on a specific trial? Close examination of the problem states to which AP's actions were selectively applied showed a recurring set of cube patterns, consistent with the construct of *perceptual* chunks often identified in expertise studies.

Macro-operator for positioning White Corners

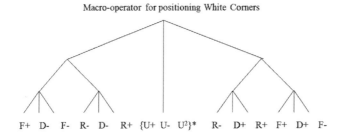

F+ D-   F- R- D-   R+ {U+ U- U²}*   R-   D+ R+ F+ D+ F-

Macro-operator for orienting Middle Slide Edge Cubes

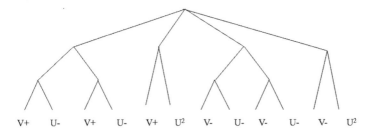

V+   U-   V+   U-   V+   U²   V-   U-   V-   U-   V-   U²

*Conditional selection of one operator

FIGURE 4.3 Hierarchical organization of multi-cubie macro-operators derived from redundancies within repeatedly appearing sequences that solve subgoals.

Perceptual Chunks

Along with the trials used to assess performance and investigate process, several sessions concluded with additional trials in which AP solved the cube under instructions to provide concurrent verbal protocols (CVPs). Given the speed with which he executed macros, there was skepticism about the utility of collecting such data. The skepticism proved *somewhat* justified; the verbal reports were extraordinarily sparse. They also greatly slowed solutions and often disrupted his normally fluent execution of macros. Nonetheless, their content, particularly some initially cryptic references that were later found to be labels for familiar local cube patterns, led to a detailed inspection of the local cube states that preceded execution of particular macros. This revealed that a small set of abstract patterns appeared on local portions of the cube, which became AP's focus of attention after prior subgoals had been achieved (e.g., the positions of the four corners relative to one another on the white face, after completion of the blue face; positions of edge cubies in the middle slice relative to one another, following completion of the white face). The local character of these patterns is illustrated in examples shown in Plate 5.

The patterns were abstract in that the common elements defining the patterns were the relations of particular cubie faces (color) on local selected types of cubies (corner or edge) on particular cube slices. Plate 6 shows several instantiations of the pattern AP referred to with the label "knight" in his verbal reports.

Rule-like consistency was found between patterns found on goal-related local portions of the cube and the execution of particular longer multi-cubie macros. Certain patterns preceded execution of certain macros, suggesting that the patterns served as triggers for macro selection and execution. In instances in which more than one macro might produce the same outcome, the shortest one was usually chosen.

Process Integration and Validation through Computational Modeling

The process analysis of AP's speeded solutions suggested that considerable order and relative simplicity were hidden under the apparent complexity of Rubik's Cube. AP seems to have managed this complexity by consistently, but not invariably, employing three mechanisms, inferred from the regularities described above: an abstract multi-level goal structure, macros that he learned to solve subproblems that arose within his dominant solution scheme, and selective perception and recognition of abstract local patterns of cubies—perceptual chunks—that guided his macro selections.

Computer simulation was employed to investigate assumptions about the functional integration of these mechanisms and their sufficiency to produce performance like the expert's. Consistent with the present effort's interest in theoretical integration, the cognitive architecture SOAR IV (Laird, 1986; Laird, Newell, & Rosenbloom, 1987) was selected as a medium for simulation. Several of SOAR's core features, especially its production system architecture and its recursive sub-goaling that produced hierarchically organized, discreet subproblem spaces, seemed particularly compatible with hypotheses about core mechanisms of AP's skill and their relations. The conceptual model included pattern-triggered macro selection and execution, global control of behavior mediated by the hierarchical goal structure shown in Figure 4.2, and the relative segregation of macro execution within subunits of AP's solution paths defined by his goal structure. RUBIK was the name given to this model instantiated using the SOAR architecture.

In brief, the goal structure shown in Figure 4.2 served as the control structure for the simulation, essentially ordering where and when perceptual evaluations of the problem states and macros were applied. Goal status changed with each goal satisfaction in the order determined by depth-first search of the goal structure. The condition portions of the program's productions incorporated the current goal and the states of a limited portion of the cube (which constituted the focus of attention). Recognition of goal-specific perceptual patterns cued retrieval and execution of particular macros. For example, if the goal is to position

TABLE 4.1 White corner orienting production set

If the goal is to orient white corners
If 2 cubies out-of-orientation

if one in FRU

if CC twist needed ➔ F+D–F–R–D–R+ {U+, U–, U²}* R–D+R+F+D+F+

else C twist needed ➔ R–D+R+R+D+F– {U+, U–, U²}* F+D–F–R–D–R+

if one in FUL

if CC twist needed ➔ L+D–L–F–D–F+ {U+, U–, U²}* F–D+F+L+D+L–

else C twist needed ➔ F–D+F+L+D+L–{U+, U–, U²}* L+D–L–F–D–F+

If 3 cubies out-of-orientation

if CC twist needed ➔ U+R² U–R–U+R–U–

else C twist needed ➔ U–L² U+L+U–L+U+

If 4 cubies out-of-orientation

if "Knight" ➔ L+U+F+U–F–U+F+U–F–L–

if "H" ➔ U– L²U+L+U–L–U+L+U–L+U+

*Selection among these options

---

white corners and three cubies are out of position and need a clockwise rotation to orient them, then execute macro L+ [L+ U– R– U+ L– U– R+] (see Table 4.1). Alternatively, if the goal is to position middle slice edges and all four edges are 180° out of correct position then execute H2 V– H2 V–.

A core assumption of the RUBIK model is that macros are triggered, indexed, and selected, by the recognition of abstract perceptual chunks found on limited portions of a cube. It is further assumed that macros are represented and executed as unitary chunks, as an uninterrupted, continuous chain of actions versus just a collection of elements executed as a sequence of primitive operators. Such macro integrity implies that problem state evaluations are not interleaved between execution of the constituent individual primitive operators that compose macros. Only after macro execution does another round of perceptual assessment of the problem state occur. This perceptual sampling of conditions occurs only at junctures of the goal structure.

Interestingly, the structure of the cube substantially constrained the number of abstract trigger states that could occur and the number of macros they triggered—once the blue face was completed. As noted earlier, however, no consistent pattern in the order of operations with which AP solved the blue face could be found, although he showed a slight tendency to finish positioning and orienting corners before edges. Therefore, a corners-first heuristic guided programming used to complete the blue face. Details of implementation of the RUBIK model can be found in Soewito (1990).

Program testing involved presentation of two sets of trials to RUBIK. One set of 27 trials used the same starting configurations as those presented to AP in the speeded trials whose solution paths were verified. This allowed a move-by-move comparison of the model's solutions with the expert's. Another test set presented 79 randomly generated starting configurations assuming that the larger sample size would more precisely reveal solution structure.

Results showed that RUBIK could solve all of the configurations with which it was presented. To what extent did its solutions resemble the expert's? Figure 4.4 shows the distributions of moves per solution produced by AP on 27 (then) verified solution problems, the program's performance on the same problems, and the program's performance on additional new problems. With the exception of the 4 trials on which AP did not use his typical solution strategy, a reasonable correspondence is observed, although RUBIK's performance on the 27 trials in the first test set shows less correspondence to AP's than the larger test sample. Operator-by-operator within trial comparisons showed that RUBIK's solution path quickly deviated from AP's in achieving the first major subgoal, completing the blue face. This early deviation stems from the unpredictability of AP's operator selections in this phase of his solution process and its effects in permuting other elements of the cube to produce quite different problem states only a move or two into solutions.

A finer-grained analysis used the same measure to evaluate RUBIK and compared the distributions of moves related to satisfaction of major subgoals. Beyond the initial subgoal, where AP's distributions suggest slightly greater efficiency than the simulation can achieve (although AP's move selections achieve that efficiency generally, the secondary mode at the high end of his blue face distribution suggests that his decision-making carries some costly risks), reasonable correspondences can be seen in Figure 4.5. Obviously, the expert's performance on the four outlier solutions recounted above and so glaringly evident in Figure 4.4 show that RUBIK falls well short of a comprehensive characterization of AP's skill. However, the correspondence between AP's and RUBIK's solution profiles on later portions of the solutions process suggests that RUBIK'S components and their functional organization reflect significant elements of AP's knowledge base. Thus, the model provides a reasonable, if somewhat incomplete, explanation of his extraordinary skill.

An Experimental Investigation of the Expert's Macro-Operators

Korf's (1985) early characterization of macro-operators and Anzai and Simon's (1979) identification of operator chunks in skilled problem-solving motivated the interpretation of AP's macros as chunks. Doing so, however, requires distinguishing the elements of chunks from just a collection of elements, or in this case, from a sequence of primitive operators. While the processing economy that chunking individual elements confers is well-established, Johnson (1970) pointed out how integration of elements into chunks also carries a cost; chunks, like suitcases, require unpacking processes to access the entities stored within

Solution Lengths: AP's vs RUBIK'S

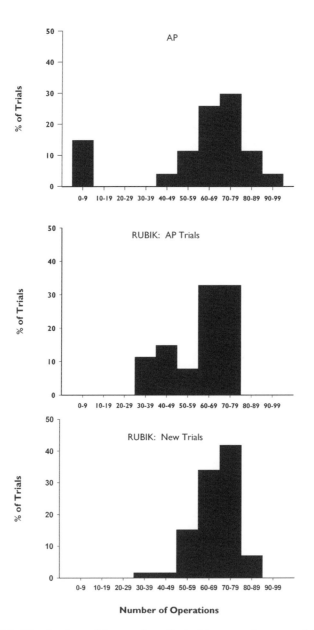

FIGURE 4.4 Distributions of the number of primitive operations per solution produced by the expert (top plot), by RUBIK on the same trials that the expert received (middle plot), and by RUBIK on a larger sample of trials not presented to the expert (bottom plot).

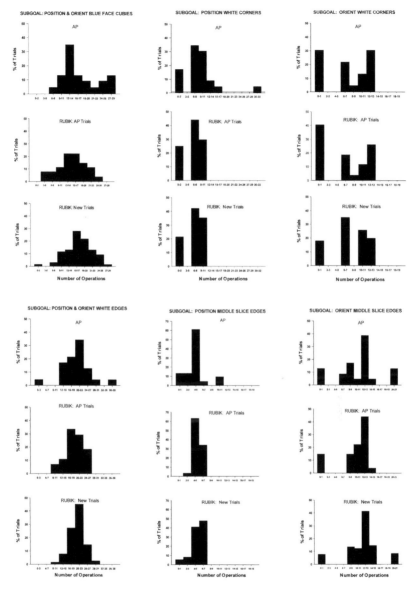

FIGURE 4.5 Distributions of the number of primitive operations used to solve specific subgoals achieved in solutions generated by the expert and the computer simulation. For each of six subgoals, the distributions produced by the expert AP (labeled AP for each subgoal), by RUBIK on the same trials that the expert received (labeled "RUBIK: AP Trials"), and by RUBIK on a larger sample of trials not presented to the expert ("RUBIK: New Trials") are shown. Note: This figure is also available online at https://osf.io/94h3f/

them. Using limited access as a means to distinguish between macros represented as chunks versus fixed associative sequences of primitive operators, the following experiment was conducted to explore the expert's representation of macros.

A core assumption of the RUBIK model is that macros are triggered, indexed, and selected, by the recognition of abstract perceptual chunks found on limited portions of a cube. After macro execution another round of perceptual assessment of the problem state occurs. However, perceptual sampling of conditions occurs only at junctures of the goal structure. It is further assumed that macros are represented and executed as unitary chunks, and state evaluations are not interleaved between execution of the primitive operators that compose macros.

To test this characterization of macros as procedural chunks, 72 experimental trials were created. For each, a randomly permuted starting configuration was solved—partially—by the experimenter. Using the understanding of AP's skill that the process analysis and the simulation results produced, each trial was

AP'S GOAL STRUCTURE

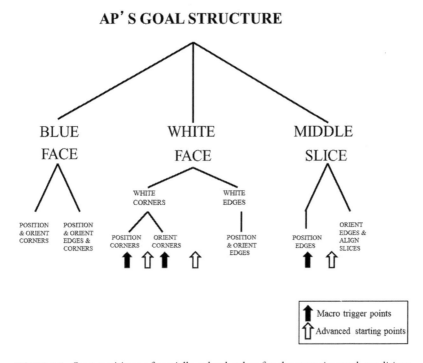

FIGURE 4.6 Start positions of partially solved cubes for the experimental conditions used to investigate the representation of the expert's macros. Solid arrows indicate the points at which cubes are solved to either (a) the junctures in AP's goal structure where trigger patterns that conditionally activate specific macros appear or (b) at more advanced locations in a predicted solution sequence, halfway into the macros predicted for execution by most recently achieved trigger patterns.

advanced from its scrambled starting configuration up to one of six systematically selected points along each solution path. The resulting cube configurations served as the starting states given to AP on each trial. Figure 4.6 shows the locations relative to AP's goals structure that were used as starting states.

The starting states were produced by a design that crossed two factors. One manipulation was the degree of completion. The least solved cubes in the trigger state condition had their blue faces completed, thus presenting the perceptual patterns whose recognition should trigger macros for positioning white corners. Another set of trials completed white corner positioning, thus presenting the patterns that should trigger white corner orienting macros. The third set completed the white face, leaving configurations that should trigger macros for positioning middle slice edges. If assumptions about AP's indexing of condition-action rules and macro representation as chunks are correct, the problem states for these "*trigger state*" trials should be easily recognized, and AP's solution activities should start quickly and proceed fluently.

A yoked set of *advanced* trials was created. Their starting states were generated by solving cubes to the three levels of completion described above and then *advancing the solution* by executing the primitive operations of the first half of the macro whose application RUBIK predicted. So, according to the theoretical model, the problem states in the advanced condition were closer to problem completion than the trials presenting the cube in the corresponding "trigger state" condition. If macro execution was triggered by familiar patterns which appeared at goal structure junctures, as the RUBIK model assumes, and macros were integrated such that problem states on advanced trials would not be recognized and solution operation would not simply continue from the advanced state, the advanced trials should be disruptive and require time-consuming evaluation of the problem state before solutions operations are initiated. This predicted slower completion times in the advanced condition despite the problem being further along the path toward the solution. Recall that macro applications temporarily move cubies from their previously solved positions and notice how the problem states in the middle of macro execution in Plates 2 and 3 have fewer cubies in their solved positions than the trigger states seen prior to macro initiation.

The trigger state condition also represented a test of RUBIK's assumptions about how AP's goal structure guided his solution processes. If the order of procedures predicted by the goal structure was correct, solution times for partially solved cubes should descend monotonically in inverse relation to the degree to which the puzzle had been pre-solved on each trial.

Experimental instructions informed AP that upcoming trials would present partially solved cubes and that his task was to solve each as quickly as possible. Order of trial presentation was randomized. Starting configurations were hidden until a start signal was issued. Trials were videotaped with timestamps for extraction of solution times and later review.

AP solved all trials successfully. His mean solution times are shown in Figure 4.7. Consistent with predictions of facile access at goal state junctures and access limitations during macro execution, times in the advanced condition were consistently slower than those for trials presenting trigger states. Qualitatively, review of the advanced trials invariably showed the expert applying operators that restored the cube to a previous trigger state before proceeding with his solutions predictably, in effect, backtracking and distancing himself from the solution state. These results are consistent with interpretation of macros represented as chunks indexed by goal states and familiar perceptual patterns and executed with impressive fluency.

As Figure 4.7 also shows, mean solutions times for the trigger-state/start point conditions showed the descending monotonic function predicted by RUBIK's control structure, adding credibility to the theoretical account the model represents.

Solution Times for Partially-Solved Cubes

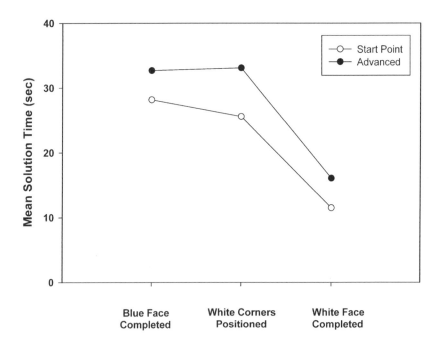

FIGURE 4.7 The expert's solution times for partially solved cubes as a function of advancement to either goal structure junctures or ahead halfway into the macros predicted to be executed at the same junctures by the trigger patterns that occur at these junctures.

Exploring Expert Flexibility

The speed and procedural fluency AP showed on 95 percent of his solutions, and especially in his execution of macros, the consistency of his solution paths, his seemingly seamless selection of macros, the disruption of these features of his behavior observed on trials for which concurrent verbal reports were requested, and experimental results suggesting limited penetrability of his macros, all suggest considerable amounts of information processing in an automatic mode (Lewandowsky & Thomas, 2009). These observations make the flexibility revealed by his deviation from his predominant solution strategy on the remaining 5 percent of trials all the more striking. These anomalous trials motivated the following exploratory efforts.

Consistent with mathematicians' and computer scientists' interest in solution optimization, a series of trials were presented to the expert with instructions to solve the cube with the minimum number of operations. Sixty-four such efficiency trials were administered with starting states generated by a dozen randomly chosen primitives.

AP's solution accuracy was 100 percent (see an efficiency trial example at scienceofexpertise.com/ch4_soe_videos). Solutions took a mean of 55.4 operations (SD = 16.4), a 21 percent reduction over solution lengths observed for trials that prioritized speed. Although this falls well short of the mathematically established optimal solution length of 12 operations, it is worth noting that finding this optimum took mathematicians several decades. The improvement and flexibility this expert showed on what is a new task for him is noteworthy and theoretically interesting, considering the inflexibility implied by phenomena associated with expertise such as domain specificity and automaticity.

The efficiency that AP achieved came at a price, however. His mean solution time increased to 188.8 sec (SD = 118.0), more than four times as long as his speeded performance on average. Qualitatively, the most obvious difference in AP's behavior on efficiency trials was the presence of long periods of inactivity punctuated by his application of macros. Otherwise, his solutions invariably followed his standard goal structure's milestones and the macros were used predictably although some were trimmed at beginnings, the ends, or both. In post-trial reports AP stated that he spent the inactive periods searching for the next move by visualizing the cube and the effects of the moves he would normally apply, looking for sequences of three or four moves containing operations that canceled each other out, and then eliminating those moves from his solution. He said he found most of these at the junctures of his solutions process corresponding to where his goals shifted. Such look-ahead search has been implicated elsewhere in the problem solving of elite chess experts (Gobet & Simon, 1996b).

Materials were also manipulated in two tests intended to explore the flexibility of the expert's skill. Two variants of Rubik's Cube were presented to AP with instructions to solve them as quickly as possible. The first was a 2×2×2 version, which he reported never having seen before. On the first trial he stared at the permuted cube briefly before solving the problem in 24.4 seconds (see science ofexpertise.com/ch4_soe_videos). In his post-trial report, AP stated that he recognized the configuration as one that appears on the corners of the cube's top surface when solving for the white corners on the 3×3×3 versions. He reported wondering if his macros for solving white corners would produce a solution and then successfully testing this hypothesis. On 35 subsequent trials, he was 100 percent successful, and his mean solution time was 19.3 seconds (SD = 9.6).

In another test session, AP was presented with a permuted 5×5×5 variant of the cube, which he reported he had heard of but had never seen. He succeeded in solving it, albeit taking over 5 minutes. The majority of solution time was spent examining the cube with individual rotations of its various slices interleaved. Like his performance in efficiency trials with the 3×3×3, more of his solution time was devoted to thought—as opposed to executing operations—which was interpreted as engagement in search for the next move.

In general, AP shows strategic and procedural flexibility, which allows him to adaptively shift between the fast, fluent, and repetitive application of stored procedures characteristic of highly practiced skills and the more controlled, search-dependent, and slower mode of cognition typical of problem solving (Newell & Simon, 1972). The flexibility observed is consistent with the recent literature showing that with experts transfer, or near-transfer at least, is more prevalent (Kimball & Holyoak, 2000; Lewandowsky & Thomas, 2009) than characterizations of expertise that (over) emphasize automaticity, limitations, and rigidity would suggest (Gobet & Campitelli, 2006).

Theoretical Linkages

How does this investigation of extraordinarily skilled problem solving on an esoteric puzzle contribute to advancing general scientific understanding of human expertise? Its links to theory on problem solving and skilled memory provide the best answer.

Expert Problem Solving

Current understanding of expert problem solving has been heavily influenced by research focused on identifying the cognitive representations and processes that expert physicists use for problem solving in that domain (Chi, Feltovich, & Glaser, 1981; Larkin *et al.*, 1980). Among the features that characterize expertise in this domain is the possession of durable hierarchical organized knowledge structures (schemata, in Larkin *et al.*'s, terms) stored in LTM that support experts' solutions. AP's goal structure, perceptual chunks, and macros are consistent with this general form of representation found in domains beyond physics. The repeated reappearances of the same general solution sequence, the same local patterns observed on local portions of the cube, and the same operator sequences over trials separated by days and weeks are evidence for LTM storage. On the basis of data generated by other methods, Larkin *et al.* (1980) and Chi *et al.* (1981) also concluded that experts possess perceptual knowledge that supports facile recognition of abstract patterns which, in turn, enable them to quickly and reliably retrieve relevant knowledge in LTM regarding which actions should be taken to solve the problem at hand.

The contiguity of specific local perceptual patterns on the cube and specific macros observed in AP's speeded solutions and applied successfully in the RUBIK model is thus consistent with the mechanisms Larkin *et al.* (1980) and Chi *et al.* (1981) have identified. The ability of RUBIK to solve all problems it was given and do so in a manner that resembled *most* of AP's solutions is also consistent with Larkin *et al.*'s conclusions that experts typically work forward in problem solving using familiar patterns to select, retrieve, and apply effective actions. Moreover, Larkin *et al.* observe that although physics experts work forward on easy problems, using strong (knowledge-based) methods, they revert to weak methods when faced with harder problems. Here, the contrast in AP's solutions for speeded trials and efficiency trials—the former showing high procedural fluency, and the latter slower, search-punctuated solution processes—resembles the procedural shift and flexibility that Larkin *et al.* (1980) observed. The evidence that AP uses look-ahead search is also consistent with its role in expert problem solving in chess (Gobet & Simon, 1996b).

The interpretation of macros as chunks is consistent with Anzai & Simon's (1979) discovery of chunked operators used in solutions to the Tower of Hanoi problem. In addition, the goal structure derived from the majority of AP's solution on speed trials is consistent with the mechanism of a goal stack that Anzai and Simon inferred in the same work.

Rubik's Cube Expertise and Skilled Memory Theory

A specific aim of this investigation was to explore the generality of the tenets of Skilled Memory Theory (Chase & Ericsson, 1981, 1982; Ericsson & Chase, 1982; Ericsson & Polson, 1988; Ericsson & Staszewski, 1989; Staszewski, 1988, 1990, 1993; Wenger & Payne, 1995). AP's performance indicated that he was able to manage the gargantuan problem space, the complexities, and the memory demands of Rubik's Cube problems. A question raised by his remarkable performance is "Would the core mechanisms linked to skilled memory and used by experts to manage high memory loads in a variety of other memory-intensive tasks also support AP's performance?"

The theoretical framework of SMT links one of the most general principles of expertise—experts' superior retention of information in the domain of their expertise—to experts' superior performance. It proposes that as experts acquire the domain content and strategic knowledge that make them experts, they also acquire memory management skills. These skills enable them to use their knowledge efficiently by relaxing the constraints on engaging large amounts of knowledge that limited capacity short-term memory imposes on novices' information storage and processing. Thus, experts can exploit the huge storage capacity of LTM with the speed and reliability associated with STM storage and retrieval. Extended deliberate task practice, particularly on tasks that impose heavy memory loads, supports development of two distinct types of knowledge structures (schemata) identified with skilled memory: chunks and retrieval structures. Evidence supporting these theoretical constructs come from information processing analyses of experts in the domains of mnemonics (Chase & Ericsson, 1981, 1982; Ericsson, 1985; Ericsson & Chase, 1982; Staszewski, 1990, 1993; Wenger & Payne, 1985), mental calculation (Chase & Ericsson, 1982; Staszewski, 1988), restaurant service (waiting table) (Ericsson & Polson, 1988), and blindfold chess (Ericsson & Staszewski, 1989).

Chunks, of course, are theoretical memory mechanisms as old as the field of cognitive psychology (Miller, 1956) and supported by a plethora of evidence. Since Chase and Simon's (1973a, 1973b) seminal studies of chess expertise, investigations that focused on explaining expert performance in terms of the cognitive mechanisms that produce it have consistently found evidence for their mediation (Chase, 1986; Chase & Ericsson, 1982; Ericsson & Staszewski, 1989; Gobet, 2015; Gobet & Simon, 1996a; Gobet et al., 2001a & 2001b, Simon, 1979). Studies using the immediate memory paradigm to demonstrate experts' domain-specific memory superiority in comparison to less skilled individuals (i.e., the Skilled Memory Effect) provide a correlational link to expert task performance.

Information processing analyses of experts' superior task performance, like those mentioned above, infer the mediation of chunks more directly from experts' behavior. For example, studies of digit-span experts showed that they encoded 3- and 4-digit segments of lists presented to them using semantic knowledge base of running times, dates, and ages. A sequence like 3492 would be coded as a running time, 3 minutes, 49.2 seconds (Chase & Ericsson, 1981). Two undergraduates who became mental calculation experts through several years of laboratory practice at mental multiplication built knowledge bases that enabled them to quickly recognize and encode multi-digit subproblems embedded in larger problem operands and rapidly retrieve their products bypassing step-by-step computation (Staszewski, 1988). Such findings led to the following generalization about experts' skilled memory: "Experts use their knowledge structures in semantic memory to store information during skilled performance" (Chase and Ericsson, 1981, p. 159), elsewhere referred to as the "meaningful encoding principle" (Ericsson & Staszewski, 1989).

Two types of theoretical mechanisms identified in AP's performance are consistent with this principle of Skilled Memory. First, the local, reoccurring abstract perceptual patterns on the cube that precede the execution of multiple different macros in the expert's solutions and serve as triggers to their execution in the RUBIK simulation are interpreted as perceptual chunks. The regularity with which they occur and evoke the same responses across trials and days, intervals far beyond the limits of STM retention, is consistent with representation in long-term memory. To the extent that meaning is referential and can be properly characterized by associations among representations that create a single relational, functional whole, the patterns in question should qualify as meaningful. They relate perceptually available element-specific faces of individual cubies, including their relative locations and orientation, to one another and also to actions and subgoals as well as in some cases linguistic labels.

Second, it is reasonable to interpret the macros repeatedly abstracted from the solution protocols as output chunks. The repeated occurrence, across trials and days, of ordered sequences of primitive operations, many of which exceed not only estimates of working memory capacity but also Miller's magical number is evidence for LTM storage. In addition, experimental results investigating the accessibility of internal elements of macros are consistent with the characterization of at least a limited sample of macros as integrated representations whose primitive components could not be readily accessed (at least at mid-point). This latter property is significant for distinguishing between expert chunks and retrieval structures in the context of Skilled Memory Theory.

Whether or not the problem-solving expertise in focus involves retrieval structures is interesting for several reasons. First, retrieval structures have been ascribed considerable significance (Gobet, 2015; Ericsson & Kintsch, 1995; Ericsson & Staszewski, 1989; Simon, 1989; Gobet & Simon, 1996a) in theorizing on human expertise. Second, evidence for the generality of these structures is limited. Finally, a mostly "within-choir" controversy appears in the literature about their characteristics (Gobet, 2000a, 2000b; Ericsson & Kintsch, 2000).

Retrieval structures are durable knowledge structures, often hierarchically organized, that experts acquire and use to store information for rapid and reliable retrieval when it is needed for task performance. Their function is analogous to filing or addressing systems that index to-be-stored information according to a pre-determined abstract organizational scheme. Cues that make up the indices are stored with the to-be-remembered information and can be regenerated reliably via this structure to retrieve material addressed by those cues. As proposed originally, a retrieval structure "can preserve the order of items to be remembered, although it is more versatile than that because it allows direct retrieval of an identifiable location" (Chase and Ericsson, 1981, p. 169).

AP's goal structure, as implemented in RUBIK, fits this description of a retrieval structure in form and function. The appearance of the same general solution sequence across trials that span weeks shows durability consistent with LTM representation. The patterns of pauses, or the absence of these pauses, in structure-transforming solution operations, which include visual inspection and reorientations of the cube along with the effects of the macros applied, serve to derive the hierarchical organization shown in Figure 4.2. The speed of invariably successful solutions is consistent with rapid and reliable access to solution information. Pause durations of a couple of seconds or less to initiate macros (see speed trial samples at scienceofexpertise.com/ch4_soe_videos) are consistent with the interpretation of direct access. Providing an example of a retrieval structure, Chase and Ericsson (1981) wrote "Chiesi, Spilich, and Voss (1979) have found that baseball fans are better able to remember sequences of baseball events because they understand the game better, which is to say, they relate the events to the game's goal structure" (p. 175).

Finally, from the perspective of discriminant validity, the results of the partial-solution experiment suggest that primitive elements of macros are not directly accessible. This leads to interpretation of macros as chunks as opposed to retrieval structures in which elements are directly accessible. The observation that the perceptual chunks and the macros they trigger change from solution to solution is compatible with Gobet's (2000a, 2000b) definition of a "*generic retrieval structure* [which] clearly allow[s] both slotted schemata (with encoding of either chunks or individual pieces of information and other encoding mechanisms" (Gobet, 2000b, p. 592). This accommodates production-like behaviors and schemata ascribed to expert problem-solving in physics (Larkin *et al.*, 1980) and is compatible with theoretical construct of a goal stack related to skilled problem solving (Anzai & Simon, 1979).

Summary and Conclusion

This work, like some research in the fields of mathematics and computer science, used the Rubik's Cube puzzle as a vehicle for investigating fundamental theoretical issues. The goals of this work were to describe and understand the skill of an expert who established his expertise in a particular domain by solving, with extraordinary speed and perfect reliability, randomly generated instantiations of a problem he received. Analyses of move-by-move descriptions of his solutions identified regularities that included (1) integrated, function-specific sequences of primitive solution operations, (2) recurring perceptual patterns defined by abstract local configurations of cube elements, (3) a sequence of problem states that occurred in 95 percent speeded test trials, and (4) linkages of local patterns to specific operator sequences. Respectively, from these regularities, macro-operators, perceptual chunks, a goal structure, and production-like condition-action contingencies were inferred. Computer simulation was used to express how these mechanisms were organized to produce the expert's performance. Computer solutions to problems showed reasonable fidelity to the solutions of the expert, which suggests the sufficiency of the proposed theoretical model of his performance. An experiment investigating the representation of the expert's macro-operators produced results (a) suggesting a structural integrity consistent with their representation as chunks instead of as simple associative strings of primitive operators and (b) converging evidence for postulated goal structure and its interpretation as a retrieval structure. In short, this effort has stitched together a theoretical explanation of our expert's performance that identifies the cognitive structures and processes and their interrelation that produce it.

This theoretical account is, however, clearly an incomplete explanation of this expert's skill. It does not address the flexibility he exhibited in (a) abandoning his usual solution strategy to solve less-scrambled problem instances, (b) solving the cube for efficiency, i.e., minimizing the number of operations, and (c) successfully solving variants of the problem that were novel to him. The expert's behavior in these contexts shows more reliance on heuristic search, a hallmark of problem solving, than on the strong knowledge-based methods associated with fluent skilled problem-solving and captured in the explanation presented. The flexibility observed cautions against over-generalizing the phenomena of specificity and automaticity characteristic of many expert skills. It is hoped that future expertise research will invest in more detailed investigation of the flexibility and transfer of expert skills to reconcile contradictory observations and refine current understanding of experts' adaptability.

The main contribution of this work lies in its links to prior theorizing on expert problem solving and skilled memory. To a large extent, this analysis of the Rubik's Cube expertise has "rounded up the usual suspects" theoretically speaking, finding evidence for the contributions of the types of mechanisms identified in prior studies of experts in other domains. If there is a surprising element, it may be that the two core mechanisms of Skilled Memory Theory were identified, especially retrieval structures, in a domain quite different than the ones in which they were proposed previously. The tasks providing the evidentiary base for SMT are consistent in imposing extraordinarily high transient memory loads upon their expert subjects; in this context, no such loads are evident that require management. Absence of such memory-demands explains this investigator's skepticism that these mechanisms would play a role in supporting AP's extraordinary performance. Their discovery suggests the broader generality of these mechanisms and bridges an understanding of skilled problem solving and skilled memory (see also Gobet and Simon (1996b).

The convergence of this work with prior theory is encouraging for expertise science. Clearly, experts constitute a special and relatively small population. If their identification and recruitment for research is challenging—and limiting— their retention for the extended laboratory analysis necessary to draw sound inferences about their cognition compounds the difficulty of building a large and diverse body of scientific principles and theory. Nonetheless, a small number of theoretical mechanisms abstracted from the current literature on expertise account surprisingly well for this investigation's findings. This indicates a broad generality and explanatory power suggestive of a sound and extensible fundamental understanding of human expertise, one on which future investigations can build.

Acknowledgements

First and foremost, AP's enthusiastic and patient contributions made this project possible. The Spencer Foundation supported this work with award number 198800082 to the author. The dedicated and meticulous efforts of Rebecca Deuser, Freddy Soewito, and John Allen contributed critically to generating the results presented here. Diane Briars, Fernand Gobet, Zach Hambrick, and Bob Siegler provided valuable and deeply appreciated comments on an earlier draft of this chapter. Finally, the debt that this work owes to the late Herb Simon, Bill Chase, and Allan Newell is vast and treasured.

Note

1 Although Figure 4.2 shows corner cubies being positioned and oriented before edge cubies, solutions showed much ordinal variability and interleaving of placement of blue face corner and edges. The expert showed a slight bias toward positioning blue corners earlier rather than later, but it appears that opportunism trumped consistent order; after placement of a blue face cube, the presence of a blue-faced cubie on either of the two visible non-blue surfaces usually led to its selection for the next placement. Such opportunistic goal-operator selection would save the time involved in changing the orientation of the cube relative to the solver to permit search for a blue target on a previously hidden face.

References

Anzai, Y., & Simon, H. A. (1979). The theory of learning by doing. *Psychological Review*, *86*(2), 124–140. http://dx.doi.org/10.1037/0033-295X.86.2.124

Banerji, R. B. (1983). GPS and the psychology of the Rubik cubist: A study in reasoning about actions. In A. Elithorn & R. Banerji (Eds.), *Artificial and Human Intelligence*. Amsterdam: North Holland.

Chase, W.G. (1986). Visual information processing. In K.R. Boff, L. Kauffman, & J.P. Thomas (Eds.), *Handbook of perception and human performance, Volume 2 Cognitive processes and performance*. (pp. 28–71). New York: John Wiley & Sons.

Chase, W. G., & Simon, H. A. (1973a). Perception in chess. *Cognitive Psychology*, *4*, 55–81.

Chase, W. G., & Simon, H. A. (1973b). The mind's eye in chess. In W. G. Chase, and Simon, H. A. (Ed.), *Visual information processing* (pp. 215–281). New York: Academic Press.

Chase, W. G., & Ericsson, K. A. (1981). Skilled memory. In J. R. Anderson (Ed.), *Cognitive skills and their acquisition* (pp. 141–189). Hillsdale, NJ: Erlbaum Associates.

Chase, W. G., & Ericsson, K. A. (1982). Skill and working memory. In G. H. Bower (Ed.) *The psychology of learning and motivation*, vol. 16 (pp. 1–58). New York: Academic Press.

Chi, M. T. H., Feltovich, P. J., & Glaser, R. (1981). Categorization and representation of physics problems by experts and novices. *Cognitive Science*, *5*(2), 121–152. doi: 10.1207/s15516709cog0502_2

Chiesi, H. L., Spilich, G. J., & Voss, J. F. (1979). Acquisition of domain-related information in relation to high and low domain knowledge. *Journal of Verbal Learning and Verbal Behavior*, *18*, 257–273.

Ericsson, K. A. (1985). Memory skill. *Canadian Journal of Psychology*, *39*, 188. doi: 10.1037/h0080059

Ericsson, K.A., & Chase, W.G. (1982). Exceptional memory: Extraordinary feats of memory can be matched or surpassed by people with average memories that have been improved by training. *American Scientist*, *70*, 607–615.

Ericsson, K. A., & Kintsch, W. (1995). Long-term working memory. *Psychological Review*, *102*, 211–245. doi:10.1037/0033-295X.102.2.211

Ericsson, K. A., & Kintsch, W. (2000). Shortcomings of generic retrieval structures with slots of the type that Gobet (1993) proposed and modelled. *British Journal of Psychology*, *91*, 571–590.

Ericsson, K. A., & Polson, P. G. (1988). Memory for restaurant orders. In M. T. H. Chi, Glaser, R., & Farr, M. J. (Ed.), *The nature of expertise* (pp. 23–70). Hillsdale, NJ: Erlbaum.

Ericsson, K. A., & Staszewski, J. J. (1989). Skilled memory and expertise: Mechanisms of exceptional performance. In D. Klahr & K. Kotovsky (Eds.), *Complex information processing: The impact of Herbert A. Simon* (pp. 235–267). Hillsdale, NJ: Erlbaum Associates.

Gobet, F. (2000a). Some shortcomings of long-term working memory. *British Journal of Psychology*, *91*, 551–570.

Gobet, F. (2000b). Retrieval structures and schemata: A brief reply to Ericsson and Kintsch. *British Journal of Psychology*, *91*, 591–594.

Gobet, F. (2015). Understanding expertise: A multidisciplinary approach. Basingstoke, UK: Palgrave-MacMillan.

Gobet, F., Lane, P. C. R., Croker, S., Cheng, P. C. H., Jones, G., Oliver, I., & Pine, J. M. (2001a). Chunking mechanisms in human learning. *Trends in Cognitive Sciences*, *5*(6), 236–243.

Gobet, F., Lane, P.C.R., Croker, S., Cheng, P.C.H., Jones, G., Oliver, I., & Pine, J.M. (2001b). Chunking mechanisms in human learning. *Trends in Cognitive Sciences*, *5*, 236–243.

Gobet, F., & Campitelli, G. (2006). Educational benefits of chess instruction: A critical review. In T. Redman (Ed.), *Chess and education: Selected essays from the Koltanowski conference* (pp. 81–97). Dallas, TX: Chess Program at the University of Texas at Dallas.

Gobet, F., & Simon, H. A. (1996a). Templates in chess memory: A mechanism for recalling several boards. *Cognitive Psychology*, *31*, 1–40. doi: 10.1006/cogp.1996.0011

Gobet, F., & Simon, H. (1996b). The roles of recognition processes and look-ahead search in time-constrained expert problem solving: Evidence from grand-master-level chess. *Psychological Science*, *7*(1), 52–55. Retrieved from http://www.jstor.org/stable/40062907

Hofstadter, D. (1985). *Metamagical themas: Questing for the essence of mind and pattern.* New York: Basic Books.

Johnson, N. F. (1970). The role of chunking and organization in the process of recall. In G. H. Bower (Ed.), *The psychology of learning and motivation*, vol. 4 (pp. 171–247). New York: Academic Press.

Kimball, D. R., & Holyoak, K. J. (2000). Transfer and expertise. In E. Tulving & F. I. M. Craik (Eds.), *The Oxford handbook of memory* (pp. 109–122). New York: Oxford University Press.

Korf, R. E. (1982, August). A program that learns to solve Rubik's Cube. In *AAAI* (pp. 164–167).

Korf, R. E. (1985). Macro-operators: A weak method for learning. *Artificial Intelligence*, *26*, 35–77. doi: 10.1016/0004-3702(85)90012-8

Korf, R. E. (1997, July). Finding optimal solutions to Rubik's cube using pattern databases. In *AAAI/IAAI* (pp. 700-705).

Kunkle, D., & Cooperman, G. (2007, July). Twenty-six moves suffice for Rubik's Cube. In *Proceedings of the 2007 international symposium on Symbolic and algebraic computation* (pp. 235–242). ACM. doi: 10.1145/1277548.1277581

Kunkle, D., & Cooperman, G. (2008). Solving Rubik's Cube: Disk is the new RAM. Communications of the ACM, 51, 31-33. doi: 10.1145/1330311.1330319

Laird, J. E. (1986). Soar User's Manual (Technical Report ISL-15) Xersox Corporation, January 1986).

Laird, J. E., Newell, A., & Rosenbloom P. S. (1987) Soar: An architecture for general intelligence. *Artificial Intelligence, 33*, 1–64.

Larkin, J., McDermott, J., Simon, D. P., & Simon, H. A. (1980). Expert and novice performance in solving physics problems. *Science, 208*(4450), 1335–1342.

Larson, M. E. (1985). Rubik's revenge: The group theoretical solution. *The American Mathematical Monthly, 92*, 381–390.

Lewandowsky, S., & Thomas, J. L. (2009). Expertise: Acquisition, limitations, and control. *Reviews of Human Factors and Ergonomics, 5*(1), 140–165.

Miller, G. A. (1956). The magical number seven, plus or minus two: Some limits on our capacity for processing information. *Psychological Review, 63*, 81–97. doi: 10.1037/h0043158

Newell, A. N., & Simon, H. A. (1972). *Human problem solving.* Englewood Cliffs, NJ: Prentice-Hall.

Palmer, J. (2008). Cube routes. *New Scientist, 199*, 40-43.

Richman, H. B., Staszewski, J. J., & Simon, H. A. (1995). Simulation of expert memory using EPAM IV. *Psychological Review, 102*, 305–330. doi: 10.1037/0033-295X.102.2.305

Simon, H. A. (1979). Information processing models of cognition. *Annual Review of Psychology, 30*, 363–396. Doi: 10.1146/annurev.ps.30.020179.002051

Simon, H. A. (1989). Memory Structures. In H. A. Simon (Ed.) *Models of thought*, vol. 2. New Haven, CT: Yale University Press.

Singmaster, D. (1980). Notes on Rubik's "Magic Cube," 5th Edition. Hillsdale, NJ: Enslow Publishers.

Soewito, F. (1990). The role of macro operators in expert problem solving skill. (Masters Thesis). Thomas Cooper Library, University of South Carolina, Columbia, SC.

Staszewski, J. (1988). Skilled memory and expert mental calculation. In M. T. H. Chi, Glaser, R., and Farr, M. J. (Ed.), *The nature of expertise* (pp. 71–128). Hillsdale, NJ: Erlbaum Associates.

Staszewski, J. (1990). Exceptional memory: The influence of practice and knowledge on the development of elaborative encoding strategies. In W. Schneider & F. E. Weinert (Ed.), *Interactions among aptitudes, strategies, and knowledge in cognitive performance* (pp. 252–285). New York: Springer-Verlag.

Staszewski, J. J. (1993). A theory of skilled memory. In *Proceedings of the 15th Annual Conference of the Cognitive Science Society* (pp. 971-975). Mahwah, NJ: Erlbaum.

Turner, E. C., & Gold, K. F. (1985). Rubik's groups. *The American Mathematical Monthly, 92*, 617–629. doi: 10.2307/2323707

Wenger, M. J., & Payne, D. G. (1995). On the acquisition of mnemonic skill: Application of skilled memory theory. *Journal of Experimental Psychology: Applied, 1*, 194–215. doi: 10.1037/1076-898X.1.3.194

5

HOW IMPORTANT IS INTELLIGENCE IN THE DEVELOPMENT OF PROFESSIONAL EXPERTISE?

Combining Prospective and Retrospective Longitudinal Data Provides an Answer

Jonathan Wai and Harrison J. Kell

Introduction

This chapter combines multiple sources of prospective and retrospective longitudinal data to show that intelligence, even at the very highest levels, matters in the development of professional expertise. At the same time, aligning these types of data sources also shows that more than talent matters to reach the top of multiple U.S. elite professions, including federal judges, CEOs, politicians, business leaders, journalists, those with extreme wealth, and the most powerful people in the world. Additionally, the importance of intelligence varies across professions, even within the extreme right tail of achievement. The science on the development of expertise in the professions requires explanations accounting for multiple interlocking factors, including both talent and practice. The best path forward to advance science is likely cross-disciplinary perspectives and synthesis.

One can become an expert in many areas (Macnamara, Hambrick, & Oswald, 2014). One of these domains is expertise in the professions (Kuncel, Hezlett, & Ones, 2004; Wai, 2014b, 2014c). Many factors contribute to eventual professional expertise, including cognitive ability, education, interests, personality, and the willingness to work long hours (Lubinski, 2004; Simonton, 2009). A large body of research has demonstrated that there are wide individual differences in general intelligence (g) in the population (Jensen, 1998), g is highly heritable (Bouchard, 2004; Neisser *et al.*, 1996), and g is highly related to the acquisition of expertise in educational and occupational domains (Kuncel *et al.*, 2004; Schmidt & Hunter, 2004; Wai, 2013, 2014a).

Although general intelligence has been shown to be highly predictive of occupational outcomes in the general population (e.g., Schmidt & Hunter, 2004), there have been few studies looking at the high end of the intelligence distribution (for example, within the top 1%). Given that one third of the cognitive ability range exists within the top 1% of the distribution alone (Lubinski & Benbow, 2000), this rare right tail segment provides one way to test the idea that ability matters in the development of professional expertise even at the high end.

This chapter draws upon both prospective and retrospective longitudinal data to examine this issue. The first section reviews prospective data from the Study of Mathematically Precocious Youth (SMPY; Lubinski & Benbow, 2006) to examine the extent to which people in the top 1% in intelligence end up as professional experts later in life. The second section reviews retrospective data from numerous extreme right tail achievement occupations (Wai, 2013, 2014a; Wai & Rindermann, 2015; Wai & Lincoln, 2016), examining the extent to which these groups were in the top 1% in intelligence in their youth. All samples are from the United States. The idea that talent matters in the development of professional expertise throughout the full range would be supported by the extent to which the link between ability and expertise can be made using multiple independent sources of prospective and retrospective data.

Prospective Longitudinal Data

The prospective data reviewed in this section are drawn from the findings of SMPY, an ongoing longitudinal study of several cohorts of individuals distinguished by possessing high cognitive abilities. Created in 1971 by Julian C. Stanley (Campbell & Stanley, 1963; Stanley, 1971) at Johns Hopkins University, SMPY is currently codirected by Camilla P. Benbow and David Lubinski at Vanderbilt University (Lubinski & Benbow, 2006; Stanley, 1996). SMPY initially used talent searches to identify young adolescents who reasoned exceptionally well mathematically and sought better ways to facilitate these adolescents' educational development (Benbow & Stanley, 1983; Stanley, 1996); selection criteria were eventually broadened to include verbal abilities. Cognitive abilities/intelligence is measured mainly by the Scholastic Assessment Test (SAT), which has been shown to measure intelligence in young adults (Frey & Detterman, 2004), but may serve as an even stronger measure of reasoning abilities for younger students less familiar with its content (e.g., Benbow, 1988). As participants have grown into adults, SMPY's emphasis has shifted from educational development and outcomes (Achter, Lubinski, Benbow, & Eftekhari-Sanjani, 1999; Benbow, 1992) to occupational ones (Lubinski & Benbow, 2000; Shea, Lubinski, & Benbow, 2001; Wai, Lubinski, & Benbow, 2005; Webb, Lubinski, & Benbow, 2002). As its oldest participants have entered midlife, SMPY is studying their creativity, embodied in accomplishments such as patents and academic publications (Kell, Lubinski, & Benbow, 2013; Kell, Lubinski, Benbow, & Steiger, 2013; Lubinski, Benbow, & Kell, 2014; Park et al., 2007, 2008; Wai et al., 2005).

SMPY consists of five cohorts but the findings reviewed here originate from studies of the first three (Lubinski & Benbow, 2006). Cohort 1 comprises individuals identified when they were 12 or 13 years old (in 1972 to 1974) and who scored in the top 1% of cognitive ability. Cohort 2 consists of participants identified when they were 12 years old (in 1976 to 1979) and who scored in the top 0.5% of cognitive ability. Cohort 3 is composed of individuals scoring in the top 0.01% of cognitive ability who were identified when they were 12 years old (in 1980 to 1983). All three cohorts have been tracked longitudinally since their initial identification and surveyed with extensive questionnaires at multiple time points. Recent follow-ups have supplemented the information provided by participants with information drawn from Web searches conducted by project staff.

Members of Cohorts 1 and 2 have recently entered midlife ($N = 1,650$; mean age = 51.5 years) and their accomplishments are extremely impressive to date. (As this chapter concerns professional expertise, which is founded on specialized educational training, we focus on achievements closely tied to educational attainment; see Lubinski *et al.* (2014) for a complete account of the two cohorts' accomplishments, including those less contingent on advanced educational credentials.) Among the top 1%, 32% earned doctoral degrees, 10% had published at least one peer-reviewed article in a science, technology, engineering or mathematics (STEM) field,[1] 8% held at least one patent, 4% had earned tenure at a research-intensive university (Carnegie Foundation, 2010), 3% had at least one National Institutes of Health (NIH) grant, and 3% had at least one National Science Foundation (NSF) grant.

The magnitude of these achievements is noteworthy on its own but especially so when contrasted with the relevant base rates in the general population of the United States: 30% of individuals earn bachelor's degrees, while slightly less than 2% earn doctoral degrees (U.S. Census Bureau 2012a, 2012b). Similarly, the base rate for holding a patent in the United States is about 1% (U.S. Patent and Trademark Office, 2011). Given that earning tenure at a research-intensive university or holding an NIH or NSF grant is a major feat for which having a doctoral degree is merely a prerequisite, the base rates for these accomplishments are minuscule.

Despite the impressive accomplishments of Cohorts 1 and 2 (top 1% and top 0.5% of ability, respectively), they are exceeded by Cohort 3 (top 0.01%). Kell, Lubinski, and Benbow (2013) surveyed the achievements of 320 members of Cohort 3, the largest group of individuals of this ability level ever assembled for psychological study. (Due to the intrinsic rarity of people scoring in the top 1 in 10,000, previous investigations of the lives of the top 0.01% consisted almost exclusively of case studies; e.g., Garrison, Burke, & Hollingworth, 1917; Hollingworth, Garrison, & Burke, 1922.) Kell and colleagues (2013) found the following: 44% held doctoral degrees, 18% had a STEM publication, 15% held a patent, 8% had tenure at a research-intensive institution, 6% held an NSF grant, and 3% held an NIH grant.[2] In all the accomplishment categories reviewed, on average, people in the top 0.01% of cognitive ability outperformed people in the top 1% of cognitive ability. (These findings were no fluke, as they were replicated in a second sample of individuals from the Duke University Talent Identification Program (Duke TIP), which identifies talented students similar to those in the SMPY sample—in the top 0.01% by Makel, Kell, Lubinski, Putallaz, and Benbow (2016).) A final detail makes this feat even more staggering: Cohort 3 participants were followed up when their mean age was less than 40.[3] Not only did the magnitude of Cohort 3's achievements outpace those of Cohort 1 and 2, those achievements were attained about 10 years earlier in participants' respective careers.

Figure 5.1 summarizes the relationship between cognitive ability and the real-world achievements previously mentioned. An aspect of Figure 5.1 worth noting is that the findings for Cohorts 1 and 2 are disaggregated, allowing for direct comparison of the real-world accomplishments across the three ability levels: top 1%, 0.5%, and 0.01%. For all achievements, the top 0.5% outperformed the top 1%, despite the fact that those scoring in the top 0.5% were, on average, five years younger than those scoring in the top 1%. The top 0.01%

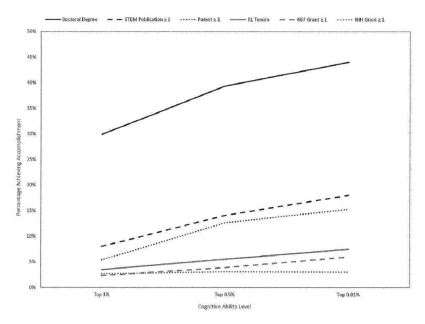

FIGURE 5.1 Percentage of individuals at three cognitive ability levels achieving six major life accomplishments. Cognitive ability levels were based on participants' scores on the SAT taken at age 12 or 13. These assessments were conducted prior to the SAT re-centering in 1995 and, at that time, cutting scores for the top 1 in 100 were SAT-M ≥ 390 or SAT-V ≥ 370, for the top 1 in 200 were SAT-M ≥ 500 or SAT-V ≥ 430, and for the top 1 in 10,000 were SAT-M ≥ 700 or SAT-V ≥ 630 (Lubinski & Benbow, 2006). Data for the top 1% and 0.5% are taken from Lubinski et al. (2014). Data for the top 0.01% are taken from Kell et al. (2013) and Makel et al. (2016).

outperformed the top 0.5% for all achievements despite being, on average, eight years younger. These results are in accordance with the linear association between ability and performance observed in the general population (Arneson, Sackett, & Beatty, 2011; Coward & Sackett, 1990). Thus, when it comes to ability, having more of it continues to make a difference even in the extreme right tail of the distribution.

Retrospective Longitudinal Data

Summary data (total $N = 11,745$) were taken from multiple publications (Wai, 2013, 2014a; Wai & Rindermann, 2015; Wai & Lincoln, 2016) and isolated to groups in the United States: Fortune 500 CEOs ($N = 500$), active federal judges ($N = 789$), World Economic Forum in Davos attendees ($N = 661$), Forbes billionaires ($N = 424$), Forbes most powerful men ($N=27$), Forbes most powerful women ($N=59$), Wealth-X 30-millionaires ($N=8,649$), U.S. Senators ($N=100$), U.S. House of Representative members ($N=441$), and The New Republic Masthead ($N=95$). Individuals invited to Davos are considered some of the world's most powerful business, political, academic, and other leaders of society. These men and women were identified based on their power and influence and included many political (e.g., U.S. presidents) and business leaders (e.g., CEOs). Wealth-X is a company that collects data on individuals with net worth of $30 million (U.S. currency) and higher and reviews hundreds of wealth identifiers from more than 1,100 intelligence sources to provide systematic information ranging from basic demographics to networks to philanthropic activity. The New Republic, an elite media outlet, was used because data were publicly and systematically available.

Utilizing retrospective longitudinal data, the importance of general intelligence in professional expertise development was assessed. Information on the college or university these individuals attended for undergraduate or graduate schools was used as a reasonable proxy for their general intelligence level (Murray, 2012), because standardized test scores on the SAT and ACT are largely required for admission and measure general intelligence to a large degree (Frey & Detterman, 2004; Koenig, Frey, & Detterman, 2008). The percentage attending an "Elite School" that had average standardized test scores on the combined SAT Math and Verbal subtests (or equivalent on the ACT) in the top 1% was examined, as well as the percentage independent of this top 1% that attended graduate school, college, or did not report or did not attend college. The impact of Harvard University alone was also examined to gauge the impact of arguably the most prestigious university. For more detail regarding the method, including a list of the colleges and universities that had average test scores in the top 1%, see the methods section, limitations section, and Table 1 of Wai (2013).

Figure 5.2 presents the percentage of each group who, according to high school standardized test scores, were in the top 1% of general ability.

"Harvard" indicates the percentage that attended Harvard for undergraduate or graduate school (likely well above the top 1% of ability). "Elite School" indicates the percentage that attended one of the schools independent of Harvard

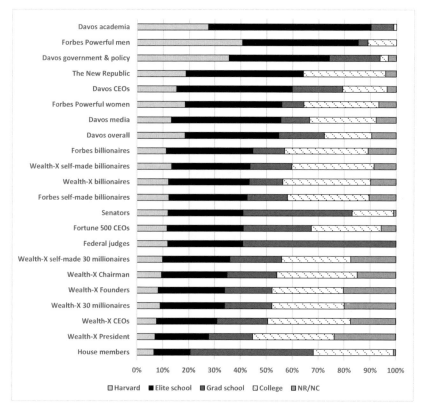

FIGURE 5.2 This figure presents the percentage of each elite U.S. occupational group who—according to high school standardized test scores—were in the top 1% of general ability. "Harvard" indicates the percentage that attended Harvard (likely well above the top 1% of ability). "Elite School" indicates the percentage that attended one of the schools with average test scores that placed them in the top 1% of ability. "Graduate School" indicates the percentage that attended graduate school independent of the Elite School category and represents a group likely in the top percentiles of ability. "College" indicates the percentage that attended college but not Graduate School or an Elite School. "NR/NC" indicates the percentage that did not report any education or had no college. These four categories are independent of one another and sum to 100%. Data were taken from multiple research papers and adapted for this figure (Wai, 2013, 2014a; Wai & Rindermann, 2015; Wai & Lincoln, 2016).

(undergraduate or graduate) with average test scores that placed them in the top 1% of ability. "Graduate School" indicates the percentage that attended graduate school independent of the Elite School category or Harvard and represents a group likely in the top percentiles of ability. "College" indicates the percentage that attended college but not Graduate School or an Elite School or Harvard. "NR/NC" indicates the remaining percentage that did not report any education or had no college. These four categories are independent of one another and sum to 100%.

Figure 5.2 shows that roughly half of the people in these positions of leadership and power were in the top 1% in ability (summing Harvard with Elite School). Harvard percentages ranged from 6.6% for U.S. House of Representatives members up through 40.7% of Forbes powerful men. Elite school percentages ranged from 20.6% for House members up through 90.1% for Davos academia. On average, 91.1% of people in these groups attended college or higher. This ranged from 76.2% for 30-millionaires who were presidents of the United States (Wealth-X President) up through 100% for Davos academia, federal judges, and Forbes powerful men.

Broadly, House members were at the bottom on brainpower and education, followed by 30-millionaire CEOs (Wealth-X CEOs), 30-millionaires overall, federal judges, Fortune 500 CEOs, senators, billionaires overall, Davos attendees overall, Davos media, Forbes powerful women, Davos CEOs, The New Republic, Forbes powerful men, and Davos academia at the top. Generally, less selective politicians, wealthy people, judges, and CEOs were in the bottom half, billionaires were in the middle, and people invited to Davos, selective journalists, selective government officials, powerful people (including heads of countries) and selective academics composed the top half of the elite occupational distribution.

Discussion

More Intelligence Matters, Even Among the Highly Select

The idea of an ability threshold hypothesis—that after a certain level more ability is no longer reliably associated with better criterion outcomes—is shown to be false by the data presented here.[4] Yet the ability threshold idea has made its way into academic and popular discourse. For example, Gladwell (2008, pp. 78–79) wrote: "The relationship between success and IQ works only up to a point. Once someone has an IQ of somewhere around 120, having additional IQ points doesn't seem to translate into any measurable real-world advantage." More recently, Ericsson & Pool (2016, pp. 234–235) wrote: "The average IQ of scientists is certainly higher than the average IQ of the general population, but among scientists there is no correlation between IQ and scientific productivity . . . among those who have become professional scientists, a higher IQ doesn't seem to offer an advantage." There is a concomitant increase of achievement with ability level within both nonrandom samples of the top 1% in general ability (SMPY: Ferriman-Robertson, Smeets, Lubinski, & Benbow, 2010; Duke TIP: Makel *et al.*, 2016), and random samples of the top 1% in general ability (Wai, 2014c). Even within highly select occupational groups, including Fortune 500 CEOs (Wai, 2013; Wai & Rindermann, 2015), billionaires (Wai, 2013), 30-millionaires (Wai & Lincoln, 2016), and senators (Wai, 2014d), higher general ability is associated with greater network power, income, and net worth. Taken together, all these sources of data robustly show that more ability matters throughout the full range.

The Importance of Intelligence Varies Widely Across Professions

Gottfredson (2003, Fig 15.1, p. 299) introduced the idea of an occupation also functioning as a general intelligence loaded mental test battery, and illustrated the wide range of cognitive ability across various occupations among the general population, ranging from a packer (21st percentile on general ability) and material handler (25th percentile) up to research analyst and attorney (91st percentile), and discussed how more socially desirable (and correspondingly prestigious) occupations recruit their workers from the upper end of the IQ distribution (Canter, 1956). Figure 5.2 illustrates that even within the extreme right tail of occupational achievement, there continues to be wide variability in the cognitive abilities of workers recruited into those occupations, with certain jobs likely placing a premium on such cognitive abilities more than others (e.g., the most powerful men and women compared to House members). For example, given that roughly half of the U.S. elite groups are at least in the top 1% in general ability, these groups are roughly centered around the 99th percentile in the general population on cognitive ability, but exhibit a wide range. This clearly shows that the importance of intelligence varies across professions, even within the extreme right tail of achievement.

Prospective and Retrospective Data Show More Talent Matters, and More than Talent Matters

When prospective and retrospective longitudinal data sources are combined as they are in Figures 5.1 and 5.2 of this chapter, we can see that talent clearly matters for occupational expertise. However, the data in Figure 5.2 serve as case controls for the prospective longitudinal data sources shown in Figure 5.1. Figure 5.2 shows that roughly 50% or more of U.S. people in highly select occupational groups are in the top 1% of cognitive ability, roughly at the cut of IQ 137 or higher. Data on students at the level of 0.01% in cognitive ability, roughly the cut of IQ 180 or higher, shows that by about age 40 many of them are in highly select occupational groups (see Kell *et al.*, 2013) but not quite at the level of the U.S. elite in Figure 5.2. Given the 0.01% group is so highly selected on ability and that the actual U.S. elite groups are not even all within the top 1% of ability, this illustrates that even though ability has a payoff throughout the range, much more than ability clearly matters to make it to the top of any elite occupation.

More Talent Matters: So Why the Belief in an Ability Threshold?

Despite this, why the belief in Gladwell's (2008) threshold hypothesis? We think it is a practically understandable, even intuitive belief: By definition, profound cognitive ability is rare, meaning it is encountered infrequently, if at all, in everyday life and then surely not with enough consistency for observers to reliably note differences between the top 0.01% and 1%, or even within the top 1% and 5%. This rarity also makes it difficult to empirically falsify the threshold effect, because, while large sample sizes are required to generate statistically stable findings, much research on expertise is on extremely small samples. Further, establishing a robust link between ability differences in the top 1% and differences in real-world accomplishment may need additional methods beyond merely large samples of the appropriate population.

The SMPY studies suggest that a threshold effect can be adequately tested with the following methods in place: (1) early identification of study participants, using tests that assess multiple abilities, not just global IQ, and that have very high ceilings; (2) longitudinally tracking participants over many decades, as it takes time for even the most able individuals to acquire the knowledge and skill needed to obtain advanced degrees and make creative contributions to the areas they have focused on; (3) choosing achievements that should be relatively rare to serve as criteria. For example, nearly all members of SMPY's Cohorts 1 through 3 earned bachelor's degrees. If this level of educational attainment were used as a criterion, there would have been no practical differences among the top 1%, top 0.5%, and top 0.01%; instead there would have been an appearance of a threshold effect. Not until doctoral degree attainment is examined do differences in the top 1% appear. However, even using retrospective longitudinal methods on highly select occupational samples shows that an ability threshold effect can also be detected (Wai, 2013; Wai, 2014d; Wai & Rindermann, 2015; Wai & Lincoln, 2016) and found to be false for a variety of outcomes including network power, income, and net worth. This suggests that the key to identifying an ability threshold effect may lie in examining such a threshold in large samples of people that have achieved rare real-world accomplishments with an early age ability indicator. Ultimately, when a threshold hypothesis for cognitive ability is posited, it is important to ask, "A threshold hypothesis *for what*?" The confirmation or falsification of that hypothesis will depend a great deal on how that question is answered.

Limitations

One limitation of this analysis may be that the way we have defined professional expertise here may not align with other definitions of what it means to be an expert (e.g., Ericsson, 2014). With acknowledgement that operational definitions can differ, we believe that our definition of an occupational expert is rare enough, quite difficult to achieve, and provides sufficient sample sizes to conduct appropriate analyses both prospectively and retrospectively (Wai, 2014c).

The prospective longitudinal synthesis may be limited in that it depends on data from nonrandom and highly select samples. However, even data on similarly select samples from a population level random sample (Wai, 2014c) has illustrated that educational outcomes are identical across both nonrandom (SMPY) and random samples (Project Talent, a nationally representative sample of U.S. high school students tracked through educational and occupational outcomes; Wise, McLaughlin, & Steel, 1979), suggesting that the findings within the nonrandom samples are likely robust when extending them to more select occupational and creative outcomes. In fact, Makel *et al.* (2016) showed replications across the SMPY sample and the Duke TIP sample, both highly select but independent nonrandom samples.

The retrospective longitudinal synthesis used average standardized test scores of a college or university according to *U.S. News & World Report* (America's Best Colleges, 2013) as an approximation for general intelligence level (Frey & Detterman, 2004; Koenig *et al.*, 2008). Although this method did not rely on individual test scores, which were not publicly available, average test scores from U.S. schools reasonably placed groups of individuals that attended one of these elite schools within the top 1% of ability. Ultimately, the method cannot disentangle education from cognitive ability. However, using this method may give an underestimate because extremely smart people may not have chosen to attend a top school for multiple reasons (e.g., financial limitations, scholarship availability, and proximity to home). Alternatively, this method may also give an overestimate because there were likely some legacies, athletic or affirmative action admits, students with political connections, or others who gained entry with lower than typical test score and academic metrics (Espenshade & Radford, 2009; Golden, 2006; Sander, 2004). It is reasonable to think factors in both directions likely counterbalance one another. The people in this study are also not fully representative of the many other individuals in the top percentiles of ability worldwide, and are likely defined by attributes not limited to ability (such as high motivation, willingness to work and engage in deliberate practice, take risks, and a desire for power, wealth, and status). Not being someone in one of these elite occupations also does not imply low cognitive ability. There are other careers for gifted people and many other factors including chance, institutional effects, and gender roles that can influence biography.

Beyond Born Versus Made: The Science of Professional Expertise

Factors other than general cognitive ability, such as specific abilities, deliberate practice, educational dosage, interests, personality, networks, and even luck likely all play a role in the development of professional expertise. We know that both genes and the environment are important in the development of professional expertise, so future research should account for the role of genes. Ultimately, the science on the development of expertise needs to account for multiple inter-locking factors (Hambrick, Macnamara, Campitelli, Ullén, & Mosing, 2016; Lubinski, 2004; Simonton, 2009) and would also benefit from synthetic perspectives that cross-disciplinary boundaries (e.g., Gobet, 2016). Thus, the age-old debates and even current media headlines asking whether experts are "born or made" should really be changed to the idea matching our current state of scientific knowledge that experts are always "born, then made" (Wai, 2014c).

Notes

1 STEM fields are the most intellectually demanding (Wai, 2015; Wai, Lubinski, Benbow, 2009).
2 For readability we have rounded to whole numbers. The precise percentage of Cohorts 1 and 2 having at least one NIH grant is 2.78% (Lubinski *et al.*, 2014), versus 3.44% for Cohort 3 (Makel *et al.*, 2016). (Numbers were also rounded in the original publications to ease readability.)
3 Information about Cohort 3's educational attainment was gathered when their mean age was 33.6 years old (Lubinski, Benbow, Webb, & Bleske-Rechek, 2006). Information about all of Cohort 3's other achievements was gathered when their mean age was 38 (Kell *et al.*, 2013; Makel *et al.*, 2016).
4 There are actually at least two "threshold hypotheses," although they are similar. The first concerns the association between intelligence and creativity and postulates that above a certain IQ score (usually 120) there is no correlation between ability and creativity (Kim, 2005). The second concerns the association between intelligence and "success" in a general sense. The modern formulation of this second version of the threshold hypothesis can be traced primarily to Gladwell's (2008) incomplete reading of Jensen (1980, p. 114), although it has precursors in the research literature (e.g., Bingham & Davis, 1924; Ghiselli, 1963).

References

Achter, J. A., Lubinski, D., Benbow, C. P., & Eftekhari-Sanjani, H. (1999). Assessing vocational preferences among gifted adolescents adds incremental validity to abilities: A discriminant analysis of educational outcomes over a 10-year interval. *Journal of Educational Psychology, 91,* 777–786.

America's Best Colleges (2013). Retrieved from www.usnews.com/rankings

Arneson, J. J., Sackett, P. R., & Beatty, A. S. (2011). Ability-performance relationships in education and employment settings critical tests of the more-is-better and the good-enough hypotheses. *Psychological Science, 22,* 1336–1342.

Benbow, C. P. (1988). Sex differences in mathematical reasoning ability among the intellectually talented: Their characteristics, consequences, and possible explanations. *Behavioral and Brain Sciences, 11*, 169–183.

Benbow, C. P. (1992). Academic achievement in math and science between ages 13 and 23: Are there differences in the top one percent of ability? *Journal of Educational Psychology, 84,* 51–61.

Benbow, C. P., & Stanley, J. C. (1983). Sex differences in mathematical reasoning ability: More facts. *Science, 222,* 1029–1031.

Bingham, W. V., & Davis, W. T. (1924). Intelligence test scores and business success. *Journal of Applied Psychology, 8,* 1–22.

Bouchard, T. J., Jr. (2004). Genetic influence on human psychological traits: A survey. *Current Directions in Psychological Science, 13,* 148–151.

Campbell, D. T., & Stanley, J. C. (1963). *Experimental and quasi-experimental designs for research.* Chicago, IL: Rand McNally.

Canter, R. R. (1956). Intelligence and the social status of occupations. *Personnel Guidance Journal, 34,* 258–260.

Carnegie Foundation. (2010). The Carnegie classification of institutions of higher education. Retrieved from http://carnegieclassifications.iu.edu

Coward, W. M., & Sackett, P. R. (1990). Linearity of ability-performance relationships: A reconfirmation. *Journal of Applied Psychology, 75,* 297–330.

Ericsson, K. A. (2014). Why expert performance is special and cannot be extrapolated from studies of performance in the general population: A response to criticisms. *Intelligence, 45,* 81–103.

Ericcson, K. A., & Pool, R. (2016). *Peak: Secrets from the new science of expertise.* Boston: Houghton Mifflin Harcourt.

Espenshade, T. J., & Radford, A. W. (2009). *No longer separate, not yet equal: Race and class in elite college admission and campus life.* Princeton, NJ: Princeton University Press.

Ferriman-Robertson, K., Smeets, S., Lubinski, D., & Benbow, C. P. (2010). Beyond the threshold hypothesis: Even among the gifted and top math/science graduate students, cognitive abilities, vocational interests, and lifestyle preferences matter for career choice, performance, and persistence. *Current Directions in Psychological Science, 19,* 346–351.

Frey, M. C., & Detterman, D. K. (2004). Scholastic assessment or *g*? The relationship between the SAT and general cognitive ability. *Psychological Science, 14,* 373–378.

Garrison, C. G., Burke, A., & Hollingworth, L. S. (1917). The psychology of a prodigious child. *Journal of Applied Psychology, 1,* 101–110.

Ghiselli, E. E. (1963). Managerial talent. *American Psychologist, 18,* 631–642.

Gladwell, M. (2008). *Outliers: The story of success.* New York: Little, Brown & Co.

Gobet, F. (2016). *Understanding expertise: A multi-disciplinary approach.* New York: Palgrave.

Golden, D. (2006). *The price of admission.* New York: Three Rivers Press.

Gottfredson, L. S. (2003). *g*, jobs, and life. In H. Nyborg (Ed.), *The scientific study of general intelligence: Tribute to Arthur R. Jensen* (pp. 293–342). New York: Pergamon.

Hambrick, D. Z., Macnamara, B. N., Campitelli, G., Ullén, F., & Mosing, M. A. (2016). Beyond born versus made: A new look at expertise. *Psychology of Learning and Motivation, 64,* 1–55.

Hollingworth, L. S., Garrison, C. G., & Burke, A. (1922). Subsequent History of E—Five Years After the Initial Report. *Journal of Applied Psychology, 6,* 205–210.

Jensen, A. R. (1980). *Bias in mental testing.* New York: Free Press.

Jensen, A. R. (1998). *The g factor: The science of mental ability.* Westport, CT: Praeger.

Kell, H., Lubinski, D., & Benbow, C. P. (2013). Who rises to the top? Early indicators. *Psychological Science, 24*, 648–659.

Kell, H. J., Lubinski, D., Benbow, C. P., & Steiger, J. H. (2013). Creativity and technical innovation: Spatial ability's unique role. *Psychological Science, 24*, 1831–1836.

Kim, K. H. (2005). Can only intelligent people be creative? *Journal of Secondary Gifted Education, 16*, 57–66.

Koenig, K. A., Frey, M. C., & Detterman, D. K. (2008). ACT and general cognitive ability. *Intelligence, 36*, 153–160.

Kuncel, N. R., Hezlett, S. A., & Ones, D. S. (2004). Academic performance, career potential, creativity, and job performance: Can one construct predict them all? *Journal of Personality and Social Psychology, 86*, 148–161.

Lubinski, D. (2004). Introduction to the special section on cognitive abilities: 100 years after Spearman's (1904) "'general intelligence', objectively determined and measured". *Journal of Personality and Social Psychology, 86*, 96–111.

Lubinski, D., & Benbow, C. P. (2000). States of excellence. *American Psychologist, 55*, 137–150.

Lubinski, D., & Benbow, C. P. (2006). Study of mathematically precocious youth after 35 years: Uncovering antecedents for the development of math-science expertise. *Perspectives on Psychological Science, 1*, 316–345.

Lubinski, D., Benbow, C. P., & Kell, H. J. (2014). Life paths and accomplishments of mathematically precocious males and females four decades later. *Psychological Science, 25*, 2217–2232.

Lubinski, D., Benbow, C. P., Webb, R. M., & Bleske-Rechek, A. (2006). Tracking exceptional human capital over two decades. *Psychological Science, 17*, 194–199.

Macnamara, B. N., Hambrick, D. Z., & Oswald, F. L. (2014). Deliberate practice and performance in music, games, sports, education, and professions: a meta-analysis. *Psychological Science, 25*, 1608–1618.

Makel, M. C., Kell, H. J., Lubinski, D., Putallaz, M., & Benbow, C. P. (2016). When lightning strikes twice: Profoundly gifted, profoundly accomplished. *Psychological Science, 27*, 1004–1018. doi: 10.1177/0956797616644735

Murray, C. (2012). *Coming apart: The state of white America, 1960-2010.* New York: Crown Forum.

Neisser, U., Boodoo, G., Bouchard, Jr., T. J., Boykin, A. W., Brody, N., Ceci, S. J., & Halpern, D. F., *et al.* (1996). Intelligence: Knowns and unknowns. *American Psychologist, 51*, 77–101.

Park, G., Lubinski, D., & Benbow, C. P. (2007). Contrasting intellectual patterns for creativity in the arts and sciences: Tracking intellectually precocious youth over 25 years. *Psychological Science, 18*, 948–952.

Park, G., Lubinski, D., & Benbow, C. P. (2008). Ability differences among people who have commensurate degrees matter for scientific creativity. *Psychological Science, 19*, 957–961.

Sander, R. H. (2004). A systemic analysis of affirmative action in American law schools. *Stanford Law Review, 57*, 367–483.

Schmidt, F. L., & Hunter, J. E. (2004). General mental ability in the world of work: Occupational attainment and job performance. *Journal of Personality and Social Psychology, 86*, 162–173.

Shea, D. L., Lubinski, D., & Benbow, C. P. (2001). Importance of assessing spatial ability in intellectually talented young adolescents: A 20-year longitudinal study. *Journal of Educational Psychology, 93*, 604–614.

Simonton, D. K. (2009). The "other IQ": Historiometric assessments of intelligence and related constructs. *Review of General Psychology, 13*, 315–326.

Stanley, J. C. (1971). Reliability. In R. L. Thorndike (Ed.) *Educational Measurement* (2nd ed., pp. 356–442). Washington, DC: American Council on Education.

Stanley, J. C. (1996). In the beginning: The study of mathematically precocious youth. In C. P. Benbow & D. Lubinski (Eds.), *Intellectual talent: Psychometric and social issues* (pp. 225–235). Baltimore, MD: Johns Hopkins University Press.

U.S. Census Bureau. (2012a). Bachelor's degree attainment tops 30 percent for first time, Census Bureau reports. Retrieved from http://www.census.gov/newsroom/releases/archives/education/cb12-33.html

U.S. Census Bureau. (2012b). Educational attainment in the United States: 2012 – detailed tables. Retrieved from http://www.census.gov/hhes/socdemo/education/data/cps/2012/tables.html

U.S. Patent and Trademark Office. (2011). U.S. patent statistics chart: Calendar years 1963 – 2011. Retrieved from http://www.uspto.gov/web/offices/ac/ido/oeip/taf/us_stat.htm

Wai, J. (2013). Investigating America's elite: Cognitive ability, education, and sex differences. *Intelligence, 41*, 203–211.

Wai, J. (2014a). Investigating the world's rich and powerful: Education, cognitive ability, and sex differences. *Intelligence, 46*, 54–72.

Wai, J. (2014b). What does it mean to be an expert? *Intelligence, 45, 122–123.*

Wai, J. (2014c). Experts are born, then made: Combining prospective and retrospective longitudinal data shows that cognitive ability matters. *Intelligence, 45*, 74–80.

Wai, J. (2014d). Are wealthier congress members also smarter? *Psychology Today.* Retrieved from https://www.psychologytoday.com/blog/finding-the-next-einstein/201401/are-wealthier-congress-members-also-smarter

Wai, J. (2015). The stubborn pattern of academic aptitude by college major: 1946-2014. *Quartz.* Retrieved from http://qz.com/334926/your-college-major-is-a-pretty-good-indication-of-how-smart-you-are/

Wai, J., Lubinski, D., & Benbow, C. P. (2005). Creativity and occupational accomplishments among intellectually precocious youth: An age 13 to age 33 longitudinal study. *Journal of Educational Psychology, 97*, 484–492.

Wai, J., Lubinski, D., & Benbow, C. P. (2009). Spatial ability for STEM domains: Aligning over fifty years of cumulative psychological knowledge solidifies its importance. *Journal of Educational Psychology, 101*, 817–835.

Wai, J., & Lincoln, D. (2016). Investigating the right tail of wealth: Education, cognitive ability, giving, network power, gender, ethnicity, leadership, and other characteristics. *Intelligence, 54*, 1–32.

Wai, J., & Rindermann, H. R. (2015). The path and performance of a company leader: An historical examination of the education and cognitive ability of Fortune 500 CEOs. *Intelligence, 53*, 102–107.

Webb, R. M., Lubinski, D., & Benbow, C. P. (2002). Mathematically facile adolescents with math/science aspirations: New perspectives on their educational and vocational development. *Journal of Educational Psychology, 94*, 785–794.

Wise, L. L., McLaughlin, D. H., & Steel, L. (1979). *The Project TALENT data bank.* Palo Alto, CA: American Institutes for Research.

6

THE LINK BETWEEN CHILD PRODIGIES AND AUTISM

Joanne Ruthsatz, Kimberly Stephens, and Mark Matthews

Introduction

Child prodigies are individuals who reach a professional level of performance in a culturally relevant domain before the age of 10 (Feldman, 1986) or adolescence (McPherson, 2006). How children can achieve so much so quickly has long been a scientific mystery. The following chapter will present evidence that child prodigies and individuals with autism (particularly autistic savants) have strikingly similar phenotypes, as well as a family and potentially a genetic link.

Early Prodigy Research

Despite significant popular interest in child prodigies, few academics have investigated the prodigy phenomenon. Partly as a result of this scientific neglect, the term "prodigy" long lacked a formal definition. In addition, there has long been little more than speculation as to how child prodigies are able to reach such astounding levels of achievement at such early ages.

The first significant prodigy investigation was an observational study of Erwin Nyiregyházi, a musical prodigy, by Révész (1925). Révész began working with Nyiregyházi when Nyiregyházi was 7 years old and closely tracked his development for several years. Révész reported that the prodigy had a remarkable memory for music and an above-average level of general intelligence. He compared his profile to that of Mozart, who was believed to have the same qualities.

Révész discussed whether Nyiregyházi was an "infant prodigy" or a "precocious child," but ultimately decided that he did not fall into either category. Instead, Révész described Nyiregyházi as a musical prodigy, but he didn't formally define that term. Nor did he put forth any explanation for the source of the young musician's extraordinary abilities.

Feldman (1986) proposed the first modern operational definition of a child prodigy. Feldman concluded that the prodigies he studied had "striking and extreme" talents, but he did not propose a theory as to the source of those talents.

Origins of the Investigation into a Prodigy-Autism Link

Autism is usually a lifelong condition. It is diagnosed based on social and communication difficulties coupled with repetitive behaviors or a narrow range of interests (American Psychiatric Association, 2013). It was first identified as an independent condition by Leo Kanner (1943) and Hans Asperger (1944).

Savants are individuals with an underlying impairment or condition combined with a domain-specific skill or skills that exceeds their overall level of abilities. Savants' abilities are typically in art, music, or mathematics. In rare instances, their savant skill may reach prodigious levels. In such instances, savants show remarkable similarities with child prodigies.

Consider, for example, James Henry Pullen. Pullen was born in 1837. Though he was deaf and spoke only a single word at the age of 7, he had extraordinary artistic abilities (Treffert, 2010). He drew and created model ships, some of which are still on display in England. His most famous work, *The Great Eastern*, was a ten-foot model ship that won first prize at the Fisheries Exhibition, a prestigious art exhibit in England. As one of his doctors noted, Pullen's "power of observation, comparison, attention, memory, will and pertinacity are extraordinary; and yet he is obviously too childish, and at the same time too emotional, unstable, and lacking in mental balance to make any headway, or even hold his own, in the outside world" (Tredgold, 1914). With the benefit of hindsight and scientific advances, modern researchers believe that Pullen was an autistic savant (Breathnach & Ward, 2005).

Child prodigies have always been treated as a group distinct from savants within the academic literature. While the abilities of Pullen and other savants may seem similar to those of child prodigies, by definition savants have an underlying disorder (usually autism), while the definition of a child prodigy is centered on individual achievement without reference to any sort of associated condition. Previous academic work has not described a link between prodigy and autism. Nor are child prodigies typically autistic. But this chapter will argue that both prodigies and savants rely on similar cognitive and neurological underpinnings to develop their special abilities, and that establishing a better understanding of child prodigies may increase our understanding of both talent and autism.

The idea that child prodigies' abilities might stem from a link with autism was born of a chance encounter with a music prodigy's autistic cousin. The 6-year-old prodigy had begun to imitate music at 2 years of age using pots and pans from around the house (Ruthsatz & Detterman, 2003). At the time of assessment, he had already performed at large venues, created two original music CDs, and been in a Disney movie. Neither of his parents played a musical instrument. At the time of the study, he had never had a formal music lesson.

Ruthsatz and Detterman used the Summation Theory (Detterman & Ruthsatz, 1999), a theory of expertise, as a framework for their investigation. According to the Summation Theory, achievement is best predicted by three factors: general intelligence, domain-specific skills, and practice time. Ruthsatz and Detterman (2003) hypothesized that general intelligence and domain-specific skills would be vital for the 6-year-old music prodigy who, given his young age, would not have had the opportunity for extended practice.

The investigator administered the Stanford-Binet 4th edition and the Gordon's Test of Music Audiation (1986). The music prodigy scored in the gifted range (X=132) on the Stanford-Binet 4th ed. His working memory was profound (X=158); his score placed him above the 99th percentile for memory. His scores on the Gordon's Test of Advanced Music Audiation (1986) revealed that he also had an extraordinary ability to recognize tone and rhythm. His results were strongly supportive of the Summation Theory.

During a break in testing, Ruthsatz had a chance encounter at a local restaurant with the prodigy's only maternal cousin, an autistic teenager. This meeting launched Ruthsatz's investigation into a possible connection between child prodigies and autism. Over the years, this line of research has generated evidence that prodigy and autism involve shared cognitive and behavioral traits, as well as a family link and potentially a genetic link.

Shared Cognitive and Behavioral Traits

IQ and Working Memory

The connection between prodigy and autism begins with shared cognitive and behavioral traits. Assessments of child prodigies' cognitive profiles have revealed that while these children do not all have exceptional full-scale IQs, they do possess extraordinary working memories. In an investigation of eight child prodigies, including math, art, and music, the prodigies had an average full-scale intelligence score in the gifted range ($M = 128$). However, their scores varied widely, from 112 to 147 (Ruthsatz & Urbach, 2012).

The prodigies, however, had extraordinary scores on the working memory subtest on the Stanford-Binet 5th ed. Each of the child prodigies in the 2012 study had a working memory score in the 99th percentile. Their average score was ($M = 147$, $SD = 5.32$).

Exceptional memory closely links prodigies and savants. Treffert has observed that extraordinary savant skills are always accompanied by "massive memory" (2010).

Attention to Detail

Studies have revealed that child prodigies have elevated attention to detail, a trait linked to autism (Baron-Cohen, Ashwin, Ashwin, Tavassoil, & Chakrabarti, 2009).

TABLE 6.1 Autism Spectrum Quotient. Table reflects means for reported scores from eight child prodigies and compares them to a study by Baron-Cohen *et al.* (2001), using established norms from the Autism Spectrum Quotient.

	Prodigy	*Control*	*HFA/AS*
	n=8	n=174	n=58
Total AQ Score	22.37	16.4	35.8
Social Skills	3.12	2.6	7.5
Attention Switching	4.75	3.9	8
Attention to Detail	8.5	5.3	6.7
Communication	2.5	2.4	7.2
Imagination	3.75	2.3	6.4

Note. HFA/AS individuals were individuals described as having high-functioning autism (HFA) or Asperger's disorder (AS).

A pilot study used the Autistic Spectrum Quotient (AQ), a test designed to measure autistic traits in individuals with normal levels of intelligence (Baron-Cohen, Wheelwright, Skinner, Martin, & Clubley, 2001), to assess the level of various autism-linked traits, including attention to detail, among the family members of child prodigies, the family members of autistic children, and the family members of children without any documented disability (Ruthsatz, 2007). In this study, the child prodigies' family members reported greater attention to detail than the family members of non-prodigious children. In a later study, child prodigies reported significantly elevated attention to detail on the AQ (Ruthsatz & Urbach, 2012). The child prodigies had an average score of 8.5 in this category, a score significantly higher than both the control sample ($X = 5.3$) and the sample for individuals with autism ($X = 6.7$).

Table 6.1 reports the results of the AQ scores from eight child prodigies and compares them to Baron-Cohen's normative sample for individuals with autism and a control group. The individuals with autism in this chart were not autistic savants. They were individuals described as having high-functioning autism or Asperger's disorder (Baron-Cohen *et al.*, 2001).

Passionate Interests

Child prodigies demonstrate extremely passionate interests. They have a rage to master their individual interests. This trait has also been linked to autism. A classic sign of autism is "highly restricted, fixated interests that are abnormal in intensity or focus" (APA, 2013). While such interests have historically received relatively less scholarly attention, they are believed to be quite common among the autistic population (Turner-Brown, Lam, Holtzclaw, Dichter, & Bodfish, 2011; South, Ozonoff, & McMahon, 2005).

Other Similarities

In addition to extraordinary working memory, heightened attention to detail, and a tendency toward passionate interests, other similarities link prodigy and autism. Both groups have a similar gender skew. The ratio of male to female child prodigies is 3.5:1 (Ruthsatz & Urbach, 2012). This ratio is mirrored among those with savant syndrome, where the ratio is 6:1 (Treffert, 2010), and autism, where the ratio is 4:1.

Additionally, both child prodigies and autistic savants excel primarily in fields based on rule-based systems, such as music, art, and mathematics (Feldman & Morelock, 2011; Young & Nettlebeck, 1995; Ruthsatz & Urbach, 2012).

A Family Link

Child prodigies frequently have autistic relatives. Among the nine prodigies investigated across two studies, over half had a first- or second-degree biological relative diagnosed with an autism spectrum disorder. Several of the prodigies had multiple close family members with autism. In one instance, an art prodigy had four close family members who were diagnosed with an autism spectrum disorder (Ruthsatz & Urbach, 2012; Ruthsatz & Detterman, 2003). Ongoing research with nine new child prodigies (Ruthsatz, Ruthsatz-Stephens, & Ruthsatz, 2014) supports the same over-representation of autism within the families of child prodigies and the similarities mentioned above.

Shared Genetic Etiology for Autism and Child Prodigies

Autism has a significant genetic component (Bailey *et al.*, 1995; Bailey, Palferman, Heavey, & LeCouteur, 1998; Bolton *et al.*, 1994; Piven, Palmer, Jacobi, Childress, & Arndt, 1997).

The results of a family-based, genome-wide linkage analysis investigated a potential genetic connection between prodigy and autism. The investigators coded both the child prodigy subjects and their biological autistic relatives as *affected*. The resulting analysis identified a significant peak on chromosome 1 (P=0.000742), indicating shared genetic etiology for autism and child prodigies. A paper with the full results was published in *Human Heredity* (Ruthsatz, Petrill, Li, Wolock, & Bartlett, 2014). This may suggest that child prodigies seem to share genetic etiology with their relatives with autism.

This finding is based on a small study, but the researchers believe that, by concentrating their DNA-collection efforts on child prodigies and their relatives, their study overcame two limitations that have hampered previous efforts to identify core phenotypes of autistic individuals. First, rather than examine members of the autistic population at large, the present study examined a specific subset of the autistic population. Because autism is a heterogeneous disorder, efforts to identify genes common to all autistic individuals have produced weak or mixed results. However, efforts to identify a genetic linkage among autistic individuals have proven more fruitful when limited to specific subsets of the autistic population that share a specific feature. For example, studies using subsets of individuals with high ratings for obsessive-compulsive traits generate stronger evidence of linkage on chromosome 1 (Buxbaum *et al.*, 2004).

Second, previous efforts to limit study to a subgroup of the autistic population have focused only on the shared impairments currently associated with the disorder (such as, in the previous example, obsessive-compulsive disorder). But limiting the search in this way resulted in examination of only some of the traits associated with autism; it neglected study of the underpinnings of the positive traits that researchers now believe are associated with autism.

The Fine Line Between Prodigies and Savants

There are several instances in which a prodigy was diagnosed with an autism spectrum disorder as a young child, but seemed to have grown out of their autism by adolescence. In these instances, the child seemed to have overcome the major social and communication challenges associated with autism while retaining prodigious abilities, an occurrence which blurs the line between prodigy and savant.

Consider, for example, the case of Jacob Barnett. Jacob was born after a difficult pregnancy (Barnett, 2013). His mother was diagnosed with preeclampsia, a condition associated with increased risk for autism (Buchmayer *et al.*, 2008), and was hospitalized nine times before her son's premature birth. Jacob was born without a soft spot on the skull. Without a soft spot, the brain does not have the proper room to grow, creating significant pressure inside of the skull. The doctors suggested surgery to relieve the pressure that was building. Jacob's parents refused the operation.

Early in his infancy, Jacob was profoundly advanced for his age. He began talking very early and could recite the alphabet forward and backward before he could walk. He was reading words by age one and had committed the entire atlas to memory by 14 months of age, demonstrating an exceptional memory.

At 16 months, Jacob began to disengage. He stopped responding to his name, refused to make eye contact, and regressed linguistically. He had obsessive interests in a very narrow range of activities, especially a preoccupation with shadows and light. At age two, he was diagnosed with autism.

Jacob's mother used a non-traditional therapy technique to help Jacob with his condition rather than following the widely used autism treatment based on the Applied Behavioral Analysis (ABA) method. The ABA method involves encouraging the patient to remediate areas of deficit, such as eye contact, attention, and speech development (Cristea, Sipos, & Iftene, 2011, p. 327), but Jacob's mother encouraged him to focus on his intense interests, such as shadows and light. Jacob quickly began to speak again, and many of the challenges associated with his autism disappeared.

He also showed exceptional abilities in math. He began college level calculus in a university at the age of 8 after teaching himself algebra, geometry, and trigonometry in the course of about three weeks on his front porch. At the age of 17, he was enrolled in a graduate program in theoretical physics. He is the youngest person ever to be accepted to The Perimeter Institute, a prestigious research institute in theoretical physics. He also won the 2013 Most Innovative People Award, prior recipients of which include Steven Hawking, Bill Gates, and Samuel Palmisando (former Chairman of IBM).

Jacob's story, and those of other children who were diagnosed with autism and then became highly prodigious, suggest a significant link between autism and prodigious abilities. The development of a number of famous historical individuals seems to follow a similar pattern. Reviewing historical cases is problematic for several reasons. But, keeping these limitations in mind, these historical examples may still prove illuminating given the extremely limited number of child prodigies.

A number of child prodigies did not begin to speak until late in childhood (Sowell, 2001). Clara Wieck Schumann, for example, was thought to be deaf as a child. At almost 5 years old, she still did not speak, a trait associated with autism (DSM-5). One day her father played a melody for Clara on their piano. After a second play, he placed Clara's hands on the piano, and she repeated the melody almost perfectly. From that moment on, Clara's ability to play the piano had an exponential effect on her development. Her ability to play was exceptional for her age, even though her father limited her practice time. The child that had first been thought to be deaf turned out to have an astounding talent for and interest in music. Clara began to play for small audiences in her home at the age of 6, and, by the age of 9, she was playing in famous concert halls. She continued as a touring pianist and composer until the age of 72 (Cotter, 2008).

Albert Einstein also had delayed speech. He did not speak until 3 years of age. He preferred solitary play and had a narrow range of interest—all potential signs of autism. He would not engage in schoolwork that did not fascinate him, and his parents and teachers feared he was mentally retarded. However, he was highly developed in mathematics and was able to master differential and integral calculus by the age of 15. He later went on to win the Nobel Prize for his work in physics (Sowell, 2001). The examples of Schumann and Einstein suggest that some of the early signs of autism may potentially be the same for prodigies, suggesting a potential connection between the two.

Acquired Savant and Acquired Prodigy

In most cases, the abilities of savants (those individuals in whom exceptional skills are combined with an underlying disability) are congenital. However, there are a significant number of cases of acquired savant abilities, in which an individual who was not born with a savant skill acquired new abilities following an illness or injury.

The same appears to be true of prodigies. While in most instances child prodigies' remarkable abilities are evident almost from birth, there are instances in which a child has acquired a prodigious skill following an illness or injury, providing another parallel between savants and prodigies. In one case, 13-year-old Zac Tiessen, a normally developing male, hit his head on a basement floor at church. After his recovery, he was given a guitar from his godmother and developed within three months to a professional level of play.

Acquired savant syndrome is most often found after either illness or injury to the left hemisphere of the brain. Neuroimaging studies of individuals with acquired savant syndrome have identified structural or functional damage or dysfunction to the left parietal region, which is also often present in individuals with autism (Treffert, 2010). A study of 12 individuals with dementia who went on to develop savant skills also identified damage in the same area of the brain using fMRIs (Miller, Boone, Cummings, & Mishkin, 2000).

Some researchers have suggested that when acquired savant abilities arise, the right hemisphere of the brain is compensating for the damage to the left hemisphere (Treffert, 2010). The usually dominant left hemisphere is specialized in language and abstract thought, while the non-dominant right hemisphere specializes in artistic and visual-spatial abilities. Both child prodigies and savants are primarily found in the same domains, which mainly rely upon right-hemisphere specialization: art, music, and mathematics.

Cognitive Underpinnings of Prodigious Abilities Differ by Specialty

Child prodigies appear to differ in significant ways according to specialty. A recent study investigated the cognitive profiles of 18 child prodigies who specialized in art, music, or math (Ruthsatz et al., 2014) using the Stanford–Binet 5th edition. The resulting analysis (see Table 6.2), offered the field's first insights into the cognitive similarities and differences among child prodigies across domains.

In this study, the average full-scale intelligence score for the group of child prodigies was in the gifted range ($X = 126$). There was, however, notable variation in these scores. This finding supports the idea put forth by Feldman that prodigious abilities do not necessarily require exceptional levels of general intelligence (Feldman & Morelock, 2011).

The prodigies' full-scale intelligence scores varied according to the domain in which they specialized. The math prodigies had significantly higher full-scale intelligence scores ($X = 140$) than both the music prodigies ($X = 129$) and the art prodigies ($X = 108$). This finding further supports Feldman and Morelock's (2011) suggestion that prodigious math abilities may require higher levels of general intelligence than prodigious abilities in music or art.

There was also significant variation in the child prodigies' scores on the subtests of the Stanford–Binet according to specialty (Ruthsatz et al., 2014), which

TABLE 6.2 Stanford-Binet 5th edition averages for child prodigies by domain.

		N	Mean	SD	Effect Size
FSIQ Standard Score★★★	art	5	108.4	6.07	
	music	7	129.14	11.23	
	math	5	139.8	5.50	
	Total	17	126.18	14.99	$\eta^2 = .74$
FR Standard Score★	art	5	100.6	3.91	
	music	7	116.14	12.29	
	math	5	125.4	19.1	
	Total	17	114.29	15.82	$\eta^2 = .39$
KN Standard Score★★	art	5	111.8	14.15	
	music	6	125.5	11.20	
	math	5	139.6	9.18	
	Total	16	125.63	15.70	$\eta^2 = .52$
QR Standard Score★★	art	5	101.6	11.76	
	music	7	119.86	12.98	
	math	5	132.8	6.87	
	Total	17	118.29	16.23	$\eta^2 = .58$
Visual Spatial Standard Score★★★	art	5	88	6.00	
	music	6	116.67	24.25	
	math	5	142.2	10.01	
	Total	16	115.69	26.88	$\eta^2 = .68$
WM Standard Score★	art	5	132	6.36	
	music	8	148.38	5.52	
	math	5	134.8	15.52	
	Total	18	140.06	11.77	$\eta^2 = .43$

Note: ★p<.05 ★★p<.01 ★★★p<.001 on One-Way ANOVA

suggests that, as previously proposed by Feldman and Morelock (2011), the interplay between general intelligence and domain-specific skills is critical in child prodigies. In the Stanford-Binet 5th edition, working memory has both a verbal and a non-verbal component. In the non-verbal section, the participants must watch as a random sequence of numbers is tapped on two different colored rows. Then the participants must repeat the numbers back in the same order that they were tapped, but first by the yellow row and then the red row. In the verbal section, participants must answer a series of questions and then recall the last word in each of the sentences in order. While all the child prodigies had exceptional working memories ($X = 140$), the music prodigies had significantly higher working memories than the art prodigies. The difference in working memory scores between the music prodigies and the math prodigies was marginally significant.

Child prodigies in the math domain had the highest scores on the visual-spatial subtest ($X = 142$). The art prodigies, on the other hand, had below-average scores on this subtest ($X = 88$). At first, the art prodigies' low visual-spatial scores may seem counterintuitive. But previous work by Milbrath (1998) offers one possible explanation for this finding. Milbrath explains that gifted young artists seem to see the world using functional processing; they attend to surface features and details. Less artistically talented children view the world from an operative processing approach. Milbrath explains that the functional processing allows for exact replication rather than categorical representations. It may turn out that art prodigies have enhanced visual memory, an ability not tested by the Stanford-Binet 5th edition, which might contribute to the talented artists' early accomplishments and advanced skills.

These specific subtests give us a first glance at how general intelligence and domain-specific skills interact to predispose a preference or ability in certain domains, at least among prodigies. They are also an excellent source of data to begin looking at neural structures and circuitry as they relate to different abilities and disabilities. These findings are ripe for exploration using fMRIs to better understand prodigies' underlying neural structures and circuitry.

Next Frontier

Future Research Area 1: General Intelligence and Domain-Specific

The question of whether intelligence is a general ability (Herrnstein & Murray, 1994; Jensen, 1998) that predicts achievement in many domains, or whether there are multiple intelligences that operate with some independence from one another (Gardner,1983), has been heavily debated. Additional research into child prodigies and savants may lead to a better understanding of the complexity of human intelligence and the relationship between intelligence and achievement.

Although child prodigies are extremely rare, research involving these extraordinary children may yield insights into how general intelligence and domain-specific skills interact to predispose not just prodigies but also more typically developing individuals.

Child prodigy research may also offer new clues as to the impact that a family link to autism may have on talent or achievement.

Future Research Area 2: Training the Talent

While a great deal of autism therapy is focused on overcoming the social and communication challenges of autism, some researchers and parents have begun to suggest that educators and parents identify and train the talents of those with autism (Grandin, 2013; Barnett, 2013; Treffert, 2010).

Future Research Area 3: Advances through Genetic Research

A recent study has found evidence that child prodigies and their autistic family members share a genetic mutation on chromosome 1 (Ruthsatz *et al.*, 2015). This locus on chromosome 1 is linked to both autism and prodigious abilities. This finding opens up new possibilities for understanding both conditions.

One possible reason that child prodigies seem to possess the strengths of autism but few of the challenges is that child prodigies possess a genetic moderator. This moderator could potentially prevent the prodigies from exhibiting the challenges typically associated with autism. This possibility can be explored by investigating the genetic differences between child prodigies and their autistic family members. The most promising research will be to identify the genetic marker or markers that allow the child prodigies to display the talent that is sometimes associated with autism, such as in the case of autistic savants without the deficits.

Conclusions

There is evidence that child prodigies and individuals with autism (and particularly savants) have significant behavioral, cognitive, familial, and potentially genetic overlap:

1. Both groups have exceptional working memories. Child prodigies typically test in the 99th percentile on the working memory subtest of the Stanford-Binet 5th edition. A "massive memory" is generally found among those with savant syndrome.
2. Attention to detail is elevated in child prodigies. This trait is also linked to autism.
3. Child prodigies show an incredible passion for their area of specialty. This is a characteristic feature of autism. "Highly restricted, fixated interests that are abnormal in intensity or focus" is included among autism's diagnostic criteria.
4. Both child prodigies and savants often exhibit their extreme abilities in the same rule-based systems: art, music, and mathematics.
5. Among child prodigies, there appears to be a gender skew: The majority of child prodigies are male. The same is true among the autistic and among autistic savants.
6. There is an over-representation of autism in the biological family members of child prodigies. In a study of 18 child prodigies, over half had a close autistic relative. Some of the prodigies had multiple close relatives with autism.
7. Several of the child prodigies had an autism spectrum disorder (ASD) diagnosis as young children but seemed to have "recovered" from the most challenging aspects of autism.

8. There is preliminary evidence that there is a genetic link between prodigy and autism. A team of investigators has found evidence that child prodigies and their autistic relatives share a mutation on chromosome 1 that their non-prodigious, non-autistic relatives do not possess.

9. In the majority of cases, prodigy and autism are both congenital conditions. There is some evidence, however, that both prodigy and savant skills can be acquired following an injury or illness.

Future child prodigy research is likely to further delineate the contours of the relationship between prodigy and autism. It may provide a novel avenue for investigating relatively new approaches to autism therapy, such as "train the talent." It may also offer an opportunity to approach autism genetics from an unexpected angle and to begin exploring why it is that child prodigies possess the strengths associated with autism but face few of the challenges.

The cognitive data across the domains of art, music, and mathematics provide a first look at the importance of both general intelligence and domain-specific skills in predisposing prodigies towards distinct developmental paths and may have implications for the general population.

References

American Psychiatric Association. (2013). *Diagnostic and statistical manual of mental disorders* (5th ed.). Arlington, VA: American Psychiatric Publishing.

Asperger, H. (1944/1991). "Autistic psychopathy" in childhood. In *Autism & Asperger Syndrome*. Trans by. Frith, U. London: Cambridge University Press.

Bailey, A., LeCouteur, A., Gottesman, I., Bolton, P., Simonoff, E., Yuzda, E., & Rutter, M. (1995). Autism as a strongly genetic disorder: Evidence from a British twin study. *Psychological Medicine: A Journal of Research in Psychiatry and the Allied Sciences*, *25*(1), 63–77.

Bailey, A., Palferman, S., Heavey, L, & LeCouteur, A. (1998). Autism: the phenotype in relatives. *Journal of Autism and Developmental Disorders*, *28*(5), 369–392.

Barnett, K. (2013). *The spark.* Random House, New York.

Baron-Cohen, S., Ashwin, E., Ashwin, C., Tavassoil, T., & Chakrabarti, B. (2009). Talent in autism: hyper-systemizing, hyper-attention to detail and sensory hyper-sensitivity. *The Royal Society*, *368*, 1377–1383.

Baron-Cohen, S., Wheelwright, S., Skinner, R., Martin, J., & Clubley, E. (2001). The Autism Spectrum Quotient (AQ): Evidence from Asperger Syndrome/High Functioning Autism, Males and Females, Scientists and Mathematicians. *Journal of Autism and Developmental Disorders*, *31*, 5–17.

Bolton, P., Macdonald, H., Pickles, A., Rios, P., Goode, S., Crowson, M., Bailey, A., & Rutter, M. (1994). A case-control family history study of autism. *Journal of Child Psychology and Psychiatry*, *35*(5), 877–900.

Breathnach, C.S., & Ward, C. (2005). The Victorian genius of Earlswood: A review of the case of James Henry Pullen. *Irish Journal of Psychological Medicine*, *22*, 151–155.

Buchmayer, S., Johansson, S., Johansson, A., Hultman, C.M., Sparen, P., & Cnattingius, S. (2008). Can association between preterm birth and autism be explained by maternal or neonatal morbidity? *Pediatrics, 5,* 817–825.

Buxbaum, J. D., Silverman, J., Keddache, M., Smith, C. J., Hollander, E., Ramoz, N., & Reichert, J. G. (2004). Linkage analysis for autism in a subset of families with obsessive-compulsive behaviors: Evidence for an autism susceptibility gene on chromosome 1 and further support for susceptibility genes on chromosome 6 and 19. *Molecular Psychiatry, 9,* 144–150.

Cotter, C. (2008). *Wonder kids: The remarkable lives of nine child prodigies.* Annick Press, USA.

Cristea, M., Sipos, R., & Iftene, F. (2011). The Parent as co-therapist in ABA therapy - alternative form of therapy for children with autism applied in the clinic of pediatric psychiatry CLUJ – NAPOCA(II). *Acta Medica Transilvanica, 16*(2), 327.

Detterman, D. K. & Ruthsatz, J. M. (1999). Toward a more comprehensive theory of exceptional abilities. *Journal for the Education of the Gifted, 22,* 148–158.

Feldman, D. H. (1986). Nature's gambit: Child prodigies and the development of human potential. New York: Basic Books.

Feldman, D. H., & Morelock, M. J. (2011). Prodigies and savants. In R. Sternberg, & S. Kaufman (Eds.), *The Cambridge handbook of intelligence* (pp. 210–234). New York, NY: Cambridge University Press.

Gardner, H. (1983). Frames of mind: the theory of multiple intelligences. New York: Basic Books, Inc.

Gordon, E. E. (1986). *Advanced measures of music audiation.* Chicago, IL: G.I.A. Publications.

Grandin, T. (2013). What's right with the autistic mind. *Time Magazine.*

Herrnstein, R. J., & Murray, C. (1994). *The bell curve.* New York: The Free Press.

Jensen, A. R. (1998). *The g factor.* Westport, CT: Praeger Publishers.

Kanner, L. (1943). Autistic disturbances of affective contact. *Nervous Child, 2,* 217–250.

McPherson, G. E. (Ed.). (2006). *The child as musician: A handbook of musical development.* Oxford, UK: Oxford University Press.

Milbrath, C. (1998). *Patterns of artistic development in children.* New York: Plenum.

Miller, B. L., Boone, K., Cummings, L. R. and Mishkin, F. (2000). Functional correlates of musical and visual ability in frontotemporal dementia. *British Journal of Psychiatry, 176,* 458–463.

Piven, J., Palmer, P., Jacobi, D., Childress, D., & Arndt, S. (1997). Broader autism phenotype: Evidence from a family history study of multiple-incidence autism families. *The American Journal of Psychiatry, 154*(2),185–190.

Revesz, G. (1925). *The psychology of a musical prodigy.* New York: Harcourt Brace.

Ruthsatz, J. (2007). Preliminary evidence: Expanding the autistic spectrum to include child prodigies. *Behavior Genetics, 37,* 790–791.

Ruthsatz, J., & Detterman, D. K. (2003). An extraordinary memory: The case study of a musical prodigy. *Intelligence, 31,* 509–518.

Ruthsatz, J., & Urbach, J. (2012). Child Prodigy: A novel cognitive profile places elevated general intelligence, exceptional working memory and attention to detail at the root of prodigiousness. *Intelligence, 40*(5), 419–426.

Ruthsatz, J., Petrill, S., Li, N., Wolock, S. & Bartlett, C. (2015). Molecular Genetic Evidence for Shared Etiology of Autism and Prodigy. *Human Heredity, 79*(2), 53–59.

Ruthsatz, J., Ruthsatz-Stephens, K., & Ruthsatz, K. (2014). Cognitive profiles for child prodigies: Similarities and differences across domains. *Intelligence, 44* (1), 44–49.

South, M., Ozonoff, S., McMahon, W. M. (2005). Repetitive behavior profiles in Asperger syndrome and high-functioning autism. *Journal of Autism and Developmental Disorders, 35* (2), 145–158.

Sowell, T. (2001). *The Einstein Syndrome*. Basic Books, New York, NY.

Tredgold, A. F. (1914). *Mental deficiency (Amentia)*. New York: William Wood.

Treffert, D. A. (2010). *Islands of genius*. Philadelphia: Jessica Kingsley.

Turner-Brown L. M., Lam K. S. L., Holtzclaw, T. N., Dichter, G. S., & Bodfish, J. W. (2011). Phenomenology and measurement of circumscribed interests in autism spectrum disorders. *Autism, 15*(4), 437–456. http://dx.doi.org/10.1177/13623613 10386507.

Young, R. L., & Nettelbeck, T. (1995). The abilities of a musical savant and his family. *Journal of Autism and Developmental Disorders, 25*(3), 231–248.

7

WHY DELIBERATE PRACTICE IS NOT ENOUGH

Evidence of Talent in Drawing

Jennifer E. Drake and Ellen Winner

Introduction

Deliberate practice (or hard work) is necessary for the achievement of high levels of expertise, but it is not sufficient. Talent—the innate proclivity to learn easily and quickly in a particular domain—is also a necessary ingredient and should not be dismissed. In this chapter, we argue for the decisive role of talent in achieving expertise in the visual arts. We argue that individual differences in innate ability exist, and that high levels of ability include a motivational component: a strong interest in a particular domain, along with a strong drive to master that domain. The same case for talent that we make here for the visual arts can also be made in many other domains. Specifically, we suggest, the case for talent can be made for any domain in which one finds childhood precocity or savants.

We use evidence from the domain of the visual arts to make the case for the role of talent in the achievement of expertise. We review what is known about the drawings of children who draw in advance of their age level, as well as what is known about other characteristics of these children. To avoid begging the question, we refer to children who draw in advance of their age as precocious rather than gifted or talented. We begin with no assumptions about whether the cause of this precocity is biological or environmental.

At the conclusion of the chapter, we evaluate the evidence that drawing precocity has an innate, biological component. We argue that although it is impossible to isolate ability from practice (because high-ability children always practice), there is converging evidence to demonstrate that practice without ability is not enough to explain expertise. First, high achievers in the visual arts have high ability before they begin to work at drawing extensively. Second, ordinary children cannot be motivated or even forced to work at drawing to the extent that a precocious child willingly does so. Third, precocious drawers display different kinds of drawing abilities than do ordinary children who simply work hard at drawing. We also argue that there are other signs besides drawing precocity that these children are atypical from birth: They are often non-right-handed, they display a variety of visual-spatial strengths, and they also tend to have linguistic deficits. This combination of factors suggests a brain-based component of drawing talent that can account for drawing precocity in savants as well as in typically developing children.

The strong role of innate talent, however, does not allow us to rule out the importance of practice and hard work. Through practice, learning occurs. Even the most prodigious show development of their skills, and this development is a function of intense work. We argue that precocious drawers, as well as children who are highly precocious in any domain, differ from the ordinary child in these four respects:

1. They learn more rapidly in the domain.
2. They are intrinsically motivated to acquire skill in the domain because of the ease with which learning occurs. We have come to call this having a "rage to master" (Winner, 1996).
3. They make discoveries in the domain without much explicit adult scaffolding. A great deal of the work is done through self-teaching, which, as pointed out by Charness, Krampe, and Mayr (1996) and Ericsson (1996), can be a form of deliberate practice.
4. They not only make discoveries on their own, but often do things in the domain that ordinary hard workers never do—inventing new solutions, thinking, seeing, or hearing in a qualitatively different way.

Does Drawing Precocity Exist?

There have been far fewer reports of reputed drawing prodigies than of prodigies in math, music, or chess. Studies searching for drawing prodigies in populations of schoolchildren have concluded that drawing talent in very young children was far rarer than talent in other domains (Goodenough, 1926; Lark-Horowitz, Lewis, & Luca, 1973). Although it is possible that drawing ability is rarer than ability in other domains, cultural factors could also account for the discrepancy. Drawing ability is far less valued in our culture than is mathematical ability; children who show ability in music are immediately given music lessons; children who show ability in chess join chess clubs and participate in competitions much as do young athletes.

Children are not routinely screened for drawing ability as they are for academic ability; nor are they typically signed up for formal lessons as they are in music. When the culture supports a particular domain, talent is more readily recognized and then nurtured; but also, such a culture makes clear what the skills are that need to be mastered for excellence to be achieved (Csikszentmihalyi & Robinson, 1986).

It is likely that many children who draw ahead of their age go unnoticed and thus unnurtured by their parents and their schools. Moreover, we now have numerous reports of children who appear to be prodigies in drawing (e.g., Drake & Winner, 2011–2012; Drake & Winner, 2012; Goldsmith, 1992; Goldsmith & Feldman, 1989; Golomb, 1992, 1995; Golomb & Hass, 1995; Milbrath, 1998; Paine, 1981; Selfe, 1977, 1983, 1985, 1995; Winner, 1996; Winner & Martino, 1993; Zhensun & Low, 1991). Thus, early high achievement in drawing is clearly possible. Whether such achievement is as common as high achievement in other domains seems less important than the fact that it does occur.

Typical Characteristics of Precocious Drawings

Our knowledge of early high achievement in drawing comes from two sources. One source is the childhood drawings of famous artists (Beck, 1928; Gordon, 1987; Gordon & Broshi, 2015; Paine, 1987; Pariser, 1987, 1991; Richardson, 1991; Vasari 1957). The problem with this kind of evidence is that it is so sparse, and we have almost no drawings by artists preserved from before the age of 9. Thus we know nothing about the first signs of drawing in those who went on to become artists. A more informative source is children who have been identified as precocious in drawing by their parents or teachers. These children do not necessarily become artists as adults, but their drawings are at least several years in advance of those of their peers. Both sources of evidence point consistently to the following set of characteristics as typical of precocious drawings.

Recognizable and Differentiated Shapes

The earliest sign of precocity in drawing is almost always (but with some exceptions discussed later in this chapter) the ability to draw recognizable shapes 1 to 2 years in advance of the normal age timetable of 3 to 4 years of age. Whereas children typically scribble until about 3 to 4, precocious children draw clearly recognizable shapes by the age of 2. Figure 7.1 contrasts a precocious and age-typical attempt at drawing apples. Both drawings were made by 2-year-olds. The age-typical child drew a slash for each apple (Figure 7.1a). For him, a slash stood for anything. The precocious child drew each apple's shape, along with the stem (Figure 7.1b). For him, the representation had to capture the apple's contour in order to represent an apple.

Fluid Contour

Whereas 3- and 4-year-olds typically represent humans by tadpoles, with a circle representing an undifferentiated head and trunk (Figure 7.2a), some precocious children draw the human figure with head and trunk differentiated by age 2 (Golomb, 1995). Preschoolers typically draw additively, juxtaposing geometric shapes (e.g., to make a human, they make a circle for a head, an oval for the body, and straight lines for arms and legs). In contrast, precocious children draw the whole object with one fluid contour line (Winner & Martino, 1993; Figure 7.2b).

Precocious drawers draw recognizable, realistic images quickly and with ease. They do not labor over and erase their lines. Picasso was reported to begin drawings from noncanonical places (e.g., drawing a dog starting with the ear), with no decrement in speed or confidence (Richardson, 1991).

Details

Precocious children do not depict a generic object, but include a rich amount of detail. For example, one child added gas tanks, axles, grills, bumpers, headlights, and brake boxes to his vehicles (Golomb, 1992). Another child drew dinosaurs with scientific accuracy, using paleontology books to acquire the needed information (Milbrath, 1995). The inclusion of detail is one way in which the drawings of precocious children achieve realism.

Techniques to Represent Depth

Precocious drawers achieve the illusion of realism not only by drawing differentiated shapes and details but also by depicting the third dimension. They use all the known Western techniques to show depth: foreshortening, occlusion, size diminution, modeling to show volume, and even the most difficult technique of all, linear perspective. In a comparison of ordinary and precocious drawers, Milbrath (1995) showed that the precocious sample used all of these techniques years earlier than did the normal sample. For instance, foreshortening was used in 50 percent of the drawings by Milbrath's precocious sample by age 7 and 8; comparable levels in the normal sample were reached only by ages 13 and 14, six years later.

Linear perspective is used by precocious drawers sometimes almost as soon as they begin to draw. But the perspective systems used are at first primitive ones, and they are applied locally to separate objects on the page, rather than in a unified fashion to the entire scene (Milbrath, 1998). Nonetheless, the invention of perspectival drawing systems by very young children is astounding to see. Linear perspective is a convention, and it is not an intuitively obvious one (Gombrich, 1960). Typically, children in the West do not begin to draw in perspective until middle childhood, and only those who have explicit instruction ever attain true geometric perspective (Willats, 1977).

Perhaps the most extreme example of the untutored invention or discovery of linear perspective is the case of Eitan reported by Golomb (1992, 1995). Eitan's parents' report that he consistently resisted instruction and insisted on working on his own. Eitan's first drawings at age 2 were flat and displayed the object from a frontal view. However, he was not satisfied with showing only canonical views, because by 2 years and 2 months he began to juxtapose different views of the same object, resulting in a feeling of solidity and depth.

Eitan discovered (or invented) three perspective systems:

1. He juxtaposed different faces of an object along the horizontal or vertical axis (horizontal and vertical oblique perspective; Figure 7.3a).
2. He drew the sides of an object with lines diverging out from the frontal plane (divergent perspective).
3. He drew the sides of an object with oblique parallel lines (Figure 7.3b). By age 4, this kind of perspective, called isometric, was his preferred strategy, and was used quite systematically by age 6 (see Figure 7.3c), but he did use converging lines to represent depth at age 3 years, 8 months.

The perspective systems that Eitan used followed a logical progression, identical to the progression followed by ordinary children. However, there are three important differences: the early age at which he began, the rapid speed with which he passed through different perspectival "stages," and the fact that he was entirely self-taught.

Orientation

Precocious drawers vary the orientation of figures, in contrast to the canonical orientation used by ordinary children. For instance, a comparison of drawings by ordinary and precocious children showed that human figures were drawn in three-quarters view only 15 percent of the time by ordinary children between 11 and 14 years. In contrast, by age 6 precocious drawers used this orientation in half of their figure drawings (Milbrath, 1995). These three-quarter views appeared abruptly between 6 and 7 years. Note that a three-quarters view is a distortion, just as is foreshortening, size diminution, occlusion, and so on. Precocious drawers are willing to distort the size and shape of objects in order to show them as they appear to the eye.

Fascination with Drawing Nature from Observation

Some precocious realists seem more interested in understanding nature than in drawing per se: Drawing is simply their tool. We have studied two children like this. Both pore over nature encyclopedias and field guides. Rocco is passionate about insects, seeds, leaves, and vegetables. He collects specimens and draws and labels each one. Figure 7.4a shows Rocco's drawing of one of the bugs he collected. Joel has memorized the *Kaufman Field Guide to Birds of North America* and makes meticulous copies of these drawings, as shown in Figure 7.4b.

These children appear to be using drawing in the service of understanding about nature. Who knows whether this early proclivity is more likely predictive of becoming a naturalist than an artist? Both fields require meticulous visual observation.

All of the characteristics just described make precocious drawings look exceptionally realistic. The ability to draw realistically at a precocious age also marks the childhoods of those who have gone on to become recognized artists. Gordon (1987) studied the childhood works of 31 Israeli artists and found that all stood out for their ability to draw realistically. Sloane and Sosniak (1985) interviewed 20 sculptors and found that most recalled drawing realistically at a very early age. Many other famous artists' early drawings have been singled out for their advanced realism: for example, Millais (Paine, 1981), Landseer (Goldsmith & Feldman, 1989), Sargent (Cox, 1992), and Klee, Picasso, and Lautrec (Pariser, 1987, 1991). Picasso recalled one of his first drawings in this way: "I was perhaps six. . . In my father's house there was a statue of Hercules with his club in the corridor, and I drew Hercules. But it wasn't a child's drawing. It was a real drawing, representing Hercules with his club" (Richardson, 1991, p. 29).

While early realism is what is typically noticed in children who draw at an advanced level, we have recently discovered a child who shows the same rage to master as precocious realists, but who eschews representation in favor of entirely abstract, detailed colorful designs (as shown in Plate 7). Arrian began to draw as he was approaching his second birthday. He is obsessed with drawing, working on large, 18 x 24-inch pages with Crayola markers. He is intense, spending up to two days on each drawing. There is nothing haphazard about his process. After putting down one marker, he carefully reviews the remaining markers before he selects the next one. He fills the entire space densely and meticulously with all kinds of lines. Whether children who start out drawing intensely in a nonrepresentational matter like Arrian are more or less likely to go on to become artists is a question we cannot answer now. We suspect that the answer to this question depends very strongly on what kind of art is valued by the culture of the child. A culture that prizes realism (as did 18th-century Western cultures) is more likely to encourage a precocious realist than an Arrian. Conversely, in the 21st century where abstract art is prized over realism, Arrian is the kind of child more likely to feel encouraged to go on and work abstractly.

The Compulsion to Draw

So far we have discussed the characteristics of the drawings produced by children who draw at a precocious level. We now turn to a pervasive characteristic of the children themselves: their compulsion to draw.

The children who draw in the manner we have described draw constantly and compulsively. When our colorist Arrian turned 3, he discovered viewfinders. For 2 weeks he carried around a comb and inspected the world through the comb (like a view finder). Around this same time, he began drawing people, right on track with typical development. While his representational skill was not advanced, the intensity with which Arrian drew was atypical. After making a drawing of a face—a circle with two eyes—he went on to draw 400 faces like this, all in one sitting. The intensity, focus, and meticulous care with which Arrian draws sets him apart from the typical 2-year-old scribbler. None of the precocious realists we have studied show anything like Arrian's interest in abstract art—they progressed rapidly to drawing representationally and show no interest in drawing abstractly.

The compulsion to draw found in precocious drawers has its parallels in many other domains. That is, any time a child is precocious in a particular activity, that child is also highly interested in and drawn to work at that activity. One can find children who spend hours every day finding and solving math problems; not surprisingly, these children also are precocious at math and are able to think about mathematical concepts far beyond the reach of their peers. The same kinds of children have been noted in music, chess, and reading (Winner, 1996).

Precocious realists certainly engage in what might be called deliberate practice. Where they differed from ordinary children was in the independence with which they worked (they needed little or no tutoring) and the ease with which they discovered the rules of their domain. This difference is one that is attributable to innate talent in the domain.

The second problem with the argument that hard work causes the high achievement is that it does not explain what motivates these children to work so hard. One cannot even cajole or force a typical child to draw all day, and the children we are talking about insisted on spending their time in this way. Indeed, they often had to be dragged away from their preferred activities in order to eat, sleep, go to school, and be sociable. The interest, drive, and desire to work on something must be part and parcel of the talent. Of course, as we have already indicated, and as Charness *et al.* (1996) and Ericsson (1996) have argued, the daily hours spent working on something lead to improvement that would not occur without the daily work. However, the desire to work so hard at something comes from within, not without, and occurs almost always when there is an ability to achieve at high levels with relative ease.

Because precocity and drive tend to co-occur, it is difficult to determine the relative contribution of each. However, the fact that precocity and drive so often co-occur is not simply a natural confound that befuddles our research efforts. This co-occurrence also tells us something of critical importance, namely that drive (or what we call the rage to master) is an ineluctable part of talent.

Occasionally one does find examples of hard work without exceptional talent. In the domain of drawing there exists a published record of drawings produced by a child who was obsessed with drawing, who drew constantly, but who never made much progress. This child, Charles, described by Hildreth (1941), provides us with a vivid example of hard work, perhaps one might say deliberate practice, without much innate ability. Charles produced over 2,000 drawings of trains from the time he was 2 until he was 11, most of them drawn between the ages of 7 and 9. Charles clearly drew 2 to 3 years ahead of his age, but as Figure 7.5 shows, although he made some progress, his drawings never reached a level anywhere near to those of Eitan.[1] True, his drawings became more complex, more realistic, and more controlled. But after age 4 his drawings showed little development, and even at age 11 his drawings were fairly schematic and did not show Eitan's mastery of perspective.

Precocious Drawers Are Not Just Ahead, They Are Different

Precocious drawers seem to be able to do things with lines on paper that are simply never mastered by ordinary children who work hard at drawing. Here are a few ways in which they differ. First, as already mentioned, they are self-taught. For example, they invent techniques such as perspective and foreshortening on their own, whereas ordinary children require instruction to arrive at these achievements. Second, they show a confidence in their line and an ability to draw a complex contour with one fluid line. Ordinary children have not been reported to arrive at this. Witness Charles's trains (Hildreth, 1941). Third, they can begin a drawing from any part of the object drawn, and draw objects from noncanonical orientations. This ability suggests a strong visual imagery ability (see the following for evidence of this). Strong visual imagery is also suggested by the way in which these children often draw something vividly that they have seen months or even years ago (Selfe, 1995; Winner, 1996). Fourth, these children are highly inventive and endlessly vary their compositions, forms, and sometimes colors. Note how Eitan varied his perspective systems.

Precocious drawers are sometimes able to draw at a level considerably higher than the typical adult. Take for instance, Arkin Rai, a 5-year-old from Singapore. By age 4 years, 7 months, he drew dinosaur scenes, shown in Figure 7.6, replete with examples of occlusion, foreshortening, and figures in motion. Arkin also shows the ability—characteristic of precocious children—to hyper focus. For example, at a restaurant he drew a complex narrative sequence on the printed paper placemat (Plate 8). He was able to tune out what was on the placemat and not allow it to interfere with his drawing. The narrative sequences he draws are the products of his imagination. It would be difficult to conceive of how a fertile imagination can be developed through practice! In any case, the notion that any child could make Arkin's progress in two and a half years simply by drawing as often as this child did does not seem plausible.

Children with precocious drawing ability are not just advanced: They are also different. We recently demonstrated that children who draw realistically at an above-average level differ in their perceptual skills and drawing strategies from typical children. We assessed children in their level of observational drawing skill and demonstrated that drawing skill (level of realism achieved) was strongly associated with the use of a local perceptual processing strategy (focusing on the parts rather than the whole; Drake, Redash, Coleman, Haimson, & Winner, 2010). For example, we administered a version of the Block Design Task once in traditional unsegmented format, and once with the blocks segmented in space from one another, making it easier to copy the designs with actual blocks. Typical children are helped by presentation of the task in segmented form, as the segmentation reveals each part (or segment) of the design to be reproduced with blocks. Individuals with autism spectrum disorder (ASD) are less helped by presentation of the task in segmented form, showing that they are able to mentally analyze the designs into their parts (Caron, Mottron, Berthiaume, & Dawson, 2006; Shah & Frith, 1993).

We demonstrated that non-autistic children precocious in drawing realism were also less helped than typical children by segmented presentation of the task. These children were also able to detect shapes hidden in complex figures more rapidly than children who drew at a typical level. Thus, like those with ASD, the children with precocious drawing skills were able to focus on the details and avoid the context. In this study, we also assessed whether children began their drawings with small details or whether the first sketched in the overall outline of what they were going to draw. We found that the greater the drawing skill, the more children began first with the details rather than the global outline.

Taken together, these findings show that children who are precocious in drawing not only are advanced but also approach drawing differently from typical children, using a local processing strategy (drawing the details of an object before drawing the overall outline). Though we do not have evidence that this processing style is innate, it seems highly unlikely that one could develop this style through practice. Rather it seems more plausible to assume that this kind of processing style is an unlearned tendency that contributes to realistic drawing skill.

Potential Biological Markers of Drawing Talent

We have thus far argued for the existence of children who draw at a precocious level and who are driven to work hard at drawing. We have argued that the drive to work at drawing, and the interest in drawing are inextricably connected to the precocity. Moreover, the precocity is seen from the outset, and thus cannot be a consequence of hard work.

We now turn to what we argue are biological markers of talent in the visual arts. The case that we make is that children who show precocity in drawing have a particular profile. These children have a higher-than-average likelihood of being non-right-handed and of having visual-spatial strengths along with linguistic deficits. The profile cut by these children can be seen in extreme and exaggerated form in the profile of abilities and disabilities seen in drawing savants. This profile of abilities and disabilities is consistent with the existence of a biological component to drawing expertise.

Higher Than Average Incidence of Non-Right-Handedness

A disproportionate number of adult artists and children who draw precociously are non-right-handed (Mebert & Michel, 1980; Peterson, 1979; Rosenblatt & Winner, 1988; Smith, Meyers, & Kline, 1989). For instance, in one study it was shown that 21 percent of art students were left-handed, compared to only 7 percent of non-art majors at the same university; 48 percent of the art students were non-right-handed (i.e., either left-handed or ambidextrous), compared to 22 percent of the non-art majors (Mebert & Michel, 1980). No environmental explanation can make sense of this finding: Artists do not need to use both hands when drawing, and even very young precocious drawers show this tendency, often drawing interchangeably with both hands (Winner, 1996).

Non-right-handedness is a marker, albeit an imperfect one, of anomalous brain dominance. It is estimated that about 70 percent of the population has standard dominance—a strong left-hemisphere dominance for language and hand (yielding right-handedness) and a strong right-hemisphere dominance for other functions such as visual-spatial and musical processing (Geschwind & Galaburda, 1985). Those remaining 30 percent with anomalous dominance have more symmetrical brains (with language and visual-spatial functions represented somewhat on both sides of the brain).

Visual-Spatial Strengths

Anomalous dominance has been argued to result in a tendency toward inborn ability in areas for which the right hemisphere is important (e.g., visual-spatial, musical, or mathematical areas; Geschwind & Galaburda, 1985), and children who draw precociously have been shown to possess other visual-spatial strengths besides the ability to render. There is also experimental evidence for advanced visual-spatial strengths in children whose drawings are unusually skilled. Such children excel in visual memory tasks of various sorts (Hermelin & O'Connor, 1986; Rosenblatt & Winner, 1988; Winner & Casey, 1992; Winner, Casey, DaSilva, & Hayes, 1991). For example, they are better able to recognize non-representational shapes that they have seen before (Hermelin & O'Connor, 1986) and to recall shapes, colors, compositions, and forms in pictures (Rosenblatt & Winner, 1988). They also show superior ability to recognize what is represented in incomplete drawings (O'Connor & Hermelin, 1983), suggesting that they have a rich lexicon of mental images. Thus, precocious drawers show the kinds of right-hemisphere skills that would be predicted by anomalous dominance. It is perhaps because of strong imaging abilities that these children are able to begin drawings from non-canonical places, and can draw from memory images they have seen long ago.

These children are not just advanced but are also different. We (Drake & Winner, 2017) studied 12 precocious children (ages 6 to 16) in drawing in order to understand what traits might underlie the ability to draw so realistically. These children came to us because their parents contacted us, asking about their child's talent. All of the children were precocious realists, as made clear by the early drawings their parents supplied. We studied these children as a group, asking what kinds of cognitive, perceptual, and personality characteristics set these children apart. We administered a battery of measures to this group and compared their performance to adult norms and on some measures to the performance of a control group of typical drawers. To determine whether these children excelled in IQ, we administered both verbal and non-verbal IQ test of the Kauffman Brief Intelligence Test (K-BIT). Because previous work (Winner & Casey, 1992; Kozbelt, 2001) has shown that adult visual artists excel in mental rotation, visual memory, and visual imagery, we administered measures of these three skills as well. Because of the strong evidence that artists possess the personality trait of openness to experience (Burch, Pavelis, Hemsley, & Corr, 2006), we sought to determine whether we could see this trait in our young prodigies. We asked parents to complete the Inventory for Children's Individual Differences (which asks questions that allowed us to code for openness, conscientiousness, extraversion, agreeableness, and neuroticism). We then assembled a control group of children matched on age and gender, and identified by us through their drawings as showing no special talent in drawing; we compared this groups' performance on the personality battery to that of our precocious realists.

Despite the recent finding that performance on the draw-a-child task (a version of the draw-a-person task) at age 4 is associated with higher intelligence at age 14 (Arden, Trzakowski, Garfield, & Plomin, 2014), our prodigies did not stand out in either kind of IQ. This discrepancy could be accounted for by several factors. First, the relationship shown by Arden *et al.* between IQ and the draw-a-child task was modest at best ($r = .20$). Second, the Arden *et al.* study did not include a wide variety of levels of drawing skills but instead included a small range of drawing abilities with children not selected for advanced drawing skill. The relationship between drawing and IQ may be very different at the positive extreme – with some level of IQ predictive of modest increases in drawing ability, but with other kinds of skills predictive of extreme levels. Further research on this topic including a large range of drawing levels is needed to determine whether IQ becomes less predictive as levels of drawing increases. Finally and perhaps most importantly, the draw-a-child task assesses the drawing for the presence and quantity of certain features (e.g., did the drawing have two eyes, mouth, hair?) rather than for level of realism. Thus, children must understand the anatomy of the body to receive a high score on the task. They do not need to represent the body realistically as precocious realists do. Consistent with other research on the weak relationship between IQ and drawing ability (Harris, 1963), the mean verbal and non-verbal IQ scores of the precocious realists were within normal range. Whereas there appears to be some relationship between drawing ability and IQ within the normal range of IQ, this relationship does not hold up when we are talking about extreme levels of drawing skill. Prodigious drawing skill apparently develops independently of IQ. This is striking.

In two respects, our precocious realists were not normal. Their scores on visual imagery and mental rotation were equivalent to adult level norms, and their visual memory was superior to adult norms. Thus underlying (or associated with) their drawing ability were superior visual skills, but not superior IQ. It is most likely, but remains to be demonstrated, that visual and visual-spatial skills (rather than hours of deliberate practice) predict level of graphic representation in typical children as well. Of course, it is likely that hours of deliberate practice improve already superior visual-spatial skills. But as already mentioned, no child is going to willingly or unwillingly engage in daily hours of work in a domain that does not come easily.

Our personality test revealed one trait distinguishing precocious realists from a group of control children: agreeableness. These children experienced more positive emotions as reported by their parents. Contrary to our hypothesis, precocious realists did not score above average on openness to experience. Openness to experience is a trait that distinguishes artists and other kinds of creative types (Burch *et al.*, 2006). Whereas early realism is the first sign of drawing talent in children who go on to become artists, very few precocious realists will go on to become adult artists (Winner, 1996). Thus it may not come as a surprise then that our precocious realists did not score higher in openness to experience: they may simply not have the temperament associated with artists.

Parents of our precocious realists described their children as obsessed with and engaged in drawing all the time. We call this a "rage to master." This is an intrinsic motivation to acquire skill in the domain because of the ease with which learning occurs (Winner, 1996). This rage to master has not been reported in typical children. We argue that rage to master does not cause talent. Rather, it is an inherent component of talent. Without this kind of intrinsic drive, talent does not develop. We speculate that children who show a rage to master experience more flow than those without such a passion, and this could explain why they scored higher in this study on agreeableness, which is associated with positive emotion traits.

Linguistic Deficits

Anomalous dominance has also been argued to lead to deficits in areas for which the left hemisphere is important, resulting in language-related problems such as dyslexia (Geschwind & Galaburda, 1985). This hypothesis can be tested either by assessing heightened right-hemisphere abilities in dyslexic children or by assessing frequencies of dyslexia in children who draw precociously. Both ways of testing the hypothesis yield a clear and consistent picture of an association between visual-spatial ability and language-related learning disorders.

Many studies have shown that on IQ tests, dyslexic children score higher on subtests assessing right-hemisphere spatial skills than on those assessing left-hemisphere sequential skills (Gordon, 1983; Gordon & Harness, 1977; Naidoo, 1972; Rugel, 1974). For instance, they score higher on constructing patterns or puzzles than on recalling sequences of numbers. These findings fit with anecdotal observations of visual-spatial talent in dyslexics (Galaburda & Kemper, 1979).

The same association shows up when either adults or children who draw at high levels are examined for verbal problems. Artists score poorly on tests of verbal fluency (Hassler, 1990), they report more reading problems as children than do other college students (Winner et al., 1991), and they make more spelling errors than do other students (Winner et al., 1991). Moreover, the kinds of spelling errors they make are just those associated with poor reading skills—nonphonetically based errors that do not preserve letter-sound relationships (Frith, 1980; Phillips, 1987). Nonphonetically based errors are ones in which wrong letters are included, correct ones are omitted, or letters are reversed (e.g., physicain for physician); in contrast, phonetically based errors are ones that when sounded out, sound right (e.g., "phisician"). This tendency to make nonphonetically based errors was found by Winner et al. (1991) even when SAT performance was partialled out. This suggests that artistically inclined individuals have problems specific to reading and spelling that are independent of the kinds of abilities measured by the SAT.

Thus individuals who show high achievement in the visual arts have a tendency toward non-right-handedness and also have heightened right-hemisphere skills and lowered left-hemisphere skills. The confluence of non-right-handedness, spatial skills, and linguistic problems has been dubbed a "pathology of superiority" by Geschwind and Galaburda (1985, p. 445). They argued that such pathologies of superiority were due to the hormonal environment of the developing fetal brain. In particular, either excess testosterone, or heightened sensitivity to testosterone, was argued to slow development of an area of the brain's left posterior hemisphere. Slowing of the left hemisphere was argued to lead to compensatory development of the right hemisphere, and thus to result in the emergence of talents associated with the right hemisphere such as music, drawing, and mathematics. This theory remains controversial (see Bryden, McManus, & Bulman-Fleming, 1994; Schachter, 1994). Nonetheless, there is as yet no other theory that can explain the established fact that ability in drawing is associated with both non-right-handedness and dyslexia. This fact lends support to the claim that children who draw precociously are different from the start.

Drawing Savants

The final piece of evidence that we present in favor of a biological component to drawing expertise is the existence of drawing savants. Savants are people who show prodigious ability in one area but severe disability in all other areas. Although such individuals are rare, generalizations about them can be drawn. They are typically found in one of four domains: music (almost always piano), mental calculation, calendar calculation, and visual arts (almost always realistic drawing). There have been numerous attempts to explain savants. Environmental explanations appeal to practice and reinforcement (Ericsson & Faivre, 1988). Psychodynamic explanations appeal to a compensatory search for a communication channel when language is lacking. However, we argue here that a biological explanation of these individuals is the only feasible one because of the rapidity with which they acquire the domain, their lack of need for scaffolding, and their drive to master. Moreover, savants can be seen as particularly extreme examples of the pathology of superiority. Savants have a highly developed skill (usually one subserved by the right hemisphere) and are deficient in everything else.[2] The severity of their pathology limits them to a restricted set of domains, and also limits what they can do in these domains.

The most famous drawing savant is Nadia, an autistic child who drew at least from the age of three (Selfe, 1977, 1983, 1985, 1995). Her drawings preserved from this age are drawn in perspective, with foreshortening, occlusion, and correct proportion. Her drawings are more advanced than those of any nonpathologically gifted child that we know of (Figure 7.7), but other autistic children have also been shown to draw at an exceptional level (Park, 1978; Sacks, 1985, 1995; Wiltshire, 1987). These savants resemble precocious drawers. They draw early and a lot, and they also stand out as different from ordinary children in the same ways as do precocious drawers. They discover perspective and foreshortening and other depth techniques on their own, they can begin a drawing from any part of the object, they draw with astounding confidence and fluidity of line, and they can draw from memory objects and pictures they have seen months or years ago.

We recently reported on the drawing ability in an autistic child, J.G., who showed clear savant-level drawing skills (Drake & Winner, 2011–2012). J.G. is able to draw in a highly realistic manner using dramatic foreshortening (e.g., see Figure 7.8), has a strong visual memory (he can recount in vivid detail what he has seen) and shows a strong local processing skill—as shown by the near equivalence of his performance on the segmented versus unsegmented Block Design Task (described above) as well as on the Embedded Figures Test. This local processing skill also manifested itself in the process by which he drew from observation. Like the savant E.C. described by Mottron and Belleville (1993), J.G. drew using a strategy of local progression. We asked him to draw a corkscrew. He did not sketch in the overall shape but rather created the corkscrew part by part, beginning at the top and working his way down.

In a study of eight precocious children across multiple domains, Ruthsatz and Urbach (2012) found that the precocious children had more autistic-like traits when compared to a control group (see Chapter 6, The Link Between

Child Prodigies and Autism). In particular, the children scored higher than the control group on attention to detail. The precocious children were also more likely to have a relative with ASD. It should be noted that three out of the eight prodigies had a diagnosis of ASD, and this may explain why there was a higher incidence of autistic traits in the prodigies Ruthsatz and Urbach studied. We have found mixed results for the relationship between drawing talent and autistic-like traits. In one study, we found that children gifted in the ability to draw realistically scored higher in repetitive and restrictive interests—one of the core symptoms of a diagnosis of ASD (Drake *et al.*, 2010). However, we did not find a heightened incidence of autistic-like traits in our precocious realists. Thus, it is unclear whether precocious realists, like children with ASD, have an exceptional ability to focus on details that may contribute to the extreme realism in their drawings.

Heightened drawing ability exists in only a small subset of autistic children (Charman & Baron-Cohen, 1993), and we do not know whether anything else differentiates this subset of autistic children from those who draw at their mental level (Selfe, 1995). Nonetheless, the existence of extraordinary drawing ability in the presence of an intellectual disability, and in the absence of any explicit instruction, calls for a biological, brain-based explanation. If the high drawing ability of savants were simply due to the fact that they draw all the time (which they do), then one would expect savants in any domain. All that would be required is compulsive practice.

The fact that savants are found only in certain domains suggests that practice cannot be the explanation. Moreover, the intense drive to draw (or play music, or calculate mentally) seen in savants is what leads to the compulsive practice. We have to explain the intense drive for mastery in a domain that we see in savants just as we see in normal children. This rage to master is part of the talent; it does not explain the talent.

Conclusion

We have tried to disentangle talent from hard work (sometimes referred to as deliberate practice, but we prefer the term "rage to master") in order to argue that talent is innate and therefore is prior to hard work. Talent is associated with a rage to master in the talent domain. A rage to master means hard work. And hard work in a domain leads to ever-increasing levels of achievement. It is useful to think in terms of four logically possible combinations of hard work and talent.

1. Most children have neither exceptional talent in drawing nor do they spend much time at drawing. These children never draw particularly realistically.
2. Some children have no really exceptional talent but they work hard at drawing (e.g., Hildreth's train drawer). These children are able to draw at a level considerably beyond their age.

3. Some children have talent but by early adolescence they disengage from their domain of talent, often because of competing demands by school and family (Csikszentmihalyi, Rathunde, & Whalen, 1993).
4. Finally, there are those with both talent and a drive to work that continues undiminished into adulthood.

What kind of further evidence would one need to conclude definitively that talent plays a decisive role in expertise in drawing or in other areas? Ideally, one would need to take a large sample of young and untutored children, selected at random, and submit them to identical levels of deliberate practice. Three conditions would have to be obtained to demonstrate that hard work began at an early age and is all that is necessary to explain the Picassos and Mozarts of the world. First, all of the children must eventually achieve the same levels of expertise with the same levels of work. Second, all children would have to learn in the same way, mastering what is given to them rather than deviating and inventing their own techniques. Third, with sufficient work and time, the levels reached must be as high as those reached by individuals we consider truly exceptional. Only then could we rule out talent as a factor in high accomplishment. We, for one, would place our bets on quite different outcomes: highly differential levels achieved despite the same amount of work; difficulty getting some of the children to work as hard as others; those that work willingly also inventing techniques on their own; and no levels achieved concomitant to those achieved by Picasso, Mozart, or Menuhin.

While the kind of study outlined above has not been done, and probably never will be done, there are now two studies that provide strong evidence that deliberate practice is not sufficient to account for extraordinary levels of performance.

A study from the domain of music demonstrates that deliberate practice is not sufficient. Meinz and Hambrick (2010) compared the relative importance of deliberate practice and working memory capacity in piano sight-reading skills in novice to expert piano players. Deliberate practice explained almost half of the variance in piano sight-reading skills. However, working memory capacity explained variance above and beyond deliberate practice. These results demonstrate that deliberate practice is not sufficient and that poor working memory capacity may limit achieving expertise. One cannot argue that working memory is simply a product of deliberate practice since working memory capacity was shown to contribute independently to the level of sight-reading reached.

The best systematic evidence disentangling nature from nurture comes from studies of chess masters (Gobet & Campitelli, 2007; Howard, 2009). These researchers were able to disentangle amount of deliberate practice from level of chess achieved, and they reported wide individual variation in the number of hours needed to reach grandmaster level. If some people reach grandmaster level with fewer hours of practice than others, we cannot account for the level they reached only by amount of deliberate practice. There must be another factor that allows some people to progress more rapidly with less practice, and that factor is most plausibly an innate proclivity to learn rapidly in the domain in question. These researchers also found players who put in huge amounts of chess time (from childhood) yet never attained master level. Thus, sheer hard work is simply not sufficient to make someone a chess master. What is true of chess is bound to be true of all kinds of great achievers, whether in the arts, the sciences, or athletics, though comparable studies have not yet been conducted.

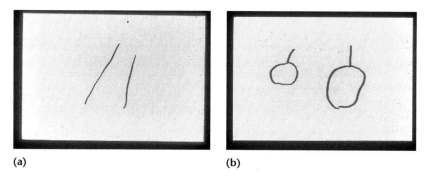

(a)   (b)

FIGURE 7.1   Apples drawn by typical 2-year-old (a) and by a precocious 2-year-old (b). From Winner (1996).

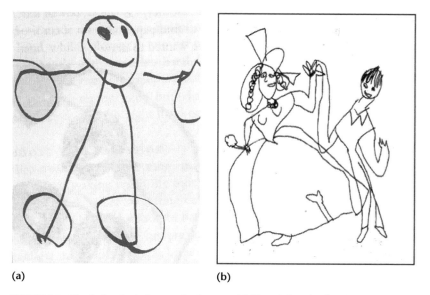

(a)   (b)

FIGURE 7.2   Typical tadpole human by 3-year-old (a) and drawing by Gracie, a precocious drawer, at age 3 (b). From private collection of Ellen Winner.

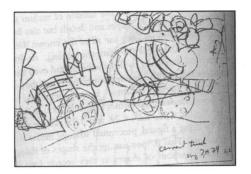

(a)

(b)

(c)

FIGURE 7.3 Examples of perspective: All drawings by Eitan from Golomb (1992).
(a) Cement truck by Eitan, age 2 yrs, 7 mths, showing the side view of the
truck, the top view of the hood, and a frontal view of grill and bumper.
(b) Truck by Eitan, age 3 yrs, 7 mths, showing isometric perspective, in
which the third dimension is represented by parallel oblique lines.
(c) Drawing entitled "Near Accident," by Eitan, age 6 yrs, 6 mths, showing
the systematic use of isometric perspective. From Golomb (1992).

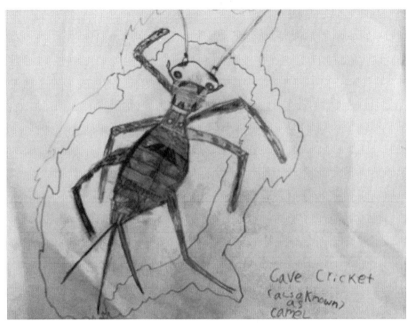

(a)

(b)

FIGURE 7.4 Drawings by precocious realists who use drawing to study biology:
(a) by Rocco, at age 6; reprinted by permission of Nigel and Amanda
Roth. (b) by Joel, at age 10; reprinted by permission of Joan Gervais.

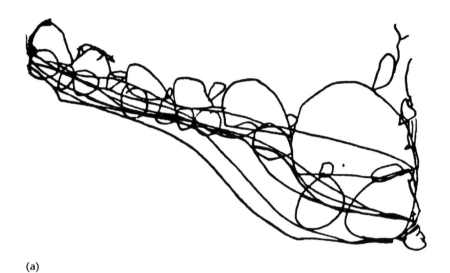

(a)

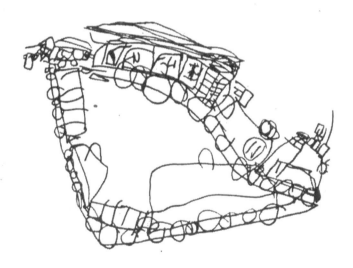

(b)

(See next page for Figure 7.5 caption.)

(c)

(d)

FIGURE 7.5 Examples of the fruits of drawing practice without much innate talent: All drawings by Charles are from Hildreth (1941). (a) Drawing of train by Charles, age 2, showing tracks and differentiation between engine and passenger cars. (b) Drawing of train by Charles, age 4, showing three-dimensional space by vertical positioning (the farther trains are placed higher up). (c) Drawing of train by Charles, age 8, in canonical side view. (d) Drawing of train by Charles, age 10, in canonical side view. From Winner (1996).

(a)

(See next page for Figure 7.6 caption.)

(b)

(c)

FIGURE 7.6 Drawings of dinosaurs by Arkin Rai at age 5 showing foreshortening, occlusion, and motion. Reprinted by permission of Dinesh Rai.

FIGURE 7.7 Drawing of horse by Nadia, at about age 5. From Selfe (1977).

FIGURE 7.8 Drawing of a jaguar by J.G., at age 9, showing dramatic foreshortening. From Drake & Winner (2011–2012).

Acknowledgements

This chapter is updated from Winner, E. (1996). The rage to master: The decisive case for talent in the visual arts. In K. A. Ericsson (Ed.), *The road to excellence: The acquisition of expert performance in the arts and sciences, sports and games* (p. 271–301). Hillsdale, NJ: Erlbaum. Reproduced by permission of Taylor and Francis.

Note

1 The second author is indebted to Rudolf Arnheim and Claire Golomb for bringing Hildreth's study to her attention as an example of what can be achieved with work but no exceptional talent.
2 Savantism in calculation, a left-hemisphere skill, can also be explained by Geschwind and Galaburda's (1985) theory. They argued that in addition to compensatory right-hemisphere development, regions next to the left posterior areas may also undergo compensatory development.

References

Arden, R., Trzakowski, M., Garfield, V., & Plomin, R. (2014). Genes influence young children's human figure drawings and their association with intelligence a decade later. *Psychological Science, 25*, 1843–1850.

Beck, W. (1928). *Self-development in drawing. As interpreted by the genius of Romano Dazzi and other children.* New York, NY: Putnam.

Bryden, M. P., McManus, I. C., & Bulman-Fleming, M. B. (1994). Evaluating the empirical support for the Geschwind-Behan-Galaburda model of cerebral lateralization. *Brain and Cognition, 26*, 103–167.

Burch, G. S. J., Pavelis, C., Hemsley, D. R., & Corr, P. J. (2006). Schizotypy and creativity in visual artists. *British Journal of Psychology, 97*, 177–190.

Caron, M. J., Mottron, L., Berthiaume, C., & Dawson, M. (2006). Cognitive mechanisms, specificity and neural underpinnings of visuospatial peaks in autism. *Brain: A Journal of Neurology, 129*, 1789–1802.

Charman, A., & Baron-Cohen, S. (1993). Drawing development in autism: The intellectual to visual realism shift. *British Journal of Developmental Psychology, 11*, 171–186.

Charness, N., Krampe, R. T., & Mayr, U. (1996). The role of practice and coaching in entrepreneurial skill domains: An international comparison of life-span chess skill acquisition. In K. A. Ericsson (Ed.), *The road to excellence: The acquisition of expert performance in the arts and sciences, sports, and games* (pp. 1–50). Mahwah, NJ: Erlbaum.

Cox, M. (1992). *Children's drawings.* London, England: Penguin.

Csikszentmihalyi, M., Rathunde, K., & Whalen, S. (1993). *Talented teenagers: The roots of success and failure.* New York, NY: Cambridge University Press.

Csikszentmihalyi, M., & Robinson, R. E. (1986). Culture, time and the development of talent. In R. J. Stembetg & J. E. Davidson (Eds.), *Conceptions of giftedness* (pp. 264–284). New York, NY: Cambridge University Press.

Drake, J. E., Redash, A., Coleman, K., Haimson, J., & Winner, E. (2010). 'Autistic' local processing bias also found in children gifted in realistic drawing. *Journal of Autism and Developmental Disorders, 40*, 762–773.

Drake, J. E., & Winner, E. (2011–2012). Superior visual analysis and imagery in an Autistic child with drawing talent. *Imagination, Cognition, and Personality, 31*, 9–29.

Drake, J. E., & Winner, E. (2012). Predicting artistic brilliance. *Scientific American Mind*, *23*(5), 42–48.

Drake, J. E., & Winner, E. (2017) Children gifted in drawing realism: Associations with visual- spatial abilities but not IQ. Unpublished.

Ericsson, K. A. (1996). The acquisition of expert performance: An introduction to some of the issues. In K. A. Ericsson (Ed.), *The road to excellence: The acquisition of expert performance in the arts and sciences, sports, and games* (pp. 1–50). Mahwah, NJ: Erlbaum.

Ericsson, K. A., & Faivre, I. A. (1988). What's exceptional about exceptional abilities? In L. K. Obler & D. A. Fein (Eds.), *The neuropsychology of talent and special abilities* (pp. 436–473). New York, NY: Guilford.

Frith, U. (1980). *Cognitive processes in spelling.* New York, NY: Academic Press.

Galaburda, A. M., & Kemper, T. L. (1979). Cytoarchitectonic abnormalities in developmental dyslexia: A case study. *Annals of Neurology*, *6*, 94–100.

Geschwind, N., & Galaburda, A. M. (1985). Cerebral lateralization: Biological mechanisms, associations, and pathology: 1. A hypothesis and a program for research. *Archives of Neurology*, *42*, 428–459.

Gobet, F., & Campitelli, G. (2007). The role of domain-specific practice, handedness, and starting age in chess. *Developmental Psychology*, *43*, 159–172.

Goldsmith, L. (1992). Stylistic development of a Chinese painting prodigy. *Creativity Research Journal*, *5*, 281–293.

Goldsmith, L., & Feldman, D. (1989). Wang Yarn: Gifts well given. In W. C. Ho (Ed.), *Wang Yani: The brush of innocence* (pp. 59–62). New York, NY: Hudson Hills.

Golomb, C. (1992). Eitan: The early development of a gifted child artist. *Creativity Research Journal*, *5*(3), 265–279.

Golomb, C. (1995). Eitan: The artistic development of a child prodigy. In C. Golomb (Ed.), *The development of gifted child artists: Selected case studies* (pp. 171–196). Hillsdale, NJ: Erlbaum.

Golomb, C., & Hass, M. (1995). Varda: The development of a young artist. In C. Golomb (Ed.), *The development of gifted child artists: Selected case studies* (pp. 71–100). Hillsdale, NJ: Erlbaum.

Gombrich, E. H. (1960). *Art and illusion.* London, England: Phaidon.

Goodenough, F. L. (1926). *Measurement of intelligence by drawings.* New York, NY: Harcourt, Brace, & World.

Gordon, A. (1987). Childhood works of artists. *The Israel Museum Journal*, *6*, 75–82.

Gordon, A., & Broshi, M. (2015). *Childhood works of artists.*

Gordon, H. W. (1983). The learning disabled are cognitively right. *Topics in Learning and Learning Disabilities*, *3*(1), 29–39.

Gordon, H. W., & Harness, B. Z. (1977). A test battery for the diagnosis and treatment of developmental dyslexia. *Journal of Speech and Hearing Disorders*, *8*, 1–7.

Harris, D. B. (1963). *Children's drawings as measures of intellectual maturity; a revision and extension of the Goodenough Draw-A-Man Test.* New York, NY: Harcourt, Brace & World.

Hassler, M. (1990). Functional cerebral asymmetric and cognitive abilities in musicians, painters, and controls. *Brain Cognition*, *13*, 1–17.

Hermelin, B., & O'Connor, N. (1986). Spatial representations in mathematically and in artistically gifted children. *British Journal of Educational Psychology*, *56*, 150–157.

Hildreth, G. (1941). *The child mind in evolution: A study of developmental sequences in drawing.* New York, NY: Kings Crown Press.

Howard, R. W. (2009). Individual differences in expertise development over decades in a complex intellectual domain. *Memory & Cognition, 37*, 194–209.

Kozbelt, A. (2001). Artists as experts in visual cognition. *Visual Cognition, 8*, 705–723.

Lark-Horowitz, B., Lewis, H., & Luca, M. (1973). *Understanding children's art for better teaching* (2nd ed.). Columbus, OH: Merrill.

Mebert, C. J., & Michel, G. F. (1980). Handedness in artists. In J. Herron (Ed.), *Neuropsychology of left-handedness* (pp. 273–279). New York, NY: Academic Press.

Meinz, E. J., & Hambrick, D. Z. (2010). Deliberate practice is necessary but not sufficient to explain individual differences in piano sight-reading skill: The role of working memory capacity. *Psychological Science, 21*, 914–919.

Milbrath, C. (1995). Germinal motifs in the work of a gifted child artist. In C. Golomb (Ed.), *The development of artistically gifted children: Selected case studies* (pp. 101–134). Hillsdale, NJ: Erlbaum.

Milbrath, C. (1998). *Patterns of artistic development.* New York, NY: Cambridge University Press.

Mottron, L., & Belleville, S. (1993). A study of perceptual analysis in a high-level autistic subject with exceptional graphic abilities. *Brain and Cognition, 23*, 279–309.

Naidoo, S. (1972). *Specific dyslexia.* New York, NY: Wiley.

O'Connor, N., & Hermelin, B. (1983). The role of general and specific talents in information processing. *British Journal of Developmental Psychology, 1*, 389–403.

Paine, S. (1981). *Six children draw.* London, England: Academic Press.

Paine, S. (1987). The childhood and adolescent drawings of Henri de Toulouse-Lautrec (1864-1901): Drawings from 6 to 18 years. *Journal of Art and Design, 6*, 297–312.

Pariser, D. (1987). The juvenile drawings of Klee, Toulouse-Lautrec and Picasso. *Visual Arts Research, 13*, 53–67.

Pariser, D. (1991). Normal and unusual aspects of juvenile artistic development in Klee, Lautrec, and Picasso. *Creativity Research Journal, 4*, 51–65.

Park, C. C. (1978). Review of "Nadia: A case of extraordinary drawing ability in an autistic child." *Journal of Autism and Childhood Schizophrenia, 8*, 457–472.

Peterson, J. M. (1979). Left-handedness: Differences between student artists and scientists. *Perceptual and Motor Skills, 48*, 961–962.

Phillips, I. (1987). *Word recognition and spelling strategies in good and poor readers.* Unpublished doctoral dissertation, Harvard Graduate School of Education, Cambridge, MA.

Richardson, J. (1991). *A life of Picasso.* New York, NY: Random House.

Rosenblatt, E., & Winner, E. (1988). Is superior visual memory a component of superior drawing ability? In L. Obler & D. Fein (Eds.), *The exceptional brain: Neuropsychology of talent and superior abilities* (pp. 341–363). New York, NY: Guilford.

Rugel, R. P. (1974). WISC subtest scores of disabled readers: A review with respect to Bannatyne's recategorization. *Journal of Learning Disabilities, 7*(1), 48–65.

Ruthsatz, J., & Urbach, J. (2012). Child Prodigy: A novel cognitive profile places elevated general intelligence, exceptional working memory and attention to detail at the root of prodigiousness. *Intelligence, 40*, 419–426.

Sacks, O. (1985, April 25). The autistic artist. *New York Review of Books*, pp. 17–21.

Sacks, O. (1995, January 9). A neurologist's notebook: Prodigies. *The New Yorker*, pp. 44–65.

Schachter, S. C. (1994). Evaluating the Bryden-McManus-Bulman-Fleming critique of the Geschwind-Behan-Galaburda model of cerebral lateralization. *Brain and Cognition, 26*, 199–205.

Selfe, L. (1977). *Nadia: A case of extraordinary drawing ability in an autistic child.* New York, NY: Academic Press.

Selfe, L. (1983). *Normal and anomalous representational drawing ability in children.* London. England: Academic Press.

Selfe, L. (1985). *Anomalous drawing development: Some clinical studies.* Cambridge, England: Cambridge University Press.

Selfe, L. (1995). Nadia reconsidered. In C. Golomb (Ed.), *The development of gifted child: Selected case studies* (pp. 197–236). Hillsdale, NJ: Erlbaum.

Shah, A., & Frith, U. (1993). Why do autistic individuals show superior performance on the block design task? *Journal of Child Psychology and Psychiatry, 34,* 1351–1364.

Sloane, K. D., & Sosniak, L. A. (1985). The development of accomplished sculptors. In B. S. Bloom (Ed.), *Developing talent in young people* (pp. 90–138). New York, NY: Ballantine Books.

Smith, B. O., Meyers, M. B., & Kline, K. (1989). For better or for worse: Left-handedness, pathology, and talent. *Journal of Clinical and Experimental Neuropsychology, 11,* 944–958.

Vasari, G. (1957). *Lives of the artists.* New York, NY: Noonday.

Willats, J. (1977). How children learn to draw realistic pictures. *Quarterly Journal of Experimental Psychology, 29,* 367–382.

Wiltshire, S. (1987). *Drawings.* London, England: J. M. Dent.

Winner, E. (1996). *Gifted children: Myths and realities.* New York, NY: Basic Books.

Winner, E., & Casey, M. B. (1992). Cognitive profiles of artists. In G. Cupchik & J. Laszlo (Eds.), *Emerging visions of the aesthetic process* (pp. 154–170). New York, NY: Cambridge University Press.

Winner, E., Casey, M. B., DaSilva, E., & Hayes, R (1991). Spatial abilities and reading deficits in visual arts students. *Empirical Studies of the Arts, 9,* 51–63.

Winner, E., & Martino, G. (1993). Giftedness in the visual arts and music. In K. Heller, F. Monks, & A. H. Passow (Eds.), *International handbook of research and development of giftedness and talent* (pp. 253–281). New York, NY: Pergamon.

Zhensun, Z., & Low, A. (1991). *A young painter: The life and paintings of Wang Yani— China's extraordinary young artist.* New York, NY: Scholastic.

8

THE DEVELOPMENT OF EXPERTISE IN THE VISUAL ARTS

Rebecca Chamberlain

Introduction

Expertise research has principally been applied to quantifiably tractable domains such as sports (e.g., Macnamara, Moreau, & Hambrick, 2016), music (e.g., Butkovic, Ullén, & Mosing, 2015) and chess (e.g., Gobet & Campitelli, 2007). The quantification of expertise enables researchers to determine the similarities between different experts, which is critical for establishing the necessary and sufficient conditions for achievement within that domain. In contrast to experts in these traditional expertise domains, artists are a highly heterogeneous group of individuals, making the study of artistic expertise especially challenging. In addition, the rules of art are in a constant state of flux, in contrast to other domains of expertise (the rules of chess have remained essentially unchanged for 200 years). Some studies have used histriometric methods to deduce the correlates of artistic expertise (Damian & Simonton, 2014) most particularly in reference to a link between artistic creativity and psychopathology (Simonton, 2014). However, this approach has limitations as information has to be gleaned retrospectively and is not collected in a controlled experimental setting.

Despite the challenges of evaluating this diverse and evolving field, a growing body of research has sought to explicate the cognitive and perceptual under-pinnings of artistic expertise. Research focus has converged on observational drawing ability, which represents the most tangible artistic skill, its goal being to create a mapping between a drawn representation and the external world. Observational drawing has many of the hallmarks of a domain of expertise, as it is characterized by domain specificity (Angelone, Hass, & Cohen, 2016), efficient processing (Perdreau & Cavanagh, 2014), and enhanced visual memory (McManus *et al.*, 2010). During the Italian Renaissance drawing was viewed as the foundation of representational art, "a seminal font from which sprang the union of theory and idea with execution" (Kenin, 1974, p.81). By contrast drawing was overlooked as a medium of expression during the twentieth century, a victim of continued post-modern attacks on traditional modes of artistic practice in favor of more conceptual approaches to art making, but the practice of drawing is beginning to resurge once again (Petherbridge, 2007).

Despite its historical primacy, drawing ability is now viewed as neither necessary nor sufficient for the kind of creative thinking that characterized artistic geniuses such as Leonardo da Vinci, Claude Monet, and Andy Warhol. However, connections between technical and creative properties of artworks have been found in past research (Kozbelt, 2004) suggesting that technical proficiency may provide a scaffold upon which creativity can thrive. In support of this, a neuroimaging study of an expert portrait artist revealed heightened activation in the frontal lobes and diminished activation in the fusiform face area (FFA) relative to control participants (Solso, 2001). This finding suggests that automated schemas created to support technical expertise free up higher-level cognitive capacities involved in creative processes. Extending this point, certain kinds of artistic training may facilitate a mode of perceiving that is conducive to discovering new ways of representing stimuli. This will be revisited in the conclusion of this chapter in an attempt to further align technical and creative skill; however, the predominant focus of this chapter will be on technical skill.

In this chapter the differences between expertise in artistic perception and production will be discussed before providing a detailed analysis of the predictors of observational drawing expertise including visual perception, visual memory, visual attention, and motor processing. The discussion will then move to the use of techniques and the role of practice in expertise development. This will be placed in the broader context of individual differences in personality and approaches to learning. In the conclusion, these various aspects of expertise development are brought together and suggestions for future research are put forward.

Similarities and Differences Between Expert Artistic Perception and Production

While the focus of this chapter is on expertise in artistic production, it is worth briefly outlining what is known about expertise in analyzing and appreciating artworks, an ability manifest in art curators, collectors, historians, and dealers as well as artists themselves. A great number of parallels can be drawn between abilities fostered by artistic production and those fostered by artistic perception, as highlighted by Tinio's mirror model of art (Tinio, 2013). In turn, by evaluating the differences between artistic practitioners and evaluators it will be possible to identify skills specific to each domain.

Knowledge-related processing is arguably critical in aesthetic evaluation, suggesting that expertise (consisting of domain-specific knowledge) has an impact on how art is perceived and appreciated (Leder, Belke, Oeberst, & Augustin, 2004). Cupchik (1992) argued that functional perception is not sufficient for aesthetic experience, which demands appreciation of often ignored sensory qualities such as shapes, colors, textures, and tones. To explore the impact of artistic expertise on perception, Augustin and Leder (2006) conducted an extensive study of lay and expert responses to artworks using a natural grouping paradigm. It was found that art history students made finer-grained classifications than novices when sorting artworks, representing a more differentiated category structure. This characteristic is common in experts across domains of perceptual expertise (Tanaka & Taylor, 1991) and falls in line with the proposition that expert artistic perception is facilitated by appreciation of non-denotative sensory qualities (Cupchik, 1992) and higher-order semantic properties (Leder *et al.*, 2004). In support, it has been shown that when viewing representational artworks artists focus more on background elements and relations between objects than novices (e.g. Vogt & Magnussen, 2007), make more global scanning eye movements (Zangemeister, Sherman, & Stark, 1995), and make eye movements that are less driven by locally salient regions (Koide, Kubo, Nishida, Shibata, & Ikeda, 2015), suggesting a reduction in the impact of stimulus-driven factors on artistic perception. This enhanced relational and semantic processing may also explain why art experts do not show the same preference for representational over abstract artworks as novices, as experts are able to extract higher-level aesthetic attributes from abstract images (e.g. van Paasschen, Bacci, & Melcher, 2015). The findings of these studies largely support the notion that experts process representational and abstract artworks with less focus on functional object-based perception and more on sensory, relational, and semantic properties.

Evidence suggests that holistic processing is characteristic of perceptual expertise (e.g. Gauthier, Curran, Curby, & Collins, 2003). However, this contrasts with empirical evidence that suggests that artistic production is associated with an enhancement of detail-focused processing and a reduction in holistic processing (Chamberlain, McManus, Riley, Rankin, & Brunswick, 2013; Zhou *et al.*, 2012). This suggests that expert aesthetic processing and expert artistic production might be characterized differently by their reliance upon either holistic or detail-based visual processing. In support of this Tso, Au and Hsiao (2014) explored the characteristics of expertise in Chinese character recognition and writing, which could be seen as analogous to the distinction between expert art perception and production. Holistic processing for Chinese characters was compared between novices, expert Chinese writers with high reading proficiency, and proficient readers who had limited experience in Chinese writing. Skilled writers perceived Chinese characters less holistically than both inexperienced writers and novices. In addition, inexperienced writers perceived characters more holistically than novices. This suggests that there is dissociation between perceptual expertise for reading and writing, with reading and writing engaging a more holistic approach and a more local approach to analysis of visual stimuli respectively. As yet, there have been no studies to examine whether such a dissociation exists for artistic expertise, therefore a comparative analysis of attentional processing in expert artists and art historians would be a valuable contribution to the literature.

Cognitive and Perceptual Correlates of Observational Drawing Expertise

Individuals with drawing expertise outperform non-experts in a range of interacting psychological domains including: perception, attention, memory, and motor processing. The main body of research in this domain concerns experts' advantages in visual perception. The relationship between individual differences in visual perception and drawing expertise can be couched in terms of the influence of illusions and delusions (Gregory, 2003). Illusions are characterized as perceptual processes that are modular from cognition including amodal completion, gestalt grouping, and perceptual constancy. Delusions are framed as perceptual processes that interact with cognition and include visual attention, canonical visual representations, and conceptual representations (Chamberlain & Wagemans, 2016a; although see Firestone & Scholl, 2016, for a discussion of this issue).

Illusory Perception

It has been proposed that individuals with drawing expertise are able to override size and shape constancy in order to access the proximal stimulus (Figure 8.1). This line of reasoning echoes the innocent eye theory of drawing put forward by historian John Ruskin (1856) and is supported by work with child drawing prodigies, which has shown that they take a figurative, surface focused approach to perception (Milbrath, 1998; Ruthsatz, Ruthsatz, & Ruthsatz-Stephens, 2014). Data from perceptual constancy tasks with adult artists are, however, highly inconsistent (Cohen & Jones, 2008; McManus, Loo, Chamberlain, Riley, & Brunswick, 2011; Ostrofsky, Kozbelt, & Seidel, 2012; Perdreau & Cavanagh, 2011; Taylor & Mitchell, 1997) and generally point to a negligible impact of illusory perception on drawing expertise (Chamberlain & Wagemans, 2016a). Similarly, inconsistent evidence is found for a link between artistic skill and the subjective strength of visual illusions which rely on constancy cues (Chamberlain & Wagemans, 2015; Ostrofsky, Kozbelt, & Cohen, 2015; Schlegel *et al.*, 2015).

The outcome of these studies appears to be dependent on the amount of stimulus overlap between the perceptual and drawing tasks used. This is likely to be a result of the tight connection between drawings and internal, canonical

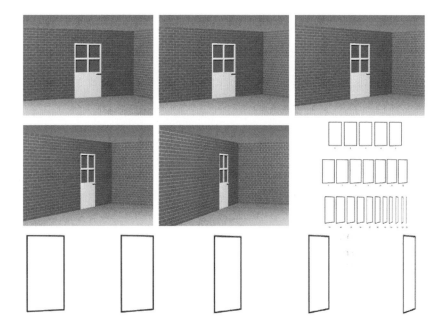

FIGURE 8.1   A task used in McManus *et al.* (2011) in which parallelograms are embedded in a computer-generated context (top two rows) or presented as simple shapes (bottom row) and then matched to a set of master parallelograms to test individual differences in the perception of shape constancy.

representations of drawn objects (Ostrofsky, 2015). This implies that the domain of drawing is confined not to particular classes of objects or scenes, as with perceptual expertise for items such as birds and cars (Bukach, Phillips, & Gauthier, 2010), but to the act of drawing itself.

Delusory Perception

Novice artists are often instructed to draw what they see rather than what they know, a heuristic upon which many "learn to draw" books are based. For example, a common piece of advice in instructional drawing texts is to invert the target object or scene in order to reduce familiarity with it; this makes an appearance in the seminal work *Drawing on the Right Side of the Brain* by Betty Edwards (Edwards, 1989). However, studies that have investigated this phenomenon have found no consistent positive impact of inverting an image on drawing accuracy (Cohen & Earls, 2010; Kozbelt, Seidel, ElBassiouny, Mark, & Owen, 2010; Ostrofsky, Kozbelt, Cohen, Conklin, & Thomson, 2016). On the other hand, it has been found that expert artists render novel and familiar items similarly, whereas non-artists show large differences in approach between the two stimulus types (Glazek & Weisberg, 2010). This suggests that the development of artistic expertise does involve an ability to see familiar objects and scenes as if they were unfamiliar in order to reduce the influence of biasing categorical schemas, but that image inversion is not the best route to this mode of perception.

While some classes of knowledge can provide a hindrance to accurate drawing, evidence suggests that certain classes of knowledge contribute to the development of drawing expertise. For example, non-artists frequently draw the eyes of a face too far up the head due to lack of conceptual knowledge about the structure of the human face, an error often explicitly corrected in drawing classes (Carbon & Wirth, 2014). These internal conceptual schemas may help to guide visual attention to appropriate aspects of the target object or scene (Kozbelt & Seeley, 2007). In support of the predictive role of top-down influences on visual attention, a robust correlation has been found between drawing expertise and enhanced local attentional processing (Chamberlain *et al.*, 2013; Chamberlain & Wagemans, 2015; Drake, 2013; Drake, Redash, Coleman, Haimson, & Winner, 2010; Drake & Winner, 2011; Pring, Ryder, Crane, & Hermelin, 2010). These findings are based upon experimental paradigms that measure the degree to which individuals can construct global representations and can extract local detail from global form. An underlying assumption in this line of research is that individuals are characterized by a certain perceptual profile or style, with variable degrees of global and local bias. In addition to enhanced local processing, it appears that artists are able to integrate local components into global forms more easily than non-artists. In support of this Kozbelt (2001) found that artists outperformed non-artists on tasks of gestalt completion, while a study by Perdreau and Cavanagh (2013) demonstrated that individuals with drawing expertise are better at identifying impossible figures when they are required to integrate local information across eye movements.

Enhancements of local and global attentional processing in relation to drawing expertise appear contradictory because a common assumption is that the two modes of processing exist in trade-off with one another. However, recent evidence suggests that artists' enhanced performance in local and global processing tasks represents attentional flexibility rather than attentional bias (Chamberlain & Wagemans, 2015; Chamberlain, Swinnen, Heeren, & Wagemans, in press). It has been proposed that artists systematically switch between proximal and distal modes of perception while creating artworks which may account for their ability to attend to holistic view-invariant properties as well as surface level detail (Lou, 2015). Here the distal mode of perception can be likened to the functional mode proposed by Cupchik (1992). In sum, expert artists develop the ability to suppress negative categorical schemas and activate positive pictorial schemas through strategic allocation of a flexible visual attentional mechanism. However, this suggests that drawing expertise does not have the hallmark of a holistic processing bias, differentiating drawing from other forms of perceptual expertise.

Visual Memory

The scope and control of visual attention are argued to be linked to visual working memory (e.g., Shipstead, Harrison, & Engle, 2012). Given that artists show increased scope of visual attention through enhanced integration and increased control through attentional flexibility, it may be expected that expert artists possess superior visuospatial working memory as a cause or consequence of this attentional enhancement. In support, studies of children who are drawing prodigies have found evidence of enhanced visual working memory (Drake & Winner, 2009, 2011; Ruthsatz, Ruthsatz-Stephens, & Ruthsatz, 2014; Ruthsatz & Urbach, 2012). Expert adult artists have been found to encode visual stimuli in central and peripheral vision more quickly and more accurately than novices (Glazek & Weisberg, 2010). This superior encoding can be used by artists to support better visual integration ability (Perdreau & Cavanagh, 2013). Expert artists are also more likely to notice masked changes to their drawings or the target object (Perdreau & Cavanagh, 2015). However, no relationship has been found between performance on a standard change detection paradigm and representational drawing skill (Perdreau & Cavanagh, 2015), suggesting that enhanced memory is domain-specific to the extent that it is harnessed only when drawing. While there is evidence to suggest art experts possess superior visuospatial memory, other researchers have suggested that expertise in drawing is underpinned by an ability to subvert the need for reliance on short-term memory mechanisms. In support, Cohen (2005) found that increasing the rate of gaze shifting between a drawing and the target object increased drawing accuracy in a group of novices. In addition, artists spend a substantial proportion of time blind drawing in which their eye does not leave the figure (Tchalenko, Nam, Ladanga, & Miall, 2014). Therefore, enhanced encoding and retention is likely to play a role in drawing expertise, but there is evidence to suggest that strategies that decrease reliance on visual memory are also important.

Representational Decisions

Some of the most compelling artworks consist of only a few marks yet they communicate information about object identity and 3D form alongside more abstract qualities such as emotion and movement (Koenderink, van Doorn, & Wagemans, 2012; Sayim & Cavanagh, 2011). As a result, expert artists must learn to select visual features that are emotionally, dynamically, or structurally salient within an object or scene. These representational decisions interact with visual attention, as attention to appropriate aspects of a stimulus will determine which features are represented, and drawing strategies will direct visual attention toward salient features. In support of the importance of representational decisions, Kozbelt et al. (2010) and Ostrofsky et al. (2012) found that artists produced more accurately than novices minimal line tracings (renderings of an object using a limited number of short pieces of tape), with artists' drawings including more features necessary for object recognition, such as junctions and occlusion barriers. This suggests that representational decisions may be driven by features for object identification, but whether these are internal object features such as the medial axis (Firestone & Scholl, 2014) or external contour-based features such as minima of curvature (De Winter & Wagemans, 2006) remains to be determined.

Motor Processing

A study by McManus, Ying, Fleming, Lee and Chamberlain (2014) failed to find a difference between art students and non-art students on the basis of fine motor control. However, there is evidence that motor processing does play a role in drawing expertise when considered in interplay with eye movements (Gowen & Miall, 2006). Kozbelt (2001) reported left-over variance discriminating artists from non-artists after perceptual differences between the two had been partialled out, suggesting differences in visuomotor integration between the two groups. To test this, Glazek (2012) measured hand and eye movements in a naturalistic drawing task and found that expert artists, when drawing, were able to produce more motor output per unit of visually encoded material than novices. Tchalenko et al. (2014) formalized this by proposing that artists utilize a Gaze Shift Strategy when drawing. This is an iterative loop in which a motor program is formulated while the artist is looking at the subject and is deployed as soon as the artist moves attention back from the paper. The eye then helps to position the beginning of the line on the paper spatially while monitoring the resulting hand movement. In an fMRI study, Miall, Gowen and Tchalenko (2009) found that the act of drawing blind remains consistent with visually guided action, despite lack of direct visual input. That artists spend periods blind drawing suggests that complex visuomotor planning is crucial for drawing expertise. This was supported by the findings of a neuroimaging study that revealed increased gray matter density in regions of the cerebellum in expert artists (Chamberlain et al., 2014).

The Role of Personality, Approaches to Learning, and Practice

The development of many forms of expertise involves the adoption of a range of training techniques for improving performance. The development of drawing expertise is no exception. Expert artists use tools and techniques for the amelioration of negative perceptual biases and the strengthening of positive pictorial schemas. For example, focusing on negative space is a tool for suppressing negative categorical schemas as it shifts attentional focus away from denotative properties of visual stimuli (Figure 8.2). On the other hand,

FIGURE 8.2 An array of objects with a region of negative space between the objects depicted in gray. Artists use negative space to shift attentional focus away from denotative aspects of vision and produce a more accurate drawing.

strategies such as plotting the pivotal points on a human body and using anatomical knowledge of musculature are examples of positive pictorial schemas which artists also engage. The key role of tools and techniques for engendering flexible attention leads into a discussion of the importance of practice on the development of artistic expertise.

An active area of debate in the expertise literature concerns the relative roles of innate factors and experience in the acquisition of expertise (Hambrick, Altmann, *et al.*, 2014; Hambrick, Oswald, *et al.*, 2014; Macnamara, Hambrick, & Oswald, 2014; Macnamara *et al.*, 2016). Because visual art expertise research is in its infancy, there is an absence of longitudinal and cross-sectional studies that could potentially pull apart the relative roles of experience and talent. Therefore, instead of reviewing existing literature of which there is very little, a recent correlational study is reported here that explored the role of a number of inter-related predictors that have been previously highlighted in the expertise literature: personality, approaches to learning, intelligence, and practice (for a more complete account of the findings reported here see Chamberlain, 2012; Chamberlain, McManus, Brunswick, Rankin, & Riley, 2015). This study provides the impetus for a number of outstanding questions in this domain which are also discussed.

In the study a large cohort of art students (*N*=682) completed questionnaires about their artistic ability, personality (Big Five Personality Scale: John, Naumann, & Soto, 2008), and approaches to learning (Study Process Questionnaire: Fox, McManus, & Winder, 2001). A subsample completed observational drawing tasks, the Rey-Osterrieth Complex Figure test (ROCFT) as a measure of visual memory, and Raven's Advanced Progressive Matrices as a measure of IQ (*n*=301). The primary aim of the study was to explore whether individual differences in personality and approaches to learning predict externally rated and self-perceived drawing ability. A secondary aim was to investigate how factors previously found to be associated with representational drawing proficiency, such as visual memory and visual imagery (McManus *et al.*, 2010), interact with individual differences in personality and approaches to learning.

Tools and Techniques for Drawing

Art students were asked to what extent they used a range of techniques and tools for improving their drawing ability (Chamberlain, 2012). The techniques most frequently reported by art students were plotting pivotal points on the image to begin the drawing, performing quick drawings to limit the inclusion of detail, and focusing on negative space. These three strategies can be cast in the light of dynamic visual attention. Plotting pivotal points on the model encourages the artist to focus on global relationships between parts of the visual stimulus. Quick drawings also do this by forcing the artist to map out the global form and ignore extraneous detail. Focus on negative space encourages the artist to ignore semantic associations of local shapes in the model, again focusing on relationships between parts. More mechanical devices such as using a frame to capture part of the visual field, or a plumb line to derive vertical axes were less popular and perhaps represent a more traditional mode of expertise, but again represent ways in which artists hone their visual attention. There was strong evidence for a single underlying factor driving use of each drawing technique; if an individual used one technique then they were more likely to use others. As a whole the extent to which art students reported using these drawing techniques correlated highly with their self-perceived drawing ability and externally rated drawing ability (Chamberlain, 2012; Chamberlain *et al.*, 2015).

The Role of Practice

Art students were asked how much time they spent drawing over the course of the last two years. This measure was positively correlated with externally rated and self-rated drawing ability (Chamberlain *et al.*, 2015), suggesting that amount of practice is predictive of drawing ability. In order to understand the interrelations between the amount of time spent drawing, the use of techniques for drawing, and self-rated and externally rated drawing skill, a path model was constructed and tested, producing what we termed the Drawing Backbone (Chamberlain *et al.*, 2015). The Drawing Backbone demonstrates that the amount of time spent drawing predicts the use of more drawing techniques, which in turn predicts higher externally rated drawing ability and self-rated drawing ability. The amount of time spent drawing and the use of more techniques had additional independent effects on self-rated drawing ability. Amount of time spent practicing did not independently predict drawing ability.

Having established the Drawing Backbone, a full path model was constructed including all predictive factors: personality, approaches to studying, IQ, visual memory, and drawing practice and technique (Figure 8.3). Surface approaches to learning related positively to time spent drawing, while an achieving (strategic) learning style positively predicted externally rated drawing ability. In addition, a surface learning style related negatively to drawing techniques and externally rated drawing ability. Several background variables exerted effects upon self-rated drawing ability, which was rated higher in males, in those with lower

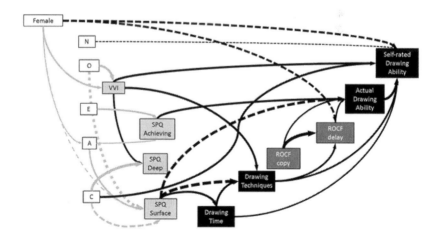

FIGURE 8.3 Full path model relating background variables to four measures of drawing and two measures of the ROCF (from Chamberlain *et al.*, 2015). Path widths are proportional to beta coefficients. Paths with positive beta coefficients are drawn as solid lines and those with negative beta coefficients as dashed lines.

neuroticism (N), higher conscientiousness (C), and with higher vividness of visual imagery (VVI). Interestingly, vividness of visual imagery was not related to externally rated drawing ability.

IQ was not included in the full path model, as it did not predict drawing expertise or any of the background variables associated with drawing, contrasting with Drake et al.'s (2010) study which found that non-verbal IQ predicted children's drawing ability. Research investigating the role of IQ in music and chess expertise has produced inconsistent findings (see Hambrick, Macnamara, Campitelli, Ullén, & Mosing, 2016). However, it has been argued that well-defined domains such as music, sports, and chess are likely to underplay the role of IQ in performance, whereas individual differences in creativity in the arts and sciences are more likely to reflect the influence of IQ and dispositional traits (Simonton, 2006, 2016a). It is critical to apply this model in another more creatively driven domain of art and design in order to test the claim that IQ is more predictive for creative domains than well-defined technical domains such as observational drawing.

Practice Doesn't Always Make Perfect

The full path model generated from this data is one in which actual drawing expertise is primarily caused by learning more drawing techniques, and having more drawing techniques is largely caused by more time spent drawing. This suggests that a large amount of practice alone is not sufficient for the development of expertise, unless the practice is associated with a flexible approach to technique usage. This conclusion is supported by the association between lower levels of actual drawing ability, higher levels of practice, and lower levels of technique use in surface learners in the full path model. The uptake of strategies for practice, rather than cumulative time spent practicing, has been shown to be a prominent predicting factor in expertise development in the domains of music (Hallam, 2001) and chess (Campitelli & Gobet, 2011), and artistic expertise is no exception.

Reported levels of practice and technique usage appeared to artificially inflate participants' self-rated drawing ability. In part, this false inflation of the role of practice may be due to the popularization of the theory of deliberate practice (Ericsson, Krampe, & Tesch-Römer, 1993) and a consequent emphasis on the amount of time spent practicing for expertise acquisition, which has been challenged (e.g. Gobet & Campitelli, 2007). In support, it has been found that retrospective reports of amount of time practicing, rather than keeping a log of practice activities, lead to larger effect sizes in terms of the contribution of deliberate practice (Hambrick et al., 2016; Macnamara et al., 2014). These data suggest that the degree to which students can effectively assess their ability and what contributes to it may also play a role in the development of expertise and should be a focus of investigation.

The development of expertise in observational drawing is underpinned by individual differences in approaches to learning, which are themselves driven by differences in personality. A surface strategy, while increasing the amount of time an individual spends practicing, discourages the novice from learning a range of techniques for expertise acquisition and results in a lower level of overall ability. An achieving strategy to learning by contrast, predicted by extroversion and agreeableness, proves the most successful for expertise development in this domain. This approach to learning involves an intention to succeed and motivation to achieve the best educational outcome, by organization of time and the learning environment (Diseth, 2002). As such it reflects an individual's ability to process the learning context and respond to task demands. This makes intuitive sense when we consider that in order to develop representational drawing expertise the sheer amount of time spent drawing is not as relevant as the strategic adoption of successful strategies for producing a convincing likeness. A strategic learning style may also be tangentially related to the concept of grit or assertiveness that has previously been found to be prevalent in eminent creators (Duckworth, Peterson, Matthews, & Kelly, 2007; Simonton, 2016b), although this assertion has yet to be tested. On the other hand, deep approaches to learning, although not implicated in the current model, may be predictive of more creative aspects of artistic practice because this learning style reflects the desire to relate ideas to one another (Diseth, 2002). It is therefore important that this model be tested in relation to other art activities with more or less creative input in order to assess its generalizability.

The Big Five personality factors were only indirectly predictive of drawing expertise, with their impact being mediated by approaches to learning, amount of time spent practicing and the uptake of techniques. Those most heavily implicated were extraversion and agreeableness, which related positively to a strategic approach to learning. In addition, conscientiousness was negatively related to surface approaches to learning, but conscientiousness was a positive predictor of a deep approach to learning, which was not associated with higher levels of practice or expertise. Drake and Winner (in Chapter 7, Why Deliberate Practice Is Not Enough: Evidence of Talent in Drawing) find higher levels of agreeableness in drawing prodigies which may be related to the enhanced experience of flow found in those with a "rage to master" (Winner, 1997). Contrary to expectation, openness to experience was not implicated in the development of drawing expertise, even though artistic individuals have been found to exhibit higher openness to experience (Burch, Pavelis, Hemsley, & Corr, 2006), and openness to experience predicts engagement in the visual arts (Chamorro-Premuzic, Reimers, Hsu, & Ahmetoglu, 2009). The lack of direct links from personality to expertise (which can be seen in the larger correlational matrix in Chamberlain *et al.*, 2015) reflects the findings of a number of expertise studies showing that deliberate practice mediates the effects of personality on expertise (Hambrick *et al.*, 2016). However, a study showing a direct link between emotional control and chess performance does suggest that there may be some aspects of personality that directly predict expertise, independently of the individuals' dispositional characteristics (Grabner, Stern, & Neubauer, 2007), and a wide variety of personality variables should be included in future cross-sectional studies.

Cognitive abilities such as visual memory appear to predict performance largely independently of other dispositional predictive factors in the current model. However, it is not possible from a correlational design to determine whether skills such as visual memory drive individuals toward development of expertise, or are themselves a product of engagement in artistic activities. Future longitudinal designs will be able to address the direction of causation between perceptual and cognitive abilities and artistic expertise. Furthermore, it is unclear whether amount of drawing practice and techniques for drawing directly predict expert performance or whether they are both underpinned by genetic factors, as has been found to be the case for musical ability (Mosing, Madison, Pedersen, Kuja-Halkola, & Ullén, 2014). Future studies investigating dispositional, practice, and talent-based predictors of artistic expertise should utilize genetic paradigms such as twin studies alongside longitudinal causal methodologies to address these gaps in our current understanding.

Conclusions and Suggestions for Further Research

The study of artistic expertise is challenging relative to other expertise domains, but this challenge is not insurmountable. The body of research reviewed here represents substantial leaps in recent years in methodology and theoretical understanding, by developing reliable and valid means for assessing artistic experience and performance and testing them against established paradigms in perceptual and cognitive domains. That being said, the study of subjective qualities of artworks such as pictorial accuracy and creativity still requires much more research focus. In addition, the relatively narrow scope of current research on observational drawing should be broadened by studying subdomains such as abstract painting, photography, sculpture, and conceptual art. Even within the domain of drawing, distinctions in practice can be drawn and are a valid focus of research. Investigating the impact of training in perceptual drawing, which focuses on surface qualities (Edwards, 1989), in comparison with design drawing which focuses on visualization (McKim, 1972), will shed light upon how engagement in different aspects of art and design facilitates different strands of perceptual expertise. Carving up the larger domain of artistic expertise therefore will be valuable and is foreseeable as the field develops.

Another way of delineating the basis of artistic expertise is to investigate the distinction between expert perception for art evaluation in contrast to perception for art production. It has been shown that the two domains have commonalities as they both engender a mode of perception that is inconsistent with functional perception for everyday purposes (Cupchik, 1992). However, they also differ in the sense that perception for aesthetic evaluation appears to favor a holistic attentional attitude, whereas artistic production appears to favor a more flexible attentional attitude. To confirm this interpretation of the existing data it is necessary to conduct cross-sectional analyses of different kinds of art professionals such as art historians in comparison with fine artists. Artistic production can also be contrasted with perceptual expertise from other domains (for cars, birds, etc.), but this too is yet to be investigated empirically. It may be possible to investigate subpopulations of artists with different perceptual expertise (for example, portrait and landscape painters) in order to assess the domain specificity of perceptual enhancements. However, at this point it can be concluded that in the case of most artists the domain of expertise is the act of art making and is intimately connected with motor processes rather than with particular classes of visual stimuli.

Substantial progress has been made in determining the perceptual and cognitive underpinnings of observational drawing expertise, as an exemplar of artistic expertise. Upon review of the available evidence it would appear that enhancement of the scope and control of visual attention is critically implicated in the development of drawing expertise, while bottom-up perceptual processing appears to be relatively unaffected by level of expertise (Chamberlain & Wagemans, 2016a). Visual attention in turn may also account for related abilities that are found to be enhanced in visual artists such as visuospatial working memory, representational decisions, and visuomotor integration. In addition, it can be proposed that top-down attentional mechanisms that enable the artist to attend to overlooked visual features could facilitate higher forms of artistic production and appreciation. Robust representational schemas could free up cognitive resources for creative processing (Solso, 2001). If these two proposals hold, one can foresee a link between technical artistic skill, artistic appreciation, and creative output. Technical artistic skill under this framework engenders a flexible and efficient perceptual system, which enables the artist to access multiple interpretations in the work of others and multiple meanings in incoming sensory and conceptual information to facilitate creative thinking.

It can be proposed that expert artists develop increased scope and control of visual attention through the use of diverse techniques for drawing that enable them to mitigate the effects of negative biases on perception and engage positive pictorial schemas. In support of this a recent study indicated that drawing expertise is developed as a result of practice that is focused not on the amount of time artists spent engaged in drawing, but in the diversity of techniques they use to develop their practice (Chamberlain et al., 2015). The adoption of techniques is driven by individual differences in personality and approaches to studying, suggesting a complex interaction of innate and learned abilities and character traits in the determination of expertise. Interestingly the only background variable that interacted with a cognitive skill (visual memory) in the aforementioned study was the uptake of drawing techniques. This suggests that there are two relatively independent routes to development of expertise in the visual arts: one through heightened cognitive and perceptual skills, and the other through motivation to learn for strategic purposes. The uptake of a diverse range of drawing techniques serves to bridge these two routes to expertise. The next logical step for research in this domain is to investigate which particular techniques lead to the development of which kinds of skills. In addition, future research should engage with work with child prodigies who demonstrate a "rage to master," in order to investigate how innate skills and traits interact with learned elements of expertise development (see Chapter 7). Research that identifies those skills that can and cannot be successfully trained in the context of artistic expertise will undoubtedly have broad implications for art and design education.

References

Angelone, B. L., Hass, R. W., & Cohen, M. (2016). Skill transfer in visual arts expertise. *Psychology of Aesthetics, Creativity, and the Arts*, *10*(2), 147–156. http://doi.org/ 10.1037/aca0000053

Augustin, D., & Leder, H. (2006). Art expertise: A study of concepts and conceptual spaces. *Psychology Science*, *48*(2), 135.

Bukach, C. M., Phillips, W. S., & Gauthier, I. (2010). Limits of generalization between categories and implications for theories of category specificity. *Attention, Perception & Psychophysics*, *72*(7), 1865–1874. http://doi.org/10.3758/APP.72.7.1865

Burch, G. S. J., Pavelis, C., Hemsley, D. R., & Corr, P. J. (2006). Schizotypy and creativity in visual artists. *British Journal of Psychology*, *97*(2), 177–190. http://doi. org/10.1348/000712605X60030

Butkovic, A., Ullén, F., & Mosing, M. A. (2015). Personality related traits as predictors of music practice: Underlying environmental and genetic influences. *Personality and Individual Differences*, *74*, 133–138. http://doi.org/10.1016/j.paid.2014.10.006

Campitelli, G., & Gobet, F. (2011). Deliberate Practice: Necessary But Not Sufficient. *Current Directions in Psychological Science*, *20*(5), 280–285. http://doi.org/10.1177/ 0963721411421922

Carbon, C.-C., & Wirth, B. E. (2014). Neanderthal paintings? Production of prototypical human (Homo sapiens) faces shows systematic distortions. *Perception*, *43*(1), 99–102. http://doi.org/10.1068/p7604

Chamberlain, R. (2012). Attitudes and approaches to observational drawing in contemporary artistic practice attitudes and approaches to observational drawing in contemporary artistic practice. *Drawing Knowledge. TRACEY Drawing and Visualisation Research*. Retrieved from http://www.lboro.ac.uk/microsites/sota/tracey/journal/ edu/old/images/Articles/Rebecca_Chamberlain-TRACEY-Journal-DK-2012.docx

Chamberlain, R., McManus, C., Brunswick, N., Rankin, Q., & Riley, H. (2015). Scratching the surface: Practice, personality, approaches to learning, and the acquisition of high-level representational drawing ability. *Psychology of Aesthetics, Creativity, and the Arts*. http://doi.org/10.1037/aca0000011

Chamberlain, R., McManus, I. C., Brunswick, N., Rankin, Q., Riley, H., & Kanai, R. (2014). Drawing on the right side of the brain: A voxel-based morphometry analysis of observational drawing. *NeuroImage*, *96*, 167–173. http://doi.org/10.1016/j.neuroimage.2014.03.062

Chamberlain, R., McManus, I. C., Riley, H., Rankin, Q., & Brunswick, N. (2013). Local processing enhancements associated with superior observational drawing are due to enhanced perceptual functioning, not weak central coherence. *The Quarterly Journal of Experimental Psychology*, *66*(7), 1448–1466. http://doi.org/10.1080/17470218.2012.750678

Chamberlain, R., Swinnen, L., Heeren, S., & Wagemans, J. (in press). Perceptual flexibility is coupled with reduced executive inhibition in students of the visual arts. *British Journal of Psychology*.

Chamberlain, R., & Wagemans, J. (2015). Visual arts training is linked to flexible attention to local and global levels of visual stimuli. *Acta Psychologica*, *161*, 185–197.

Chamberlain, R., & Wagemans, J. (2016). The genesis of errors in drawing. *Neuroscience & Biobehavioral Reviews*, *65*, 195–207. http://doi.org/10.1016/j.neubiorev.2016.04.002

Chamorro-Premuzic, T., Reimers, S., Hsu, A., & Ahmetoglu, G. (2009). Who art thou? Personality predictors of artistic preferences in a large UK sample: The importance of openness. *British Journal of Psychology*, *100*(3), 501–516. http://doi.org/10.1348/000712608X366867

Cohen, D. J. (2005). Look little, look often: The influence of gaze frequency on drawing accuracy. *Perception & Psychophysics*, *67*(6), 997–1009.

Cohen, D. J., & Earls, H. (2010). Inverting an image does not improve drawing accuracy. *Psychology of Aesthetics, Creativity, and the Arts*, *4*(3), 168–172. http://doi.org/10.1037/a0017054

Cohen, D. J., & Jones, H. E. (2008). How shape constancy relates to drawing accuracy. *Psychology of Aesthetics, Creativity, and the Arts*, *2*(1), 8–19. http://doi.org/10.1037/1931-3896.2.1.8

Cupchik, G. C. (1992). From perception to production: A multilevel analysis of the aesthetic process. In *Emerging Visions of the Aesthetic Process: Psychology, Semiology, and Philosophy* (pp. 83–99). Cambridge University Press.

Damian, R., & Simonton, D. K. (2014). Diversifying experiences in the development of genius and their impact on creative cognition. In *The Wiley handbook of genius* (pp. 375–393). John Wiley & Sons, Inc.

De Winter, J., & Wagemans, J. (2006). Segmentation of object outlines into parts: A large-scale integrative study. *Cognition*, *99*(3), 275–325. http://doi.org/10.1016/j.cognition.2005.03.004

Diseth, Å. (2002). The relationship between intelligence, approaches to learning and academic achievement. *Scandinavian Journal of Educational Research*, *46*(2), 219–230. http://doi.org/10.1080/00313830220142218

Drake, J. E. (2013). Is superior local processing in the visuospatial domain a function of drawing talent rather than autism spectrum disorder? *Psychology of Aesthetics, Creativity, and the Arts*, *7*(2), 203–209. http://doi.org/10.1037/a0030636

Drake, J. E., Redash, A., Coleman, K., Haimson, J., & Winner, E. (2010). "Autistic" local processing bias also found in children gifted in realistic drawing. *Journal of Autism and Developmental Disorders*, *40*(6), 762–773. http://doi.org/10.1007/s10803-009-0923-0

Drake, J. E., & Winner, E. (2009). Precocious realists: Perceptual and cognitive characteristics associated with drawing talent in non-autistic children. *Philosophical Transactions of the Royal Society B: Biological Sciences*, *364*(1522), 1449–1458. http://doi.org/10.1098/rstb.2008.0295

Drake, J. E., & Winner, E. (2011). Realistic drawing talent in typical adults is associated with the same kind of local processing bias found in individuals with ASD. *Journal of Autism and Developmental Disorders, 41*(9), 1192–1201. http://doi.org/10.1007/s10803-010-1143-3

Duckworth, A. L., Peterson, C., Matthews, M. D., & Kelly, D. R. (2007). Grit: Perseverance and passion for long-term goals. *Journal of Personality and Social Psychology, 92*(6), 1087–1101. http://doi.org/10.1037/0022-3514.92.6.1087

Edwards, B. (1989). *Drawing on the right side of the brain.* New York: Putnam.

Ericsson, K. A., Krampe, R., & Tesch-Römer, C. (1993). The role of deliberate practice in the acquisition of expert performance. *Psychological Review, 100*, 363–406.

Firestone, C., & Scholl, B. J. (2014). "Please tap the shape, anywhere you like": Shape skeletons in human vision revealed by an exceedingly simple measure. *Psychological Science, 25*(2), 377–386.

Firestone, C., & Scholl, B. (2016). Cognition does not affect perception: Evaluating the evidence for "top-down" effects. *Behavioral and Brain Sciences, 39.* doi:10.1017/S0140525X15000965.

Fox, R. A., McManus, I. C., & Winder, B. C. (2001). The shortened Study Process Questionnaire: An investigation of its structure and longitudinal stability using confirmatory factor analysis. *British Journal of Educational Psychology, 71*(4), 511–530.

Gauthier, I., Curran, T., Curby, K. M., & Collins, D. (2003). Perceptual interference supports a non-modular account of face processing. *Nature Neuroscience, 6*(4), 428–432.

Glazek, K. (2012). Visual and motor processing in visual artists: Implications for cognitive and neural mechanisms. *Psychology of Aesthetics, Creativity, and the Arts, 6*(2), 155–167. http://doi.org/10.1037/a0025184

Glazek, K. J., & Weisberg, R. W. (2010). Expertise in visual art is associated with altered perceptual strategies within and across domains: Evidence from eye tracking. In *Proceedings of the 32nd Annual Conference of the Cognitive Science Society* (pp. 417–422). Retrieved from http://csjarchive.cogsci.rpi.edu/proceedings/2010/papers/0070/paper0070.pdf

Gobet, F., & Campitelli, G. (2007). The role of domain-specific practice, handedness, and starting age in chess. *Developmental Psychology, 43*(1), 159–172. http://doi.org/10.1037/0012-1649.43.1.159

Gowen, E., & Miall, R. C. (2006). Eye–hand interactions in tracing and drawing tasks. *Human Movement Science, 25*(4–5), 568–585. http://doi.org/10.1016/j.humov.2006.06.005

Grabner, R. H., Stern, E., & Neubauer, A. C. (2007). Individual differences in chess expertise: A psychometric investigation. *Acta Psychologica, 124*(3), 398–420. http://doi.org/10.1016/j.actpsy.2006.07.008

Gregory, R. L. (2003). Delusions. *Perception, 32*(3), 257–261. http://doi.org/10.1068/p3203ed

Hallam, S. (2001). The development of expertise in young musicians: Strategy use, knowledge acquisition and individual diversity. *Music Education Research, 3*(1), 7–23. http://doi.org/10.1080/14613800020029914

Hambrick, D. Z., Altmann, E. M., Oswald, F. L., Meinz, E. J., Gobet, F., & Campitelli, G. (2014). Accounting for expert performance: The devil is in the details. *Intelligence, 45*, 112–114. http://doi.org/10.1016/j.intell.2014.01.007

Hambrick, D. Z., Macnamara, B. N., Campitelli, G., Ullén, F., & Mosing, M. A. (2016). Beyond born versus made. In *Psychology of Learning and Motivation* (Vol. 64, pp. 1–55). Elsevier. Retrieved from http://linkinghub.elsevier.com/retrieve/pii/S0079742115000328

Hambrick, D. Z., Oswald, F. L., Altmann, E. M., Meinz, E. J., Gobet, F., & Campitelli, G. (2014). Deliberate practice: Is that all it takes to become an expert? *Intelligence, 45,* 34–45. http://doi.org/10.1016/j.intell.2013.04.001

John, O., Naumann, L. P., & Soto, C. J. (2008). Paradigm shift to the integrative big five trait taxonomy: History, measurement, and conceptual issues. In *Handbook of personality: Theory and research* (pp. 114–158). New York: Guilford Press.

Kenin, R. (1974). *The art of drawing: From the dawn of history to the era of the Impressionists.* New York: Paddington Press.

Koenderink, J., van Doorn, A., & Wagemans, J. (2012). Picasso in the mind's eye of the beholder: Three-dimensional filling-in of ambiguous line drawings. *Cognition, 125*(3), 394–412. http://doi.org/10.1016/j.cognition.2012.07.019

Koide, N., Kubo, T., Nishida, S., Shibata, T., & Ikeda, K. (2015). Art expertise reduces influence of visual salience on fixation in viewing abstract-paintings. *PLOS ONE, 10*(2), e0117696. http://doi.org/10.1371/journal.pone.0117696

Kozbelt, A. (2001). Artists as experts in visual cognition. *Visual Cognition, 8*(6), 705–723. http://doi.org/10.1080/13506280042000090

Kozbelt, A. (2004). Originality and technical skill as components of artistic quality. *Empirical Studies of the Arts, 22*(2), 157–170.

Kozbelt, A., & Seeley, W. P. (2007). Integrating art historical, psychological, and neuro-scientific explanations of artists' advantages in drawing and perception. *Psychology of Aesthetics, Creativity, and the Arts, 1*(2), 80–90. http://doi.org/10.1037/1931-3896.1.2.80

Kozbelt, A., Seidel, A., ElBassiouny, A., Mark, Y., & Owen, D. R. (2010). Visual selection contributes to artists' advantages in realistic drawing. *Psychology of Aesthetics, Creativity, and the Arts, 4*(2), 93–102. http://doi.org/10.1037/a0017657

Leder, H., Belke, B., Oeberst, A., & Augustin, D. (2004). A model of aesthetic apprecia-tion and aesthetic judgments. *British Journal of Psychology, 95*(4), 489–508.

Lou, L. (2015). *Observational visual depiction involves interplays of proximal and distal modes of seeing.* Presented at the Visual Science of Art Conference, Liverpool, UK.

Macnamara, B. N., Hambrick, D. Z., & Oswald, F. L. (2014). Deliberate practice and performance in music, games, sports, education, and professions: A meta-analysis. *Psychological Science, 25*(8), 1608–1618. http://doi.org/10.1177/0956797614535810

Macnamara, B. N., Moreau, D., & Hambrick, D. Z. (2016). The relationship between deliberate practice and performance in sports a meta-analysis. *Perspectives on Psychological Science, 11*(3), 333–350.

McKim, R. (1972). *Experiences in visual thinking.* Belmont, CA: Brooks/Cole Publishing Company.

McManus, I. C., Chamberlain, R., Loo, P.-W., Rankin, Q., Riley, H., & Brunswick, N. (2010). Art students who cannot draw: Exploring the relations between drawing ability, visual memory, accuracy of copying, and dyslexia. *Psychology of Aesthetics, Creativity, and the Arts, 4*(1), 18–30. http://doi.org/10.1037/a0017335

McManus, I. C., Loo, P.-W., Chamberlain, R., Riley, H., & Brunswick, N. (2011). Does shape constancy relate to drawing ability? Two failures to replicate. *Empirical Studies of the Arts, 29*(2), 191–208.

McManus, I. C., Ying, B. T. Z., Fleming, E., Lee, P., & Chamberlain, R. (2014). *Testing Ruskin: seeing, drawing and remembering complex curves.* Presented at the Visual Science of Art Conference, Belgrade, Serbia.

Miall, R. C., Gowen, E., & Tchalenko, J. (2009). Drawing cartoon faces – a functional imaging study of the cognitive neuroscience of drawing. *Cortex, 45*(3), 394–406. http://doi.org/10.1016/j.cortex.2007.10.013

Milbrath, C. (1998). *Patterns of artistic development in children: Comparative studies of talent.* New York: Cambridge University Press.

Mosing, M. A., Madison, G., Pedersen, N. L., Kuja-Halkola, R., & Ullén, F. (2014). Practice does not make perfect: No causal effect of music practice on music ability. *Psychological Science*, 956797614541990.

Ostrofsky, J. (2015). Developmental and Geographic Analyses of Spatial Biases in Face Drawings Produced by Children. *Empirical Studies of the Arts, 33*(1), 3–17. http://doi.org/10.1177/0276237415569978

Ostrofsky, J., Kozbelt, A., & Cohen, D. J. (2015). Observational drawing biases are predicted by biases in perception: Empirical support of the misperception hypothesis of drawing accuracy with respect to two angle illusions. *The Quarterly Journal of Experimental Psychology, 68*(5), 1007–1025. http://doi.org/10.1080/17470218.2014.973889

Ostrofsky, J., Kozbelt, A., & Seidel, A. (2012). Perceptual constancies and visual selection as predictors of realistic drawing skill. *Psychology of Aesthetics, Creativity, and the Arts, 6*(2), 124–136. http://doi.org/10.1037/a0026384

Ostrofsky, J., Kozbelt, A., Cohen, D. J., Conklin, L., & Thomson, K. (2016). Face inversion impairs the ability to draw long-range, but not short-range, spatial relationships between features. *Empirical Studies of the Arts, 34*(2), 221–233. http://doi.org/10.1177/0276237416634851

Perdreau, F., & Cavanagh, P. (2011). Do artists see their retinas? *Frontiers in Human Neuroscience, 5.* http://doi.org/10.3389/fnhum.2011.00171

Perdreau, F., & Cavanagh, P. (2013). The artist's advantage: Better integration of object information across eye movements. *I-Perception, 4*(6), 380–395. http://doi.org/10.1068/i0574

Perdreau, F., & Cavanagh, P. (2014). Drawing skill is related to the efficiency of encoding object structure. *I-Perception, 5*(2), 101–119. http://doi.org/10.1068/i0635

Perdreau, F., & Cavanagh, P. (2015). Drawing experts have better visual memory while drawing. *Journal of Vision, 15*(5), 5. http://doi.org/10.1167/15.5.5

Petherbridge, D. (2007). On the moving line and the future subjunctive of drawing in a post-Duchampian age. *Futures, 39*(10), 1191–1200. http://doi.org/10.1016/j.futures.2007.05.004

Pring, L., Ryder, N., Crane, L., & Hermelin, B. (2010). Local and global processing in savant artists with autism. *Perception, 39*(8), 1094–1103. http://doi.org/10.1068/p6674

Ruskin, J. (1856). *The elements of drawing.* Mineola, NY: Dover Publications Inc.

Ruthsatz, J., Ruthsatz, K., & Ruthsatz-Stephens, K. (2014). Putting practice into perspective: Child prodigies as evidence of innate talent. *Intelligence, 45*, 60–65. http://doi.org/10.1016/j.intell.2013.08.003

Ruthsatz, J., Ruthsatz-Stephens, K., & Ruthsatz, K. (2014). The cognitive bases of exceptional abilities in child prodigies by domain: Similarities and differences. *Intelligence, 44*, 11–14. http://doi.org/10.1016/j.intell.2014.01.010

Ruthsatz, J., & Urbach, J. B. (2012). Child prodigy: A novel cognitive profile places elevated general intelligence, exceptional working memory and attention to detail at the root of prodigiousness. *Intelligence, 40*(5), 419–426. http://doi.org/10.1016/j. intell.2012.06.002

Sayim, B., & Cavanagh, P. (2011). What line drawings reveal about the visual brain. *Frontiers in Human Neuroscience, 5.* http://doi.org/10.3389/fnhum.2011.00118

Schlegel, A., Alexander, P., Fogelson, S. V., Li, X., Lu, Z., Kohler, P. J., ... Meng, M. (2015). The artist emerges: Visual art learning alters neural structure and function. *NeuroImage, 105*, 440–451. http://doi.org/10.1016/j.neuroimage.2014.11.014

Shipstead, Z., Harrison, T. L., & Engle, R. W. (2012). Working memory capacity and visual attention: Top-down and bottom-up guidance. *The Quarterly Journal of Experimental Psychology, 65*(3), 401–407. http://doi.org/10.1080/17470218.2012.65 5698

Simonton, D. K. (2006). Presidential IQ, Openness, Intellectual Brilliance, and Leadership: Estimates and Correlations for 42 U.S. Chief Executives. *Political Psychology, 27*(4), 511–526.

Simonton, D. K. (2014). More method in the mad-genius controversy: A historiometric study of 204 historic creators. *Psychology of Aesthetics, Creativity, and the Arts, 8*(1), 53–61. http://doi.org/10.1037/a0035367

Simonton, D. K. (2016a). Intelligence, inheritance, motivation and expertise: Review of "Grit: The power of passion and perseverance" A. Duckworth and "Peak: Secrets from the new science of expertise" A. Ericsson and R. Pool. *Intelligence, 58.* http:// doi.org/10.1016/j.intell.2016.05.005

Simonton, D. K. (2016b). Reverse engineering genius: Historiometric studies of superlative talent. *Annals of the New York Academy of Sciences.* http://doi.org/10.1111/nyas. 13054

Solso, R. L. (2001). Brain activities in a skilled versus a novice artist: An fMRI study. *Leonardo, 34*(1), 31–34.

Tanaka, J. W., & Taylor, M. (1991). Object categories and expertise: Is the basic level in the eye of the beholder. *Cognitive Psychology, 23*, 457–482.

Taylor, L. M., & Mitchell, P. (1997). Judgments of apparent shape contaminated by knowledge of reality: Viewing circles obliquely. *British Journal of Psychology, 88*(4), 653–670.

Tchalenko, J., Nam, S.-H., Ladanga, M., & Miall, R. C. (2014). The gaze-shift strategy in drawing. *Psychology of Aesthetics, Creativity, and the Arts, 8*(3), 330–339. http://doi. org/10.1037/a0036132

Tinio, P. P. L. (2013). From artistic creation to aesthetic reception: The mirror model of art. *Psychology of Aesthetics, Creativity, and the Arts, 7*(3), 265–275. http://doi. org/10.1037/a0030872

Tso, R. V.-y., Au, T. K.-f., & Hsiao, J. H.-w. (2014). Perceptual expertise: Can sensorimotor experience change holistic processing and left-side bias? *Psychological Science, 25*(9), 1757–1767. http://doi.org/10.1177/0956797614541284

van Paasschen, J., Bacci, F., & Melcher, D. P. (2015). The influence of art expertise and training on emotion and preference ratings for representational and abstract artworks. *PLOS ONE, 10*(8), e0134241. http://doi.org/10.1371/journal.pone.0134241

Vogt, S., & Magnussen, S. (2007). Expertise in pictorial perception: Eye-movement patterns and visual memory in artists and laymen. *Perception, 36*(1), 91–100. http://doi. org/10.1068/p5262

Winner, E. (1997) *Gifted children: Myths and realities*. New York, NY: Basic Books

Zangemeister, W. H., Sherman, K., & Stark, L. (1995). Evidence for a global scanpath strategy in viewing abstract compared with realistic images. *Neuropsychologia, 33*(8), 1009–1025.

Zhou, G., Cheng, Z., Zhang, X., & Wong, A. C.-N. (2012). Smaller holistic processing of faces associated with face drawing experience. *Psychonomic Bulletin & Review, 19*(2), 157–162. http://doi.org/10.3758/s13423-011-0174-x

9

THE DELIBERATE PRACTICE VIEW

An Evaluation of Definitions, Claims, and Empirical Evidence

Brooke N. Macnamara, David Z. Hambrick, David J. Frank, Michael J. King, Alexander P. Burgoyne, and Elizabeth J. Meinz

Introduction

The question of how people acquire high levels of skill in complex domains such as music, games, sports, and science has long been of interest to psychologists. Nearly 25 years ago, in their classic article, Ericsson, Krampe, and Tesch-Römer (1993) introduced the highly influential *deliberate practice view* in an attempt to answer this question. This view proposes that individual differences in expertise are largely accounted for by differential amounts of "deliberate practice"—effortful training activities specially designed to improve performance.

To test this view, Ericsson *et al.* (1993) asked violin students to retrospectively estimate their lifetime hours of *practice alone*—the time they spent practicing music on their own to improve their skills. Ericsson *et al.* found that the average number of accumulated hours of practice alone was higher for the "best" violinists than for the "good" violinists. Furthermore, the combined average of these two groups was higher than the average for the least accomplished "music teachers." In a second study, Ericsson *et al.* found that "expert" pianists had accumulated thousands of hours more practice alone than "amateur" pianists.

Ericsson *et al.* (1993) concluded that "individual differences in ultimate performance can largely be accounted for by differential amounts of past and current levels of practice," (p. 392) and that "[i]ndividual differences, even among elite performers, are closely related to assessed amounts of deliberate practice" (p. 363). They further argued, "Our theoretical framework can also provide a *sufficient account* of the major facts about the nature and scarcity of exceptional performance. Our account does not depend on scarcity of innate ability (talent)" (p. 392, emphasis added). Making exceptions only for height and body size, they added, "[W]e reject any important role for innate ability" (p. 399).

The deliberate practice view has had tremendous impact on both scientific and popular views on expertise. Cited more than 6,600 times (source: Google Scholar as of December 19, 2016) since its publication, the Ericsson *et al.* (1993) article is one of the most referenced articles in the psychological literature. Moreover, numerous popular books have been inspired by the deliberate practice view, including Geoff Colvin's (2008) *Talent Is Overrated* and Malcolm Gladwell's (2008) *Outliers,* where Gladwell describes his "10,000-hour rule"— the idea that it takes 10,000 hours of practice to become an expert. No one has had a greater impact on scientific and popular views of expertise than Ericsson.

Why is the deliberate practice view so popular? Even though the view is not so simplistic, a likely reason is that it reinforces the idea that through hard work and determination, anyone can accomplish anything they set their mind to—an idea many people embrace. This was the case with professional photographer Dan McLaughlin, who after reading Colvin's and Gladwell's books quit his job to complete 10,000 hours of deliberate practice in golf (see thedanplan.com). With consultation from Anders Ericsson, McLaughlin's goal was to make it to the PGA Tour—the highest level of competitive golf. In a report on the first half of the project, he wrote, "It would be a lot easier to just . . . say it takes 'natural talent' to make it, but we here at The Plan don't believe in that attitude. Anything is possible with enough determination, hard work and proper guidance" (McLaughlin, 2014, p. 913). McLaughlin recalls Ericsson telling him, "I think you're the right astronaut for this mission" (see http://www.thedanplan.com/theplan.php).

Deliberate practice is clearly an important factor in becoming an expert. Obviously, no one can become an expert in a field like music, science, golf, or chess without extensive training. That is, people are not born with the sort of specialized knowledge that underpins success in these domains. Additionally, there is also no reason to doubt that virtually any healthy person will benefit from deliberate practice. Dan McLaughlin is a case in point: After nearly 6,000 hours of deliberate practice his handicap (an index of golf skill) was about 4, putting him in the top 5 percent of amateur golfers (see Figure 9.1). Regardless of whether he reaches the PGA Tour, this is a level of performance that few golfers ever achieve. Furthermore, some forms of training have a greater impact on performance than others. For example, as psychologists have long known, immediate feedback is generally beneficial for learning (McGehee, 1958; McKeachie, 1961).

In more technical terms, deliberate practice very clearly contributes to *intra*-individual variability in skill level—that is, an individual's improvement in a domain. However, in recent years, expertise researchers have questioned Ericsson and colleagues' central claim that deliberate practice largely accounts for *inter*-individual variability in performance—that is, performance differences across individuals (e.g., Gobet & Campitelli, 2007; Hambrick, Macnamara, Campitelli, Ullén, & Mosing, 2016). The fact that training is necessary for an

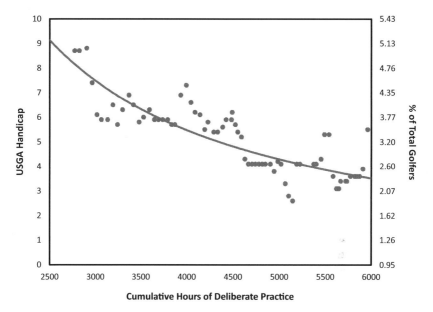

FIGURE 9.1   Illustration of intra-individual variability in skill; relationship between accumulated deliberate practice and golf skill in Dan McLaughlin (data obtained from http://www.thedanplan.com).

individual to acquire skill does not imply that individuals acquire skills at the same rate (or have the same starting points or asymptotes in their performance). That is, the necessity of training for individual improvement does not mean that training must also largely account for skill differences *between individuals*. In fact, evidence from recent meta-analyses (Macnamara, Hambrick, & Oswald, 2014; Macnamara, Moreau, & Hambrick, 2016) reveals that deliberate practice leaves the majority of the inter-individual variability in performance unexplained and potentially explainable by other factors. The view that has emerged from this evidence is that deliberate practice is an important piece of the expertise puzzle— but not the only piece.

In this chapter, focusing on our own research but highlighting findings from others' research, we briefly review empirical tests of the deliberate practice view. We then discuss Ericsson's response to these challenges, focusing on discrepancies between claims and empirical evidence, and inconsistent definitions of theoretical terms. We then discuss how these discrepancies and inconsistencies limit progress in scientific research on expertise.

Empirical Tests of the Deliberate Practice View

Does deliberate practice *largely* explain individual differences in expertise as Ericsson and colleagues have claimed? It does not appear so. Searching more than 9,300 documents, Macnamara, Hambrick, and Oswald (2014) conducted the most extensive systematic review of deliberate practice to date—a meta-analysis across all major domains in which deliberate practice had been investigated. On average, deliberate practice accounted for 12 percent of the variance in performance across individuals. The average contribution of deliberate practice varied considerably by domain—26 percent for games, 21 percent for music, 18 percent for sports, 4 percent for education, and less than 1 percent in other professions. However, across all domains, the evidence indicated that deliberate practice leaves a large amount of variance in performance unexplained, even after correcting for measurement error (see also Hambrick, Oswald, *et al.*, 2014).

More recently, Macnamara, Moreau, and Hambrick (2016) investigated the contribution of deliberate practice to sports performance. The effect of deliberate practice was very similar to the overall average (18 percent) for studies that measured solitary practice (22 percent), those that measured performance via objective measures (e.g., race time; 20 percent), and those that measured performance via group membership (e.g., an athlete on a national team vs. a state team; 25 percent). However, the relationship between deliberate practice and expertise varied by skill level: Deliberate practice explained 19 percent of the variance in performance among sub-elite athletes (e.g., recreational athletes, athletes competing at the state level), but explained only 1 percent of the variance in performance among elite athletes (e.g., athletes competing in the NCAA championship, international competitors, Olympians). This finding suggests that deliberate practice may lose its predictive power at a high level of skill, contrary to Ericsson *et al.*'s (1993) claim that "[i]ndividual differences, even among elite performers, are closely related to assessed amounts of deliberate practice" (p. 363). That is, factors other than deliberate practice may differentiate who merely reaches a high level of skill and who becomes a top-ranked athlete in a sport.

Overall, these results indicate that people require very different amounts of deliberate practice to acquire complex skills. For example, in Ericsson *et al.*'s (1993) study of violinists, the 95 percent confidence interval around the mean of accumulated deliberate practice at age 18 for the 'best' violinists ranged from 2,894 hours to 11,926 hours (Ericsson, 2014c). Similarly, Sloboda, Davidson, Howe, and Moore (1996) studied the practice habits of music students across different skill levels and found there were some students who attained each skill level by practicing less than 20 percent of the mean amount for that group. As another example, in Gobet and Campitelli's (2007) study of chess players, the amount of deliberate practice (including both individual and group activities) to reach "master" status ranged from 3,016 hours to 23,608 hours—a difference of nearly a factor of 8.

Results of a training study provide an additional illustration to this point. Sakakibara (2014) enrolled children from a music school in a training program

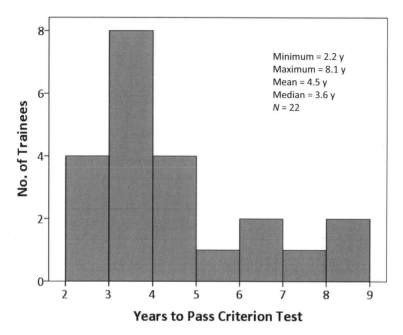

Minimum = 2.2 y
Maximum = 8.1 y
Mean = 4.5 y
Median = 3.6 y
N = 22

FIGURE 9.2 Frequency distribution for time to reach criterion for AP in Sakakibara's (2014) pitch training study (data obtained from Sakakibara's Table 2; $N = 22$).

designed to train absolute pitch (AP). Colloquially known as "perfect pitch," AP is the ability to name the pitch of a tone without hearing another tone for reference. With a trainer playing a piano, the children learned to identify chords. Then, the children were tested on their ability to identify the pitches of individual notes until they reached a criterion level of proficiency. Nearly all of the children (22 of 24) completed the training and reached the criterion. However, there was a large amount of variability in the amount of time it took them to reach criterion—from around 2 years to 8 years (see Figure 9.2). Based on this finding, Sakakibara concluded that "the possibility of a genetic predisposition in AP cannot be denied" (p. 101).

In short, there is now a large amount of evidence to indicate that deliberate practice does not *largely* account for individual differences in expertise. Based on this evidence, we have argued that deliberate practice is one, but not the only, important factor contributing to inter-individual variability in expertise. More to the point, we have argued that deliberate practice is an important predictor of individual differences (i.e., *inter*-individual variability) in expertise—just not as important as Ericsson *et al.* (1993) originally argued it is.

Ericsson's Response

In response, Ericsson has mounted a vigorous defense of the deliberate practice view. However, as we have noted elsewhere (Hambrick, Altmann, *et al.*, 2014; Macnamara, Moreau, & Hambrick, 2016), this defense is undermined by contradictions and inconsistencies in Ericsson's arguments. Here, we highlight some of these contradictions and inconsistencies, focusing on shifting definitions of the key theoretical terms *deliberate practice* and *expert performance*.

Definitions of Deliberate Practice

Ericsson has argued that many of the studies that we included in our meta-analyses did not measure *actual* deliberate practice. For example, in an unpublished commentary Ericsson (2014a, 2014b) claimed many of the studies we included "used operational definitions of practice that violate our [Ericsson et al.'s, (1993)] original definition of deliberate practice" (2014a, p. 4), even though we used operational definitions of deliberate practice used by Ericsson, including his original operational definition (see Ericsson *et al.*, 1993). In a similar vein, in their recent book *Peak: Secrets from the New Science of Expertise*, Ericsson and Pool (2016) claimed that the "major problem with this meta-analysis [Macnamara *et al.*, 2014] was that few of the studies the researchers examined were actually looking at the effects of the type of practice on performance that we had referred to as deliberate practice" (p. 276).

However, Ericsson and colleagues have multiple definitions of "deliberate practice" that sometimes contradict one another. As one example, Ericsson and colleagues have been inconsistent about whether a teacher (or coach) must design training activities for them to qualify as deliberate practice (see Table 9.1): Krampe and Ericsson (1996) explained that "Ericsson et al. defined *deliberate practice* as a very specific activity designed for an individual by a skilled teacher" (p. 333), but Ericsson (1998) later explained that "Ericsson et al. (1993) proposed the term deliberate practice to refer to those training activities that were designed solely for the purpose of improving individuals' performance by a teacher *or the performers themselves*" (p. 84, emphasis added; see also Keith & Ericsson, 2007). Thus, Ericsson and colleagues have claimed both that involvement of a teacher *is* and *is not* necessary for an activity to qualify as deliberate practice. (In our own meta-analyses, we used the latter definition of deliberate practice, particularly given that we could find no record in any study Ericsson has authored on accumulated deliberate practice where his operational definition limited practice estimates to only teacher-designed activities.) As another example, in the seminal study of deliberate practice, Ericsson *et al.* (1993) operationally defined deliberate practice as estimates of "practice alone," yet in the commentary on the Macnamara *et al.* (2014) meta-analysis, Ericsson stated that

TABLE 9.1 Inconsistent definitions of Deliberate Practice

Deliberate Practice Must Involve a Teacher:

"In distinction from leisurely or normal job-related experience, Ericsson et al. defined *deliberate practice* as a very specific activity designed for an individual by a skilled teacher explicitly to improve performance."

Krampe & Ericsson (1996, p. 333, emphasis original)

"Ericsson et al. (1993) used the term 'deliberate practice for the individualized training activities specially designed by a coach or teacher to improve specific aspects of an individual's performance through repetition and successive refinement.' (Ericsson & Lehmann, 1996, pp. 278–279)."

Ericsson (2014a, p. 3, emphasis original)★

Deliberate Practice Usually Involves a Teacher:

"When individuals engage in a practice activity (typically designed by their teachers), with full concentration on improving some aspect of their performance, we call that activity *deliberate practice.*"

Ericsson (2007, p. 14, emphasis original)

"Expert performance can . . . be traced to active engagement in deliberate practice (DP), where training (often designed and arranged by their teachers and coaches) is focused on improving particular tasks."

Ericsson (2008, p. 988)

Deliberate Practice Need Not Involve a Teacher:

"Ericsson et al. (1993) proposed the term deliberate practice to refer to those training activities that were designed solely for the purpose of improving individuals' performance by a teacher or the performers themselves."

Ericsson (1998, p. 84)

"Ericsson et al. (1993) introduced the term *deliberate practice* to describe focused and effortful practice activities that are pursued with the explicit goal of performance improvement. Deliberate practice implies that well-defined tasks are practiced at an appropriate level of difficulty and that informative feedback is given to monitor improvement. These activities can be designed by external agents, such as teachers or trainers, or by the performers themselves."

Keith & Ericsson (2007, p. 136, emphasis original)

Note. ★Ericsson (2014a) misquotes Lehmann and Ericsson's (1996) definition of deliberate practice: ". . .specially designed by a coach or teacher" should be ". . .*especially* designed by a coach or teacher" (emphasis added).

at present "it is *not possible* to estimate the proportion of deliberate practice from estimates of practice alone" (Ericsson, 2014a, p. 5, emphasis added).

In the commentary on our meta-analysis, Ericsson (2014a, 2014b) rejected 87 of the 88 studies.[1] He even rejected studies that he has used in the past to argue explicitly for the importance of "deliberate practice," including some of his own studies (see Table 9.2). For example, he rejected his own study of darts (Duffy, Baluch, & Ericsson, 2004) because the practice was not supervised by a teacher. However, he and his colleagues explicitly referred to the practice activities they measured in their study as "deliberate practice" and concluded that the results of the study supported "one of the main tenets of Ericsson et al.'s (1993) theory whereby expertise is acquired through a vast number of hours spent engaging in activities purely designed to improve performance, i.e., deliberate practice" (Duffy *et al.*, 2004, p. 243). For the same reason, Ericsson rejected his own study of Spelling Bee contestants (Duckworth, Kirby, Tsukayama, Berstein, & Ericsson, 2011) for not actually measuring deliberate practice. However, in criticizing a journalist for his portrayal of the study, Ericsson was emphatic that deliberate practice was, in fact, measured in the study, stating:

> To argue that deliberate practice needs to be augmented, he [Jaffe, 2012] explicitly cites an article, which includes deliberate practice in its title, "Deliberate practice spells success." In that study we (as I was also one of the co-authors) collected data on "deliberate practice." (Ericsson, 2012, pp. 5–6)

We do not believe it is scientifically defensible to claim that a study measured deliberate practice and then to claim, without explanation for the shift, that the *same* study did *not* measure deliberate practice. Shifting definitions allows evidence to be accepted as valid when arguing it supports a view, but rejected as invalid when arguing against others' use of the same evidence.

TABLE 9.2 Illustrations of inconsistent definitions of "Deliberate Practice" from Ericsson's (2014a, 2014b) Commentary on Macnamara *et al.*'s (2014) Meta-Analysis

Study rejected by Ericsson (2014b) because practice activity does not meet criteria for "deliberate practice"	*Previous use of the same study (in the left column) by Ericsson to argue for the importance of "deliberate practice"*
Charness, Tuffiash, Krampe, Reingold, & Vasyukova (2005)[a]	"This paper reports the most compelling and detailed evidence for how designed training (**deliberate practice**) is the crucial factor in developing expert chess performance." Ericsson (2005, p. 237)
deBruin, Rikers, & Schmidt (2007)[a]	"this study showed that the amount of **deliberate practice** was related to the development of performance for all players." Ericsson & Towne (2010, p. 410)[*]
Duckworth, Kirby, Tsukayama, Berstein, & Ericsson (2011)[a]	"Grittier spellers engaged in deliberate practice more so than their less gritty counterparts, and hours of **deliberate practice** fully mediated the prospective association between grit and spelling performance." Duckworth *et al.* (2011, p. 178)

Duffy, Baluch, & Ericsson (2004)[a]	"In short, the present study revealed that the single major factor contributing to professional level dart playing performance is **deliberate practice.**" Duffy, Baluch, & Ericsson (2004, p. 244)
Helsen, Starkes, & Hodges (1998)[b]	"Several studies and reviews have found a consistent association between the amount and the quality of solitary **deliberate practice** and performance . . . in different types of sports (. . .Helsen, Starkes, & Hodges, 1998. . .)." Ericsson, Nandagopal, & Roring (2005, p. 295)
Hodges, Kerr, Starkes, Weir, & Nananidou (2004)[b]	"Research conducted in several domains such as . . . sports (. . . Hodges, Kerr, Starkes, Weir, & Nananidou, 2004) . . . suggests that the amount of accumulated **deliberate practice** is closely related to an individual's attained level of performance." Keith & Ericsson (2007, p. 136)
Hodges & Starkes (1996)[b]	"Several studies and reviews have since found a consistent relation between performance and amount and quality of **deliberate practice** . . . in sports (. . . Hodges & Starkes, 1996 . . .)." Ericsson (1998, p. 87)
Sonnentag & Kleine (2000)[a]	"In a study of insurance agents Sonnentag and Kleinc [sic] (2000) found that engagement in **deliberate practice** predicted higher performance ratings." Ericsson (2006, p. 695)
Tuffiash, Roring, & Ericsson (2007)[a]	"Several researchers have reported a consistent association between the amount and quality of solitary activities meeting the criteria of **deliberate practice** and performance in different domains of expertise, such as . . . Scrabble (Tuffiash *et al.*, 2007)." Ericsson, Perez, et al. (2009, p. 9)
Ward, Hodges, Starkes, & Williams (2007)[b]	"Several researchers have reported a consistent association between the amount and quality of solitary activities meeting the criteria of **deliberate practice** and performance in different domains of expertise, such as . . . sports (Ward, Hodges, Starkes, & Williams, 2007. . .)." Ericsson et al. (2009, p. 9)

Note. In each quotation, the emphasis on "deliberate practice" is added.

[a] *Study rejected by Ericsson (2014b) because it did not "record a teacher or coach supervising and guiding all or most of the practice." See Ericsson (2014b), Table 2.*

[b] *Study rejected by Ericsson (2014b) because it did not "record assigned individualized practice tasks with immediate feedback and goals for practice." See Ericsson (2014b), Table 3.*

[*] *Ericsson and Towne (2010) cite deBruin, Smits, Rikers, and Schmidt (2008), but the data are the same as in deBruin, Rikers, and Schmidt (2007).*

What are the implications of these inconsistent definitions of deliberate practice for the claim that accumulated deliberate practice largely accounts for variance in performance? If one accepts the definition of deliberate practice requiring a teacher, there is little to no evidence remaining to support the claim that deliberate practice largely accounts for individual differences in expertise. If, on the other hand, one accepts the definition of deliberate practice not requiring a teacher, then the available evidence does not support the claim. Specifically, the available evidence suggests that deliberate practice, as it has been operationally defined and measured by Ericsson and others, is a statistically and practically important predictor of individual differences in expertise but does not *largely* account for individual differences in performance.

Definitions of Expert Performance

Ericsson and colleagues have further criticized studies challenging their view for not capturing *actual* expert performance—in other words, for not including *true* experts. However, as with deliberate practice, it is not clear what qualifies as "expert performance." In particular, Ericsson and colleagues have defined expert performance as "reproducibly superior performance on representative, authentic tasks" (Ericsson, 2006, p. 688, see also Ericsson & Smith, 1991), but the requirements for "superior performance" have been inconsistent.

As one example, Ericsson and Charness (1994) proposed that "if someone is performing at least two standard deviations above the mean level in the population, that individual can be said to be performing at an expert level" (p. 731), whereas Ericsson (2014c) suggested that the expert performance framework applies to "less than [a] handful [of] individuals" (p. 100). By the former standard, it would be reasonable to consider, say, any golfer who has qualified for the PGA Tour or LPGA Tour or any chess player at the rank of "master" or higher an expert. By the latter standard, very few professional golfers or chess masters would qualify as experts. As another example, when arguing against the results of two behavioral genetic studies that included amateurs (Hambrick & Tucker-Drob, 2015; Mosing, Madison, Pedersen, Kuja-Halkola, & Ullén, 2014), Ericsson (2016) claimed the results "cannot be generalized to expert[s]" (p. 352) and that "[e]xperts have acquired skills and mechanisms . . . that allow them to perform tasks that amateurs are unable to perform successfully" (p. 352). Yet he classified *amateur* music students in Ericsson *et al.*'s (1993) study of violinists and *amateur* collegiate bowlers in Harris's (2012) study of bowlers as "experts" (see Ericsson, 2006; Ericsson, 2016; Ericsson *et al.*, 1993). These inconsistencies allow favorable evidence to be accepted under some definitions, and unfavorable evidence to be rejected under other definitions.

Furthermore, an inherent problem with defining expert performance as "superior" performance is that what qualifies as superior will depend on the number of performers in a domain. For example, there are tens of millions of golfers in the world, but perhaps only a few thousand digit memorizers. Thus, superior performance in golf probably reflects a higher level of skill than superior performance in digit memorizing. Moreover, as the preceding discussion illustrates, any judgment about what qualifies as "superior" is ultimately arbitrary. One could, for example, define a "superior" baseball player as a member of a major league team, a member of a major league All-Star team, or a top-10 player in history—and all of these definitions would seem reasonable. In short, "superior" is not a discrete, naturally occurring category—it is an artificial label. In light of these problems, our view is that expertise (or skill) should be treated as the continuous variable that it is in research.

It also bears noting that Ericsson and colleagues have made contradictory claims about the existence of evidence for expert performance as measured by representative laboratory tasks. As a case in point, Ericsson, Roring, and Nandagopal (2007) claimed that "representative tasks have been found to capture expertise in . . . simultaneous translations of languages" (p. 10), and as evidence for this claim cited a review of the literature on expertise in language interpreting authored by Ericsson (2000/2001). However, in that review, Ericsson actually concluded that *no* representative laboratory tasks have successfully captured expertise in the interpreting domain, stating that "in the domain of interpreting researchers have not identified such demonstrations of consistently superior performance" (p. 211) and that "[o]nly future research will tell whether the application of the expert-performance approach to interpreting will advance our understanding of language comprehension and production, translation, and interpreting." (p. 216). When a person with authority in a field makes contradictory claims, it can lead to confusion in the literature, making it difficult to draw conclusions and to identify unanswered questions for future research.

Other Claims of the Deliberate Practice View

In addition to the claim that deliberate practice largely explains individual differences in expertise—where depending on one's definition of deliberate practice the evidence is either lacking or does not support this claim—other key claims of the deliberate practice view are problematic. Here, we mention three.

The 10-Year Rule

The first is the claim that at least 10 years of deliberate practice are required to reach an elite level in a domain. Ericsson and colleagues have endorsed this idea numerous times in the literature. For example, Ericsson et al. (1993) concluded that "expert performance is not reached with less than 10 years of deliberate practice" (p. 372). Similarly, Ericsson and Lehmann (1996) argued, "The highest levels of human performance in different domains can only be attained after around ten years of extended, daily amounts of deliberate practice activities" (p. 273). As another example, Ericsson, Prietula, and Cokely (2007) claimed that "our research shows that even the most gifted performers need a minimum of ten years (or 10,000 hours) of intense training before they win international competitions (p. 119), and Ericsson (2008) stated, "To reach a level where one can win international competitions, it is estimated that over 10,000 hours of DP [deliberate practice] have been generated for several domains" (p. 992). As a final example, Ericsson, Prietula, and Cokely (2007) declared, "It will take you *at least* a decade to achieve expertise, and you will need to invest that time wisely, by engaging in 'deliberate' practice—practice that focuses on tasks beyond your current level of competence and comfort" (p. 116, emphasis added). Later, however, Ericsson (2013) stated:

> In direct violation of the alleged necessity of 10,000 h in 10 years for becoming an expert, our original study [Ericsson *et al.*, 1993] estimated that one of our four groups of expert violinists had only *averaged* around 5,000 h of solitary practice (the activity most closely matching the criteria for deliberate practice) at age 20—as a consequence more than half of them had actually accumulated less than 5,000 h. (p. 534).

It is difficult to discern from these statements what, exactly, Ericsson and colleagues' position actually is on the necessity of at least 10 years (or 10,000 hours) of practice for achieving expertise.

Ericsson and colleagues' position aside, what does the available evidence indicate about the 10-year rule and the 10,000-hour rule? In short, it indicates that they are unfounded. For example, a number of chess players have obtained the grandmaster level in fewer than 10 years, including Magnus Carlsen who achieved the title after around 5 years of serious study while others have accumulated more than 25,000 hours of deliberate practice over many years and have not reached master status (Gobet & Campitelli, 2007). As another example, Lombardo and Deaner (2014) used archival records to document the 20 fastest American male sprinters in history, and found that eight of the 12 sprinters for whom data were available were found to reach world-class status in fewer than 10 years ($M = 8.7$, SD = 3.8). The 10-year rule may serve as a reminder to laypeople that expertise is acquired only after extensive training, but as a scientific proposition, it appears to be false.

Deliberate Practice vs. Other Forms of Domain-Relevant Experience

The second claim is that deliberate practice is a stronger predictor of individual differences in performance than other forms of domain-specific experience—namely, engaging in activities for external reward ("work") and for pleasure ("play"). As

Ericsson (2013) stated, "[I]t is now quite clear that the number of hours of merely engaging in activities, such as playing music, chess and soccer, or engaging in professional work activities has a much lower benefit for improving performance than deliberate practice" (p. 534). However, evidence suggests that this might not be the case. For example, in a study of pianists' accompanying and sight-reading performance, Lehmann and Ericsson (1996) measured actual accompanying experience (i.e., a work activity) as well as accumulated piano practice. They found that accompanying experience was more strongly correlated with all performance measures (rs = .63, .72, .67; all ps < .01) than was practice (rs = .32, .42, .36; all ns). As another example, in a study of insurance agents, Sonnentag and Kleine (2000) measured the number of cases handled (i.e., work activities) as well as deliberate practice. They found that the number of cases handled was a better predictor of job performance (r = .37, p = .01) than was cumulative deliberate practice (r = .13, ns). In short, there is evidence to suggest that (1) deliberate practice is not the only form of domain-relevant experience that is an important predictor of expertise, and (2) other types of experience may be more important predictors of expertise than deliberate practice in some domains.

The Role of Genetic Factors in Expert Performance

Evoking Watson's (1930) famous guarantee that he could take a "dozen healthy infants" and take "any one at random and train him to become any type of specialist I might select . . . regardless of his talents" (p. 104), the third—and boldest—claim of the deliberate practice view is that "the distinctive characteristics of elite performers are adaptations to extended and intense practice activities that selectively activate dormant genes that *all healthy children's DNA contain*" (Ericsson, 2007, p. 4, emphasis added). To argue for this view, Ericsson, Roring, and Nandagopal (2007) cited the results of a study by Carson, Nettleton, and Reecy (2001), claiming that "when humans engage in intense physical activity, several hundred genes are activated from their dormant state in the DNA (Carson *et al.*, 2001)" (p. 22). It should be noted, however, that the Carson *et al.* study made no mention of human expertise at all, nor of extended practice; it examined initial changes to microRNA over three days of physical work overload in rats. We can find no empirical evidence that can reasonably be interpreted as support for Ericsson and colleagues' idea that extended practice activities "selectively activate dormant genes that *all healthy children's DNA contain*" (Ericsson, 2007, p. 4, emphasis added). This claim would seem to be highly speculative.

Summary and Conclusions

Some people are better—*much* better—at complex tasks than other people. The question of why they are has been a topic of scientific inquiry for as long as psychology has been a field. The pendulum has swung on the question between "nature"—the view that experts are "born"—and "nurture"—the view that experts are "made." The latter view has been dominant in the scientific literature since the early 1970s (Chase & Simon, 1973), and particularly since Ericsson and colleagues proposed the deliberate practice view (Ericsson *et al.*, 1993).

Ericsson and colleagues' efforts to identify optimal conditions for complex learning are highly commendable. Their work has highlighted the importance of environmental factors in acquiring expertise and brought worldwide attention to the study of expertise, including to the public. Described in numerous pop psychology and self-help books, the deliberate practice view affects people's decisions from child rearing and personal development—including career changes—to how to allocate personal, institutional, and organizational resources. However, inconsistent definitions and contradictory interpretations of evidence are problematic for the viability of a scientific theory. That is, conclusions concerning a theory are susceptible to bias if conflicting definitions of a variable can be used interchangeably so as to use the same evidence to either support or reject a theory. Accordingly, we think it is critical for proponents of the deliberate practice view to clearly and consistently define key variables in their framework.

Most importantly, the central claim that individual differences in expertise can largely be accounted for by deliberate practice is not supported by the available evidence. Under some definitions of deliberate practice (see e.g., Krampe & Ericsson, 1996; Ericsson, 2014a, 2014b), there is little to no evidence to support this claim. Under other definitions of deliberate practice (see e.g., Keith & Ericsson, 2007; Ericsson, 1998), the available evidence indicates that deliberate practice is important but does not largely account for individual differences in performance (e.g., Macnamara *et al.*, 2014).

In sum, it seems clear that deliberate practice is one important predictor of expertise. However, it seems equally clear that other experiential factors, genetic factors, task factors, and their interactions must also be considered, lest we commit the single cause fallacy. We believe the challenge now for researchers interested in advancing the science of expertise is to develop consistently testable hypotheses and models that take into account multiple relevant factors. By putting the nature–nurture debate to rest, scientific research on the origins of expertise can move forward.

Note

1 Moreover, the one study Ericsson (2014a, 2014b) did not reject—Ericsson *et al.* (1993) Study 2—also appears to violate the criteria he set forth because can we can find no record that participants were asked to restrict their practice estimates *only* to teacher-designed activities. See instructions to participants in Appendix A, Krampe (1994).

References

Carson, J. A., Nettleton, D., & Reecy, J. M. (2001). Differential gene expression in the rat soleus muscle during early work overload-induced hypertrophy. *FASEB Journal,* *15*, U261–U281.

Charness, N., Tuffiash, M., Krampe, R., Reingold, E., & Vasyukova, E. (2005). The role of deliberate practice in chess expertise. *Applied Cognitive Psychology,* *19*, 151–165. doi:10.1002/acp.1106

Chase, W. G., & Simon, H. A. (1973). Perception in chess. *Cognitive Psychology,* *4*(1), 55–81. doi:10.1016/0010-0285(73)90004-2

Colvin, G. (2008). *Talent is overrated: What really separates world-class performers from everybody else.* New York, NY: Penguin Group.

de Bruin, A. B. H., Rikers, R. M. J. P., & Schmidt, H. G. (2007). The influence of achievement motivation and chess-specific motivation on deliberate practice. *Journal of Sport & Exercise Psychology,* *29*, 561–583.

de Bruin, A. B. H., Smits, N., Rikers, R. M. J. P., & Schmidt, H. G. (2008). Deliberate practice predicts performance over time in adolescent chess players and drop-outs: A linear mixed model analysis. British Journal of Psychology, 99, 473-497. doi: 10.1348/000712608X295631

Duckworth, A. L., Kirby, T. A., Tsukayama, E., Berstein, H., & Ericsson, K. A. (2011). Deliberate practice spells success: Why grittier competitors triumph at the national spelling bee. *Social Psychological and Personality Science,* *2*(2), 174–181. doi: 10.1037/0022-3514.92.6.1087.

Duffy, L. J., Baluch, B., & Ericsson, K. A. (2004). Dart performance as a function of facets of practice amongst professional and amateur men and women players. *International Journal of Sport Psychology,* *35*, 232–245.

Ericsson, K. A. (1998). The scientific study of expert levels of performance: General implications for optimal learning and creativity. *High Ability Studies,* *9*(1), 75–100. doi: 10.1080/1359813980090106

Ericsson, K. A. (2000/2001). Expertise in interpreting: An expert-performance perspective. *Interpreting,* *5*, 187–220.

Ericsson, K. A. (2005). Recent advances in expertise research: A commentary on the contributions to the special issue. *Applied Cognitive Psychology,* *19*, 233–241. doi: 10.1002/acp.1111

Ericsson, K. A. (2006). The influence of experience and deliberate practice on the development of superior expert performance. In K. A. Ericsson, N. Charness, P. J. Feltovich, & R. R. Hoffman (Eds.), *The Cambridge handbook of expertise and expert performance* (pp. 683–703). New York: Cambridge University Press.

Ericsson, K. A. (2007). Deliberate practice and the modifiability of body and mind: Toward a science of the structure and acquisition of expert and elite performance. *International Journal of Sport Psychology,* *38*, 4–34.

Ericsson, K. A. (2008). Deliberate practice and acquisition of expert performance: A general overview. *Academic Emergency Medicine,* *15*, 988–994. doi: 10.1111/j.1553-2712.2008.00227.

Ericsson, K. A. (2012). The danger of delegating education to journalists: Why the APS Observer needs peer review when summarizing new scientific developments. Unpublished commentary. Retrieved from: https://psy.fsu.edu/faculty/ericsson/ericsson.hp.html

Ericsson, K. A. (2013). Training history, deliberate practice and elite sports performance: an analysis in response to Tucker and Collins review—what makes champions? *British Journal of Sports Medicine, 47*(9), 533–535.

Ericsson, K. A. (2014a). Challenges for the estimation of an upper-bound on relations between accumulated deliberate practice and the associated performance of novices and experts: Comments on Macnemara [sic], Hambrick, and Oswald's (2014) published meta analysis. Unpublished commentary. Retrieved from: https://psy.fsu.edu/faculty/ericsson/ericsson.hp.html

Ericsson, K. A. (2014b). Supplemental online materials for "A challenge to estimates of an upper-bound on relations between accumulated deliberate practice and the associated performance in domains of expertise: Comments on Macnemara [sic], Hambrick, and Oswald's (2014) published meta-analysis." Unpublished supplemental materials to unpublished commentary. Retrieved from: https://psy.fsu.edu/faculty/ericsson/ericsson.hp.html

Ericsson, K. A. (2014c). Why expert performance is special and cannot be extrapolated from studies of performance in the general population: A response to criticisms. *Intelligence, 45,* 81–103. doi:10.1016/j.intell.2013.12.001

Ericsson, K. A. (2016). Summing up hours of any type of practice versus identifying optimal practice activities: Comments on Macnamara, Moreau, and Hambrick (2016). *Perspectives on Psychological Science, 11*(3), 351–354.

Ericsson, K. A., & Charness, N. (1994). Expert performance: Its structure and acquisition. *American Psychologist, 49*(8), 725–747. 10.1037/0003-066X.49.8.725

Ericsson, K. A., Krampe, R. T., & Tesch-Römer, C. (1993). The role of deliberate practice in the acquisition of expert performance. *Psychological Review, 100,* 363–406. doi:10.1037/0033-295X.100.3.363

Ericsson, K. A., & Lehmann, A. C. (1996). Expert and exceptional performance: Evidence of maximal adaptation to task constraints. *Annual Review of Psychology, 47*(1), 273–305. doi:10.1146/annurev.psych.47.1.273

Ericsson, K. A., Nandagopal, K., & Roring, R. W. (2005). Giftedness viewed from the expert-performance perspective. *Journal of the Education of the Gifted, 28,* 287–311.

Ericsson, K. A., Nandagopal, K., & Roring, R. W. (2009). Toward a science of exceptional achievement. *Annals of the New York Academy of Sciences, 1172*(1), 199–217. doi:10.1196/annals.1393.001

Ericsson, K. A., Perez, R. S., Eccles, D. W., Lang, L., Baker, E. L., Bransford, J. D., VanLehn, K., & Ward, P. (2009). The measurement and development of professional performance: An introduction to the topic and a background to the design and origin of this book. In K. A. Ericsson (Ed.), *Development of professional expertise: Toward measurement of expert performance and design of optimal learning environments* (pp. 1–27). New York: Cambridge University Press.

Ericsson, K. A., & Pool, R. (2016). *Peak: Secrets from the new science of expertise.* Boston: Houghton-Mifflin Harcourt.

Ericsson, K. A., Prietula, M. J. & Cokely, E. T. (2007). The making of an expert. *Harvard Business Review, 85* (7/8), 114-121.

Ericsson, K. A., Roring, R. W., & Nandagopal, K. (2007). Giftedness and evidence for reproducibly superior performance: An account based on the expert-performance framework. *High Ability Studies, 18,* 3–56.

Ericsson, K. A., & Smith, J. (1991). Prospects and limits in the empirical study of expertise: An introduction. In K. A. Ericsson & J. Smith (Eds.), *Toward a general theory of expertise: Prospects and limits* (pp. 1–38). Cambridge: Cambridge University Press.

Ericsson, K. A., & Towne, T. J. (2010). Expertise. *Wiley Interdisciplinary Reviews: Cognitive Science, 1*, 404–416. doi: 10.1002/wcs.47

Gladwell, M. (2008). *Outliers: The story of success.* New York, NY: Little, Brown.

Gobet, F., & Campitelli, G. (2007). The role of domain-specific practice, handedness, and starting age in chess. *Developmental Psychology, 43*, 159–172. doi:10.1037/0012-1649.43.1.159

Hambrick, D. Z., Altmann, E. M., Oswald, F. L., Meinz, E. J., Gobet, F., & Campitelli, G. 2014). Accounting for expert performance: The devil is in the details. *Intelligence, 45*, 112-114. doi: 10.1016/j.intell.2014.01.007

Hambrick, D. Z., Macnamara, B. N., Campitelli, G., Ullén, F., & Mosing, M. A. (2016). Beyond born versus made: A new look at expertise. In B. H. Ross (Ed.), *Psychology of Learning and Motivation* (pp. 1–55). Cambridge, MA: Academic Press.

Hambrick, D.Z., Oswald, F.L., Altmann, E.M., Meinz, E.J., Gobet, F., & Campitelli, G. (2014).Deliberate practice: Is that all it takes to become an expert? *Intelligence, 45*, 34-45. doi: 10.1016/j.intell.2013.04.001

Hambrick, D. Z., & Tucker-Drob, E. M. (2015). The genetics of music accomplishment: evidence for gene–environment correlation and interaction. *Psychonomic Bulletin & Review, 22*, 112–120. doi:10.3758/s13423-014-0671-9

Harris, K. R. (2008). *Deliberate practice, mental representations, and skilled performance in bowling* (Doctoral dissertation). Florida State University. Electronic Theses, Treatises and Dissertations, Diginole Commons. (Paper No. 4245)

Helsen, W. F., Starkes, J. L., & Hodges, N. J. (1998). Team sports and the theory of deliberate practice. *Journal of Sport & Exercise Psychology, 20*, 12–34.

Hodges, N. J., Kerr, T., Starkes, J. L., Weir, P. L., Nananidou, A. (2004). Predicting performance times from deliberate practice hours for triathletes and swimmers: What, when, and where Is practice important? *Journal of Experimental Psychology: Applied, 10*, 219–237. doi: 10.1037/1076-898X.10.4.219

Hodges, N. J., & Starkes, J. L. (1996). Wrestling with the nature expertise: A sport specific test of Ericsson, Krampe and Tesch-Römer's (1993) theory of "deliberate practice". *International Journal of Sport Psychology, 27*, 400–424.

Jaffe, E. (2012). Piecing together performance. *APS Observer, 25*(7), 13–16.

Keith, N., & Ericsson, K. A. (2007). A deliberate practice account of typing proficiency in everyday typists. *Journal of Experimental Psychology: Applied, 13*(3), 135–145. doi: 10.1037/1076-898X.13.3.135

Krampe, R. T. (1994). *Maintaining excellence: Cognitive-motor performance in pianists differing in age and skill level.* Doctoral dissertation. Max-Planck-Institut für Bildungsforschung.

Krampe, R. T., & Ericsson, K. A. (1996). Maintaining excellence: Deliberate practice and elite performance in young and older pianists. *Journal of experimental psychology: General, 125*(4), 331–359. doi: 10.1037/0096-3445.125.4.331

Lehmann, A. C., & Ericsson, K. A. (1996). Performance without preparation: Structure and acquisition of expert sight-reading and accompanying performance. *Psychomusicology, 15*, 1–29. doi: 10.1037/h0094082

Lombardo, M. P., & Deaner, R. O. (2013). You can't teach speed: Sprinters falsify the deliberate practice model of expertise. *PeerJ, 2*, e445. doi: 10.7717/peerj.445

Macnamara, B. N., Hambrick, D. Z., & Oswald, F. L. (2014). Deliberate practice and performance in music, games, sports, professions, and education: A meta-analysis. *Psychological Science, 25*, 1608–1618. doi:10.1177/0956797614535810

Macnamara, B. N., Moreau, D. & Hambrick, D. Z. (2016). The Relationship Between Deliberate Practice and Performance in Sports: A Meta-Analysis. *Perspectives in Psychological Science, 11*, 333–350. doi: 10.1177/1745691616635591

McGhee, W. (1958). Are we using what we know about training? Learning theory and training. *Personnel Psychology, 11*, 1–12. doi: 10.1111/j.1744-6570.1958.tb00001.x

McKeachie, W. J. (1961). Motivation, teaching methods, and college learning. In M. R. Jones, (Ed.), *Current theory and research m motivation.* Lincoln: University of Nebraska Press.

McLaughlin, D. (2014). *The first half of a journey in human potential: Half way to the 10,000 hour goal, four years of a blog by Dan McLaughlin (the Dan plan).* [Kindle]. Retrieved from: http://www.amazon.com/First-Half-Journey-Human-Potential-ebook/dp/B00MTC0NJA.

Mosing, M. A., Madison, G., Pedersen, N. L., Kuja-Halkola, R., & Ullén, F. (2014). Practice does not make perfect: No causal effect of music practice on music ability. *Psychological Science, 25*, 1795–1803. doi:10.1177/0956797614541990

Sakakibara, A. (2014). A longitudinal study of the process of acquiring absolute pitch: A practical report of training with the 'chord identification method'. *Psychology of Music, 42*, 86–111.

Sloboda, J. A., Davidson, J. W., Howe, M. J. A., & Moore, D. G. (1996). The role of practice in the development of performing musicians. *British Journal of Psychology, 87*, 287–309.

Sonnentag, S., & Kleine, B. M. (2000). Deliberate practice at work: A study with insurance agents. *Journal of Occupational and Organizational Psychology, 73*(1), 87–102.

Tuffiash, M., Roring, R. W., & Ericsson, K. A. (2007). Expert performance in SCRABBLE: Implications for the study of the structure and acquisition of complex skills. *Journal of Experimental Psychology: Applied, 13*, 124–134. doi: 10.1037/1076-898X.13.3.124

Ward, P., Hodges, N. J., Starkes, J. L., & Williams, M. A. (2007). The road to excellence: deliberate practice and the development of expertise. *High Ability Studies, 18*, 119–153. doi: 10.1080/13598130701709715

Watson, J. B. (1930). *Behaviorism.* Chicago, IL: The University of Chicago Press.

PART II
Neural Approach

10

Primer

NEURAL APPROACHES IN RESEARCH ON EXPERTISE

Alessandro Guida, Audrey Noël, and Pierre-Yves Jonin

Introduction

To study the neurophysiology of expertise, neuro-imaging techniques can be very convenient tools. The aim of this chapter is to provide an overview of these methodologies used to study the neural bases of expertise and briefly present the main pattern of results found in the literature, along with their interpretation, and the associated conceptual issues. This primer chapter is specially addressed to newcomers in this domain, as we introduce what one needs to know to begin the neural study of expertise. Importantly, this is not a technical chapter; the scope is larger, as it also encompasses conceptual issues. Therefore, we only briefly present each technique and what it can achieve; but we direct the interested reader toward more technical articles or books. The chapter begins with a brief description of the main neuro-imaging techniques that have been used to study expertise and concludes with a presentation of the neural patterns of results often found in studies of expertise.

Neuro-Imaging Techniques to Scrutinize the Brain

Nowadays several techniques are used by researchers to study the cerebral activations and structures that undergird expertise. These neuro-imaging techniques can be divided into two categories: (1) those that allow studying the activations that occur in the brain—*functional techniques*—and (2) those that allow uncovering the structure of the brain—*structural techniques*.

Functional Techniques: EEG, MEG, PET, fMRI

Among the functional techniques, *electroencephalography* (EEG) and *magnetoencephalography* (MEG) allow the most direct measures based on neurophysiology.

Because EEG and MEG have a high temporal resolution (in terms of milliseconds) but a modest spatial resolution of 1 to 3 cm, (e.g., Siebenhühner, Lobier, Wang, Palva, & Palva, 2016), these are appropriate tools if one is interested in the time course of fairly fast processes.

EEG records the electrical activity of the brain allowing measurement of fluctuations in the electrical voltage via electrodes placed on the scalp. The electrocortical activity is measured in microvolts (μV) and then amplified by a 10^6 factor (e.g., Marcuse, Fields, & Yoo, 2015).

MEG also allows a direct measure of neural activity, but while EEG records the potential distribution caused by the currents on the scalp, MEG measures the magnetic fields produced by the currents' activity (e.g., Hari & Salmelin, 2012). Compared to EEG, MEG systems are expensive and cumbersome, but spatio-temporal resolution is reached without using complex head models; moreover, MEG does not require a reference because it is an absolute measure (Supek & Aine, 2014).

If one is more interested in the source of the neural signal and thus in "where" kinds of questions, *positron emission tomography* (PET) and *functional magnetic resonance imaging* (fMRI) are the tools of choice. In effect, what these techniques lack in temporal resolution (in terms of seconds), they make up for in spatial resolution (5 mm to 1 mm).

PET allows the detection of weak brain metabolic and blood flow changes (Buckner & Logan, 2001). Blood flow provides the necessary energy to neurons making it a good index of neural activity. In PET, radioactive tracers injected in the bloodstream accumulate where metabolic demand increases. Via a chain reaction involving positrons and electrons, the disintegration of the radioactive tracer causes the emission of two photons in opposite directions which induces an ionizing radiation. PET allows accurate quantification of radiotracer distribution in the brain. Then a map of brain activations (location and intensity) can be drawn. PET has a good spatial resolution, although lower than that of fMRI.

The technique of fMRI indirectly measures neural activity through the so-called "BOLD" signal (Blood-Oxygen-Level Dependent). Sensory or cognitive processing is associated with local firing of neurons, which results in increased local cerebral metabolism. This requires more oxygen, so that locally the ratios between oxygenated and deoxygenated hemoglobin are modified. These changes increase the BOLD signal (Jezzard, Matthews, & Smith, 2001). In short, acquisition of the BOLD signal in response to a given task allows localization of the area of the brain involved in the task.

Structural Techniques: VBM and DTI

This second category of neuro-imaging techniques enables observation of the structure of the brain. While structural and functional techniques do not measure the same substratum, the pattern of activation measured with functional techniques is thought to be linked to the structure of the brain; for the moment, however, how the linkage occurs is not clear (e.g., Wang, Dai, Gong, Zhou, & He, 2014). Moreover, concerning expertise, very few studies have investigated how practice does or does not differentially impact structure and function.

Two types of neural structures can be observed: (1) gray matter of the brain (neurons) using *voxel-based morphometry* (VBM), or (2) white matter using *diffusion tensor imaging* (DTI).

Voxel-based Morphometry

VBM which involves *magnetic resonance imaging* (MRI), allows obtaining three-dimensional images of the brain, including gray matter, white matter, and cerebrospinal fluid. MRI relies on the magnetic proprieties of hydrogen nuclei in water molecules (present in large quantities in the brain). In the absence of a magnetic field, protons are oriented randomly, but when subjected to a strong magnetic field, they align on the same axis. The return of protons to equilibrium state engenders a radio signal that can be used to achieve detailed images of brain tissues (Brown & Semelka, 2010). VBM allows analysis of the whole brain. It compares the local density of gray matter, white matter, or cerebrospinal fluid between several groups of subjects. This process involves the spatial normalization of all images into the same stereotactic space (to create a template), the segmentation (i.e., assigning each voxel to gray matter, white matter or cerebrospinal fluid) and the smoothing of data. Finally, statistical analyses are carried out in order to localize differences between groups.

Diffusion Tensor Imaging

This is a specific kind of modeling for *diffusion weighted imagery* (DWI), which is a variant of conventional MRI based on the tissue-water diffusion rate. In a barrier-free environment, diffusion is isotropic (the probability of displacements is the same for every direction), however it is anisotropic in white matter. Direction and amount of diffusion enables computation of a "tensor," which is an estimate of the local diffusion directions, thus leading to the so-called "DTI." Different methods are used to quantify the tensors in each point of the brain (a common method uses fractional anisotropy). A classical application of DTI is *fiber tractography* (Stieltjes *et al.*, 2001).

How to Use These Neuro-Imaging Techniques

Once one has access to these techniques, how should they be used to study expertise? The best way to understand this is to see how these techniques have been used and what kinds of patterns have been reported. As in the behavioral approach, two kinds of approach exist: (1) *cross-sectional*, where experts are compared to novices, and (2) *longitudinal*, where one measures the same individuals while they are gaining expertise. We will not go into details concerning the pros and cons of each approach, as they have already been covered in chapters on the behavioral approach. Of interest here is the specificity of the neural approach; therefore we will present two scanning paradigms used in the longitudinal approach and tease apart their respective advantages and disadvantages.

The most classic paradigm is *scanning-training-scanning* (S–T–S) (for a review of studies adopting this paradigm, see Guida, Gobet, Tardieu, & Nicolas, 2012). In S–T–S, the brain is scanned before training (*novice condition*) and after training (*practiced condition*), or additionally in between.

In contrast, some authors (e.g., Moore, Cohen, & Ranganath, 2006) prefer using a *training-scanning* (T–S) paradigm where participants are first trained concerning a task and a type of material and scanned only after training; however, participants are scanned twice after training: (1) while executing the task for which they have been trained and with the same material used during the training—the *practiced condition*, and (2) while executing the task for which participants have been trained *but* with a novel kind of material for which they have no expertise—the *(pseudo)novice condition*.

Importantly, these paradigms measure the effect of practice in different ways. First, whereas studies using the S–T–S paradigm compare a physiological state before training and a physiological state after training, in the T–S studies the physiological state before practice is unknown and is not part of the experimental contrast. The two physiological states that are compared in the T–S paradigm are the (pseudo)novice condition and the practiced condition, both of which are post-training. This can be a shortcoming, because the training can also affect the (pseudo)novice condition, especially since the same task is used in the practiced condition and in the (pseudo)novice condition. Therefore, while the S–T–S paradigm seems to engender an authentic "trained vs. untrained" contrast, the T–S paradigm seems more likely to show a "trained in a task with very familiar object vs. trained in a task with less familiar object" contrast. The T–S paradigm also has interesting features compared with the S–T–S paradigm. In fact, with the S–T–S paradigm there are two confounds that do not appear in the T–S paradigm: *time and training*.

In the S–T–S paradigm, the time factor is confounded with the *practice* factor. One way of controlling this is to use a control/placebo group and to scan it twice exactly the same as the experimental group. Due to the cost of the scanning process this is rarely done. In the T–S paradigm, the time factor is not confounded, because the two scanning sessions occur at the same moment, after the training.

The second confound in the S–T–S paradigm is the training procedure once its content has been removed. Let us imagine that the training can be divided into two parts: (a) the content of the training and (b) the training without its content. In this way, an effect of training could be due to the content of that particular training (the "a" part) or just because training occurred, meaning that even an irrelevant training would cause an effect (the "b" part).

Summing up, it appears that the S-T-S paradigm has fewer methodological problems only if a control/placebo group is used. However, if one wants to avoid using controls/placebos, a solution would be to merge the two paradigms; that is, (1) scan all the participants (like in S-T-S); (2) train them (like in S-T-S); and finally (3) after the training, give them a novel material and the familiar material (used in the training), in order to scan the participants in the "untrained" situation (the novice condition, like in T-S) and scan the participants in the trained situation (the practice condition, like in S-T-S and T-S).

Now that we know more about the scanning paradigms that are used, let us turn to the changes in the brain that co-occur with the acquisition of expertise. Logically, if one compares two moments on a continuum of expertise, two changes in the brain can take place when considering one location of the brain: increase or decrease. However, when one takes into account multiple locations in the brain, then one must add *reorganization*, which can be defined as a combined pattern of increases and decreases across brain areas (Kelly & Garavan, 2005).

In the following sections, from the literature, we present and interpret the three cerebral change-patterns that are observed through functional and structural neuro-imaging techniques.

Interpreting Cerebral Patterns

Brain Decrease

Brain decrease can be functionally or structurally observed. This decrease has been reported indirectly by comparing experts vs. novices (cross-sectional studies) or directly (longitudinal studies). In the latter case, most authors use the S-T-S paradigm. No matter the techniques or comparisons, when studying the effect of expertise, the decreasing pattern is the most observed pattern, with, as we will see later, one exception—motor tasks.

Several interpretations of the decreasing pattern exist; nonetheless, there seems to be almost a consensus. As reviewed by Guida *et al.* (2012), authors tend to describe the decreasing pattern in terms of neural efficiency of the brain. This hypothesis (e.g., Buschkuehl, Jaeggi, & Jonides, 2012), which can be linked to Haier and colleagues' neural efficiency theory (Haier *et al.*, 1988) postulates that the ratio between information processing and cerebral resources can increase with practice, leading to a more efficient cortical functioning. Interestingly, Poldrack (2000) suggested that in order to speak about "neural efficiency" the brain decrease must be associated with a behavioral improvement, otherwise the decrease can be caused by other (confounded) factors rather than by efficiency.

Though this suggestion is appealing, Poldrack (2015) recently warned against the use of this concept in an explanatory fashion, as it is insufficient and necessitates a more mechanistic explanation. And, indeed, at least three cognitive explanations of brain decrease have been proposed. For Beauchamp, Dagher, Aston, and Doyon (2003) for example, the decrease of activation they detected in the orbitofrontal cortex areas suggested that skill in solving Tower-of-London problems became increasingly implicit with practice. A second way of interpreting efficiency is in terms of flexibility. Landau, Garavan, Schumacher, and D'Esposito (2007) have shown, for example, that practice impacts more unimodal and multimodal regions than primary sensory and motor regions. The first two types of regions are more flexible because they participate in top-down "modulatory and selection processes," while the latter are involved in bottom-up perceptual and motor processes, which are less susceptible to adaptation. A third way of explaining efficiency is by appealing to the concept of *chunks*. Guida *et al.* (2012) proposed that with practice there is a gradual buildup of chunks (*chunk creation*). These chunks can then be used (*chunk retrieval*) to represent and process the world with fewer cognitive and neural resources (see also Guida, Gobet, & Nicolas, 2013).

Finally, increased efficiency may be accounted for by more physiological oriented explanations such as reduction in the number of activated neurons (e.g., Garavan, Kelley, Rosen, Rao, & Stein, 2000) or by neural efficiency (e.g., Kelly & Garavan, 2005).

As noted above, decreased efficiency seems to be found in almost all the expert activities, especially at the early stages as postulated by Guida *et al.* (2012, 2013) in their two-stage framework of expertise acquisition, except specifically for motor-sensory activities where brain increase is more often observed. So let us turn to this pattern.

Brain Increase

The physiological features of increase can be considered as the reverse pattern of decrease. If one considers that activation decrease is the contraction of a neural representation, increase can be seen as an expansion of the cortical representation (Pascual-Leone, Amedi, Fregni, & Merabet, 2005). For example, in tasks such as long-term motor training that tap the primary cortices, there is a modification in horizontal connectivity (e.g., Buonomano & Merzenich, 1998) that suggests an extension of the representation. However, according to Poldrack (2000), the increase in activation can have at least one other interpretation, i.e., a strengthening of the response activation (see also Kelly, Foxe, & Garavan, 2006), and it is difficult to distinguish between the two possibilities.

No matter the technique, studies on motor expertise almost always trigger a neural pattern of increase when comparing the neuro-imaging data of experts versus that of novices. This pattern has been evident since the first study on the subject (Elbert, Pantev, Wienbruch, Rockstroh, & Taub, 1995), which showed that string-player musicians had a larger cortical finger representation of the left hand that correlated with musical expertise (starting age). Reviews by Buschkuehl *et al.* (2012) and Kelly and Garavan (2005) confirmed this pattern, showing for example that increased brain activation can be observed almost systematically in motor-sensory tasks (e.g., Ungerleider, Doyon, & Karni, 2002). Conversely, expertise in more complex tasks does not seem related to an increase of activation (Buschkuehl *et al.*, 2012; Guida *et al.*, 2012; but see Klingberg, 2010), although it is important to note that the only meta-analysis on motor tasks is not clear-cut (Yang, 2015).

Concerning structural techniques, the same pattern of increase is found. For example, in their review, Zatorre, Fields, and Johansen-Berg (2012) (see also Zatorre, Chen, & Penhune, 2007) showed that there consistently seem to be a greater gray matter volume and cortical thickness in auditory cortices of expert musicians. Bengtsson *et al.* (2005) also showed that extensive piano practice had specific effects on white matter development in the spinothalamic tract. And Zatorre *et al.* (2012) reported that generally in all the studies reviewed, the effects increased as a function of years of musical practice. This pattern was also reported by Debarnot, Sperduti, Di Rienzo, and Guillot (2014) in their review. However, given the cross-sectional nature of these studies, the link is only correlational. The same is true in various domains such as basketball (Park *et al.*, 2011), typing (Cannonieri, Bonilha, Fernandes, Cendes, & Li, 2007), or golf (Jäncke, Koeneke, Hoppe, Rominger, & Hänggi, 2009).

But more direct longitudinal evidence does exist. For example, using a longitudinal design Draganski *et al.* (2004) observed an increase of gray matter density—in mid-temporal regions and in the left posterior intra-parietal sulcus—when individuals trained at juggling for three months. A comparable result was obtained after seven days (Driemeyer, Boyke, Gaser, Büchel, & May, 2008). Interestingly, this increase can also alter white matter pathways as shown by Scholz, Klein, Behrens, and Johansen-Berg (2009) using DTI.

Zatorre *et al.* (2012) listed the candidate mechanisms for explaining these structural changes.[1] For gray matter, the major candidates are *neurogenesis*, *gliogenesis*, and *synaptogenesis* changes in neuronal morphology and even vascular changes. For white matter, the major candidates are *activity-dependent axonal sprouting*, *pruning or re-routing*, and *myelination* (Fields, 2015).

Co-occurrence of Brain Decrease and Increase

Interestingly, structural techniques have also detected more complex results, with co-occurring increase and decrease. For example, using VBM, James *et al.* (2014) compared expert musicians and novices. They reported a decreasing pattern in motor-sensory areas which co-occurred with a gray matter density increase in higher-order regions. This type of pattern is not unique; for example, when compared to individuals who do not drive taxis, taxi drivers usually exhibit greater volume in the posterior hippocampus with less volume in the anterior hippocampus (Maguire *et al.*, 2000). As noted above, this pattern of combined increase and decrease may be termed *reorganization* in studies utilizing functional techniques (Kelly & Garavan, 2005). However, in other research using structural techniques (especially in the domain of rehabilitation), reorganization is considered more synonymous with *plasticity*, and the term may be employed to designate change, which can be a simple decrease or increase.

Functional Reorganization

In this section, we present and interpret the special status of functional reorganization as a combined pattern of activation increases and decreases across brain areas (Kelly & Garavan, 2005). At present, two types of functional reorganization have been pinpointed: *scaffolding* (Petersen, van Mier, Fiez, & Raichle, 1998) and *true reorganization* (Kelly & Garavan, 2005).

The concept of scaffolding is the idea that a set of brain regions can be used by unskilled individuals in effortful performance to cope with novel task demands when attentional and control processes are needed. After a period of practice, the activation of the brain areas involved in scaffolding decreases while the activation of other brain areas may increase. Kelly and Garavan (2005) contrasted scaffolding, which fades away with practice, to true reorganization, which does not occur immediately. Two recent reviews (Guida *et al.* 2012; Neumann, Lotze, & Eickhoff, 2016) are compatible with the idea that reorganization occurs only at a late stage of practice; that is, when sufficient time has been available to practice. Guida *et al.* (2012) have tied this physiological process to the development of knowledge structures; that is, cognitive structures that allow increasing the cognitive context around incoming information, with a consequent increase in mnemonic capacities.

Relevant here is the concept of *neural context* (e.g., Bressler & McIntosh, 2007), which suggests that the context of activation around a particular brain area is also crucial. From this perspective, it is easy to understand how a brain region can have different functions if there is variation in its interaction with different brain areas. Related to expertise, this concept translates as follows: Even if an expert and a novice have exactly the same pattern of activation in one brain region, this region could be processing information in a completely different manner because its interactions with other regions could be different. In terms of functional reorganization, neural context seems therefore to be crucial, although its application still needs to be taken further.

Conclusion

This chapter has shown that no matter the kind of techniques—functional or structural—similar cerebral patterns are found in expertise acquisition. When comparing increasing and decreasing patterns, the latter is the most commonly found, especially when people start practicing (e.g., Guida *et al.*, 2012), no matter the domain, with the exception of motor-sensory tasks. In this case, an increasing pattern is often observed (Buschkuehl *et al.*, 2012; Kelly & Garavan, 2005). Finally, when sufficient time is available, reorganization tends to take place, and has been linked by Guida *et al.* (2012) with the development and utilization of knowledge structures. These three patterns—decrease, increase, and reorganization—that co-occur with expertise acquisition are fundamental for the understanding of neural research on expertise.

Note

1 Not all results are systematically in favor of an increase in structure with expertise in motor tasks (e.g., Bengtsson *et al.*, 2005). Zatorre *et al.* (2012) suggested that the contradiction may not be due to genuine white matter decrease but could be caused by axon diameters increase (or if a secondary fiber population matures in a region of fiber crossing).

References

Beauchamp, M. H., Dagher, A., Aston, J. A., & Doyon, J. (2003). Dynamic functional changes associated with cognitive skill learning of an adapted version of the Tower of London task. *Neuroimage, 20*, 1649–1660.

Bengtsson, S. L., Nagy, Z., Skare, S., Forsman, L., Forssberg, H., & Ullén, F. (2005). Extensive piano practicing has regionally specific effects on white matter development. *Nature Neuroscience, 8*(9), 1148–1150.

Bressler, S. L., & McIntosh, A. R. (2007). The role of neural context in large-scale neurocognitive network operations. In Viktor K. Jirsa & A. R. McIntosh (Eds.), *Handbook of brain connectivity* (pp. 403–419). Berlin; Heidelberg: Springer Verlag.

Brown, M. A., & Semelka, R. C. (2010). *MRI basic principles and applications. Fourth Edition.* New York: Wiley-Liss.

Buckner, R. L., & Logan, J. M. (2001). Functional neuroimaging methods: PET and fMRI. In R. Cabeza & A. Kingstone (Eds), *Handbook of functional neuroimaging of cognition* (pp. 27–48). Cambridge, MA: MIT Press.

Buonomano, D. V., & Merzenich, M. M. (1998). Cortical plasticity: From synapses to maps. *Annual Review of Neuroscience, 21*, 149–186.

Buschkuehl, M., Jaeggi, S. M., & Jonides, J. (2012). Neuronal effects following working memory training. *Developmental Cognitive Neuroscience, 2*, S167–S179.

Cannonieri, G. C., Bonilha, L., Fernandes, P. T., Cendes, F., & Li, L. M. (2007). Practice and perfect: length of training and structural brain changes in experienced typists. *Neuroreport, 18*(10), 1063–1066.

Debarnot, U., Sperduti, M., Di Rienzo, F., & Guillot, A. (2014). Experts bodies, experts minds: How physical and mental training shape the brain. *Frontiers in Human Neuroscience, 8*, 280. doi:10.3389/fnhum.2014.00280

Draganski, B., Gaser, C., Busch, V., Schuierer, G., Bogdahn, U., & May, A. (2004). Neuroplasticity: changes in grey matter induced by training. *Nature, 427*(6972), 311–312.

Driemeyer, J., Boyke, J., Gaser, C., Büchel, C., & May, A. (2008). Changes in gray matter induced by learning—revisited. *PLoS One, 3*(7), e2669.

Elbert, T., Pantev, C., Wienbruch, C., Rockstroh, B., & Taub, E. (1995). Increased cortical representation of the fingers of the left hand in string players. *Science, 270* (5234), 305.

Fields, R. D. (2015). A new mechanism of nervous system plasticity: Activity-dependent myelination. *Nature Reviews Neuroscience, 16*(12), 756–767.

Frutiger, S. A., Strother, S. C., Anderson, J. R., Sidtis, J. J., Arnold, J. B., & Rottenberg, D. A. (2000). Multivariate predictive relationship between kinematic and functional activation patterns in a PET study of visuomotor learning. *Neuroimage, 12*, 515–27.

Garavan, H., Kelley, D., Rosen, A., Rao, S. M., & Stein, E. A. (2000). Practice-related functional activation changes in a working memory task. *Microscopy Research and Techniques, 51*, 54–63.

Guida, A., Gobet, F., & Nicolas, S. (2013). Functional cerebral reorganization: A signature of expertise? Reexamining Guida, Gobet, Tardieu, and Nicolas' (2012) two-stage framework. *Frontiers in Human Neuroscience, 7*. doi:10.3389/fnhum.2013.00590

Guida, A., Gobet, F., Tardieu, H., & Nicolas, S. (2012). How chunks, long-term working memory and templates offer a cognitive explanation for neuroimaging data on expertise acquisition: A two-stage framework. *Brain and Cognition, 79*(3), 221–244.

Haier, R. J., Siegel, B. V., Nuechterlein, K. H., Hazlett, E., Wu, J. C., Paek, J., … Buchsbaum, M. S. (1988). Cortical glucose metabolic rate correlates of abstract reasoning and attention studied with positron emission tomography. *Intelligence, 12*(2), 199–217.

Hari, R., & Salmelin, R. (2012). Magnetoencephalography: from SQUIDs to neuroscience: Neuroimage 20th anniversary special edition. *Neuroimage, 61*(2), 386–396.

James, C. E., Oechslin, M. S., Van De Ville, D., Hauert, C.-A., Descloux, C., & Lazeyras, F. (2014). Musical training intensity yields opposite effects on grey matter density in cognitive versus sensorimotor networks. *Brain Structure and Function, 219*(1), 353–366.

Jäncke, L., Koeneke, S., Hoppe, A., Rominger, C., & Hänggi, J. (2009). The architecture of the golfer's brain. *PloS One, 4*(3), e4785.

Jezzard, P., Matthews, P. M., & Smith, S. M. (2001). *Functional Magnetic Resonance Imaging: An introduction to methods.* Oxford: Oxford University Press, 2001.

Kelly, A. C., & Garavan, H. (2005). Human functional neuroimaging of brain changes associated with practice. *Cerebral Cortex, 15*(8), 1089–1102.

Kelly, C., Foxe, J. J., & Garavan, H. (2006). Patterns of normal human brain plasticity after practice and their implications for neurorehabilitation. *Archives of Physical Medicine and Rehabilitation, 87*(12), 20–29.

Klingberg, T. (2010). Training and plasticity of working memory. *Trends in Cognitive Sciences, 14*(7), 317–324.

Landau, S. M., Garavan, H., Schumacher, E. H., & D'Esposito, M. (2007). Regional specificity and practice: Dynamic changes in object and spatial working memory. *Brain Research 1180*, 78–89.

Maguire, E. A., Gadian, D. G., Johnsrude, I. S., Good, C. D., Ashburner, J., Frackowiak, R. S., & Frith, C. D. (2000). Navigation-related structural change in the hippocampi of taxi drivers. *Proceedings of the National Academy of Sciences, 97*(8), 4398–4403.

Marcuse, L. V., Fields, M. C., & Yoo, J. J. (2015). *Rowan's Primer of EEG.* Elsevier - Health Sciences Division, United States.

Moore, C. D., Cohen, M. X., & Ranganath, C. (2006). Neural mechanisms of expert skills in visual working memory. *The Journal of Neuroscience, 26*(43), 11187–11196.

Neumann, N., Lotze, M., & Eickhoff, S. B. (2016). Cognitive Expertise: An ALE Meta-Analysis. *Human Brain Mapping, 37*(1), 262–272.

Park, I. S., Lee, K. J., Han, J. W., Lee, N. J., Lee, W. T., Park, K. A., & Rhyu, I. J. (2009). Experience-dependent plasticity of cerebellar vermis in basketball players. *The Cerebellum, 8*(3), 334–339.

Park, I. S., Lee, K. J., Han, J. W., Lee, N. J., Lee, W. T., Park, K. A., & Rhyu, I. J. (2011). Basketball training increases striatum volume. *Human Movement Science, 30*(1), 56–62.

Pascual-Leone, A., Amedi, A., Fregni, F., & Merabet, L. B. (2005). The plastic human brain cortex. *Annual Review of Neuroscience, 28*, 377–401.

Petersen, S. E., van Mier, H., Fiez, J. A., & Raichle, M. E. (1998). The effects of practice on the functional anatomy of task performance. *Proceedings of the National Academy of Sciences of the United States of America, 95*, 853–860.

Poldrack, R. A. (2000). Imaging brain plasticity: Conceptual and methodological issues – a theoretical review. *NeuroImage, 12*(1), 1–13.

Poldrack, R. A. (2015). Is "efficiency" a useful concept in cognitive neuroscience? *Developmental Cognitive Neuroscience, 11*, 12–17.

Scholz, J., Klein, M. C., Behrens, T. E., & Johansen-Berg, H. (2009). Training induces changes in white-matter architecture. *Nature Neuroscience, 12*(11), 1370–1371.

Siebenhühner, F., Lobier, M., Wang, S. H., Palva, S., & Palva, J. M. (2016). Measuring large-scale synchronization with human MEG and EEG: Challenges and solutions. In Palva Satu (Ed.), *Multimodal Oscillation-based Connectivity Theory* (pp. 1–18). Springer International Publishing, Switzerland.

Stieltjes, B., Kaufmann W. E., van Zijl, P. C., Fredericksen, K., Pearlson, G. D., Solaiyappan, M., & Mori, S. (2001) Diffusion tensor imaging and axonal tracking in the human brainstem. *Neuroimage, 14*, 723–735.

Supek, S., & Aine, C. J. (Eds.) (2014). *Magnetoencephalography: From signals to dynamic cortical networks*. Berlin; Heidelberg: Springer Verlag.

Taubert, M., Draganski, B., Anwander, A., Müller, K., Horstmann, A., Villringer, A., & Ragert, P. (2010). Dynamic properties of human brain structure: Learning-related changes in cortical areas and associated fiber connections. *The Journal of Neuroscience, 30*(35), 11670–11677.

Ungerleider, L. G., Doyon, J., & Karni, A. (2002). Imaging brain plasticity during motor skill learning. *Neurobiology of Learning and Memory, 78*(3), 553–564.

Wang, Z., Dai, Z., Gong, G., Zhou, C., & He, Y. (2014). Understanding structural-functional relationships in the human brain a large-scale network perspective. *The Neuroscientist, 21*(3), 290–305. doi: 10.1177/1073858414537560.

Yang, J. (2015). The influence of motor expertise on the brain activity of motor task performance: A meta-analysis of functional magnetic resonance imaging studies. *Cognitive, Affective, & Behavioral Neuroscience, 15*(2), 381–394.

Zatorre, R. J., Chen, J. L., & Penhune, V. B. (2007). When the brain plays music: Auditory-motor interactions in music perception and production. *Nature Reviews Neuroscience, 8*(7), 547–558.

Zatorre, R. J., Fields, R. D., & Johansen-Berg, H. (2012). Plasticity in gray and white: neuroimaging changes in brain structure during learning. *Nature Neuroscience, 15*(4), 528–536.

11

THE NEURAL UNDERPINNINGS OF EXPERTISE IN GAMES

Merim Bilalić, Anna Conci, Mario Graf, and Nemanja Vaci

Introduction

Most of the games that we will examine here, especially the board games, are deceptively simple. The space is clearly defined and the rules are fixed and so simple that even children can learn them. Yet, as anybody who has tried their hand at the games of chess or Go (also called Baduk) knows, it takes years to become merely competent, let alone to master these games. This simplicity of environment, which still leads to complex games, has been appealing to scientists investigating the human mind. The constrained environment allows experimental manipulations, while the complexity mimics the real world, making it possible to investigate phenomena of interest without reducing their complexity (Bilalić, 2016). Here we will first examine how board games have been used in scientific investigations. We will then move on to illuminate how cognitive processes, such as memory, attention and perception, enable expertise at board games. Finally, we will look at how the brain implements skilled performance at board games.

The Expertise Approach

The complexity of board games enables two different research approaches. Both of these investigate experts' performance, but one focuses on performance in its full complexity, while the other looks at simple components of complex performance. The main idea behind the first approach, called the *expert performance approach* (Ericsson & Smith, 1991), is to capture the essence of the expertise under investigation within a laboratory setting. This is achieved by identifying representative tasks, activities that represent the core of skill, but are simple enough to be executed in the laboratory. For example, the fundamental skill of expert chess players is that they find the right solution among numerous possibilities over and over again in the course of a game. Instead of asking chess experts to play a whole game in the laboratory, researchers choose to present them with an unfamiliar position from a normal game between two masters and ask them to find the best move. Once the laboratory task has been established, researchers can manipulate factors such as *skill* (Bilalić, McLeod, & Gobet, 2008a) and *familiarity* (Bilalić, McLeod, & Gobet, 2009) and see what processes mediate experts' outstanding performance.

The other research approach, called the *expertise approach* (Bilalić, Turella, Campitelli, Erb, & Grodd, 2012; Rennig, Bilalić, Huberle, Karnath, & Himmelbach, 2013), exploits the presence of experts,[1] people who possess large amounts of domain-specific knowledge, and novices, who lack that knowledge, for investigating single components of performance. Finding a good solution in the sea of possibilities may be the pinnacle of board expertise, but that skill encompasses numerous other simpler skills. They may be trivial from the board game aspect, but they feature important cognitive processes, which can be investigated. For example, at the most basic level, one needs to recognize the individual objects, then to retrieve their function, and eventually connect that function with other objects on the board. None of these components would be mistaken for the essence of expertise, but they all involve cognitive processes of general interest. The expertise approach investigates these cognitive processes by comparing the performance of experts and novices on simple domain-related tasks. It seeks to understand how domain-specific knowledge influences human cognition. In that sense, the contrasting expertise approach is not unlike the approach in neuropsychology where patients are compared to healthy controls. In the expertise approach, novices are controls, and they enable us to check whether the results obtained on experts are indeed the consequence of domain-specific knowledge. In other words, the expertise approach enables us to get a better picture of the nature of cognitive processes, even though the tasks employed may represent trivial aspects of expertise.

The expertise performance approach may be more idiosyncratic because its goal is to explain how experts manage to achieve their incredible feats. In contrast, the expertise approach may seem more general as it aims to provide additional insight into the workings of the human mind by manipulating the presence of domain-specific knowledge. The two approaches, however, are complementary in nature. In the following sections, we will see how they are frequently employed together.

Cognitive Mechanisms of (Board) Game Expertise

Before we move to the main topic of the chapter, the neural underpinnings of game expertise, it is necessary to consider the cognitive processes behind experts' outstanding performance in board games. As mentioned above, there are many aspects of skilled performance, some of them absolutely elementary, such as recognizing individual objects (see Chapter 12, The Neural Underpinnings of Perceptual Expertise). Chess experts are better at recognizing individual chess objects, called pieces, than novices and especially than beginners, people who have just started to play the game (Saariluoma, 1995). The differences are rather small, but they increase as the tasks begin to include additional cognitive processes. For example, the usual task where players need to recognize an object, retrieve the function, and put it in relation with other objects, is to examine whether there is a "check" in a chess position. In the case of this task, the experts' advantage becomes greater (Kiesel, Kunde, Pohl, Berner, & Hoffmann, 2009). The reason for this advantage is that experts retrieve the function of an object automatically and in parallel with its identity (Reingold, Charness, Schultetus, & Stampe, 2001). This is particularly on display when there is more than one piece that may give check to the king. Typically, novices need to check each of the objects and see if they connect to the king. Experts grasp the situation with three objects in a single glance (Bilalić, Kiesel, Pohl, Erb, & Grodd, 2011).

Experts' extraordinary familiarity with the objects from their domain and the relations between those objects is evident in the *subliminal priming and stroop paradigms*. It is possible, for example, to prime chess experts subliminally in order to detect more quickly the check relation between a king and a piece on a 3 × 3 board (Kiesel *et al.*, 2009). Similarly, when there are two pieces that may give check to the king, experts cannot ignore their presence even if they are told to, which results in a *stroop-like* interference (Reingold *et al.*, 2001). The recognition of domain-specific objects, retrieval of their function, and relations to other objects are overlearned to such an extent that those automatic and parallel processes may be used to investigate subliminal and stroop phenomena.

These basic level skills are inevitably the building blocks of board game expertise. Quickly identifying objects and relations on a board full of objects is the main ingredient of board game expertise. Indeed, even when they are presented with a board full of objects, experts almost instantly direct their focus to the relevant aspects (Sheridan & Reingold, 2014). When the players need to examine the situation in detail, the main differences between greater and lesser experts consist in where they look for answers (Bilalić, McLeod, & Gobet, 2008b; De Groot, 1978). The very best experts may not search more thoroughly than their less skilled colleagues, but they certainly examine the more promising solution. Plenty of evidence indicates that experts' almost instant focus on the important aspects of the situation is a consequence of their vast domain-specific knowledge. For example, when asked to look for certain pieces in a normal mid-game position, experts immediately focus on the relevant pieces, whereas novices need to examine the whole board to identify the objects of interest (see Figure 11.1, upper panel).

Given the stable nature of board games, with rules that hardly ever change, certain constellations of objects often recur. Players pick up on things that appear

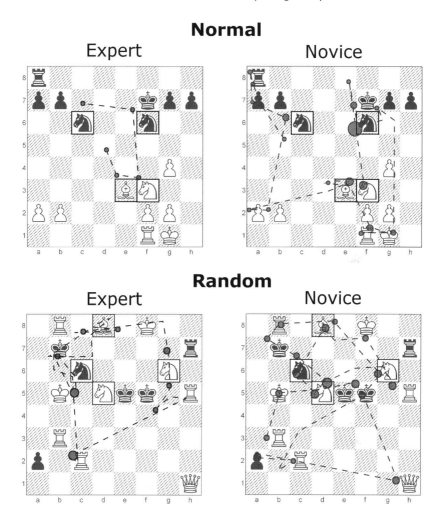

FIGURE 11.1 Perception in Experts. Experts quickly identify knights and bishops (objects highlighted by black squares) in normal positions, whereas novices need to examine the whole board (upper panel). When the position is randomized (lower panel), experts suddenly struggle at the same task (again, the objects of interest are in black squares). They still retain a small edge over novices because they do not need to focus on the objects directly to grasp their identity. Adapted from Bilalić *et al.* (2010).

together frequently, as well as ways of dealing with such constellations, and store them in their long-term memory (LTM). Once similar constellations reappear on the board, they can draw on their LTM to recognize the situation and quickly orient themselves by retrieving typical ways of dealing with the situation at hand (Chase & Simon, 1973; Gobet & Simon, 1996). If the same domain-specific material is used, but the relations between them have been distorted by placing the objects randomly on the board, experts' advantage disappears almost completely (Gobet & Simon, 1996). The randomization manipulation renders the acquired knowledge structures in experts' LTM incompatible with the new patterns on the board. Experts still exhibit better memory and orientation (see Figure 11.1, lower panel) in these random positions, but that is because they still can fall back on their superior knowledge about individual objects (Bilalić, Langner, Erb, & Grodd, 2010).

There are a few theories of expertise, some in the *system production tradition* (Chase & Simon, 1973; Ericsson & Kintsch, 1995; Gobet & Simon, 1996), and others in the *connectionist tradition* (Harré, Bossomaier, & Snyder, 2012). We will not go into the details about their differences here (see also Chapter 3, Cognitive Processes in Chess), but they all propose that experts match the situation on the board with the stored knowledge in LTM. This inevitably leads to the activation of all the knowledge connected to the matched structure, including plans for dealing with the situation. Novices may not necessarily have inferior general cognitive abilities, but they lack domain-specific knowledge that would enable them to grasp the essence of the situation quickly.

Here it is important to understand that experts' strategies, although highly efficient and mostly automated, are in no way simpler than those of novices. They require the retrieval of a large amount of knowledge, which then influences how the situation will be perceived and dealt with. They are not just a quicker version of the steps involved in the strategies of novices. Experts' strategies are qualitatively different because they rely on domain-specific knowledge that enables complex interaction between a number of cognitive processes, such as memory, perception, and attention. As we will see in the next section, the differences between the complexity of experts' and novices' strategies have a profound effect on the way the brain accommodates the performance of experts and novices.

Neural Underpinnings of Expertise in (Board) Games

As with the cognitive mechanisms in the previous section, we will consider the neural underpinning of simpler aspects such as object recognition and then slowly move towards more complex processes such as decision making and problem solving. In all cases presented here, we will see that the brain implementation closely follows the processes involved in the strategies of experts and novices.

Skilled Object Recognition

The first study we will examine comes from one of us (Bilalić, Kiesel, Pohl, Erb, & Grodd, 2011) and investigates how the brain accommodates skilled object recognition. A miniature 3 x 3 board with the fixed position of the king in the upper left corner was used (see Figure 11.2). The first task was to indicate the type of the second object on the miniature board, when both location and type were varied. Unsurprisingly, experts were better at this simple task, confirming the previous findings (Saariluoma, 1995). The recorded eye movements showed that this was due to familiarity with the domain-specific objects – experts did not have to move their eyes and directly fixate on the object (remember that the location was varied and players could not know where the object would appear), instead remaining in the center of the board. Novices, on the other hand, had to fixate the object directly to identify it correctly. The differences were even more pronounced in the check task where the players needed to indicate if the object was giving check to the king in the corner. Here novices not only had to fixate the object to identify it and retrieve its function, but also to see whether the object was spatially connected with the king. Experts again only needed a single fixation in the center, which was sufficient to grasp the identity of the object and its relation to the other object. The advantage of experts disappeared when they had to identify squares and circles on the same miniature board instead of chess pieces. This is more evidence that experts parse the relations between objects in a highly parallel and automatic manner (Reingold *et al.*, 2001; Sheridan & Reingold, 2014).

Skilled object perception has a specific neuronal signature too (Bilalić, Kiesel, *et al.*, 2011). Both experts and novices engaged a large network of brain areas, starting from frontal and spreading over parietal to temporal areas (see Figure 11.2). Most of the brain areas, however, were task-related and were activated in the control task with squares and circles. Only the posterior middle temporal gyrus (pMTG) seemed to be important for object recognition. Its left part was engaged to a similar extent in both experts and novices. However, its equivalent on the opposite side was only engaged in experts. As a matter of fact, novices showed almost no activation above the baseline in the right pMTG. The same pattern of bilateral engagement of the pMTG in experts and unilateral engagement in novices was found in the check task. Here, in addition to the pMTG activation, another bilateral activity in the supramarginal gyrus (SMG) was evident in experts while it was absent in novices.

We can therefore assume that the pMTG is important for recognition of objects, especially its right part, while the SMG additionally codes its function and relates them to other objects in space. These lateral brain areas are well known to be responsible for the perception of manmade objects such as tools (Johnson-Frey, 2004). Now, chess pieces are not common tools, but, not unlike tools, they have a clearly defined function that is based on movement. The pMTG may then be responsible for identification of objects and their function whereas the SMG may deal with explicit retrieval of the physical action of the objects (Johnson-Frey, 2004). It remains unclear why the SMG was not greatly activated in experts even in the identity task, given experts' automatic

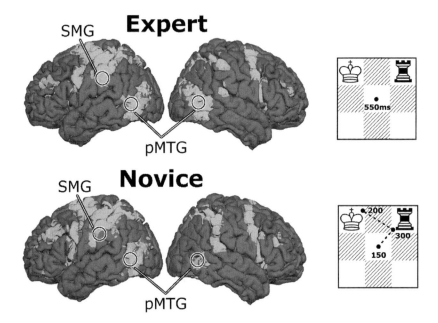

FIGURE 11.2 Object Recognition in Experts. Experts could grasp the relations between the two objects in the chess tasks with a single glance (right upper panel). Novices had to fixate on each object individually (right lower panel). The dots represent fixations and the adjacent numbers indicate the duration of the fixation (rounded). The posterior middle temporal gyrus (pMTG) was more active in experts and novices when they had to identify the object. Experts, however, engaged both pMTG areas whereas novices only engaged the pMTG in the left hemisphere. In the check task, where they had to retrieve a function of the object to examine if the king was in check, the left supramarginal gyrus (SMG) was more active in experts in addition to the pMTG. Novices showed no activation in the SMG. From Bilalić, Kiesel, *et al.* (2011).

response of parsing the relations between domain-specific objects. One possibility is that the tested experts, who were certainly very good players, but nowhere near professional level, were not of sufficient proficiency. The other is that the involvement of the additional brain areas, that is the SMG, is necessary to achieve the efficient performance which is characteristic of experts. The performance may seem automated, but its execution may require additional neural resources.

The above study is an example of the expertise approach. Identifying quickly and correctly the objects and their function on the board is hardly going to be mistaken for board game expertise. Skilled object recognition, however, represents a relevant topic in cognitive neuroscience. The expertise aspect provides insight into how the brain accommodates highly efficient object recognition. We know from the literature on the perception of manmade objects that their neural implementation is left lateralized (Noppeney, 2008). Here we have corroborated that finding but added another detail. The pMTG and SMG in the left hemisphere were indeed activated in experts and partly in novices, but the real differences were in the same areas in the right hemisphere, not known to be particularly relevant for the perception of handmade objects. The skilled perception of objects requires additional engagement of the same brain areas in the opposite hemisphere. This neural expansion, termed the *double take of expertise* (Bilalić, Kiesel *et al.*, 2011, Bilalić *et al.*, 2012), is the consequence of the complex cognitive machinery behind skilled perception of objects. Sharing the computational burden along both hemispheres is a standard way in which the human brain accommodates demanding activities (Weissman & Banich, 2000). Expertise, even its simple aspects such as object recognition, certainly involves the retrieval of a large amount of domain-specific knowledge, which then influences other cognitive processes, such as perception.

The double take of expertise reminds us that the cognitive implementation of experts' and novices' strategies are qualitatively different. It also represents a neural signature of expertise because the brain's double engagement is evident in other expertise domains where one needs to retrieve and manipulate domain-specific knowledge, such as mental (Pesenti *et al.*, 2001) and abacus calculations (Hanakawa, Honda, Okada, Fukuyama, & Shibasaki, 2003). In the next section we will see that more complex processes, such as skilled pattern recognition, also leave the typical neural signature in experts' brains.

Skilled Pattern Recognition

As we mentioned in the section on cognitive mechanisms, the differences between experts and novices are particularly pronounced when they deal with a board full of pieces. This was evident in a series of experiments where experts and novices had to identify a number of particular pieces (Bilalić *et al.*, 2010) or threats (Bilalić *et al.*, 2012) in positions that occurred in normal chess games. In order to do so, one needs to examine the whole position. This is what we find in novices when their eye movements are recorded; they need to examine every corner of the board to ascertain whether it contains the target pieces or threats. In contrast, experts quickly identify the objects of interest without wandering around the board. When the same pieces on the board were randomly placed, the manipulation that distorts the common patterns in the game, experts' performance dropped significantly (see Figure 11.1). They were still better at finding objects and threats in random positions, but mostly because they were drawing on their familiarity with individual pieces for quicker identification. The random positions did not have much effect on novices: Their performance remained the same as on normal positions. The pattern of results indicates that novices were not able to exploit the common game patterns in normal positions, whereas most of the advantage of experts was in skilled pattern recognition.

The fMRI data showed that the same lateral brain areas that are important for skilled object recognition were also relevant for pattern recognition. Experts engaged both pMTG to a greater extent than novices when they had to find particular pieces in both normal and random positions. When they needed to identify threats, experts engaged the left SMG in addition to the bilateral pMTG more than novices. Again, the differences were present in both normal and random positions. The randomization may not have had an effect on the lateral brain areas, but some medial brain areas were significantly affected. The brain areas around the middle of both collateral sulci (CoS), which divide the fusiform and parahippocampal gyri (PHG) in the inferotemporal cortex, demonstrated the expertise effect; that is, more activation in experts (see Figure 11.3). However, experts had more activation in the same areas when they were dealing with normal positions than when they were looking for objects and threats in random positions. Novices, on the other hand, had hardly any activation above the visual control (chess board with the pieces in the starting position) in either kind of position. The same pattern of results was found in the bilateral posterior cingulate cortex, the area also often called the retrosplenial cortex (RSC). It is important to emphasize that the parahippocampal place area (PPA) and RSC were related to the parsing of patterns on the board and not the visual feature. When the same positions were used, but the experts' task was to count all the pieces, essentially having to pay attention to every object, the PHG and RSC were not significantly more active in experts than novices, nor were there any differences between normal and random positions.

The results depict how the brain divides labor for different components of the board skills among its areas. The lateral areas (pMTG and SMG) are responsible for the recognition of individual objects and the explicit retrieval of their function. These areas are not affected by the randomization because the recognition of objects is the common component in both normal and random positions. The randomization affects the CoS and RSC in both hemispheres, but only in experts, which indicates that these areas are responsible for pattern recognition. We have seen that pMTG and SMG are implicated in the perception of everyday stimuli such as manmade objects. The CoS and RSC are connected to perception, but their function is connected rather to stimuli encompassing numerous objects, such as scenes, than individual objects. The CoS, which is essentially a part of the PPA, is responsible for the perception of layout (Epstein, 2008) and relations between objects (Aminoff, Kveraga, & Bar, 2013), while RSC is implicated in spatial navigation (Epstein, 2008).

A few other studies using different paradigms confirmed the involvement of the PHG and RSC in board game expertise. When the recall paradigm in chess was employed, the PHG was the area that was differentiated between normal and random positions (Campitelli, Gobet, Head, Buckley, & Parker, 2007; Campitelli, Gobet, & Parker, 2005). Passively observing normal and random chess positions also induced the differences between experts and novices in RSC (Bartlett, Boggan, & Krawczyk, 2013; Krawczyk, Boggan, McClelland, & Bartlett, 2011).

Another study (Wan et al., 2011), which employed shogi, a board game similar to chess, examined the neural response of experts and novices when they passively observed domain-specific (shogi) constellations and other neutral stimuli, such as faces and places. The pMTG in both hemispheres were engaged for the perception of shogi positions in both experts and novices. The PHG and the RSC (Epstein, 2008), were also important for shogi perception but were activated only in experts. These areas were not only engaged when shogi positions were compared to visually distinctive stimuli such as faces and places, but also when more visually similar stimuli such as Western and Chinese chess positions were used. Somewhat surprisingly, another area also distinguished between normal and random shogi positions among experts. The posterior precuneus was more activated when experts watched normal positions than when they watched random positions. The other medial shogi-related areas, the PHG and RSC, also reacted more strongly to normal shogi constellations than random ones, but these differences did not quite reach statistical significance. Shogi and chess therefore share a common neural implementation, with shogi additionally engaging the posterior precuneus.

At the moment, it is unclear how these areas come together to enable efficient orientation in a complex environment like that of board games. One possibility is that the PPA and RSC are necessary for the activation of stored patterns similar to the incoming stimulus, which is important for forming an initial impression of the situation. This initial impression may then guide attention to important aspects of the stimulus where the SMG and pMTG would be engaged for object identification and retrieval of their function. Obviously, the other way of information direction, starting from lateral areas for individual object recognition and leading to the CoS and RSC, is also possible. Future research, possibly using other techniques such as functional connectivity and neurostimulation, may provide more information on the exact information exchange between these areas.

Problem Solving

It is true that expert (board game) players can recognize isolated objects, retrieve their function, and find particular objects among numerous other similar objects on the board faster than novice players. However, this is more an additional effect of their core expertise; that is, finding an adequate way of continuing the game among the sea of possibilities.

A couple of studies have investigated the way the brain accommodates decision making and problem solving in board game practitioners, but these studies were either conducted with novices only (Atherton, Zhuang, Bart, Hu, & He, 2003) or featured complex designs where it was difficult to pinpoint the exact processes at hand (e.g., Amidzic, Riehle, Fehr, Wienbruch, & Elbert, 2001). Other recent studies (Bilalić, 2016; Bilalić, Langner, Ulrich, & Grodd, 2011) employed the expertise approach to tackle the issue of brain modularity (see Chapter 12, The Neural Underpinnings of Perceptual Expertise). However, the study on shogi that we examined in the previous section (Wan et al., 2011), also featured a task where the players were asked to find the best move in a position presented for only a second. Obviously, this would have been an extremely difficult task for even the best players, but the position presented involved only a quarter of the board and featured well-known motifs. Although skilled practitioners could recognize these motifs, they could not investigate the whole sequence and check to see if it led to the desired effect within a single second. In other words, they had to base their quick intuitive decisions on the pattern recognition processes.

Not surprisingly, experts were better than novices at finding the solution within such a short period of exposure. However, the brain areas engaged in the task were rather similar in both groups. Besides the already mentioned posterior precuneus, the dorsolateral prefrontal cortex (DLPFC) as well as premotor and motor areas were all activated, with no differences between experts and novices in the extent of engagement. Only the head of the *nucleus caudatus* (CaudNuc), a part of the basal ganglia situated in the middle of the brain, was significantly more activated in experts than novices during the quick decision. A number of control experiments demonstrated that the activation of the nucleus caudatus is most likely responsible for fast and efficient decision making in experts. First, spotting a particular piece (e.g., the king) in the same positions, a task that requires the same processes as the previous task except for the final move decision, did activate the well-known areas (precuneus, motor and premotor, and DLPFC) but not the nucleus caudatus (see Figure 11.3). Similarly, longer deliberation of 8 seconds for a decision also activated the common areas except the nucleus caudatus. Finally, the better the experts were at quick decisions, the more their nucleus caudatus was activated. Even novices demonstrated the activation of the nucleus caudatus in rare problems that they could solve. However, when the problems became too difficult for one-second decisions, the activation disappeared.

The nucleus caudatus does seem to be responsible for quick problem solving, because it is not implicated when players have more time or when they just look for an object. It is well known that the basal ganglia, the structure where the nucleus caudatus is situated, is important in the formation and execution of the typical responses that constellations of stimuli elicit (Poldrack, Prabhakaran, Seger, & Gabrieli, 1999). It is therefore possible, according to the authors (Wan *et al.*, 2011), that the typical and good solutions were triggered by the recognition of the well-known constellation. It remains unclear how the nucleus caudatus is able to match the incoming input with constellations stored in memory. Most likely, the constellations are retrieved from the precuneus (and possibly the PHG and RSC) and fed to the nucleus caudatus for a quick response. Not only is the precuneus sensitive to normal and random positions, it is in general implicated in imagery of visuo-spatial stimuli as well as episodic memory retrieval (Cabeza, Ciaramelli, Olson, & Moscovitch, 2008). It is also directly connected through brain tracts to the very same head of the nucleus caudatus, the area engaged in finding quick solutions (Leichnetz, 2001). As it happens, the activation levels in the precuneus and nucleus caudatus fluctuate in the same manner. When more activation is found in the precuneus at one point in time, more activation is available in the nucleus caudatus at the same time.

The final piece of evidence for the role of the nucleus caudatus in quick decisions comes from a training study by the same group (Wan *et al.*, 2012). Shogi novices were trained for 15 weeks and after the training somewhat improved their performance, solving four problems out of ten compared to three before the training. Again, a number of the same brain areas were involved in the

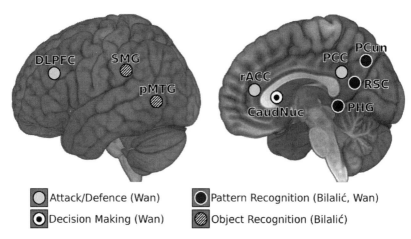

Attack/Defence (Wan)   ◉ Pattern Recognition (Bilalić, Wan)
Decision Making (Wan)   ◈ Object Recognition (Bilalić)

FIGURE 11.3   Overview of Neural Basis of Expertise in Board Games. Experts engage lateral areas for skilled object recognition (SMG and pMTG) whereas they need medial areas for pattern recognition (PHG, RSC, and PCun). The nucleus caudatus (CaudNuc) is important for skilled decision making, while the rostral anterior cingulate cortex (rACC) and posterior cingulate cortex (PCC) parse defense and attack relations between the objects on the board, respectively. The DLPFC is implicated in deciding between attack and defense options. Adapted from Bilalić *et al.* (2010, 2012), Bilalić, Kiesel, *et al.* (2011) and Wan *et al.* (2011, 2012, 2015).

performance (precuneus, premotor and motor areas, and DLPFC) but none of them changed due to training. The only area that had increased the activation after the training was the nucleus caudatus. The nucleus caudatus also predicted the improvement after the training. The more the nucleus caudatus was activated after the training compared to the beginning of the training, the more the player improved the performance.

One plausible explanation of the two studies is that the medial areas process the incoming stimuli for patterns, sending the information to the nucleus caudatus for the generation of suitable solutions. The precuneus–nucleus caudatus connection may act as the equivalent of the cognitive mechanisms where knowledge structures enable pattern recognition, thereby automatically triggering common ways of dealing with the situation at hand. The problem with this explanation is that the nucleus caudatus was not activated when experts had more time at their disposal and mentally played through possibilities. This is at odds with the current cognitive theories of expertise (Gobet & Simon, 1996), which suppose that the same mechanism of triggering the solution is at work in both deliberate search and decision making. In other words, once the first solution to a position has been triggered, it is implemented in the "mind's eye," which then again leads to the triggering of the next move (solution). The recurring process of triggering solutions, which is the essence of deliberate problem solving, does not seem to be reflected in the activation of the nucleus caudatus, the area that is apparently responsible for the generation of quick solutions.

Similarly, a recent study by the same group (Wan, Cheng, & Tanaka, 2015), did not quite lead to the resolution of the inconsistent results. In the study, expert players had to indicate within a second whether the position required a strategy associated with attack or defense, two typical broad approaches to problems in shogi. Experts were better than chance in the task and again a number of areas were activated which we have previously encountered (e.g., Wan et al., 2011). However, other areas were crucial for the quick decisions on strategy. The posterior cingulate cortex (PCC), more anterior to the RSC, was particularly activated if the position required attack but not when defense was the best way to proceed. In contrast, the rostral anterior cingulate cortex (rACC) was engaged in the positions where defense was the best strategy (see Figure 11.3). Therefore, it seems that the PCC and rACC were parsing the relations in presented positions for attack and defense strategies, respectively. It seems that the values were then sent to the dorsolateral prefrontal cortex (DLPFC) for the decision. The activation in the DLPFC was particularly associated with the difference in the values for attack and defense. When the experts chose attack, the DLPFC was more connected to the PCC. When defense was chosen, the activation in the DLPFC was more associated with that in the rACC.

The above-mentioned brain areas are indeed important for decision making in general. The rACC is often implicated in decision making, but its rostral part most likely encodes subjective values of the situation (Nicolle *et al.*, 2012). The PCC is near to the other areas associated with expertise, RSC, and PCun, but is sometimes activated in decision-making settings (McCoy & Platt, 2005). The DLPFC is important for cognitive control (Lee, Shimojo, & O'Doherty, 2014) and decision making based on explicit rules (Hyafil, Summerfield, & Koechlin, 2009). However, the rACC, PCC, and DLPFC did not play an important role in the previous studies on board games expertise. One way to reconcile the results is to look at the paradigm used. Deciding on the strategy in shogi is the first step in solving the problem (i.e., finding the right solution). As a matter of fact, experts in the study were not very good at finding the best moves in the positions; that is, the full board of pieces, rather than the section used in the previous study (Wan *et al.*, 2011), and the short time allowed made the task nearly impossible. The nucleus caudatus, together with other areas (precuneus [PCun], RSC, PHG) may be important for quickly finding the solution, which is in reality only the second step in the problem-solving process in shogi. One needs to decide first on the strategy and then on the actual way to proceed.

The game of shogi seems to be one of the rare board games where the question of whether to attack or defend plays such a crucial role. It is unclear how this paradigm could be implemented with other games. Nevertheless, the inconsistencies between the findings of different studies, as well as between the theoretical cognitive considerations and the current neural evidence, point out the need for further examination of the phenomenon.

Structural Changes

We have seen that the brain adapts to the demands of expertise by additionally engaging brain areas. Here we will look at whether the neural requirements necessary in expert performance result in anatomical changes in experts' brains.

The studies examined above could not establish or did not report morphological differences between the brains of experts and those of novices. However, other studies with more participants found differences even though the findings were somewhat inconsistent over the studies. For example, Baduk (Go) experts had a larger nucleus caudatus, the structure important in experts' decision making (Wan *et al.*, 2011), than novices in one study (Jung *et al.*, 2013), but the opposite pattern was found in another study (Duan *et al.*, 2012). The most recent study (Hänggi, Brütsch, Siegel, & Jäncke, 2014) could find no differences between the experts and novices, although admittedly this related to chess and not Go. That study did find differences in the pMTG, the brain area important for skilled recognition (Bilalić *et al.*, 2010, 2012; Bilalić, Kiesel *et al.*, 2011). However, chess players had a rather smaller pMTG than non-chess players. Non-chess players also displayed increased cortical thickness not only in the pMTG, but also in the SMG and precuneus, all of these areas being implicated in (chess) expertise, compared to chess players. On the other hand, chess players displayed a denser and more compact superior longitudinal fasciculus, a pathway that connects the temporal lobe with the parietal and frontal lobes. Given the importance of temporal and parietal areas in skilled perception in board games, it may not come as a big surprise that the brains of board game experts have reacted by improving the connections between these two areas.

Most likely, the smaller brain areas and thinner cortex are products of the pruning of neurons and neuronal connections that may not be necessary for experts' performance. In any case, the fMRI activation does not have to be smaller in these restricted areas (Lu *et al.*, 2009). In board game expertise it seems to be the case that fMRI activation is instead an indication that the performance is more efficient. For example, recent studies on Chinese chess (Duan *et al.*, 2012, 2014) demonstrated that the activation in the nucleus caudatus in experts was better synchronized with activation in the inferotemporal and parietal areas, the parts of the brain important for skilled object and pattern recognition.

Conclusion

We have seen that board games offer plenty of possibilities for investigating the human mind and brain. The mere presence of differently skilled practitioners enables the expertise approach, where the focus may not be the essence of the board game expertise, but rather the investigation of cognitive processes. Board game expertise also offers a glimpse into the functioning of the human brain at its best, when it needs to perceive a large amount of information present in the environment and connect it with previously acquired knowledge.

One of the recurring themes in this chapter is how domain-specific knowledge modifies the human cognition. The way experts deal with stimuli from their domain of expertise is heavily influenced by the knowledge they have previously stored in the LTM. Their strategies may look effortless compared to those of novices, but they require an immense amount of cognitive resources. This is reflected in the way the brain accommodates the complex interplay between perception, memory, and attention in experts' performance. The double take of expertise is a hallmark of the neural implementation of expertise and further evidence that domain-specific knowledge results in qualitatively different ways of processing information from the environment. Similarly, it demonstrates a close connection between cognitive and neural processing of stimuli.

The neuroscience of expertise (Bilalić, 2017) is a relatively new field of research that offers a unique insight into the functioning of the human brain. We hope that our chapter provides another incentive for researchers to use the expertise approach in investigating cognitive processes and their neural implementation.

Acknowledgement

The writing of this chapter was supported by OeNB Project (#16449) to Merim Bilalić and scholarship Talent Austria to Nemanja Vaci. We are grateful to Anna Stylianopoulou for making the figures in the chapter.

Note

1 Here we define experts as people who consistently and reliably perform clearly above the average in a domain of their specialization (Ericsson & Smith, 1991). In the studies presented in this chapter, experts are at least more than 2 standard deviations above the average player. In contrast, novices perform clearly worse than the average practitioner, but are better than beginners who have just started playing.

References

Amidzic, O., Riehle, H. J., Fehr, T., Wienbruch,C., & Elbert, T. (2001). Pattern of focal γ-bursts in chess players. *Nature, 412*(6847), 603.

Aminoff, E. M., Kveraga, K., & Bar, M. (2013). The role of the parahippocampal cortex in cognition. *Trends in Cognitive Sciences, 17*(8), 379–390.

Atherton, M., Zhuang, J., Bart, W. M., Hu, X., & He, S. (2003). A functional MRI study of high-level cognition. I. The game of chess. *Brain Research. Cognitive Brain Research, 16*(1), 26–31.

Bartlett, J., Boggan, A. L., & Krawczyk, D. C. (2013). Expertise and processing distorted structure in chess. *Frontiers in Human Neuroscience, 7*, 825.

Bilalić, M. (2016). Revisiting the role of the fusiform face area in expertise. *Journal of Cognitive Neuroscience, 28*(9), 1345–1357.

Bilalić, M. (2017). *The neuroscience of expertise*. Cambridge: Cambridge University Press.

Bilalić, M., Kiesel, A., Pohl, C., Erb, M., & Grodd, W. (2011). It takes two–skilled recognition of objects engages lateral areas in both hemispheres. *PLoS ONE, 6*(1), e16202.

Bilalić, M., Langner, R., Erb, M., & Grodd, W. (2010). Mechanisms and neural basis of object and pattern recognition: A study with chess experts. *Journal of Experimental Psychology: General, 139*(4), 728–742.

Bilalić, M., Langner, R., Ulrich, R., & Grodd, W. (2011). Many faces of expertise: fusiform face area in chess experts and novices. *The Journal of Neuroscience, 31*(28), 10206–10214.

Bilalić, M., McLeod, P., & Gobet, F. (2008a). Expert and "novice" problem solving strategies in chess: Sixty years of citing de Groot (1946). *Thinking & Reasoning, 14*(4), 395–408.

Bilalić, M., McLeod, P., & Gobet, F. (2008b). Inflexibility of experts—reality or myth? Quantifying the Einstellung effect in chess masters. *Cognitive Psychology, 56*(2), 73–102.

Bilalić, M., McLeod, P., & Gobet, F. (2009). Specialization effect and its influence on memory and problem solving in expert chess players. *Cognitive Science, 33*(6), 1117–1143.

Bilalić, M., Turella, L., Campitelli, G., Erb, M., & Grodd, W. (2012). Expertise modulates the neural basis of context dependent recognition of objects and their relations. *Human Brain Mapping, 33*(11), 2728–2740.

Cabeza, R., Ciaramelli, E., Olson, I. R., & Moscovitch, M. (2008). The parietal cortex and episodic memory: an attentional account. *Nature Reviews. Neuroscience, 9*(8), 613–625.

Campitelli, G., Gobet, F., Head, K., Buckley, M., & Parker, A. (2007). Brain localization of memory chunks in chessplayers. *The International Journal of Neuroscience, 117*(12), 1641–59.

Campitelli, G., Gobet, F., & Parker, A. (2005). Structure and stimulus familiarity: A study of memory in chess-players with functional magnetic resonance imaging. *The Spanish Journal of Psychology, 8*(2), 238–45.

Chase, W. G., & Simon, H. A. (1973). Perception in chess. *Cognitive Psychology, 4*(1), 55–81.

De Groot, A. (1978). *Thought and choice in chess* (2nd ed.). The Hague: Mouton De Gruyter.

Duan, X., He, S., Liao, W., Liang, D., Qiu, L., Wei, L., … Chen, H. (2012). Reduced caudate volume and enhanced striatal-DMN integration in chess experts. *NeuroImage, 60*(2), 1280–1286.

Duan, X., Long, Z., Chen, H., Liang, D., Qiu, L., Huang, X., … Gong, Q. (2014). Functional organization of intrinsic connectivity networks in Chinese-chess experts. *Brain Research, 1558*, 33–43.

Epstein, R. A. (2008). Parahippocampal and retrosplenial contributions to human spatial navigation. *Trends in Cognitive Sciences, 12*(10), 388–396.

Ericsson, K. A., & Kintsch, W. (1995). Long-term working memory. *Psychological Review, 102*(2), 211.

Ericsson, K. A., & Smith, J. (1991). *Toward a general theory of expertise: Prospects and limits.* Cambridge University Press.

Gobet, F., & Simon, H. A. (1996). Templates in chess memory: A mechanism for recalling several boards. *Cognitive Psychology, 31*(1), 1–40.

Hanakawa, T., Honda, M., Okada, T., Fukuyama, H., & Shibasaki, H. (2003). Neural correlates underlying mental calculation in abacus experts: A functional magnetic resonance imaging study. *NeuroImage, 19*(2 Pt 1), 296–307.

Hänggi, J., Brütsch, K., Siegel, A. M., & Jäncke, L. (2014). The architecture of the chess player's brain. *Neuropsychologia, 62*, 152–162.

Harré, M., Bossomaier, T., & Snyder, A. (2012). The perceptual cues that reshape expert reasoning. *Scientific Reports, 2*.

Hyafil, A., Summerfield, C., & Koechlin, E. (2009). Two mechanisms for task switching in the prefrontal cortex. *The Journal of Neuroscience, 29*(16), 5135–5142.

Johnson-Frey, S. H. (2004). The neural bases of complex tool use in humans. *Trends in Cognitive Sciences, 8*(2), 71–78.

Jung, W. H., Kim, S. N., Lee, T. Y., Jang, J. H., Choi, C.-H., Kang, D.-H., & Kwon, J. S. (2013). Exploring the brains of Baduk (Go) experts: Gray matter morphometry, resting-state functional connectivity, and graph theoretical analysis. *Frontiers in Human Neuroscience, 7*, 633.

Kiesel, A., Kunde, W., Pohl, C., Berner, M. P., & Hoffmann, J. (2009). Playing chess unconsciously. *Journal of Experimental Psychology. Learning, Memory, and Cognition, 35*(1), 292–298.

Krawczyk, D. C., Boggan, A. L., McClelland, M. M., & Bartlett, J. C. (2011). The neural organization of perception in chess experts. *Neuroscience Letters, 499*(2), 64–69. http://doi.org/10.1016/j.neulet.2011.05.033

Lee, S. W., Shimojo, S., & O'Doherty, J. P. (2014). Neural computations underlying arbitration between model-based and model-free learning. *Neuron, 81*(3), 687–699.

Leichnetz, G. R. (2001). Connections of the medial posterior parietal cortex (area 7m) in the monkey. *The Anatomical Record*, *263*(2), 215–236.

Lu, L. H., Dapretto, M., O'Hare, E. D., Kan, E., McCourt, S. T., Thompson, P. M., … Sowell, E. R. (2009). Relationships between brain activation and brain structure in normally developing children. *Cerebral Cortex*, *19*(11), 2595–2604.

McCoy, A. N., & Platt, M. L. (2005). Risk-sensitive neurons in macaque posterior cingulate cortex. *Nature Neuroscience*, *8*(9), 1220–1227.

Nichelli, P., Grafman, J., Pietrini, P., Alway, D., Carton, J. C., & Miletich, R. (1994). Brain activity in chess playing. *Nature*, *369*(6477), 191.

Nicolle, A., Klein-Flügge, M. C., Hunt, L. T., Vlaev, I., Dolan, R. J., & Behrens, T. E. (2012). An agent independent axis for executed and modeled choice in medial prefrontal cortex. *Neuron*, *75*(6), 1114–1121.

Noppeney, U. (2008). The neural systems of tool and action semantics: A perspective from functional imaging. *Journal of Physiology-Paris*, *102*(1–3), 40–49.

Pesenti, M., Zago, L., Crivello, F., Mellet, E., Samson, D., Duroux, B., … Tzourio-Mazoyer, N. (2001). Mental calculation in a prodigy is sustained by right prefrontal and medial temporal areas. *Nature Neuroscience*, *4*(1), 103–107.

Poldrack, R. A., Prabhakaran, V., Seger, C. A., & Gabrieli, J. D. (1999). Striatal activation during acquisition of a cognitive skill. *Neuropsychology*, *13*(4), 564–574.

Reingold, E. M., Charness, N., Schultetus, R. S., & Stampe, D. M. (2001). Perceptual automaticity in expert chess players: Parallel encoding of chess relations. *Psychonomic Bulletin & Review*, *8*(3), 504–510.

Rennig, J., Bilalić, M., Huberle, E., Karnath, H.-O., & Himmelbach, M. (2013). The temporo-parietal junction contributes to global gestalt perception-evidence from studies in chess experts. *Frontiers in Human Neuroscience*, *7*, 513.

Saariluoma, P. (1995). *Chess players' thinking: A cognitive psychological approach*. London: Routledge.

Sheridan, H., & Reingold, E. M. (2014). Expert vs. novice differences in the detection of relevant information during a chess game: Evidence from eye movements. *Cognition*, *5*, 941.

Wan, X., Cheng, K., & Tanaka, K. (2015). Neural encoding of opposing strategy values in anterior and posterior cingulate cortex. *Nature Neuroscience*, *18*(5), 752–759.

Wan, X., Nakatani, H., Ueno, K., Asamizuya, T., Cheng, K., & Tanaka, K. (2011). The neural basis of intuitive best next-move generation in board game experts. *Science*, *331*(6015), 341–346.

Wan, X., Takano, D., Asamizuya, T., Suzuki, C., Ueno, K., Cheng, K., … Tanaka, K. (2012). Developing intuition: Neural correlates of cognitive-skill learning in caudate nucleus. *Journal of Neuroscience*, *32*(48), 17492–17501.

Weissman, D. H., & Banich, M. T. (2000). The cerebral hemispheres cooperate to perform complex but not simple tasks. *Neuropsychology*, *14*(1), 41.

12

THE NEURAL UNDERPINNINGS OF PERCEPTUAL EXPERTISE

Mackenzie Sunday and Isabel Gauthier

Introduction

A *perceptual expert* is someone who performs exceptionally well in certain perceptual decision-making tasks because he or she benefited from experience in a particular domain. Here we focus on visual expertise in object recognition. Experts typically invest hours upon hours of hard work and practice to excel in their fields. Given the human brain's remarkable plasticity, it is unsurprising that the behavioral products of such an investment are accompanied by measurable neural changes. It is also expected that the brain reflects differences in perceptual task performance, regardless of whether these differences emerge from training or inherent predispositions in visual ability. The neural correlates of perceptual expertise have been studied with neuroimaging, most often using functional magnetic resonance imaging (fMRI) in which brain activation is measured via changes in blood flow indexed by the blood-oxygen-level dependent signal (BOLD signal). This method has particularly good spatial resolution (compared for instance to EEG), which has been especially important in perceptual expertise research because it allows researchers to localize visual areas recruited by expertise in different domains and the degree to which different domains overlap (McGugin, Gatenby, Gore, & Gauthier, 2012a).

Indeed, neuroimaging research on perceptual expertise grew from questions surrounding the domain-specificity of a cortical region sensitive to faces located on the ventral part of the temporal cortex. A landmark fMRI study found that a portion of the fusiform gyrus, termed the fusiform face area (FFA), preferentially responded to visually presented face stimuli (Kanwisher, McDermott, & Chun, 1997). Subsequent work began to question if the FFA responds solely to faces or if the region processes a wider range of objects. The first evidence that the FFA responds to non-face objects came from a study in which subjects were trained to become experts with a

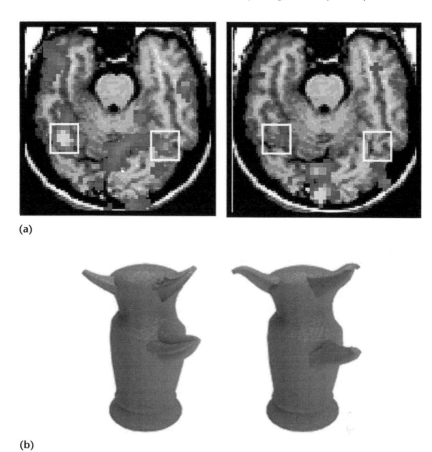

(a)

(b)

FIGURE 12.1 MRI scans showing functional activation in the fusiform gyrus of a Greeble expert. A. Left image shows response to faces; right, to Greebles. The FFA is within the white squares in both images. B. Example Greeble stimuli (Gauthier *et al.*, 1999). Figures in color at https://osf.io/94h3f/.

novel object category called Greebles. Subjects were trained to individuate Greebles as well as categorize Greebles into "families" defined by their body shape and were considered experts once they were able to classify individuals as quickly as they could families, similar to bird experts who identify the specific species as fast as they can spot a bird (Tanaka & Taylor, 1991). After training, there was an increase in these subjects' right fusiform responses (Gauthier, Tarr, Anderson, Skudlarski, & Gore, 1999). This suggested that the FFA is not a face-specific module, but rather is a region that responds to object domains with which an individual has extensive experience (Figure 12.1). More specifically, the FFA could be best described as a region engaged when a person learns to individuate exemplars within a domain in which objects share a common configuration of parts.

Subsequent studies examined various domains of real-world expertise to ask if fusiform activity was also engaged with naturally acquired (as opposed to experimentally learned) visual expertise. Behavioral performance in matching tasks with cars and birds correlated with car and bird activation, respectively, in the right FFA (Gauthier *et al.*, 2000; Xu, 2005). This has since been replicated several times (e.g. McGugin, Newton, Gore, & Gauthier, 2014; van der Linden, Murre, & van Turennout, 2008; but see Grill-Spector, Knouf, & Kanwisher, 2004, for a failure to replicate). A related line of work has demonstrated that children with high levels of interest in the Pokémon çard game show greater FFA activation when viewing Pokémon characters relative to those who were less interested in the game (James & James, 2013). In addition to these studies demonstrating that experience with a particular non-face stimuli category can shape neural responses, similar effects have also been found for faces: There is more activation in the FFA when subjects view faces belonging to their own race than when they view other-race faces (Golby, Gabrieli, Chiao, & Eberhardt, 2001). Because behaviorally measured differences between own-race and other-race face recognition abilities are thought to be at least partially driven by differences in exposure to same and other races (De Heering, De Liedekerke, Deboni, & Rossion, 2010), the increased activation to own- relative to other-race faces suggests experience moderates FFA activation. Therefore, one view emerging from neuroimaging research on visual expertise is that experience may be a common denominator in driving neural responses in the FFA, for both faces and non-face objects.

While research in this area was, to a large extent, originally driven by questions surrounding whether the FFA is dedicated only to face recognition, the research focus recently shifted to studying the neural correlates of perceptual expertise for their own sake. As a result, we now have a better idea of what brain areas support perceptual expertise, what happens in these areas, and what drives the domain of expertise specificity in these regions. Studies have explored the effect that different object categories, training tasks, and testing tasks levels have on the cortical regions and activation patterns associated with perceptual expertise. More recent work provides insight into the structural changes accompanying perceptual expertise gain, and new hypotheses have emerged proposing mechanistic explanations for these structural and functional correlates.

Where in the Brain Do We Find Perceptual Expertise Effects?

An obvious question when discussing the neural correlates of any behavior is to ask *where* in the brain we find differences in activation corresponding to the behavior. Do we only see differences in a specific brain region or over a distributed network throughout the brain? Are these neural correlates lateralized to a hemisphere or do they always occur bilaterally? In the case of perceptual expertise, is this a singular concept with a singular neural signature or are there many possible kinds of skill acquisitions that engage the brain in different ways? As previously mentioned, many neuroimaging studies of perceptual expertise have been (and still are) focused on the FFA. This is not without reason, as there is strong evidence that the FFA plays a critical role in visual expertise. Indeed, a recent study used high-resolution imaging to locate precisely where car expertise correlates reside within the fusiform. The results show that car expertise-related activation is found in the peak of the FFA and this activation disappears further away from the face-selective peaks (McGugin et al., 2012a). This study suggests that previously reported standard-resolution expertise correlates in the FFA cannot be explained by spatial blurring due to low spatial resolution, and more importantly, that expertise and face-selective functions recruit overlapping neuronal populations in the fusiform. Though in principle different neurons could be selective for faces and cars within the very center of the FFA, neurophysiological work in non-human primates revealed that almost all neurons in that region are face selective (Tsao, Freiwald, Tootell, & Livingstone, 2006), suggesting that expertise effects are driven by face neurons. Any new research will also need to incorporate a recent distinction between two FFA sub-regions. Two distinct clusters (one posterior and one more anterior) appear to form what was once considered a single region and have been named FFA-1 and FFA-2 respectively (Pinsk et al., 2009). Because there is some evidence that these sub-regions may have slightly different functionality (McGugin, Van Gulick, Tamber-Rosenau, Ross, & Gauthier, 2015b), analyses in a single FFA Region of Interest (ROI) are becoming difficult to defend and may very likely conflate responses from truly different areas.

The dozens of studies that report activation changes in the FFA associated with expertise make a strong case for the FFA as an important neural correlate of perceptual expertise. However, perceptual expertise is arguably associated with a diverse and complex set of skills, only some of which are engaged by face processing. The FFA may be critical for expertise that depends on one particular strategy, namely *holistic individuation*. Objects are processed holistically when all parts are processed together. This is often measured by asking subjects to focus on a single part while ignoring the rest of the object and showing they cannot do so (Richler & Gauthier, 2014). Early work examining the FFA's response to objects of expertise found that FFA activation is stronger for upright than inverted stimuli (Gauthier et al., 1999; Gauthier et al., 2000), suggesting that FFA activation is sensitive to configuration. While inverted objects of expertise, such as faces, may sometimes be processed holistically, inversion dramatically impacts and slows processing efficiency (Richler, Mack, Palmeri, & Gauthier, 2011; Curby & Gauthier, 2009). There are likely other strategies that can be used to develop perceptual expertise, and these different strategies likely recruit different networks involving the FFA to varying extents.

Few, if any, studies conclude that expertise recruits the FFA exclusively and many studies report expertise-related activation outside the fusiform

(Wong & Gauthier, 2009; Bilalić, Langner, Erb, & Grodd, 2010; Bilalić, Langner, Ulrich, & Grodd, 2011; Bilalić, Turella, Campitelli, Erb, & Grodd, 2012; Bilalić, 2016; Behrmann & Plaut, 2013; Brants, Wagemans, & de Beeck, 2011; de Beeck, Baker, DiCarlo, & Kanwisher, 2006; Harel *et al.*, 2010; Krawczyk, Boggan, McClellan, & Bartlett, 2011). For example, a recent study presented medical students and experienced x-ray technicians with images of x-rays and other objects in the MRI scanner. The researchers then looked throughout the brain to find where they were able to classify the neural activation patterns for x-rays and the other images above chance level, using a technique called *searchlight analysis*. They were able to successfully classify activation patterns in many regions, such as the posterior middle temporal gyrus, posterior cingulate gyrus, inferior and medial frontal gyri, and bilateral lingual gyri (as well as the FFA, Bilalić *et al.*, 2014). Some studies even reported stronger expertise correlates in object-selective regions outside the fusiform than inside the fusiform (de Beeck *et al.*, 2006) or no overlap between where these correlates are found and face-selective regions (Krawczyk *et al.*, 2011, though see McGugin *et al.*, 2012a). Collectively, these studies provide strong evidence that while the FFA may be central to holistic individuation, it is not the only region that correlates with perceptual expertise.

So what determines which areas are engaged during perceptual expertise tasks? The visual similarity of stimuli could play a role in determining which cortical areas are active. A concern with the initial expertise work is that the object stimuli (for example Greebles, or the front view of cars) have features resembling faces that drive the FFA activation (de Beeck *et al.*, 2006; Brants *et al.*, 2011). To address this, several studies investigated expertise effects using stimuli that are drastically different from faces, such as chessboards and x-ray images, and still found expertise correlates in the FFA (Bilalić, 2016; Bilalić *et al.*, 2014). However, it is still possible that visual similarity may determine the engagement of some cortical regions. When scanning car experts, a recent study found that sofas engaged the FFA despite the fact that no car experts showed behavioral signs of sofa expertise (McGugin *et al.*, 2014). Since sofas are visually similar to profiles of cars in their global shape, this finding suggests the global similarity may be sufficient to engage the FFA. However, this does not mean that expertise generalizes to globally similar objects, since there was no evidence that car experts were particularly above average in their perceptual abilities with sofas!

Different perceptual experts can excel in a variety of tasks and the process engaged by a specific kind of perceptual expertise might determine the specific brain regions recruited. At the most basic level, practice making perceptual decisions about objects affects the visual system relative to mere exposure to these objects. For instance, after learning to categorize novel objects, subjects showed increased fusiform activity, as compared with subjects who did not learn any category information (van der Linden *et al.*, 2008). An ensuing study found that while individuation training produced relatively focal activation differences in the right FFA, basic level categorization training produced more distributed changes in medial areas of the ventral occipito-temporal cortex (Wong, Palmeri, Rogers, Goer, & Gauthier, 2009). Further work has found that using perceptual learning tasks versus perceptual expertise tasks during training induces differing neural changes (Wong, Folstein, & Gauthier, 2012). In this study, subjects were trained with novel objects using either a visual search task typically used in perceptual learning studies or an object-labeling task typically used in perceptual expertise studies. Subjects who were trained in the perceptual learning condition showed increased activation in early visual cortex while subjects from the perceptual expertise training condition showed increased activation in the ventral temporal cortex (Wong et al., 2012). Therefore, while some authors have suggested that learning in visual cortex tends to be limited to a modest modulation of a map determined by bottom-up image statistics (de Beeck & Baker, 2010), these studies suggest that the kind of experience one has with an object category has a profound influence on the changes that accompany learning.

This is also supported by studies reporting different cortical regions engaged when real-world experts engage in their domain of interest. For example, the game of chess requires players to manipulate the spatial positions of a set of pieces on a checkered array. It is thus not solely a categorization or individuation problem, since the game requires much more of its players than just quick recognition or identification of pieces. Moreover, chess involves a myriad of cognitive processes, including working memory, spatial reasoning, and decision-making. The neural underpinnings of chess expertise are often more distributed than novel object expertise effects (Krawczyk et al., 2011; Bilalić et al., 2010), which is consistent with the finding that less individuation-driven training results in more distributed activation (Wong, Palmeri et al., 2009).

Though there is debate as to exactly which cortical regions correspond to perceptual expertise acquisitions, the laterality of these correlates is less disputed. In particular, though objects of expertise often recruit the fusiform bilaterally, they do not do so uniformly. The right FFA responds strongly to faces and objects of expertise such as cars, whereas a region in the left fusiform gyrus has an affinity for words and letters (Cohen et al., 2000). Stronger right hemisphere responses have been reported for objects with category training (van der Linden et al., 2008), radiological images (Bilalić et al., 2014, Harley et al., 2009), Pokémon characters (James & James, 2013), cars (Gauthier et al., 2000; McGugin et al., 2012a), birds (Gauthier et al., 2000; Xu, 2005), and chess images (Bilalić et al., 2011; Bilalić, 2016).

Conversely, words and letters appear to be lateralized to the left fusiform gyrus, although not in the same area that is face selective. The word-selective area in the left fusiform has been called the Visual Word Form Area (VWFA) (Cohen et al., 2000). This region responds more strongly to written words than consonant strings (Cohen et al., 2002), line drawings and false fonts (Ben-Shachar,

Dougherty, Deutsch, & Wandell, 2007), auditorily presented words (Dehaene, Le Clec'H, Poline, Le Bihan, & Cohen, 2002), and line drawings of objects (Szwed *et al.*, 2011). Moreover, the VWFA has been found to be invariant to which hemifield the words are presented (Cohen *et al.*, 2000), word case (lower or upper; Dehaene *et al.*, 2001), language used (Liu *et al.*, 2008), and word style (typed or handwritten; Qiao *et al.*, 2010), though there is some evidence this region becomes engaged during tasks other than word recognition as well (Price & Devlin, 2003).

There is strong evidence that the development of the VWFA, can, at least partially, be explained using the perceptual expertise hypothesis. VWFA activation correlates with accuracy on a letter recognition task (Garrett *et al.*, 2000) and with reading ability (Dehaene *et al.*, 2010). This activation is specific to a writing system in which the perceiver is fluent (Baker *et al.*, 2007; Wong, Jobard, James, K., James, T., & Gauthier, 2009), suggesting that extensive experience is necessary to engage the VWFA. Not only does orthographic experience influence VWFA activation, but there is also evidence that experience with the specific letter combinations can influence activation, as VWFA activation is sensitive to bigram frequency (Binder, Medler, Westbury, Liebenthal, & Buchanan, 2006; Vinckier *et al.*, 2007). Interestingly, experts at the game of Scrabble (a game that requires players to create words out of tiles with printed letters on them) show increased fusiform activity, though this activity was not lateralized to the left hemisphere and occurred concurrently with activity increases in many other regions (Protzner *et al.*, 2016).

Some VWFA studies extend beyond a correlational approach by attempting to directly manipulate word experience. Though the results have been variable (Xue, Chen, Jin, & Dong, 2006; Xue & Poldrack, 2007; Callan, A., Callan, D., & Masaki, 2005), a recent study provides striking evidence that perceptual expertise accounts for some of the word-specialization found in the VWFA. In this study, subjects were trained to recognize pseudowords, and neural VWFA selectivity before and after training was compared using an fMRI rapid adaptation method. The results showed that after training with pseudowords, the neural VWFA selectivity became more narrowly tuned and more closely resembled the tuning of real words (Glezer, Kim, Rule, Jiang, & Riesenhuber, 2015). These results further support that VWFA activation is influenced by experience, becoming more tightly tuned as experience with certain words increase. Interestingly, the VWFA is also engaged when blind subjects read braille, suggesting the area has some multi-modal functionality (Reich, Szwed, Cohen, & Amedi, 2011). Though this might be interpreted as evidence that the VWFA serves a functionally different purpose than the FFA, it is worth noting that similar multi-modal functioning in the blind has been found in the right FFA (Goyal, Hansen, & Blakemore, 2006).

Neuroimaging work on perceptual expertise has provided much insight into which brain regions correspond to different perceptual expertise levels.

One important issue with this work that is gaining attention concerns the reliability of the behavioral and functional measures used. Most neuroimaging studies correlate fMRI BOLD activation with behavioral measures. As a result, the correlations are affected by the reliability of both the neural signal and the behavioral measures. For example, if both the behavioral and neural measures have reliabilities of 0.5 and the true correlation between the two measures is 0.9, then we would observe an attenuated correlation of only 0.45 (Nunnally, 1970). Until recently, the reliability of both behavioral perceptual expertise measures and neural responses were often not considered or reported (this reliability of individual differences is not the same as showing that the FFA reliability shows up in the same spatial location, Engell & McCarthy, 2013), but new work has started to explore these reliabilities. In one study, the face-selective responses in FFA1 and FFA2 produced high split-half reliabilities (0.7–0.9) that was highest in the peak voxel and not significantly improved by increasing ROI size (McGugin & Gauthier, 2015c). On the behavioral side, efforts have been devoted to create new tests with good psychometric properties. For instance, the Vanderbilt Expertise Test is a battery of tests in several domains (e.g., cars, birds, mushrooms, planes) that can produce reliable measurements of expertise (McGugin *et al.*, 2012b). Reliable behavioral and neural measures improve power and precision in measuring correlations between behaviorally measured constructs and brain activation. Importantly, reliability is not an intrinsic test property but is instead dependent on the sample used, so while scientists may choose measures that often produce high reliability, they need to ensure that high reliability is achieved in the given sample.

What Causes Certain Brain Regions to Become Selective for Objects of Expertise?

Establishing exactly where expertise-related functional responses occur in the brain is an important pursuit, but it begs the question of why these regions become selective for objects of expertise. The emergence of a face-selective region in the human brain is often explained through evolutionary means. Because faces are critical to effective social interactions, developing a face-specific brain region devoted to tackling the face identification problem would be evolutionarily advantageous. However, this evolutionary account does not explain all the neural correlates of expertise. It is implausible for brain regions selective to words, and certainly cars, to have been naturally selected, given the relatively short amount of time these domains have existed. One explanation that attempts to be consistent with the perceptual expertise literature is the *neuronal recycling hypothesis* (Dehaene, 2005). According to this hypothesis, when presented with a novel task, the brain will recruit neurons that currently perform similar tasks and repurpose these neurons for the new task. In this way, specialization in brain regions like the VWFA could result from repurposing neuron populations that were initially used for face recognition to instead accomplish the similar recognition task presented by words. Thus, when confronted with the reoccurring problem of classifying letters, cars, or other similar visual stimuli, the brain reuses regions that are already performing comparable functions (Dehaene & Cohen, 2007). In this way, the brain recycles the circuitry initially devoted solely to face recognition to accomplish the other object discrimination tasks that characterize perceptual expertise. This hypothesis seems plausible given the economical plasticity of the human brain, though there is evidence of perceptual expertise-related neural activation in at least one individual with autism, who showed no prior face specialization (Grelotti et al., 2005).

So why do faces and other objects of expertise more strongly correlate with right hemisphere activation but words show stronger left hemisphere activation? One reason may be a right hemisphere bias for global processing and a left hemisphere advantage for part-based, more featural processing (Robertson, Lamb, & Knight, 1988; Yovel, G., Yovel, I., & Levy, 2001). Others have proposed that because face, object of expertise, and word identification are all overlearned skills requiring foveal visual information, these problems compete with one another for brain resources (Plaut & Behrmann, 2011). Accomplishing word identification requires proximity to the brain's language centers in the left hemisphere, so the VWFA develops more strongly in the left, and consequently the FFA becomes right lateralized (Plaut & Behrmann, 2011). These theories are not mutually exclusive and may both give rise to the lateralization often seen in neuroimaging work.

What Differences Between Experts and Novices Account for the Neural Correlates of Expertise?

One theory offered to explain the functional correlates of perceptual expertise focuses on *attention*. This postulates that the neural correlates of perceptual expertise are actually due to attention, as experts may allocate more attention to objects within their domain of expertise (Harel, Gilaie-Dotan, Malach, & Bentin, 2010). This idea is supported by a study finding that when car experts complete a task where car images are shown but are irrelevant, the expertise effects usually found in the brain decrease (Harel et al., 2010). However, a recent study investigated whether varying the attentional load of the task performed in the scanner (either a low-load condition demanding little attention or high-load condition demanding more attention) would modulate the neural activation associated with perceptual expertise (McGugin et al., 2015b). When the subjects were under a low attentional load, the expertise correlates were widely distributed. However, under the high-load condition, the expertise effects were more focused in the right FFA2 – in fact, in contrast to most other areas engaged in the low-load condition, this area showed a relation with behavioral expertise that was not impacted by attentional load. This suggests that while attention modulates expertise effects in visual areas, which should not come as a surprise given the pervasive effects of attention (Ungerleider & Kastner, 2000), the category-selectivity that we observe for faces and objects of expertise in the FFA is not entirely explained by attention.

New research investigating structural changes corresponding to perceptual expertise (discussed in depth below) may also undermine the attentional theory because the structural correlates found cannot be accounted for by something as transient as different attentional allocations. Structural correlates of perceptual expertise are likely given that initial work found structural correlates of other abilities. For example, individual differences in intelligence correlate with cortical thickness (Narr et al., 2007; Choi et al., 2008; Karama et al., 2011). Moreover, it is possible to train behavioral performance on a certain perceptual task and observe a corresponding structural change in the brain (Haier et al., 2009).

Most work investigating how cortical thickness relates to expertise has not focused on higher-level visual abilities specifically. One of the first studies to show structural differences relating to experience is the famous London cab driver study, which found that London cab drivers had increased hippocampal volume relative to controls (Maguire, Woollett, & Spiers, 2006). Since then, differences in the cortical thickness of brain regions associated with the processing of music have been found between groups with great musical abilities and novices (Bermudez, Lerch, Evans, & Zatorre, 2008; Sato et al., 2015). Professional perfumers exhibit different cortical volume in olfactory regions (Delon-Martin, Plailly, Fonlupt, Veyrac, & Royet, 2013), and these differences can also be found in subjects who have better "general olfactory performance" (Seubert, Freiherr, Frasnelli, Hummel, & Lundström, 2013). Developmental prosopagnosics (individuals who have been face-blind since birth) show reduced grey matter volume in various cortical areas associated with face perception (Garrido et al., 2009) and people with congenital amusia (who show musical deficits since birth) also present with different cortical thickness in the right inferior frontal gyrus (Hyde et al., 2007).

What structural changes accompany expertise in the visual modality? After three months' training with the puzzle-like game Tetris, girls showed increased cortical thickness in left frontal eye fields and temporal pole (Broadmann's areas 6 and 22/38, Haier et al., 2009). Grey matter volume also correlates with car expertise in both the pre-frontal cortex (Gilaie-Dotan, Harel, Bentin, Kanai, & Rees, 2012) and FFA (McGugin et al., 2015a). See Figure 12.2. The latter of these studies also found that subjects who were better at recognizing faces and living objects (butterflies, leaves, mushrooms, owls, wading birds) had thinner cortices in the FFA (McGugin et al., 2015a). A thinner left fusiform cortex also predicts greater improvement in a face discrimination task (Bi, Chen, Zhou, He, & Fang, 2014). One possible explanation provided by McGugin et al. (2015a) is that performance with faces vs. objects reflects different ages of expertise acquisition, arguably with faces and perhaps also some living objects being learned

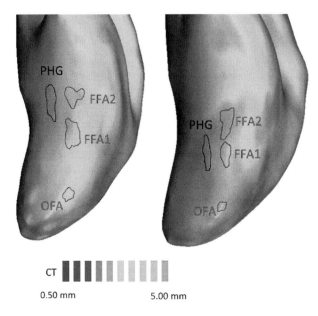

FIGURE 12.2 Inflated left hemispheres showing cortical thickness. FFA1, FFA2, occipital face area and object-selective parahippocampal gyrus are outlined and labeled. Left image from an individual with lower living-object recognition ability; right, from an individual with high living-object recognition ability (McGugin et al., 2015a). See figure in color at https://osf.io/94h3f/.

earlier than vehicles. Different mechanisms of plasticity can operate at these different ages. Face recognition is learned early in life when pruning of large fiber tracts is taking place (Bourgeois, Jastreboff, & Rakic, 1989). By contrast, thickening of cortex might accompany visual skill learning in adulthood (Maguire, Woollett, & Spiers, 2006; Mårtensson et al., 2012). While it is clear that perceptual expertise relates not only to functional changes in the brain, but also to structural changes, more work is needed for a complete picture, including a link between the functional and structural correlates of expertise.

In sum, there are both functional and structural results that suggest an expert's attention to objects of expertise during scanning does not completely account for the neural correlates of expertise. So what other explanations have been proposed? The bulk of perceptual expertise neuroimaging work has used traditional fMRI analysis methods to compare brain activation between conditions or subjects. However, new analysis methods allow researchers to explore new questions about the changes in representations that may support perceptual expertise.

The development of multi-voxel pattern analysis (MVPA) allows researchers to go beyond the mean activity level in an area to examine how activation patterns differ and relate to behavior. If an algorithm trained on activation patterns from one experimental condition can classify activation patterns from another experimental condition, then we can infer that the information used in those two conditions is similarly represented in the brain. This analysis method can provide different information from a conventional univariate analysis, which is useful in expertise research when the aim is to assess distributed coding in the cortex (Bilalić *et al.*, 2014). In one study, a classifier was trained to calculate the probability a subject perceived either a car or face using activation patterns in the right FFA. The outputted probabilities negatively correlated with subjects' behaviorally measured car expertise, suggesting that as car expertise increases, cars and faces are represented more similarly in the right FFA (McGugin *et al.*, 2015b).

Future Directions

Several questions remain about the neural correlates of perceptual expertise. An important question is how variability in abilities to learn from experience can account for these effects. It is possible that neural correlates of expertise are entirely experience driven, but it appears likely that in perceptual learning, as in other forms of learning, some individuals are better able to benefit from experience than others. Studies investigating how brain connectivity relates to face processing have found that congenital prosopagnosics show disrupted white-matter fiber tracts in the ventral pathway (Thomas *et al.*, 2008). Moreover, white-matter properties correlate with behaviorally measured face recognition ability (Gomez *et al.*, 2015). These connectivity differences between individuals may reflect individual differences in learning abilities. If this is the case, then neural correlates of perceptual expertise in specific regions may in part be due to learning differences via differences in connectivity. To address what role individual differences in learning play in perceptual expertise, it is important that both domain-general and domain-specific abilities are measured. Since domain-specific abilities are arguably associated with differences in experience, separate measures of subjects' abilities to identify objects from any domain and objects from a specific domain will help tease apart the roles of experience and learning ability in perceptual expertise. Doing so requires measures from several domains that produce reliable scores, optimally with both familiar domains with which many people have at least some experience and with novel domains with which no one has experience.

New research should also determine if the engagement of a brain region correlated with perceptual expertise is necessary for expert level performance, and what patterns of activity are less essential. Though neuroimaging work has revealed many cortical regions that correlate with behaviorally measured expertise, there are now methods that allow experiments to extend beyond correlational results into more causal determinations. With the growing popularity of methods like transcranial magnetic stimulation (TMS) and transcranial direct current stimulation (TDCS), brain activity can be directly manipulated, which would allow researchers to determine if reducing activation in certain regions also reduces behavioral performance on expertise measures (similar to what is done in Parvizi *et al.*, 2012). This would not only provide great insight into which brain regions are necessary for perceptual expertise, but would also open the door to innovative applications of the field.

References

Baker, C. I., Liu, J., Wald, L. L., Kwong, K. K., Benner, T., & Kanwisher, N. (2007). Visual word processing and experiential origins of functional selectivity in human extrastriate cortex. *Proceedings of the National Academy of Sciences, 104*(21), 9087–9092. http://doi.org/10.1073/pnas.0703300104

Behrmann, M., & Plaut, D. C. (2013). Distributed circuits, not circumscribed centers, mediate visual recognition. *Trends in Cognitive Sciences, 17*(5), 210–219. http://doi.org/10.1016/j.tics.2013.03.007

Ben-Shachar, M., Dougherty, R. F., Deutsch, G. K., & Wandell, B. A. (2007). Differential sensitivity to words and shapes in ventral occipito-temporal cortex. *Cerebral Cortex, 17*(7), 1604–1611. http://doi.org/10.1093/cercor/bhl071

Bermudez, P., Lerch, J. P., Evans, A. C., & Zatorre, R. J. (2009). Neuroanatomical correlates of musicianship as revealed by cortical thickness and voxel-based morphometry. *Cerebral Cortex, 19*(7), 1583–1596. http://doi.org/10.1093/cercor/bhn196

Bi, T., Chen, J., Zhou, T., He, Y., & Fang, F. (2014). Function and structure of human left fusiform cortex are closely associated with perceptual learning of faces. *Current Biology, 24*(2), 222–227. http://doi.org/10.1016/j.cub.2013.12.028

Bilalić, M. (2016). Revisiting the role of the fusiform face area in expertise. *Journal of Cognitive Neuroscience, 28*(9), 1345–1357. http://doi.org/10.1162/jocn_a_00974

Bilalić, M., Grottenthaler, T., Nägele, T., & Lindig, T. (2014). The faces in radiological images: Fusiform face area supports radiological expertise. *Cerebral Cortex, 26*(3), 1004–1014. http://doi.org/10.1093/cercor/bhu272

Bilalić, M., Langner, R., Erb, M., & Grodd, W. (2010). Mechanisms and neural basis of object and pattern recognition: A study with chess experts. *Journal of Experimental Psychology: General, 139*(4), 728–742. http://doi.org/http://dx.doi.org.proxy.library.vanderbilt.edu/10.1037/a0020756

Bilalić, M., Langner, R., Ulrich, R., & Grodd, W. (2011). Many faces of expertise: Fusiform face area in chess experts and novices. *The Journal of Neuroscience, 31*(28), 10206–10214. http://doi.org/10.1523/JNEUROSCI.5727-10.2011

Bilalić, M., Turella, L:, Campitelli, G., Erb, M., & Grodd, W. (2012). Expertise modulates the neural basis of context dependent recognition of objects and their relations. *Human Brain Mapping, 33*, 2728–2740.

Binder, J. R., Medler, D. A., Westbury, C. F., Liebenthal, E., & Buchanan, L. (2006). Tuning of the human left fusiform gyrus to sublexical orthographic structure. *NeuroImage, 33*(2), 739–748. http://doi.org/10.1016/j.neuroimage.2006.06.053

Bourgeois, J. P., Jastreboff, P. J., & Rakic, P. (1989). Synaptogenesis in visual cortex of normal and preterm monkeys: Evidence for intrinsic regulation of synaptic overproduction. *Proceedings of the National Academy of Sciences, 86*(11), 4297-4301.

Brants, M., Wagemans, J., & de Beeck, H. P. O. (2011). Activation of fusiform face area by greebles is related to face similarity but not expertise. *Journal of Cognitive Neuroscience, 23*(12), 3949–3958. http://doi.org/10.1162/jocn_a_00072

Callan, A. M., Callan, D. E., & Masaki, S. (2005). When meaningless symbols become letters: Neural activity change in learning new phonograms. *NeuroImage, 28*(3), 553–562. http://doi.org/10.1016/j.neuroimage.2005.06.031

Choi, Y. Y., Shamosh, N. A., Cho, S. H., DeYoung, C. G., Lee, M. J., Lee, J.-M., … Lee, K. H. (2008). Multiple bases of human intelligence revealed by cortical thickness and neural activation. *The Journal of Neuroscience, 28*(41), 10323–10329. http://doi.org/10.1523/JNEUROSCI.3259-08.2008

Cohen, L., Dehaene, S., Naccache, L., Lehéricy, S., Dehaene-Lambertz, G., Hénaff, M.-A., & Michel, F. (2000). The visual word form area. *Brain, 123*(2), 291–307. http://doi.org/10.1093/brain/123.2.291

Cohen, L., Lehéricy, S., Chochon, F., Lemer, C., Rivaud, S., & Dehaene, S. (2002). Language-specific tuning of visual cortex? Functional properties of the visual word form area. *Brain, 125*(5), 1054–1069. http://doi.org/10.1093/brain/awf094

Curby, K. M., & Gauthier, I. (2009). The temporal advantage for individuating objects of expertise: Perceptual expertise is an early riser. *Journal of Vision, 9*(6), 7–7.

Dehaene, S. (2005). *From monkey brain to human brain: A Fyssen Foundation Symposium.* Camridge, MA.: MIT Press.

Dehaene, S., & Cohen, L. (2007). Cultural recycling of cortical maps. *Neuron, 56*(2), 384–398. http://doi.org/10.1016/j.neuron.2007.10.004

Dehaene, S., Le Clec'H, G., Poline, J.-B., Le Bihan, D., & Cohen, L. (2002). The visual word form area: A prelexical representation of visual words in the fusiform gyrus. *Neuroreport, 13*(3), 321–325.

Dehaene, S., Naccache, L., Cohen, L., Bihan, D. L., Mangin, J.-F., Poline, J.-B., & Rivière, D. (2001). Cerebral mechanisms of word masking and unconscious repetition priming. *Nature Neuroscience, 4*(7), 752–758. http://doi.org/10.1038/89551

Dehaene, S., Pegado, F., Braga, L. W., Ventura, P., Filho, G. N., Jobert, A., … Cohen, L. (2010). How learning to read changes the cortical networks for vision and language. *Science, 330*(6009), 1359–1364. http://doi.org/10.1126/science.1194140

de Beeck, H. P. O., Baker, C. I., DiCarlo, J. J., & Kanwisher, N. G. (2006). Discrimination training alters object representations in human extrastriate cortex. *The Journal of Neuroscience, 26*(50), 13025–13036. http://doi.org/10.1523/JNEUROSCI.2481-06.2006

de Beeck, H. P. O., & Baker, C. I. (2010). The neural basis of visual object learning. *Trends in Cognitive Sciences, 14*(1), 22–30.

De Heering, A., De Liedekerke, C., Deboni, M., & Rossion, B. (2010). The role of experience during childhood in shaping the other-race effect. *Developmental Science, 13*(1), 181–187. http://doi.org/10.1111/j.1467-7687.2009.00876.x

Delon-Martin, C., Plailly, J., Fonlupt, P., Veyrac, A., & Royet, J.-P. (2013). Perfumers' expertise induces structural reorganization in olfactory brain regions. *NeuroImage, 68*, 55–62. http://doi.org/10.1016/j.neuroimage.2012.11.044

Engell, A. D., & McCarthy, G. (2013). Probabilistic atlases for face and biological motion perception: An analysis of their reliability and overlap. *NeuroImage, 74*, 140–151.

Garrett, A. S., Flowers, D. L., Absher, J. R., Fahey, F. H., Gage, H. D., Keyes, J. W., … Wood, F. B. (2000). Cortical activity related to accuracy of letter recognition. *NeuroImage, 11*(2), 111–123. http://doi.org/10.1006/nimg.1999.0528

Garrido, L., Furl, N., Draganski, B., Weiskopf, N., Stevens, J., Tan, G. C.-Y., ... Duchaine, B. (2009). Voxel-based morphometry reveals reduced grey matter volume in the temporal cortex of developmental prosopagnosics. *Brain*, *132*(12), 3443–3455. http://doi.org/10.1093/brain/awp271

Gauthier, I., Skudlarski, P., Gore, J. C., & Anderson, A. W. (2000). Expertise for cars and birds recruits brain areas involved in face recognition. *Nature Neuroscience*, *3*(2), 191–197. http://doi.org/10.1038/72140

Gauthier, I., Tarr, M. J., Anderson, A. W., Skudlarski, P., & Gore, J. C. (1999). Activation of the middle fusiform "face area" increases with expertise in recognizing novel objects. *Nature Neuroscience*, *2*(6), 568–573. http://doi.org/10.1038/9224

Gilaie-Dotan, S., Harel, A., Bentin, S., Kanai, R., & Rees, G. (2012). Neuroanatomical correlates of visual car expertise. *NeuroImage*, *62*(1), 147–153. http://doi.org/10.1016/j.neuroimage.2012.05.017

Glezer, L. S., Kim, J., Rule, J., Jiang, X., & Riesenhuber, M. (2015). Adding words to the brain's visual dictionary: Novel word learning selectively sharpens orthographic representations in the VWFA. *The Journal of Neuroscience*, *35*(12), 4965–4972. http://doi.org/10.1523/JNEUROSCI.4031-14.2015

Golby, A. J., Gabrieli, J. D. E., Chiao, J. Y., & Eberhardt, J. L. (2001). Differential responses in the fusiform region to same-race and other-race faces. *Nature Neuroscience*, *4*(8), 845–850. http://doi.org/10.1038/90565

Gomez, J., Pestilli, F., Witthoft, N., Golarai, G., Liberman, A., Poltoratski, S., ... & Grill-Spector, K. (2015). Functionally defined white matter reveals segregated pathways in human ventral temporal cortex associated with category-specific processing. *Neuron*, *85*(1), 216–227.

Goyal, M. S., Hansen, P. J., & Blakemore, C. B. (2006). Tactile perception recruits functionally related visual areas in the late-blind. *Neuroreport*, *17*(13), 1381–1384.

Grelotti, D. J., Klin, A. J., Gauthier, I., Skudlarski, P., Cohen, D. J., Gore, J. C., ... & Schultz, R. T. (2005). fMRI activation of the fusiform gyrus and amygdala to cartoon characters but not to faces in a boy with autism. *Neuropsychologia*, *43*(3), 373–385.

Grill-Spector, K., Knouf, N., & Kanwisher, N. (2004). The fusiform face area subserves face perception, not generic within-category identification. *Nature Neuroscience*, *7*(5), 555–562. http://doi.org/10.1038/nn1224

Haier, R. J., Karama, S., Leyba, L., & Jung, R. E. (2009). MRI assessment of cortical thickness and functional activity changes in adolescent girls following three months of practice on a visual-spatial task. *BMC Research Notes*, *2*, 1–7. http://doi.org/10.1186/1756-0500-2-174

Harel, A., Gilaie-Dotan, S., Malach, R., & Bentin, S. (2010). Top-down engagement modulates the neural expressions of visual expertise. *Cerebral Cortex*, *20*(10), 2304–2318. http://doi.org/10.1093/cercor/bhp316

Harley, E. M., Pope, W. B., Villablanca, J. P., Mumford, J., Suh, R., Mazziotta, J. C., ... Engel, S. A. (2009). Engagement of fusiform cortex and disengagement of lateral occipital cortex in the acquisition of radiological expertise. *Cerebral Cortex*, *19*(11), 2746–2754. http://doi.org/10.1093/cercor/bhp051

Hyde, K. L., Lerch, J. P., Zatorre, R. J., Griffiths, T. D., Evans, A. C., & Peretz, I. (2007). Cortical thickness in congenital amusia: When less is better than more. *The Journal of Neuroscience*, *27*(47), 13028–13032. http://doi.org/10.1523/JNEUROSCI.3039-07.2007

James, T. W., & James, K. H. (2013). Expert individuation of objects increases activation in the fusiform face area of children. *NeuroImage*, *67*, 182–192. http://doi.org/10.1016/j.neuroimage.2012.11.007

Kanwisher, N., McDermott, J., & Chun, M. M. (1997). The fusiform face area: A module in human extrastriate cortex specialized for face perception. *The Journal of Neuroscience*, *17*(11), 4302–4311.

Karama, S., Colom, R., Johnson, W., Deary, I. J., Haier, R., Waber, D. P., … Evans, A. C. (2011). Cortical thickness correlates of specific cognitive performance accounted for by the general factor of intelligence in healthy children aged 6 to 18. *NeuroImage*, *55*(4), 1443–1453. http://doi.org/10.1016/j.neuroimage.2011.01.016

Krawczyk, D. C., Boggan, A. L., McClelland, M. M., & Bartlett, J. C. (2011). The neural organization of perception in chess experts. *Neuroscience Letters*, *499*(2), 64–69. http://doi.org/10.1016/j.neulet.2011.05.033

Liu, C., Zhang, W.-T., Tang, Y.-Y., Mai, X.-Q., Chen, H.-C., Tardif, T., & Luo, Y.-J. (2008). The visual word form area: Evidence from an fMRI study of implicit processing of Chinese characters. *NeuroImage*, *40*(3), 1350–1361. http://doi.org/10.1016/j.neuroimage.2007.10.014

Maguire, E. A., Woollett, K., & Spiers, H. J. (2006). London taxi drivers and bus drivers: A structural MRI and neuropsychological analysis. *Hippocampus*, *16*(12), 1091–1101. http://doi.org/10.1002/hipo.20233

Mårtensson, J., Eriksson, J., Bodammer, N. C., Lindgren, M., Johansson, M., Nyberg, L., & Lövdén, M. (2012). Growth of language-related brain areas after foreign language learning. *NeuroImage*, *63*(1), 240–244.

McGugin, R. W., Gatenby, J. C., Gore, J. C., & Gauthier, I. (2012a). High-resolution imaging of expertise reveals reliable object selectivity in the fusiform face area related to perceptual performance. *Proceedings of the National Academy of Sciences*, *109*(42), 17063–17068. http://doi.org/10.1073/pnas.1116333109

McGugin, R. W., & Gauthier, I. (2015c). The reliability of individual differences in face-selective responses in the fusiform gyrus and their relation to face recognition ability. *Brain Imaging and Behavior*, *10*(3), 1–12.

McGugin, R. W., Newton, A. T., Gore, J. C., & Gauthier, I. (2014). Robust expertise effects in right FFA. *Neuropsychologia*, *63*, 135–144. http://doi.org/10.1016/j.neuropsychologia.2014.08.029

McGugin, R. W., Richler, J. J., Herzmann, G., Speegle, M., & Gauthier, I. (2012b). The Vanderbilt Expertise Test reveals domain-general and domain-specific sex effects in object recognition. *Vision Research*, *69*, 10–22. http://doi.org/10.1016/j.visres.2012.07.014

McGugin, R. W., Van Gulick, A. E., & Gauthier, I. (2015a). Cortical thickness in fusiform face area predicts face and object recognition performance. *Journal of Cognitive Neuroscience*, *28*(2), 282–294. http://doi.org/10.1162/jocn_a_00891

McGugin, R. W., Van Gulick, A. E., Tamber-Rosenau, B. J., Ross, D. A., & Gauthier, I. (2015b). Expertise effects in face-selective areas are robust to clutter and diverted attention, but not to competition. *Cerebral Cortex*, *25*(9), 2610–2622.

Narr, K. L., Woods, R. P., Thompson, P. M., Szeszko, P., Robinson, D., Dimtcheva, T., … Bilder, R. M. (2007). Relationships between IQ and regional cortical gray matter thickness in healthy adults. *Cerebral Cortex*, *17*(9), 2163–2171. http://doi.org/10.1093/cercor/bhl125

Nunnally, J. C. (1970). *Introduction to psychological measurement*. New York, NY: McGraw-Hill.

Parvizi, J., Jacques, C., Foster, B. L., Withoft, N., Rangarajan, V., Weiner, K. S., & Grill-Spector, K. (2012). Electrical stimulation of human fusiform face-selective regions distorts face perception. *The Journal of Neuroscience, 32*(43), 14915–14920.

Pinsk, M. A., Arcaro, M., Weiner, K. S., Kalkus, J. F., Inati, S. J., Gross, C. G., & Kastner, S. (2009). Neural representations of faces and body parts in Macaque and human cortex: A comparative fMRI study. *Journal of Neurophysiology, 101*(5), 2581–2600. http://doi.org/10.1152/jn.91198.2008

Plaut, D. C., & Behrmann, M. (2011). Complementary neural representations for faces and words: A computational exploration. *Cognitive Neuropsychology, 28*(3–4), 251–275.

Price, C. J., & Devlin, J. T. (2003). The myth of the visual word form area. *NeuroImage, 19*(3), 473–481. http://doi.org/10.1016/S1053-8119(03)00084-3

Protzner, A. B., Hargreaves, I. S., Campbell, J. A., Myers-Stewart, K., van Hees, S., Goodyear, B. G., … Pexman, P. M. (2016). This is your brain on Scrabble: Neural correlates of visual word recognition in competitive Scrabble players as measured during task and resting-state. *Cortex, 75*, 204–219. http://doi.org/10.1016/j.cortex.2015.03.015

Qiao, E., Vinckier, F., Szwed, M., Naccache, L., Valabrègue, R., Dehaene, S., & Cohen, L. (2010). Unconsciously deciphering handwriting: Subliminal invariance for handwritten words in the visual word form area. *NeuroImage, 49*(2), 1786–1799. http://doi.org/10.1016/j.neuroimage.2009.09.034

Reich, L., Szwed, M., Cohen, L., & Amedi, A. (2011). A ventral visual stream reading center independent of visual experience. *Current Biology, 21*(5), 363–368. http://doi.org/10.1016/j.cub.2011.01.040

Richler, J. J., & Gauthier, I. (2014). A meta-analysis and review of holistic face processing. *Psychological Bulletin, 140*(5), 1281.

Richler, J. J., Mack, M. L., Palmeri, T. J., & Gauthier, I. (2011). Inverted faces are (eventually) processed holistically. *Vision Research, 51*(3), 333–342.

Robertson, L. C., Lamb, M. R., & Knight, R. T. (1988). Effects of lesions of temporal-parietal junction on perceptual and attentional processing in humans. *The Journal of Neuroscience, 8*(10), 3757–3769.

Sato, K., Kirino, E., & Tanaka, S. (2015). A voxel-based morphometry study of the brain of university students majoring in music and nonmusic disciplines. *Behavioural Neurology*, e274919. http://doi.org/10.1155/2015/274919.

Seubert, J., Freiherr, J., Frasnelli, J., Hummel, T., & Lundström, J. N. (2013). Orbitofrontal cortex and olfactory bulb volume predict distinct aspects of olfactory performance in healthy subjects. *Cerebral Cortex, 23*(10), 2448–2456. http://doi.org/10.1093/cercor/bhs230

Szwed, M., Dehaene, S., Kleinschmidt, A., Eger, E., Valabrègue, R., Amadon, A., & Cohen, L. (2011). Specialization for written words over objects in the visual cortex. *NeuroImage, 56*(1), 330–344. http://doi.org/10.1016/j.neuroimage.2011.01.073

Tanaka, J. W., & Taylor, M. (1991). Object categories and expertise: Is the basic level in the eye of the beholder? *Cognitive Psychology, 23*(3), 457–482.

Thomas, C., Avidan, G., Humphreys, K., Jung, K. J., Gao, F., & Behrmann, M. (2008). Reduced structural connectivity in ventral visual cortex in congenital prosopagnosia. *Nature Neuroscience, 12*, 29–31.

Tsao, D. Y., Freiwald, W. A., Tootell, R. B., & Livingstone, M. S. (2006). A cortical region consisting entirely of face-selective cells. *Science, 311*(5761), 670–674.

Ungerleider, L. G., & Kastner S. (2000). Mechanisms of visual attention in the human cortex. *Annual Review of Neuroscience*, *23*(1), 315–341.

van der Linden, M., Murre, J. M. J., & van Turennout, M. (2008). Birds of a feather flock together: Experience-driven formation of visual object categories in human ventral temporal cortex. *PLOS ONE*, *3*(12), e3995. http://doi.org/10.1371/journal.pone.0003995

Vinckier, F., Dehaene, S., Jobert, A., Dubus, J. P., Sigman, M., & Cohen, L. (2007). Hierarchical coding of letter strings in the ventral stream: Dissecting the inner organization of the visual word-form system. *Neuron*, *55*(1), 143–156. http://doi.org/10.1016/j.neuron.2007.05.031

Wong, A. C.-N., Jobard, G., James, K. H., James, T. W., & Gauthier, I. (2009). Expertise with characters in alphabetic and nonalphabetic writing systems engage overlapping occipito-temporal areas. *Cognitive Neuropsychology*, *26*(1), 111–127. http://doi.org/10.1080/02643290802340972

Wong, A. C.-N., Palmeri, T. J., Rogers, B. P., Gore, J. C., & Gauthier, I. (2009). Beyond shape: How you learn about objects affects how they are represented in visual cortex. *PLOS ONE*, *4*(12), e8405. http://doi.org/10.1371/journal.pone.0008405

Wong, Y. K., Folstein, J. R., & Gauthier, I. (2012). The nature of experience determines object representations in the visual system. *Journal of Experimental Psychology: General*, *141*(4), 682–698. http://doi.org/10.1037/a0027822

Wong, Y. K., & Gauthier, I. (2009). A multimodal neural network recruited by expertise with musical notation. *Journal of Cognitive Neuroscience*, *22*(4), 695–713. http://doi.org/10.1162/jocn.2009.21229

Xue, G., Chen, C., Jin, Z., & Dong, Q. (2006). Language experience shapes fusiform activation when processing a logographic artificial language: An fMRI training study. *NeuroImage*, *31*(3), 1315–1326. http://doi.org/10.1016/j.neuroimage.2005.11.055

Xue, G., & Poldrack, R. A. (2007). The neural substrates of visual perceptual learning of words: Implications for the visual word form area hypothesis. *Journal of Cognitive Neuroscience*, *19*(10), 1643–1655. http://doi.org/10.1162/jocn.2007.19.10.1643

Xu, Y. (2005). Revisiting the role of the fusiform face area in visual expertise. *Cerebral Cortex*, *15*(8), 1234–1242. http://doi.org/10.1093/cercor/bhi006

Yovel, G., Yovel, I., & Levy, J. (2001). Hemispheric asymmetries for global and local visual perception: Effects of stimulus and task factors. *Journal of Experimental Psychology: Human Perception and Performance*, *27*(6), 1369.

13

THE NEUROSCIENCE OF MOTOR EXPERTISE IN REAL-WORLD TASKS

Ellen M. Kok and Anique B. H. de Bruin

Introduction

Ever since the seminal publication by Ericsson and Smith (1991), the *expert performance approach* has dominated expertise research and has led to increased insight into the mechanisms causing expert performance. From identifying criterion tasks at which expert performers excel (Stage 1), to unraveling the mediating mechanisms that explain expert performance (Stage 2), to analyzing how learning and practice contribute to these mechanisms and identifying implications for effective coaching and teaching (Stage 3), the expert performance approach provides an all-encompassing framework that informs expertise theory and educational practice.

One of the expertise domains in which the expert performance approach has proven particularly valuable is the area of *motor expertise*. Motor expertise includes all physical sports (e.g., soccer, athletics; see Naito & Hirose, 2014; Olsson, Jonsson, Larsson, & Nyberg, 2008) but also professional skills such as driving, flying, and surgery (Bahrami *et al.*, 2014; Callan *et al.*, 2013; Lappi, 2015). Research in soccer has, for example, revealed that expert soccer players are superior to non-experts in anticipating the trajectory of a ball (Williams, Ward, Knowles, & Smeeton, 2002), and outperform their less proficient peers in picking up contextual cues based on the opponent's posture (Williams & Burwitz, 1993).

Fitts and Posner's (1967) *stage theory* of motor learning describes how individuals proceed through three stages when acquiring novel motor skills. In the first or *cognitive* stage, individuals identify and develop the component parts of the skill, make numerous errors, and attentional demands to complete (part of) the skill are high. In the second or *associative* stage, performance becomes more persistent and individuals' ability to detect the cause of errors improves. In the final or *autonomous* stage, performance is fluent, there is low demand on working memory, and errors are rare. Not all individuals reach the final stage, though, and the amount of deliberate practice exerted proves to be an indicator of ultimate attainment of motor expertise (Hodge & Deakin, 1998; Starkes *et al.*, 1996).

The vast amount of research on motor expertise has concerned sport expertise, but interest in professional areas such as surgery is growing (Morris, Frodl, D'Souza, Fagan, & Ridgway, 2015). Recently, a methodological innovation has enabled a novel line of research dedicated to unearthing the brain correlates of expert performance. Although this line of research is relatively new, a preliminary overview of its findings will help determine how it contributes to central issues in expertise research. Where the focus in other chapters in this volume lies in visual expertise and cognitive expertise, this chapter emphasizes motor expertise.

Specifically, we will provide an overview of neuroscience research and findings related to motor expertise. We will focus mostly but not exclusively on fMRI (functional magnetic resonance imaging) studies on motor expertise in real-world tasks (see also Chapter 10, Neural Approaches in Research on Expertise.). While doing so, we report on research contrasting experts and novices (Bilalić, Langner, Erb, & Grodd, 2010). Building on the expert performance approach, these studies assume that expertise is domain-specific, and they therefore identify and study expertise in domain-specific, real-world tasks. Note that motor tasks always require perceptual (visual, touch, and/or auditory) skills. The focus in this chapter, however, lies on the motor aspect of expertise. Real-world tasks that are typically studied in motor expertise research include music (e.g., pianists, Meister *et al.*, 2004), dance (e.g., Calvo-Merino, Glaser, Grèzes, Passingham, & Haggard, 2005), sports (e.g., tennis, Balser *et al.*, 2014) and professional tasks such as driving (Lappi, 2015), flying (Callan *et al.*, 2013), and laparoscopic surgery (Bahrami *et al.*, 2014).

In sum, in the current chapter, we provide a narrative review of the neural correlates of motor expertise. We focus on expertise in real-world tasks and exclude findings from artificial tasks. We will describe research designs, theory, and research findings. We make a distinction between structural and functional neural differences, although we are aware that these two factors are related to a certain extent in part of the cases. A related question is to what extent neuroscience research contributes to theory development in motor expertise, or mainly represents a methodological innovation. While we discuss general motor expertise theories, designs, and findings, it should be noted that more task-specific changes are also found. For example, Debarnot, Sperduti, Di Rienzo, and Guillot (2014) report structural changes in balance-related brain regions in short-track ice skaters. This type of task-specific finding is not captured by this general overview.

A Short Summary of the Motor System

The motor system is a complex, extensive system that coordinates a range of tasks like regulating balance, executing reflexes, as well as executing domain-specific movements. An in-depth discussion of the motor system is beyond the

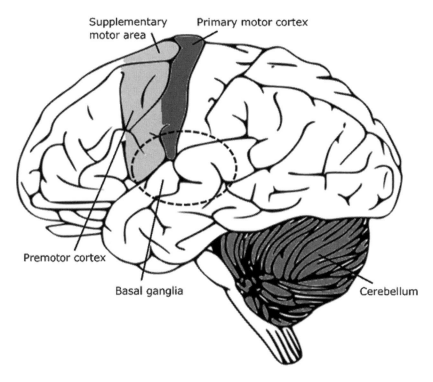

FIGURE 13.1 Motor system

scope of this chapter, but we will address some basics of motor control in the central nervous system. The three major regions of the central nervous system that are involved with movement are the basal ganglia, the cerebellum and the motor cortex (see Figure 13.1).

The basal ganglia lie deep within the brain. They play a role in monitoring and updating movement execution and early stages of skill learning (Turner & Pasquereau, 2014), as well as inhibition of movement (Kalet, 2013).

The cerebellum is located at the back of the brain. It is thought to serve as a predictive model for motor control, integrating sensory information with motor commands. Furthermore, it plays a role in error-based learning (Diedrichsen & Bastian, 2014). Cerebellar damage can result in problems with rapid movements and initiation of movement (Kalet, 2013). The cerebellum plays a role in the coordination of accurate movements and the integration of movements into a coordinated movement. It also helps to fine-tune complex movements and timing (Kolb & Whishaw, 2009).

The motor cortex is the region in the frontal lobe of the cortex, which is involved in motor planning and execution (Kalet, 2013). It is located anterior of the central sulcus and consists of the primary motor region, the premotor cortex and the supplementary motor region.

The primary motor cortex (M1) is located just anterior of the central sulcus, at the precentral gyrus (Brodmann's area 4). It elicits motion by sending signals into the brainstem and spinal cord (Kalet, 2013). M1 is organized in a somatotopic way, meaning that cells that serve similar regions of the body are located close to each other in the brain. Body parts that require finer motor control (such as the hand and the tongue) have a larger region of the M1 dedicated to them. While M1 generates movement, planning movements is mostly done by the premotor cortex and supplementary motor cortex (Kalet, 2013).

The premotor cortex (PMC) is located anterior to M1, and corresponds to Brodmann's area 6 (Kalet, 2013). It is thought to be involved in motor planning under sensory-motor control (Binkofski & Buccino, 2006). The supplementary motor area (SMA) is also located anterior to M1, but more towards the medial surface of the cortex, in the dorso-medial frontal gyrus (Nachev, Kennard, & Husain, 2008). It is thought to be involved in planning and integrating complex motor tasks and rapid sequences (Kalet, 2013). The SMA seems to be more involved in the generation of self-initiated actions rather than in actions in response to external signals (Nachev et al., 2008). Other cortical regions involved in planning movements are the posterior parietal cortex, which is involved in keeping track of the body relative to the world, and the prefrontal cortex, which is involved in organizing movement (Kalet, 2013).

The Challenge of Investigating Motor Expertise in an fMRI Scanner

How does Tiger Woods prepare a golf swing? How does a surgeon cut around a tumor without hurting healthy tissue? How does a pianist play an up-tempo piece of classical music? Expertise research has a long tradition of developing experiments that accurately represent the task of the expert. Staying within this tradition, research into the neural correlates of motor expertise requires such ecologically valid, domain-specific tasks just as well. However, as Mann, Dicks, Canal-Bruland, and van der Kamp (2013) point out, "It is difficult to make meaningful inferences about perceptual-motor expertise from experiments where participants cannot move" (p. 78). fMRI research typically requires participants to remain completely still in the scanner: Head-movement as small as several millimeters can deteriorate data quality. Still, researchers have been able to come up with several solutions to this issue. Three different types of experimental paradigms have been employed to investigate motor expertise in an fMRI scanner: *action observation*, *motor imagery*, and *task execution*.

In action observation tasks, participants are required to watch video clips of domain-specific movements. These videos show either a first-person perspective (e.g., Cosic et al., 2012) or a third-person perspective (e.g., Calvo-Merino et al., 2005). Some studies employ anticipation tasks, in which participants observe a movement from a third-person perspective that will be occluded sometime during or after the movement and then are asked to anticipate direction. For example, Wimshurst, Sowden, and Wright (2016) required their participants to judge the direction that a hockey ball or badminton shuttlecock will be traveling. Balser *et al.* (2014) compared participants' brain activity when making either a direction judgement or observing videos of volleyball and tennis movements. Studies that take such an approach typically rely on theory about the action observation network in the brain (Milton, Small, & Solodkin, 2008; Rizzolatti & Craighero, 2004).

Other studies investigate motor expertise by asking motor experts to imagine task execution (Olsson & Nyberg, 2010). Mental imagery or kinetic motor imagery refers to the covert mental rehearsal of movement without overt movements, usually from a first-person perspective (Milton *et al.*, 2008). The rationale here is that imagining and executing a movement recruit similar cortical circuits (Jeannerod, 2001), including the supplementary motor area (SMA), premotor cortex (PMC) and cerebellum (Munzert, Lorey, & Zentgraf, 2009). Involvement of the primary motor cortex (M1) in motor imagery is controversial. While it has been argued that M1 sends motor commands to the periphery and should thus not be active in mere imagery, several studies do find M1 activity during motor imagery (Munzert *et al.*, 2009).

The most ecologically valid approach is to have participants actually execute a (part of a) domain-specific task in the scanner. Some studies have managed to do just that. For example, Bahrami *et al.* (2011) built a MRI-compatible laparoscopic surgery training simulator to investigate motor expertise in laparoscopic surgery (Bahrami *et al.*, 2014). Callan *et al.* (2013) made participants fly a plane using a simulated flying task employing joysticks as well as rudder (foot) pedals. Lappi (2015) reports several studies that use simulated car driving tasks in which participants actually control the steering or speed of a vehicle. A special case of task execution in the fMRI scanner is the so-called pre-shot routine. In sports such as shooting and golf, elite athletes execute a pre-shot routine before executing the movement, in order to accurately aim for the target. It is a critical step in superior task performance (Kim *et al.*, 2014; Milton *et al.*, 2008). During a pre-shot routine, the athlete programs the movement before executing it. Those routines typically take several seconds to execute and are executed in the absence of overt movement, while at the same time eliciting brain activation in regions such as M1. This makes pre-shot routines a very suitable task for investigating motor expertise in an fMRI scanner (Milton *et al.*, 2008).

Finally, in studies on structural (or anatomical changes) to the brain, resting state MRI scans are typically used and the size of specific regions involved in the expertise task at hand is literally measured. Areas usually include (part of) M1, the planum temporale, and the corpus callosum. The voxel-based morphometry protocol is often applied to determine the actual size of the relevant regions (see Bernardi *et al.*, 2014, for a measurement example, which is beyond the scope of this chapter).

While actually executing a domain-specific task might be the most eco-logically valid approach, for many domains this is simply impossible, and motor imagery and action observation approaches are required. It is important to keep in mind that the employed experimental paradigm and theoretical framework influence findings, and that, in order to get a comprehensive understanding of motor expertise, we should investigate motor expertise using several different paradigms. Below, we discuss the most common outcomes from studies that take the different theoretical approaches.

Structural (Anatomical) Neuroplasticity

Only 7½ hours after his death, Einstein's brain was removed from his body to enable research into possible observable structural irregularities. Several studies were conducted, some suggesting that areas related to mathematical reasoning were larger, and that areas related to language ability were smaller compared to the average adult brain. Others suggested he had an increased number of glial cells, and a thicker corpus callosum (Men et al., 2014) allowing for better communication between the hemispheres. In essence, researchers studying the anatomy of Einstein's brain assume that exceptional cognitive abilities should be identifiable by measuring the size of specific brain regions involved in the execution of the cognitive tasks. In a similar vein, MRI research is used to determine the exact size of the brain regions that relate to expert performance. These measurements are usually compared with those of novice performers, to establish how extensive practice has structurally altered the brain. Just as intense physical exercise changes the body physiologically (e.g., by increasing the maxi-mum oxygen consumption rate or improving muscular blood flow; Ericsson & Ward, 2007), cognitive and visuo-motor practice are known to change the brain anatomically. Note that the brain regions that are measured need to be deduced either from the motor task at hand (e.g., the anatomical representation of the hands in pianists) or through functional research that shows what brain areas are involved in performing the expertise task.

In this section, we provide a comprehensive overview of research related to effects of motor expertise development on the structural aspects of the brain. We limit the overview to studies that examined physically measurable enlargements of specific brain areas related to expertise criterion tasks, although some of these studies in fact investigated how structural differences were related to functional adaptations. These studies are based on the principle of neuroplasticity; that is, the assumption that the size and the spatial organization of brain representa-tions when performing certain tasks are continuously (re)shaped by experience (Munte, Altenmuller, & Jäncke, 2002). Changes to the brain may occur in different time frames (Gruber, Jansen, Marienhagen, & Altenmueller, 2010). In a matter of seconds or minutes of practice, the size and efficiency of syn-apses can improve. After hours to days, new synapses and dendrites are formed.

After weeks, gray and white matter growth can be observed, as well as growth of blood vessels needed to support the enlarged structure of the brain. The principle of neuroplasticity is closely in line with the theory of *deliberate practice* (Ericsson, Krampe, & Tesch-Römer, 1993), which poses that the amount of "deliberate" or dedicated practice that is solely focused on improving skill level is the foremost contributor to current expertise level. Alternatively, this principle also fits with the more recently posited practice-plasticity-processes model (Campitelli, Gobet, & Bilalić, 2014), which describes expertise development as the result of the interaction between practice and individual differences in neural plasticity. That is, individuals with higher plasticity are predicted to acquire expertise faster, given equal practice. Most of the studies reviewed in this chapter were conducted in the domain of music, but in recent years the number of studies incorporating physical sports has grown.

Evidence from Musical Expertise

The earliest study dating back to the mid-nineties revealed that expert string players had a greater cortical representation of the index to small fingers on the left hand compared to the thumb and compared to non-expert controls (Elbert, Pantev, Wienbruch, Rockstroh, & Taub, 1995). The finding that the cortical sensorimotor representation of the hands or fingers enlarges with practice has become widespread over the years. Amunts and colleagues (1997), for instance, replicated these findings and added that the typical left-larger-than-right asymmetry in hand representation found in right-handed non-experts was reduced in expert keyboard players. The length of the posterior wall of the precentral gyrus bordering the central sulcus (intrasulcal length of the precentral gyrus, ILPG) was measured as an approximation of the cortical representation of the hand. Not only was this area relatively larger in experts, the size of the ILPG was negatively correlated with the age starting to play keyboard in the experts. This provided early evidence for a sensitive period in neuroplasticity of the brain during development. Schwenkreis and colleagues (2007) showed that in violinists the enlargement of the left-hand representation in the motor cortex was not visible in general hand motor tasks, indicating that the structural reorganization is task-specific.

Apart from increases in the representation of the hands or fingers on the motor cortex, the corpus callosum has been shown to alter due to prolonged practice. Both pianists and violinists were found to have larger anterior portions of the corpus callosum, in particular when experts had started practice before the age of 7 (Schlaug, Jäncke, Huang, Staiger, & Steinmetz, 1995). This was interpreted as resulting from the high demands on coordination between the hands during music making, which stimulates nerve fiber growth in the connection between the hemispheres. Bengtsson and colleagues (2005) discovered that posterior parts of the corpus callosum were enlarged in pianists, presumably as a result of more effective connectivity between the left and right auditory regions of the temporal lobes. Moreover, the planum temporale was shown to be more asymmetrical (left larger than right) in musicians with absolute pitch compared to those without absolute pitch (Keenan, Thangaraj, Halpern, & Schlaug, 2001). Building on the evidence for structural adaptations to auditory and motor areas of the brain through acquiring musical expertise, James and colleagues (2014) studied the involvement of higher-order cognitive processes and their neuroanatomical substrates in amateur and expert musicians. They observed both an increase and a decrease in gray matter density in experts compared to amateurs, depending on the underlying function of the supporting brain area. In particular, areas involved in higher-order cognitive processing such as syntactic processing, executive function (i.e., the left inferior frontal gyrus), and visuo-motor coordination (i.e., the left intraparietal sulcus) showed higher gray matter density in experts compared to amateurs. Areas related to automation of motor skills (i.e., bilateral perirolandic and striatal areas) showed reduced gray matter density. Apparently, expertise in music expresses itself in the brain as neural extension and neural efficiency at the same time (for a more extensive description of research on neural efficiency, see this chapter, section on Neural Efficiency).

Evidence from Sports and Arts

The last decade has been marked by a rapid increase in studies examining the structural characteristics of sports (and to a smaller extent artistic) expertise in the brain. Similar to musical expertise, increased gray matter volume was found in auditory, sensorimotor and premotor cortex as well as in the cerebellum in expert typists (Cannonieri, Bonilha, Fernandes, Cendes, & Li, 2007), basketball players (Park et al., 2009, 2011), and golf players (Jäncke, Koeneke, Hoppe, Rominger, & Hänggi, 2009). Parallel to the work by James in musicians, *reduced* gray matter density was observed in women ballet dancers in certain brain areas, possibly those areas that are related to automated skill execution (in particular, the left premotor cortex, the SMA, the putamen, the superior frontal gyrus). Longitudinal research in which novices were trained daily over a three-month period to learn to juggle showed a bilateral expansion of the mid-temporal area and the left inferior parietal sulcus from pre- to post-training scans (Draganski et al., 2004). Without doubt, longitudinal research will provide the strongest evidence for plasticity of the brain, and improved availability of MRI scanning will possibly increase its use.

In professional racing-car drivers, Bernardi et al. (2014) found evidence for extensive structural brain differences compared to non-experts (e.g., the basal ganglia, the sensorimotor cortex, the inferior frontal gyrus). What is more, the gray matter density in the retrosplenial cortex correlated with drivers' success in actual racing competition. In a similar manner, but in an observational drawing task, Chamberlain *et al.* (2014) showed that gray matter density in the left anterior cerebellum and the right medial frontal gyrus was related to observational drawing skill (as judged by external raters) in a sample of art and non-art students. The amount of artistic training (in years) was correlated with gray matter density in the precuneus.

Summary: Structural Changes with Motor Expertise

In both musical and sports expertise, over the last two decades a rather robust evidence base has been established for structural adaptations to the brain as a result of prolonged, intense practice. These structural adaptations can be traced back to the nature of the expertise task at hand, and the underlying cognitive and perceptual-motor functions it relies on. These adaptations are typically highly task-specific, mostly involve increased gray matter density, and in certain cases correlate with objective performance standards such as competitions or rater judgments. At the same time, evidence for reduced gray matter density as a result of experience indicates that the brain abides by the principle of neural efficiency as well, to allow for automated skill execution. Clearly, there is a need for more longitudinal research to unravel the issue of nature versus nurture, an issue that cannot be resolved through cross-sectional, contrastive research alone.

Functional Neuroplasticity

So far, we have discussed *anatomical* changes with increased expertise. Expertise has also been found to impact brain activation patterns, as has been investigated using *functional* MRI. Studies that investigate functional changes together suggest that with increased expertise, there seems to be a decrease in overall brain activation (i.e., neural efficiency) as well as increases in specific cortical circuits (Callan & Naito, 2014; Debarnot *et al.*, 2014; Yang, 2015), as suggested by theory regarding action observation and mental imagery. We will discuss these three sets of findings in the context of theories and their related design-choices.

Neural Efficiency

The sheer speed of hand movements required to play Chopin's "Fantasia Impromptu" is likely to overwhelm the brain of a novice piano player. Expert pianists, however, are not likely to be overwhelmed by this piece because they have automated playing the piano, and might thus use less brain activation to do the same task. Neural efficiency refers to a (general) decrease in brain activation with increased motor expertise (Callan & Naito, 2014; Debarnot *et al.*, 2014; Diedrichsen & Kornysheva, 2015; Jäncke, Shah, & Peters, 2000; Munte *et al.*, 2002). Novices show activity in a wider range of regions, which has been interpreted as inefficient processing (Kim *et al.*, 2014). Callan and Naito (2014) discuss that neural efficiency could reflect two different processes: decreased energy expenditure and increased automaticity.

First, expertise could cause metabolic changes, reflecting less energy expenditure (Callan & Naito, 2014; Debarnot et al., 2014; Diedrichsen & Kornysheva, 2015). This would typically mean lower activation in task-related regions such as M1 with increased expertise. For example, Naito and Hirose (2014) asked participants (including the Brazilian soccer player Neymar da Silva Santos Júnior) to continuously rotate their ankle, and found decreased M1 activation with increased soccer expertise. Bernardi et al. (2013) asked naïve and professional drivers to execute a basic motor reaction task, and found decreased activity in task-related regions such as M1 and premotor regions. Several studies investigated neural efficiency in pianists and musically naïve control subjects while executing finger tapping tasks (Jäncke et al., 2000; Koeneke, Lutz, Wüstenberg, & Jäncke, 2004; Krings et al., 2000). They found decreased activity in task-related regions such as motor and premotor regions and the cerebellum. Note that in these studies, participants did not execute a domain-specific task, but rather a simplified task that could be executed equally well by both groups. In contrast, several studies have investigated neural efficiency in pre-shot routines in golf and shooting (Chang et al., 2011; Kim et al., 2014; Milton, Solodkin, Hlustik, & Small, 2007). All three studies found decreases in overall brain activity with increased expertise, specifically in regions such as the premotor and motor regions.

Alternatively, neural efficiency is thought to reflect increased automaticity and decreased (prefrontal) control (Callan & Naito, 2014; Debarnot et al., 2014; Diedrichsen & Kornysheva, 2015; Patel, Spreng, & Turner, 2013). Increased automaticity is a key concept in motor learning (Debarnot et al., 2014; Diedrichsen & Kornysheva, 2015; Fitts & Posner, 1967). Increased automaticity predicts decreased activity in control regions, and this is indeed found in several studies (e.g., Jäncke et al., 2000; Vogt et al., 2007). For example, both Kim et al. (2014) and Milton et al. (2007) investigated pre-shot routines, respectively in archery and golf, and found decreased overall activation with increased expertise, with specific decreases in control regions such as the basal ganglia. Similarly, Milton, Small, and Solodkin (2004) pose that the inverse relationship between limbic system activation and expertise that has been found in some studies suggests that experts no longer need intentional effort to control the movement. Debarnot et al. (2014) sum up the evidence as a decrease in activation of the fronto-parietal and dorsal attention networks. Both Debarnot et al. (2014) and Diedrichsen and Kornysheva (2015) point out, however, that systematic reviews find evidence for both increased and decreased activity in motor and premotor areas, and that findings might depend on the phase of learning.

The Mirror Neuron System and Action Observation

Venus Williams is ready for the opponents' return of her serve. She looks at the movements of her opponent to anticipate where the ball will go next, and plans her movements accordingly. What happens in her brain when she plans her movement in response to the movements of the opponent? Action observation is an important aspect of motor expertise (Caspers, Zilles, Laird, & Eickhoff, 2010). Action observation plays a role in anticipating your opponents' movements and planning a response to that (Savelsbergh, Williams, Kamp, & Ward, 2002). It has been argued that in fast sports such as tennis, volleyball, and hockey, motor planning occurs concurrently with seeing the opponents' movements (Milton *et al.*, 2008). Action observation is thought to be situated in the mirror neuron system (Rizzolatti & Craighero, 2004). Mirror neurons were originally discovered in the monkey premotor cortex. Neurons in this region were found to fire both when an action was performed, as well as when the monkey observed someone else perform the action (Gallese, Fadiga, Fogassi, & Rizzolatti, 1996). While the role of mirror neurons in functions such as empathy and speech perception is highly debated (e.g., Hickok, 2009), their role in action observation and imitation is more established. In humans, the mirror neuron system is thought to consist of a complex network of occipital, temporal and parietal visual regions, and two motor regions: the rostral part of the inferior parietal lobule (rostral IPL), and the lower part of the precentral gyrus plus the posterior part of the inferior frontal gyrus (IFG) (Caspers *et al.*, 2010; Rizzolatti & Craighero, 2004).

An elegant experimental paradigm that has been employed includes experts in one of two similar sports, such as tennis and volleyball, (see Balser *et al.*, 2014), or capoeira, a Brazilian martial art, and ballet, (see Calvo-Merino *et al.*, 2005), who act as novices in the other sport. Stimuli are videos from both sports. This 2x2 mixed design should yield a cross-over interaction in performance data, with either group doing best on tasks in their domain. This experimental paradigm typically yields increased activity in the mirror neuron system/action observation network (AON) for experts compared to novices in the domain-specific task. Balser *et al.* (2014) report increased activation in the superior parietal lobe (SPL), presupplementary motor area (preSMA), and the cerebellum. Calvo-Merino *et al.* (2005) found increased activity in experts compared to novices in the premotor area, the intraparietal sulcus (IPS), the superior parietal lobe (SPL), and the superior temporal sulcus (SPS).

Similar, but less clear-cut findings are found when novices and experts in only one sport are included. Olsson and Lundstrom (2013) found that expert ice-hockey players showed increased activations in the superior and middle temporal gyri and the premotor area, while novices recruited visual and frontal regions. Wimshurst *et al.* (2016) found increased activation in the AON in hockey experts compared to novices, but did not find an interaction with video-type (videos of badminton and hockey), so the increased activation might not be domain-specific. Diersch *et al.* (2013) found that expert figure skaters showed increased activity in the bilateral caudate and thalamus as compared to novice figure skaters on figure-skating tasks. Callan *et al.* (2013) studied pilots and non-pilots watching a glider plane landing in a simulated environment. They found that experts, as compared to novices, showed increased activation in the premotor cortex, inferior frontal gyrus (IFG), anterior insula, parietal cortex, superior temporal gyrus, and middle temporal MT area.

A special case is the study of Liew, Sheng, Margetis, and Aziz-Zadeh (2013), who, instead of studying sport experts, studied an individual with limb amputations in a similar experimental paradigm. Liew *et al.* (2013) compared a participant with amputations, participants without amputations, and occupational therapists, who were familiar with seeing people with amputations, so they would have visual but not motor experience. Participants observed videos of actions such as turning a book page, performed by an individual born without arms, and goal-matched actions by a typically developed individual. They found highest AON activation in novices and the individual with amputations. After novices were shown videos of the movements for extended periods of time, their AON activation decreased, which suggests that novelty is also correlated with increased AON activation. Thus, motor expertise seems to be related with domain-specific brain activity in regions related to the action observation network: The brain seems to respond more strongly to movements that are part of the motor repertoire (i.e., that the participant can actually execute) (Turella, Wurm, Tucciarelli, & Lingnau, 2013). Findings by Liew *et al.* (2013) suggest that the AON also responds to novel movements. Likewise, Vogt *et al.* (2007) found that when novice guitar players imitated new or practiced guitar chords, they showed increased activation in the inferior parietal and ventral premotor areas when observing new chords. Typical expertise studies only focus on the contrast between novices (for whom the movement is usually not completely novel, although it is not part of the motor repertoire) and experts, and thus miss out on the findings reported by Liew *et al.* (2013).

Mental Imagery

Imagine preparing for a high jump, Fosbury flop-style. You start running toward the bar, faster and faster until you are right next to the bar. You thrust your arms and knees upwards and arch your back over the bar. At the very last moment, you pull your legs over the bar and land backwards on the mat. Did you see yourself doing the high jump? As discussed above, the rationale of mental imagery studies is that the act of mentally imagining movements recruits brain networks that are very similar to those recruited by actual movement. This makes it a useful paradigm to investigate movements that are hard to execute in the scanner, such as diving, dancing, and high jumping.

Designs of studies that employ mental imagery as a framework either ask participants to observe and subsequently imagine movement, or ask participants to imagine movements in response to a (visual) cue. For example, Wei and Luo (2010) asked expert divers and non-divers to observe and subsequently imagine diving and simple gymnastic (e.g., jumping) movements. They found that experts showed increased activations as compared to novices in the left parahippocampal gyrus (BA 36) and left medial frontal gyrus (BA 10) when imagining diving movements. Olsson, Jonsson, Larsson, & Nyberg (2008) compared high jumping novices and experts while performing first-person motor imagery of a high jump. They found that expert high jumpers activated mostly motor regions such as the premotor cortex and cerebellum, while novices activated visual regions such as the superior occipital cortex.

An important issue of using motor imagery to investigate expertise is summarized in the title of a paper by Olsson and Nyberg (2010): "If you can't do it, you won't think it: Expertise impacts the ability to perform mental imagery of motor execution." Indeed, novices in the study by Olsson, Jonsson, and Nyberg (2008) seemed to perform visual instead of motor imagery. Similarly, Tomasino, Maieron, Guatto, Fabbro, and Rumiati (2013) found that expert volleyball players have stronger responses in motor areas (M1 and the left premotor cortex) when imagining feasible versus non-feasible movements. An inherent disadvantage of the use of mental imagery is that manipulation checks are typically hard to perform (Munzert et al., 2009), and the "degree" of mental imagery is often impossible to establish. Often, post-experiment questionnaires are used to get some insight into the subjective experience of mental imagery (e.g., Wei & Luo, 2010).

Mental imagery is widely used as a way of mental training in many sports (Munzert et al., 2009), but also in surgery (Immenroth et al., 2007) and piano playing (Meister et al., 2004). The pre-shot routine described previously could be considered mental imagery, although it is used to improve performance rather than learning. The finding that motor imagery performance increases with expertise suggests that motor imagery for training motor skills is mostly effective when some sort of motor representation is present, and not so much for training motor skills de novo (Milton et al., 2008).

Summary: Functional Changes with Motor Expertise

Research on functional changes related with motor expertise has employed several different theoretical perspectives to explain those changes. Studies that take the neural efficiency perspective have findings reflecting either decreased energy expenditure (showing task-specific changes in regions such as M1) or increased automaticity (showing task-specific changes in control regions such as the basal ganglia). These studies have mostly employed action execution tasks. Studies that take the action observation network as a starting point typically ask participants to observe videos of movements, or anticipate movement direction from videos. Typically, these studies show increased activation in the action observation network with increased expertise. Finally, studies that take mental imagery as a starting point find higher activity in motor regions such as the PMC with increased expertise.

Implications and Further Questions

After two decades of research, MRI and fMRI studies into motor expertise development are still considered in their infancy, and we can only begin to imagine the research paradigms that will be designed in the near future and the results these studies will deliver. It is premature to draw up the balance in terms of what MRI and fMRI studies on motor expertise have contributed theoretically and practically, but here we would like to put forward a number of issues. Generally speaking, MRI and fMRI research on motor expertise is considered valuable (1) if it results in confirmation, adaptation of creation of theory with regard to motor expertise or, more broadly, motor learning, and/ or (2) if it leads to adaptation or expansion of training and/or selection of individuals for practice. So far, it is clear that the abundant functional and structural changes in the brain observed through fMRI and MRI research support behavioral theories of expertise development in which the effect of deliberate practice is considered paramount to exceptional performance. At the same time, neural efficiency findings help explain how automation in skill execution is reflected in the brain. Connectivity analyses are considered promising to help unravel how the brain moves from elaborate, conscious processing to automated, nonconscious processing. Severe adaptations to existing theories or formulation of new theories on motor expertise based on MRI and fMRI research have not occurred, although specific insights have shifted our knowledge of the brain significantly (e.g., the finding that learning to juggle alters the grey matter in the occipito-temporal cortex after a mere 7 days of training; Driemeyer, Boyke, Gaser, Büchel, & May, 2008). We expect that fMRI research will continue to be particularly insightful for expertise aspects that are not readily captured in behavioral research, such as movement planning, action observation, mental imagery, and anticipation skill. Note though that manipulation checks for purely mental tasks such as imagery are virtually impossible.

In order for the full scope of fMRI research to reach its potential in influencing expertise theory and training, certain shifts or expansions in paradigm, task, and domain would be needed. First, longitudinal research is required to contribute to the nature–nurture debate. Current cross-sectional studies delineate differences between the novice and expert brain in highly specific brain regions. While these findings render a strong "nature" view of motor expertise development unlikely (i.e., the assumption that motor expertise is chiefly if not entirely determined by individuals' genetic endowment), it is largely unknown when morphometric changes to the brain are detected and how long they last. Longitudinal research commencing with novice participants can provide neuroscientific evidence to the nature–nurture debate of expertise. Second, a more consistent conceptualization and operationalization of expertise and exceptional performance would be needed to enable comparison and conclusions across studies and across domains. Expertise is often approached in a relative manner in both behavioral and MRI and fMRI research; those who have been performing in a domain for a significant number of years (often more than 10 years) are considered experts and those who only recently started or have no experience in the domain form the control comparison group. These criteria tend to be arbitrarily chosen and can trouble comparison between studies. Clearer criteria for expertise based on criterion task performance will provide a more reproducible basis for conclusions about the nature of expertise. On the other hand, certain studies incorporate exceptional (internationally renowned) performers as experts, taking an absolute stance in assigning expertise. The question whether and how experts' brains in terms of relative versus absolute standards are comparable is unresolved and warrants further research.

Finally, the domains studied in neuroscience research on motor expertise have mostly focused on music and sports expertise. Expanding the paradigm to professional domains such as surgery will not only augment our knowledge of surgical skill development but will also broaden the scope of motor expertise theory development in general. Little is known about the neuroscience of surgical skills (but see Morris *et al.*, 2015, for a feasibility study). This line of research will launch new questions, such as the effect of starting age: In professional development such as surgical residency, training commences at a much later age compared to sports practice (typically residents start in their early- to mid-20s). What are the implications for neuroplasticity for this later starting age? And how do older surgeons cope with rapid changes in complexity of surgical instruments? As in sports and music research, fMRI research in professional domains suffers from the limitation of reduced or no possibility for movement in the scanner. Alternative paradigms, such as viewing video clips or making behavioral decisions, should be chosen carefully, and their value as an expertise criterion task should be validated first outside of the scanner.

Conclusions

This chapter attempts to provide a comprehensive overview of findings from MRI and fMRI research on neural aspects of motor expertise development. The overview is by no means meant to be exhaustive, but our goal was to incorporate and discuss the dominant contemporary issues and findings in this domain. To mark the scope, research based on alternative neuroscientific methods such as EEG, fNIRS, or PET was omitted from this chapter, but is included in other reviews such as those by Debarnot *et al.* (2014) and Gruber and colleagues (2010). Although gross alterations to theory and implications for practice are not expected, neuroscience research is by now an intrinsic part of expertise development research and continuously contributes to our knowledge of motor expertise development. Given the multidisciplinary nature of expert performance (i.e., expert performance usually contains perceptual, cognitive, social, and other characteristics, and is often highly contextual), a multimethod approach combining neuroscientific, behavioral, and qualitative research paradigms is necessary to fully unearth the complexity of experts' minds and the exceptionality of their performance.

References

Amunts, K., Schlaug, G., Jäncke, L., Steinmetz, H., Schleicher, A., Dabringhaus, A., & Zilles, K. (1997). Motor cortex and hand motor skills: Structural compliance in the human brain. *Human Brain Mapping, 5*(3), 206–215.

Bahrami, P., Graham, S. J., Grantcharov, T. P., Cusimano, M. D., Rotstein, O. D., Mansur, A., & Schweizer, T. A. (2014). Neuroanatomical correlates of laparoscopic surgery training. *Surg Endosc, 28*(7), 2189–2198. doi:10.1007/s00464-014-3452-7

Bahrami, P., Schweizer, T. A., Tam, F., Grantcharov, T. P., Cusimano, M. D., & Graham, S. J. (2011). Functional MRI-compatible laparoscopic surgery training simulator. *Magnetic Resonance in Medicine, 65*(3), 873–881. doi:10.1002/mrm.22664

Balser, N., Lorey, B., Pilgramm, S., Naumann, T., Kindermann, S., Stark, R., … Munzert, J. (2014). The influence of expertise on brain activation of the action observation network during anticipation of tennis and volleyball serves. *Frontiers in Human Neuroscience, 8*, 568. doi:10.3389/fnhum.2014.00568

Bengtsson, S. L., Nagy, Z., Skare, S., Forsman, L., Forssberg, H., & Ullén, F. (2005). Extensive piano practicing has regionally specific effects on white matter development. *Nature Neuroscience, 8*(9), 1148–1150.

Bernardi, G., Cecchetti, L., Handjaras, G., Sani, L., Gaglianese, A., Ceccarelli, R., … Pietrini, P. (2014). It's not all in your car: Functional and structural correlates of exceptional driving skills in professional racers. *Frontiers in Human Neuroscience*: 888/ doi:10.3389/fnhum.2014.00888

Bernardi, G., Ricciardi, E., Sani, L., Gaglianese, A., Papasogli, A., Ceccarelli, R., … Pietrini, P. (2013). How skill expertise shapes the brain functional architecture: An fMRI study of visuo-spatial and motor processing in professional racing-car and naive drivers. *Plos One, 8*(10). doi:10.1371/journal.pone.0077764

Bilalić, M., Langner, R., Erb, M., & Grodd, W. (2010). Mechanisms and neural basis of object and pattern recognition: A study with chess experts. *Journal of Experimental Psychology: General, 139*(4), 728–742. doi: 10.1037/a0020756

Binkofski, F., & Buccino, G. (2006). The role of ventral premotor cortex in action execution and action understanding. *Journal of Physiology-Paris, 99*(4), 396–405. doi:10.1016/j.jphysparis.2006.03.005

Callan, D. E., & Naito, E. (2014). Neural processes distinguishing elite from expert and novice athletes. *Cognitive and Behavioral Neurology, 27*(4), 183–188. doi:10.1097/ WNN.0000000000000043

Callan, D. E., Terzibas, C., Cassel, D. B., Callan, A., Kawato, M., & Sato, M.-a. (2013). Differential activation of brain regions involved with error-feedback and imitation based motor simulation when observing self and an expert's actions in pilots and non-pilots on a complex glider landing task. *Neuroimage, 72*, 55–68. doi:10.1016/j. neuroimage.2013.01.028

Calvo-Merino, B., Glaser, D. E., Grèzes, J., Passingham, R. E., & Haggard, P. (2005). Action observation and acquired motor skills: An fMRI study with expert dancers. *Cerebral Cortex, 15*(8), 1243–1249. doi:0.1093/cercor/bhi007

Campitelli, G. J., Gobet, F., & Bilalic, M. (2014). Cognitive processes and development of chess genius: An integrative approach. In D. K. Simonton (Ed.), *The Wiley handbook of genius* (pp. 350–374). England: Wiley-Blackwell.

Cannonieri, G. C., Bonilha, L., Fernandes, P. T., Cendes, F., & Li, L. M. (2007). Practice and perfect: Length of training and structural brain changes in experienced typists. *Neuroreport, 18*(10), 1063–1066. doi:10.1097/WNR.0b013e3281a030e5

Caspers, S., Zilles, K., Laird, A. R., & Eickhoff, S. B. (2010). ALE meta-analysis of action observation and imitation in the human brain. *Neuroimage, 50*(3), 1148–1167. doi:10.1016/j.neuroimage.2009.12.112

Chamberlain, R., McManus, I. C., Brunswick, N., Rankin, Q., Riley, H., & Kanai, R. (2014). Drawing on the right side of the brain: A voxel-based morphometry analysis of observational drawing. *Neuroimage, 96,* 167–173. doi:10.1016/j.neuroimage. 2014.03.062

Chang, Y., Lee, J.-J., Seo, J.-H., Song, H.-J., Kim, Y.-T., Lee, H. J., ... Kim, J. G. (2011). Neural correlates of motor imagery for elite archers. *NMR in Biomedicine, 24*(4), 366–372. doi:10.1002/nbm.1600

Cosic, K., Popovic, S., Fabek, I., Kovac, B., Rados, M., Rados, M., ... Simic, G. (2012). Pilot fMRI study of neural activation patterns induced by professional military training. *Translational Neuroscience, 3*(1), 46–50. doi:10.2478/s13380-012-0012-2

Debarnot, U., Sperduti, M., Di Rienzo, F., & Guillot, A. (2014). Experts bodies, experts minds: How physical and mental training shape the brain. *Frontiers in Human Neuroscience, 8.* doi:10.3389/fnhum.2014.00280

Diedrichsen, J., & Bastian, A. (2014). Cerebellar function. In M. S. Gazzaniga & G. R. Mangun (Eds.), *The Cognitive Neurosciences* (5 ed., pp. 451–460). Cambridge, Massachusetts: MIT Press.

Diedrichsen, J., & Kornysheva, K. (2015). Motor skill learning between selection and execution. *Trends in Cognitive Sciences, 19*(4), 227–233. doi:10.1016/j.tics.2015.02.003

Diersch, N., Mueller, K., Cross, E. S., Stadler, W., Rieger, M., & Schuetz-Bosbach, S. (2013). Action prediction in younger versus older adults: Neural correlates of motor familiarity. *Plos One, 8*(5). doi:10.1371/journal.pone.0064195

Draganski, B., Gaser, C., Busch, V., Schuierer, G., Bogdahn, U., & May, A. (2004). Neuroplasticity: Changes in grey matter induced by training. *Nature, 427*(6972), 311–312. doi:10.1038/427311a

Driemeyer, J., Boyke, J., Gaser, C., Büchel, C., & May, A. (2008). Changes in gray matter induced by learning—revisited. *Plos One, 3*(7), e2669. doi: 10.1371/journal. pone.0002669

Elbert, T., Pantev, C., Wienbruch, C., Rockstroh, B., & Taub, E. (1995). Increased cortical representation of the fingers of the left hand in string players. *Science, 270*(5234), 305–307.

Ericsson, K. A., Krampe, R. T., & Tesch-Römer, C. (1993). The role of deliberate practice in the acquisition of expert performance. *Psychological Review, 100*(3), 363–406. doi:10.1037/0033-295x.100.3.363

Ericsson, K. A., & Smith, J. (1991). Prospects and limits of the empirical study of expertise: An introduction. *Toward a general theory of expertise: Prospects and limits* (pp. 1–38). Cambridge: Cambridge University Press.

Ericsson, K. A., & Ward, P. (2007). Capturing the naturally occurring superior performance of experts in the laboratory toward a science of expert and exceptional performance. *Current Directions in Psychological Science, 16*(6), 346–350.

Fitts, P. M., & Posner, M. I. (1967). *Human performance*. Belmont, CA: Brooks/Cole Pub. Co.

Gallese, V., Fadiga, L., Fogassi, L., & Rizzolatti, G. (1996). Action recognition in the premotor cortex. *Brain, 119*(2), 593–609. doi:10.1093/brain/119.2.593

Gruber, H., Jansen, P., Marienhagen, J., & Altenmueller, E. (2010). Adaptations during the acquisition of expertise. *Talent Development & Excellence, 2*(1), 3–15.

Hickok, G. (2009). Eight problems for the mirror neuron theory of action understanding in monkeys and humans. *Journal of Cognitive Neuroscience, 21*(7), 1229–1243. doi:10.1162/jocn.2009.21189

Hodge, T. Y., & Deakin, J. M. (1998). Deliberate practice and expertise in the martial arts: The role of context in motor recall. *Journal of Sport & Exercise Psychology, 20*, 260–279.

Immenroth, M., Bürger, T., Brenner, J., Nagelschmidt, M., Eberspächer, H., & Troidl, H. (2007). Mental training in surgical education: a randomized controlled trial. *Annals of Surgery, 245*(3), 385–391. doi:10.1097/01.sla.0000251575.95171.b3

James, C. E., Oechslin, M. S., Van de Ville, D., Hauert, C.-A., Descloux, C., & Lazeyras, F. (2014). Musical training intensity yields opposite effects on grey matter density in cognitive versus sensorimotor networks. *Brain Structure & Function, 219*(1), 353–366. doi:10.1007/s00429-013-0504-z

Jäncke, L., Koeneke, S., Hoppe, A., Rominger, C., & Hänggi, J. (2009). The architecture of the golfer's brain. *Plos One, 4*(3), e4785. doi: 10.1371/journal.pone.0004785

Jäncke, L., Shah, N., & Peters, M. (2000). Cortical activations in primary and secondary motor areas for complex bimanual movements in professional pianists. *Cognitive Brain Research, 10*(1), 177–183. doi:10.1016/S0926-6410(00)00028-8

Jeannerod, M. (2001). Neural simulation of action: A unifying mechanism for motor cognition. *Neuroimage, 14*(1), S103–S109. doi:10.1006/nimg.2001.0832

Kalet, J. W. (2013). *Biological Psychology*. Belmont, CA, USA: Wadsworth.

Keenan, J. P., Thangaraj, V., Halpern, A. R., & Schlaug, G. (2001). Absolute pitch and planum temporale. *Neuroimage, 14*(6), 1402–1408.

Kim, W., Chang, Y., Kim, J., Seo, J., Ryu, K., Lee, E., … Janelle, C. M. (2014). An fMRI study of differences in brain activity among elite, expert, and novice archers at the moment of optimal aiming. *Cognitive and Behavioral Neurology, 27*(4), 173–182. doi:10.1097/WNN.0000000000000042

Koeneke, S., Lutz, K., Wüstenberg, T., & Jäncke, L. (2004). Long-term training affects cerebellar processing in skilled keyboard players. *Neuroreport, 15*(8), 1279–1282. doi:10.1097/01.wnr.0000127463.10147.e7

Kolb, B., & Whishaw, I. Q. (2009). *Fundamentals of human neuropsychology*. Basingstoke: Macmillan.

Krings, T., Töpper, R., Foltys, H., Erberich, S., Sparing, R., Willmes, K., & Thron, A. (2000). Cortical activation patterns during complex motor tasks in piano players and control subjects. A functional magnetic resonance imaging study. *Neuroscience Letters, 278*(3), 189–193. doi:0.1016/S0304-3940(99)00930-1

Lappi, O. (2015). The racer's brain – how domain expertise is reflected in the neural substrates of driving. *Frontiers in Human Neuroscience, 9*, 635. doi:10.3389/fnhum.2015.00635

Liew, S.-L., Sheng, T., Margetis, J. L., & Aziz-Zadeh, L. (2013). Both novelty and expertise increase action observation network activity. *Frontiers in Human Neuroscience, 7*, 541. doi:10.3389/fnhum.2013.00541

Mann, D., Dicks, M., Canal-Bruland, R., & van der Kamp, J. (2013). Neurophysiological studies may provide a misleading picture of how perceptual-motor interactions are coordinated. *i-Perception*, *4*(1), 78–80. doi:10.1068/i0569ic

Meister, I. G., Krings, T., Foltys, H., Boroojerdi, B., Müller, M., Töpper, R., & Thron, A. (2004). Playing piano in the mind—an fMRI study on music imagery and performance in pianists. *Cognitive Brain Research*, *19*(3), 219–228. doi:10.1016/j. cogbrainres.2003.12.005

Men, W., Falk, D., Sun, T., Chen, W., Li, J., Yin, D., … Fan, M. (2014). The corpus callosum of Albert Einstein's brain: Another clue to his high intelligence? *Brain*, 137 (4), e268. http://doi.org/10.1093/brain/awt252.

Milton, J., Small, S. S., & Solodkin, A. (2004). On the road to automatic: Dynamic aspects in the development of expertise. *Journal of Clinical Neurophysiology*, *21*(3), 134–143. doi:10.1097/00004691-200405000-00002

Milton, J., Small, S. L., & Solodkin, A. (2008). Imaging motor imagery: Methodological issues related to expertise. *Methods*, *45*(4), 336–341. doi:10.1016/j.ymeth. 2008.05.002

Milton, J., Solodkin, A., Hlustik, P., & Small, S. L. (2007). The mind of expert motor performance is cool and focused. *Neuroimage*, *35*(2), 804–813. doi:10.1016/j.neuroimage.2007.01.003

Morris, M. C., Frodl, T., D'Souza, A., Fagan, A. J., & Ridgway, P. F. (2015). Assessment of competence in surgical skills using functional magnetic resonance imaging: A feasibility study. *Journal of Surgical Education*, *72*(2), 198–204. doi:10.1016/j. jsurg.2014.09.007

Munte, T. F., Altenmuller, E., & Jancke, L. (2002). The musician's brain as a model of neuroplasticity. *Nature Reviews Neuroscience,* *3*(6), 473–478. doi:10.1038/nrn843

Munzert, J., Lorey, B., & Zentgraf, K. (2009). Cognitive motor processes: The role of motor imagery in the study of motor representations. *Brain Research Reviews*, *60*(2), 306–326. doi:10.1016/j.brainresrev.2008.12.024

Nachev, P., Kennard, C., & Husain, M. (2008). Functional role of the supplementary and pre-supplementary motor areas. *Nature Reviews Neuroscience,* *9*(11), 856–869. doi:10.1038/nrn2478

Naito, E., & Hirose, S. (2014). Efficient foot motor control by Neymar's brain. *Frontiers in Human Neuroscience*, 8, 594. doi:10.3389/fnhum.2014.00594

Olsson, C. J., Jonsson, B., Larsson, A., & Nyberg, L. (2008). Motor representations and practice affect brain systems underlying imagery: An fMRI study of internal imagery in novices and active high jumpers. *The Open Neuroimaging Journal*, *2*, 5–13. doi:10.2174/1874440000802010005

Olsson, C. J., Jonsson, B., & Nyberg, L. (2008). Internal imagery training in active high jumpers. *Scandinavian Journal of Psychology*, *49*(2), 133–140. doi:10.1111/j.1467-9450.2008.00625.x

Olsson, C. J., & Lundstrom, P. (2013). Using action observation to study superior motor performance: A pilot fMRI study. *Frontiers in Human Neuroscience*, 7. doi:10.3389/fnhum.2013.00819

Olsson, C. J., & Nyberg, L. (2010). Motor imagery: If you can't do it, you won't think it. *Scandinavian Journal of Medicine & Science in Sports*, *20*(5), 711–715. doi:10.1111/j.1600-0838.2010.01101.x

Park, I. S., Lee, K. J., Han, J. W., Lee, N. J., Lee, W. T., & Park, K. A. (2009). Experience-dependent plasticity of cerebellar vermis in basketball players. *The Cerebellum*, *8*(3), 334–339.

Park, I. S., Lee, K. J., Han, J. W., Lee, N. J., Lee, W. T., & Park, K. A. (2011). Basketball training increases striatum volume. *Human Movement Science*, *30*(1), 56–62. doi: 10.1016/j.humov.2010.09.001

Patel, R., Spreng, R. N., & Turner, G. R. (2013). Functional brain changes following cognitive and motor skills training: a quantitative meta-analysis. *Neurorehabilitation and Neural Repair*, *27*(3), 187–199. doi:10.1177/1545968312461718

Rizzolatti, G., & Craighero, L. (2004). The mirror-neuron system. *Annual Review of Neuroscience.*, *27*, 169–192. doi:10.1146/annurev.neuro.27.070203.144230

Savelsbergh, G. J., Williams, A. M., Kamp, J. V. D., & Ward, P. (2002). Visual search, anticipation and expertise in soccer goalkeepers. *Journal of Sports Sciences*, *20*(3), 279–287. doi:10.1080/026404102317284826

Schlaug, G., Jäncke, L., Huang, Y., Staiger, J. F., & Steinmetz, H. (1995). Increased corpus callosum size in musicians. *Neuropsychologia*, *33*(8), 1047–1055.

Schwenkreis, P., El Tom, S., Ragert, P., Pleger, B., Tegenthoff, M., & Dinse, H. R. (2007). Assessment of sensorimotor cortical representation asymmetries and motor skills in violin players. *European Journal of Neuroscience*, *26*(11), 3291–3302.

Starkes, J. L., Deakin, J., Allard, F., Hodges, N., Hayes, A., & Ericsson, K. (1996). Deliberate practice in sports: What is it anyway. In K. A. Ericsson (Ed.), *The road to excellence: The acquisition of expert performance in the arts and sciences, sports, and games* (pp. 81–106). Mahwah, NJ: Erlbaum.

Tomasino, B., Maieron, M., Guatto, E., Fabbro, F., & Rumiati, R. I. (2013). How are the motor system activity and functional connectivity between the cognitive and sensorimotor systems modulated by athletic expertise? *Brain Research*, *1540*, 21–41. doi:10.1016/j.brainres.2013.09.048

Turella, L., Wurm, M. F., Tucciarelli, R., & Lingnau, A. (2013). Expertise in action observation: Recent neuroimaging findings and future perspectives. *Frontiers in Human Neuroscience*, *7*, 637. doi:10.3389/fnhum.2013.00637

Turner, R. S., & Pasquereau, B. (2014). Basal ganglia function. In M. S. Gazzaniga & G. R. Mangun (Eds.), *The cognitive neurosciences* (5 ed., pp. 435–450). Cambridge, MA, USA: MIT Press.

Vogt, S., Buccino, G., Wohlschlaeger, A. M., Canessa, N., Shah, N. J., Zilles, K., … Fink, G. R. (2007). Prefrontal involvement in imitation learning of hand actions: Effects of practice and expertise. *Neuroimage*, *37*(4), 1371–1383. doi:10.1016/j.neuroimage.2007.07.005

Wei, G., & Luo, J. (2010). Sport expert's motor imagery: Functional imaging of professional motor skills and simple motor skills. *Brain Research*, *1341*, 52–62. doi:10.1016/j.brainres.2009.08.014

Williams, A. M., & Burwitz, L. (1993). Advance cue utilization in soccer. In T. Reilly, J. Clarys, & A. Stibbe (Eds.), *Science and Football II* (pp. 239–244). London: E & FN Spon.

Williams, A. M., Ward, P., Knowles, J. M., & Smeeton, N. J. (2002). Anticipation skill in a real-world task: Measurement, training, and transfer in tennis. *Journal of Experimental Psychology: Applied*, *8*(4), 259–270. doi: 10.1037/1076-898X.8.4.259

Wimshurst, Z. L., Sowden, P. T., & Wright, M. (2016). Expert-novice differences in brain function of field hockey players. *Neuroscience*, *315*, 31–44. doi:10.1016/j.neuroscience.2015.11.064

Yang, J. (2015). The influence of motor expertise on the brain activity of motor task performance: A meta-analysis of functional magnetic resonance imaging studies. *Cognitive Affective & Behavioral Neuroscience*, *15*(2), 381–394. doi:10.3758/s13415-014-0329-0

PART III

Genetic Approach

14

Primer

THEORETICAL CONCEPTS IN THE GENETICS OF EXPERTISE

Elliot M. Tucker-Drob

Introduction

What does it mean for a behavioral tendency or skill to be heritable? This basic question is perhaps one of the most vexing and debated issues in all of the social sciences (for a thoughtful discussion of this topic, see Turkheimer, 1998). To many scientists and laypersons alike, the concept of heritability is haunted by the twin specters of predetermination and immutability, specifically, that the more heritable a phenotype is, the less experience matters. However, the fallacy of this logic becomes clear when one considers the realm of expertise. Levels of expertise in a wide variety of specialized domains, ranging from playing a musical instrument to performing quantum physics, necessarily rely on the (typically effortful) acquisition of both declarative and procedural knowledge that can only occur through experience. At the same time, a growing body of behavioral genetic research reports moderate genetic effects on interindividual variation in empirical indices of expert skill (Hambrick, Macnamara, Campitelli, Ullén, & Mosing, 2016).

Given that experience is necessary for the acquisition of expertise and that expertise in a wide range of domains is heritable, the intuition that genetic effects compete with experiential effects is clearly flawed. How can genetic and experiential influences on expertise be reconciled? Contemporary work in behavioral genetics has come to use the term *gene-environment interplay* as an umbrella term to refer to several dynamic processes through which genetic and experiential factors work together to influence development. In this chapter, I describe how such dynamic processes may be relevant to understanding the development of expertise and to making sense of heritable variation in behavioral phenotypes more generally. I begin by describing what, statistically, heritability refers to.

Estimation and Interpretation of Genetic Influences

Genetic material (DNA) contains the code for creating proteins that are critical to the functions of cells and the tissues and organs that they compose. (DNA also contains sequences that do not code for proteins, but may serve other functions, such as regulation of when and how other segments of DNA are read and turned into proteins.) An overwhelming proportion of the code contained in the DNA of an individual is exactly the same as that of all other humans in the world. It is this commonality that serves as the basis for the physiological and psychological phenotypes that we as a species have in common (e.g., having 10 fingers, 10 toes, and the capacity for language). However, a small proportion of the code in DNA varies from person to person. The heritability of a characteristic refers to the extent to which this within-species *variation* in genetic code (DNA sequence variation) is statistically associated with *variation* in that phenotype. As it is exclusively an index of association between DNA variation and phenotypic variation, heritability itself is not directly concerned with the genetic basis (or lack thereof) for human universals.

Classical methods in behavioral genetics, such as twin and extended-family studies capitalize on the fact that interindividual differences in DNA sequence variation are not entirely random. Mendel's laws of inheritance (Mendel, 1865) dictate that individuals who are more closely related, in the familial sense, are more genetically similar. (Whether individuals are more similar on a phenotype under study is an empirical question on which the phenotype's heritability estimate is based; see below.) Monozygotic (MZ) twins are nearly perfectly genetically similar; dizygotic (DZ) twins and full siblings share, on average, about half of the genetic variants that differ within the general population; first cousins share, on average, about 12.5 percent of these variants, and so on. The magnitude of genetic influence on a phenotype (e.g., musical expertise) is inferred from the extent to which, holding amount of shared rearing constant,[1] individuals who are more genetically similar (e.g. MZ twins compared to DZ twins) are also more similar on that characteristic. Other sources of variation are also typically estimated. For instance, a shared environmental effect on a characteristic refers to the extent to which individuals raised together (e.g., siblings) resemble one another on that characteristic to a greater extent than can be attributed to their genetic similarity alone. For instance, the extent to which similar-aged, biologically unrelated, adoptive siblings tend to resemble one another on the characteristic under study can be taken as an index of the shared environmental effect on that characteristic, because adoptive siblings share a common rearing environment but are expected to be no more genetically similar, on average, than they are to individuals chosen at random out of the population. A nonshared environmental influence refers to the extent to which individuals nearly perfectly matched on their genes and their shared upbringing (i.e., identical twins reared together) are still not perfectly concordant on that characteristic. The nonshared environment may reflect measurement error, as well as environmental effects uniquely experienced by individuals reared together (e.g., different friend groups, different perceptions of the same event).

Newer methods use measured DNA from unrelated individuals to estimate the magnitude of genetic effects on a phenotype. For instance, recently developed methods (e.g., Yang et al., 2011) estimate the magnitude of genetic influence on a characteristic from the extent to which unrelated individuals who are slightly more genetically similar also tend to be more similar on that characteristic. Progress has been made in identifying some of the specific genetic variants that account for heritable variation in complex behavioral traits and psychiatric disorders, but it has become clear that many different variants distributed widely across the genome are together responsible for the majority of genetic variation in such traits (Visscher et al., 2012). In other words, it is not the case that only a handful of genetic variants account for the totality of genetic variation in complex behavioral phenotypes.

Regardless of the method used to estimate heritability or individual effects of specific genetic variants, genetic effects by themselves are nothing more than statistical associations, i.e., regression effects. For instance, the heritability of a characteristic can be directly interpreted as the proportion of variance (R^2) in that characteristic when it is entered as the dependent variable in a regression equation in which the independent variable is genetic variation. This is, in fact, exactly how structural equation models that estimate heritability are specified, with one caveat being that the independent variable (genetic variation) is a latent variable that is not directly measured, but inferred from cross-relative covariance information on the characteristic under study. Similarly, genetic associations involving specific DNA measures, whether these be in the context of a *polygenic score* formed as a weighted composite of many different variants or in the context of a score on a single genetic variant (e.g., a single nucleotide polymorphism, or SNP), are also nothing more than regression associations with genes as the predictor variables and the characteristic of interest as the outcome. (Control variables are also typically included to remove confounds between sociocultural stratification and DNA variation associated with racial and ethnic ancestry; Hamer, 2000.)

Because genetic associations are simply squared correlations (i.e., R^2), maxims regarding the ambiguous link between correlation and causation apply. As is the case in any observational study, once a correlate of an outcome is detected, much work remains to identify the potentially circuitous pathways of causation, including determining direction(s) of causation, and mediating and moderating mechanisms. Indeed, contemporary research in gene-environment interplay focuses on how environmental experiences moderate the effects of genotype (or, alternatively put, how genotypes moderate the effects of environment) on the development of psychological outcomes and how environmental experiences relevant for this development come to be correlated with genotypes over time. In the following section I discuss how such processes may apply to the developmental of expert skill.

Classical Concepts of Reaction Range

Of all realms of psychological function, it is perhaps most clear that the development of expert skill results from learning through experience. The scientific study of learning is foundational to the field of psychology, at least dating back to Ebbinghaus's (1885) work on memory retention and forgetting. Ebbinghaus introduced mathematical functions relating the strength of memory retention to the amount of repetition and retention interval. Importantly, these are some of the same factors commonly examined in modern studies of associations between practice and expert skill acquisition, with intensity of practice constituting a third major factor (Ericsson, 2004; Ullén, Hambrick, & Mosing, 2015). One simplified representation of the relationship between amount of practice and skill level is depicted in Figure 14.1, in which the skill increases with amount of practice, albeit at a decreasing rate.

One straightforward conceptualization of the role of genetics in learning is that genetic variation is related to the *slope* of the practice-skill function. This is represented in Figure 14.2, which closely resembles the reaction ranges originally depicted by Gottesman in 1963, based on earlier work from the early 1900s.

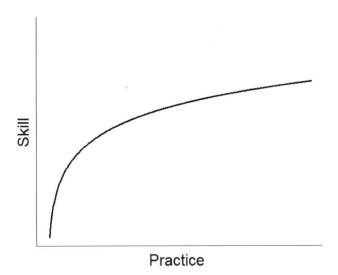

FIGURE 14.1 A stylized example of a hypothetical learning curve relating skilled performance to amount of practice.

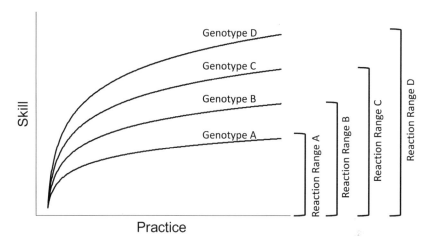

FIGURE 14.2 A stylized adaptation of Gottesman's (1963) concept of reaction range to the development of skilled performance with practice.

Gottesman hypothesized that the function relating the level of the phenotype to environmental quality (e.g., amount or quality of training or practice) might differ according to genotype, such that genotypes differed in the range (distribution) of probable levels on the phenotype (e.g., skill) under study. Under this framework, the genotype-specific ranges of skill often overlap, and where within the genotype-specific range a skill level is manifest depends on the quality of the environment, or in this case, the amount of practice. Moreover, the reaction range only applies to the range of environmental experience (practice) observed in the empirical data. While extrapolation to unobserved ranges of quality or amount of environmental experience is possible, there are no guarantees that such extrapolation may be accurate.

We can extend the stylized learning curve presented in Figures 14.1 and 14.2 by situating the accrual of practice within time, thereby allowing for time intervals between repetitions (e.g., practice sessions). As originally described by Ebbinghaus (1885) and depicted in Figure 14.3, some degree of loss may occur during these intervals. This stepwise, or sawtooth, pattern of skill development resembles patterns that feature prominently both in contemporary developmental models of skill development (e.g., Siegler, 1999), and in classical Piagetian models of assimilation of accommodation (Piaget, 1952).

Allowing for the benefit of each individual experience (e.g., practice session) to be differential by genotype creates a pattern of differential accrual of skill over time, illustrated in Figure 14.4. In this example, genotypes engage in equal frequency of practice and differ in the benefit of each practice session. This pattern of initial differences magnifying over time, such that "the rich get richer," has been referred to as a *Matthew Effect* (Stanovich, 1986).

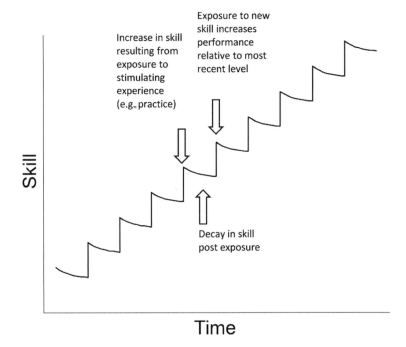

FIGURE 14.3 A stylized hypothetical example of learning response to discrete practice sessions separated in time, and forgetting during the inter-practice interval.

Developmental Concepts of Gene-Environment Transaction

In controlled experiments on learning, the schedule of training and practice is determined by the researcher, and differences between individuals in the pace of learning can be cleanly separated into components associated with manipulation of the training regime (typically the active training condition vs. no-training control), components associated with naturally occurring (oftentimes pre-existing) individual differences in skill, and components associated with individual differences in response to the training or intervention (Tucker-Drob, 2011). However, outside of the laboratory, where most expert skill acquisition actually occurs, the amount, frequency, and intensity of training and practice are nonrandomly experienced by individuals. From a classical experimental perspective, such selection effects are inconveniences that muddle the strength of causal inferences that can be made from observational research. However, selection effects may not simply be methodological nuisances, but rather key mechanisms of the differentiation of phenotypes by genotype "in the wild."

Plomin, DeFries, and Loehlin (1977) described a conceptual taxonomy of genotype-environment correlation, the tendency for exposure to environmental

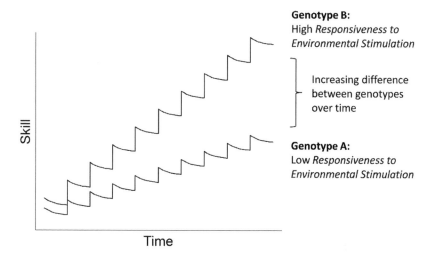

FIGURE 14.4 A stylized hypothetical example of genetic differences in learning response to discrete practice sessions separated in time. Both genotypes are exposed to the same schedule of practice.

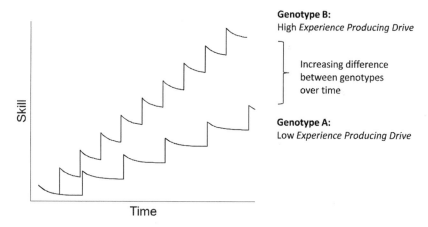

FIGURE 14.5 A stylized hypothetical example of genetic differences in drive to engage in discrete practice. Both genotypes respond equivalently to each discrete practice session, but the genotypes differ in the frequency of practice.

experience to differ systematically by genotype. Passive gene–environment correlation refers to situations in which offspring inherit genes from their biological parents that also influence those parents to provide the rearing environment that they provide to their children. For instance, a parent who has passion for and skill at playing musical instruments may both raise his or her child in an environment that is particularly conducive to fostering the development of musical expertise, and also pass on to that child genetic dispositions for passion and talent for music. Active gene-environment correlations refer to situations in which individuals seek out certain environmental experiences on the basis of their genetically influenced characteristics. For instance, children genetically disposed toward a passion for music may actively pursue musical training. Evocative gene-environment correlation refers to situations in which individuals evoke environmental experiences based on genetically influenced traits from the people and institutions around them. For instance, children who show an early aptitude for playing a musical instrument in the context of a music course that is offered to all students might be encouraged by classmates or selected by teachers to join extracurricular musical training, join a band, or enroll in specialized music coursework.

Active and evocative genotype-environment correlations may serve as the base for dynamic feedback processes in which individuals differentially select and evoke environmental experiences, such as practice, on the basis of their genetically influenced characteristics, and these experiences in turn affect the development of expert skill, while at the same time reinforcing the original characteristics that drove the selection and evocation. Such dynamic feedback processes have come to be termed *gene-environment transactions* (Tucker-Drob, Briley, & Harden, 2013). Characteristics that lead people to differentially select and evoke environmental experiences such as training and practice have been termed *experience-producing drives* (EPDs; Bouchard, 1997; Hayes, 1962; Johnson, 2013). Experience-producing drives may include interests, proclivities, motivations, goals, and aptitudes for the skills being acquired (Tucker-Drob & Harden, in press). As dynamic processes unfold, experience and the skills that benefit from experience are expected to become increasingly differentiated by genotype, again producing a *Matthew Effect* in which the "rich get richer." This is illustrated in Figure 14.5. Importantly, Figure 14.5 illustrates a situation in which the increment in skill that is associated with each specific learning experience (e.g., practice session) is equivalent across genotype, as is the rate of decay of skill post exposure. The genotypes differ only in their frequency of exposure to the learning experience. In other words, the amount of experience comes to be correlated with genotype, such that environmental experience itself is "heritable."

Multiple Processes May Simultaneously Differentiate Skill by Genotype

The processes described above have the potential net effect of differentiating skill by genotype over time. Figure 14.4 depicts a situation in which genotypes differentially benefit from a given practice or training session, but the frequency of practice and training is held constant across genotypes. Figure 14.5 depicts a situation in which genotypes equally benefit from a given practice or training session, but—as a result of differences in motivational factors—the frequency of practice and training is differential by genotype. These processes may of course co-occur, leading to even more rapid differentiation of skill by genotype over time. Additionally, I have cast the former situation in terms of differences in responsivity to environmental stimulation, which lends itself to conceptualizing the different genotypes as corresponding to different inherent aptitudes. However, the former scenario may also stem from genetically influenced individual differences in motivational factors or experience-producing drives leading to differences in the extent to which individuals effortfully engage with the training material or practice. By the same token, the latter scenario could result from feedback processes in which individuals who experience training or practice as being particularly difficult or producing minimal results become less motivated to pursue frequent or intensive practice or training. Thus, both genetically influenced aptitudes and experience-producing drives may play roles in the hypothetical patterns depicted in both Figures 14.4 and 14.5.

Growing Differences Between Genotypes Over Time Imply Increasing Heritability

Thus far, I have characterized genetic effects in terms of differential profiles of skill development by genotype. Importantly, interindividual differences in genetic propensities and aptitudes are unlikely to be distributed into a few discrete categories, but are better described by continuous distributions. I have chosen discrete genotype values for illustrative purposes, in the same way that specific levels of a continuous moderator are chosen for plotting simple slopes in a linear regression with an interaction term. Particularly when one bears in mind that genotypes are continuously distributed, it becomes clear that the patterns of diverging means by genotype that are depicted in Figures 14.2, 14.4, and 14.5 imply increasing heritability of skill over time. As described earlier, heritability refers to the amount of variation in a phenotype (e.g., skill) statistically accounted for by genetic variation, expressed as a proportion of total variation in the phenotype. For instance, in Figure 14.2, it can be seen that mean skill levels for each genotype become increasingly separated as practice accrues, such that genetic differences statistically account for increasing amounts of variation in skill with the accrual of practice. Unless environmental variation unique of the practice itself also explains an increasing amount of variation in skill as practice accrues (such that the relative proportion of genetic variation to total variance remains constant or decreases), the patterns depicted in Figures 14.2, 14.4, and 14.5 directly imply that heritability will increase with the accrual of practice. Indeed, in the area of cognitive ability (which one might consider a form of expertise), there is strong evidence for increasing heritability over child development (Tucker-Drob et al., 2013; Briley & Tucker-Drob, 2013). In the realm of motor learning, Fox and colleagues (1996) reported genetic influences on rate of learning for a rotary pursuit task that resulted in increasing heritability on task performance over the course of practice. More recently, Hambrick and I (Hambrick & Tucker-Drob, 2015) reported evidence of higher heritability of music accomplishment (e.g., performing with a professional orchestra, receiving a high rating in a musical contest) among adolescents who reported regularly practicing a musical instrument, compared to those who reported not practicing. Other patterns are, of course, possible. For instance, if mean skill levels for different genotypes converge after prolonged practice, the implication would be decreasing heritability over time. Ackerman (2007) for instance, proposed that whether a task is *open* (such that there is no upper limit to the skill level that can be attained with further practice or training) or *closed* (such that there is a finite upper level of skill that can be attained) is the major determinant of whether interindividual differences in skill levels will converge or diverge over time.

The "Cafeteria" of Experience and Gene × Environment Interaction

The "cafeteria of experience" (Lykken, Bouchard, McGue, & Tellegen, 1993) refers to the assorted variety of possible experiences to which individuals have access, just as in a dining hall cafeteria where an assortment of food options is available from which to choose. Each individual may choose a different set of experiences (or food items) from the cafeteria, but in a given cafeteria, the same experiences (or food items) are available to everyone.

Scarr and McCartney (1983) proposed that, as infants develop into children, children into adolescents, and adolescents into adults, increasing autonomy to select and evoke environments within their surroundings may lead to increasing differentiation of experience and skill by genotype. Keeping with the cafeteria analogy, we would anticipate that the diversity of experiences from which to choose increases over child development. However, not all individuals have access to the same cafeteria or variety of experiences from which to choose. For instance, some children are never given the opportunity to take piano lessons, or even place their fingers on a piano. In such a case, no matter what an individual's drive, desire, or aptitude for learning piano may be, it is highly unlikely that she or he will be able to engage in piano training or to practice to the extent necessary to become an expert pianist. Thus, one would expect that genetic influences on skilled performance would be most expressed in contexts of high access to the experiences and resources necessary for accruing expertise in the domain under study (Briley & Tucker-Drob, 2015). Indeed there is some evidence that such a pattern applies to the heritability of cognitive ability as a function of socioeconomic opportunity (Tucker-Drob & Bates, 2016). Importantly, the availability of experiences and resources does not guarantee that expertise will be attained (genetically influenced drives and aptitudes are likely to be the other key ingredients), but without a sufficient cafeteria of experience, attaining expert skill levels is predicted to be exceedingly unlikely.

When the differentiation of a phenotype by genotype differs systematically with the quality or amount of environmental experience (such that heritability of that phenotype systematically differs with the quality or amount of environmental experience), this is termed *Gene × Environment interaction.*

Conclusions

In this chapter I have provided a conceptual framework for research into genetic effects on expert skill. This framework explicitly specifies a central role for environmental experience on skill development. I have proposed that genetic variation may relate to skill development both in its relationship to heterogeneity in the effect of training and practice on skill development, and in its relationship to experience-producing drives that lead people to differentially engage in frequent effortful training and practice necessary for high levels of skill development. Further, I have proposed that genetic effects on variation in expert skill level depend on the availability of a cafeteria of experience that includes access to opportunities for training and practice relevant for the skill under investigation.

Acknowledgements

Paige Harden and Laura Engelhardt provided valuable feedback on previous drafts of this chapter.

Note

1 I return to the question of whether more genetically similar people experience more similar environments later in this chapter. As has been discussed in detail elsewhere, behavioral genetic methods rely on the "equal environments" assumption that the average range of experiences to which more genetically similar individuals have access (e.g., MZ twins) have access is no more similar than that to which less genetically similar individuals have access (e.g., DZ twins). As a result of more similar preferences, motivations, and aptitudes, more genetically similar individuals may seek out and evoke more similar experiences from that range over time. This increased similarity of experience among more genetically related similar individuals is not a violation of the equal environments assumption, but potentially a central mechanism of the translation of genetic variation into phenotypic variation.

References

Ackerman, P. L. (2007). New developments in understanding skilled performance. *Current Directions in Psychological Science, 16,* 235–239.

Bouchard, T. J. (1997). Experience producing drive theory: How genes drive experience and shape personality. *Acta Paediatrica, 86*(S422), 60–64.

Briley, D. A., & Tucker-Drob, E. M. (2013). Explaining the increasing heritability of cognition over development: A meta-analysis of longitudinal twin and adoption studies. *Psychological Science, 24,* 1704–1713.

Briley, D. A. & Tucker-Drob, E. M. (2015). Comparing the developmental genetics of cognition and personality over the life span. *Journal of Personality, 85*(1), 51–64.

Ebbinghaus, H. (1885). *Memory: A contribution to experimental psychology.* New York: Dover.

Ericsson, K. A. (2004). Deliberate practice and the acquisition and maintenance of expert performance in medicine and related domains. *Academic Medicine, 79,* S70–S81.

Fox, P. W., Hershberger, S. L., & Bouchard, T. J. (1996). Genetic and environmental contributions to the acquisition of a motor skill. *Nature, 384,* 356–358.

Gottesman, I. I. (1963). Genetic aspects of intelligent behavior. In N. R. Ellis (Ed.), *Handbook of mental deficiency: Psychological theory and research* (pp. 253–296). New York: McGraw-Hill.

Hambrick, D. Z., Macnamara, B. N., Campitelli, G., Ullén, F., & Mosing, M. A. (2016). Chapter One – Beyond born versus made: A new look at expertise. *Psychology of Learning and Motivation, 64,* 1–55.

Hambrick. D. Z., & Tucker-Drob, E. M. (2015). The genetics of music accomplishment: Evidence for gene-environment interaction and correlation. *Psychonomic Bulletin and Review, 22,* 112–120.

Hamer, D. H. (2000). Beware the chopsticks gene. *Molecular Psychiatry, 5*(1), 11–13.

Hayes, K. K. (1962). Genes, drives, and intellect. *Psychological Reports, 10*(2), 299–342.

Johnson, W. (2013). Greatness as a manifestation of experience-producing drives. In S. B. Kaufman (Ed.), *The Complexity of Greatness* (pp. 3–16). Oxford: Oxford University Press.

Lykken, D. T., Bouchard, T. J., McGue, M., & Tellegen, A. (1993). Heritability of interests: A twin study. *Journal of Applied Psychology, 78,* 649–661.

Mendel, J. G. (1865). "Versuche über Pflanzenhybriden", *Verhandlungen des naturforschenden Vereines in Brünn,* Bd. IV für das Jahr, 1865, *Abhandlungen:* 3–47, [1]. For the English translation, see: Druery, C. T., & Bateson, William (1901). Experiments in plant hybridization. *Journal of the Royal Horticultural Society, 26,* 1–32.

Piaget, J. (1952). *The origins of intelligence in children* (Vol. 8, No. 5, pp. 18–1952). New York: International Universities Press.

Plomin, R., DeFries, J. C., & Loehlin, J. C. (1977). Genotype-environment interaction and correlation in the analysis of human behavior. *Psychological Bulletin, 84,* 309.

Scarr, S., & McCartney, K. (1983). How people make their own environments: A theory of genotype→ environment effects. *Child Development, 54*(2), 424–435.

Siegler, R. S. (1999). Strategic development. *Trends in Cognitive Sciences, 3,* 430–435.

Stanovich, K. E. (1986). Matthew effects in reading: Some consequences of individual differences in the acquisition of literacy. *Reading Research Quarterly, 21*(4), 360–407.

Tucker-Drob, E. M. (2011). Individual differences methods for randomized experiments. *Psychological Methods, 16,* 298–318.

Tucker-Drob, E. M., & Bates, T. C. (2016). Large cross-national differences in gene × socioeconomic status interaction on intelligence. *Psychological Science, 27,* 138–149.

Tucker-Drob, E. M., Briley, D. A., & Harden, K. P. (2013). Genetic and environmental influences on cognition across development and context. *Current Directions in Psychological Science, 22,* 349–355.

Turkheimer, E. (1998). Heritability and biological explanation. *Psychological Review, 105,* 782–791.

Ullén, F., Hambrick, D. Z., & Mosing, M. A. (2015). Rethinking expertise: A multifactorial gene–environment interaction model of expert performance. *Psychological Bulletin, 142*(4), 427–446.

Visscher, P. M., Brown, M. A., McCarthy, M. I., & Yang, J. (2012). Five years of GWAS discovery. *The American Journal of Human Genetics, 90,* 7–24.

Yang, J., Lee, S. H., Goddard, M. E., & Visscher, P. M. (2011). GCTA: A tool for genome-wide complex trait analysis. *The American Journal of Human Genetics, 88,* 76–82.

15

THE ETIOLOGY OF READING AND MATH EXPERTISE

The Western Reserve Reading and Math Project

Lee A. Thompson, Carol A. Gross, Susan I. Gross, Sarah Lukowski, and Stephen A. Petrill

Introduction

During childhood and adolescence, academic skills are perhaps the most frequently practiced of all skills. Typical 12-year-olds in the United States spend over 1,000 hours each year in school receiving formal instruction and another 60–90 minutes per night engaged in homework practicing what they learned in school (National Education Association Research Department, 2006). Formal schooling in the United States has heavily emphasized core skills required for reading and arithmetic. Long-term occupational success, socioeconomic status, and health are all influenced by academic performance (Geary, 2011). Behavioral geneticists have made significant progress discovering the etiology of individual differences in reading and math skills, and genetic and environmental influences are known to create variability across the ability continuum for both (Petrill, 2013). More recently, significant effort has been applied to delineating genetic and environmental contributions to low reading ability, including reading disability, and increasing attention has been paid to the development of math skills and the implications for math disability. At the same time, little attention has been paid to understanding the etiology of exceptionally high reading or math ability.

In 2002, we began the Western Reserve Reading and Math Project (WRRMP), a longitudinal twin study in Ohio focused on the etiology of individual differences in reading and math skill development, e.g., Petrill *et al.*, 2010. Initially we were motivated to conduct the study by the dearth of information on how environmental influences impact individual differences in reading acquisition while simultaneously assessing genetic influences. Previous work had demonstrated the overall importance of genetic influences on reading ability and disability, but a longitudinal behavioral genetic study across the early school years had yet to focus on detailed assessments of the reading environment. Over the last

15 years, we broadened the scope of the study to include math achievement and math cognition, transitioned from reading acquisition to reading comprehension, added an additional emphasis on reading and math disabilities, and added collaborators and information from twins in the United Kingdom and Boulder, Colorado (Harlaar, Kovas, Dale, Petrill, & Plomin, 2012; Hart, Petrill, Thompson, & Plomin, 2009; Soden *et al.*, 2015; Willcutt *et al.*, 2013).

The primary goal for this chapter is to build on the results published thus far on the WRRMP twins and extend the findings to explore specifically genetic and environmental contributions to reading and math expertise in children and adolescents. We will also discuss several key issues important for research on expertise. First, how should expertise be defined particularly in the context of the development of reading and math expertise? Second, do reading and math expertise simply represent the high extreme on a continuum of behaviors or can these areas of expertise be best characterized as distinct traits? Third and related to the preceding question, when the etiology of expertise is explored, do genetic and environmental influences operate in a generalist or specialist role? In other words, can we identify specific genes that contribute only to reading or math expertise, or do the same genes contribute to multiple areas of expertise? And is the same true for environmental influences?

A model reflecting the current consensus of empirical work identifying factors contributing to the development of expertise was recently proposed (Ullén, Hambrick, & Mosing, 2016). The Multifactorial Gene-Environment Interaction Model (MGIM) of expert performance encompasses the contribution of traits ranging from physical characteristics, neurobiology, cognitive abilities, personality, interests and motivation, to deliberate practice (see Chapter 21, The Multifactorial Gene-Environment Interaction Model [MGIM] of Expert Performance). Genetic and environmental influences including genotype-environment covariation can contribute directly to expertise and/or to any or all the other characteristics. The model was developed in response to a widely publicized theory of expertise, the deliberate practice theory, which emphasizes the primacy of deliberate practice in determining expert performance across all domains of behavior (Ericsson, 2007, 2014). Ullén and colleagues state, "In short, deliberate practice theory appears incompatible with the findings of a growing number of studies, which show that variables other than deliberate practice are highly relevant to expert performance" (Ullén *et al.*, 2016, p. 433). Clearly, the MGIM resonates much more readily than the deliberate practice theory with what behavioral geneticists have discovered over the last century about the etiology of individual differences in human behavior. This chapter will take what we have learned thus far about reading and math abilities and apply the information to the MGIM to set the stage for future work.

Overview of the Western Reserve Reading and Math Project

Twins in the WRRMP were initially recruited through school nominations, birth records of the state of Ohio, and media advertisements in the Greater

Cleveland Metropolitan area. Once the project was underway, additional twins were added from the entire state. We secured the cooperation of 293 schools across Ohio. The schools sent our packet of information to parents of twins, and the parents contacted us to participate. Since 2002, we have completed 10 waves of assessment. Table 15.1 provides information on the ages for each assessment wave (see supplemental online material (https://osf.io/94h3f/) for a complete list of the assessments administered at each wave). The initial three waves, administered roughly one year apart, began when the twins were in kindergarten or first grade, and these waves primarily assessed early reading and reading-related skills.

Starting with the fourth visit when the twins were approximately 8.5 years of age, we added assessments of math achievement and math cognition. At this point, we added our collaborators working on the Twins Early Development Study led by Robert Plomin (TEDS; Kovas et al., 2007). The TEDS followed longitudinally a sample of over 3,500 pairs of twins recruited from all twins born in England and Wales in 1994, 1995, and 1996 (Trouton, Spinath, & Plomin, 2002). More details on the TEDS will be provided later in this chapter.

We have continued testing the children in the WRRMP across additional visits, which focused on both reading and mathematics. The first nine assessments were conducted in the twins' homes where separate testers were assigned to each twin. The tenth assessment included measures of brain structure, function, and neural connectivity requiring access to magnetic resonance imaging facilities and thus was conducted in laboratory settings in Cleveland or Columbus, Ohio. Overall 468 pairs of same-sex twins and their families have participated in at least one wave of assessment. We determined twins' zygosity using DNA analysis via a cheek swab or saliva samples. For the cases where parents did not consent to genotyping ($n = 76$), we determined zygosity using a parent questionnaire to assess twins' physical similarity (Goldsmith, 1991). Parent education levels varied widely and were similar for fathers and mothers: 12% had a high school education or less, 18% had attended some college, 30% had a bachelor's degree, 24% had some postgraduate training or a degree, and 5% did not specify. Most families were two-parent households (92%) and nearly all self-identified as White (92% of mothers, 94% of fathers).

This chapter will first review what we have learned about genetic and environmental influences on reading and math skills across the continuum. We will then focus on how these influences affect twins selected for a high level of expertise in reading or math. For those unfamiliar with behavioral genetic quantitative analysis approaches, the next section will provide a brief summary (see also Chapter 14, Theoretical Concepts in the Genetics of Expertise).

Quantitative Genetic Methodology: The Twin Study Design

Quantitative genetic methods allow individual differences or variability in a trait to be decomposed into *genetic*, *shared family environment*, and *nonshared* environmental influences (Plomin, DeFries, Knopik, & Neiderhiser, 2013). Genetic

TABLE 15.1 Mean age in years for each assessment and univariate estimates for heritability (h²), shared environment (c²), and nonshared environment (e²) influences for reading achievement and mathematics achievement composite scores.

Assessment Wave	Mean Age in Years	Reading Achievement			Mathematics Achievement		
		h²	c²	e²	h²	c²	e²
1	6.09 ± 0.69	.58 (.44, .73)	.26 (.12, .39)	.16 (.13, .19)	.39 (.15, .59)	.13 (0, .33)	.48 (.40, .56)
2	7.16 ± 0.67	.48 (.34, .63)	.35 (.20, .47)	.17 (.14, .22)	.17 (0, .43)	.16 (0, .34)	.68 (.56, .78)
3	8.21 ± 0.82	.63 (.48, .79)	.20 (.04, .34)	.17 (.14, .21)	.00 (0, .28)	.24 (.01, .31)	.76 (.69, .84)
4	8.57 ± 0.50	.41 (.16, .65)	.33 (.11, .51)	.27 (.20, .37)	.15 (0, .35)	.58 (.40, .72)	.27 (.20, .37)
5	9.81 ± 0.98	.85 (.81, .88)	0 (0, .13)	.15 (.12, .19)	.39 (.27, .53)	.46 (.33, .57)	.15 (.12, .18)
6	10.90 ± 1.01	.67 (.50, .83)	.13 (0, .29)	.20 (.16, .25)	.20 (.05, .35)	.56 (.43, .68)	.24 (.19, .30)
7	12.21 ± 1.20	.67 (.47, .87)	.07 (0, .24)	.27 (.22, .33)	—	—	—
8	12.25 ± 1.20	—	—	—	.39 (.26, .54)	.43 (.29, .55)	.18 (.14, .22)
9	15.05 ± 1.45	.49 (0, .75)	.11 (0, .49)	.40 (.25, .66)	.36 (.23, .53)	.50 (.34, .63)	.13 (.10, .17)

influences are represented statistically by the term "heritability" or "h^2" which is defined as the proportion of the total variance in a trait explained by genetic variance. Many behavioral genetic studies substitute the term "a^2" in place of "h^2" to reflect that only additive genetic influences are represented. Shared family environment or "c^2" captures aspects of the environment that family members experience together making them more alike than two individuals randomly drawn from a population. Finally, nonshared environment, or "e^2," represents environmental factors that each individual uniquely experiences, thus creating phenotypic differences among family members. Measurement error is also included in estimates of "e^2." Traditionally, behavioral geneticists have primarily relied on family, twin, and adoption designs whereby comparisons of the resemblance between family members who share different proportions of genetic material allow statistical modeling approaches to estimate the contributions of genetic and environmental influences. As molecular genetic techniques have advanced and individual genotypes for a large number of polymorphic loci can be determined quickly and affordably in samples of unrelated individuals, Genome-wide Complex Trait Analysis (GCTA) has been applied to the study of complex human traits. GCTA directly measures the genetic similarity of individuals by genotyping thousands (Petrill & Kovas, 2016) of loci across the genome for each individual in the sample and can then compare phenotypic similarity to genetic similarity. This chapter will focus primarily on the twin study approach (Petrill, 2013) which has been the most frequently applied to the study of reading and math ability. Briefly, identical or *monozygotic* (MZ) twins develop when, not long after conception during the cell division process, a fertilized egg splits into two separate sets of cells and each continues to develop into a separate embryo; therefore, MZ twins share all of the same genetic material. In contrast, fraternal or *dizygotic* (DZ) twins develop when two sperm fertilize two separate eggs which gestate at the same time. DZ twins share the same degree of genetic resemblance as full-siblings and share on average 50% of their additive genes. When MZ twin-within-pair comparisons are more alike than DZ twin-within-pair comparisons, genetic influences are implicated. To the extent that within-pair resemblance for both MZ and DZ twins is greater than what would be expected by heritability alone, shared family environmental effects are implicated. Finally, when MZ twin resemblance is less than 100%, the effect of nonshared environmental influences are estimated. Twin variances and covariances are typically analyzed with structural equation modeling packages such as Mx (Neale, Boker, Xie, & Maes, 2003) which provide an overall goodness-of-fit index and allow for comparison of reduced models to determine the individual significance of contributions from heritability, shared, and nonshared environment, respectively. Table 15.1 provides estimates of heritability, shared, and nonshared environment for composites representing reading and math across all of the assessment waves in the WRRMP.

Genetic and Environmental Influences on Academic Achievement in Reading and Reading-Related Skills

Behavior genetics analyses using data from the WRRMP and TEDS have evaluated the role of genetics, shared environment, and nonshared environment on individual differences in reading outcomes for children across the range of reading achievement and across age. When examining individual differences in reading, a fundamental shift occurs in the core skills needed around the third grade (Hart, Petrill, & Thompson, 2010) when children switch from the acquisition of core skills—*phonological awareness, rapid automatized naming, orthographic coding*—needed to read fluidly where they apply their reading skill to understand information conveyed by text, in other words, *reading comprehension*. In general, genetic contributions to reading and reading acquisition are significant across the school years. In contrast, shared environmental factors account for a majority of the variation in reading skills prior to and upon first entering school (Hart & Petrill, 2009). After children enter school and begin engaging in the standard curriculum where school environments are relatively and consistently similar, genetics begin to account for more variation than the shared environment, with an increasing share of the variance accounted for by genetics as the child develops.

The early school years appear to be an essential time of skill development in reading. To examine the stability of particular foundational skills, Stephen Petrill and colleagues (Petrill *et al.*, 2007) examined scores for children at 6 and 7 years old in the WRRMP on *phonological awareness, rapid automatized naming, expressive vocabulary, letter knowledge, word knowledge, phonological decoding*, and *passage comprehension*. They found that genetic influences accounted for the stability of all variables except for rapid automatized naming, and shared environment effects influenced stability in phonological awareness, expressive vocabulary, and letter knowledge. Therefore, foundational skills that are thought to precede reading comprehension appear to have stable influences from early shared environments.

Overall, Petrill and colleagues (2007) found that stability in most reading skills was influenced by both genetic and shared environmental factors, but is that also the case for growth in reading skills? To determine the general trends of reading over time and also to examine how growth in reading is related to genetics and shared environment, Logan and colleagues (Logan *et al.*, 2013) used latent growth curve modeling to examine, over a six-year period, word attack, word identification, reading comprehension, and rapid naming in children from age 6 to age 12 in the WRRMP sample. Overall, children showed growth in reading from age 6 to 12, but the reading achievement growth slowed over time so that children tended to make rapid gains in reading early and smaller gains later. The direction of the trends showed that children who began the study with high scores on reading measures had lower growth rates than children with low scores because the early high achievers did not have as much room to grow over time.

Because the study included twin pairs, Logan and colleagues examined the genetic factors that influenced at what reading level the children began and the genetics that influenced how quickly their reading improved. They found that the genetics that determined where children began in their level of reading were different from the genetics that determined their improvement. Therefore, once children enter school, genes different from those that determined their starting point then become relevant for predicted growth in reading. The shared environment showed a different pattern, in which the shared environment effects at 6 years old (i.e., print exposure, home literacy environment) were also influential on the growth trajectory of the child, indicating that early environments continue to have an effect on later growth even after the child enters school.

To encourage growth in reading skills, teachers and parents encourage students to read as much as they can, since it is widely known that higher frequency of reading is associated with higher reading achievement. However, it has not been clear in past research if children have better reading skills because of more frequent reading or if children who perform highly on reading tests have positive experiences reading and thus engage in the behavior more often. Harlaar and colleagues (Harlaar, Deater-Deckard, Thompson, Dethorne, & Petrill, 2011) attempted to dissect the direction of the relationship between the two variables in children age 10 and 11 in the WRRMP study. They found that frequency of independent reading at age 11, as measured by a child's self-report and a parent's report, was associated with reading achievement (passage comprehension and word identification) at age 10 (after controlling for independent reading at age 10) but frequency of independent reading at age 10 was not associated with reading achievement at age 11 (after controlling for reading achievement at age 10). In addition, independent reading at age 11 and reading achievement at age 10 shared a genetic component. Therefore, the relationship between independent reading and reading achievement is partly due to common genetic influences.

Reading comprehension is the ultimate goal of teaching children to read. After children can fluently read and understand the written word, they begin to use reading as a tool for learning. To find out how genetics and shared environment contribute to reading comprehension during the critical elementary school period, Soden and colleagues (2015) examined data from the WRRMP and International Longitudinal Twin Study (ILTS; Byrne *et al.*, 2009) in first through sixth grade and first, second, and fourth grade, respectively, on their performance on the Woodcock Reading Mastery Test-Revised Passage Comprehension subtest (Woodcock, 1987). A stable genetic influence was shown in both samples, and new genetic influence was significant only in Grade 1, indicating that reading comprehension has a strong genetic influence that is consistent from Grades 1 through 6. Shared environment was most influential at Grades 1 and 2 but was not significant in Grades 3 through 6. New unshared environment and error and stable genetic influences accounted for most of the variance in Grades 2 through 6.

In general, reading skill development is influenced largely by genetics once children enter school, but does that general trend hold for children at the ends of the distribution? Logan and colleagues (Logan *et al.*, 2012) developed a quantile regression method in order to answer this question and found differences in the contribution of genetics, shared environment, and nonshared environment/ error for different reading components and across the skill distribution. First grade twins in the WRRMP study were given tests to assess reading fluency for real words (how quickly they could read real words), reading fluency for non-words, phonological awareness (phonemic segmentation and deletion) and vocabulary using the Woodcock Reading Mastery Test Word Identification subtest (Woodcock, 1987), Woodcock Reading Mastery Test Word attack subtest, Phonological Awareness Test (Robertson & Salter, 1997), and Stanford Binet Vocabulary subtest (Thorndike, Hagen, & Sattler, 1986), respectively. The estimated heritability of phonological awareness did not change based upon the level of skill ($h^2 = .57$, $c^2 = .26$). In contrast, as scores increased on word attack and word identification, heritability estimates decreased, and shared environment increased. The estimates for heritability of the whole sample may differ when you restrict the range to a certain portion (either low or high), and there is evidence in our data that vocabulary, word identification, and word attack— but not phonological awareness—have a pattern of higher heritability across the whole distribution compared to the tails, and the tails have higher shared environmental variance. That phonological awareness is showing a different pattern compared to the other reading components is interesting and may be attributed to the role of phonological awareness as a precursor of the other skills.

Genetic and Environmental Influences on Academic Achievement in Mathematics

Compared to the study of individual differences in reading achievement, behavioral genetic studies of achievement in mathematics have been sparse (Petrill & Kovas, 2016). Prior to 2004, only a handful of twin and adoption studies reported estimates of heritability and of shared and nonshared environmental influences on math achievement. The studies varied widely in terms of the age of participants within each sample, as well as the measures used (Hart, Petrill, Thompson & Plomin, 2009), making it difficult to form generalizable conclusions. In the last decade, two longitudinal twin studies have provided considerable information on the etiology of individual differences in math achievement: the TEDS (Kovas *et al.*, 2007) and the WRRMP (Hart, Petrill, Thompson & Plomin, 2009).

Several reports on the TEDS include in-depth assessments of math collected via online testing on over 2,600 pairs of twins (Harlaar *et al.*, 2012; Kovas *et al.*, 2007) and based on items from the National Foundation for Educational Research 5–14 Mathematics Series (nferNelson, 2001). When the twins were assessed at approximately 10 years of age, the impact of genetic factors on all math achievement measures ranged from .32 to .45; the impact of shared environment ranged from .07 to .23; and the impact of nonshared environment ranged from .42 to .48 (Kovas *et al.*, 2007). At 12 years of age, 1,627 pairs of MZ twins and 2,092 pairs of DZ twins were assessed and the impact of genetic influences ranged from .42 to .50, shared environment ranged from .08 to.16, and nonshared environment from .37 to.44.

In the WRRMP, all twins were assessed in person by a trained tester on a wide range of math achievement and math cognition measures beginning in the 4th assessment wave when the twins were approximately 8.5 years of age. In contrast to the results in the TEDS, heritability estimates for measures collected at approximately ages 8.5 and 10 were somewhat lower ranging from .00 to .63, shared family environmental influences were somewhat higher ranging from .15 to .50 and nonshared environmental influences ranged from .14 to.50 (Hart, Petrill, Thompson & Plomin, 2009).

Etiology of High Reading and Math Performance

The literature on expertise presents differing views on how "expertise" should be defined and studied. In this chapter, we choose to define expertise, along the same lines as Plomin, Shakeshaft, McMillan, & Trzaskowski (2014, p. 47), as "exceptional performance." As we ask questions about the attributes and experiences that distinguish experts from non-experts in the real world, we posit, much like Plomin and colleagues, that studying the development of reading and math expertise in twins provides a perfect testing ground for hypotheses seeking to explain the origins of expertise. Typically, for at least 12 consecutive years, children spend 9 months or more every year receiving in-depth instruction and engagement in a significant amount of dedicated practice with the goal of mastering reading and math skills. Thus far, we have focused on the etiology of individual differences across the continuum for reading and math achievement measures. Typically, we assume that the same proportion of genetic and environmental influences affecting the majority of individuals in the middle of the distribution affect the individuals at the low and high extremes of the continuum. However, it is not hard to imagine plausible scenarios where genetic or environmental factors may differ in their impact at the low and high extreme. For example, the low end of the distribution for reading and math often includes individuals diagnosed with specific learning disabilities or intellectual disabilities and several large twin studies have set out to understand the etiology of reading disability (Hart & Petrill, 2009). In fact, one of the first successful quantitative genetic studies, which was searching for specific genes associated with a complex polygenic trait, identified a gene on chromosome 6 which contributes to the risk for reading disability (Cardon *et al.*, 1994). This link has since been replicated in several additional studies suggesting that specific genes may impact the low end of the reading ability continuum differently than the rest of the distribution. While fewer studies have targeted math disability, there is some evidence that individuals diagnosed with genetic disorders demonstrate specific deficits in math ability (Baker & Reiss, 2016; Libertus, Feigenson, Halberda, & Landau, 2014). One example is Turner's Syndrome, the chromosomal anomaly involving a missing X chromosome where females diagnosed with the syndrome consistently perform more poorly than those without the syndrome in cognitive tests requiring visuo-spatial thinking (Baker & Reiss, 2016).

When the tails of a continuous distribution are selected for analysis as in the case of reading and math ability, standard twin analyses involving the decomposition of variances and covariances are not appropriate due to the restriction in range and violations of normality in the distribution of scores (DeFries & Fulker, 1985). Behavioral geneticists have developed several different analytic approaches to allow for the estimation of genetic and environmental influences on traits in highly selected samples (Bailey & Revelle, 1991; Cherny, Cardon, Fulker, & DeFries, 1992). The most popular approaches include an analysis of twin-pair concordances (Kovas *et al.*, 2007), liability threshold analysis (Kovas *et al.*, 2007), DeFries-Fulker (DeFries & Fulker, 1985), and most recently quantile regression (Logan *et al.*, 2012). Each approach has strengths and weaknesses, and we have decided to focus on applications of the DF analysis approach because the approach balances the ability to examine genetic and environmental contributions to the average ability of extreme groups despite violations of normality and restriction of range with adequate power when the sample size is relatively small.

For any continuously distributed phenotype, DF analyses essentially compare selected MZ and DZ co-twin means (DeFries & Fulker, 1985). If the DZ co-twin mean regresses toward the unselected population mean more than the MZ co-twin mean, then genetic influences are presumed to contribute to the difference between the selected group's mean and the unselected population mean. As with classical twin analysis which decomposes variances and covariances, the DF approach capitalizes on the fact that, from a genetic perspective, MZ twins share 100% of their additive genetic variance and DZ twins only share on average 50%. Therefore, if the MZ and DZ co-twin means regress equally toward the sample mean, then there are shared environmental effects on achievement among experts. Conversely, if the MZ and DZ co-twin means are not significantly different from the unselected population mean, then nonshared environmental influences are contributing to the extreme group. While a t-test can determine whether the MZ and DZ co-twin means are significantly different, the DF approach applies the multiple regression equation $C = B_1P + B_2R = A$, where C = Co-twin score, P = Proband score, R = coefficient of relationship (MZ=1, DZ = .5), A = constant. The use of double-entered twin data allows for each individual in the twin pair to be selected as the proband such that concordant pairs are used twice in the analysis. When all the scores are transformed by dividing each by the proband mean prior to applying the regression analysis, B_2 directly estimates group heritability (h^2_g); however, standard errors must be corrected for the true sample size.

To explore the etiology of reading and math expertise in our sample, we opted to focus on measures collected in the 7th and 8th assessment waves when twins were approximately 12 years of age. These assessments provided the most complete reading and math information on the largest subset of the WRRMP twins at the highest grade level thus far in our longitudinal study. Furthermore, work in previous studies looking at reading and math expertise in twins included assessments collected at about the same age.

The genetic and environmental influences underlying reading and math achievement in expert groups were calculated using the basic DF model (DeFries & Fulker, 1985). The experts were selected to fall in the top 15% for achievement in either math or reading and their co-twins' scores were analyzed. When creating extreme groups within an unselected sample for a continuous trait, the determination of cut-off scores is always somewhat subjective. We chose the top 15%, approximately 1 standard deviation above the mean, because it provided a reasonably sized sample for the extreme group and because previous studies also applied this threshold (Petrill, Kovas, Hart, Thompson, & Plomin, 2009). Figure 15.1 presents the results for math achievement, the MZ co-twin mean is .94 and the DZ co-twin mean is .49. Again, the DZ co-twin mean regresses to the unselected sample mean of zero more than the MZ co-twin mean.

The group heritability of math expertise is estimated to be .78 ± .27; therefore, approximately 78% of the mean difference between math experts and non-experts in math is accounted for by genetic factors. Individual-differences heritability for math achievement in the entire unselected sample is 39%. The results of DF analyses for reading achievement were similar to those for math achievement. The MZ co-twin mean is 1.08 and the DZ co-twin mean is .49. Because the DZ co-twin mean regresses toward the sample mean of zero more than the MZ co-twin mean, reading achievement has genetic influences within the expert group. Group heritability for reading expertise is estimated at .72 ± .28, meaning about 72% of the mean difference in reading achievement between the reading experts and the reading non-experts is the result of genetic differences between the two groups. Individual-differences heritability of reading achievement for the entire sample is .67 ±.20.

Taken together, these results indicate that genetic influences on reading expertise are similar across the distribution. This finding is consistent with previous reports from other studies examining high and low reading ability (Plomin et al., 2014). Reading ability is highly heritable across age and across the ability continuum. In contrast, the difference between h^2_g and h^2 for math expertise in the WRRMP is quite a bit larger; however, we have limited statistical power to detect differences unless they are extremely large.

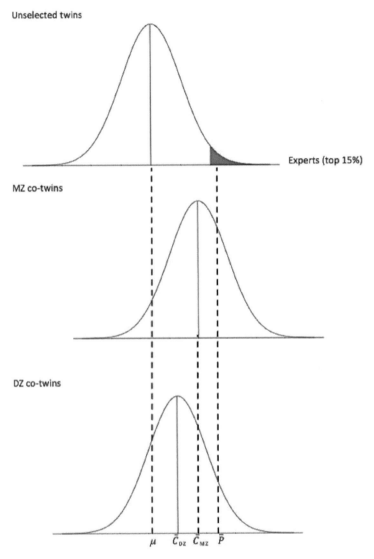

FIGURE 15.1 Proband and co-twin means for math in the unselected and selected for 85th percentile and above samples where the Proband mean is 1.50, the MZ co-twin mean is .94, and the DZ co-twin mean is .49.

From a developmental perspective, we can take a first pass at examining longitudinal stability and change for high math performance. We had a total of 794 children participating in the study at age 6 years, and 90 of these children were in the top 15% for math. Of these 90 children, 18 were in the top 15% 6 years later when they were on average 12 years old. Furthermore, within this group of 18, 7 were from DZ twin pairs and none of the pairs were concordant while 5 of the 6 MZ pairs were concordant. Although the sample size is very small and provides limited power to detect even moderate effect sizes, the pattern of higher developmental stability for MZ twin pairs compared to DZ twin pairs is compatible with the hypothesis that genetic influences play at least a partial role in determining high math performance throughout the early school years.

How does a higher heritability for high math performance translate to the real world in terms of improving education? Group heritability for high math accounts for 78% of the mean difference between the unselected sample and the top 15%, while shared environmental influences are not significant for the selected group. In contrast, shared environmental influences contribute to individual differences in math for the unselected sample. A reasonable explanation for this pattern of results is that for the selected high-performing sample, the environment has been optimally configured for the development and execution of math ability such that the environment is a constant for the top 15% of the sample allowing genes to be more fully expressed. Environmental influences for the unselected sample are more variable in nature and operate to limit gene expression.

The results from the WRRMP consistently demonstrate the importance of genetic factors for determining individual differences across the ability range for both reading and math. Interestingly, our examination of the top 15% of the children for math performance may indicate that genetic factors are even more important for math expertise. However, we have also consistently demonstrated that genes are not the sole influence on either reading or math abilities. Historically, the developmental psychology literature had focused a great deal on the age-old "nature versus nurture controversy" and until recently not enough on a more balanced perspective that recognizes the complex interplay between genes and environment including genotype-environment interaction and correlation (Plomin *et al.*, 2013).

The literature on expert performance has paralleled developmental psychology and lagged slightly behind (Ullén *et al.*, 2016) with a heavy emphasis on the role of the environment in the form of deliberate practice (Ericsson, 2014). We were delighted to discover that Ullén and colleagues (2016) address the need to incorporate a more complete view of factors that likely impact the development of expert performance with the MGIM. Of particular note, this model not only includes genetic and environmental contributions and GxE covariation, it recognizes that multiple phenotypes can contribute to expert performance along with their respective sets of genes and environments. For example, other phenotypes that likely impact math performance include general cognitive ability, visuo-spatial skills, magnitude estimation, impulsivity and/or anxiety, motivation, number of years in school, and neural efficiency. Individual variation in each of these phenotypes will be impacted by "specialist" genes and environments and also by genes and environments that are shared across all or subsets of phenotypes therefore operating in a "generalist" fashion (for details, see Plomin, Kovas, & Haworth, 2007). While we are not yet to the point where we can test the full MGIM in the WRRMP, we have examined specific portions of the model.

Just as univariate behavioral genetic models decompose phenotypic similarity for identical and fraternal twins into genetic and environmental parameters, multivariate behavioral genetic models decompose phenotypic variances and covariances to estimate genetic and environmental contributions that are overlapping or independent among phenotypes (Plomin *et al.*, 2013). We wondered how much of the genetic and environmental influences affecting math also impacted reading and general cognitive ability? When we looked at the first five assessment waves analyzed together, in general, multivariate analyses suggest that general cognitive ability and math are influenced in part by overlapping genes and environment and that the same is true for reading and math performance (Hart, Petrill, Thompson & Plomin, 2009). A strength of the WRRMP is the depth and breadth of the assessments conducted because multivariate analyses can compare similarities and differences across specific math and reading skills. For example, in contrast to math calculation (WJ-III Calculation), problem solving (WJ-III Applied Problems), and conceptual understanding of math (WJ-III Quantitative Concepts), math fluency (WJ-III Fluency) had significant independent genetic influences (Woodcock, McGraw, & Mather, 2001). In addition, the overlap between math measures and reading decoding (Word ID, WRMT; Woodcock, 1987) and reading fluency (Rapid Letter Naming and Rapid Digit Naming subtests from the CTOPP; Wagner, Torgesen, & Rashotte, 1999) varied such that math measures requiring reading shared significant genetic overlap with reading decoding and general cognitive ability, while math measures not requiring reading did not. In contrast, overlapping shared environmental influences were identified for general cognitive ability and reading decoding across all of the math measures, but no overlapping shared environmental influences were found for general cognitive ability and reading fluency with any of the math measures. Results from these analyses (Hart, Petrill, Thompson & Plomin, 2009) in relation to the MGIM model call for additional work exploring the mix of cognitive phenotypes for math experts affected by overlapping genetic and shared environmental factors.

Research on educational outcomes has explored in great depth the role of noncognitive traits on academic success, most notably motivation, temperament and personality, and affect. In the WRRMP we have been particularly intrigued by the role of specific math anxiety on math achievement (Wang *et al.*, 2014). In assessment wave 8 when the twins were about 12 years old, we asked the twins to complete the Math Anxiety Rating Scale of Elementary Students (Suinn, Taylor, & Edwards, 1988) and the Spence Children's Anxiety Scale (Spence, 1998) to assess math-specific anxiety and general anxiety, respectively. Genetic influences accounted for roughly 40% of the variation in math anxiety, with the remaining accounted for by specific environmental factors. Multivariate genetic analyses indicated that math anxiety was impacted by genetic and nonfamilial environmental risk factors associated with general anxiety and with independent genetic influences associated with math-based problem solving. The development of math anxiety may involve not only exposure to negative experiences with mathematics, but also likely involves genetic risks related to both anxiety and math cognition. While the literature is clear that high math anxiety negatively impacts math performance, the opposite relationship—low math anxiety leads to high math performance—cannot be assumed. Lyons and Beilock (2012) suggest that a U-shaped curve can best describe the relationship between math anxiety and performance with moderate levels of anxiety resulting in the best performance. This finding may implicate that anxiety level impacts motivation, where moderate anxiety acts as an "energizer" to engage in challenging cognitive tasks. In the WRRMP, using the same assessment wave and measures detailed in the previous section with the addition of three questionnaire items assessing math motivation taken from a larger motivation scale (Chiu & Xihua, 2008), we explored the relationship between math anxiety and motivation in regard to the impact on math performance (Wang *et al.*, 2015). In summary, children who were intrinsically motivated in math demonstrated an inverted-U relation between math anxiety and performance. Children who were less intrinsically motivated in math demonstrated a negative linear relation between math anxiety and performance. While we did not specifically explore whether this pattern can be extrapolated to the subgroup of children who score exceptionally high on math assessments, the results suggest that the ideal mix of phenotypes would be high intrinsic motivation and moderate anxiety.

Currently, the twins in the WRRMP are participating in our 10th wave of assessment, and the average age for this wave is 15.5 years. In this assessment, the twins visited neuroimaging labs at either the Ohio State University or at Case Western Reserve University, whichever location was more convenient. We are in the process of collecting fMRI data while the twins engage in tasks representing working memory, numerical estimation, and reading comprehension. Additional scans were also conducted to allow us to assess resting state connectivity and neural networks via diffusion tensor imaging (DTI). In the near future, we will be able to provide insight on aspects of brain function and structure, and neural networks affecting the variance and covariance in working memory, math, and reading for the entire unselected sample and for selected twins in the top 15% for math and reading. Just as behavioral phenotypes can be analyzed through the application of twin models to estimate genetic and environmental influences, the etiology of neuroimaging phenotypes can also be explored. If neuroimaging phenotypes operate as *endophenotypes*—biologically based traits that are closer to the genotype—they may provide really interesting information on the foundations of math and reading expertise.

Conclusions

The framework proposed by Ullén *et al.*'s (2016) MGIM model provides an extremely useful big-picture map for future research on the etiology of expertise. Behavioral genetic research and, in particular, twin research can address almost every category of influences identified in the model. In this chapter, we have provided an in-depth look at the impact of genes and environment on reading and math expertise, and have shown how our previously published work on other traits lends support to the applicability of the full model for further work on reading and math expertise. We hope that our continued work on the WRRMP will allow us to simultaneously analyze and describe the role that each category of influences depicted in the MGIM plays in determining reading and math expertise.

Acknowledgement

This work was supported by National Institute of Child Health and Human Development (NICHD) Grants HD38075, HD046167, HD0592, HD075460.

References

Bailey, J. M., & Revelle, W. (1991). Increased heritability for lower IQ levels? *Behavior Genetics*, *21*(4), 397–404.

Baker, J. M., & Reiss, A. L. (2016). A meta-analysis of math performance in Turner syndrome. *Developmental Medicine & Child Neurology*, *58*(2), 123–130. doi:10.1111/dmcn.12961

Byrne, B., Coventry, W. L., Olson, R. K., Samuelsson, S., Corley, R., Willcutt, E. G., ... DeFries, J. C. (2009). Genetic and environmental influences on aspects of literacy and language in early childhood: Continuity and change from preschool to grade 2. *Journal of Neurolinguistics*, *22*(3), 219–236. doi:10.1016/j.jneuroling.2008.09.003

Cardon, L. R., Smith, S. D., Fulker, D. W., Kimberling, W. J., Pennington, B. F., & DeFries, J. C. (1994). Quantitative trait locus for reading disability on chromosome 6. *Science*, *266*(5183), 276–279. doi:10.1126/science.7939663

Cherny, S. S., Cardon, L. R., Fulker, D. W., & DeFries, J. C. (1992). Differential heritability across levels of cognitive ability. *Behavior Genetics*, *22*(2), 153–162.

Chiu, M. M., & Xihua, Z. (2008). Family and motivation effects on mathematics achievement: Analyses of students in 41 countries. *Learning and Instruction*, *18*(4), 321–336. http://dx.doi.org/10.1016/j.learninstruc.2007.06.003

DeFries, J. C., & Fulker, D. W. (1985). Multiple regression analysis of twin data. *Behavior Genetics*, *15*(5), 467–473. doi:10.1007/BF01066239

Ericsson, K. A. (2007). Deliberate practice and the modifiability of body and mind: Toward a science of the structure and acquisition of expert and elite performance. *International Journal of Sport Psychology*, *38*(1), 4–34.

Ericsson, K. A. (2014). Why expert performance is special and cannot be extrapolated from studies of performance in the general population: A response to criticisms. *Intelligence*, *45*, 81–103. doi:10.1016/j.intell.2013.12.001

Geary, D. C. (2011). Cognitive predictors of achievement growth in mathematics: A 5-year longitudinal study. *Developmental Psychology, 47*(6), 1539–1552. http://dx.doi.org/10.1037/a0025510

Goldsmith, H. H. (1991). A zygosity questionnaire for young twins: A research note. *Behavior Genetics, 21*(3), 257–269. doi:10.1007/BF01065819

Harlaar, N., Deater-Deckard, K., Thompson, L. A., Dethorne, L. S., & Petrill, S. A. (2011). Associations between reading achievement and independent reading in early elementary school: A genetically informative cross-lagged study. *Child Development, 82*(6), 2123–2137. doi:10.1111/j.1467-8624.2011.01658.x

Harlaar, N., Kovas, Y., Dale, P. S., Petrill, S. A., & Plomin, R. (2012). Mathematics is differentially related to reading comprehension and word decoding: Evidence from a genetically sensitive design. *Journal of Educational Psychology, 104*(3), 622–635. doi:10.1037/a0027646

Hart, S. A., & Petrill, S. A. (2009). The genetics and environments of reading: A behavioral genetic perspective. In Y. Kim (Ed.), *Handbook of behavior genetics* (1st ed., pp. 113). New York, NY: Springer.

Hart, S. A., Petrill, S. A., DeThorne, L. S., Deater-Deckard, K., Thompson, L. A., Schatschneider, C., & Cutting, L. E. (2009). Environmental influences on the longitudinal covariance of expressive vocabulary: Measuring the home literacy environment in a genetically sensitive design. *Journal of Child Psychology and Psychiatry, and Allied Disciplines, 50*(8), 911–919. doi:10.1111/j.1469-7610.2009.02074.x

Hart, S. A., Petrill, S. A., & Thompson, L. A. (2010). A factorial analysis of timed and untimed measures of mathematics and reading abilities in school aged twins. *Learning and Individual Differences, 20*(2), 63–69. doi:10.1016/j.lindif.2009.10.004

Hart, S. A., Petrill, S. A., Thompson, L. A., & Plomin, R. (2009). The ABCs of math: A genetic analysis of mathematics and its links with reading ability and general cognitive ability. *Journal of Educational Psychology, 101*(2), 388–402. doi:10.1037/a0015115

Kovas, Y., Haworth, C. M. A., Harlaar, N., Petrill, S. A., Dale, P. S., & Plomin, R. (2007). Overlap and specificity of genetic and environmental influences on mathematics and reading disability in 10-year-old twins. *Journal of Child Psychology and Psychiatry, and Allied Disciplines, 48*(9), 914–922.

Libertus, M. E., Feigenson, L., Halberda, J., & Landau, B. (2014). Understanding the mapping between numerical approximation and number words: Evidence from Williams syndrome and typical development. *Developmental Science, 17*(6), 905–919. doi:10.1111/desc.12154

Logan, J. A. R., Hart, S. A., Cutting, L., Deater-Deckard, K., Schatschneider, C., & Petrill, S. (2013). Reading development in young children: Genetic and environmental influences. *Child Development, 84*(6), 2131–2144. doi:10.1111/cdev.12104

Logan, J. A. R., Petrill, S. A., Hart, S. A., Schatschneider, C., Thompson, L. A., Deater-Deckard, K., … Bartlett, C. (2012). Heritability across the distribution: An application of quantile regression. *Behavior Genetics, 42*(2), 256–267. doi:10.1007/s10519-011-9497-7

Lyons, I. M., & Beilock, S. L. (2012). When math hurts: Math anxiety predicts pain network activation in anticipation of doing math. *PLoS ONE, 7*(10), 1–6. doi:10.1371/journal.pone.0048076

National Education Association Research Department. (2006). *Bridging the great homework divide: A solutions guide for parents of middle school students.* (No. ED496302). Washington DC: National Education Association.

Neale, M., Boker, S. M., Xie, G., & Maes, H. H. (2003). *MX: Statistical modeling* (6th ed.). Richmond, VA: Department of Psychiatry, Virginia Commonwealth University.

nferNelson. (2001). *Mathematics 5-14 series*. London: nferNelson Publishing Company.

Petrill, S. A. (2013). Behavioral genetics, learning abilities, and disabilities. In H. L. Swanson, K. R. Harris, & S. Graham (Eds.), *Handbook of learning disabilities*, (pp. 293–306). New York: Guilford Press

Petrill, S. A., Deater-Deckard, K., Thompson, L. A., Schatschneider, C., DeThorne, L. S., & Vandenbergh, D. J. (2007). Longitudinal genetic analysis of early reading: The western reserve reading project. *Reading and Writing: An Interdisciplinary Journal, 20*(1–2), 127–146. http://dx.doi.org/10.1007/s11145-006-9021-2

Petrill, S. A., Hart, S. A., Harlaar, N., Logan, J., Justice, L. M., Schatschneider, C., … Cutting, L. (2010). Genetic and environmental influences on the growth of early reading skills. *Journal of Child Psychology and Psychiatry, and Allied Disciplines, 51*(6), 660–667. doi:10.1111/j.1469-7610.2009.02204.x

Petrill, S. A., & Kovas, Y. (2016). Individual differences in mathematics ability: A behavioral genetic approach. In D. B. Berch, D. C. Geary, K. Mann Koepke (Eds.), *Development of mathematical cognition: Neural substrates and genetic influences* (Vol. 2, *Mathematical Cognition and Learning*) (pp. 299–332). San Diego, CA, US: Elsevier Academic Press. doi:10.1016/B978-0-12-801871-2.00011-3

Petrill, S. A., Kovas, Y., Hart, S. A., Thompson, L. A., & Plomin, R. (2009). The genetic and environmental etiology of high math performance in 10-year-old twins. *Behavior Genetics, 39*(4), 371–379. doi:10.1007/s10519-009-9258-z

Plomin, R., Kovas, Y., & Haworth, C. A. (2007). Generalist genes: Genetic links between brain, mind, and education. *Mind, Brain, And Education, 1*(1), 11–19. doi:10.1111/j.1751228X.2007.00002.x

Plomin, R., DeFries, J. C., Knopik, V., & Neiderhiser, J. (2013). *Behavioral genetics* (6th ed.). New York, NY: Worth.

Plomin, R., Shakeshaft, N. G., McMillan, A., & Trzaskowski, M. (2014). Nature, nurture, and expertise. *Intelligence, 45*, 46–59. doi:10.1016/j.intell.2013.06.008

Robertson, C., & Salter, W. (1997). *The phonological awareness test*. East Moline, IL: LinguiSystems.

Soden, B., Christopher, M. E., Hulslander, J., Olson, R. K., Cutting, L., Keenan, J. M., … Petrill, S. A. (2015). Longitudinal stability in reading comprehension is largely heritable from grades 1 to 6. *PLoS ONE, 10*(1).

Spence, S. H. (1998). A measure of anxiety symptoms among children. *Behaviour Research and Therapy, 36*(5), 545–566. doi:10.1016/S0005-7967(98)00034-5

Suinn, R. M., Taylor, S., & Edwards, R. W. (1988). Suinn mathematics anxiety rating scale for elementary school students (MARS-E): Psychometric and normative data. *Educational and Psychological Measurement, 48*(4), 979–986. doi:10.1177/001316448 8484013

Thorndike, R. L., Hagen, E. P., & Sattler, J. M. (1986). *Stanford-binet intelligence scale* (4th ed.). Chicago, IL: Riverside.

Trouton, A., Spinath, F. M., & Plomin, R. (2002). Twins Early Development Study (TEDS): A multivariate, longitudinal genetic investigation of language, cognition and behavior problems in childhood. *Twin Research, 5*(5), 444–448. doi:10.1375/136905202320906255

Ullén, F., Hambrick, D. Z., & Mosing, M. A. (2016). Rethinking expertise: A multi-factorial gene–environment interaction model of expert performance. *Psychological Bulletin, 142*(4), 427–446. doi:10.1037/bul0000033; 10.1037/bul0000033.supp (Supplemental)

Wagner, R. K., Torgesen, J. K., & Rashotte, C. A. (1999). *Comprehensive test of phonological processing.* Austin, TX: PRO-ED.

Wang, Z., Hart, S. A., Kovas, Y., Lukowski, S., Soden, B., Thompson, L. A., & ... Petrill, S. A. (2014). Who is afraid of math? Two sources of genetic variance for mathematical anxiety. *Journal of Child Psychology and Psychiatry, 55*(9), 1056–1064. doi:10.1111/jcpp.12224

Wang, Z., Lukowski, S. L., Hart, S. A., Lyons, I. M., Thompson, L. A., Kovas, Y., & ... Petrill, S. A. (2015). Is math anxiety always bad for math learning? The role of math motivation. *Psychological Science, 26*(12), 1863–1876. doi:10.1177/0956797615602471

Willcutt, E. G., Petrill, S. A., Wu, S., Boada, R., DeFries, J. C., Olson, R. K., & Pennington, B. F. (2013). Comorbidity between reading disability and math disability: Concurrent psychopathology, functional impairment, and neuropsychological functioning. *Journal of Learning Disabilities, 46*(6), 500–516. doi:10.1177/0022219413477476

Woodcock, R. (1987). *Woodcock reading mastery tests - revised.* Circle Pines, MN: American Guidance Service.

Woodcock, R., McGraw, K. S., & Mather, N. (2001). *Woodcock Johnson III tests of achievement.* Itasca, IL: Riverside.

16

GENETIC INFLUENCES ON MUSIC EXPERTISE

Miriam A. Mosing, Isabelle Peretz, and Fredrik Ullén

Introduction

Music plays a central role in human societies and can be traced back approximately 50,000 years on the basis of an old bone "flute" found in Slovenia (McDermott & Hauser, 2005). Music not only forms part of many cultural events such as weddings and funerals, but musical engagement at an amateur level is also very common in society. Many individuals invest a considerable amount of time and resources in listening to music or learning to play an instrument (Eurostat, 2011). Further, music can evoke emotions and therefore has become a central part of the advertisement and film industry (DeNora, 2001). For these reasons, among others, music has been the center of much research interest over the last few decades, not only as a fascinating phenomenon in itself but also as a model for expertise research. While much research has focused on environmental factors, the underlying genetic architecture of *musicality* has only recently gained attention (Gingras, Honing, Peretz, Trainor, & Fisher, 2015; Tan, McPherson, Peretz, Berkovic, & Wilson, 2014). Indication for musicality as a biological phenomenon has come from different directions. In this chapter we will review recent empirical findings on its genetic basis.

Do Genes Contribute? General Findings Suggesting a Biological Basis for Musicality

Universality

Although there are large individual differences in musicality and music skills among individuals in the human population, music is a universal feature of human culture (McDermott & Hauser, 2005). Auditory brain circuits of modern humans are likely similar to those of the very first primates who lived millions of years ago (Langner, 2005). Even without formal music training, humans have the ability to perceive, produce, and appreciate music and some basic cognitive components underlying musicality such as *relative pitch, tonal encoding of pitch, beat induction* and *metrical encoding of rhythm* may be universal and tend to develop spontaneously and early during child development (for a detailed review see McDermott & Hauser, 2005). In line with this, newborns and infants show natural interest in music (Trehub & Hannon, 2006) and exhibit signs of early music memory (e.g., Saffran, Loman, & Robertson, 2000). Furthermore, neuroscience research suggests that although there are no neural circuits exclusively dedicated to music perception, there are at least some distinct mechanisms that appear to be specialized for processing musical sounds (McDermott & Hauser, 2005). Together these observations strongly suggest that music, to some degree, is a biological phenomenon hardwired in our genetic makeup.

Familial Aggregation

A general observation in the literature is that musical *talent* (as well as *giftedness* in other domains) appears to run in families, which is often interpreted as support for underlying genetics (Galton, 1869; Mjöen, 1925). A famous example of such a remarkable *familial aggregation* of musical talent is the Bach family. Of course, single case studies are not sufficient to draw any conclusions about the relative importance of genes and environment for musicality. Using many families and cases though, familial aggregation can address the question whether a trait clusters in a family more than expected by chance; that is, the trait is more prevalent in the family of a *proband* than in the general population (Naj, Park, & Beaty, 2012). Well-known music-related examples of familial aggregation are *congenital amusia* and *absolute pitch* (AP). Congenital amusia, a specific impairment in processing of music also referred to as *tone deafness*, has been shown to aggregate in families, with siblings of individuals with the impairment having a 10.8 times higher risk of having amusia (*sibling recurrence risk ratio*) than an unrelated individual in the general population (Peretz, Cummings, & Dube, 2007). Offspring of those with amusia had a risk ratio of 2.3, so increased risk, but much less so than for siblings. Similarly, several studies have shown that AP, the ability to identify pitches without relying on external reference notes, aggregates in families, with a sibling recurrence risk ratio of 7.5 to 15.1, even when controlling for music training (Baharloo, Johnston, Service, Gitschier, & Freimer, 1998; Baharloo, Service, Risch, Gitschier, & Freimer, 2000; Gregersen, Kowalsky, Kohn, & Marvin, 1998). What remains to be seen is the distinction between genetic and non-genetic (cultural or shared family environment) influences in familial clustering in music-related traits.

Large Variability in Hours of Training Among Music Experts

Debate has arisen around the fact that *expert* musicians (as well as experts in any other domain) vary widely in the hours of *deliberate practice* they have accumulated over time (Ericsson, 2013; Ericsson, Krampe, & Tesch-Römer, 1993; Meinz & Hambrick, 2010). It now seems clear that in addition to deliberate practice, genetic influences and *talent* may play a considerable role in musicality. As compared to others, some individuals may need fewer practice hours to reach a specific skill level in a given domain, suggesting that either some individuals were considerably more talented from the outset, or that they learn quicker and thus benefit more from each hour of practice than others (suggesting *gene by environment interactions*).

Genetic Syndromes and Altered Musicality

In the context of musicality, two known genetic syndromes have been studied because those diagnosed with one or the other of these syndromes reportedly show altered musical skills. The first one, Williams-Beuren syndrome (WBS), is a genetic disorder known to be caused by heterozygous gene deletions on chromosome 7q11.23. Despite often serious deficits in various cognitive domains, affected individuals may have surprisingly good musical skills including increased *auditory sensitivity, high musical interest, creativity*, along with strong emotional responses to music (e.g., Martens, Wilson, & Reutens, 2008; Martinez-Castilla & Sotillo, 2014; Ng, Lai, Levitin, & Bellugi, 2013). Interestingly, the heightened music skills of these individuals correlated with increased *social drive* and *emotionality*, suggesting potential shared genetic variants underlying these traits (e.g., Ng *et al.*, 2013). However, given the large phenotypic variability between patients with WBS, the findings are not as straight forward (for a detailed discussion see Lense, Shivers, & Dykens, 2013). Similarly, a rare mutation known to disrupt a regulatory gene also on chromosome 7 reportedly causes severe speech and language problems as well as reduced musical ability (e.g., Fisher & Scharff, 2009; Lai, Fisher, Hurst, Vargha-Khadem, & Monaco, 2001). In both syndromes the causal genes can clearly be pinpointed and musicality seems to be altered, suggesting that these genes on chromosome 7 are to some degree likely involved in musical development.

To summarize, the four observations discussed above—(1) music is a universal feature of human culture, (2) musical talent tends to aggregate in families, (3) practice seems, although important, insufficient to explain individual differences in musical ability, and (4) some known genetic syndromes may alter musicality—all suggest that underlying genetic variants explain at least some of the individual differences we see in musicality on the population level. In the next section we will review studies trying to quantify genetic influences on such individual differences in musicality observed in the population.

Quantifying Genetic Influences on Individual Differences in Music Expertise in the General Population – Heritability and Twin Studies

A method to quantify genetic influences underlying individual differences in human traits, which has gained much popularity over the last few decades, is the *classical twin design* (Rijsdijk & Sham, 2002). The classical twin design utilizes the fact that monozygotic (MZ) twins share 100% of their segregating genes, while dizygotic (DZ) twins share only 50% on average. Importantly though, both twins of a pair (regardless of zygosity) share their home environment with each other. This so-called *shared environment* will typically include teachers, friends, school, family and all other factors which are shared between the twins and tend to make them more similar to each other. In addition, there are *nonshared environmental influences*; that is, all environmental influences which make the twins more different from each other. In *twin modeling*, this term will also include measurement error. Examples of nonshared environmental influences are all *idiosyncratic experiences* (e.g., one twin experiences a trauma while the other twin is not affected, different school experiences, or friends which are not shared), as well as *stochastic biological effects*. So if variance in a trait were due to shared genes only, we would expect a *twin correlation*, roughly defined as resemblance between the two twins of a pair averaged over many pairs, of 1 for MZ pairs and 0.5 for DZ pairs. If all variance in the trait were due to shared environment we would expect to see the same resemblance (correlation of 1) within both MZ and DZ twin pairs. And finally, if all variance were due to nonshared environmental influences, we would see a twin correlation of zero both within MZ and DZ twins. Based on these peculiarities of twin pairs and the advancement of complex statistical methods (*structural equation modeling*), we can partition the variance of a single trait as well as the covariance between two or more traits (multivariate twin modeling; Rijsdijk & Sham, 2002) into components that are explained by genetic, shared, and nonshared environmental influences, respectively. Since twin modeling gained widespread recognition as a field of research (Plomin, DeFries, Knopik, & Neiderheiser, 2013), evidence is accumulating that essentially all complex human traits are partly heritable (Polderman *et al.*, 2015). And, not surprisingly, in the last few years more and more evidence has come from twin studies, suggesting that individual differences in music expertise and related traits are also to a considerable part genetically influenced (Ullén, Hambrick, & Mosing, 2015).

Self-Reported Measures of Musicality

A very early twin study on music-related traits was performed by Coon and Carey (1989) on a sample of over 800 same-sex twin pairs. This study assessed self-reported musical achievement (out-of-school music performances) and reported a heritability (i.e., the proportion of total variance explained by genetic influences) of 38% for males and 20% for females. In line with these estimates, a more recent twin study reported a heritability of 26% for self-reported music accomplishment with some additional shared environmental influences (61%; Hambrick & Tucker-Drob, 2014). Another recent study (Vinkhuyzen, van der Sluis, Posthuma, & Boomsma, 2009) using a much larger sample of 1,685 twin pairs explored the heritability of self-rated musical *aptitude* (three categories: *less competent than most people*, *as competent as most people*, and *more competent than most people*) and exceptional musical *talent* (comparing ability in the *normal range* vs. *exceptionally skilled*). This study revealed heritability estimates for self-rated musical aptitude of 66% for males and 30% for females with some additional shared environmental influences of 8% and 54%, respectively. For exceptional musical talent Vinkhuyzen and colleagues (2009) reported a heritability as high as 86%. Last, the largest twin study in this domain (Mosing *et al.*, 2015) measured *self-perceived success* in the music world in more than 10,000 twins on a seven-point scale ranging from *not involved in music* to *(inter)nationally acclaimed* and reported a heritability of 57% in males and only 9% (and not statistically significant) with an additional 46% of shared environmental influences in females. These four studies suggest that individual differences in self-rated musicality or musical achievement are at least partly genetically influenced, potentially somewhat stronger in males than in females.

Objective Measures of Musicality

Several twin studies to date have also explored the genetic architecture of individual differences in more objective music-related measures. For example, Theusch and Gitschier (2011) reported a significantly higher concordance rate for Absolute Pitch (AP) in MZ than in DZ twins suggesting some genetic influences for the development of AP. However, the sample was very small (14 MZ and 31 DZ pairs) and the rare occurrence of AP makes it hard to capture the trait even in a large twin study (Theusch & Gitschier, 2011). Exploring individual differences in pitch processing in the general population, Drayna *et al.* (2001) reported that 80% of the variation in performance on the Distorted Tunes Test, where participants have to identify incorrect pitches in familiar melodies, was due to genetic influences. Slightly lower heritability estimates of 50%, 59%, and 12–30% for individual differences in rhythm, melody and pitch discrimination skills (based on the Swedish Musical Discrimination Test), respectively, were recently reported by a large Swedish twin study of more than 10,000 twins (Ullén, Mosing, Holm, Eriksson, & Madison, 2014). Finally, a recent smaller twin study of 384 twins used the scale, out-of-key and off-beat tests from an online test (Peretz *et al.*, 2007) and reported greatly varying heritability estimates (50%, 3%, and 24%, respectively) and some shared environmental influence (59%) for the out-of-key test (Seesjarvi *et al.*, 2016).

Interestingly, recent and much debated evidence from twin studies suggests that the predisposition to engage in music practice also seems to be partly heritable, with two recent studies reporting genetic influences of 38% and 70% for individual differences in music practice (Hambrick & Tucker-Drob, 2014; Mosing, Madison, Pedersen, Kuja-Halkola, & Ullén, 2014). These findings suggest that individual differences in music practice hours are genetically influenced. Interestingly, Mosing and colleagues could also show that the association between practice and music discrimination skills were largely explained by shared underlying genes (Mosing et al., 2014). In line with this, there was no skill difference between the more trained twins and their less trained, genetically identical co-twins for either musical discrimination (Mosing et al., 2014) or accuracy of motor timing (Ullén, Mosing, & Madison, 2015), suggesting that the associations between practice and these types of skills was not causal. Similarly, it seems, contrary to previous proposals (Ericsson, 2014; Ericsson et al., 1993), that genetic influences on self-reported musical accomplishment (Hambrick & Tucker-Drob, 2014) tend to increase, rather than decrease, with music practice, indicating that genetic influences become more important with accumulated practice hours.

In summary, individual differences in objectively measured musicality are significantly heritable, depending on the trait measured, on the measure used, and the sample size, with even higher estimates for some self-rated measures. Further, heritability of musicality tends to increase with accumulated practice hours, rather than decrease. Last and maybe most unexpectedly, even variation in time spent in music practice seems to be to a large part influenced by genes, and these genes tend to be shared with those underlying variants in musicality. In the next section we will discuss and review the genetic variants potentially important for music-related traits.

Gene Finding Studies—Getting at the Exact Genes

A number of studies have tried to pinpoint the exact genes underlying music-related traits using *linkage* and *association analyses*. Linkage analysis observes how different chromosomal regions (indicated by *polymorphic genetic markers*) co-segregate with the phenotype of interest among family members (Pulst, 1999). Music-related traits explored using linkage analyses include AP (Gregersen et al., 2013; Theusch, Basu, & Gitschier, 2009), pitch and rhythm perception (Oikkonen et al., 2015; Pulli et al., 2008), singing (Park et al., 2012), and creative activities in music (Oikkonen et al., 2016). However, recent findings in genetic research suggest that most complex traits, and as such most likely also musicality, are influenced by many genetic variants of very small effect, which are difficult to detect using linkage analysis (Gingras et al., 2015).

Association analysis, on the other hand, tests for correlations between some or even all genetic variants (polymorphisms) and a trait at the population level (Lewis & Knight, 2012). Most association studies on musicality were candidate gene studies based on findings from linkage studies or hypotheses about the biology of the trait, exploring traits such as musical aptitude (Ukkola, Onkamo, Raijas, Karma, & Järvelä, 2009), music memory (Granot et al., 2007), music listening (Ukkola-Vuoti et al., 2011), and choir participation (Morley et al., 2012). To our knowledge, only three studies to date have conducted genome-wide association or copy number variation (CNV) analyses of music ability/aptitude/creativity which allows for hypothesis free association testing across the genome (Oikkonen et al., 2015; Park et al., 2012; Ukkola-Vuoti et al., 2013). Unfortunately, most linkage and association studies on music-related traits lack replication, which is likely due to the small sample sizes, among other reasons (Ott, 2004). Therefore, in the following paragraph we will only briefly summarize the general findings of the music-genetics literature.

Several studies have independently reported associations between different music-related traits with loci on chromosome 8q (AP and music perception; Pulli et al., 2008; Theusch et al., 2009; Ukkola-Vuoti et al., 2013) and chromosome 4 (musical aptitude, pitch perception accuracy, composing, and pitch accuracy during singing; Oikkonen et al., 2015; Oikkonen et al., 2016; Park et al., 2012; Pulli et al., 2008). Further, associations have been reported for the gene AVPR1A on chromosome 12q with music perception (Ukkola et al., 2009), music listening (Ukkola-Vuoti et al., 2011), and music memory (Granot et al., 2007) and the gene SLC6A4 with choir participation (Morley et al., 2012) as well as music memory (Granot et al., 2007). Both genes may also play a role in social behavior, raising the possibility of a shared neurobiological basis (Tan et al., 2014).

However, as mentioned above, some studies failed to replicate the associations reported above; for example, Oikkonen and colleagues (2015) could not confirm the association between AVPR1A with music perception, and similarly Morley and colleagues (2012) could not replicate the association with choir participation. To identify variants of small effect in complex traits using genome-wide association studies, very great power is needed, which recently has resulted in the formation of large consortia in order to combine samples to increase power (e.g., Okbay et al., 2016). It is important to keep in mind that although very large genome-wide studies on complex traits have been able to successfully identify specific genetic variants (e.g., Okbay et al., 2016), these studies tend to explain relatively little of the heritability of the complex traits in question (Maher, 2008). Given what we know about musicality and its many facets we can conclude that for music-related traits there also will be many genetic variants of small effect involved which will be challenging to identify even with large samples and excellent measures.

Conclusions—Importance of Genes and Environment in Musicality and Expertise in General

In this chapter we reviewed the current knowledge of genetic influences on individual differences in musicality. What we can conclude is that for all studied music-related traits and even for music practice, genetic influences play a significant role. However, the range of reported heritabilities varies largely between the measured traits and between studies (even on similar traits). Apart from reflecting true differences in heritability for different music-related traits, heritabilities can differ due to several other factors such as measurement error (high measurement error will result in a lower heritability), lack of power, true differences in heritability between different aspects of musical competence, population differences, and gene-environment interaction. Notably, although genes seem to play an important role, past research using correlational data (not reviewed here) as well as twin studies show that environmental influences also explain a large part of the variance in music-related traits.

Given the importance of both genes and environment, we can expect that gene-environment interactions as well as gene-environment correlations are of importance for musical expertise. For example, one hour of music practice may be much more beneficial for a musically talented individual than for a less talented one. Similarly, it is possible that individuals who are genetically predisposed to be musically endowed may be more likely to be exposed to environments which facilitate musical development during upbringing, as their family members (e.g., parents) may also be interested or involved in music and hence created a musically stimulating environment.

To date, still very little is known about the interplay between genes and environment in musicality as well as expertise in general. In determining musicality and expertise, only very recently has the interplay of genes and environment gained attention and resulted in a new model of expertise: the Multifactorial Gene-Environment Interaction Model (MGIM), see Chapter 21. The MGIM proposes effects of genetic and environmental factors as well as gene-environment interactions on practice behavior, expert performance, other expertise related traits, and the covariations between these variables. The MGIM is the first expertise model that can explain all previous findings on expertise research using musicality as a model. The challenge for music and expertise research over the next decade will be not only to identify the genetic variants underlying individual differences in musicality (Gingras *et al.*, 2015), but also to gain a better understanding of the gene-environment interplay, which would allow optimizing musical training based on an individual's genetic predispositions and talent.

References

Baharloo, S., Johnston, P. A., Service, S. K., Gitschier, J., & Freimer, N. B. (1998). Absolute pitch: An approach for identification of genetic and nongenetic components. *American Journal of Human Genetics*, 62(2), 224–231.

Baharloo, S., Service, S. K., Risch, N., Gitschier, J., & Freimer, N. B. (2000). Familial aggregation of absolute pitch. *American Journal of Human Genetics*, 67(3), 755–758.

Coon, H., & Carey, G. (1989). Genetic and environmental determinants of musical ability in twins. *Behavior Genetics*, 19(2), 183–193.

DeNora, T. (2001). Aesthetic agency and musical practice: New directions in the sociology of music and emotion. In P. N. Juslin & J. A. Sloboda (Eds.), *Music and emotion: Theory and research* (pp. 71–104). Oxford, England: Oxford University Press.

Drayna, D., Manichaikul, A., de Lange, M., Snieder, H., & Spector, T. (2001). Genetic correlates of musical pitch recognition in humans. *Science, 291*(5510), 1969–1972.

Ericsson, K. A. (2013). Training history, deliberate practice and elite sports performance: an analysis in response to Tucker and Collins review – what makes champions? *British Journal of Sports Medicine, 47*(9), 533–535. doi: 10.1136/bjsports-2012-091767

Ericsson, K. A. (2014). Why expert performance is special and cannot be extrapolated from studies of performance in the general population: A response to criticisms. *Intelligence, 45,* 81–103. doi: http://dx.doi.org/10.1016/j.intell.2013.12.001

Ericsson, K. A., Krampe, R. T., & Tesch-Römer, C. (1993). The role of deliberate practice in the acquisition of expert performance. *Psychological Review, 100*(3), 363–406.

Eurostat. (2011). *Cultural statistics.* Luxembourg: Publications Office of the European Union.

Fisher, S. E., & Scharff, C. (2009). FOXP2 as a molecular window into speech and language. *Trends in Genetics, 25*(4), 166–177. doi: 10.1016/j.tig.2009.03.002

Galton, F. (1869). *Hereditary genius: An inquiry into its laws and consequences.* London: Macmillan.

Gingras, B., Honing, H., Peretz, I., Trainor, L. J., & Fisher, S. E. (2015). Defining the biological bases of individual differences in musicality. *Philosophical Transactions of the Royal Society of London. Series B, Biological Sciences. B Biol Sci, 370*(1664), 20140092. doi: 10.1098/rstb.2014.0092

Granot, R. Y., Frankel, Y., Gritsenko, V., Lerer, E., Gritsenko, I., Bachner-Melman, R., … Ebstein, R. P. (2007). Provisional evidence that the arginine vasopressin 1a receptor gene is associated with musical memory. *Evolution and Human Behavior, 28*(5), 313–318. doi: http://dx.doi.org/10.1016/j.evolhumbehav.2007.05.003

Gregersen, P. K., Kowalsky, E., Kohn, N., & Marvin, E. W. (1998). Absolute pitch: Prevalence, ethnic variation, and estimation of the genetic component. *American Journal of Human Genetics, 65*(3), 911–913.

Gregersen, P. K., Kowalsky, E., Lee, A., Baron-Cohen, S., Fisher, S. E., Asher, J. E., … Li, W. (2013). Absolute pitch exhibits phenotypic and genetic overlap with synesthesia. *Human Molecular Genetics, 22*(10), 2097–2104.

Hambrick, D. Z., & Tucker-Drob, E. M. (2014). The genetics of music accomplishment: Evidence for gene-environment correlation and interaction. *Psychonomic Bulletin & Review, 22*(1), 112–120.

Lai, C. S., Fisher, S. E., Hurst, J. A., Vargha-Khadem, F., & Monaco, A. P. (2001). A forkhead-domain gene is mutated in a severe speech and language disorder. *Nature, 413*(6855), 519–523. doi: 10.1038/35097076

Langner, G. (2005). Neuronal mechanisms underlying the perception of pitch and harmony. *Annals of the New York Academy of Sciences, 1060*(1), 50–52.

Lense, M. D., Shivers, C. M., & Dykens, E. M. (2013). (A)musicality in Williams syndrome: Examining relationships among auditory perception, musical skill, and emotional responsiveness to music. *Frontiers in Psychology, 4,* 525. doi: 10.3389/fpsyg.2013.00525

Lewis, C. M., & Knight, J. (2012). Introduction to genetic association studies. *Cold Spring Harbor Protocols, 2012*(3), 297–306. doi: 10.1101/pdb.top068163

Maher, B. (2008). Personal genomes: The case of the missing heritability. *Nature, 456*(7218), 18–21. doi: 10.1038/456018a

Martens, M. A., Wilson, S. J., & Reutens, D. C. (2008). Research Review: Williams syndrome: A critical review of the cognitive, behavioral, and neuroanatomical phenotype. *Journal of Child Psychology and Psychiatry, 49*(6), 576–608. doi: 10.1111/j.1469-7610.2008.01887.x

Martinez-Castilla, P., & Sotillo, M. (2014). Pitch processing in children with Williams syndrome: Relationships between music and prosody skills. *Brain Science, 4*(2), 376–395. doi: 10.3390/brainsci4020376

McDermott, J., & Hauser, M. D. (2005). The origins of music: Innateness, uniqueness, and evolution. *Music Perception, 23*(1), 29–59. doi: citeulike-article-id:738251

Meinz, E. J., & Hambrick, D. Z. (2010). Deliberate practice is necessary but not sufficient to explain individual differences in piano sight-reading skill: The role of working memory capacity. *Psychological Science, 21*(7), 914–919.

Mjöen, J. A. (1925). Zur Erbanalyse der musikalischen Begabung. *Hereditas, 7*, 109–128.

Morley, A. P., Narayanan, M., Mines, R., Molokhia, A., Baxter, S., Craig, G., … Craig, I. (2012). AVPR1A and SLC6A4 polymorphisms in choral singers and non-musicians: A gene association study. *PLoS One, 7*(2), e31763. doi: 10.1371/journal.pone.0031763

Mosing, M. A., Madison, G., Pedersen, N. L., Kuja-Halkola, R., & Ullén, F. (2014). Practice does not make perfect: No causal effect of musical practice on musical ability. *Psychological Science, 25*(9), 1795–1803.

Mosing, M. A., Verweij, K. J. H., Madison, G., Pedersen, N. L., Zietsch, B. P., & Ullén, F. (2015). Testing predictions from the sexual selection hypothesis of music evolution using a large genetically informative sample of over 10,000 twins. *Evolution and Human Behavior, 36*(5), 359–366.

Naj, A. C., Park, Y. S., & Beaty, T. H. (2012). Detecting familial aggregation. *Methods of Molecular Biology, 850*, 119–150. doi: 10.1007/978-1-61779-555-8_8

Ng, R., Lai, P., Levitin, D. J., & Bellugi, U. (2013). Musicality correlates with sociability and emotionality in Williams syndrome. *Journal of Mental Health Research in Intellectual Disabilities, 6*(4), 268–279. doi: 10.1080/19315864.2012.683932

Oikkonen, J., Huang, Y., Onkamo, P., Ukkola-Vuoti, L., Raijas, P., Karma, K., … Jarvela, I. (2015). A genome-wide linkage and association study of musical aptitude identifies loci containing genes related to inner ear development and neurocognitive functions. *Molecular Psychiatry, 20*, 275–282.

Oikkonen, J., Kuusi, T., Peltonen, P., Raijas, P., Ukkola-Vuoti, L., Karma, K., … Jarvela, I. (2016). Creative activities in music—A genome-wide linkage analysis. *PLoS One, 11*(2), e0148679. doi: 10.1371/journal.pone.0148679

Okbay, A., Baselmans, B. M., De Neve, J. E., Turley, P., Nivard, M. G., Fontana, M. A., … Cesarini, D. (2016). Genetic variants associated with subjective well-being, depressive symptoms, and neuroticism identified through genome-wide analyses. *Nature Genetics, 48*(6), 624–633. doi: 10.1038/ng.3552

Ott, J. (2004). Association of genetic loci: Replication or not, that is the question. *Neurology, 63*(6), 955–958.

Park, H., Lee, S., Kim, H. J., Ju, Y. S., Shin, J. Y., Hong, D., … Seo, J. S. (2012). Comprehensive genomic analyses associate UGT8 variants with musical ability in a Mongolian population. *Journal of Medical Genetics, 49*(12), 747–752.

Peretz, I., Cummings, S., & Dube, M. P. (2007). The genetics of congenital amusia (tone deafness): A family-aggregation study. *American Journal of Human Genetics, 81*(3), 582–588.

Plomin, R., DeFries, J. C., Knopik, V. S., & Neiderheiser, J. M. (2013). *Behavioral genetics* (6 ed.). New York: Worth Publishers.

Polderman, T. J., Benyamin, B., de Leeuw, C. A., Sullivan, P. F., van Bochoven, A., Visscher, P. M., & Posthuma, D. (2015). Meta-analysis of the heritability of human traits based on fifty years of twin studies. *Nature Genetics, 47*(7), 702–709. doi: 10.1038/ng.3285

Pulli, K., Karma, K., Norio, R., Sistonen, P., Goring, H. H., & Jarvela, I. (2008). Genome-wide linkage scan for loci of musical aptitude in Finnish families: Evidence for a major locus at 4q22. *Journal of Medical Genetics, 45*(7), 451–456.

Pulst, S. M. (1999). Genetic linkage analysis. *Archives of Neurology, 56*(6), 667–672.

Rijsdijk, F. V., & Sham, P. C. (2002). Analytic approaches to twin data using structural equation models. *Briefings in Bioinformatics, 3*(2), 119–133.

Saffran, J. R., Loman, M. M., & Robertson, R. R. (2000). Infant memory for musical experiences. *Cognition, 77*(1), B15–23.

Seesjarvi, E., Sarkamo, T., Vuoksimaa, E., Tervaniemi, M., Peretz, I., & Kaprio, J. (2016). The nature and nurture of melody: A twin study of musical pitch and rhythm perception. *Behavior Genetics, 46*(4), 506–515. doi: 10.1007/s10519-015-9774-y

Tan, Y. T., McPherson, G. E., Peretz, I., Berkovic, S. F., & Wilson, S. J. (2014). The genetic basis of music ability. *Frontiers in Psychology, 5*, 658.

Theusch, E., Basu, A., & Gitschier, J. (2009). Genome-wide study of families with absolute pitch reveals linkage to 8q24.21 and locus heterogeneity. *American Journal of Human Genetics, 85*(1), 112–119.

Theusch, E., & Gitschier, J. (2011). Absolute pitch twin study and segregation analysis. *Twin Research and Human Genetics, 14*(2), 173–178.

Trehub, S. E., & Hannon, E. E. (2006). Infant music perception: Domain-general or domain-specific mechanisms? *Cognition, 100*(1), 73–99.

Ukkola, L. T., Onkamo, P., Raijas, P., Karma, K., & Järvelä, I. (2009). Musical aptitude is associated with AVPR1A-haplotypes. *PLoS One, 4*(5), e5534. doi: 10.1371/journal.pone.0005534

Ukkola-Vuoti, L., Kanduri, C., Oikkonen, J., Buck, G., Blancher, C., Raijas, P., … Jarvela, I. (2013). Genome-wide copy number variation analysis in extended families and unrelated individuals characterized for musical aptitude and creativity in music. *PLoS One, 8*(2). doi: 10.1371/journal.pone.0056356

Ukkola-Vuoti, L., Oikkonen, J., Onkamo, P., Karma, K., Raijas, P., & Jarvela, I. (2011). Association of the arginine vasopressin receptor 1A (AVPR1A) haplotypes with listening to music. *Journal of Human Genetics, 56*(4), 324–329.

Ullen, F., Hambrick, D. Z., & Mosing, M. A. (2015). Rethinking expertise: A multifactorial gene-environment interaction model of expert performance. *Psychological Bulletin, 142*(4), 427–446. doi: 10.1037/bul0000033

Ullén, F., Mosing, M. A., Holm, L., Eriksson, H., & Madison, G. (2014). Psychometric properties and heritability of a new online test for musicality, the Swedish Musical Discrimination Test. *Personality and Individual Differences, 63*, 87–93.

Ullén, F., Mosing, M. A., & Madison, G. (2015). Associations between motor timing, music practice, and intelligence studied in a large sample of twins. *Annals of the New York Academy of Sciences, 1337*, 125–129. doi: 10.1111/nyas.12630

Vinkhuyzen, A. A., van der Sluis, S., Posthuma, D., & Boomsma, D. I. (2009). The heritability of aptitude and exceptional talent across different domains in adolescents and young adults. *Behavior Genetics, 39*(4), 380–392.

17

THE MOLECULAR GENETIC BASIS OF MUSIC ABILITY AND MUSIC-RELATED PHENOTYPES

Yi Ting Tan, Gary E. McPherson, and Sarah J. Wilson

Introduction

In the past decade, researchers have sought to uncover potential genes that underlie various musical traits through molecular genetic approaches once the genetic basis of a musical trait has been established using behavioral genetic methods. Since the 1980s, progress in molecular genetic technology and bioinformatics has brought about the advent of human molecular genetic approaches, especially for elucidating the genetic mechanisms of complex diseases. In contrast, the investigation of the molecular genetic basis of music ability only began to surface in recent years, with Irma Järvelä, a clinical geneticist at the University of Helsinki, Finland, and her collaborators contributing a sizeable and significant research output on this topic. Although this field is still in its infancy, some exciting and converging results are already beginning to emerge.

This chapter provides an overview of the main findings from molecular genetic studies on musical traits, which are broadly organized according to the categories shown in Table 17.1.

Music Perception

As shown in Table 17.1, a majority of the molecular genetic studies have focused primarily on traits pertaining to music perception—the perception of musical pitches, melodies, and rhythms, music listening behavior, and the uncommon music perception ability of Absolute Pitch (AP). The molecular genetic findings for each of these traits are discussed in the sections below.

TABLE 17.1 The number of molecular genetic studies investigating various music-related phenotypes

Category	Music subskill	No. of studies	Authors
Music perception	Basic music perception abilities	2	Pulli et al. (2008); Oikkonen et al. (2015)
	Higher level music perception abilities	6	Alcock et al. (2000); Pulli et al. (2008); Ukkola et al. (2009); Ukkola-Vuoti et al. (2013); Oikkonen et al. (2015); Liu et al. (2016)
	Music memory	2	Granot et al. (2007); Granot et al. (2013)
	Music listening	2	Ukkola-Vuoti et al. (2011); Kanduri, Raijas, et al. (2015)
	Absolute pitch	4	Theusch, Basu, & Gitschier (2009); Theusch & Gitschier (2011); Gregersen et al. (2013); Gervain et al. (2013)
Music production	Music performance	1	Kanduri, Kuusi, et al. (2015)
	Music creativity	3	Ukkola et al. (2009); Ukkola-Vuoti et al. (2013); Oikkonen et al. (2016)
	Singing participation	1	Morley et al. (2012)
	Singing accuracy	1	Park et al. (2012)
	Rhythm production	1	Alcock et al. (2000)
Music culture		2	Pamjav et al. (2012); Brown et al. (2014)

Basic Music Perception Abilities

Possible genetic substrates underlying basic music perception abilities have been investigated by Järvelä and her collaborators in several large molecular genetic studies (Oikkonen et al., 2015; Pulli et al., 2008). In these studies, basic music perception abilities were measured using the pitch and time tests from the Seashore Measures of Musical Talents, in which participants were asked to detect differences in the pitch and note duration of 50 paired tones (Seashore, Lewis, & Saetveit, 1960).

Genome-wide linkage analysis revealed some evidence of linkage on chromosome 10 (LOD = 1.67) for pitch discrimination, and on chromosome 4q (LOD = 1.18) for note duration discrimination (Pulli et al., 2008). A subsequent larger-scaled genome-wide linkage and association study (Oikkonen et al., 2015) has also found evidence that chromosome 4 was implicated in music perception. For pitch discrimination, the best linkage was obtained at 4p14, with some evidence of linkage also observed at 22q11.21. In addition, the region 3q21.3

was associated with pitch and note duration discrimination. Interestingly, some of these implicated chromosomal loci contain genes that are expressed in the auditory pathway. For instance, the *PCDH7* gene is located next to 4p14, and is known to be expressed in the developing cochlea of chicken and the amygdala of mice (Hertel, Redies, & Medina, 2012; Lin *et al.*, 2012), which provides tentative evidence for the gene's role in music perception and music-evoked emotions. On the other hand, located close to 3q21.3 is the *GATA2* transcription factor, which likely plays an important role in the development of cochlear hair cells and the inferior colliculus (Haugas *et al.*, 2010). The inferior colliculus is a core structure in the peripheral auditory pathways for music perception, supporting the initial integration of pitch, direction, and loudness information (McLachlan & Wilson, 2010). Moreover, *GATA2* is expressed in dopaminergic neurons (Scherzer *et al.*, 2008), which release dopamine during pleasure-evoking activities such as music listening and performance (Salimpoor, Benovoy, Larcher, Dagher, & Zatorre, 2011). Finally, the region 22q11.21 is linked to DiGeorge syndrome (also known as 22q11.2 deletion syndrome), which typically includes symptoms of conductive and sensorineural hearing losses (Digilio, Marino, Capolino, & Dallapiccola, 2005).

Higher Level Music Perception Abilities

The abilities to perceive tonal or rhythmic structures in music are more cognitively advanced forms of music perception than the pairwise discrimination of pitches or note durations. Because of this, Järvelä's research team has also investigated the ability to discern melodic and rhythmic patterns (referred to as auditory structuring ability) using the Karma Music Test (KMT) in two family pedigree studies (Oikkonen *et al.*, 2015; Pulli *et al.*, 2008). In the earlier study, genome-wide linkage analysis revealed promising evidence of linkage at 4q22 for the KMT (LOD = 2.91) and significant evidence of linkage (LOD = 3.33) for the combined score of the KMT and Seashore's pitch and time tests (Pulli *et al.*, 2008). The subsequent genome-wide linkage and association study also found some evidence of linkage for 4q21.23–22.1 and 4q24 being linked to the KMT (Oikkonen *et al.*, 2015). A possible candidate gene at 4q22 is the netrin receptor *UNC5C*. Netrins are responsible for directing axon extension and cell migration during neural development, with studies demonstrating interactions between netrins and robo family receptors (Stein & Tessier-Lavigne, 2001). One such receptor, *ROBO1*, is a candidate gene for dyslexia (Carrion-Castillo, Franke, & Fisher, 2013). Such results indicate possible shared molecular substrates between music and language, an assertion that is further strengthened by previous behavioral findings demonstrating that the KMT significantly predicts dyslexia (Karma, 2002).

Oikkonen *et al.*'s (2015) genome-wide linkage and association study has also found potential linkage evidence for the KMT at 16q21-22.1, which overlaps with a previously proposed hearing impairment locus (Basit et al., 2011). Furthermore, association analysis conducted in this study revealed that the KMT was associated with 5q31.3, 1p31.1, and 11q21. While the associations at 1p31.1 and 11q21 were not linked to any known gene near these loci, the gene NDFIP1 is located at 5q31.3 and has a function in immune signaling regulation (Wang, Tong, & Ye, 2012). In addition, this study also revealed that some of the chromosomal regions showing evidence of linkage for the combined score (KMT and Seashore's pitch and time tests) contain genes implicated in the auditory pathway. For instance, the linked region 18q12.3-21.1 contains the gene LOXHD1 which is expressed in the inner-ear hair cells and results in auditory defects in the case of mutation (Grillet et al., 2009). In another linked region, 4p12-q12, the gene PDGFRA is expressed in the cochlea of mice (Ballana et al., 2008), and the gene KCTD8 is expressed in the spiral ganglion, a group of nerve cells in the cochlea.

In a genome-wide copy number variation (CNV) analysis, Järvelä and her collaborators detected several copy number variable regions containing genes that influence neurodevelopment, learning, and memory (Ukkola-Vuoti et al., 2013). Notably, a deletion on 5q31.1 was present in some participants with a low combined score on the KMT and Seashore's pitch and time tests. This particular region covers the protocadherin-α gene cluster (Pcdha 1-9), which is involved in the synaptogenesis and maturation of serotonergic projection neurons, as well as learning and memory (Fukuda et al., 2008). The authors proposed Pcdha as a plausible candidate for music perception since learning and memory are important for music perception and the development of musical expertise (McLachlan, Marco, Light, & Wilson, 2013). Also noteworthy is the identification of a large duplicated region on 8q24.22 in an individual with a low combined score, which happens to overlap with a major linkage region for AP (Theusch, Basu, & Gitschier, 2009). Thus, duplication in the putative AP linkage region may have a negative impact on pitch perception, since large duplications are known to be potentially detrimental to neurodevelopment (Almal & Padh, 2012).

Extending these findings, a candidate gene study by Järvelä and her team has demonstrated significant associations between the haplotype RS1 and RS3 of the AVPR1A gene on chromosome 12q and the combined score for the KMT and Seashore's pitch and time tests (Ukkola et al., 2009). Arginine vasopressin (AVP) has previously been implicated in social cognition and behavior (Bielsky et al., 2004; Ferguson et al., 2002) and in social and spatial memory (Aarde & Jentsch, 2006; Ferguson et al., 2002). Its association with auditory structuring ability therefore suggests a potential link between music perception and human social functioning.

Recently, Järvelä's team conducted a genome-wide positive selection analysis on the music perception ability of 148 Finnish participants, as measured by the combined score for the KMT and Seashore's pitch and time tests (Liu et al., 2016). Using a case-control design (cases: > 125/150 for combined score vs.

controls: < 117.25/150 for combined score; as determined from the residuals of a fitted linear regression between the combined score and age of participants), these researchers identified numerous chromosomal regions that show differential positive selection signals between cases and controls using several haplotype-based and frequency-based selection methods. Because a large number of positive selection regions were identified, it was difficult to interpret the functional importance of these regions. As such, the researchers described in detail only the genes important in brain function, hearing, and the singing network of songbirds.

Several genes found within the positive selection regions are involved in inner-ear development and auditory perception. *GPR98* at 5q14.3, for example, is necessary for proper development of auditory hair bundles (McGee *et al.*, 2006) and has a possible function in birdsong (Pfenning *et al.*, 2014). *USH2A* at 1q32.3-41 is also required in the development of cochlear hair cells, which influence hearing sensitivity (Liu *et al.*, 2007). Both *GRP98* and *USH2A* have also been associated with Usher syndrome, which includes symptoms of deafness. These findings are in line with an earlier molecular genetic study on music perception ability which implicated genes associated with inner-ear development and cognition (Oikkonen *et al.*, 2015). Some genes found within the positive selection regions were also implicated in cognition and memory. For instance, *GRIN2B* at 12p13.1 is involved in learning and neural plasticity in the temporal lobe (Milnik *et al.*, 2012). It is also one of the expressed genes in the singing control network of the zebra finch (Pfenning *et al.*, 2014). Moreover, *IL1B* at 2q14 is linked to cognition and working memory (Benke *et al.*, 2011) and *RAPGEF5* at 7p15.3 may also have implications for learning and memory (Ostroveanu *et al.*, 2010). On the other hand, one of the selection regions contains *GZMA* (at 5q11.2), a gene associated with neurodegeneration that has previously been noted to be downregulated after music listening (Kanduri *et al.*, 2015).

The study by Liu *et al.* (2016) also reported that the positive selection region on chromosome 17 contained the *RGS9* gene (17q24). One variant of the gene (*RGS9-2*) is putatively associated with reward mechanisms because it interacts with dopamine receptors in the striatum (Taymans, Leysen, & Langlois, 2003). This finding is in keeping with previous studies that have noted an association between dopamine release and music-induced reward (Salimpoor *et al.*, 2011). Another gene from the RGS family, *RGS2*, which was reported to be upregulated after performing and listening to music (Kanduri, Kuusi, *et al.*, 2015; Kanduri, Raijas, *et al.*, 2015), has also been previously implicated in the vocal learning of songbirds. Thus, this research suggests that RGS proteins may be potential candidate genes for the evolution of music. In fact, approximately 5% of the identified candidate genes (e.g. *FOXP1*, *RGS9*, *GRIN2B*, *GPR98*, *VLDLR*) in the positive selection regions are related to song perception and production in songbirds (Pfenning *et al.*, 2014), which suggests a possible cross-species evolutionary conservation of genes associated with auditory perception. Among these candidate genes, *FOXP1* at 3p13 and *VLDLR* at 9p24.2 are also known to be involved in language development (Chen *et al.*, 2013), pointing to a possible common genetic and evolutionary background for music and language.

As for a possible genetic substrate underlying rhythm perception, the study of a three-generation family pedigree (KE family) with multiple probands of severe speech and language disorder has shown that the affected individuals also demonstrated an impairment in rhythm perception and production, while their pitch perception and production abilities remained intact (Alcock *et al.*, 2000). Subsequent gene sequencing has demonstrated that the affected KE family members has a point mutation in the *FOXP2* gene (Lai, Fisher, Hurst, Vargha-Khadem, & Monaco, 2001). Taken together, these findings suggest a possible shared genetic basis for speech and rhythm, in contrast to pitch-based music abilities which seem likely to be influenced by other genetic factors (Peretz, 2009).

Music Memory

Granot and colleagues (2007) have investigated the possible association of phonological and music memory with the genes *AVPR1A* and *SLC6A4*. The grounds for interest in this association come from previous research indicating a possible epistatic relationship between *AVPR1A*, which is a receptor for AVP, and *SLC6A4*, a serotonin transporter (Albers, Karom & Smith, 2002), in addition to the association of AVP with spatial and social memory (Aarde & Jentsch, 2006; Ferguson *et al.*, 2002). In this study, 82 university students with minimal music training were genotyped for the *AVPR1A* (RS1 and RS3 haplotypes) and the *SLC6A4* (HTTLPR) polymorphisms using population-based and family-based association analyses. The music memory performance of the participants was assessed using four melodic memory tests and two rhythmic memory tests. Results revealed significant gene-by-gene epistatic interactions between the *AVPR1A* and *SLC6A4* polymorphisms for two of the melodic memory tests (the Gordon melodic imagery subtest from the Musical Aptitude Profile, and the interval subtest from the Montreal Battery of Evaluation of Amusia [MBEA]), one of the rhythmic memory tests (Seashore's rhythm perception task), and one phonological memory task. These results remained robust even after applying conservative Bonferroni corrections for multiple testing. They provide initial evidence for an epistatic relationship between *AVPR1A* and *SLC6A4* polymorphisms that may be linked to short-term memory for music, or more generally, to phonological memory.

In a follow-up study, AVP was administered intranasally to 50 male adults with little or no music training in a double-blind, placebo-controlled, crossover study (Granot *et al.*, 2013). At the end of each session (AVP/placebo), the participants' music working memory was assessed using the melodic imagery subtest from Gordon's Musical Aptitude Profile and the interval subtest from the MBEA, while verbal working memory was assessed with digits forward and backwards from the Digit Span task. Although AVP administration was not found to affect digit span performance significantly, a complex pattern emerged for the music memory tasks. Specifically, for the MBEA test, in both sessions, the group that received AVP first performed more poorly than the group that received the placebo first. For Gordon's melodic imagery subtest, both groups performed significantly better in the second session, with the group that received placebo first marginally outperforming those who received AVP first. Findings also showed that for the group who received AVP first, their music memory scores were significantly positively correlated with their affective state scores. On the basis of these findings, the researchers argued that the apparent detrimental effects of AVP on music memory may be mediated by mood, attention, and arousal, such that only those who scored low on happiness and attentiveness were negatively affected by AVP in terms of their music working memory. In light of music's propensity for modulating arousal and AVP's influence on mood and arousal, the researchers deemed it conceivable that the documented associations between AVP and music perception, creativity, and memory might reflect individual differences in arousal and attention modulation rather than individual differences in cognitive or social abilities per se.

Music Listening

Listening to music is a prevalent behavior in all known human cultures. To investigate this human attribute, Järvelä's team examined the role of *AVPR1A* gene polymorphisms in the active and passive music listening behavior of 31 Finnish families using family-based association analysis (Ukkola-Vuoti *et al.*, 2011). Findings indicate that current active music listening was significantly associated with the RS1 and AVR haplotype, whereas lifelong active music listening was significantly associated with the RS1 and RS3 haplotype. A possible shared genetic basis for the frequency of lifelong active music listening and music perception ability was proposed by the authors, given that the same haplotype (RS1 and RS3) was previously demonstrated to be associated with music perception (Ukkola *et al.*, 2009). Given the well-established role of AVP in mediating social behavior (Bielsky *et al.*, 2004), the researchers proposed that these findings provide tentative evidence that music listening may share common neurobiological substrates with social attachment and communication.

The above research has been extended to investigate the effect of listening to classical music on human transcriptome using genome-wide transcriptional profiling (Kanduri, Raijas, *et al.*, 2015). It was found that in participants with high musical experience (based on years of music training or music perception ability), several genes implicated in dopamine secretion, transport, and signaling were upregulated, converging with previous evidence that showed that music listening induces dopaminergic release and transmission (Salimpoor *et al.*, 2011). Notably, one of the most upregulated gene *SNCA* is a known risk gene for Parkinson's disease (Scherzer *et al.*, 2008), and is located on the most significant linkage region for music perception ability, 4q22.1 (Oikkonen *et al.*, 2015; Pulli *et al.*, 2008). In addition, *SNCA* is regulated by *GATA2*, a transcription factor which has a possible association with music perception ability (Oikkonen *et al.*, 2015). Other upregulated genes in participants with high musical experience included those associated with learning, memory and cognition (e.g. *SNCA, NRGN, NPTN*), synaptic function and neurotransmission (e.g. *SNCA, HDAC4, FKBP8*), neuroprotection and neurogenesis (e.g. *SNCA, KLF4*), and auditory cortical activation and absolute pitch (e.g. *FAM49B, HDAC4*). Importantly, some of the upregulated genes (e.g. *SNCA, NRGN, RGS2*) are also known to be associated with song perception and production in songbirds (Wada *et al.*, 2006), suggesting a potential cross-species shared evolutionary background for sound perception. On the other hand, several of the downregulated genes (e.g. *ATP5J, ATP5L, GZMA, CASP8*) are involved in neurodegenerative processes. Collectively, the downregulation of genes implicated in neurodegeneration and the upregulation of genes involved in neurogenesis and neuroprotection indicate that music listening may have a neuroprotective role, supporting the use of music therapy in people with neurodegenerative diseases.

Absolute Pitch

Absolute pitch (AP) or "perfect pitch" is the rare musical ability to identify or produce pitches without relying on an external reference tone. It has an estimated prevalence of less than 1 in 10,000 (Bachem, 1955), although more recent studies have suggested the prevalence could be closer to 1 in 1,500 (Profita & Bidder, 1988).

A genome-wide linkage study of 73 AP families (each with ≤ 2 AP possessors) of European, East Asian, Ashkenazi Jewish, and Indian descent in the United States and Canada revealed suggestive linkage evidence on chromosomes 8q24.21 (LOD = 2.33) and 8q21.11 (LOD = 2.07) for the European/Ashkenazi Jewish/Indian combined dataset (Theusch *et al.*, 2009). Notably, the gene *ADCY8* is located near the linkage peak on 8q24.21, which is expressed almost exclusively in the brain and is implicated in learning and memory processes (De Quervain & Papassotiropoulos, 2006; Ludwig & Seuwen, 2002; Wong *et al.*, 1999). When only the subset of 45 European AP families was examined, there was strong evidence of linkage on 8q24.21 (LOD = 3.46) for AP, suggesting that genes such as *FAM49B* and *ADCY8* within this linkage region could potentially predispose individuals of European descent. Other linkage peaks were also found in the European AP families, namely on loci 8q21.11 (LOD = 2.24), 7q22.3 (LOD = 2.07) and 9p21.3 (LOD = 2.05). These peaks suggest that multiple genetic factors may underpin the etiology of AP, even within the same population. Interestingly, the linkage region on 7q22.3 was also observed in a subset of 19 AP families of East Asian ancestry, albeit with a smaller linkage peak (LOD ≈ 1-1.5). Taken together, these findings support a strong and possibly heterogeneous genetic contribution to AP, both within and across populations of different ancestries.

Another genome-wide linkage study investigated the genetic relationship between AP and synesthesia in 53 multiplex families with AP (i.e., families with multiple AP possessors) and 36 multiplex families with synesthesia (Gregersen *et al.*, 2013). Notably, approximately 22% of the AP possessors from the AP families reported synesthesia, while eight synesthesia families also had AP possessors within each family. Non-parametric linkage analyses conducted separately on the AP and synesthesia datasets revealed overlaps in several linkage regions (LOD > 2), especially on chromosomes 2 and 6. Given this overlap and the hypothesis that the two phenotypes may be jointly influenced by genes underpinning brain structural and functional connectivity, the AP and synesthesia datasets were combined for further linkage analysis. Significant linkage evidence was found at 6q14.1-6q16.1 (LOD = 4.68), which coincided with the small linkage peak (LOD = 1.72) previously reported for AP families of European ancestry (Theusch *et al.*, 2009). Upon sequencing several potential candidate genes in this region, Gregersen and colleagues found that AP possessors from four of the AP multiplex families shared one or more of three non-synonymous variants of the gene *EPHA7* at 6q16.1. *EPHA7* has been implicated in brain development, particularly establishing neural connectivity between auditory cortex and other cortical regions with the thalamus (North, Clifford, & Donoghue, 2013; Torii, Hackett, Rakic, Levitt, & Polley, 2013). Since neuroimaging studies have reported that both AP and synesthesia are marked by atypical structural and functional connectivity (Dovern *et al.*, 2012; Loui, Kroog, Zuk, Winner, & Schlaug, 2011; Rouw & Scholte, 2007), it is conceivable that *EPHA7* variants may underpin these two traits. A more complex pattern of linkage was also observed on chromosome 2 in the combined AP and synesthesia dataset, with a heterogeneity LOD score of 4.7 on 2q24.1. When only the AP families were considered, a maximum heterogeneity LOD score of 3.93 was observed on 2q22.1.

Apart from one documented case of a non-musically trained AP possessor (Ross, Olson, & Gore, 2003), most AP possessors report early onset of music training (Levitin & Zatorre, 2003; Miyazaki & Ogawa, 2006; Russo, Windell, & Cuddy, 2003), which suggests a possible critical time window for the development of AP. Previous studies have reported that the inhibition of *HDAC* (histone-deacetylase), an enzyme which serves as a "brake" to critical-period neuroplasticity, could reopen the critical window and alter music preference or enable recovery from amblyopia in adult mice (Putignano *et al.*, 2007; Silingardi, Scali, Belluomini, & Pizzorusso, 2010; Yang, Lin, & Hensch, 2012). Based on this evidence, Gervain *et al.* (2013) investigated whether the administration of valproate, a *HDAC* inhibitor may potentially reopen the critical period for AP development and facilitate pitch naming ability in 24 non-musically trained adult males. Using a randomized, double-blind, placebo-controlled crossover study, during each treatment arm, the participants took either valproate or placebo capsules over the course of 15 days and underwent daily 10-minute pitch association online training from days 8 to 14 before taking the AP assessment task on day 15. Results showed that in the first treatment arm, the valproate group performed significantly above chance level while the placebo group performed at chance. Intriguingly, in the second treatment arm, no significant difference in performance was observed between the two groups as both performed at chance level. It was suggested that the worse performance in both groups during the second treatment arm could be due to a memory conflict whereby the set of pitches learned in the first treatment interfered with those learned in the second treatment. The researchers therefore concluded that the significant findings from the first treatment arm offered a preliminary, proof-of-concept demonstration that valproate has an effect on AP perception, potentially by reactivating critical-period learning through *HDAC* inhibition. It is important to note, however, that no significant correlation between AP performance and valproate levels in the blood was observed.

Music Production Abilities

Music Performance

Using genome-wide transcriptional profiling, Järvelä's research team have investigated the effect of performing music on the human transcriptome in 10 professional musicians (Kanduri, Kuusi, *et al.*, 2015). Peripheral blood samples from the musicians before and after a 2-hour concert performance were compared to those of 10 musician controls before and after a 2-hour session without music exposure. Similar to their transcriptome study on music listening (Kanduri, Raijas, *et al.*, 2015), music performance was observed to upregulate several genes involved in dopaminergic neurotransmission, one of which was *SNCA*, a gene on chromosome 4q22.1 previously identified as a strong candidate for music perception ability (Oikkonen & Järvelä, 2014; Pulli *et al.*, 2008), music listening (Kanduri, Raijas, *et al.*, 2015), and a possible early biomarker for Parkinson's disease (Scherzer *et al.*, 2008). In addition, other motor behavior-related genes including *CCR4* and *FOS* were also upregulated, which may potentially shed light on the molecular mechanisms for executing music-related fine motor skills. Other upregulated genes included those implicated in learning and memory (e.g., *FOS, HDC, CLN8, DOPEY2*), and biological processes crucial for neuronal survival and neuroprotection, such as calcium ion and iron ion homeostasis (e.g., *SNCA, FOS, CLN8*).

It is noteworthy that this study also found that some genes known to be involved in song perception and production in songbirds (e.g., *SNCA*, *FOS*, *DUSP1*) were upregulated in music performance. This suggests a possible evolutionary conservation in sound perception and production molecular mechanisms. In addition, several of the upregulated genes such as *SNCA*, *FOS*, *CLN8* and *DOPEY2* have been implicated in neuropsychiatric or neurode-generative disorders (Byun *et al.*, 2013; Scherzer *et al.*, 2008; Smith *et al.*, 1997; Vantaggiato *et al.*, 2009). The researchers therefore speculated that modulation of these genes by music performance may serve to explain music's therapeutic effects (Conrad, 2010).

Music Creativity

The genetic basis of music creativity was first investigated in a candidate gene study involving 19 Finnish musical families who were assessed using a web-based questionnaire. This consisted of questions about music background and participation in creative music activities, such as music composition, improvisation or arrangement (Ukkola *et al.*, 2009). Findings suggest that creative functions in music have a strong genetic component, with a heritability estimate of .84 reported for this sample. While a significant positive association between music creativity and high music perception test scores was observed, no significant associations between music creativity and the polymorphisms of candidate genes such as *TPH1*, *COMT* and *AVPR1A* were found.

Ukkola-Vuoti *et al.* (2013) performed a subsequent CNV analysis on five multigenerational Finnish families and 172 unrelated individuals using the same music creativity questionnaire. A "creative phenotype" was characterized by engagement in at least one creative music activity (i.e., composing, improvising, or music arranging). Results showed that a deletion on 5p15.33 was present in 48% of family members and 28% of unrelated participants who exhibited the creative phenotype, while a duplication on 2p22.1 was present in 27% of the creative family members. On the other hand, deletions in three CNV regions (2p12, 3p14.1 and 3q28) occurred in 19% to 31% of family members who did not engage in creative music activities. The researchers speculated that the link between 2p22.1 and music creativity may be due to the gene *GALM* found at that locus, which is associated with serotonin transporter binding potential in the human thalamus (Liu *et al.*, 2011). The medial geniculate nucleus of the thalamus forms part of the auditory pathways, and more generally has been implicated in music-related functions such as beat perception (McAuley, Henry, & Tkach, 2012), sensorimotor synchronization (Krause, Schnitzler, & Pollok, 2010), and musical imagery (Goycoolea *et al.*, 2007). Other studies have also found a link between the serotonin transporter gene (*SLC6A4*) and music-related functions such as choir participation (Morley *et al.*, 2012) and creative dance (Bachner-Melman *et al.*, 2005).

Using an expanded version of their original questionnaire, the same Finnish research group recently performed genome-wide linkage analysis on a large sample consisting of 474 participants from 79 families and 103 unrelated individuals to investigate engagement in three forms of music creativity, namely, composing, arranging, and improvising (Oikkonen et al., 2016). The heritabilities for the various phenotypes estimated from the family data were moderate in general (composing: 33.3%; arranging: 33.4%; non-musically creative phenotype [defined as musically trained individuals who neither compose nor arrange]: 28.9%), with the exception of improvising which had a low heritability estimate of 11.6%. The phenotypes with moderate heritability were then selected for genome-wide linkage analysis. For arranging, suggestive linkage evidence was observed at 16p12.1-q12.1 (LOD = 2.75), which is near the previously identified chromosomal region for music perception (Oikkonen et al., 2015). The best linkage evidence in the region was obtained at 16p12.1 (LOD = 4.22), in the intron of the GSG1L gene, which is implicated in fast synaptic transmission in the central nervous system (Shanks et al., 2012). Suggestive linkage evidence at 4q22.1 was found for composing (LOD = 2.15), which overlaps with the previously identified loci (4q22-23) for music perception ability (Oikkonen et al., 2015; Pulli et al., 2008) and is in the vicinity of the implicated locus (4q26) for vocal pitch-matching accuracy (Park et al., 2012). Furthermore, the locus 4q22.1 also contains the gene SNCA, which was previously observed to be one of the most upregulated genes after music listening and music performance (Kanduri, Kuusi, et al., 2015; Kanduri, Raijas, et al., 2015). The converging findings therefore add credence to the chromosome 4 region being a candidate region for various music-related traits and point to a common genetic background for these traits. Functional analysis of putative genes in the implicated chromosomal region for composing indicated an overrepresentation of the cerebellar long-term depression (LTD) pathway: 17 out of the 141 known genes involved in the LTD pathway were found in the analysis for genes suggestively associated with composing. The LTD pathway is purportedly a cellular model for synaptic plasticity and memory (Collingridge, Peineau, Howland, & Wang, 2010), which are cognitive attributes arguably relevant to creatively composing music from existing knowledge structures. In addition, the LTD pathway contains the aforementioned GSG1L gene which is suggestively linked to arranging. This implies that individual differences in genes affecting the LTD pathway may potentially influence music creativity.

Interestingly, at 18q21, there was significant linkage evidence (LOD = 3.09) for the non-musically creative phenotype, with the best linkage evidence in the vicinity of the CDH7 and CDH19 genes from the cadherin family. These genes have been linked to neuropsychiatric conditions such as schizophrenia (Redies, Hertel, & Hübner, 2012), and CDH7 is also implicated in the vocal development of songbirds (Matsunaga & Okanoya, 2008). The significant linkage region at 18q21 has also been associated with the 18q deletion syndrome which may cause hearing loss and intellectual disability, and is adjacent to a previously identified loci (18q23-21.1) for music perception ability (Oikkonen *et al.*, 2015).

A major limitation of the above studies is that the creative phenotypes were not defined quantitatively by objective testing nor were they indicative of actual creative ability. Therefore, there is a possibility that these phenotypes may reflect a willingness or motivation to engage in music creativity rather than the actual ability itself. Furthermore, by defining the non-musically creative phenotype as musically trained individuals who do not actively compose or arrange music appears to be dismissive of other manifestations of music creativity that do not involve composing or arranging. A more carefully considered characterization of various music creativity phenotypes is thus warranted.

Singing

Using a single note vocal pitch-matching task, Park *et al.* (2012) investigated the genetic factors underpinning singing ability by conducting family-based linkage and association analyses on 1,008 participants from 73 extended Mongolian families. Genome-wide linkage analysis revealed that the most significant linkage peak for singing accuracy was on 4q23 (LOD = 3.1), which overlaps with other regions on chromosome 4q implicated in music perception ability (Oikkonen *et al.*, 2015; Pulli *et al.*, 2008). The researchers also utilized exome sequencing to find other potential candidate SNPs and discovered a non-synonymous SNP (rs4148254) in *UGT8* on 4q26 that was significantly associated with singing accuracy. *UGT8* encodes *UDP* glycosyltransferase 8, a protein highly expressed in the brain (especially the substantia nigra) which catalyzes the transfer of galactose to ceramide. In addition, CNV analysis using an array comparative genomic hybridization (aCGH) platform has shown that a copy number loss at 5.6kb (5,600 base pairs) upstream of *UGT8* may be negatively associated with singing accuracy. This study thus provides promising evidence that singing accuracy may be heritable and possibly associated with the gene *UGT8* on chromosome 4q.

A candidate gene association study by Morley *et al.* (2012) investigated the relationship between singing participation and allelic variants of the genes *AVPR1A* and *SLC6A4*. An overall association with choir participation was observed at the STin2 (intron 2) polymorphism in the *SLC6A4* gene, with the STin2 9-repeat and 12-repeat alleles being more common in choral singers, and the 10-repeat alleles more common in controls (defined as individuals with no regular participation in any organized musical activity; e.g., choir, dance class, orchestra, or rock band). No significant differences in allele frequencies were observed between the two groups for other *SLC6A4* and *AVPR1A* polymorphisms. Previous studies have reported possible involvement of STin2 in personality traits and reward behavior (Kazantseva *et al.*, 2008; Saiz *et al.*, 2010;

Zhong et al., 2009). *SLC6A4* polymorphisms (together with *AVPR1A*) have also been linked to participation in creative dance (Bachner-Melman et al., 2005). As several studies have observed associations between *AVPR1A* polymorphisms and certain musical traits such as music memory, music perception ability and music listening behavior (Granot et al., 2007; Ukkola-Vuoti et al., 2011; Ukkola et al., 2009), the non-significant *AVPR1A* association in this study led the authors to speculate that the observed STin2 effect may be related to social behavioral characteristics (i.e., a "predisposed to group activity" phenotype) rather than being music-related per se.

Rhythm Production

So far, no genetic studies have focused specifically on rhythm production ability. As noted previously in this chapter, a study investigating speech and language disorder in a family pedigree showed that the affected family members were impaired in rhythm perception and production (Alcock et al., 2000), and all of them had a mutated copy of the *FOXP2* gene (Lai et al., 2001)

Music Culture

An association between music culture and genes has been demonstrated in several recent studies, even though music culture is typically viewed as an environmental factor that influences musical ability. In one study, traditional songs from 39 African cultures were classified by their music characteristics such as yodeling and tempo (Callaway, 2007). When the music styles of the various African cultures were compared with a database of African genotypes, a correlation between genes and music culture was found, which suggests that cultures that are musically similar also exhibit greater genetic similarity. Importantly, the researchers also found that the correlation between music culture and geographical distance was weaker than the correlation between music culture and genes, supporting this interpretation.

Similarly, in the first comparative phylogenetic study of genetics and folk music, Pamjav et al. (2012) established a relationship between folk music styles in 31 Eurasian cultures and genetic distance, with maternal lineages more strongly linked to folk music traditions than paternal lineages. Specifically, they found that significantly similar folk music cultures could predict significant genetic connections in 82% of the cases examined. However, the reverse was not true; close genetic connections were able to predict similar folk music styles in only 28% of the cases. Based on these results, the researchers speculated that a close genetic relation between two populations is indicative of prior physical and biological contact between ancestors of both populations, which may have in turn brought about an interaction and transmission of musical cultures between the two groups and resulted in the similar folk music styles. This work has also identified a common musical style that was prevalent in a large subset of the cultures studied, most of which were closely related genetically. It also leads to the possibility of the existence of a common musical "parent language" from which various folk music traditions branched out and evolved.

Brown *et al.* (2014) demonstrated a statistically significant correlation between folk song structure and mitochondrial DNA variation in nine indigenous Taiwanese populations, even after controlling for geographical proximity. Notably, although a significant correlation between language and genes in the populations studied was also found, the correlation became insignificant after controlling for geographical proximity. In addition, the correlation between music and language was insignificant, which indicates that the genetic components of music and language may be partially distinct. In particular, an examination of the population structure for genes, music, and language for the nine indigenous populations revealed greater similarities in the population structures between music and genes as compared to language and genes. Taken together, these findings suggest the possibility of the coevolution of music and genes, and they promote the use of music as a novel cultural marker for the study of population migration history, which can serve to complement existing markers such as language.

Collectively, convergent findings from diverse cultural samples as described above give credence to a link between music culture and genes and highlight the importance of genetic influences in shaping the music environment of a human culture and challenges the common perception of music culture purely as an environmental factor.

Summary

Our goal in this chapter has been to describe the molecular genetic bases of various music-related traits, which can now be grouped together and summarized in Plate 9. For the genome-wide transcriptome and positive selection analysis studies (Kanduri, Kuusi, *et al.*, 2015; Kanduri, Raijas, *et al.*, 2015; Liu *et al.*, 2016), the only genes listed are those known to be important in brain function, hearing, the singing network of songbirds, or previously implicated in other music studies.

To date, some promising and converging findings have begun to emerge from the molecular genetic studies of musical traits. Most notably, the locus 4q22 has been consistently implicated in music-related traits, including music perception ability and music composing. The implication of neighboring loci 4q23 and 4q26 in vocal pitch-matching provide further support of the involvement of this chromosomal region in influencing music-related traits. In addition, the locus 4q22.1 harbors the gene *SNCA*, which has emerged in recent transcriptome studies as a potential candidate gene for music listening and music performance in musically experienced individuals. Given the role of *SNCA* in dopamine-related functions and music's association with dopamine release, as well as *SNCA*'s implication in song perception, learning, and production in songbirds, it appears that *SNCA* is a strong contender for influencing music behavior. Moreover, the putative links between *SNCA* and other songbird-related genes (e.g., *GRIN2B, FOXP1, VLDLR, RGS9, FOS*) and various music traits suggest the possibility of cross-species evolutionary conservation for auditory perception and vocal production.

Apart from *SNCA, FAM49B* at 8q24.21 was another gene noted to be upregulated in musically experienced participants after classical music listening. This finding is in line with past research evidence showing that the locus 8q24 and nearby locus 8q21 were linked to music perception and AP.

The gene polymorphisms of *AVPR1A* on chromosome 12q has also been consistently implicated in music listening, music perception ability, and music memory. On the other hand, the gene *SLC6A4* has been associated with music memory and choir participation. The role of *AVPR1A* in social cognition and behavior has been well-investigated, as has the possible interaction between *AVPR1A* and *SLC6A4* in communicative behavior. The associations of these two genes with various music functions raises the intriguing possibility of an overlap in the neurobiological basis of music functions and social behavior, which appears to be consistent with the evolutionary adaptive role of music in promoting social bonding some researchers have proposed (e.g., Huron, 2001; Tarr, Launay, & Dunbar, 2014).

In conclusion, given the pervasive influence of genetic factors on a vast array of human traits (Polderman *et al.*, 2015), it is not surprising to observe a growing body of genetic evidence for music ability and music-related traits. Future research would benefit from a more precise delineation of music phenotypes, so as to facilitate the identification of specific genetic factors underlying each music phenotype. As the molecular genetic basis of musical traits becomes increasingly elucidated, it is likely that this will bring new insights into the biological basis of music. Furthermore, the exciting developments and emerging evidence in music genetics research make the stance of radical environmentalism increasingly implausible. It is understandable that some may feel uncomfortable with the notion of music ability being influenced by genes, given their concern about the ethical implications that potentially arise if genetic makeup is used as a basis to reserve music learning resources for a select few and exclude the less endowed from having the opportunity to learn. It is our strong view however, that both biological determinism and radical environmentalism are problematic, and that a complete account of music ability and the development of musical expertise requires both genetic and environmental factors and their interaction to be understood thoroughly.

Note

The chapter is adapted from the first author's doctoral dissertation (Tan, 2016). Readers are encouraged to refer to the thesis for further information.

References

Aarde, S. M., & Jentsch, J. D. (2006). Haploinsufficiency of the arginine-vasopressin gene is associated with poor spatial working memory performance in rats. *Hormones and Behavior, 49*(4), 501–508.

Albers, H. E., Karom, M., & Smith, D. (2002). Serotonin and vasopressin interact in the hypothalamus to control communicative behavior. *NeuroReport, 13*(7), 931–933.

Alcock, K. J., Passingham, R. E., Watkins, K., & Vargha-Khadem, F. (2000). Pitch and timing abilities in inherited speech and language impairment. *Brain and Language, 75*(1), 34–46.

Almal, S. H., & Padh, H. (2012). Implications of gene copy-number variation in health and diseases. *Journal of Human Genetics, 57*(1), 6–13.

Bachem, A. (1955). Absolute pitch. *Journal of the Acoustical Society of America, 11*, 434–439.

Bachner-Melman, R., Dina, C., Zohar, A. H., Constantini, N., Lerer, E., Hoch, S., ... Ebstein, R. P. (2005). AVPR1a and SLC6A4 gene polymorphisms are associated with creative dance performance. *PLos Genetics, 1*(3), e42.

Ballana, E., Wang, J., Venail, F., Estivill, X., Puel, J. L., Arbonès, M. L., & Bosch, A. (2008). Efficient and specific transduction of cochlear supporting cells by adeno-associated virus serotype 5. *Neuroscience Letters, 442*(2), 134–139.

Basit, S., Lee, K., Habib, R., Chen, L., Umm, E. K., Santos-Cortez, R. L. P., ... Leal, S. M. (2011). DFNB89, a novel autosomal recessive nonsyndromic hearing impairment locus on chromosome 16q21-q23.2. *Human Genetics, 129*(4), 379–385.

Benke, K. S., Carlson, M. C., Doan, B. Q., Walston, J. D., Xue, Q. L., Reiner, A. P., ... Fallin, M. D. (2011). The association of genetic variants in interleukin-1 genes with cognition: Findings from the cardiovascular health study. *Experimental Gerontology, 46*(12), 1010–1019.

Bielsky, I. F., Hu, S. B., Szegda, K. L., Westphal, H., & Young, L. J. (2004). Profound impairment in social recognition and reduction in anxiety-like behavior in vasopressin V1a receptor knockout mice. *Neuropsychopharmacology, 29*(3), 483–493.

Brown, S., Savage, P. E., Ko, A. M. S., Stoneking, M., Ko, Y. C., Loo, J. H., & Trejaut, J. A. (2014). Correlations in the population structure of music, genes and language. *Proceedings of the Royal Society B: Biological Sciences, 281*(1774), 2013–2072.

Byun, K., Kim, D., Bayarsaikhan, E., Oh, J., Kim, J., Kwak, G., ... Lee, B. (2013). Changes of calcium binding proteins, c-Fos and COX in hippocampal formation and cerebellum of Niemann-Pick, type C mouse. *Journal of Chemical Neuroanatomy, 52*, 1–8.

Callaway, E. (2007). Music is in our genes. *Nature News.* Retrieved from http://www.nature.com/news/2007/071210/full/news.2007.359.html

Carrion-Castillo, A., Franke, B., & Fisher, S. E. (2013). Molecular genetics of dyslexia: An overview. *Dyslexia, 19*(4), 214–240.

Chen, Q., Heston, J. B., Burkett, Z. D., & White, S. A. (2013). Expression analysis of the speech-related genes FoxP1 and FoxP2 and their relation to singing behavior in two songbird species. *Journal of Experimental Biology, 216*(19), 3682–3692.

Collingridge, G. L., Peineau, S., Howland, J. G., & Wang, Y. T. (2010). Long-term depression in the CNS. *Nature Reviews Neuroscience, 11*(7), 459–473.

Conrad, C. (2010). Music for healing: From magic to medicine. *The Lancet, 376*(9757), 1980–1981.

De Quervain, D. J. F., & Papassotiropoulos, A. (2006). Identification of a genetic cluster influencing memory performance and hippocampal activity in humans. *Proceedings of the National Academy of Sciences of the United States of America, 103*(11), 4270–4274.

Digilio, M. C., Marino, B., Capolino, R., & Dallapiccola, B. (2005). Clinical manifestations of Deletion 22q11.2 syndrome (DiGeorge/Velo-Cardio-Facial syndrome). *Images in Paediatric Cardiology, 7*(2), 23–34.

Dovern, A., Fink, G. R., Fromme, A. C. B., Wohlschläger, A. M., Weiss, P. H., & Riedl, V. (2012). Intrinsic network connectivity reflects consistency of synesthetic experiences. *Journal of Neuroscience, 32*(22), 7614–7621.

Ferguson, J. N., Young, L. J., & Insel, T. R. (2002). The neuroendocrine basis of social recognition. *Frontiers in Neuroendocrinology, 23*(2), 200–224.

Fukuda, E., Hamada, S., Hasegawa, S., Katori, S., Sanbo, M., Miyakawa, T., … Yagi, T. (2008). Down-regulation of protocadherin-α A isoforms in mice changes contextual fear conditioning and spatial working memory. *European Journal of Neuroscience, 28*(7), 1362–1376.

Gervain, J., Vines, B. W., Chen, L. M., Seo, R. J., Hensch, T. K., Werker, J. F., & Young, A. H. (2013). Valproate reopens critical-period learning of absolute pitch. *Frontiers in Systems Neuroscience, 7*, 102. http://doi.org/10.3389/fnsys.2013.00102.

Goycoolea, M. V., Mena, I., Neubauer, S. G., Levy, R. G., Grez, M. F., & Berger, C. G. (2007). Musical brains: A study of spontaneous and evoked musical sensations without external auditory stimuli. *Acta Oto-Laryngologica, 127*(7), 711–721.

Granot, R. Y., Frankel, Y., Gritsenko, V., Lerer, E., Gritsenko, I., Bachner-Melman, R., … Ebstein, R. P. (2007). Provisional evidence that the arginine vasopressin 1a receptor gene is associated with musical memory. *Evolution and Human Behavior, 28*(5), 313–318.

Granot, R. Y., Uzefovsky, F., Bogopolsky, H., & Ebstein, R. P. (2013). Effects of Arginine Vasopressin on musical short-term memory. *Frontiers in Psychology, 4*, 712.

Gregersen, P. K., Kowalsky, E., Lee, A., Baron-Cohen, S., Fisher, S. E., Asher, J. E., … Li, W. (2013). Absolute pitch exhibits phenotypic and genetic overlap with synesthesia. *Human Molecular Genetics, 22*(10), 2097–2104.

Grillet, N., Schwander, M., Hildebrand, M. S., Sczaniecka, A., Kolatkar, A., Velasco, J., … Müller, U. (2009). Mutations in LOXHD1, an evolutionarily conserved stereociliary protein, disrupt hair cell function in mice and cause progressive hearing loss in humans. *American Journal of Human Genetics, 85*(3), 328–337.

Haugas, M., Lilleväli, K., Hakanen, J., & Salminen, M. (2010). Gata2 is required for the development of inner ear semicircular ducts and the surrounding perilymphatic space. *Developmental Dynamics, 239*(9), 2452–2469.

Hertel, N., Redies, C., & Medina, L. (2012). Cadherin expression delineates the divisions of the postnatal and adult mouse amygdala. *Journal of Comparative Neurology, 520*(17), 3982–4012.

Huron, D. (2001) Is music an evolutionary adaptation? *Annals of the New York Academy of Sciences, 930*, 43–61.

Kanduri, C., Kuusi, T., Ahvenainen, M., Philips, A. K., Lähdesmäki, H., & Järvelä, I. (2015). The effect of music performance on the transcriptome of professional musicians. *Scientific Reports, 5*, 9506.

Kanduri, C., Raijas, P., Ahvenainen, M., Philips, A. K., Ukkola-Vuoti, L., Lähdesmäki, H., & Järvelä, I. (2015). The effect of listening to music on human transcriptome. *PeerJ, (3)*, e830.

Karma, K. (2002). Auditory structuring in explaining dyslexia. In P. McKevitt, S. Nuallain, & C. Mulvihill (Eds.), *Language, vision and music* (pp. 221–230). Amsterdam/Philadelphia: John Benjamins Publishing Company.

Kazantseva, A. V., Gaysina, D. A., Faskhutdinova, G. G., Noskova, T., Malykh, S. B., & Khusnutdinova, E. K. (2008). Polymorphisms of the serotonin transporter gene (5-HTTLPR, A/G SNP in 5-HTTLPR, and STin2 VNTR) and their relation to personality traits in healthy individuals from Russia. *Psychiatric Genetics*, *18*(4), 167–176.

Krause, V., Schnitzler, A., & Pollok, B. (2010). Functional network interactions during sensorimotor synchronization in musicians and non-musicians. *NeuroImage*, *52*(1), 245–251.

Lai, C. S. L., Fisher, S. E., Hurst, J. A., Vargha-Khadem, F., & Monaco, A. P. (2001). A forkhead-domain gene is mutated in a severe speech and language disorder. *Nature*, *413*(6855), 519–523.

Levitin, D. J., & Zatorre, R. J. (2003). On the nature of early music training and absolute pitch: A reply to Brown, Sachs, Cammuso, and Folstein. *Music Perception: An Interdisciplinary Journal*, *21*(1), 105–110.

Lin, J., Yan, X., Wang, C., Guo, Z., Rolfs, A., & Luo, J. (2012). Anatomical expression patterns of delta-protocadherins in developing chicken cochlea. *Journal of Anatomy*, *221*(6), 598–608.

Liu, X., Bulgakov, O. V., Darrow, K. N., Pawlyk, B., Adamian, M., Liberman, M. C., & Li, T. (2007). Usherin is required for maintenance of retinal photoreceptors and normal development of cochlear hair cells. *Proceedings of the National Academy of Sciences of the United States of America*, *104*(11), 4413–4418.

Liu, X., Cannon, D. M., Akula, N., Moya, P. R., Knudsen, G. M., Arentzen, T. E., … McMahon, F. J. (2011). A non-synonymous polymorphism in galactose mutarotase (GALM) is associated with serotonin transporter binding potential in the human thalamus: Results of a genome-wide association study. *Molecular Psychiatry*, *16*(6), 584–594.

Liu, X., Kanduri, C., Oikkonen, J., Karma, K., Raijas, P., Ukkola-Vuoti, L., … Järvelä, I. (2016). Detecting signatures of positive selection associated with musical aptitude in the human genome. *Scientific Reports*, *6*, 21198.

Loui, P., Kroog, K., Zuk, J., Winner, E., & Schlaug, G. (2011). Relating pitch awareness to phonemic awareness in children: Implications for tone-deafness and dyslexia. *Frontiers in Psychology*, *2*, 111.

Ludwig, M. G., & Seuwen, K. (2002). Characterization of the human adenylyl cyclase gene family: cDNA, gene structure, and tissue distribution of the nine isoforms. *Journal of Receptors and Signal Transduction*, *22*(1–4), 79–110.

Matsunaga, E., & Okanoya, K. (2008). Expression analysis of cadherins in the songbird brain: Relationship to vocal system development. *Journal of Comparative Neurology*, *508*(2), 329–342.

McAuley, J. D., Henry, M. J., & Tkach, J. (2012). Tempo mediates the involvement of motor areas in beat perception. *Annals of the New York Academy of Sciences*, *1252*(1), 77–84.

McGee, J., Goodyear, R. J., McMillan, D. R., Stauffer, E. A., Holt, J. R., Locke, K. G., … Richardson, G. P. (2006). The very large G-protein-coupled receptor VLGR1: A component of the ankle link complex required for the normal development of auditory hair bundles. *Journal of Neuroscience*, *26*(24), 6543–6553.

McLachlan, N., Marco, D., Light, M., & Wilson, S. (2013). Consonance and pitch. *Journal of Experimental Psychology: General*, *142*(4), 1142–1158.

McLachlan, N., & Wilson, S. (2010). The central role of recognition in auditory perception: A neurobiological model. *Psychological Review*, *117*(1), 175–196.

Milnik, A., Heck, A., Vogler, C., Heinze, H. J., de Quervain, D. J. F., & Papassotiropoulos, A. (2012). Association of KIBRA with episodic and working memory: A meta-analysis. *American Journal of Medical Genetics, Part B: Neuropsychiatric Genetics, 159* B(8), 958–969.

Miyazaki, K., & Ogawa, Y. (2006). Learning absolute pitch by children: A cross-sectional study. *Music Perception: An Interdisciplinary Journal, 24*(1), 63–78.

Morley, A. P., Narayanan, M., Mines, R., Molokhia, A., Baxter, S., Craig, G., … Craig, I. (2012). AVPR1A and SLC6A4 polymorphisms in choral singers and non-musicians: A gene association study. *PLoS ONE, 7*(2), e31763. doi: 10.1371/journal. pone.0031763

North, H. A., Clifford, M. A., & Donoghue, M. J. (2013). 'Til Eph do us part': Intercellular signaling via Eph receptors and ephrin ligands guides cerebral cortical development from birth through maturation. *Cerebral Cortex, 23*(8), 1765–1773.

Oikkonen, J., Huang, Y., Onkamo, P., Ukkola-Vuoti, L., Raijas, P., Karma, K., … Jarvela, I. (2015). A genome-wide linkage and association study of musical aptitude identifies loci containing genes related to inner ear development and neurocognitive functions. *Molecular Psychiatry, 20*(2), 275–282.

Oikkonen, J., & Järvelä, I. (2014). Genomics approaches to study musical aptitude. *BioEssays, 36*(11), 1102–1108.

Oikkonen, J., Kuusi, T., Peltonen, P., Raijas, P., Ukkola-Vuoti, L., Karma, K., … Järvelä, I. (2016). Creative activities in music ? A genome-wide linkage analysis. *PLoS ONE, 11*(2), e0148679.

Ostroveanu, A., Van Der Zee, E. A., Eisel, U. L. M., Schmidt, M., & Nijholt, I. M. (2010). Exchange protein activated by cyclic AMP 2 (Epac2) plays a specific and time–limited role in memory retrieval. *Hippocampus, 20*(9), 1018–1026.

Pamjav, H., Juhász, Z., Zalán, A., Németh, E., & Damdin, B. (2012). A comparative phylogenetic study of genetics and folk music. *Molecular Genetics and Genomics, 287*(4), 337–349.

Park, H., Lee, S., Kim, H. J., Ju, Y. S., Shin, J. Y., Hong, D., … Seo, J. S. (2012). Comprehensive genomic analyses associate UGT8 variants with musical ability in a Mongolian population. *Journal of Medical Genetics, 49*(12), 747–752.

Peretz, I. (2009). Music, language and modularity framed in action. *Psychologica Belgica, 49*(2–3), 157–175.

Pfenning, A. R., Hara, E., Whitney, O., Rivas, M. V., Wang, R., Roulhac, P. L., … Jarvis, E. D. (2014). Convergent transcriptional specializations in the brains of humans and song-learning birds. *Science, 346*(6215).

Polderman, T. J. C., Benyamin, B., De Leeuw, C. A., Sullivan, P. F., Van Bochoven, A., Visscher, P. M., & Posthuma, D. (2015). Meta-analysis of the heritability of human traits based on fifty years of twin studies. *Nature Genetics, 47*(7), 702–709.

Profita, J., & Bidder, T. G. (1988). Perfect pitch. *American Journal of Medical Genetics, 29*(4), 763–771.

Pulli, K., Karma, K., Norio, R., Sistonen, P., Göring, H. H. H., & Järvelä, I. (2008). Genome-wide linkage scan for loci of musical aptiatde in Finnish families: Evidence for a major locus at 4q22. *Journal of Medical Genetics, 45*(7), 451–456.

Putignano, E., Lonetti, G., Cancedda, L., Ratto, G., Costa, M., Maffei, L., & Pizzorusso, T. (2007). Developmental downregulation of histone posttranslational modifications regulates visual cortical plasticity. *Neuron, 53*(5), 747–759.

Redies, C., Hertel, N., & Hübner, C. A. (2012). Cadherins and neuropsychiatric disorders. *Brain Research, 1470*, 130–144.

Ross, D. A., Olson, I. R., & Gore, J. C. (2003). Absolute pitch does not depend on early musical training. *Annals of the New York Academy of Sciences, 999*, 522–526.

Rouw, R., & Scholte, H. S. (2007). Increased structural connectivity in grapheme-color synesthesia. *Nature Neuroscience, 10*(6), 792–797.

Russo, F. A., Windell, D. L., & Cuddy, L. L. (2003). Learning the 'special note': Evidence for a critical period for absolute pitch acquisition. *Music Perception: An Interdisciplinary Journal, 21*(1), 119–127.

Saiz, P. A., Garcia-Portilla, M. P., Herrero, R., Arango, C., Corcoran, P., Morales, B., ... Bobes, J. (2010). Interactions between functional serotonergic polymorphisms and demographic factors influence personality traits in healthy Spanish Caucasians. *Psychiatric Genetics, 20*(4), 171–178.

Salimpoor, V. N., Benovoy, M., Larcher, K., Dagher, A., & Zatorre, R. J. (2011). Anatomically distinct dopamine release during anticipation and experience of peak emotion to music. *Nature Neuroscience, 14*(2), 257–264.

Scherzer, C. R., Grass, J. A., Liao, Z., Pepivani, I., Zheng, B., Eklund, A. C., ... Schlossmacher, M. G. (2008). GATA transcription factors directly regulate the Parkinson's disease-linked gene α-synuclein. *Proceedings of the National Academy of Sciences of the United States of America, 105*(31), 10907–10912.

Seashore, C. E., Lewis, D., & Saetveit, J. G. (1960). *Seashore measures of musical talents manual* (2nd ed.). New York: Psychological Corporation.

Shanks, N. F., Savas, J. N., Maruo, T., Cais, O., Hirao, A., Oe, S., ... Nakagawa, T. (2012). Differences in AMPA and kainate receptor interactomes facilitate identification of AMPA receptor auxiliary subunit GSG1L. *Cell Reports, 1*(6), 590–598.

Silingardi, D., Scali, M., Belluomini, G., & Pizzorusso, T. (2010). Epigenetic treatments of adult rats promote recovery from visual acuity deficits induced by long-term monocular deprivation. *European Journal of Neuroscience, 31*(12), 2185–2192.

Smith, D. J., Stevens, M. E., Sudanagunta, S. P., Bronson, R. T., Makhinson, M., Watabe, A. M., ... Rubin, E. M. (1997). Functional screening of 2 Mb of human chromosome 21q22.2 in transgenic mice implicates minibrain in learning defects associated with Down syndrome. *Nature Genetics, 16*(1), 28–36.

Stein, E., & Tessier-Lavigne, M. (2001). Hierarchical organization of guidance receptors: Silencing of netrin attraction by slit through a Robo/DCC receptor complex. *Science, 291*(5510), 1928–1938.

Tan, Y. T. (2016). The genetic basis of singing ability: A twin study. Unpublished doctoral dissertation. The University of Melbourne, Australia.

Tarr, B., Launay, J., & Dunbar, R. I. M. (2014). Music and social bonding: 'Self-other' merging and neurohormonal mechanisms. *Frontiers in Psychology, 5*(SEP), 1096.

Taymans, J. M., Leysen, J. E., & Langlois, X. (2003). Striatal gene expression of RGS2 and RGS4 is specifically mediated by dopamine D1 and D2 receptors: Clues for RGS2 and RGS4 functions. *Journal of Neurochemistry, 84*(5), 1118–1127.

Theusch, E., & Gitschier, J. (2011). Absolute pitch twin study and segregation analysis. *Twin Research and Human Genetics, 14*(2), 173–178. doi 10.1375/twin.14.2.173

Theusch, E., Basu, A., & Gitschier, J. (2009). Genome-wide study of families with absolute pitch reveals linkage to 8q24.21 and locus heterogeneity. *American Journal of Human Genetics, 85*, 112–119.

Torii, M., Hackett, T. A., Rakic, P., Levitt, P., & Polley, D. B. (2013). EphA signaling impacts development of topographic connectivity in auditory corticofugal systems. *Cerebral Cortex, 23*(4), 775–785.

Ukkola-Vuoti, L., Kanduri, C., Oikkonen, J., Buck, G., Blancher, C., Raijas, P., … Järvelä, I. (2013). Genome-wide copy number variation analysis in extended families and unrelated individuals characterized for musical aptitude and creativity in music. *PLoS ONE, 8*(2), e56356. https://doi.org/10.1371/journal.pone.0056356

Ukkola-Vuoti, L., Oikkonen, J., Onkamo, P., Karma, K., Raijas, P., & Järvelä, I. (2011). Association of the arginine vasopressin receptor 1A (AVPR1A) haplotypes with listening to music. *Journal of Human Genetics, 56*(4), 324–329.

Ukkola, L. T., Onkamo, P., Raijas, P., Karma, K., & Järvelä, I. (2009). Musical aptitude is associated with AVPR1A-haplotypes. *PLoS ONE, 4*(5), e5534. https://doi.org/10.1371/journal.pone.0005534

Vantaggiato, C., Redaelli, F., Falcone, S., Perrotta, C., Tonelli, A., Bondioni, S., … Bassi, M. T. (2009). A novel CLN8 mutation in late-infantile-onset neuronal ceroid lipofuscinosis (LINCL) reveals aspects of CLN8 neurobiological function. *Human Mutation, 30*(7), 1104–1116.

Wada, K., Howard, J. T., McConnell, P., Whitney, O., Lints, T., Rivas, M. V., … Jarvis, E. D. (2006). A molecular neuroethological approach for identifying and characterizing a cascade of behaviorally regulated genes. *Proceedings of the National Academy of Sciences of the United States of America, 103*(41), 15212–15217.

Wang, Y., Tong, X., & Ye, X. (2012). Ndfip1 negatively regulates RIG-I-dependent immune signaling by enhancing E3 ligase smurf1-mediated MAVS degradation. *Journal of Immunology, 189*(11), 5304–5313.

Wong, S. T., Athos, J., Figueroa, X. A., Pineda, V. V., Schaefer, M. L., Chavkin, C. C., … Storm, D. R. (1999). Calcium-stimulated adenylyl cyclase activity is critical for hippocampus-dependent long-term memory and late phase LTP. *Neuron, 23*(4), 787–798.

Yang, E. J., Lin, E. W., & Hensch, T. K. (2012). Critical period for acoustic preference in mice. *Proceedings of the National Academy of Sciences of the United States of America, 109*(SUPPL.2), 17213–17220.

Zhong, S., Israel, S., Xue, H., Sham, P. C., Ebstein, R. P., & Chew, S. H. (2009). A neurochemical approach to valuation sensitivity over gains and losses. *Proceedings of the Royal Society B: Biological Sciences, 276*(1676), 4181–4188.

PART IV
Integrative Models

18

EXPERTISE DEVELOPMENT FROM AN IMTD PERSPECTIVE

Françoys Gagné

Let's start with two questions. First, what does the IMTD acronym mean? It identifies the *Integrative (formerly Comprehensive) Model of Talent Development* (see Figure 18.1). The expression *talent development* means that it focuses on the progressive construction of outstanding achievements, labeled *talents* within that model; the term *integrative* indicates that it purports to identify and classify all significant causal influences of outstanding outcomes, from the more distal genetic influences to the more proximal behavioral and environmental sources. Figure 18.1 not only identifies all the components and subcomponents of the IMTD but illustrates their structural organization and interrelations. It also shows that the IMTD was born from the merging of two other models: the *Developmental Model for Natural Abilities (DMNA, columns 1-2-3)* and the long-standing and well-known *Differentiating Model of Giftedness and Talent (DMGT, columns 3-4-5)*. The DMGT was created over 30 years ago within the field of education (Gagné, 1985); it progressively evolved in breadth and complexity, even gaining some notoriety in arts (McPherson & Williamon, 2006) and sports (Tranckle & Cushion, 2006). The DMNA appeared much more recently (Gagné, 2013), and it immediately became clear that I could easily merge them to produce a comprehensive and seamless theoretical description of the complex talent development process.

Second, how is the IMTD relevant to the study of expertise? The answer is simple: thanks to the fuzzy terminology that afflicts the social sciences, the concepts of talent and expertise largely overlap, as both do with other closely related labels, such as *professional, specialist, eminent,* and even *prodigy* or *genius*. Indeed, such is the overlap between the *talent* and *expertise* labels that we could substitute expertise for talent in the acronym—thus creating the IMED—without modifying substantially the nature of the model. All these labels represent diverse forms

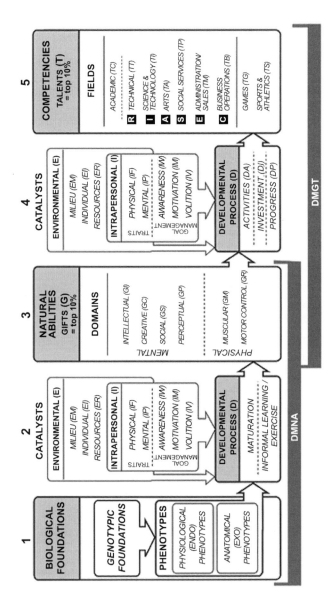

FIGURE 18.1 Gagné's Integrative Model of Talent Development (IMTD)

Reproduced from "From Genes to Talent: The DMGT/CMTD Perspective," Gagné, 2015b, p. 34, Figure 4, © Ministry of Education, Culture and Sport. General Technical Secretariat. Also from "Analyzing Musical Prodigiousness Using Gagné's Integrative Model of Talent Development," Gagné and McPherson, 2016, p. 18. ©2016, Oxford University Press.

and/or levels of excellence or outstanding achievements. I will examine each of these models according to their chronological emergence, inserting, when relevant, precisions more specific to the field of expertise research.

Introducing the DMGT

Defining the Key DMGT Constructs

The DMGT was created to bring some logic and consistency to a perceived terminological and definitional chaos over the meaning of the *giftedness* and *talent* constructs, two key concepts in the field of gifted education.

Giftedness and Talent

Scholars and practitioners who employ the term giftedness almost unanimously acknowledge, although most of the time implicitly, that the concept of gifted-ness represents two distinct realities: early emerging forms of giftedness with strong biological roots, often called *innate/natural talent*, as opposed to fully developed adult forms of giftedness. Scholars express that distinction through pairs of labels such as *potential/realization, aptitude/achievement,* or *promise/fulfillment*; we find them in many common expressions such as "Education's goal is to maximize each student's potential," or "Realizing one's potential is each per-son's lifelong challenge" (Gagné, 2009). Since two labels, giftedness and talent respectively, were available to describe outstanding abilities, it seemed logical to attach a distinct label to each of these two concepts. Thus were born the two basic definitions that constitute the core of the DMGT framework, presented below in their current form.

GIFTEDNESS designates the possession and use of untrained and spontane-ously expressed outstanding *natural abilities* or *aptitudes* (called *gifts*), in at least one ability *domain*, to a degree that places an individual at least among the *top 10 percent* of age peers.

TALENT designates the outstanding mastery of *systematically developed competencies* (knowledge and skills) in at least one *field* of human activity to a degree that places an individual at least among the *top 10 percent* of *learning peers* (those having accumulated a similar amount of learning time from current or past training).

Note how the DMGT clearly distinguishes the concepts of giftedness, potential, aptitude, and natural ability on the one hand, from those of talent, performance, achievement, systematically developed ability, as well as expertise, eminence, and prodigiousness; it is one of its unique qualities. Note also the use of the term *ability* as an umbrella construct that covers both natural abili-ties (aptitudes) and systematically developed abilities (competencies). Note finally that for the sake of common sense—but contrary to a current usage inspired by

Csikszentmihalyi's proposal (see Gagné, 1999, p. 226)—I chose the label *field* for categories of occupations, reserving the label *domain* for types of natural abilities.

Differential Assessment of Aptitudes and Achievements

Even though we call an aptitude a *potential*, assessing their level involves measuring some form of performance; for instance, IQ tests represent well-recognized measures of intellectual potential. How can we distinguish aptitude measures from achievement measures if both rely on some form of performance? The differences are not qualitative: There are no "pure" measures of aptitude on one side and achievement on the other. Ability measures range over a continuum from indices much more typical of natural abilities to clearly accepted achievement measures. Angoff (1988) proposed ten differentiating characteristics between aptitude and achievement measures (see Table 18.1), all of them worded as *quantitative* differences between types of instruments; they simply lean in opposite directions with regard to each criterion. The disparities will appear strikingly if we compare well-known examples in each category, for instance an IQ test as opposed to any semester exam in a school subject. The specificity (A) and recency (B) of contents differ markedly; the abilities assessed with an IQ test will apply to the learning of any subject, whereas any school curriculum focuses on a particular subject (C). Similar clear differences will emerge as we continue down the list in Table 18.1. Is there any hierarchy among these ten characteristics? The labels used in the DMGT (*natural* vs. *systematically developed*) point at our common choice for the overarching differentiator, namely the strength of genetic input in the case of aptitudes as opposed to the capital role of practice in the case of competencies/talents (see Gagné, 2009, for a detailed discussion).

The Prevalence Issue

How many people are gifted and/or talented? The "how many" question has no absolute answer; nowhere will we find a magical number that automatically separates gifted or talented individuals from the rest of the population. The establishment of a proper threshold requires a partially subjective professional consensus, just like nutritionists did when they established the various category thresholds for the body mass index (BMI). Unfortunately, no such consensus has yet been achieved in the various fields of talent development (Gagné, 1998). Yet the prevalence question is crucial for both theoretical and practical reasons. From a theoretical standpoint, a prevalence estimate represents an important contribution toward a more precise definition of any *normative* construct (e.g., poverty, tallness, weight, most neurotic syndromes) that targets—as is the case with giftedness and talent—a specific subgroup within a population. Practically speaking, adopting for instance a threshold of 10% instead of 1%—a *tenfold* difference in estimated prevalence—has a huge impact on selection practices, talent development

TABLE 18.1 Differentiating characteristics between aptitudes and competencies (adapted from Angoff, 1988)

Aptitudes (natural abilities)	Competencies (systematically developed abilities)
Content	
A More *general* content	More *specific* content
B "*Old formal*" learning	*Recent* acquisitions
C More widely *generalizable*	*Narrower* transfer to other situations
Processes	
D Major *genetic* substratum	Major *practice* component
E *Slow* growth	*Rapid* growth
F *Resistance* to stimulation	*Susceptibility* to stimulation
G *Informal* learning	More *formal* learning
Purpose	
H *Prospective* use (predicting future learning)	*Retrospective* use (assessing amount learned)
I Usable for *general population* evaluation	Limited to *systematically exposed individuals*
J Usable before any formal learning	Assessment requires formal learning

services, and their associated funding. These reasons no doubt explain why, according to my experience, the "how many" question is the second most common question—after "What do you mean by gifted (or talented)?"—that media people and the general public address to specialists in the field.

Because that question is so important, the DMGT proposes its own clear answer (Gagné, 1998): "Outstanding" means individuals who belong to the top 10% of the relevant reference group in terms of natural ability (for giftedness) or achievement (for talent). This generous choice for the initial threshold is counterbalanced by the recognition of degrees of giftedness or talent. The DMGT's metric-based (MB) system of levels has five hierarchically structured levels, with each successive level including the top 10% of the preceding one; they are labeled *mildly* (top 10%), *moderately* (top 1%), *highly* (top 1:1,000), *exceptionally* (top 1:10,000), and *extremely or profoundly* (top 1:100,000). These levels apply to every domain of giftedness and every field of talent.

Expertise Versus Talent

If we were to substitute expertise for talent in the DMGT's official definition, most scholars and professionals (experts?) in this field would probably endorse it. For instance, K. Anders Ericsson, the acknowledged "father" of expertise research, recently stated: "I will use the definition of Ericsson and Lehmann (1996, p. 227) and refer to expert performance 'as consistently superior performance on a specified set of representative tasks for a domain' without any age conditions" (2014, p. 83). Who would argue that there is a significant difference between "outstanding" and "superior"? Yet we observe significant definitional disagreements between various researchers, which seem to focus around two main points of contention: (a) the MB system's adoption of a top 10% minimum threshold for the recognition of talent or expertise; (b) the qualitative versus quantitative nature of the differences in competencies between experts and non-experts. Without surprise we observe the same two points of contention among scholars in gifted education. Let's briefly examine each of them.

Minimal Expertise

My earlier discussion of the prevalence issue applies here equally well. What proposals do we observe with respect to expertise? Just like in gifted education, muteness is the norm! In spite of its crucial role as a component of a clear definition, I have found no systematic discussion concerning the exceptionality of experts within any occupational field. Ericsson himself, within the very same 2014 text quoted above, shows little consistency by introducing other much more selective criteria. For instance, he describes experts "as exceptional individuals whose performance in sports, the arts, and science is vastly superior to that of the rest of the population" (p. 82). And further still in that same text, he describes expertise as "the very highest levels of performance—a level of performance attained by less than a handful individuals" (p. 100). We have moved within a few pages from a DMGT-like view to an extremely select fraternity! These very different estimates of the prevalence of experts illustrate how little importance "experts" in the field of expertise give to a question so crucial in my view for a proper definition of their key concept.

Even in chess, a sport/game extremely structured hierarchically thanks to the Elo system of ratings, we can count experts by either dozens or thousands. For instance, the World chess federation (FIDE in French) has created four levels of excellence: FIDE Master (FM, Elo rating ≥ 2300), International Master (IM, Elo rating ≥ 2400), Grandmaster (GM, Elo rating ≥ 2500), and Super Grandmaster (Elo rating ≥ 2700). As of a few years ago, the levels numbered approximately 5,700; 3,600; 1,500; and 50 respectively. The 3,600 or so IM players represent approximately 0.25% of the 1 million or so tournament players worldwide (see "Chess title" rubric in Wikipedia), which places them in the "highly" category of the MB system. Who among them should we consider experts? Should we include all 5,700 FIDE Masters, or strictly the 50 or so Super Grandmasters? Aren't they all vastly superior to the rest of the population of chess players? In fact, could we consider still lower ratings as worthy of expertise? At least, that is what the United States Chess Federation (USCF) has decided, attributing the label *chess expert* to players reaching an Elo ranking of "just" 2,000. There are approximately 2,000 of them within a population of about 50,000 players with USCF rankings; they represent approximately the top 5% of all USCF tournament chess players, all amateurs excluded (see "Chess title" item in Wikipedia). Would researchers in this field hesitate to endorse the USCF criterion? And why not go down further and consider regional champions as experts even if their Elo rating remains below the USCF 1,900+ threshold? That single occupational field illustrates perfectly (a) the impossibility of finding an objective answer, and (b) the need for a consensus among scholars to bring clarity to that issue.

Quality or Quantity

The human tendency to bipolarize (Manichaeism) continuous characteristics is ubiquitous. Thus we create subgroups deemed qualitatively distinct, like gifted/non-gifted, or experts/non-experts. For instance, Morelock (1996) defined giftedness as "asynchronous development in which advanced cognitive abilities and heightened intensity combine to create inner experiences and awareness that are qualitatively different from the norm" (p. 8), a view that I strongly contested (Gagné, 1997). More recently, I examined this question in depth in the case of musical prodigies (see Gagné & McPherson, 2016). Since their first publications, Ericsson and his colleagues have strongly defended a qualitative view of expertise, as evidenced in this early quote: "We agree that expert performance is qualitatively different from normal performance and even that expert performers have characteristics and abilities that are qualitatively different from or at least outside the range of normal adults" (Ericsson, Krampe, & Tesch-Römer, 1993, p. 400). Note the last part of the sentence, where they leave open some small possibility of a quantitative interpretation—"at least outside the range"—for these differences; but ulterior publications did anchor the qualitative perspective.

Of course, if we compare novices with professionals, primary school children with graduate students, or young Suzuki students with music conservatory violinists, huge qualitative disparities in processing skills will jump to the eye! But, the slow passage from initial involvement into a field of study manifests itself essentially through almost imperceptible modifications in knowledge and skill mastery. Which brings us to the prevalence question discussed above: Is there any sudden transformation that will mark the passage from non-experts to expert, or from one level of expertise to the next? As I argued in the prevalence section above, all normative concepts require some professional consensus to establish thresholds of access, and then thresholds of progress within. This conundrum confirms the quantitative nature of the growth processes within any occupational field.

The Talent Development Trio

Keeping in mind the large overlap in meaning between the DMGT's definition of talent and the concept of expertise as it is generally understood, let us proceed with our overview of the DMGT. As illustrated in more detail in Figure 18.2,

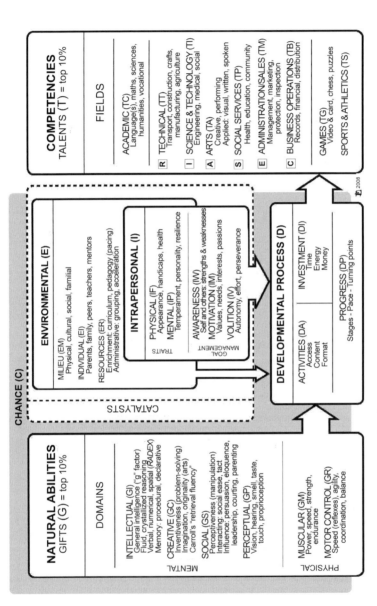

FIGURE 18.2 Gagné's Differentiating Model of Giftedness and Talent (DMGT)

Reproduced from "From Genes to Talent: The DMGT/CMTD Perspective," Gagné, 2015b, p. 19, Figure 1, © Ministry of Educatión, Culture and Sport. General Technical Secretariat. Also from Gagné and McPherson, 2016, "Analyzing Musical Prodigiousness Using Gagné's Integrative Model of Talent Development," p. 7, © Oxford University Press.

it brings together five components: gifts (*G*), talents (*T*), the talent development process (*D*), intrapersonal (*I*), and environmental catalysts (*E*). The first three constitute the core of the DMGT; their interaction summarizes the essence of the DMGT's conception of talent development, namely the progressive transformation of gifts into talents. Each component is subdivided into a variable number of *subcomponents*; that number is set within the theory. We also find a diversity of *facets* within each subcomponent; as we will see below through some examples, their sheer diversity makes any definitive structuring utopic.

Gifts (G)

The DMGT proposes six natural ability domains; four of them belong to the mental realm (intellectual-*GI*, creative-*GC*, social-*GS*, perceptual-*GP*), and the other two to the physical realm (muscular-*GM*, motor control-*GR*). Natural abilities are not innate; they do develop, especially during childhood, through maturational processes and informal exercise (see page 320, this chapter). That natural development and its level of expression are partially controlled by the individual's genetic endowment. We observe major individual differences in natural abilities in all children, both at home and at school. For instance, think of the intellectual abilities needed to learn to read, speak a foreign language, or understand new mathematical concepts; the creative abilities needed to solve a diversity of daily problems and produce original work in the visual and performing arts, literature, and science; the physical abilities involved in sports, music, and sculpture; the social abilities essential in interactions with classmates, teachers, and parents. We can observe gifts more easily and directly in young children because environmental influences and systematic learning have not yet exerted their moderating influence in a significant way. However, they still show themselves in older children, and even in adults through the facility and speed with which they acquire new competencies in any field of human activity. Said differently, ease and speed in learning are the trademarks of giftedness: They contribute strongly to the learners' differential pace of progress.

Talents (T)

Talents progressively emerge from the transformation of these outstanding natural abilities into the well-trained and systematically developed competencies that define a particular field of human activity. On a potential-performance continuum, talents occupy the performance pole, thus the outcome of the talent development process. Talent fields can be extremely diverse. Figure 18.2 shows nine talent subcomponents, with a myriad of facets within each of them. Six of them correspond to the American College Testing's World-of-Work classification of occupations. It has its source in John Holland's classification of work-related personality types: Realistic, Investigative, Artistic, Social,

Enterprising, and Conventional (RIASEC; see Anastasi & Urbina, 1997). Three additional subcomponents complement the RIASEC taxonomy: pre-occupational academic (K-12) subjects, games, and sports. A particular natural ability can express itself in many different ways depending on the field(s) of activity adopted by an individual. For example, motor control (GR) can be modeled into the particular skills of a pianist, a painter, or a video game player. Similarly, cognitive processes can be modeled into the scientific reasoning of a chemist, the memorization and game analysis of a chess player, or the strategic planning of an athlete.

Developmental Process (D)

Natural abilities serve as the "raw materials" or constituent elements of talents; they act through the talent development process. I define talent development as the systematic pursuit by *talentees*, over a significant period of time, of a structured program of activities leading to a specific excellence goal (Gagné, 2015a). The neologism *talentee* describes anyone actively involved in a systematic talent development program, whatever the field. The D component has three subcomponents (see Figure 18.2): activities (DA), investment (DI), and progress (DP), each of them subdivided into multiple *facets*. Talent development begins when a child or adult gains access, through an identification or selection process (DAA), to a systematic program of activities, defined by a specific content (DAC) and learning environment (DAF). The investment (DI) subcomponent quantifies the intensity of the talent development process in terms of time (DIT), psychological energy (DIE), or money (DIM). Ericsson's (2002) concept of *deliberate practice* perfectly overlaps the DIT and DIE facets. Finally, we can break down the progress (DP) of talentees from initial access to peak performance into a series of stages (DPS; e.g., novice, advanced, proficient, expert). Its main quantitative representation is pace (DPP), or how fast—compared to learning peers—talentees are progressing toward their predefined excellence goal. The long-term developmental course of a talentee will be marked by a series of more or less crucial turning points (DPT) (e.g., being spotted by a teacher or a coach, receiving an important scholarship, accidents, death of a family member or close friend).

The "Supporting Cast"

Two large sets of catalysts, respectively labeled *intrapersonal* and *environmental* (see Figure 18.2) affect the talent development process, either positively or negatively.

Intrapersonal Catalysts (I)

The I component has five subcomponents grouped into two main dimensions: stable traits (physical-IF, mental-IP), and goal management processes (self-awareness-IW, motivation-IM, and volition-IV). Within the mental or personality (IP) category, we find an extremely long list of descriptive qualities. The concept of *temperament* refers to behavioral predispositions with a strong hereditary component, whereas the term *personality* encompasses a large diversity of positive or negative acquired styles of behavior (Rothbart, 2012). The most widely accepted structure for personality attributes is called the Five-Factor Model, or FFM. These factors are respectively labeled Extraversion (E), Neuroticism versus emotional stability (N), Agreeableness versus Antagonism (A), Conscientiousness (C), and Openness to experience (O). Extensive research has shown that each factor has significant biological roots (McCrae, 2009).

The term motivation usually brings to mind both the idea of what motivates us (IM) and how motivated (IV) we are; that is, how much effort we are ready to invest in order to reach a particular goal. Within the framework of their *Action Control Theory*, two German scholars (Kuhl & Beckmann, 1985; see also Corno, 1993) proposed to differentiate the goal-seeking process into distinct goal-setting activities, which would receive the label motivation (IM), and goal-attainment activities, which they labeled *volition* or *will power (IV)*. Talentees will first examine their values and their needs, as well as determine their interests or be swept by a sudden passion; these will serve to identify the specific talent goal they will be aiming for (IM). The loftier that goal, the more efforts talentees will need to reach it (IV). Long-term goals placed at a very high level require intense dedication, as well as daily acts of will power to maintain practice through obstacles, boredom, and occasional failure.

Environmental Catalysts (E)

Figure 18.2 represents the E component as partially hidden behind the I component. This partial overlap signals the crucial filtering role that the I component plays with regard to environmental influences. The arrow at left indicates some limited direct E influences on the developmental process (e.g., social pressures, rules, or laws). But the bulk of environmental stimuli have to pass through the sieve of an individual's needs, interests, or personality traits. Talentees continually pick and choose which stimuli will receive their attention. The E component comprises three distinct subcomponents. The first one (EM) includes a diversity of environmental influences, from physical ones (e.g., climate, rural vs. urban living) to social, political, financial, or cultural ones. The second subcomponent (EI) focuses on the psychological influence of significant persons in the talentees' immediate environment. It includes, of course, parents and siblings, but also the larger family, teachers and trainers, peers, mentors, and even public figures adopted as role models by talentees. The third subcomponent (ER) covers all forms of talent development resources (e.g., courses, special schools, summer camps, mentorship). Here we adopt the broader perspective of what is available in talentees' environments, rather than examine resources from the subjective outlook of a given talentee's talent development course as the DA subcomponent does.

Note on the Chance Factor (C)

Chance used to play the role of a fifth causal factor associated with the environment (e.g., the chance of being born into a particular family; the chance of the school in which the child is enrolled developing a program for talented students). But, strictly speaking it is *not* a causal factor. Just like the positive or negative value influences can take, chance characterizes the *predictability* (controllable *vs.* uncontrollable) of elements belonging to three other components (G, I, or E). Chance's crucial involvement is well summarized by Atkinson's (1978) belief that all human accomplishments can be ascribed to "two crucial rolls of the dice over which no individual exerts any personal control. These are the accidents of birth and background. One roll of the dice determines an individual's heredity; the other, his formative environment" (p. 221). These two impacts alone give a powerful role to chance in sowing the bases of a person's talent development possibilities.

Dynamic Interactions

Complex Patterns

The four groups of causal factors entertain a large diversity of complex dynamic interactions, between components as well as within them. Space does not allow a detailed survey, but consider for example that all efforts by teachers, coaches or parents to modify the characteristics of talentees (e.g., interests, personality, beliefs, deviant behavior) illustrate E → I influences; of course, you can easily imagine influences in the opposite direction (e.g., talentees' passions influencing positively the behavior of parents or teachers). The most fundamental pattern of interactions involves of course the five components: As stated earlier, talent development involves all four causal components in a myriad of ways over long periods of time. Even talent, the outcome, can have a motivating impact on students: success breeds success! It can also influence environmental sources, parents as well as teachers. In summary, no causal component stands alone. They all interact with each other and with the learning process in very complex ways, and these interactions will differ very significantly from one person to the next.

What Makes the Difference?

Even though all four causal components are active, it does not mean that they are equally powerful as agents of talent emergence. This is no doubt a truism at the individual level since each talented person follows a unique path toward excellence. But what can we say about averages? Are some factors generally recognized as more powerful predictors of outstanding performance? For all those involved in the talent development of gifted individuals, the question of "what makes the difference" is THE ultimate question, since a precise circumscription of the best predictors increases substantially the efficacy and efficiency of the talent development process. Scholars and lay people entertain, more or less consciously, a personal set of beliefs—an implicit theory—about the hierarchy of these four groups of influences. With respect to the prediction of academic achievement, I analyzed the relevant literature and proposed (Gagné, 2004) the following decreasing order of influence: Gifts, Intrapersonal catalysts, Developmental activities, and Environmental influences (G, I, D, E). Recent research (Macnamara, Hambrick, & Oswald, 2014) on the limited power of deliberate practice in education (study and homework) would suggest an inversion of the last two components. Of course, this hierarchy might change if we analyzed the causal influences of talent emergence in other fields, just as I did in much detail with respect to the phenomenon of musical prodigiousness (Gagné & McPherson, 2016).

Introducing the DMNA and IMTD

The DMGT constitutes a strictly behavioral representation of the numerous influences facilitating or blocking the growth of competencies in general, including their outstanding manifestations as talents. This behavioral focus omits a large group of more distal influences, namely recognized biological influences on the growth of natural abilities (e.g., neurophysiological activity, type of muscle fibers) or the expression of intrapersonal catalysts (e.g., neurotransmitter action, genetic foundations of personality traits). The extraordinary growth of the neurosciences, thanks in large part to neuroimaging techniques, shows also how brain structures and processes significantly correlate with individual differences in cognitive, social or physical abilities, interests, and other major behavioral functions. As described and illustrated, the DMGT leaves no specific room for such distal sources of talent emergence. These observations led to four consecutive theoretical developments: (a) identifying the main categories and levels for the biological underpinnings of the main DMGT components; (b) integrating these biological basements with the existing DMGT framework; (c) determining the dynamic interactions between these biological bases and other influences responsible for the development of natural abilities, thus creating the *Developmental Model for Natural Abilities* (DMNA); and (d) creating the *Integrative Model of Talent Development* (IMTD) as a natural fusion of the two existing models. Let us look more closely at this evolution.

Biological Underpinnings of Talent Development

Science takes for granted some form of hierarchical organization of explanations, moving progressively from behavioral phenomena, down to physiology, microbiology, chemistry, then physics. For instance, Plomin, DeFries, Craig, and McGuffin (2003) describe functional genomics as "a bottom-up strategy in which the gene product is identified by its DNA sequence and the function of the gene product is traced through cells and then cell systems and eventually the brain" (p. 14). The expression "bottom-up" makes clear that such biological underpinnings would occupy a basement level under the strictly behavioral DMGT framework. The large number of levels of analysis indicates a need for more than one basement. But how many should there be? Strictly speaking, identifying the proper number of levels is not crucial; it is also highly probable that experts in these fields would argue *ad infinitum* about the right number of explanatory levels. A brief survey of the literature suggested three basic underground levels.

Consequently, if we use a "house" metaphor, we have the DMGT occupying the ground floor (see Figure 18.3), with three distinct basements underneath. The bottom basement (B-3) has been reserved for genotypic foundations (e.g., gene identification, mutations, gene expression, epigenetic phenomena, protein production, and so forth). We could label that third basement the *chemistry* level. The second basement, the *biology* level (B-2), is essentially devoted to microbiological and physiological processes. This second basement moves us from genotypic to phenotypic phenomena; but their hidden nature, at least to the naked eye, justifies labeling them *endophenotypes*; they correspond to physical traits—phenotypes—that are not externally visible but are measurable. Gottesman and Gould (2003) explain that in the case of phenomena having multi-gene origins endophenotypes provide "a means for identifying the 'downstream' traits or facets of clinical phenotypes, as well as the 'upstream' consequences of genes" (p. 637). Finally, the basement closest to ground level (B-1) includes anatomical or morphological characteristics that have been shown to impact abilities or intrapersonal catalysts. Most of these characteristics are observable *exophenotypes*, either directly (e.g., tallness in basketball, physical template in gymnastics) or indirectly (e.g., brain size through neuroimaging, muscle type through biopsy). Both endophenotypes and morphological traits are part of the complex hierarchical causal chain joining genes to physical abilities, and ultimately to systematically developed competencies and skills.

A Developmental Model for Natural Abilities (DMNA)

The creation of the DMNA pursued two goals: (a) Correct the wrong image of natural abilities given by well-meaning users of the DMGT who describe gifts as innate and talents as acquired; (b) Respond to scholars who question the relevance of the concept of giftedness. That simplistic bipolar view is wrong: Gifts are not innate, they develop during the course of childhood, and sometimes continue to do so during adulthood. Of course, this developmental view of natural abilities has to fight its way through a host of common language expressions

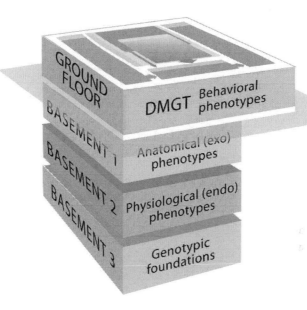

FIGURE 18.3 Biological underpinnings of the DMGT.

that maintain the ambiguity, such as "she is a born musician," or "it's God's gift," or "either you have it or you don't!" So, if all these uses of the label *innate* are incorrect, what should that label really mean?

The Proper Meaning of "Innate"

When we say that Mary is a "born" pianist, we are certainly not implying that she began playing the piano in the nursery, nor that she was able to play a concerto within weeks of beginning her piano lessons. Describing her talent as innate only makes sense metaphorically. It will convey the idea that Mary progressed rapidly and seemingly effortlessly through her music curriculum, at a much more rapid pace than that of her learning peers. The same applies to any natural ability. Intellectually precocious children do not suddenly manifest an exceptional vocabulary or highly logical reasoning processes; they develop these cognitive abilities by going through the same developmental stages as any other child. The difference resides in the ease and speed with which they advance through these successive stages. The term "precocious" says it all: The children reach a given level of knowledge and reasoning before the vast majority of learning peers. And the higher their intellectual giftedness, the more rapidly they will pass through these successive stages.

Researchers in behavioral genetics have given the term "innate" a very specific definition. At the behavioral level, it implies "hard-wired, fixed action patterns of a species that are impervious to experience. Genetic influence on abilities and other complex traits does not denote the hard-wired deterministic effect of a single gene but rather probabilistic propensities of many genes in multiple-gene systems" (Plomin, 1998, p. 421). When we use that term to qualify the DMGT's natural abilities, we convey two false interpretations: (a) that the observed individual differences are immutable, and (b) that they are present at birth or, if not, appear suddenly with minimal training. Because of its restricted meaning, very few scientists use the term innate to describe any type of natural ability or temperamental characteristic. Consequently, the term "innate talent" should disappear from our technical vocabulary; indeed, it is a clear oxymoron within the IMTD framework just as "innately gifted" would be!

If natural abilities by themselves cannot be considered innate as defined above, what exactly is innate? Where does the "gift" in giftedness reside? It is certainly not in the upper basement of Figure 18.3, since these anatomical structures require extensive development: Most do not achieve their maturity until late childhood, adolescence, or even adulthood. If we go down to the level of neurophysiological or biological processes, we might be in a gray zone where it becomes difficult to differentiate innate processes from those that result from developmental activities. For example, most stages of embryogenesis are governed by genetic rules. If the development was strictly maturational, then we could probably speak of innateness. Most importantly, however, it is clear that the lowest basement, devoted to gene activity, is almost completely—but not totally, according to the new field of epigenetics—under inborn control.

Describing the DMNA

If natural abilities do develop, as we have just argued, how does their development proceed? The left side of Figure 18.1 illustrates that process through the *Developmental Model for Natural Abilities (DMNA)*. At first glance, it looks very similar to the DMGT, but a closer analysis reveals major differences between the two, both at the component and the subcomponent levels. The main difference is of course a transfer of the G component from the left side to the right side; aptitudes—and their outstanding expression in gifts—now become the result of this particular developmental process. Here, the three levels of biological underpinnings, structural elements as well as processes, serve as building blocks for the phenotypic behavioral abilities. Genotypic foundations (B-3) are isolated with an arrow showing their action on both endo- (B-2) and exo- (B-1) phenotypes. The two upper basements are linked because of their parallel influences on the growth and manifestation of outstanding aptitudes.

The developmental process specific to the DMNA appears here in summary form, with just two macro processes identified. The label maturation covers of course a diversity of biological processes at each of the three basement levels, from embryogenesis upward, which govern the growth of mental and physical abilities. These maturational processes have no direct relationship with the talent development process itself; their role is to mold the natural abilities that will become, in turn, the building blocks of talents. As for the learning sub-component, it is called "informal" because it lacks the structured organization (e.g., curriculum, access rules, systematic schedule, formal assessment) typical of talent development activities. It takes the form of spontaneous learning acquired mostly subconsciously, with little daily or weekly attention to its growth. We could subdivide that informal process into the three subcomponents—activities, investment, progress—adopted in the case of talent development, but the lack of systematization would make these elements difficult to assess in any system-atic way. Of course, parents will be able to identify their children's physical or mental activities, the approximate amount of weekly investment, as well as their approximate standing among same-sex age peers. Beyond that, we would be moving into talent development territory.

We should not think of any developmental process without catalytic influ-ences, both intrapersonal and environmental. The two sets of catalysts appear here structurally unchanged, that is with the same subcomponents and facets. Of course, the exact contents within each element will differ, as well as their relative causal significance. For example, we cannot expect young children to show the same level of awareness (IW) toward their strengths and weaknesses as older individuals. But we can expect strong interests and passions (IM) to manifest themselves very early, fostering intense—although non-systematic—involvement in a particular set of activities. Similarly, within the realm of mental traits (IP), very large individual differences appear as soon as we start assessing any of them, either through self, parent, or teacher/coach ratings. For example, in a famous research program, Jerome Kagan was able to distinguish inhibited toddlers from uninhibited ones (Kagan, 1989), and follow their development for a number of years. Children express very early their desire—or lack of it!—to engage in all kinds of daily activities: physical exercise, reading, playing a musi-cal instrument, video games, playing with friends, and so forth. To some extent, their level of interest will influence their amount of investment, as well as their eventual decision to participate in a talent development program.

Finally, environmental catalysts also play a significant role in fostering or hindering the development of human aptitudes; and all three subcomponents are involved, although Resources play a much less significant role for obvious reasons. For example, recent studies have clearly shown that the degree of herit-ability of cognitive abilities varies with the socio-economic level of the families; the H component's explanatory power decreases significantly in low-income families (Harden, Turkheimer, & Loehlin, 2007; Tucker-Drob & Harden, 2012). In fact, the whole area of gene by environment interactions belongs to the E component. In the case of the EI subcomponent, any interventions by the parents to create a specific family environment, propitious either to general knowledge learning, to musical activities, or to athletic ones, could impact the development of related natural abilities. The same applies to their active efforts to involve their children in such activities, like visits to museums or concerts, winter or summer family sports activities, or any other activities that could foster a child's mental or physical natural gifts. In the case of the Resources (ER) subcomponent, public programs aimed at improving the school preparedness (a.k.a. cognitive abilities) of at-risk children represent an interesting example of efforts to build up these natural abilities (Haskins, 1989). But, since most of these programs target children with average or below average abilities, their relevance for the emergence of cognitive giftedness remains doubtful.

In sum, natural abilities proceed through a developmental process somewhat similar to the talent development process. The same basic ingredients are involved in fostering or hindering their growth. Of course, as Angoff (1988) perceptively highlighted, the most significant distinction between gifts and talents remains the amount of direct genetic contribution. The DMNA makes that point clear in its choice of building blocks.

Merging the DMGT/DMNA into the IMTD

As soon as the DMNA was conceived, it became clear that joining the two developmental models into an *Integrative Model of Talent Development (IMTD)* would bring closure to my theoretical efforts. As already pointed out, Figure 18.1 illustrates the result, with the G component's central position ensuring the linkage between the development of outstanding natural abilities on the left side and the talent development process itself on the right side. The IMTD argues that talent development has its distal origins in the progressive growth of natural abilities, as early as through the chance meeting of a sperm cell and an ovum. This produces a unique genotype in the fertilized egg. Through the complex process of embryogenesis, that single egg will multiply, its descendants will diversify into hundreds of different cell types, each with millions of exemplars, in a coordinated developmental process closely supervised by the genotype that will lead to the birth of a new baby. The maturation process will continue after birth as the various natural abilities, mental and physical, progressively take form at different levels from one individual to the next, thanks to the contribution of the two sets of catalysts, as well as innumerable daily occasions for informal learning and exercise. At some point, usually during childhood or early adolescence depending on the type of talent chosen, some gifted individuals, or those not too far from the DMGT's cut-off threshold of top 10 percent, will choose a talent field that fits their perceived profile of natural abilities and interests, and begin the long and complex journey leading to outstanding performance, as described through the DMGT framework. Some will go far beyond the basic 10 percent threshold of minimal talent, others will not, and the reasons behind the level of expertise achieved by these talentees will be as numerous as the facets that comprise the DMGT.

Summing Up

It should be clear from the above description that the IMTD stands out among existing talent development models with its large number of unique characteristics. Let's focus first on its most basic and long-standing unit, the *Differentiating Model of Giftedness and Talent* (DMGT).

1. The DMGT stands alone among talent development theories with its clear differentiation between outstanding potentialities (gifts) and remarkable achievements (talents, expertise). That differentiation allows a unique definition of talent development, namely the progressive transformation of gifts in one or more domains into expertise/talent in a particular occupational field with constant positive or negative inputs from intrapersonal and environmental catalysts. In this view, natural abilities act as building blocks for the systematically developed outstanding abilities characteristic of specific talents.

2. The DMGT offers a detailed three-level structure, with its 5 components (G, T, D, I, E), 26 subcomponents (6 G, 9 T, 3 D, 5 I, 3 E), and innumerable facets made available for individual personalization. This detailed structure becomes a virtual geographical map of all potential causal influences of talent-expertise emergence.

3. The DMGT's six giftedness domains and nine talent fields offer a comprehensive, all-encompassing view of these two large groups of abilities.

4. The DMGT proposes a clear answer to the prevalence issue, the "how many" question, through its metric-based (MB) system of five levels that applies to any giftedness domain or talent field. It helps maintain a constant awareness of differences *within* the subpopulations of gifted and talented individuals.

5. By adopting the core constructs of *Action Control Theory*, the DMGT adds a clear differentiation between goal *identification* processes (IM – Motivation) and goal *attainment* processes (IV – Volition).

6. The DMGT clarifies the role of Chance as a significant index of the degree of controllability of specific causal influences. It thus introduces an important modulator of developmental interactions.

7. Finally, we do find in the DMGT alone an explicit attempt to discuss in detail the complex modalities of the hierarchical contributions of various causal influences, a subject referred to as the "what makes a difference" (WMD) question.

   When we switch to its recent companion, the *Developmental Model for Natural Abilities* (DMNA), we can add a few unique characteristics.

8. The DMNA clarifies the origin and circumscribed status of innate influences, and thus shows the erroneous nature of the concept of innate talent.

9. The DMNA clearly situates the distal position of biological foundations within the global developmental process, as well as their indirect influence, through natural abilities—and intrapersonal catalysts—on the emergence of talents or expertise.

10. The DMNA shows that the developmental path of natural abilities is a very complex one, and that it largely parallels the talent development path through its diverse sources of influence.

Finally, the merging of the DMNA and DMGT into the *Integrative Model of Talent Development* (IMTD) demonstrates that the slogan "from genes to talents" summarizes correctly the long developmental pathway of all talents.

Note

On the author's website (gagnefrancoys.wixsite.com/dmgt-mddt), interested readers will find additional materials on the DMGT/IMTD and related subjects.

References

Anastasi, A., & Urbina, S. (1997). *Psychological testing* (7th ed.). Upper Saddle River, NJ: Prentice-Hall.

Angoff, W. H. (1988). The nature-nurture debate, aptitudes, and group differences. *American Psychologist, 41,* 713–720.

Atkinson, J. W. (1978). Motivational determinants of intellective performance and cumulative achievement. In J. W. Atkinson & J. O. Raynor (Eds.), *Personality, motivation, and achievement* (pp. 221–242). New York: Wiley.

Corno, L. (1993). The best-laid plans: Modern conceptions of volition and educational research. *Educational Researcher, 22,* 14–22.

Ericsson, K. A. (2002) Attaining excellence through deliberate practice: Insights from the study of expert performance. In C. Desforges & R. Fox (Eds.), *Teaching and learning: The essential readings.* Oxford: Blackwell Publishers Ltd.

Ericsson, K. A. (2014). Why expert performance is special and cannot be extrapolated from studies of performance in the general population: A response to criticisms. Intelligence, 45, 81–103.

Ericsson, K. A., Krampe, R. T., & Tesch-Römer, C. (1993). The role of deliberate practice in the acquisition of expert performance. *Psychological Review, 100,* 363–406.

Gagné, F. (1985). Giftedness and talent: Reexamining a reexamination of the definitions. *Gifted Child Quarterly, 29,* 103–112.

Gagné, F. (1997). Critique of Morelock's (1996) definitions of giftedness and talent. *Roeper Review, 20,* 76–85.

Gagné, F. (1998). A proposal for subcategories within the gifted or talented populations. *Gifted Child Quarterly, 42,* 87–95.

Gagné, F. (1999). Is there any light at the end of the tunnel? *Journal for the Education of the Gifted, 22,* 191–234.

Gagné, F. (2004). Transforming gifts into talents: The DMGT as a developmental theory. *High Ability Studies, 15,* 119–147.

Gagné, F. (2009). Debating giftedness: Pronat vs. Antinat. In L. V. Shavinina (Ed.), *International handbook on giftedness* (pp. 155–198). Dordrecht, Netherlands: Springer.

Gagné, F. (2013). The DMGT: Changes within, beneath, and beyond. *Talent Development and Excellence*, *5*, 5–19.

Gagné, F. (2015a). Academic talent development programs: A best practices model. *Asia-Pacific Education Review*, *16*, 281–295. DOI: 10.1007/s12564-015-9366-9

Gagné, F. (2015b). From genes to talent: the DMGT/CMTD perspective. *Revista de Educacion*, *368*, 12–37, DOI: 10.4438/1988-592X-RE-2015-368-289. Madrid, Spain: Ministry of Educatión, Culture and Sport. General Tecnhicall Secretariat.

Gagné, F., & McPherson, G. E. (2016). Analyzing musical prodigiousness using Gagné's Integrative Model of Talent Development. In G. E. McPherson (Ed.), *Musical prodigies: Interpretations from psychology, education, musicology and ethnomusicology* (pp. 3–114). Oxford, UK: Oxford University Press.

Gottesman, I. I., & Gould, T. D. (2003). The endophenotype concept in psychiatry: Etymology and strategic intentions. *American Journal of Psychiatry*, *160*, 636–645.

Harden, K. P., Turkheimer, E., & Loehlin, J. C. (2007). Genotype by environment interaction in adolescents' cognitive aptitude. *Behavioral genetics*, *37*, 273–283.

Haskins, R. (1989). Beyond metaphor: The efficacy of early childhood education. *American Psychologist*, *44*, 274–282.

Kagan, J. (1989). *Unstable ideas: Temperament, cognition, and self.* Cambridge, MA: Harvard University Press.

Kuhl, J., & Beckmann, J. (Eds.) (1985). *Action control: From cognition to behavior.* New York: Springer Verlag.

Macnamara, B. N., Hambrick, D. Z., & Oswald, F. L. (2014). Deliberate practice and performance in music, games, sports, education, and professions: A meta-analysis. *Psychological Science*, *25*(8), 1608–1618. doi: 10.1177/0956797614535810.

McCrae, R. B. (2009). The Five-Factor Model of personality traits: Consensus and controversy. In P. J. Corr & G. Matthews (Eds.), *The Cambridge handbook of personality psychology* (pp. 148–161). Cambridge, England: Cambridge University Press.

McPherson, G. E., & Williamon, A. (2006). Giftedness and talent. In G. E. McPherson (Ed.), *The child as musician: A handbook of musical development* (pp. 239–256). New York: Oxford University Press.

Morelock, M. (1996). On the nature of giftedness and talent: Imposing order on chaos. *Roeper Review*, *19*, 4–12.

Plomin, R. (1998). Genetic influence and cognitive abilities. *Behavioral and Brain Sciences*, *21*, 420–421.

Plomin, R., DeFries, J. C., Craig, I. W., & McGuffin, P. (2003). *Behavioral genetics.* In R. Plomin, J. C. DeFries, I. W. Craig, & P. McGuffin, P. (Eds.), *Behavioral genetics in the postgenomic era* (pp. 3–15). Washington, D.C.: APA.

Rothbart, M. K. (2012). Advances in temperament: History, concepts, and measures. In M. Zentner & R. L. Shiner (Eds.), *Handbook of temperament* (pp. 3–20). New York: Guilford Press.

Tranckle, P., & Cushion, C. J. (2006). Rethinking giftedness and talent in sport. *Quest*, *58*, 265–282.

Tucker-Drob, E. M., & Harden, K. P. (2012). Intellectual interest mediates gene x socioeconomic status interaction on adolescent academic achievement. *Child Development*, *83*, 743–757.

19

CREATIVITY AND EXPERTISE

Creators are Not Equivalent to
Domain-Specific Experts!

Dean Keith Simonton

Introduction

What is creativity? Is it domain specific? If so, does creativity constitute just a form of domain-specific expertise? Are the most creative people also the greatest experts? In more concrete terms, was Albert Einstein the most knowledgeable and skilled theoretical physicist of his day? Did he become *Time* magazine's "Person of the [20th] Century" in part because he knew so much more physics and mathematics than any other contemporary? Or did Einstein's exceptional creativity entail something more than just domain-specific expertise? After all, his revolutionary ideas overthrew classical physics and thereby helped establish modern physics. The old, outdated expertise had been replaced with an entirely new expertise. For example, Newtonian and Maxwellian concepts of absolute space and time were superseded by the relativistic concept of four-dimensional space-time—yielding the famous $E = mc^2$ as one necessary implication!

Now some psychologists would argue that creativity, even creative genius, is just a guise of supreme domain-specific expertise (Ericsson, 2014). Indeed, exceptional creativity is so expertise driven that we do not even have to speak of a distinctly creative process: Ordinary thinking, when applied to relevant expertise, produces extraordinary outcomes (Weisberg, 2014). According to this expertise view, any one of us could have become an Einstein if we were just a bit more assiduous in doing the problem sets assigned in our math and physics courses.

One obstacle to accepting this flattering notion, unfortunately, is that Einstein was not a superlative student. Indeed, he so irregularly attended his undergraduate math classes that one professor called him a "lazy dog" (Hoffman, 1972, p. 85). In fact, it is unlikely that Einstein would have passed his exams were it not for his classmate Marcel Grossmann, who lent him his meticulous lecture notes.

Much later, when Einstein got in over his head with the mathematics necessary for developing his general theory of relativity, Grossmann was taken on as an essential collaborator to "do the math." It's highly doubtful that Einstein was merely the most expert mathematician and physicist of his time. Something here seems amiss.

This enigma can be resolved only by thinking deeply about what we mean by "creativity" and "expertise." In this chapter, in fact, I propose to provide a formal definition of both concepts with the aim of proving, logically, that the two psychological phenomena cannot possibly be identical. Given that analytical proof, it naturally follows that creators are *not* equivalent to domain-specific experts. Any such supposed equivalence leads to a logical contradiction. I start with creativity before turning to expertise—after which I can relate the two.

Creativity

Creativity researchers have a tendency to conflate two distinct levels of analysis: the personal and the consensual. The personal level concerns what is actually happening inside an individual's head, and thus is purely psychological. In contrast, the consensual level requires the involvement of others besides the individual, such as co-workers and colleagues, editors and referees, patent examiners and festival jurors, audiences and connoisseurs, or critics and scholars. These two levels are sometimes represented as the distinction between "little-c" and "Big-C" creativity (Simonton, 2013c). In the former case, creators judge for themselves whether an idea or behavior is creative, whereas in the latter case, that creativity assessment requires a consensus of those most in position to judge—often but not always domain-specific experts. Although personal creativity is most commonly the prerequisite for consensual creativity, the latter often introduces interpersonal, social, cultural, and even economic and historical factors that need not involve psychology at all. Hence, I begin with personal creativity before turning to consensual creativity.

Personal Creativity

For a long time, creativity researchers have operated with what has been called the "standard definition," that is, "Creativity requires both originality and effectiveness" (Runco & Jaeger, 2012, p. 92). This agreement notwithstanding, the standard definition has recently been shown to be totally inadequate to the task of defining the corresponding phenomena (Simonton, 2016b). Indeed, the standard definition cannot fully distinguish the diverse ways that ideas can be noncreative. The main reason for this conceptual deficiency is that creativity requires the satisfaction of *three* criteria, not just two. Happily, a modified version of the standard definition plus one addition does the trick. To demonstrate this requirement, I must first define three parameters and then show how these yield the fully adequate definition of personal creativity.

Three Parameters

Suppose an individual is put in a situation that is expected to evoke a response, whether an idea or a behavior. For example, the situation might involve a specific problem that requires a solution. At that singular moment, any particular response can be described by the following three parameters (Simonton, 2016b): (a) the *initial probability* (or "response strength") given by p; (b) the *final utility* represented by u; and (c) the *prior knowledge* of that utility symbolized by v.[1] All three parameters can assume values ranging between 0 and 1, like probabilities or proportions. Thus, if $p = 0$, the particular response will have no chance of immediate generation, whereas if $p = 1$, that same response will have the highest possible likelihood, even to the degree of automaticity (Simonton, 2016b). Values between these two limits indicate middling levels. For instance, $v \approx .5$ would indicate that the person has some "feeling of knowing," "hunch," or "informed guess" regarding the utility, but without enough confidence to "bet the house on it." Similarly, $u \approx .5$ might not prove adequately useful for an optimizer, but turn out acceptable for someone merely engaged in satisficing, and accordingly willing to accept a solution meeting only half of the specified utility criteria. The unsatisfied criteria that remain are then just relegated to "pie in the sky" or "maybe someday" wishes.

Importantly, the three parameters are completely orthogonal to each other and therefore can assume any values whatsoever between 0 and 1 inclusively. For example, $v = 0$ could indicate that the individual is entirely ignorant about whether $u = 0$ or 1, whereas $v = 1$ could say that the individual is 100% confident about whether $u = 0$ or 1. Likewise, when p and v are considered jointly, while ignoring u, then the value of p does not constrain the value of v one iota, and vice versa. Even so, certain combinations of the three parameter values are much more likely than are others. Two combinations are particularly unlikely: (a) $u \rightarrow 1$ and $v \rightarrow 1$ but $p \rightarrow 0$; and (b) $u \rightarrow 0$ and $v \rightarrow 1$ but $p \rightarrow 1$, where "$\rightarrow$" signifies "approaches" or "nears." In fact, the former has been called "irrational suppression" and the latter "irrational perseveration" (Simonton, 2016a). In the first case a response is suppressed even when it is already known to have a high utility, whereas in the second case a response is emitted when it is already known to have a low utility. Both responses are not rational. Indeed, the second set of parameters formalizes the common saying (often incorrectly attributed to Albert Einstein in online inspirational posters) that "The definition of insanity is doing the same thing over and over and expecting it to come out different."

One final point: New terms can be derived from both p and v that will prove extremely useful in the next section. The two parameters are just subtracted from 1, yielding parameters that also vary from 0 to 1, but inversely. First, $1 - p$ defines the *originality* of the response because the most original responses are the least probable in the person's mind. Second, $1 - v$ defines the *surprise* elicited by the response upon learning the actual utility because the most surprising responses are those that contribute the most to the person's a posteriori knowledge (i.e., lowers the individual's prior ignorance about *u*'s actual value by the biggest amount). Because knowledge acquisition can go two ways—learning that a response is useless or learning that it is useful—the surprise can also go both ways. A person can be surprised that something actually works, and also surprised that it doesn't work.

Multiplicative Integration

Given the foregoing definitions, I can now define the *personal creativity* of a given response by the following equation:

$$c = (1 - p)u(1 - v), \text{ where again } 0 \le c \le 1.$$

In words, creativity is a multiplicative function of originality, utility, and surprise (Simonton, 2016b). If $c = 0$, response creativity is nil, but if $c = 1$, creativity is maximal, values between those extremes representing variable degrees of creativity. Hence, the above formal definition specifies that $c \to 1$ as $p \to 0$, $u \to 1$, and $v \to 0$.

As noted earlier, the standard two-criterion definition of creativity requires the addition of a third criterion to become truly adequate. Here the addition is *surprise*, an inverse measure of the person's prior knowledge of the utility. This three-criterion definition closely parallels other definitions that largely add a third criterion to the standard definition. To illustrate, the correspondence is clearly apparent in Boden's (2004) criteria of novel, valuable, and surprising as well as the United States Patent and Trademark Office criteria of new, useful, and nonobvious (Simonton, 2012b), where surprising means $(1 - v) \to 1$ and obvious means $(1 - v) \to 0$.

But why are the three factors multiplied rather than added? Simply put, the multiplicative integration enables each of the three factors to become necessary but not sufficient determinants of creativity. Additive integration does not. For example, a jet fighter constructed out of cinderblocks and shooting soap bubble bullets would be totally useless as an offensive or defensive weapon (assuming enemy fighter pilots don't laugh themselves to death), and yet it might still have some degree of creativity owing to the idea being so original. In contrast, because zero times any number is always zero, the multiplicative function guarantees that all three criteria must assume nonzero values for the response to have any creativity whatsoever. Each criterion exerts veto power over the others.

By now I hope it has become apparent why the standard definition must be considered a necessary but not sufficient basis for defining creativity. If the standard definition is translated into the above formal representation, we obtain $c = (1 - p)u$, omitting the third factor, and then specifying that $p \to 0$ and $u \to 1$ for $c \to 1$. Yet this two-criterion definition must elicit the following question:

Why is the response strength so low when the utility is so high? Only by adding the third factor $(1 - v)$ do we get the answer: Because the person didn't know the utility value in advance. Indeed, if the individual did already know the utility value, so that $v \rightarrow 1$, then these parameters would yield what was previously identified as irrational suppression; the person did not emit a response despite knowing that it was useful (Simonton, 2016b). Once more, the standard definition is only necessary, not sufficient, to capture creativity's precise meaning.

Consensual Creativity

Personal creativity can certainly take place at the purely psychological level. It happens every time an animal or human engages in creative problem solving (Simonton, 2015a). For example, the famous insight experiments that Köhler (1925) conducted dramatically illustrate how chimpanzees can generate original, useful, and surprising behaviors (see also Epstein, 2015). However, for creativity to attain importance beyond the individual organism, it must be subjected to a consensual evaluation (Simonton, 2013c). In many domains of creativity, for example, the evaluators are those who have the requisite expertise in the field. In scientific disciplines, these domain-specific experts are most likely colleagues working in the same specialty area who make their consensual assessments via peer review and citation decisions. In any case, we can hypothetically define the resulting evaluation of consensual creativity as a mean assessment across all evaluators (for the definitional formulas, see Simonton, 2013c).

Although seemingly straightforward, this conception of consensual creativity contains many hidden complexities. Perhaps the following four are the most significant:

First, field consensus should probably be founded on a weighted mean that acknowledges that the opinions of some assessors are worth more than those of others. Thus, in theoretical physics, the judgments of Nobel laureates in the same specialty area may matter far more than the evaluations of rank and file physicists—particularly given that laureates also become Nobel nominators! That's why the young Einstein having received Max Planck's early endorsement was a really big deal.

Second, fields vary substantially in the magnitude of consensus. For instance, scientific disciplines can be arranged in a hierarchy from the natural sciences to the social sciences, the former exhibiting far greater agreement in peer evaluations than seen in the latter (Simonton, 2015b). Accordingly, consensual creativity is assessed with far greater reliability in physics than in psychology, with biology falling roughly between. In particular, as one descends the hierarchy, peer reviewers exhibit appreciably less agreement when evaluating submitted manuscripts or grant proposals.

Third, fields differ in the degree to which the consensus is necessarily heterogeneous rather than homogeneous. A particularly striking example is cinematic creativity (Simonton, 2011b). The success of a film can be gauged by critical acclaim, movie awards, and box office performance, that is, by three groups—media critics, industry professionals, and consumers, respectively—who seldom agree with each other even if the consensus within each of the three groups is fairly strong. Think how often blockbusters have been panned by the critics and ignored by the award ceremonies!

Fourth and last, fields can exhibit temporal instability in their assessments, rendering consensual creativity a volatile variable (Weisberg, 2015). Einstein had to wait many years, and endure several failed nominations, before he finally received the 1921 Nobel Prize for work he had published in 1905. More dramatic examples come from the inventory of so-called "neglected geniuses," such as Emily Dickinson and Gregor Mendel, whose creativity had to await posthumous acknowledgment—decades after their personal creativity had ceased.

These four complexities demonstrate quite conclusively that consensual creativity cannot possibly represent a purely psychological phenomenon. Too much of what underlies any consensus involves processes extraneous to the individual.

Expertise

Just as creativity can be either personal or consensual, so can expertise be considered either personal or consensual.

Personal Expertise

Although expertise is often associated with a particular domain, as when we mentioned domain-specific expertise, the same term can be used in a general sense that reflects its etymological connections with the same Latin root that yielded not just *expert* but also *experience* and *experiment* (viz., *experiri*, meaning "try" or "attempt"). Personal expertise indicates knowledge or skill acquired through "trial and error" interactions with the environment. For example, a rat or pigeon subjected to operant "Skinnerian" conditioning can be said to have acquired a form of expertise by learning how to attain food by pushing a lever or pecking a disk (Skinner, 1981). Similarly, a human being might discover that an unusual spice pleasantly enhances the flavor of an otherwise dull food. Needless to say, expertise can also involve learning what *not* to do, such as not touching fire. Both of these cases can be conceived in terms of the same three parameters used in defining creativity (cf. Simonton, 2016a).

First, a potential response might have the values $p \rightarrow 1$, $u \rightarrow 1$, and $v \rightarrow 1$. In words, the response has a very high utility, and the organism has near perfect if not perfect prior knowledge of that high utility through past experience, that prior knowledge then leading rationally and directly to the maximization of its probability. Responses with these parameter values can be labeled "routine, reproductive, or habitual" (Simonton, 2016b). Most of the thoughts and behavior that we all engage in every day of our lives are precisely of this nature. We just do what we know works. That's what rational creatures do.

Second, a potential response might have the values $p \to 0$, $u \to 0$, and $v \to 1$. Again expressed in words, because the response has a zero utility and that utility is already known, the probability becomes nil. Not surprisingly, responses with these values have been styled "rational suppression" (Simonton, 2016b). It represents what an individual should not do instead of the irrational perseveration defined earlier. Rational beings do not do what they know doesn't work.

Before advancing to the consensual level, I need to mention a third possibility because it has significant consequences for delineating the boundaries of personal expertise. These are responses with the parameter values $p \to 1$, $u \to 0$, and $v \to 0$. In this case, a response has a high probability because it has always worked in the past, but the individual fails to notice that the current situation actually differs from past situations in an unforeseen manner that renders the response useless (cf. "discriminative stimuli" in operant conditioning or "boundary conditions" in mathematical modeling). In some contexts, this violation of an expertise-driven expectation can then be called "problem finding" because the person has learned that a solution reasonably thought to solve a given problem fails to do so, mandating the quest for a solution that does work (Simonton, 2016b). Should the resulting search lead to a solution, including knowledge of the conditions specifying when to use the new and old solutions, then the individual's personal expertise has appreciably grown.

Consensual Expertise

Like personal creativity, personal expertise operates solely at the individual level and requires no comparisons or assessments involving other individuals, expert or otherwise. Likewise, just as consensual creativity requires the introduction of social evaluations, so does consensual expertise. For example, suppose a young basketball player has been practicing free throws to the point that she can make as many as 60 percent in any given session. If she is content with just knowing her "personal best," then that percentage defines her current skill level. But if she wants to know how she compares with professional players in the Women's National Basketball Association, she may become sorely disappointed. The best free throwers hit 80 percent or more. If she aspires to go pro, she may have to practice many more shots from the line. A similar social comparison process operates in track and field events in which there are well-established benchmarks, such as running times.

More obviously, consensual expertise is often established via direct competition rather than just social comparison. Sometimes this competition is head to head, as in tennis and chess, and other times the competition may involve a large field of competitors, such as happens in golf, where the winner and the runner up might not have even played opposite each other on the course.

In any event, these competitive matches are often frequent enough to support rankings that purport to represent the relative degrees of expertise on an ordinal or even interval scale. A classic example of the latter is the Elo rating of chess players (Elo, 1986).

When it comes to creative domains, such as the arts and sciences, the assessment of expertise is far more complex and varied. Certainly, competitive methods are much less common, albeit they do happen from time to time. For example, Renaissance mathematicians would often compete to solve publicized problems, and film festivals today will sometimes have juries assign awards in a manner roughly comparable to the scoring in Olympic figure skating competitions. Of course, in those creative domains that are strongly academic, such as the sciences, expertise can be assessed using scholastic performance and psychometric achievement tests. Once a scientist begins submitting grant proposals and publishing in peer-reviewed journals, the assessments of consensual expertise become more pointed at the particulars of relevant specialty areas. For instance, referees are often specifically instructed to evaluate the adequacy of a researcher's literature review and the proposed or applied methods and analyses. Although the number of evaluators always represents a small subset of the entire field, the journal editors or program directors do their best to select referees who possess the requisite expertise.

It should be manifest to anyone who has served at either end of the peer-review process that personal and consensual expertise seldom overlap perfectly (Simonton, 2003). Investigators might have thought that the literature review omitted nothing essential, only to have at least one referee chide them for overlooking a mandatory reference (viz. some publication of the referee). Or the investigators learn to their chagrin that the analytical technique that they had thought represented the state of the art was already rendered obsolete years earlier. In general, what an investigator views as having the parameters $p = u = v = 1$, a referee might condemn as having the parameters $p = 0$ and $u = 0$, but $v = 1$. The investigators are not only obviously wrong, but they clearly should have known better.

Given the inconsistencies between personal and consensual assessments regarding both creativity and expertise, might there also appear conflicts between creativity and expertise themselves, however evaluated?

Creativity-Expertise Relations

An essential conflict between creativity and expertise would seem to follow naturally from the three criteria that the United States Patent and Trademark Office uses to assess applications for the possible legal protection of patents: As noted earlier, besides novel and useful the invention must also be nonobvious. Significantly, the assessment of the third criterion is supposed to be determined by someone having "ordinary skill in the art," that is, a person who has the applicable domain-specific expertise (http://www.uspto.gov/web/offices/pac/

mpep/documents/2100_2141_03.htm). If anyone with the requisite knowledge or skill could invent the same thing, then it cannot be patentable. To provide a straightforward example, if experts know that material A has exactly the same physical properties as material B, such as two interchangeable plastics, and a product made out of B has received patent protection, a new patent for the exact same product made out of A should not be accepted. The substitution would be obvious to anybody with ordinary expertise in materials science.

As might be expected, the creativity-expertise relation is far more complex than this illustration implies. Besides having to maintain the distinction between personal and consensual meanings of the two phenomena, we also have to distinguish relations that are just necessary from those that are both necessary and sufficient. To anticipate a little, even when expertise is necessary for creativity, it may not be sufficient as well (see also Simonton, 2014).

Expertise as Necessary for Creativity

Creativity does not entail any particular process or procedure, but rather a large set of processes and procedures that can operate in any creative domain (Simonton & Damian, 2013). A partial list includes cognitive disinhibition, divergent thinking, remote association, analogy, conceptual reframing, broadening perspective, reversal, tinkering, play; Janusian, homospatial, and sep-con articulation processes; and both systematic and heuristic searches (e.g., Ness, 2013; Rothenberg, 2015). Whether voluntary and deliberate (such as systematic searches) or involuntary and haphazard (such as cognitive disinhibition), these processes and procedures share one and only one characteristic: They all provide various means for generating ideational or behavioral combinations. It is for this reason that all creativity must be considered combinatorial (Simonton, 2010). For example, every major discovery and invention in the history of science and technology can ultimately be analyzed into various kinds of combinations (Thagard, 2012). Better yet, combinatorial models both mathematical and computational have proven successful in explicating the central features of creativity across a diversity of domains (e.g., Simonton, 1997, 2010; Thagard & Stewart, 2011). Combinatorial creativity alone explains how the new can originate from the old.

Yet what undergoes combination? What represents the old that is combined into the new? The answer is where expertise enters the picture. Because expertise can operate at both personal and consensual levels, this prerequisite must be discussed at both levels, too.

Personal Level

Without a single exception, classic laboratory experiments concerning creative problem solving all require that the participant generate a solution that entails a combinatorial product from acquired expertise. For instance, the well-known two-strings problem presumes that the participant knows how to (a) tie two strings together, (b) attach a string to a chair, pole, extension cord, or pliers, (c) shorten a string so that it no longer hangs all the way to the floor, and (d) propel a string into a pendulum motion using a weight tied at the end (Maier, 1931). None of this knowledge or skill is innate but rather had to be learned one way or another, whether through operant conditioning, observational learning, reading, or direct instruction. This prior expertise can most often be taken for granted. The nine-dot problem presumes that the participant already knows how to connect dots with straight lines just as Duncker's candle problem presupposes that the participant can tack cardboard to a wall.

The necessity of prior expertise before combinatorial creativity can even begin becomes more evident when researchers can control the experience acquired before entering the situation. A case in point is Epstein's (2015) research testing his Generativity Theory of creativity, an explicitly combinatorial model. Using pigeons under complete experimental control, Epstein was able to replicate Köhler's (1925) insight experiments that used chimpanzees. However, the pigeons could have the insight—such as the need to maneuver a box to use as a stool to peck at an object hanging over the cage—only when they had acquired prior skills in the component behaviors (such as moving boxes in a specific direction across a surface). Expressed in more formal terms, combinatorial processes and procedures can operate only on a sizable inventory of potential responses having the parameter values $p = u = v = 1$, such as reaching for food or pushing objects away. That inventory defines the available personal expertise from which to generate new responses.

Of course, most often there is no reason to generate new responses if the old ones work just fine. Yet, as already noted, sometimes they don't. Instead of the parameters given for routine or habitual responses, the individual discovers that the actual parameter values are $p = 1$, $u = 0$, and $v = 0$. The most likely response may prove useless, an outcome of which the individual is ignorant until the response is actually emitted and found to fail. Hence, a chimpanzee's most immediate response to seeing a banana just outside the cage is to reach for it—only to discover that the fruit has been placed just out of reach! Similarly, the most immediate response of a participant in the two-strings experiment is just to grab one string, walk over to the other string, and attempt to tie them together as the experimenter instructed—only to learn that the first string is not long enough! Having encountered a boundary to their respective accumulated expertise, these two primates have inadvertently stumbled into problem finding. At this point, if they still seek the same goal, they must search for some other solution, a condition that may then require the implementation of combinatorial creativity (Epstein, 2015). For example, the chimpanzee will have to get the banana using a stick, or perhaps even two sticks manually attached together (Köhler, 1925).

I must emphasize that the foregoing illustrations truly entail personal expertise. Although the examples involve experimenters who have put the organism in an artificial problem-finding situation, no consensual evaluation is required for a solution to be considered successful or not. Either the chimp or the human might be stranded alone in the middle of the wilderness, the former trying to get a banana just out of reach, the latter trying to tie two cords together between two trees in order to hang a makeshift tent to provide shelter through the night. The processes involved remain purely psychological. If either one discovers a solution with the parameter values $p \to 0$, $u \to 1$, and $v \to 0$, then an act of personal creativity results, based on the requisite personal expertise.

Consensual Level

Let me return to the human stranded in the wilderness (Simonton, 2015a). Suppose she's lost for several days and must muster the maximum ingenuity before a helicopter comes to her rescue. During that time she exploits whatever skills and knowledge she possesses to devise (via various combinatorial processes and procedures) a set of new survival techniques to allay thirst, hunger, and the cold. When the rescue team finally arrives, she excitedly tells them about all of the creative ways she stayed alive. For her each solution to various ramifications of this urgent problem had the parameters $p \to 0$, $u \to 1$, and $v \to 0$.

At this juncture, we can imagine two alternative scenarios. On the one hand, the rescue crew can listen in amazement to her narrative, finally advising her that she definitely needs to write her story for some outdoors magazine for the benefit of others who might ever encounter the same misfortune. On the other hand, the crew might almost immediately start yawning and rolling their eyes until one member finally informs her that she merely reinvented the wheel. The techniques she was so proud of would be routinely detailed in any decent wilderness survival guide. Notice that her personal expertise and creativity are identical in both scenarios, but her consensual expertise and creativity are dramatically different.

Now conceive an altogether different, third scenario: The stranded person just so happens to be one of the world's leading experts in wilderness survival techniques, having written the definitive guide on that very subject. The unexpected event now affords her the opportunity to apply her prodigious personal and consensual expertise in a real-life test. Perhaps she confirms that many of her routine adaptations work as exactly as planned, indicating that each technique has the parameter values $p = u = v = 1$, but maybe she also discovers that some well-known adaptations do not actually work, yielding $p = 1$ but $u = 0$ and $v = 0$ (e.g., a certain plant is actually quite inedible no matter how it's prepared). Perhaps in recoil from such problem-finding episodes, she comes up with several creative responses in which $p = 0$, $u = 1$, and $v = 0$. She then has created ample material for a new edition of her best-selling manual—one that will receive more rave reviews in all the best outdoors magazines!

This last scenario is most representative of the typical domain of creativity, whether in the arts or the sciences. An individual's personal expertise corresponds closely with the consensual expertise represented by the field, and thus personal creativity will receive validation as consensual creativity. What the creator views as original, useful, and surprising will tend to be seen the same way by colleagues and other adepts in the field. To be sure, it is certainly conceivable for an individual who lacks any expertise whatsoever to make a contribution that can earn consensual validation as creative—as was illustrated in the first wilderness scenario—but the odds of that happening are very small. The more minimal the expertise, the lower those odds. At best, a certain minimum level of consensual expertise is required for consensual creativity. For instance, Einstein may not have been the most expert mathematician and physicist of his age, yet he knew enough mathematics and physics to produce a doctoral dissertation that would not even be understood by anyone lacking sufficient training in both subjects (to wit, see http://e-collection.library.ethz.ch/eserv/eth:30378/eth-30378-01.pdf). His expertise was just sufficient to work out the revolutionary ideas that he had visualized in his famous "thought experiments." Even then, he at times needed outside help, as in the case of general relativity mentioned earlier.

The obvious question is as follows: What is the threshold level of consensual expertise necessary before a person can expect to engage in consensual creativity? That turns out to be a very difficult issue. It largely depends on the nature of the contribution (cf. Sternberg, 1999). If a creator is building upon the work of predecessors, as Einstein was, then the minimum must be to understand thoroughly that prior work, an understanding that enables the person to "stand on the shoulders of giants," as Isaac Newton put it, rather than sit at their feet. Yet on other occasions an individual is creating an entirely new expertise largely from scratch. Two striking examples are Galileo Galilei's invention of telescopic astronomy and Antonie van Leeuwenhoek's creation of microscopic biology (Simonton, 2012a). Their breakthroughs were so out of line with contemporary consensual expertise that many of their discoveries were ridiculed by the reigning experts. The moon couldn't possibly have mountains, nor could animals exist that were invisible to the naked eye. Otherwise Aristotle would have mentioned these possibilities. The newfangled devices must be producing optical illusions instead. It should come as no surprise, then, that Galileo was a college dropout sans higher degrees while Leeuwenhoek had no formal education at all, his entire training consisting of an apprenticeship with a draper (fabric merchant).

Expertise as Necessary but Not Sufficient for Creativity

Having established that a certain minimal amount of expertise is required for creativity, we must now ask whether expertise suffices to produce creativity, whether at personal or consensual levels. Actually, I can now take advantage of a logical necessity. If personal creativity is a necessary but not sufficient basis for consensual creativity, then all I need to demonstrate is that personal expertise is a necessary but not sufficient basis for personal creativity. My argument can thus focus on the personal level.

At that personal level, creativity is defined by those responses (ideas or behaviors) that have the following parameter values: $p \rightarrow 0$, $u \rightarrow 1$, and $v \rightarrow 0$. These values yield a response that is original, useful, and surprising (viz. $c \rightarrow 1$). In contrast, personal expertise is defined by those responses that have the values $p \rightarrow 1$, $u \rightarrow 1$, and $v \rightarrow 1$. In words, the response has a high probability of generation because it is known to be highly useful. The contradiction between these two definitions should be apparent at once. Although both assume a high utility, the other two parameters must go in the opposite direction, so to the extent that a response is routine, habitual, or reproductive, it cannot possibly be creative (cf. Simonton, 2013b). Hence, the expertise component of creativity has been reduced to just response utility. A creative response must add useful ideas or behaviors to the repertoire that defines personal expertise. Indeed, when a highly useful response is finally discovered, its probability and knowledge value will both change to unity (Simonton, 2013a). Of course, both revised parameters are now a posteriori rather than the initial probability or the prior knowledge values.

To illustrate these differences, we can return to the two-string experiment (Maier, 1931). After the participant learned that the highest probability response had a zero utility, the experimenter advised that several objects in the lab could be used to solve the problem. One of those objects was a chair. At this point, most participants immediately walked over to the chair, moved it to a spot about midway between the strings, brought one string over and attached it to the chair, then brought over the second string, removed the first string from the chair, and tied the strings together. So many participants quickly arrived at this solution that Maier considered it routine rather than creative. A chair is often used to hold things. Such uses are part of our expertise regarding chairs. Hence, this obvious solution has the parameters $p = u = v = 1$.

After the participants had exhausted the obvious solutions, such as using the extension cord and the pole, the experimenter then tried to elicit a truly creative response to the problem. Maier (1931) started with a subtle hint by "accidentally" setting the cord in motion when nonchalantly walking toward the window. If that didn't work, the experimenter became more direct: "the subject was handed a pair of pliers and told 'With the aid of this and no other object there is another way of solving the problem'" (p. 183). Some participants immediately thought of using the pliers as tongs, but quickly realized that the tool was not long enough. If no solution resulted, the experimenter would repeat the first hint, and if that repetition failed to inspire a solution, the participants were shown the solution. The solution entailed shortening the string in the center of the room, attaching the pliers to the shortened string, and then setting the makeshift pendulum into motion. The other string could then be brought over and tied to the first string once it swung toward the participant. Mission accomplished!

Given how few participants arrived at this solution, and how long it took even for the successful participants to attain the insight, Maier quite rightly considered this response creative. As he put it, the pliers-as-pendulum solution added "an element of surprise and a change in meaning since the tool changes to a weight and the string, which was too short, suddenly becomes too long and must be shortened" (Maier, 1940, p. 52). In formal terms, we can say that $u = 1$ but that $v \rightarrow 0$ and hence $p \rightarrow 0$. Indeed, with respect to the prior knowledge value for this solution, even participants who were given earlier experience with standard (rigid) pendulums remained unlikely to think of the pliers as weights (Maier, 1940). Using this tool that way clearly represented an "unusual use" (cf. the Alternative Uses Test in Guilford, 1967). Pliers-as-bob is not a combination that very likely comes to mind, the experimenter's first and second hints notwithstanding.

To sum up, personal expertise is necessary but not sufficient basis for personal creativity, and hence personal expertise is a necessary but not sufficient basis for consensual creativity, given that personal creativity is a necessary but not sufficient basis for consensual creativity.[2]

Discussion

If expertise is necessary but not sufficient for creativity, then what supplies the sufficient condition? The answer is implied by the parameters that define a highly creative response, namely, $p \rightarrow 0$, $u \rightarrow 1$, and $v \rightarrow 0$. Somehow a person must come up with a low probability but highly useful thought or behavior even though the prior knowledge of that utility approaches zero if not being totally absent. Indeed, by definition the most creative response requires that $p = v = 0$ while $u = 1$, a seemingly impossible situation. When $p = 0$, the individual cannot possibly respond at the outset but instead must enter some perhaps very prolonged incubation period before the response attains a nonzero probability—very likely as a "flash of insight" or "Eureka" experience. And when $v = 0$, the person has absolutely no prior idea whether the response would be useful or not even if it could be hypothetically generated. Consequently, the individual's only option is to engage in some kind of "generate and test" or "trial and error" process or procedure in which highly original combinations are first produced and then evaluated to determine their actual utilities. In brief, the individual, whether animal or human, has no other choice but to rely on what Campbell (1960) called "blind variation and selective retention," or what later became abbreviated as BVSR (Nickles, 2003).

It must be noted that the modifier "blind" does not mean that responses must be generated randomly or that they are necessarily equiprobable, nor does the adjective imply that the generated responses stupidly ignore any applicable expertise (Simonton, 2011a). In the latter case, a response with $p \to 0$ because $u \to 1$ and $v \to 1$ would certainly not be entered into the selection filter because it already would have been ruled out by personal expertise (i.e. BVSR pre-selection discussed in Simonton, 2011a). Still, any time that $v \to 0$, so that the utility is largely if not entirely unknown in advance, then a two-stage "produce and assess" operation becomes mandatory. That mandate includes all $v \to 0$ "blind variations" with the following values for the remaining two parameters: (a) $p \to 1$ but $u \to 0$ (problem finding, as mentioned earlier), (b) $p \to 1$ and $u \to 1$ (a fortuitous response bias or "lucky guess"), (c) $p \to 0$ and $u \to 0$ (fruitless dreaming, fantasy, mind wandering, exploration, tinkering, or play), and (d) $p \to 0$ but $u \to 1$ (the only truly creative idea or behavior; Simonton, 2016b).[3] By definition, these four distinct blind variations cannot be separated into the creative and the not creative without some evaluation of the utility u, thus implementing BVSR, whether implicit or explicit.

Sad to say, although expertise plus BVSR are necessary to produce creativity, whether personal or consensual, the two together remain not sufficient. A response with the parameters $u = 1$ and $v = 0$ will never undergo a generation and test (or trial and error) episode if $p = 0$ for all creators throughout all eternity. Nobody will ever know what magnificent masterworks of science or art never saw the light of day because no creator ever thought to try out some impossibly improbable idea. Creators are great risk takers, but there are practical limits to risk taking (but see Charles Darwin's amazing "fool's experiments" discussed in Darwin, 1892/1958).

This implication helps us understand why serendipity often plays a crucial role in the advancement of science (e.g., Kantorovich & Ne'eman, 1989). Courtesy of chance, hypotheses are implicitly tested that would never have been explicitly conceived. The history of science and technology is replete with serendipitous discoveries, such as animal electricity (Galvani), classical conditioning (Pavlov), D-line in the solar spectrum (Kirchhoff), dynamite (Nobel), electromagnetism (Oersted), geometric laws of crystallography (Haüy), interference of light (Grimaldi), laughing gas anesthesia (Davy), ozone (Schönbein), phonograph (Edison), photography (Daguerre), radioactivity (Becquerel), saccharin (Fahlberg), sulfa drugs (Domagk), synthetic coal-tar dyes (Perkin), Teflon (Plunkett), vaccination (Pasteur), Velcro (de Maestral), and X-rays (Röntgen). Notable instances run into the hundreds if not thousands.

But perhaps the prototypical example is Alexander Fleming's serendipitous discovery of penicillin. Although he had been studying anti-bacterial agents for many years, he never would have dreamed of testing the world's first antibiotic by deliberately introducing *Penicillium notatum* mold spores into his staphylococci cultures. That epochal event had to take place quite by accident—owing to his somewhat messy lab practices. Obviously, Fleming possessed the expertise to recognize the potential utility implied by the mold colony's destruction of the surrounding bacteria. As Louis Pasteur famously said, "In the fields of observation chance favors only the prepared mind." Yet in the absence of happenstance, his expertise would not have sufficed to overcome the fundamental a priori constraints, namely, $p = v = 0$, exactly, despite $u = 1$. How many other great discoveries are still waiting for analogous serendipitous events to happen?

Even when we account for serendipity, another variable underlying creativity must be included in the analysis that is unrelated to domain-specific expertise— and might even be considered antithetical to any highly specialized expertise. That variable is *openness to experience*, the dimension of the Big Five Factor Model that is most strongly correlated with actual creative achievement (McCrae & Greenberg, 2014). Rather than obsessively focus on a narrow topic, such as is required for expertise acquisition, individuals who score highly on this factor tend to exhibit much broader interests and a wider range of avocations. This breadth often supports insights that cannot be attributed to domain-specific expertise alone. For example, Galileo's artistic interests, especially his training in chiaroscuro, enabled him to observe—and draw—the lunar mountains that others, using comparable telescopes, had literally overlooked (Simonton, 2012a). The light and dark at the crescent's edge implied peaks and valleys—not mere blotches on the perfectly smooth spherical surface advocated in Aristotelian cosmology.

Just as significantly, open persons are also more likely to display cognitive disinhibition, a disposition that inclines them to notice things that others simply filter out (Carson, 2014). Such an inclination would clearly give them the advantage in spotting potential utilities in seemingly trivial events—such as staphylococci cultures ruined by a commonplace mold. Fleming was not the first to experience this otherwise inconvenient event. Yet as the physicist Ernst Mach (1896) pointed out in his classic essay, many great discoveries "were *seen* numbers of times before they were *noticed*" (p. 169). So it was left to Fleming to become the first to draw the inference that revolutionized medicine and earned him a Nobel Prize. Therefore, openness to experience represents yet another mediating factor between expertise and creativity.[4]

To repeat for one last time, expertise is necessary but not sufficient for creativity. Creators must be far more than domain-specific experts—and sometimes can even be far less than fully expert!

Notes

1 The concept of v might seem to bear a superficial resemblance to the "prior probability" used in Bayesian inference. Yet any Bayesian statistician would easily notice that the "priors" used here are not the same (Press, 1989). Indeed, the Bayesian prior is more similar to the initial probability p (albeit no distribution is specified). In contrast, v is more closely related to the concept of "justification" in the epistemological theory of "justified true belief" that can be traced back to Plato's dialogue *Theaetetus*, where v directly quantifies the degree to which the "true belief" (viz. regarding response utility or nonutility) is in fact "justified" (cf. Campbell, 1974). If completely justified, $v = 1$, if completely unjustified, $v = 0$.

2 Some more nerdy members of my own baby-boom generation might rightly infer that this chapter's author was a teenage aficionado of the 1960s WFF 'N Proof board game. This idiosyncratic component of my personal expertise may or may not have contributed to any consensual creativity. But for the uninitiated, a "WFF" is a "well-formed formula," and the sentence culminating in the superscript identifying this note represents a "proof" given what was posited at the beginning of the section. With a little review I could translate this argument by lining up the die marked with the signs of symbolic logic. I still possess the game!

3 An astute reader might reckon, correctly, that an intimate connection exists between the mind wandering or behavioral exploration, as represented by $p \to 0$, $u \to 0$, and $v \to 0$, and actual personal creativity, as represented by $p \to 0$, $u \to 1$, and $v \to 0$ (Simonton, 2016b). Although the former cannot guarantee the emergence of the latter, because of the very likely low utility, neither does the former exclude the latter, because of the low prior knowledge value for that same utility. Hence, it occasionally happens that a creative idea will inadvertently pop into awareness in the reverie or play taking place during the incubation period (Smallwood & Schooler, 2015). In neuroscience terms, this possible even if extremely rare outcome would often be associated with the "default mode network" (Kühn et al., 2014).

4 Openness to experience is not the only individual-difference variable associated with creativity, just the most important one both empirically and theoretically (cf. Feist, Reimer-Palmon, & Kaufman, in press). It is worthwhile to note that an "innate talent" for achievement in a particular domain can be defined by a profile of the entire set of participatory traits weighted by their corresponding heritabilities and predictive validities with respect to the sets of deliberate practice and performance criteria (see Simonton, 2014, for detailed discussions).

References

Boden, M. A. (2004). *The creative mind: Myths & mechanisms* (2nd ed.). New York: Routledge.

Campbell, D. T. (1960). Blind variation and selective retention in creative thought as in other knowledge processes. *Psychological Review, 67*, 380–400.

Campbell, D. T. (1974). Unjustified variation and selective retention in scientific discovery. In F. Ayala & T. Dobszhansky (Eds.), *Studies in the philosophy of biology: Reduction and related problems* (pp. 139–161). London: Macmillan.

Carson, S. H. (2014). Cognitive disinhibition, creativity, and psychopathology. In D. K. Simonton (Ed.), *The Wiley handbook of genius* (pp. 198–221). Oxford, UK: Wiley.

Darwin, F. (Ed.). (1958). *The autobiography of Charles Darwin and selected letters.* New York: Dover. (Original work published 1892)

Einstein, A. (1905). *Eine neue Bestimmung der Moleküldimensionen.* Bern: Wyss

Elo, A. E. (1986). *The rating of chessplayers, past and present* (2nd ed.). New York: Arco.

Epstein, R. (2015). Of course animals are creative: Insights from Generativity Theory. In A. B. Kaufman & J. C. Kaufman (Eds.). *Animal creativity and innovation* (pp. 375–390). San Diego, CA: Academic Press.

Ericsson, K. A. (2014). Creative genius: A view from the expert-performance approach. In D. K. Simonton (Ed.), *The Wiley handbook of genius* (pp. 321–349). Oxford, UK: Wiley.

Feist, G. J., Reimer-Palmon, R., & Kaufman, J. C. (Eds.). (in press). *Cambridge handbook of creativity and personality research.* New York: Cambridge University Press.

Guilford, J. P. (1967). *The nature of human intelligence.* New York: McGraw-Hill.

Hoffmann, B. (1972). *Albert Einstein: Creator and rebel.* New York: Plume.

Kantorovich, A., & Ne'eman, Y. (1989). Serendipity as a source of evolutionary progress in science. *Studies in History and Philosophy of Science, 20,* 505–529.

Köhler, W. (1925). *The mentality of apes* (E. Winter, Trans.). New York: Harcourt, Brace.

Kühn, S., Ritter, S. M., Müller, B. C. N., van Baaren, R. B., Brass, M., & Dijksterhuis, A. (2014). The importance of the default mode network in creativity—A structural MRI study. *Journal of Creative Behavior, 48,* 152–163.

Mach, E. (1896, January). On the part played by accident in invention and discovery. *Monist, 6,* 161–175.

Maier, N. R. F. (1931). Reasoning in humans: II. The solution of a problem and its appearance in consciousness. *Journal of Comparative and Physiological Psychology, 12,* 181–194.

Maier, N. R. F. (1940). The behavioral mechanisms concerned with problem solving. *Psychological Review, 47,* 43–58.

McCrae, R. R., & Greenberg, D. M. (2014). Openness to experience. In D. K. Simonton (Ed.), *The Wiley handbook of genius* (pp. 222–243). Oxford, UK: Wiley.

Ness, R. B. (2013) *Genius unmasked.* New York: Oxford University Press.

Nickles, T. (2003). Evolutionary models of innovation and the Meno problem. In L. V. Shavinina (Ed.), *The international handbook on innovation* (pp. 54–78). New York: Elsevier Science.

Press, S. J. (1989). Bayesian statistics: principles, models, and applications. New York: Wiley.

Rothenberg, A. (2015). *Flight from wonder: An investigation of scientific creativity.* Oxford, UK: Oxford University Press.

Runco, M., & Jaeger, G. J. (2012). The standard definition of creativity. *Creativity Research Journal, 21,* 92–96.

Simonton, D. K. (1997). Creative productivity: A predictive and explanatory model of career trajectories and landmarks. *Psychological Review, 104,* 66–89.

Simonton, D. K. (2003). Scientific creativity as constrained stochastic behavior: The integration of product, process, and person perspectives. *Psychological Bulletin, 129,* 475–494.

Simonton, D. K. (2010). Creativity as blind-variation and selective-retention: Combinatorial models of exceptional creativity. *Physics of Life Reviews, 7,* 156–179.

Simonton, D. K. (2011a). Creativity and discovery as blind variation: Campbell's (1960) BVSR model after the half-century mark. *Review of General Psychology, 15,* 158–174.

Simonton, D. K. (2011b). *Great flicks: Scientific studies of cinematic creativity and aesthetics.* New York: Oxford University Press.

Simonton, D. K. (2012a). Foresight, insight, oversight, and hindsight in scientific discovery: How sighted were Galileo's telescopic sightings? *Psychology of Aesthetics, Creativity, and the Arts, 6,* 243–254.

Simonton, D. K. (2012b). Taking the US Patent Office creativity criteria seriously: A quantitative three-criterion definition and its implications. *Creativity Research Journal, 24,* 97–106.

Simonton, D. K. (2013a). Creative problem solving as sequential BVSR: Exploration (total ignorance) versus elimination (informed guess). *Thinking Skills and Creativity, 8,* 1–10.

Simonton, D. K. (2013b). Creative thought as blind variation and selective retention: Why sightedness is inversely related to creativity. *Journal of Theoretical and Philosophical Psychology, 33,* 253–266.

Simonton, D. K (2013c). What is a creative idea? Little-c versus Big-C creativity. In J. Chan & K. Thomas (Eds.), *Handbook of research on creativity* (pp. 69–83). Cheltenham Glos, UK: Edward Elgar.

Simonton, D. K. (2014). Creative performance, expertise acquisition, individual-differences, and developmental antecedents: An integrative research agenda. *Intelligence, 45,* 66–73.

Simonton, D. K. (2015a). Defining animal creativity: Little-c, often; Big-C, sometimes. In A. B. Kaufman & J. C. Kaufman (Eds.). *Animal creativity and innovation* (pp. 390–393). San Diego, CA: Academic Press.

Simonton, D. K. (2015b). Psychology as a science within Comte's hypothesized hierarchy: Empirical investigations and conceptual implications. *Review of General Psychology, 19,* 334–344.

Simonton, D. K. (2016a). Creativity, automaticity, irrationality, fortuity, fantasy, and other contingencies: An eightfold response typology. *Review of General Psychology, 20,* 194–204.

Simonton, D. K. (2016b). Defining creativity: Don't we also need to define what is *not* creative? *Journal of Creative Behavior.* Early view. DOI: 10.1002/jocb.137

Simonton, D. K., & Damian, R. I. (2013). Creativity. In D. Reisberg (Ed.), *Oxford handbook of cognitive psychology* (pp. 795–807). New York: Oxford University Press.

Skinner, B. F. (1981, July 31). Selection by consequences. *Science, 213,* 501–504.

Smallwood, J. & Schooler, J. W. (2015). The science of mind wandering: Empirically navigating the stream of consciousness. *Annual Review of Psychology, 66,* 487–518.

Sternberg, R. J. (1999). A propulsion model of types of creative contributions. *Review of General Psychology, 3,* 83–100.

Thagard, P. (2012). Creative combination of representations: Scientific discovery and technological invention. In R. Proctor & E. J. Capaldi (Eds.), *Psychology of science: Implicit and explicit processes* (pp. 389–405). New York: Oxford University Press.

Thagard, P., & Stewart, T. C. (2011). The AHA! experience: Creativity through emergent binding in neural networks. *Cognitive Science: A Multidisciplinary Journal, 35,* 1–33.

Weisberg, R. W. (2014). Case studies of genius: Ordinary thinking, extraordinary outcomes. In D. K. Simonton (Ed.), *The Wiley-Blackwell handbook of genius* (pp. 139–165). Oxford, UK: Wiley-Blackwell.

Weisberg, R. W. (2015). On the usefulness of "value" in the definition of creativity. *Creativity Research Journal, 27,* 111–124.

20

COMPUTATIONAL MODELS OF EXPERTISE

Fernand Gobet, Martyn Lloyd-Kelly, and Peter C. R. Lane

Introduction

Expertise is a complex phenomenon. Not only do many cognitive mechanisms operate simultaneously, but they also operate at different levels of analysis (e.g., micro-mechanisms with perception, macro-mechanisms with decision making) and at different timescales (from seconds to years). How can we provide good explanations of expert behavior in spite of this complexity? How can we develop theories that satisfy the requirements of good scientific practice, such as lack of ambiguity, parsimony, and testability? This chapter will argue that computational modeling is one of the few methods powerful enough to do so. Whereas most psychological theories are expressed verbally, this type of representation is unsatisfactory for answering these questions successfully and explaining a behavior as complex as expertise, particularly because it often leads to vague, unspecified, and self-contradictory theories.

After providing a few definitions, the chapter will briefly discuss the strengths and weaknesses of computational modeling. Mathematical modeling is a close cousin of computational modeling, and we will provide an overview of this approach. We will then review computational models developed to account for phenomena linked to expertise, discussing in turn the following: models of heuristic search, models based on the mechanism of chunking, connectionist models and production systems. The CHREST (Chunk Hierarchy and REtrieval STructures) architecture, which has led to many models of expertise, is then discussed in some detail. The chapter concludes with a discussion of why computational modeling, despite considerable advantages, has not enjoyed the same popularity as other methods for studying expertise, and provides recommendations for future research.

Some Definitions

Scientific theories can be divided into several categories (e.g. Gobet, Chassy, & Bilalić, 2011). *Informal theories* are expressed in natural language such as English; *formal theories* use some form of formalism, which can be defined as a system of rigorously defined rules. The majority of theories in psychology—and the study of expertise is no exception—are formulated informally. Formal theories can further be divided into *computational theories*, stated as computer programs, and *non-computational theories,* expressed, for example, in mathematics. The boundary between these two types can be fuzzy; for example, a theory might start as a mathematical theory but then be implemented as a computer program.

A popular classification divides computational modeling into *symbolic modeling*, which assumes that the manipulation of symbols is central to cognition, *neural modeling* (or *connectionism*), which uses biological neurons as an analogy for cognition, and *hybrid modeling*, where symbolic modeling is combined with neural modeling. Another classification considers the scope of models. Most models in psychology are *micro-models*, addressing only one experimental paradigm. Some *macro-models* are more ambitious and cover phenomena across different experimental paradigms. At the extreme, we have *cognitive architectures*, which provide a blueprint for simulating a wide range of phenomena across different subfields of psychology, such as perception, memory, expertise, and language acquisition, as is the case with the CHREST architecture (see below).

Other classifications are possible, for example, distinguishing models that learn and those that do not, or differentiating between deterministic and probabilistic models. Computational theories in psychology are often closely related to programs written in artificial intelligence (AI). However, computational modeling emphasizes comparisons with human data.

Strengths of Computational Modeling

It is generally accepted that computational modeling has a number of strengths (for discussion, see Gobet *et al.*, 2011; Lane & Gobet, 2012b; Ritter *et al.*, 2003), and it is worth discussing those particularly relevant for the study of expertise. A natural starting point is to set computational modeling against informal theorizing. A common criticism leveled at informal theories is that they do not really explain the data, but rather just re-describe them with fancy labels. Another criticism is that they make predictions that are not testable because they do not offer enough constraints, and thus allow an indefinite number of possible interpretations. By contrast, computational modeling requires that the mechanisms and parameters of a theory be rigorously specified; if this is not done, the computer program will not run. Clarity and unambiguity are the *sine qua non* condition for a valid scientific theory, as repeatedly emphasized by philosophers of science. If these criteria are not satisfied, it is not possible to derive testable predictions from a theory. For example, when the informal long-term working memory theory (Ericsson & Kintsch, 1995), which aimed to account for data in expertise and reading, was implemented as a computer model, it explained nothing because it predicted nearly all possible outcomes (Gobet, 2000a).

Another important strength is that computer programs make it possible to model and understand complex behaviors, even when many variables are involved (see Figure 20.1). Note that this is impossible with all but the simplest informal theories, because cognitive limitations impinge upon humans' ability to keep track of all the constraints involved. A related advantage is that computer models afford the possibility of systematically manipulating mechanisms and parameters to establish their effects on behavior. Similarly, the characteristics and the statistics of the task environment can be altered. Such explorations often lead to better understanding of a system, particularly when its dynamics are complex, non-linear, and characterized by multiple interactions. Note that computer models allow one to manipulate not only numerical parameters, such as the capacity of short-term memory (STM), but also qualitative parameters such as the heuristics used by participants.

Finally, a unique feature of computational models is that they offer explanations that are "sufficient" (Newell, Shaw, & Simon, 1958): They can not only provide input–output relationships, but also carry out the behavior of interest.

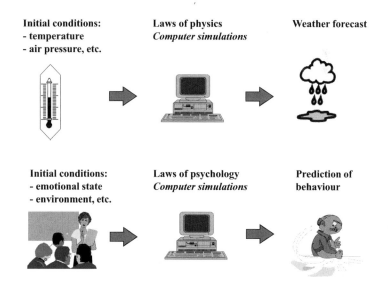

FIGURE 20.1 Simulating complex phenomena. There is no principled difference between computational modeling in psychology and in the physical sciences. In both cases, it is possible to predict complex phenomena by specifying initial conditions and the postulated mechanisms (laws) of the domain.

Thus, as we will discuss later in this chapter, a model of chess players' memory recall simulates eye movements when players look at the position, the kind of pieces they remember, the way pieces are grouped during recall, and even the errors made. This allows detailed predictions to be made about differences at the macro (group) and micro (individual) level.

Criticisms of Computational Modeling

Like any scientific method, computational modeling is not perfect. Indeed, there has been some debate in the field of expertise research about the (putative) drawbacks of using computational modeling (e.g., Ericsson & Kintsch, 2000; Gobet, 2000b; Simon & Gobet, 2000). A common criticism is that research in psychology has not reached a stage providing the precision required of computational modeling. As we will see later, this analysis is too pessimistic because detailed and accurate models of expert behavior have been developed. A second criticism concerns the difficulty of comparing models that might differ with respect to coverage, goodness of fit and complexity (e.g. Ritter *et al.*, 2003). For example, one theory might simulate a small number of phenomena with great precision, using many free parameters that can be fine-tuned to allow the simulations to fit the data. Another theory might simulate many phenomena with reasonable but not perfect fit, using few free parameters. At the moment, there is no definite way to decide which theory is objectively correct, although Occam's razor would suggest the latter.

A third criticism is that it is sometimes difficult to distinguish between theoretical claims and features that are required to implement the model as a computer program (e.g., Lane & Gobet, 2003). For example, connectionist models are implemented with a particular number of units. Is this an arbitrary decision or a component of the theory? A final criticism is that there is no accepted methodology for developing, comparing, and evaluating models (e.g., Ritter *et al.*, 2003). However, much progress has been made in this respect. For example, Lane and Gobet (2012b) recently proposed a methodology based on systematic testing of code and continuously improving the program's design.

In general, the same criticisms we have just discussed can also be leveled against verbal theories, sometimes with a vengeance. However, because verbal theories are frequently under-specified, researchers seem unaware of this. It is as if, due to its stringent requirement of specifying everything in detail, computational modeling magnifies the features required by a good scientific theory.

Mathematical Models of Expert Behavior

A close cousin of computational modeling is mathematical modeling, which typically consists of building a system of equations based on theoretical assumptions, and solving it. Often, the system has no closed solution, and computer simulations are used to study the behavior of the system; for example, the behavior of a set of differential equations as a function of time can be simulated on the computer. Mathematical modeling shares with computational modeling the requirements of precision and unambiguity.

Mathematical modeling has been used occasionally in expertise research. De Groot, Gobet, and Jongman (1996) used information theory to compute the amount of information contained in chess positions likely to occur in master games. They concluded that the amount of information in such positions was at most 50 bits, which is much smaller than the number of bits for the set of all chess positions (143 bits). Simon and Gilmartin (1973) used a combination of computer modeling and mathematical analysis to estimate the number of chunks necessary to reach master level, obtaining 50,000 as a first approximation. Gobet (1997) describes SEARCH, an abstract computer model of template theory, which successfully reproduced key phenomena in chess problem solving, including the fact that the average depth of search follows a power function of skill. Finally, Campitelli, Gobet, and Bilalić (2014) developed the *practice-plasticity-processes model*, which accounted for key phenomena in chess expertise, including the presence of prodigies and the effect of aging on chess skill. The model uses twelve variables, such as the level of intelligence and the amount of practice, whose relations are described by equations. Simulations show how performance varies as a function of time in a large sample of players (17,250 at the end of the simulations).

There are two main disadvantages of mathematical modeling. First, as soon as many relations are described, psychologically unrealistic assumptions and constraints (such as linearity) have to be made to enable the system to be solved (Simon, 1967). Second, all values and responses must be translated into numbers, which can lead to loss of information (e.g., Simon, 1967), for example with respect to the similarity of respective stimuli. Interestingly, this weakness is not shared with computational models (in particular, symbolic models), which can process more realistic stimuli and produce behavior, including verbal protocols, directly comparable to that of humans.

Models of Heuristic Search

We now present a variety of computational models aimed at explaining (aspects of) expert behavior. These models will be organized using the main data structures they use. Interestingly, many of these models are dedicated to chess expertise, probably because this task is relatively easy to formalize and because one of the most vocal champions of computational modeling, Herbert A. Simon, was interested in chess. Note that some important theoretical debates in the field of expertise focused on chess.

Early models were interested in the way humans carry out a search when trying to select a move in a chess position. One of their key theoretical contributions is to have formalized and shed light on the issue of bounded rationality

(Simon, 1956). How is it possible for humans to find reasonably good solutions in complex domains, in spite of their cognitive limitations (e.g., limited span of attention, small working-memory capacity, and low learning rates)? How can they become experts in combinatorial tasks? These models address the issues of heuristic and selective search, the use of goals, the dynamic adjustment of expectations, and satisficing (i.e., selecting solutions that are good enough even though they are not optimal). In some cases, the output of the models was compared to human players' verbal protocols. Unlike other contemporary chess programs, these models aimed to simulate human problem-solving behavior rather than playing at a high level.

The NSS chess program (Newell, Shaw, & Simon, 1963) carries out search in chess using goals such as the maintenance of material equilibrium or control of the center. These goals inform two move generators that run independently; the first one handles base moves (moves immediately playable in the problem situation at hand), and the second one generates moves taking place during the analysis of a branch in the search tree. The acceptability of moves is evaluated by an independent process. The program implements Simon's (1956) idea of satisficing by selecting the first move whose value is above the current expectation. NSS could play only weak chess, but it demonstrated that reasonable moves could be chosen with modest search trees (around 100 nodes).

Baylor and Simon (1966) also focused on selective search with MATER, a chess mating combination program. Selectivity was obtained by directing search to situations with "forced moves" (i.e., situations where only one move is possible) and to situations where the opponent has only a handful of moves. These heuristics allowed MATER to play well in positions where a checkmate combination was possible but also meant that it could not play beyond this kind of position, which represents only a small subset of the set of possible chess positions met in games.

In sport, Alain and Sarrazin (1990) developed a model of decision making in squash. The strategy of the defending player was represented as an algorithm assumed to be stored in long-term memory (LTM) and activated as a function of the information present in STM. The strategy could be influenced by several factors such as the level of expertise, time pressure, and expectations.

Chunking Networks

An important class of models is built around the idea of *chunking networks*. The central assumption is that knowledge is built incrementally and can be formalized as the growth of a network, where each node represents a piece of knowledge. This idea was first implemented in the Elementary Perceiver and Memorizer (EPAM) program, one of the first computational models, and has led to the very influential *chunking theory*. We briefly discuss EPAM and chunking theory below, before discussing specific models of expertise.

The Foundations: EPAM and Chunking Theory

A *chunk* can be defined as "a meaningful unit of information built from smaller pieces of information" (Gobet & Lane, 2012, p. 541), and *chunking* as the creation of such units.[1] The earliest computational implementation of this idea is Feigenbaum and Simon's EPAM theory of perception and memory (Simon & Feigenbaum, 1964), which was used to simulate data on "verbal learning" (essentially, how one learns lists or pairs of nonsense syllables). The theory is quite versatile and has been used to simulate other tasks such as children learning how to spell (Simon & Simon, 1973) and concept formation (Gobet, Richman, Staszewski, & Simon, 1997).

EPAM stores information using a discrimination network, a sequential network of tests applying to the features of the input. Learning consists of creating new nodes (*discrimination*) and elaborating existing nodes (*familiarization*). In line with Simon's idea of satisficing, learning is parsimonious and occurs incrementally; that is, new nodes are created only when it is necessary to distinguish between two stimuli. EPAM also makes assumptions about the attentional strategies used by the participants, and about STM capacity and mechanisms. Each cognitive operation incurs a time cost in EPAM, which makes it possible to make predictions about the time it takes to learn or recognize a stimulus.

Chase and Simon's (1973) chunking theory is a verbal theory applying and extending EPAM to expertise in chess. (Note that the informal theory had much more impact than the formal theory.) The key postulate is that chess expertise requires the acquisition of a large number of perceptual chunks, which denote patterns of pieces on the chess board. In line with EPAM, chunks are nodes in a discrimination net, which is an index to long-term procedural and semantic memory. When players practice and study classic chess games, they acquire new chunks, add information to existing chunks, and create links associating information to these chunks. Information includes potential moves, strategies, and tactical motifs. Cognition is bounded, for players of all skill levels, by limits in STM capacity (about seven chunks) and learning rate (around eight seconds to create a new chunk in LTM).

PERCEIVER and MAPP

PERCEIVER (Simon & Barenfeld, 1969) is a program written as a reply to Tikhomirov and Poznyanskaya's (1966) study of chess players' eye movements, which concluded that expert perception is holistic. Rather, Simon and Barenfeld wanted to show through computer simulations that expert perception could be accounted for by simple and local mechanisms. PERCEIVER was able to simulate a player's eye movements relatively well. The program did not learn but was considered as a perceptual interface for an EPAM-like learner. It used a number of routines from MATER (Baylor & Simon, 1966), in particular to compute trajectories of pieces (relations of attack and defense). The key hypothesis—supported by the simulations, according to the authors—was that information gathered during the perceptual phase concerns relations between pairs of pieces or relations between pieces and squares.

In their program MAPP (Memory-Aided Pattern Perceiver), Simon and Gilmartin (1973) implemented aspects of the chunking theory. Specifically, they used the idea that the human information processing system is character-ized by limits that apply equally to novices and experts. Learning is realized by the growth of a discrimination network and follows (slightly simplified) EPAM mechanisms. Once learned, chunks are accessed by perceptual cues. MAPP simulated De Groot's (1946) classic memory task: A chess position is presented for a few seconds, and, after it has been hidden, participants have to reconstruct it on an empty board. During the presentation of the board position, MAPP attempts to identify LTM chunks using its discrimination net-work. When a chunk has been successfully recognized, a pointer to it is placed in STM. During the recall phase, MAPP simply goes through all the pointers stored in STM, accesses the relevant LTM chunks, and places the pieces they contain on the board. MAPP was able to simulate the recall performance of a good amateur, but not of a master. A shortcoming of the model was that the chunks to learn were created by the programmers and not automatically and autonomously identified by the program.

Extrapolating from the MAPP simulations using mathematical techniques, Simon and Gilmartin (1973) estimated that expertise in chess required between 10,000 and 100,000 chunks. More recent simulations with CHREST suggest that this number is closer to 300,000 to simulate grandmaster-level performance (Gobet & Simon, 2000).

EPAM-IV

One weakness of chunking theory, and its MAPP implementation as a com-puter program, was that it underestimated LTM access speed. Charness (1976) demonstrated this by interpolating a task between the presentation of a chess position and its recall. According to the theory, the interpolated task should erase the STM pointers, and therefore recall should be severely hampered. However, the data showed that the interference had only a minimal effect (a recall loss of around 10 percent). Research into mnemonics also showed that access speed had been underestimated. In a series of influential experiments, Chase and Ericsson (1982) trained a participant to recall up to 81 digits, each presented for a second. (Without special training, most people can recall only about seven digits.) Chase and Ericsson argued that this could not be accounted for by the recognition of chunks, as the sequence of digits was essentially random, and thus that access to LTM should be rapid with experts. Two computer models based on EPAM were developed to address this and other issues. This section discusses EPAM-IV, which simulated the digit span task. CHREST will be covered in a later section.

EPAM-IV simulated in detail the progress of DD, another participant. After 865 practice sessions over more than three years, DD was able to recall 104 digits, despite the fact that his digit span was initially 7–9 digits. Richman, Staszewski and Simon (1995) aimed to account for this progression. Like the participants studied by Ericsson and Chase, DD had a good semantic knowledge of numbers (e.g., historical dates, running times, etc.) and used a "retrieval structure." This structure is a set of memory cues that have been consciously learned so that they facilitate storage and retrieval of information. Many mnemonics lead to the acquisition of such structures, most notably the method of loci (also known as memory palaces), where one puts the material to recall in previously learned locations, such as the rooms of a house (Yates, 1966).

EPAM-IV added the concept of a retrieval structure to EPAM. In addition, STM was modeled in more detail, and was divided into two components. The visual component combines a limited number of chunks with a visuo-spatial representation. Similarly, the auditory component combines a limited number of chunks with the idea of the articulatory loop (Baddeley & Hitch, 1974). LTM is divided into a semantic and a procedural component. Retrieval structures are considered as schemata, and thus belong to semantic LTM. The model precisely specifies the way chunks are learned, retrieval structures are constructed, and different types of knowledge are incrementally connected. Since each cognitive process has a time parameter associated with it, it is possible to simulate in detail the timing of the experiment, both with respect to the presentation phase and the recall phase. EPAM-IV was able to account for the development of DD's expertise in detail, both quantitatively and qualitatively.

Non-Hierarchical Chunking

While still using the idea of chunking in chess, Saariluoma and Laine (2001) used a flat, modular representation of LTM rather than the kind of hierarchical structure characterizing EPAM's discrimination net. They described simulations with two learning algorithms: one based on neighborhood information, and one using frequency of co-occurrences. The simulations were aimed at replicating the behavior of two novices trained to memorize chess positions for six months, from 15 to 30 minutes a day (a total of 45–90 hours), and accounted for the two main results. First, for both participants, learning was well described by a power law: Improvement is rapid at the beginning, but then slows and the rate of learning decreases. Second, participants improved not only with the recall of game positions, but also with the recall of random positions. Note that these data are also simulated successfully by CHREST (Gobet, 2001a).

Production Systems

In the formalism of production systems, all knowledge is expressed as productions (condition-action rules). For example, a production rule in experimental psychology could be stated as follows: "If the design has two independent variables, then assign a value to both." Since this formalism is very flexible for encoding knowledge, it has often been used to model early stages of expertise acquisition and, somewhat less often, later stages.

In physics, the model developed by Bhaskar and Simon (1977) addresses the semantically complex domain of thermodynamics as taught in engineering classes. Another model (Larkin & Simon, 1981), ABLE, accounts for the change in search strategy observed during the transition from novice to expert, where forwards, data-driven search replaces backwards, goal-directed search. ABLE also accounts for how declarative statements can be used to derive new results and how these can be used later to solve new problems. In economics, Tabachnek-Schijf, Leonardo and Simon (1997) were interested in the way experts can use different types of visual and verbal internal representations, and how they could coordinate internal representations with external representations, such as diagrams. Their model used a hybrid architecture combining parallel mechanisms for low-level vision with a production system and a semantic network. Langley, Simon, Bradshaw, and Zytkow (1987) use production systems to replicate several important scientific discoveries, such as Kepler's Third Law of Planetary Motion. Finally, Kulkarni and Simon (1988) wrote a production system replicating the key steps in Krebs's discovery of the urea cycle in 1932. The program's heuristics allowed it not only to draw theoretical inferences and evaluate the acceptability of its knowledge base, but also to propose new experimental tests of its theories.

Two cognitive architectures might be mentioned here, although they have typically been used to simulate early acquisition of skill rather than high levels of expertise. In Soar (Newell, 1990), all knowledge is stored as productions. Soar was able to reach high levels of performance in designing computer chips and flying fighter jets, although its behavior was not directly compared to that of humans. ACT-R (Anderson et al., 2004) is a hybrid system where procedural knowledge is coded as productions, and declarative knowledge as chunks, which are snippets of knowledge. (Note that here "chunk" has a different meaning than in chunking theory and template theory; see Gobet et al., 2016.) Skill acquisition in various domains has been simulated in ACT-R, including driving, geometry, and algebra.

Connectionist Models

Several authors (e.g., Dreyfus & Dreyfus, 1988) have argued that connectionist models offer a better alternative than symbolic models (such as chunking networks and production systems) to account for experts' behavior, in particular the intuitive way in which they solve problems. However, the impact of connectionism on our understanding of expertise has been rather limited since these optimistic claims. Two models (Hyötyniemi & Saariluoma, 1998; Lories, 1992) tried to simulate the recall of chess positions, without much success. These models tend to do well with the recall of pieces on their starting squares and more poorly with pawns and pieces on central squares, while the opposite occurs with chess masters. The program developed by Mireles and Charness (2002) explored how knowledge might protect against the negative effects of aging, but did not directly compare the output of the simulations with human data. Chassy (2013) trained a three-layer feed-forward neural network to classify chess positions into six different openings. The model closely replicated the performance of novice and expert human players.

Beyond chess, Raufaste, Eyrolle and Mariné (1998) were interested in radiological diagnosis and investigated experts' generation of relevant hypotheses with a connectionist model. Glöckner et al. (2012) used a neural net model to simulate how eye-movement measures can predict the kind of action selected by handball players. In general, it seems fair to conclude that connectionism fairs better with simulations of perception and memory than problem solving and decision making. In this respect, it is likely that new developments in deep learning algorithms (Silver *et al.*, 2016), exemplified by AlphaGo's victory over one of the top Go grandmasters in March 2016, will lead to new models of expert behavior.

The CHREST Model

Template Theory

Just as chunking theory is the informal version of EPAM/MAPP, template theory is the informal version of CHREST (Chunk Hierarchy and REtrieval STructures). Gobet and Simon (1996b) developed template theory to expand chunking theory in various ways, in particular to remove two weaknesses of the earlier theory: an overestimation of the time taken by experts to encode information in LTM (Charness, 1976), and a neglect of the kind of high-level knowledge structures, such as schemata, that experts seem to use in many domains of expertise (e.g. Gobet, 2015). A central idea in template theory is that frequently used chunks evolve into more complex structures known as templates. Templates are schema-like structures with both a non-changeable core (similar to the chunks of chunking theory) and slots where information can be stored swiftly (about 250 milliseconds). Slots are formed with information that often recurs in an expert's experience but with a number of small variations. For example, in chess, a slot may be created for a Rook that is placed on different squares in similar board positions. Templates thus explain how experts can encode classes of situations efficiently. Whereas the quickest encoding time was 2 seconds with chunking theory—the time to familiarize an LTM node—templates make it possible to encode information in a quarter of a second, and thus help explain experimental results such as Charness's (1976) that were recalcitrant to chunking theory. Another important contribution of template theory was to propose mechanisms more precise than chunking theory for eye movements, autonomous learning of chunks, and creation of productions. All these mechanisms are implemented in the CHREST model.

Components and Mechanisms

In its initial implementation (Gobet, 1993), CHREST was a combination of two models we have discussed: PERCEIVER and MAPP. Key additions were mechanisms for the creation and use of templates, mechanisms for directing eye movements using LTM knowledge and more realistic ways of acquiring chunks. Rather than being selected by the programmer, as was the case with MAPP, chunks are autonomously acquired by having the program scan databases of master games using simulated eye movements. In addition, time parameters are systematically used, not only for learning mechanisms such as chunk creation, but for every single cognitive process (e.g., time to encode a chunk into STM, time to match two patterns). The presence of these time parameters enables very precise simulations; for example, about the average time taken by eye fixations. In general, CHREST can be seen as the complement of EPAM-IV for domains in which there is no deliberate intention to improve one's memory. Thus, CHREST is a model of *implicit learning*. See Figure 20.2.

Mechanisms for automatically creating productions (Gobet & Jansen, 1994) were later additions. Thus, CHREST has mechanisms for augmenting both semantic and procedural memory. Moves are selected by pure pattern recognition: Given a constellation of pieces on a chess board, a move (or a sequence of moves) is proposed. A complication is that several chunks can be recognized in a position and that some of the chunks might suggest several moves. In these cases, a simple conflict resolution scheme is applied, combining

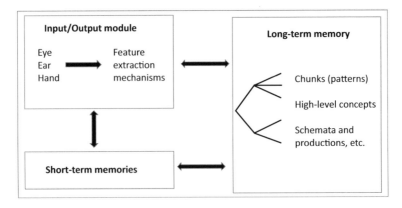

FIGURE 20.2 Key components of the CHREST architecture.

information about frequency and chunk size. The program's ability was reasonable in strategic positions but weak in tactical positions, where the program lacked search mechanisms for exploring the implications of moves suggested by pattern recognition.

Simulations of Chess Expertise

CHREST has reproduced a considerable number of phenomena in chess expertise. Many data from De Groot's memory task and its variants have been simulated with success. Perceptually, CHREST accounts for weak and strong players' eye movements when looking at a position for five seconds (De Groot, Gobet, & Jongman, 1996). With respect to memory, it accounts for the role of presentation time, the modification of positions by mirror image, the type of errors made (both by commission and omission), and the kind of piece configurations replaced, including the pattern of relationships that statistically distinguish pairs of pieces within a chunk and between chunks (Gobet, 1993, 2001b; Gobet & Simon, 2000). In many cases, the simulations closely match the human data, from novice to grandmaster.

An important contribution of CHREST was the prediction that experts' superiority over novices during the recall task should be present not only with game positions, but also with random positions (Gobet & Simon, 1996a). This prediction was counterintuitive, as reflected at the time by textbooks of psychology and cognitive science. It was proven correct with presentation times ranging from 1 to 60 seconds (Gobet & Simon, 2000) and with different randomization types (Gobet & Waters, 2003). A recent meta-analysis has shown that the prediction is correct over a wide range of domains of expertise (Sala & Gobet, 2017).

CHREST also simulated the results of a training experiment where novices learned to memorize chess positions (Gobet & Jackson, 2002), and the effects of aging on memory (Smith, Lane, & Gobet, 2008). It can categorize positions as a function of the opening they are likely to come from (Lane & Gobet, 2012a). CHREST has also been used to account for the phenomenon of intuition—in chess and other domains—showing how apparently holistic behavior can be accounted for by incremental, local mechanisms (Gobet & Chassy, 2009).

Simulations of Expert Behavior Beyond Chess

Although CHREST was originally developed for chess expertise, it is not specifically tailored for this domain and has been applied to several others. In a rare application of computer modeling to cross-cultural psychology, CHREST has accounted for data on memory and problem solving in the African game of Awalé (Gobet, 2009). It has also been used for move prediction in the Asian game of Go (Bossomaier, Traish, Gobet, & Lane, 2012).

Beyond board games, Gobet and Oliver (2016) demonstrated that CHREST could reproduce the skill effect found with humans memorizing random computer programs. In physics, it has simulated the acquisition of multiple representations by novices when learning about electricity (Lane, Cheng, & Gobet, 2001). It has also simulated some of the verbal learning data accounted for by EPAM and simulated experiments on implicit learning and concept formation (e.g., Lane & Gobet, 2012a).

Finally, variants of CHREST have been used to simulate children's vocabulary development (Jones, Gobet, & Pine, 2007) and grammatical development (Freudenthal, Pine, Aguado-Orea, & Gobet, 2007). The direct conclusion—unpalatable for mainstream, Chomskyan linguistics—is that language acquisition does not rely on innate universal grammar, but is a type of expertise acquisition.

Conclusions

Research on expertise has been hampered by the presence of many theories that lack precision and specification. This has often led to unproductive debates, with considerable disagreement due to the fact that theories were poorly specified. A recent example of this sorry state of affairs is the 2014 debate about "deliberate practice" (Ericsson, Krampe, & Tesch-Römer, 1993) in a special issue of *Intelligence*. The aim of this chapter has been to argue that it is possible to develop precise and well-specified theories of expert behavior, using as a medium the rigorous methodology of computational modeling.

An interesting issue concerns the very small number of modelers active in expertise research, despite the clear advantages of this methodology. Part of the answer is that modeling is time-consuming and requires specific skills, which are typically not mastered by psychologists. Related to this point, developing models of expertise is harder than developing models of simpler phenomena, such as experiments in short-term memory research, due to the complexity of the phenomena under study. Answering the question of the limited popularity of modeling also requires one to reflect on the empirical slant of much expertise research, which often holds the naïve expectation that more empirical data will lead to better understanding without needing to develop detailed theories.

We believe that the future is bright for computational models of expertise. Partly due to the unprecedented computational resources currently available, ambitious and adventurous research is now possible, and we mention some of the possible lines of research. The role of emotions can be studied in computational models, a topic otherwise neglected in our field. Agent modeling, where several instances of a model interact, could be used to study social aspects of expertise and explore the effect of complex and dynamic environments. Finally, more complex models could be developed, simulating both neuroscientific and psychological data. Indeed, we expect more modeling at the intersection of several disciplines (e.g., between psychology, education, and sociology). These interdisciplinary models may lead to applications on instructional methods and decision-making support systems.

Note

1 Other meanings include the use of mnemonics for recoding the information in STM; see Gobet, Lloyd-Kelly, and Lane (2016) for a discussion.

References

Alain, C., & Sarrazin, C. (1990). Study of decision-making in squash competition: A computer-simulation approach. *Canadian Journal of Sport Sciences, 15*, 193–200.

Anderson, J. R., Bothell, D., Byrne, M. D., Douglass, S., Lebiere, C., & Qin, Y. L. (2004). An integrated theory of the mind. *Psychological Review, 111*, 1036–1060.

Baddeley, A. D., & Hitch, G. J. (1974). Working memory. In G. Bower (Ed.), *The psychology of learning and motivation: Advances in research and theory* (pp. 47–90). New York, NY: Academic Press.

Baylor, G. W., & Simon, H. A. (1966). A chess mating combinations program. In *1966 Spring Joint Computer Conference* (Vol. 28, pp. 431–447). Boston.

Bhaskar, R., & Simon, H. A. (1977). Problem solving in semantically rich domains: An example from engineering thermodynamics. *Cognitive Science, 1*, 193–215.

Bossomaier, T., Traish, J., Gobet, F., & Lane, P. C. R. (2012). Neuro-cognitive model of move location in the game of Go., *International Joint Conference on Neural Networks (IJCNN 2012)* (pp. 1–7). New York: IEEE.

Campitelli, G., Gobet, F., & Bilalić, M. (2014). Cognitive processes and development of chess genius: An integrative approach. In D. K. Simonton (Ed.), *The Wiley handbook of genius* (pp. 350–374). Chichester, UK: Wiley-Blackwell.

Charness, N. (1976). Memory for chess positions: Resistance to interference. *Journal of Experimental Psychology: Human Learning and Memory, 2*, 641–653.

Chase, W. G., & Ericsson, K. A. (1982). Skill and working memory. *The Psychology of Learning and Motivation, 16*, 1–58.

Chase, W. G., & Simon, H. A. (1973). The mind's eye in chess. In W. G. Chase (Ed.), *Visual information processing* (pp. 215–281). New York: Academic Press.

Chassy, P. (2013). The role of memory templates in experts' strategic thinking. *Psychology Research, 3*, 276–289.

De Groot, A. D. (1946). *Het denken van den schaker*. Amsterdam: Noord Hollandsche.

De Groot, A. D., Gobet, F., & Jongman, R. W. (1996). *Perception and memory in chess*. Assen: Van Gorcum.

Dreyfus, H. L., & Dreyfus, S. E. (1988). *Mind over machine: The power of human intuition and expertise in the era of the computer* (2nd ed.). New York: Free Press.

Ericsson, K. A., & Kintsch, W. (1995). Long-term working memory. *Psychological Review, 102*, 211–245.

Ericsson, K. A., & Kintsch, W. (2000). Shortcomings of generic retrieval structures with slots of the type that Gobet (1993) proposed and modelled. *British Journal of Psychology, 91*, 571–590.

Ericsson, K. A., Krampe, R. T., & Tesch-Römer, C. (1993). The role of deliberate practice in the acquisition of expert performance. *Psychological Review, 100*, 363–406.

Freudenthal, D., Pine, J. M., Aguado-Orea, J., & Gobet, F. (2007). Modeling the developmental patterning of finiteness marking in English, Dutch, German and Spanish using MOSAIC. *Cognitive Science, 31*, 311–341.

Glöckner, A., Heinen, T., Johnson, J. G., & Raab, M. (2012). Network approaches for expert decisions in sports. *Human Movement Science, 31*, 318–333.

Gobet, F. (1993). *Les mémoires d'un joueur d'échecs [Chess players' memories].* Fribourg: Editions universitaires.

Gobet, F. (1997). A pattern-recognition theory of search in expert problem solving. *Thinking and Reasoning, 3*, 291–313.

Gobet, F. (2000a). Long-term working memory: A computational implementation for chess expertise. In N. Taatgen & J. Aasman (Eds.), *Proceedings of the Third International Conference on Cognitive Modeling* (pp. 150–157). Veenendaal, The Netherlands: Universal Press.

Gobet, F. (2000b). Retrieval structures and schemata: A brief reply to Ericsson and Kintsch. *British Journal of Psychology, 91*, 591–594.

Gobet, F. (2001a). Chunk hierarchies and retrieval structures. Comments on Saariluoma and Laine. *Scandinavian Journal of Psychology, 42*, 149–155.

Gobet, F. (2001b). Is experts' knowledge modular? In *Proceedings of the 23rd Meeting of the Cognitive Science Society* (pp. 336–431). Mahwah, NJ: Erlbaum.

Gobet, F. (2009). Using a cognitive architecture for addressing the question of cognitive universals in cross-cultural psychology: The example of Awalé. *Journal of Cross-Cultural Psychology, 40*, 627–648.

Gobet, F. (2015). *Understanding expertise: A multidisciplinary approach.* London: Palgrave.

Gobet, F., & Chassy, P. (2009). Expertise and intuition: A tale of three theories. *Minds & Machines, 19*, 151–180.

Gobet, F., Chassy, P., & Bilalić, M. (2011). *Foundations of cognitive psychology.* London: McGraw Hill.

Gobet, F., & Jackson, S. (2002). In search of templates. *Cognitive Systems Research, 3*, 35–44.

Gobet, F., & Jansen, P. J. (1994). Towards a chess program based on a model of human memory. In H. J. van den Herik, I. S. Herschberg & J. W. H. M. Uiterwijk (Eds.), *Advances in Computer Chess* 7 (pp. 35–60). Maastricht: University of Limburg Press.

Gobet, F., & Lane, P. C. R. (2012). Chunking mechanisms and learning. In N. M. Seel (Ed.), *Encyclopedia of the sciences of learning* (pp. 541–544). New York: Springer.

Gobet, F., Lloyd-Kelly, M., & Lane, P. C. R. (2016). What's in a name? The multiple meanings of "chunk" and "chunking." *Frontiers in Psychology, 7*, 102. http://doi.org/10.3389/fpsyg.2016.00102

Gobet, F., & Oliver, I. (2016). Memory for the random: A simulation of computer program recall. In *Proceedings of the 38th Annual Meeting of the Cognitive Science Society.* Philadelphia: Cognitive Science Society.

Gobet, F., Richman, H. B., Staszewski, J. J., & Simon, H. A. (1997). Goals, representations, and strategies in a concept attainment task: The EPAM model. *The Psychology of Learning and Motivation, 37*, 265–290.

Gobet, F., & Simon, H. A. (1996a). Recall of random and distorted positions. Implications for the theory of expertise. *Memory & Cognition, 24*, 493–503.

Gobet, F., & Simon, H. A. (1996b). Templates in chess memory: A mechanism for recalling several boards. *Cognitive Psychology, 31*, 1–40.

Gobet, F., & Simon, H. A. (2000). Five seconds or sixty? Presentation time in expert memory. *Cognitive Science, 24*, 651–682.

Gobet, F., & Waters, A. J. (2003). The role of constraints in expert memory. *Journal of Experimental Psychology: Learning, Memory & Cognition, 29*, 1082–1094.

Hyötyniemi, H., & Saariluoma, P. (1998). Simulating chess players' recall: How many chunks and what kind can they be? In F. Ritter & R. Young (Eds.), *Second European Conference on Cognitive Modelling* (pp. 195–196). Nottingham: Nottingham University Press.

Jones, G., Gobet, F., & Pine, J. M. (2007). Linking working memory and long-term memory: A computational model of the learning of new words. *Developmental Science, 10*, 853–873.

Kulkarni, D., & Simon, H. A. (1988). The processes of scientific discovery: The strategy of experimentation. *Cognitive Science, 12*, 139–176.

Lane, P. C. R., Cheng, P. C. H., & Gobet, F. (2001). Learning perceptual chunks for problem decomposition. In *Proceedings of the 23rd Meeting of the Cognitive Science Society* (pp. 528–533). Mahwah, NJ: Erlbaum.

Lane, P. C. R., & Gobet, F. (2003). Developing reproducible and comprehensible computational models. *Artificial Intelligence, 144*, 251–263.

Lane, P. C. R., & Gobet, F. (2012a). CHREST models of implicit learning and board game interpretation. *Lecture Notes in Computer Science (including subseries Lecture Notes in Artificial Intelligence and Lecture Notes in Bioinformatics), 7716 LNAI*, 148–157.

Lane, P. C. R., & Gobet, F. (2012b). A theory-driven testing methodology for developing scientific software. *Journal of Experimental and Theoretical Artificial Intelligence, 24*, 421–456.

Langley, P., Simon, H. A., Bradshaw, G. L., & Zytkow, J. M. (1987). *Scientific discovery*. Cambridge, MA: MIT press.

Larkin, J. H., & Simon, H. A. (1981). Learning through growth of skill in mental modeling. In *Proceedings of the Third Annual Conference of the Cognitive Science Society* (pp. 106–111). Berkeley: Cognitive Science Society.

Lories, G. (1992, July). *Using a neural network to pre-process chess positions*. Paper presented at the XXVth International Congress of Psychology, Brussels.

Mireles, D. E., & Charness, N. (2002). Computational explorations of the influence of structured knowledge on age-related cognitive decline. *Psychology and Aging, 17*, 245–259.

Newell, A. (1990). *Unified theories of cognition*. Cambridge, MA: Harvard University Press.

Newell, A., Shaw, J. C., & Simon, H. A. (1958). Elements of a theory of human problem solving. *Psychological Review, 65*, 151–166.

Newell, A., Shaw, J. C., & Simon, H. A. (1963). Chess-playing programs and the problem of complexity. In E. A. Feigenbaum & J. Feldman (Eds.), *Computers and thought* (pp. 39–70). New York: McGraw-Hill.

Raufaste, E., Eyrolle, H., & Mariné, C. (1998). Pertinence generation in radiological diagnosis: Spreading activation and the nature of expertise. *Cognitive Science, 22*, 517–546.

Richman, H. B., Staszewski, J. J., & Simon, H. A. (1995). Simulation of expert memory with EPAM IV. *Psychological Review, 102*, 305–330.

Ritter, F. E., Shadbolt, N. R., Elliman, D., Young, R. M., Gobet, F., & Baxter, G. D. (2003). *Techniques for modeling human performance in synthetic environments: A supplementary review*. Wright-Patterson Air Force Base, OH: Human Systems Information Analysis Center.

Saariluoma, P., & Laine, T. (2001). Novice construction of chess memory. *Scandinavian Journal of Psychology, 42*, 137–146.

Sala, G., & Gobet, F. (2017). Experts' memory superiority for domain-specific random material generalizes across fields of expertise: A meta-analysis. *Memory & Cognition, 45*, 183–193.

Silver, D., Huang, A., Maddison, C. J., Guez, A., Sifre, L., van den Driessche, G., *et al.* (2016). Mastering the game of Go with deep neural networks and tree search. *Nature, 529*, 484–489.

Simon, D. P., & Simon, H. A. (1973). Alternative uses of phonemic information in spelling. *Review of Educational Research, 43*, 115–137.

Simon, H. A. (1956). Rational choice and the structure of the environment. *Psychological Review, 63*, 129–138.

Simon, H. A. (1967). The use of information processing languages in psychology. In P. Fraisse (Ed.), *Les modèles de la formalisation du comportement* (pp. 303–326). Paris: CNRS-Editions.

Simon, H. A., & Barenfeld, M. (1969). Information processing analysis of perceptual processes in problem solving. *Psychological Review, 7*, 473–483.

Simon, H. A., & Feigenbaum, E. A. (1964). An information processing theory of some effects of similarity, familiarity, and meaningfulness in verbal learning. *Journal of Verbal Learning and Verbal Behavior, 3*, 385–396.

Simon, H. A., & Gilmartin, K. J. (1973). A simulation of memory for chess positions. *Cognitive Psychology, 5*, 29–46.

Simon, H. A., & Gobet, F. (2000). Expertise effects in memory recall: Comments on Vicente and Wang (1998). *Psychological Review, 107*, 593–600.

Smith, L., Lane, P. C. R., & Gobet, F. (2008). Modeling the relationship between visual short-term memory capacity and recall ability. *European Modelling Symposium 2008 (EMS2008)*. Liverpool: Institute of Electrical and Electronics Engineers.

Tabachnek-Schijf, H. J. M., Leonardo, A. M., & Simon, H. A. (1997). CaMeRa: A computational model of multiple representations. *Cognitive Science, 21*, 305–350.

Tikhomirov, O. K., & Poznyanskaya, E. D. (1966). An investigation of visual search as a means of analyzing heuristics. *Soviet Psychology, 5*, 2–15.

Yates, F. A. (1966). *The art of memory.* Chicago: University of Chicago Press.

21

THE MULTIFACTORIAL GENE-ENVIRONMENT INTERACTION MODEL (MGIM) OF EXPERT PERFORMANCE

Fredrik Ullén, Miriam A. Mosing, and David Z. Hambrick

Introduction

A dominating paradigm in expertise research during the last decades has been the deliberate practice theory, developed in particular by K. Anders Ericsson and colleagues (Ericsson, Krampe, & Tesch-Römer, 1993; Ericsson & Pool, 2016; Ericsson & Smith, 1991; Ericsson & Ward, 2007; Feltovich, Prietula, & Ericsson, 2006). Essentially, this is a single-factor theory of expert performance: With a few exceptions, such as effects of disease or injury, or of physical variables such as body size and height in certain sports, expert performance in a domain is assumed to reflect one factor—the amount of deliberate practice an individual has accumulated (Ericsson, 2007; Ericsson *et al.*, 1993; Ericsson & Pool, 2016). Deliberate practice is here defined as explicit, effortful, goal-directed activities that are specifically designed to improve performance. Other variables (e.g., cognitive abilities or genetic constitution) may matter for performance differences among beginners, but with sufficient deliberate practice, the effects of such factors are assumed to be bypassed (Ericsson, 2007; Ericsson *et al.*, 1993).

Recent years have witnessed dramatic empirical and theoretical progress in expertise research. An important reason for this development is methodological. Research in the deliberate practice theory tradition has naturally tended to focus on correlations between long-term deliberate practice and performance. Such an approach obviously has limited possibilities to reveal the full range of factors that influence expertise and its neural underpinnings. Today, expertise and its biological basis are being studied with a broad range of techniques and designs that include neuroimaging studies of the neural mechanisms of expertise, behavioral studies that incorporate measures of both practice and other relevant trait variables, and, not least, large-scale studies of expert performance in genetically informative samples (for comprehensive reviews see Hambrick, Macnamara, Campitelli, Ullén, & Mosing, 2016; Ullén, Hambrick, & Mosing, 2016). The results of these studies have provided fascinating new insights into the nature of expertise, but also serious challenges for deliberate practice theory.

First, several recent meta-analyses have provided quantitative estimates of the proportion of variance in expert performance that is, in reality, explained by deliberate practice (Hambrick *et al.*, 2014; Macnamara, Hambrick, & Oswald, 2014; Platz, Kopiez, Lehmann, & Wolf, 2014). The obtained estimates were surprisingly low, ranging from less than 1 percent for professional expertise in Macnamara *et al.* (2014), to 36 percent for music in Platz *et al.* (2014). Contrary to predictions from deliberate practice theory, most of the variance in expert performance was found to be unrelated to deliberate practice. The clear implication of this evidence is that deliberate practice is only one piece of the expertise puzzle.

Second, evidence is accumulating that this practice-independent variance may instead be related to individual differences in both global (e.g., intelligence) and specific traits of relevance for the particular domain of expertise. In music, for example, sight-reading ability is related to working memory capacity (Meinz & Hambrick, 2010), while musical auditory discrimination correlates genetically with intelligence (Mosing, Pedersen, Madison, & Ullén, 2014).

Third, twin studies have confirmed substantial genetic effects on both long-term practice (Hambrick & Tucker-Drob, 2014; Mosing, Madison, Pedersen, Kuja-Halkola, & Ullén, 2014), sensory and motor aspects of musical expertise (Drayna, Manichaikul, de Lange, Snieder, & Spector, 2001; Mosing, Madison, *et al.*, 2014; Mosing, Pedersen, *et al.*, 2014; Mosing, Verweij, Madison, & Ullén, 2016), and self-rated expertise in various domains (Vinkhuyzen, van der Sluis, Posthuma, & Boomsma, 2009). Furthermore, Mosing and coworkers found associations between music practice and musical aptitude to be driven mainly by genetic pleiotropy, rather than causal effects of music practice (Mosing, Madison, *et al.*, 2014).

It is thus evident that deliberate practice theory is unable to account for a number of recent empirical findings. To summarize, deliberate practice explains only a modest proportion of the variance in expert performance. One reason for this is that other traits influence expert performance, over and above practice. Furthermore, research indicates that practice itself, as well as its covariation with expertise-related traits, is influenced by genetic factors. Associations between practice and performance may thus reflect genetic pleiotropies as well as causal effects in either direction on the phenotypic level.

Accordingly, expertise research has started to move away from the overly simplistic, single-factor model of deliberate practice theory to multifactorial frameworks that allow for a systematic investigation of all factors that influence expert performance and that can give rise to novel, testable hypotheses. We have recently proposed one such model: The Multifactorial Gene-Environment Interaction model (the MGIM).

Main Features of the MGIM

Key features of the MGIM are schematically illustrated in Figure 21.1. Variables in italics are examples of factors that have been shown empirically to be involved in various forms of expertise.

In line with ample empirical evidence, the MGIM assumes that deliberate practice is an important predictor of expert performance (Macnamara *et al.*, 2014), and that a main reason for this association, although not the only one (Mosing, Madison, *et al.*, 2014), is causal effects of deliberate practice on expert performance. Long-term deliberate practice may lead to extensive anatomical and functional reorganizations of brain circuits that control performance (Ullén *et al.*, 2016). These plastic processes involve different brain systems and can include more efficient interactions between long-term memory and working memory (LTM-WM) and improved domain-specific sensorimotor skills (Figure 21.1).

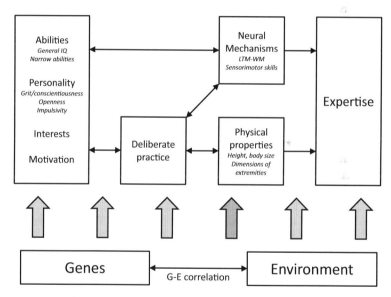

FIGURE 21.1 Main elements of the Multifactorial Gene-Environment Interaction Model (MGIM). Upper part: At the phenotypic level, practice is associated with psychological traits such as abilities, personality, interests, and motivation. Specific examples of variables involved in various forms of expertise are italicized. Practice may influence neural mechanisms and physical body properties relevant for expertise, but such trait differences may also impact expertise independently of practice. Lower part: The variables involved in expertise at the phenotypic level are influenced by genetic and non-genetic factors. These influences are likely to include gene-environment interactions and covariation between genes and environment. Reprinted with permission from Ullén et al (2016).

Generally, the neural reorganizations accompanying expertise acquisition appear to lead to an increased degree of specialization rather than improvements of general capacity; transfer effects to other tasks are typically small or negligible (Ericsson, Chase, & Faloon, 1980; Ericsson & Lehmann, 1996; Singley & Anderson, 1989).

A second feature of the MGIM is that deliberate practice can be influenced by a multitude of variables (abilities, personality, interests, motivation) that impact which domain an individual elects to invest time in, as well as the quantity and quality of practice itself. Empirically supported examples of such influences are shown in Figure 21.1. Amount of deliberate practice in different domains has been shown to be related to personality traits, with *openness* predicting music practice (Butković, Ullén, & Mosing, 2015; Corrigall, Schellenberg, & Misura, 2013), and *grit*—a personality construct which is strongly related to conscientiousness—predicting practice in a spelling competition (Duckworth, Kirby, Tsukayama, Berstein, & Ericsson, 2010). For music, other personality dimensions such as *impulsivity* have been shown to influence practice quality (Miksza, 2006, 2011). These aspects of the MGIM are similar to other models of how achievement in different domains is related to specific clusters of traits in various individual difference modalities (see Ackerman, 1996; Ackerman, Chamorro-Premuzic, & Furnham, 2011; Kell, Lubinski, & Benbow, 2013).

A third feature of the MGIM is that it assumes that expert performance can be influenced by numerous variables other than deliberate practice. As discussed above, recent data suggest that it is essential to consider a wide range of trait variables in relation to expertise, over and above effects of practice. These could involve psychological variables, as well as physical traits (Figure 21.1, upper part), with considerable variation in the effects of specific variables across domains. For example, intelligence and related constructs such as working memory are important in domains such as music (Meinz & Hambrick, 2010; Mosing, Pedersen, *et al.*, 2014) and chess (Grabner, 2014). Physical traits matter primarily for forms of expertise that involve skilled sensorimotor control, such as sports, music, and dance.

Finally, the MGIM takes into account genetic influences on practice, expert performance, and related traits (Figure 21.1, lower part). This includes practice-independent genetic effects on traits that are relevant for expert performance, such as intelligence and physical body properties. Genetic influences are likely to be important also for more narrow abilities of relevance for expert performance. For music, one example is musical auditory discrimination ability, which shows genetic overlaps with intelligence and motor accuracy, as well as more specific genetic influences (Mosing, Pedersen, *et al.*, 2014; Mosing *et al.*, 2016). Other genetic factors affect expertise indirectly by influencing deliberate practice and its covariates. This highlights the potential importance of both gene-environment interactions (Kennedy *et al.*, 2011; Schellenberg, 2015) and various forms of gene-environment covariation (Scarr, 1996) for expertise.

The MGIM and Future Empirical Work on Expertise

When judging the relative merits of competing models, it is important to consider how well they can explain existing data as well as the extent to which they give rise to novel, testable predictions (Lakatos, 1978). To summarize the previous discussion, the single-factor framework of deliberate practice theory is directly contradicted by three recent sets of empirical findings: (1) Meta-analyses demonstrate weak to modest overall effects of practice on expert performance; (2) For some domains, specific traits have been shown to influence expert performance even when controlling for practice; (3) Both practice and its covariation with expert performance are subject to substantial genetic influences.

In contrast, these findings are readily explained by the MGIM, which assumes as a basic tenet of the model that the acquisition of expertise depends on a multitude of phenotypic variables, each of which is influenced by both genetics and environment. Notably, it has sometimes been argued that for deliberate practice theory to be falsified it would have to be demonstrated that variables other than deliberate practice limit the ultimate level of expertise that an individual hypothetically could achieve (Ericsson, Roring, & Nandagopal, 2007). However, in our view, this line of argument must be rejected for two reasons. First, proving that something never could take place under any circumstances is typically impossible in principle, since it would require the investigation of a practically infinite number of counterfactual scenarios. If this suggestion is taken seriously, it would therefore be doubtful whether deliberate practice theory qualifies as an empirically testable scientific theory (Ullén et al., 2016). Second, the argument involves an unreasonable shift of the burden of proof. Lack of evidence that something is impossible is not evidence that it is possible. In this case, it is clearly the radical, positive claim that practice alone limits expert performance that would require empirical support—for example, by the demonstration that randomly selected novices can be trained to reach the highest levels of competence in fields such as chess, mathematics, and music, regardless of their intelligence, personality, and other relevant traits. Unsurprisingly, such empirical evidence is wanting.

The MGIM can readily be seen to suggest a number of possible directions for future empirical research, where it and deliberate practice theory give rise to differing predictions. One key question when evaluating the two models is how genetic influences on expert performance are modulated by practice. According to deliberate practice theory, genetic factors may influence performance in beginners, but with prolonged practice the genetic impact on skilled performance will decrease and ultimately approach zero (Ericsson, 2014; Ericsson et al., 1993). Since the MGIM assumes that genetic factors influence both practice itself and various other traits that impact expert performance, independently of practice, a prediction of this theory is rather that genetic factors will remain important for expert performance, even after extensive practice.

Second, the MGIM predicts that both psychological and physical traits may influence expert performance, even when controlling statistically for deliberate practice. For specific cases, this has already been demonstrated empirically. As mentioned before, Meinz and Hambrick found a partial correlation of $r = .37$ between sight-reading ability in musicians and working memory capacity, after controlling for deliberate practice (Meinz & Hambrick, 2010). Other studies have found that intelligence correlates with Elo rating in tournament chess players (Grabner, Stern, & Neubauer, 2007). However, relatively few studies have so far modeled directly how expert performance depends on practice as well as other traits, and further work using experimental designs that allow such analyses will be an important task for future research.

In general, one would predict that cognitive abilities will remain important even at high levels of practice in those domains where expert performance includes tasks that require complex processing of novel information (i.e. have low predictability). One reason for this is that such tasks are difficult or impossible to fully automate, and therefore tax attention and working memory even in experienced experts. This prediction is in line with the work of Ackerman and colleagues which demonstrates that correlations between performance and intelligence remain—or even increase—during several hours of training of complex, low-predictability tasks (Ackerman, 2014; Ackerman & Cianciolo, 2000). Still, further investigations of the role of cognitive abilities and executive functions for expert performance in samples of experts with extensive training would be important.

Personality may also influence expert performance. Personality correlates with interests (Ackerman & Heggestad, 1997; Harris, Vernon, Johnson, & Jang, 2006; Holland, 1997; McKay & Tokar, 2012) and is therefore likely to influence vocational choices and which domains of expertise an individual chooses to engage in. Several studies have also found associations between personality and amount of practice (Butković *et al.*, 2015; Corrigall *et al.*, 2013; Duckworth *et al.*, 2010; Grabner *et al.*, 2007). An interesting question for future research is whether personality may also have a direct influence on expert performance, when statistically controlling for deliberate practice. Conceivably, extraversion and neuroticism could influence expert performance in domains that involve public performance, and personality traits related to emotional competence could play a role for expertise in domains that require interpersonal interaction and an empathetic understanding of others.

Physical traits can influence expert performance, most obviously so in domains that involve physical activity, such as sports, dance, and music. One reason for this is that physical performance is influenced by anthropometric variables that influence the biomechanical properties of the body, such as body size, height, and the proportions and morphology of the extremities (Anderson, 1996; Debanne & Laffaye, 2011; Epstein, 2013). In music, the importance of physical traits is likely to vary between musician groups, with, for example, properties of the voice apparatus being critical for singers, and hand size and morphology influencing the probability of acquiring a high level of technical skill in pianists and other instrumentalist groups (Wagner, 1987, 1988).

The above considerations highlight an important aspect of the MGIM—that it is a generic meta-model or framework for expertise studies, rather than a specific model of expert performance in a particular domain. While some predictions of the MGIM are indeed general and domain-independent—for example, that phenotypic variables impact expert performance over and above practice, and that genetic factors influence individual differences in expert performance even after extensive deliberate practice—the specific relations between various traits and expert performance are bound to differ between domains of expertise. Importantly, this also implies that any individual will have a higher probability of acquiring a high level of expertise in some domains than in others, depending on how well the traits of the individual match the demands of the domain. Conversely, experts in different domains would be predicted to have different typical clusters of traits, similarly to what has been shown for academic achievement in different fields (Ackerman, Bowen, Beier, & Kanfer, 2001; Ackerman & Heggestad, 1997).

Finally, an important property of the MGIM is that it allows both additive and multiplicative effects of the various variables that influence expertise. In general, a prediction from the MGIM is that the acquisition of expert performance may depend on interaction effects between time spent on practice and other moderating variables that influence the efficacy of the practice. These moderator variables are likely to include specific psychological and physical traits that affect the rate of skill learning in a particular domain. However, there is also reason to believe that there are more domain-general interactions effects between practice, intelligence, and personality. As discussed above, intelligence would be predicted to impact expert performance independently of practice, in domains with high demands on processing of novel information. However, deliberate practice is itself a cognitively demanding, goal-oriented process characterized by a conscious search for strategies to improve performance (Ericsson, 2007). This type of practice evidently requires sustained attention and metacognition, both of which are associated with intelligence (Schweizer & Moosbrugger, 2004; Schweizer, Moosbrugger, & Goldhammer, 2005; Stankov, 2000). Accordingly, it appears reasonable to predict that general intelligence may influence expertise also through its correlation with the efficacy of long-term practice itself; that is, there are intelligence × practice interaction effects on expert performance.

Similarly, one would predict that personality traits related to impulse control and motivation influence the capacity to engage in efficient practice for longer time periods. Here, more research using designs that include measures of both personality and actual practicing behaviors would be of interest; however, in line with the hypothesis, Miksza (2006, 2011) found impulsivity in musicians to be related to less well-organized practice with correlations in the range $r = -.2$ to $-.4$ between impulsivity and behavioral measures.

The potential importance of non-linear interactions between predictors of expertise is perhaps seen most clearly when one considers exceptional achievement and the phenomenon of prodigies, who rapidly reach stunning levels of performance. Biographical studies of exceptional achievers provide ample evidence that eminent individuals in many cases perform at an exceptional level at an early age, as compared to other experts in the same field (see Cox, 1926). Such findings appear virtually impossible to explain if one assumes that practice is the only predictor of expertise and, indeed, detailed case studies support that top-level achievers may even outperform other individuals with considerably more practice. One example is the current number one chess player, the Norwegian Magnus Carlsen, who has had the highest chess rating in history, as well as world-record Elo ratings also for rapid chess and Blitz chess (see https://ratings.fide.com/). Strikingly, a recent analysis of practicing data demonstrated that Carlsen had *fewer* accumulated years of practice than the average of the ten following best players in the world (Gobet & Ereku, 2014).

Conclusion

Expertise research has traditionally been characterized by a strong focus on practice and its associations with performance. This approach has been fruitful, and resulted in important new insights into how long-term, deliberate practice can lead to optimization of performance and dramatic improvements of the trained skills. However, expertise research is currently in a dynamic phase where it is becoming increasingly clear that the acquisition of expert performance is a complex process that depends on multiple factors besides practice. The MGIM represents an attempt to synthesize recent findings into a domain-general model for expert performance that takes into account both the multifactorial influences on expertise at the phenotypic level and the influence of genetic factors. We hope that this generic framework will serve as a useful basis for the formulation of more specific models of expertise in particular domains, which in turn can guide further empirical work on both domain-specific and domain-general mechanisms of expert performance. At the phenotypic level, important areas for further research include practice-independent effects of trait variables and specific environmental influences, as well as interactions between practice and other variables. Studies on expertise in genetically informative samples have only started to be performed in recent years, and many interesting questions remain to be explored. Key questions here include the role of specific genes for different forms of expert performance, as well as how the acquisition of expertise is influenced by gene-environment interactions and gene-environment covariation.

It already appears clear that the adoption of multivariate frameworks such as the MGIM, as well as interdisciplinary empirical approaches that combine methods from differential and experimental psychology, behavior genetics, and neuroimaging have been important reasons for the exciting current developments in expertise research. We are convinced that continued work along these lines will lead to important new insights into how competence in a particular domain is acquired through complex interactions between genes, environment, practice, and traits of the individual.

Acknowledgements

This work was supported by the Bank of Sweden Tercentenary Foundation (M11-0451:1) and the Sven and Dagmar Salén Foundation.

References

Ackerman, P. L. (1996). A theory of adult intellectual development: Process, personality, interests, and knowledge. *Intelligence, 22*(2), 227–257.

Ackerman, P. L. (2014). Nonsense, common sense, and science of expert performance: Talent and individual differences. *Intelligence, 45*, 6–17.

Ackerman, P. L., Bowen, K. R., Beier, M. B., & Kanfer, R. (2001). Determinants of individual differences and gender differences in knowledge. *Journal of Educational Psychology, 93*, 797–825.

Ackerman, P. L., Chamorro-Premuzic, T., & Furnham, A. (2011). Trait complexes and academic achievement: Old and new ways of examining personality in educational contexts. *British Journal of Educational Psychology, 81*(1), 27–40.

Ackerman, P. L., & Cianciolo, A. T. (2000). Cognitive, perceptual-speed and psychomotor determinants of individual differences during skill acquisition. *Journal of Experimental Psychology: Applied, 6*, 259–290.

Ackerman, P. L., & Heggestad, E. D. (1997). Intelligence, personality, and interests: Evidence for overlapping traits. *Psychological Bulletin, 121*(2), 219–245.

Anderson, T. (1996). Biomechanics and running economy. *Sports Medicine, 22*(2), 76–89.

Butković, A., Ullén, F., & Mosing, M. A. (2015). Personality and related traits as predictors of music practice: Underlying environmental and genetic influences. *Personality and Individual Differences, 74*, 133–138.

Corrigall, K. A., Schellenberg, E. G., & Misura, N. M. (2013). Music training, cognition, and personality. *Frontiers of Psychology, 4*, 222. doi: 10.3389/fpsyg.2013.00222

Cox, C. M. (1926). *Early mental traits of three hundred geniuses.* Stanford, CA: Stanford University Press.

Debanne, T., & Laffaye, G. (2011). Predicting the throwing velocity of the ball in handball with anthropometric variables and isotonic tests. *Journal of Sports Science, 29*(7), 705–713.

Drayna, D., Manichaikul, A., de Lange, M., Snieder, H., & Spector, T. (2001). Genetic correlates of musical pitch recognition in humans. *Science, 291*(5510), 1969–1972. doi:10.1126/science.291.5510.1969

Duckworth, A. L., Kirby, T. A., Tsukayama, E., Berstein, H., & Ericsson, K. A. (2010). Deliberate practice spells success: Why grittier competitors triumph at the National Spelling Bee. *Social Psychology and Personality Science, 2*, 174–181.

Epstein, D. (2013). *The sports gene: Inside the science of extraordinary athletic performance.* New York, NY: Penguin.

Ericsson, K. A. (2007). Deliberate practice and the modifiability of body and mind: Toward a science of the structure and acquisition of expert and elite performance. *International Journal of Sport Psychology, 38*, 4–34.

Ericsson, K. A. (2014). Why expert performance is special and cannot be extrapolated from studies of performance in the general population: A response to criticisms. *Intelligence, 45*, 81–103.

Ericsson, K. A., Chase, W. G., & Faloon, S. (1980). Acquisition of a memory skill. *Science, 208*, 1181–1182.

Ericsson, K. A., Krampe, R. T., & Tesch-Römer, C. (1993). The role of deliberate practice in the acquisition of expert performance. *Psychological Review, 100*(3), 363–406.

Ericsson, K. A., & Lehmann, A. C. (1996). Expert and exceptional performance: Evidence of maximal adaptation to task constraints. *Annual Review of Psychology, 47*, 273–305.

Ericsson, K. A., & Pool, R. (2016). *Peak. Secrets from the new science of expertise.* New York, NY: Houghton Mifflin Harcourt.

Ericsson, K. A., Roring, R. W., & Nandagopal, K. (2007). Misunderstandings, agreements, and disagreements: Toward a cumulative science of reproducibly superior aspects of giftedness. *High Ability Studies, 18*(1), 97–115.

Ericsson, K. A., & Smith, J. (Eds.). (1991). *Toward a general theory of expertise: Prospects and limits.* New York, NY: Cambridge University Press.

Ericsson, K. A., & Ward, P. (2007). Capturing the naturally occurring superior performance of experts in the laboratory: Toward a science of expert and exceptional performance. *Current Directions in Psychological Science, 16*(6), 346–350.

Feltovich, P. J., Prietula, M. J., & Ericsson, K. A. (2006). Studies of expertise from psychological perspectives. In K. A. Ericsson, N. Charness, P. J. Feltovich, & R. R. Hoffman (Eds.), *The Cambridge handbook of expertise and expert performance* (pp. 41–68). New York, NY: Cambridge University Press.

Gobet, F., & Ereku, M. H. (2014). Checkmate to deliberate practice: The case of Magnus Carlsen. *Frontiers in Psychology, 5*, 878. doi: 10.3389/fpsyg.2014.00878.

Grabner, R. H. (2014). The role of intelligence for performance in the prototypical expertise domain of chess. *Intelligence, 45*, 26–33. doi:10.1016/j.intell.2013.07.023

Grabner, R. H., Stern, E., & Neubauer, A. C. (2007). Individual differences in chess expertise: A psychometric investigation. *Acta Psychol, 124*, 398–420.

Hambrick, D. Z., Macnamara, B. N., Campitelli, G., Ullén, F., & Mosing, M. A. (2016). A new look at expertise: Beyond the experts are born vs made debate. *Psychology of Learning and Motivation, 64*, 1–55.

Hambrick, D. Z., Oswald, F. L., Altmann, E. M., Meinz, E. J., Gobet, F., & Campitelli, G. (2014). Deliberate practice: Is that all it takes to become an expert? *Intelligence, 45*(1), 34–45. DOI: 10.1016/j.intell.2013.04.001

Hambrick, D. Z., & Tucker-Drob, E. M. (2014). The genetics of music accomplishment: Evidence for gene-environment correlation and interaction. *Psychonomic Bulletin and Review, 22*(1), 112–120. doi: 10.3758/s13423-014-0671-9.

Harris, J. A., Vernon, P. A., Johnson, A. M., & Jang, K. L. (2006). Phenotypic and genetic relationships between vocational interests and personality. *Personality and Individual Differences, 40*(8), 1531–1541.

Holland, J. L. (1997). *Making vocational choices: A theory of vocational personalities and work environments.* Odessa, FL: Psychological Assessment.

Kell, H. J., Lubinski, D., & Benbow, C. P. (2013). Who rises to the top? Early indicators. *Psychological Science, 24*, 648–658.

Kennedy, Q., Taylor, J. L., Noda, A., Adamson, M., Murphy, G. M., Zeitzer, J. M., & Yesavage, J. A. (2011). The roles of COMT val158met status and aviation expertise in flight simulator performance and cognitive ability. *Behavior Genetics, 41*(5), 700–708.

Lakatos, I. (1978). *The methodology of scientific research programmes. Philosophical Papers Volume 1.* Cambridge, UK: Cambridge University Press.

Macnamara, B. N., Hambrick, D. Z., & Oswald, F. L. (2014). Deliberate practice and performance in music, games, sports, education, and professions: A meta-analysis. *Psych Sci, 25*(8), 1608–1618.

McKay, D. A., & Tokar, D. M. (2012). The HEXACO and five-factor models of personality in relation to RIASEC vocational interests. *Journal of Vocational Behavior, 81*(2), 138–149.

Meinz, E. J., & Hambrick, D. Z. (2010). Deliberate practice is necessary but not sufficient to explain individual differences in piano sight-reading skill: The role of working memory capacity. *Psychological Science, 21*(7), 914–919.

Miksza, P. (2006). Relationships among impulsiveness, locus of control, sex, and music practice. *Journal of Research in Music Education, 54*, 308–323.

Miksza, P. (2011). Relationships among achievement goal motivation, impulsivity, and the music practice of collegiate brass and woodwind players. *Psychology of Music, 39*(1), 50–67.

Mosing, M. A., Madison, G., Pedersen, N. L., Kuja-Halkola, R., & Ullén, F. (2014). Practice does not make perfect: No causal effect of music practice on music ability. *Psychological Science, 25*(9), 1795–1803.

Mosing, M. A., Pedersen, N. L., Madison, G., & Ullén, F. (2014). Genetic pleiotropy explains associations between musical auditory discrimination and intelligence. *PLoS One, 9*(11), e113874.

Mosing, M. A., Verweij, K. J. H., Madison, G., & Ullén, F. (2016). The genetic architecture of correlations between perceptual timing, motor timing, and intelligence. *Intelligence, 57*, 33–40.

Platz, F., Kopiez, R., Lehmann, A. C., & Wolf, A. (2014). The influence of deliberate practice on musical achievement: A meta-analysis. *Frontiers in Psychology, 5*, 646. doi:10.3389/fpsyg.2014.00646

Scarr, S. (1996). How people make their own environments: Implications for parents and policy makers. *Psychology, Public Policy, and Law, 2*, 204–228.

Schellenberg, E. G. (2015). Music training and speech perception: A gene-environment interaction. *Neurosciences and Music V: Cognitive Stimulation and Rehabilitation, 1337*, 170–177.

Schweizer, K., & Moosbrugger, H. (2004). Attention and working memory as predictors of intelligence. *Intelligence, 32*(4), 329–347.

Schweizer, K., Moosbrugger, H., & Goldhammer, F. (2005). The structure of the relationship between attention and intelligence. *Intelligence, 33*, 589–611.

Singley, M., & Anderson, J. R. (1989). *The transfer of cognitive skill.* Cambridge, MA: Harvard University Press.

Stankov, L. (2000). Complexity, metacognition, and fluid intelligence. *Intelligence, 28*(2), 121–143.

Ullén, F., Hambrick, D. Z., & Mosing, M. A. (2016). Rethinking expertise: A multifactorial gene-environment interaction model of expert performance. *Psychological Bulletin, 142*(4), 427–446. doi:10.1037/bul0000033

Wagner, C. (1987). Manual demands in instrumental playing. *Handchirurgie Mikrochirurgie Plastische Chirurgie, 19*(1), 23–32.

Wagner, C. (1988). The pianist's hand – anthropometry and biomechanics. *Ergonomics, 31*(1), 97–131.

Vinkhuyzen, A. A., van der Sluis, S., Posthuma, D., & Boomsma, D. I. (2009). The heritability of aptitude and exceptional talent across different domains in adolescents and young adults. *Behavior Genetics, 39*, 380–392.

22

THE ROLE OF PASSION IN THE DEVELOPMENT OF EXPERTISE

A Conceptual Model

Arielle Bonneville-Roussy and Robert J. Vallerand

> *Nothing is as important as passion.*
> *No matter what you do with your life, be passionate.*
>
> Jon Bon Jovi

Introduction

In many achievement domains, such as sports, music, and the arts, in the professions, and amongst academics, when experts are asked about what carried them to excellence, most talk about their enduring passion for their activity. Indeed, several personalities over the years, such as Jon Bon Jovi, the American rock musician quoted above, have celebrated the role of passion in persistence and high levels of performance. From ancient Greece up to this day, the concept of passion for an activity has fascinated scientists interested in the study of human flourishing (for a brief history of research on passion for an activity, see Vallerand, 2015). For instance, the German philosopher Hegel (1770–1831) claimed that "Nothing great in this world has ever been accomplished without passion." So it is in this chapter, that we, as "fascinated scientists," propose that passion represents a key motivational force that leads individuals to persist, develop, and succeed in their preferred activity, from their initial contact with the activity through full mastery of their skills.

This chapter is divided into four main sections. The first section examines the definitions and current developmental models of expertise. In the second section, we present the Dualistic Model of Passion (DMP; Vallerand, 2015; Vallerand *et al.*, 2003). Then, drawing from past research, the third section proposes a new conceptual model linking passion to the development of expertise.

Finally, the fourth section explores the practical implications of the model and suggests avenues for future research.

The Development of Expertise

A Definition of Expertise

According to the Oxford English Dictionary (OED), an expert is defined as (1) "One who is expert or has gained skill from experience," and (2) "One whose special knowledge or skill causes him to be regarded as an authority; a specialist"(Oxford English Dictionary, 2016). This definition mirrors early psychological research in the area, where expertise entailed the distinctions of experts and non-experts as a function of experience (Simon & Chase, 1973).

More recently, Chi (2006), has proposed a taxonomy to account for the diverse ways in which expertise was categorized in past research. The two main approaches to expertise have been conceptualized as being "absolute" or "relative." The absolute approach attempts to understand exceptional expert skills, those that are attained by only a handful of individuals per generation (and is associated with the second OED definition presented above). Early research divided experts and non-experts with regard to this absolute approach, by looking at the acquisition of exceptional levels of expertise as measured by objective performance criteria (Baker, Côté, & Abernethy, 2003; Ericsson & Charness, 1994; Helsen, Hodges, Van Winckel, & Starkes, 2000; Krampe & Ericsson, 1996). The relative approach posits that experts are the most proficient individuals in a gradient of skills ranging from novice to experts (Chi, 2006). For instance, using a relative approach, skills can be compared between international or national sports teams and regional teams, between doctoral students and under-graduate students, or even between senior and junior staff in a company. Chi outlines specific criteria to define expertise using this relative approach that can be summarized as follows: Experts generate the best answers to a problem, with the best strategy possible, and with the least amount of cognitive (or physical) effort. Adopting the relative perspective allows us to examine, at a macro-level, how individuals develop their skills to become experts. Most importantly, this relative approach assumes that expertise can be generalized to almost any field.

The Development of Expertise

Current models of expertise development—for instance, development of talent in young people (Bloom, 1985), talent in sports (Côté, 1999; Macnamara, Button, & Collins, 2010a, 2010b), expert skills acquisition (Ericsson, Krampe, & Tesch-Römer, 1993), and the novice-to-expert continuum (Dreyfus & Dreyfus, 1980)—have focused on describing the set of cognitive and, to some extent, physical skills needed to reach the highest levels of expertise. One developmental model stands out by the richness of the investigation that led to its conceptualization. Using the absolute approach, Bloom (1985) and his team interviewed 120 exceptional performers in the arts, sciences, and sports, along with their parents and their teachers, in order to understand how talent and skills develop from childhood up until early adulthood.

From this research, Bloom (1985) concluded that the development of expert skills mainly encompasses three stages: the *early*, *middle*, and *final years*. This developmental model stipulates that the stages are distinguishable in three key areas: (1) early successes and interests; (2) social influences; (3) time and effort invested in the activity. This section summarizes the stages described by Bloom (1985); later sections will expand the model further. The first stage of development of expertise, the early years, is characterized by the exploration of various activities, in which fostering interest is the main focus. Time and effort is split between various activities and the amount of formal involvement in a single activity is limited. The middle years of expertise development are marked by an increased commitment to mainly one activity. The transition between the middle and the later years is again marked by an increased amount of time doing the activity. Finally, in the later years stage, individuals make a full-time investment in the activity of interest. The main goal of this phase is to practice and improve the required skills to attain the expert level. Côté (1999) later revised and applied Bloom's (1985) model to the sports domain. Côté's model of expertise defined the three stages of age-specific expertise development as the *sampling* (6–12 years old), *specialization* (13–15 years old), and *investment* (16 years old and older) stages (for more on this model, see Chapter 23, Play During Childhood and the Development of Expertise in Sport).

The models of development of talent in young people (Bloom, 1985; Côté, 1999) have served as a foundation to empirical research that explains the developmental processes that lead people to become experts (Ericsson *et al.*, 1993; Macnamara *et al.*, 2010a, 2010b). Those studies investigated the types of activities that lead people to become experts in a given area, what skills distinguish experts from non-experts, and who is influential in this development. Although the aforementioned models have acknowledged the key role of motivation in developing skills, they make little direct reference to the type of psychological drive that people need in order to become experts. We believe that passion for an activity can explain the determination that leads people to become experts.

Passion as the Motor Underlying the Development of Expertise

A Definition of Passion

Surprisingly, until recently, there has been very little theorizing and research on the psychology of passion (see Vallerand, 2015). Although there has been research on passionate love (e.g., Hatfield, Walster, & Reading, 1978), no theoretical analysis of passion for activities has been formulated until Vallerand and colleagues (2003) proposed a Dualistic Model of Passion (DMP; see also Vallerand, 2015). The DMP defines passion as a strong inclination toward a *self-defining* activity that one loves (or strongly likes), finds important, and in which one invests time and energy (Vallerand *et al.*, 2003). Such an activity comes to be so self-defining that it represents a central feature of one's identity. Playing tennis, playing a musical instrument (e.g., the piano), or one's work represent examples of activities that one can be passionate about and help define identity.

On the Harmonious and Obsessive Passions

The DMP further posits that there are two types of passion, *harmonious* and *obsessive*, that can be distinguished in terms of how the passionate activity has been internalized into one's identity. Obsessive passion results from a controlled internalization (Ryan & Deci, 2000) in identity of the activity that one loves. Such a controlled internalization process leads the activity representation to be part of the person's identity thereby preventing access to optimal self-processes. With obsessive passion, people can experience an uncontrollable urge to partake in the activity. Consequently, although they may display task persistence, with obsessive passion such persistence is rigid and people risk experiencing conflicts and other negative affective, cognitive, and behavioral consequences during and after activity engagement.

Conversely, harmonious passion results from an autonomous internalization of the activity into the person's identity. An autonomous internalization occurs when individuals have freely accepted the activity as important for them without any contingencies attached to it. When harmonious passion is at play, the activity occupies a significant but not overpowering space in the person's identity, is in harmony with other aspects of the person's self and life, and is experienced as volitional. This type of passion is conducive to flexible persistence and positive outcomes. In sum, with harmonious passion, the person controls one's passion, while with obsessive passion, one is controlled by the passion. Although both types of passion are expected to be very powerful, harmonious passion is hypothesized to be more adaptive than obsessive passion and should therefore lead to more optimal outcomes.

Research on Passion

The Vallerand *et al.* (2003) article opened up a new area of research on passion for activities. Since then, well over 200 studies have been conducted on the passion construct. Such research has been typically conducted in field settings with a variety of real-life participants such as athletes, musicians, actors, dancers, painters, teachers, nurses, administrators, video gamers, and others. In most studies, participants are asked to complete the Passion Scale, which contains two sub-scales assessing obsessive (e.g., "I almost have an obsessive feeling toward this activity") and harmonious passion (e.g., "This activity is in harmony with other activities in my life"). There is also another subscale that assesses the general passion criteria (e.g., love, valuation, and regular engagement in the activity) and thus helps determine whether participants are passionate or not with respect to their favorite activity (e.g., painting). Such research has used a variety of methodological designs (e.g., cross-sectional, longitudinal, diary study), and psychological and behavioral outcomes as well as responses from various informants (see Vallerand, 2015 for a review). In other studies, the harmonious and obsessive passions have been experimentally induced (the results with these procedures and the Passion Scale are remarkably similar).

On the Prevalence of Passion

Using the criteria reflecting the definition of passion (see above), several studies have shown that a majority of the population is either highly passionate (75 percent; Philippe et al., 2009) or at least moderately passionate (84 percent; Stenseng, 2008; Vallerand et al., 2003, Study 1) for at least one activity in their life. Of importance, such passion is not fleeting but rather persistent as people typically engage in their passionate activity on average eight hours per week and have been doing so for several years (see Vallerand et al., 2003). As long as activities include some interesting elements, they have the potential to become passionate for a given individual.

On the Development of Passion

The DMP posits that people engage in various activities throughout life in the hope of satisfying the basic psychological needs of autonomy (to feel a sense of personal initiative), competence (to interact effectively with the environment), and relatedness (to feel connected to significant others) (see Ryan & Deci, 2000). Of these activities, a limited few (one or two) will eventually be perceived as particularly enjoyable and important, and to have some resonance with how we see ourselves. Such valuation and identification for these activities will lead them to be internalized in identity, and passion for these activities will develop.

According to the DMP, there are at least three processes involved in the transformation of an interesting activity into a passion: *activity valuation, identification with the activity*, and *internalization of the activity in one's identity*. Activity valuation refers to the importance one gives to an activity. Activity identification takes place when one feels that the activity defines him or her. Finally, activity internalization is the process through which the activity becomes part of the person's sense of self and identity. In line with past research (Deci, Eghrari, Patrick, & Leone, 1994), an activity is likely to be internalized when it is highly valued and meaningful. In line with self-determination theory (Ryan & Deci, 2000), to the extent that one's social environment (e.g., parents, teachers, coaches, school principals) is autonomy supportive (provides some choices within reasonable limits), an autonomous internalization is likely to take place leading to harmonious passion. Conversely, to the extent that one's social environment is controlling (coercing people to engage in behavior), a controlled internalization will take place, leading to obsessive passion. Parents, teachers, coaches, supervisors, managers, and mentors all play an important role in individuals' valuation of a given activity (e.g., Eccles & Wigfield, 2002).

Results reveal that all three processes are important in the development of passion. For instance, Mageau *et al.* (2009, Study 3) showed that first-year high school students who had never played a musical instrument before and who later became passionate for music at the end of a semester (36 percent of the sample) were those who valued music, identified with it, and interacted with autonomy-supportive parents and music teachers. Furthermore, among the passionate music students, those who developed a harmonious passion reported experiencing higher levels of autonomy support than those who developed an obsessive passion. When an interesting activity becomes so important that it contributes to one's identity or has the potential to do so in the future, individuals are more likely to become passionate. Indeed, enjoying music and having the perception that one may become a musician later on should make this potential identity element salient, facilitate its internalization in identity (Houser-Marko & Sheldon, 2006), and should lead to the development of passion. This internalization process, facilitated by autonomy support provided by the social environment, represents à crucial factor leading to passion development (see also Mageau *et al.*, 2009).

The processes discussed above pertain to activities where participants have engaged in the activity for just a few months or even from time zero (Mageau *et al.*, 2009, Study 3). Thus, these studies relate more to the initial development of passion. However, once developed, passion can also undergo ongoing development as it is affected by a variety of social factors (Vallerand, 2015). Because internalization is never 100 percent autonomous or controlled in nature, both types of internalization processes are at play and elements of the two types of passion are internalized to different degrees. Depending on the type of social factors present in one's environment, it is possible to subsequently trigger one type of passion or the other. For instance, in a study with music students and with an average of over seven years of musical experience (Bonneville-Roussy, Vallerand, & Bouffard, 2013), it was found that students who interacted with autonomy-supportive music teachers displayed higher levels of harmonious passion toward music than those with controlling teachers. Other social factors such as task autonomy and task resources (support) have been found to facilitate the development of a more harmonious passion (Trépanier, Fernet, Austin, Forest, & Vallerand, 2014).

Individual differences may also play a role in the development of specific types of passion. Vallerand et al. (2006) showed that athletes' activity valuation (the subjective importance of the activity) coupled with an autonomous internalization style predicted harmonious passion. Obsessive passion, on the other hand, was predicted by activity valuation coupled with a controlled internalization style. Other research has shown that using signature strengths (one's most positive core attributes) leads one to experience increases in harmonious passion for work (Forest et al., 2012). In sum, the development of passion is related to contextual influences, social factors, and, to some extent, personal dispositions, that shape how the passionate activity is internalized into one's identity and leads to the initial or ongoing development of passion.

Passion and Psychological Outcomes

Most studies conducted on passion have looked at the role of the two types of passion in a variety of outcomes. The results of these studies yield remarkably similar findings (see Curran et al., 2015 for a recent meta-analysis). Germane to this chapter, passion has been found to predict behavioral engagement, persistence, and performance. In this case, both harmonious passion and obsessive passion have been typically found to predict positively the sustained engagement in the passionate activity (e.g., Parastatidou, Doganis, Theodorakis, & Vlachopoulos, 2012; Vallerand et al., 2007; Vallerand et al., 2008). In addition, both harmonious and obsessive passions have been found to predict positively the engagement in highly demanding task activities aimed at improving on the activity, such as deliberate practice (see Bonneville-Roussy et al., 2011; Vallerand et al., 2007; Vallerand et al., 2008). It is through regular engagement in deliberate practice activities that long-term improvement in performance takes place. However, Bonneville-Roussy et al. (2013) have found that only harmonious passion predicted long-term persistence in an activity. That is, obsessively passionate individuals may be more likely than their harmoniously passionate counterparts to drop out of an activity. Finally, both types of passion affect the display of performance through their positive effects on various cognitive mediators such as concentration and absorption (e.g., Ho, Wong, & Lee, 2011). Thus, because both the harmonious and obsessive passions lead one to engage in deliberate practice to a similar extent, they both facilitate the development of long-term performance and its display in the short term.

Of additional importance, harmonious passion leads to higher levels of optimal functioning both at the intrapersonal (e.g., concentration, psychological well-being, health, engagement, motivation, etc.) and interpersonal levels (e.g., relationships; see Vallerand, 2015). On the contrary, obsessive passion positively predicts maladaptive outcomes (e.g., general negative affect, life conflicts, burnout), whereas harmonious passion is either unrelated or even negatively associated with these negative outcomes. In other words, harmonious passion for a given activity may protect one against negative outcomes and ill-being. Conversely, with obsessive passion, individuals seem to be on a "see-saw pattern" where their well-being goes up and down as a function of their performance on the activity that they are passionate about (see Lafrenière, St-Louis, Vallerand, & Donahue, 2012; Mageau, Carpentier, & Vallerand, 2011). It should also be emphasized that the adaptive outcomes engendered by harmonious passion are experienced on a recurrent basis. Thus, contrary to the often reported "treadmill effect" where gains are not sustained, the positive effects due to harmonious passion are indeed sustainable (see Vallerand, 2015).

Finally, although the long-term performance effects of the two types of passion may be similar, it should be noted that the process leading to performance appears to be quite different. Specifically, because harmonious passion also facilitates the experience of more adaptive on-task cognitive and affective as well as life outcomes, the harmonious road to excellence would appear to be much more adaptive than the obsessive road that is devoid of such a positive process and may include emotional suffering along the way (Vallerand, 2015).

Toward a Conceptual Model Linking Passion to Expertise Development

Building on past research on passion and expertise, we propose a model of the long-term development of expertise that examines how passion can serve as a drive to this development. Research has demonstrated that experts are in general highly passionate about their dedicated activity (e.g. Bonneville-Roussy et al., 2011; Vallerand et al., 2007). As such, passion can be considered as the fuel that individuals need in order to engage, persist, and succeed in their preferred activity, and eventually become experts. This model also expands prior models of expertise development (Bloom, 1985; Côté, 1999), as it takes a lifespan developmental perspective (Baltes, Staudinger, & Lindenberger, 1999) and assumes that expertise, and passion towards an activity, can be developed and maintained at almost any stage in life.

Figure 22.1 illustrates our conceptual model in which the former stages serve as the foundation to the next stage of development. We propose four stages of expertise in which passion plays a major role. The first three stages are based on Bloom (1985b), and Côté's (1999) models of development of expertise described above, and are the *exploration* (early years or sampling, Bloom, 1985, and Côté, 1999, respectively), *specialization* (Côté, 1999; the middle years for Bloom, 1985), and *investment* (final years, Bloom, 1985) stages of development. To these three stages, we add a fourth one, namely the *refinement stage* of expertise that happens when experts have acquired their skills and need to maintain

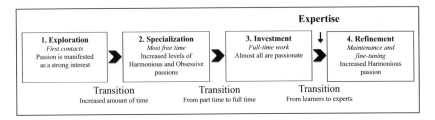

FIGURE 22.1 Conceptual model on the relations between passion and the development of expertise. The first three stages are adapted from Bloom (1985) and Côté (1999).

and refine them. Table 22.1 summarizes the most important findings on the role of passion in the developmental stages of expertise that are described below.

Passion and the Exploration Stage of Expertise Development

This first stage roughly encompasses the first few years of involvement in an activity, from the complete start up until one or a few preferred activities become more formally chosen. The main developmental goal of the exploration stage of expertise acquisition is to promote interest and passion in one or many activities (Bloom, 1985; Côté, Baker, & Abernethy, 2003). Children usually explore activities, such as music, mathematics, reading, and sports informally and formally at school and during extracurricular activities. Families can also create a climate that is conducive to exploration, through continuing exposition to varied activities and promoting growth within them (Bloom, 1985; Vallerand, 2015). Young adults may sample different study and career choices in secondary school and college. Adults may also explore a variety of activities as hobbies, or during work transitions. The key feature of this stage is that many activities are often explored simultaneously, and mostly informally, according to the availability of the activities and initial interests. Individuals at this stage of development find out that some activities are more valuable to them than others. At any age, role models can be influential in the selection of activities, and individuals repeatedly report that role models play an important part in the initiation of a new activity (Bloom, 1985; Gibson, 2004).

At the exploration stage, the type of passion that is developed is strongly influenced by the levels of involvement of social agents, such as family, friends, coaches, and mentors (Mageau et al., 2009) and also culture (Vallerand, 2015). For instance, Mageau et al. (2009) have found that, in the exploration stage of expertise development, only 36 percent of individuals develop a passion towards a specific activity presented in a school context. In addition, harmonious and obsessive passions appear to be malleable at this stage of development, and highly influenced by the social context (Mageau et al., 2009). As seen in a previous section, autonomy support from social agents tends to influence the development of passion in general. Without freedom to engage and to explore in the activity,

TABLE 22.1 Summary of the key characteristics of passion at each stage of the development of expertise.

Stages of Development / Associated Passion Characteristics	Development of passion	Contextual factors	Outcomes
Exploration *The activity is new and is explored on its own or in combination with other similar activities*	• Around 30% of people develop a passion for a specific activity • Harmonious and obsessive passions may be less differentiated	• Strong contextual influences • Autonomy-support fosters the development of harmonious passion • Psychological control fosters the development of obsessive passion	• Non-passionate individuals are likely to drop out of the activity
Specialization *The activity is valued and chosen as the area of concentration. More time is spent on the activity.*	• Passion towards one specific activity starts to develop • Early preference for activity specialization is associated with obsessive passion • Beginning of the integration of the activity into the identity	• An environment that supports the needs for autonomy and competence promotes passion • Autonomy-support fosters the development of harmonious passion • Psychological control fosters the development of obsessive passion	• Boredom hinders the development of a passion, and may lead to a drop out
Investment *Full-time investment in the activity, the main focus of skills mastery and control. At the end of this stage, individuals are experts.*	• Almost all individuals at this stage are passionate • High levels of both harmonious and obsessive passion	• Important influence of the activity-related peers and mentors • Autonomy support or psychological control from mentors lead to the development of a harmonious or an obsessive passion, respectively • Individuals may be more immune to contextual influences	• Harmonious passion promotes performance, persistence, and well-being • Obsessive passion may promote performance, but hinders persistence and well-being
Refinement *The skills are mastered and the focus is on preservation and fine-tuning of such skills.*	• Higher levels of harmonious passion may be more prevalent • Individuals may develop a more harmonious passion with time • The most obsessively passionate performers may drop out		• Harmonious passion is linked with more positive affect, and a greater life satisfaction and well-being • Obsessive passion is associated with more negative affect, burnout, and physical injuries

only external regulation will develop for a given activity. The activity is then engaged only when one feels that he or she has to do it (e.g., practicing a musical instrument only when told "go to your room and practice!"). However, sustained autonomy support from one's social environment is key in leading to the further differentiation of passion into harmonious passion, whereas further controlling behaviors from social agents lead to the development of obsessive passion (Bonneville-Roussy et al., 2013; Mageau et al., 2009).

The supportive role of family and friends, as well as mentors and teachers, is also acknowledged in talent development theories (e.g. Bloom, 1985; Côté, 1999). For instance, Peter, an Olympic swimmer cited in Bloom's (1985) research, indirectly summarizes the difference between autonomy-supportive parents and controlling parents, and the consequences they had for the desire to swim: "They weren't oppressive—a lot of parents are oppressive in their support. [. . .] My parents were very encouraging [and] smart enough to know not to overencourage me or not to be oppressive, because a lot of people will rebel and just back away" (Bloom, 1985, p.196). Therefore, adequate support fosters the growth of healthy passion and interest in the activity, whereas psychological control or "oppression" hinders it and leads to obsessive passion (see Mageau et al., 2009).

Two main outcomes may arise from the development of passion and of expertise at the end of the exploration stage. It is likely that an activity that is not interesting enough or not considered important may never develop into a passion. It is also likely that this non-passionate activity will be dropped before the next stage of expertise development. If the activity is highly valued, loved, and starting to form an integral part of one's identity, providing that the person invests a sufficient amount of time doing it, this activity can eventually become a passion. Regardless of whether individuals developed an obsessive or harmonious passion, as long as they are at least moderately passionate for an activity, it is expected that individuals will carry on to the next stage of expertise development.

In operational terms, the exploration phase should be characterized by (a) the sampling of various activities; (b) a focus on enjoyment and informal training rather than deliberate practice and formal training; (c) a strong influence of the social environment seen through autonomy support and control that promote or hinder harmonious or obsessive passion, respectively; and finally (d) lower levels, or fluctuating levels, of passion towards the activity. A successful transition between the first stage and the next stages of development should be seen through a greater identification towards the activity, higher levels of passion, and a greater amount of time and energy spent in the activity.

Passion and the Specialization Stage of Expertise Development

During the specialization stage of expertise development, individuals choose one or sometimes two areas of specialization (Bloom, 1985; Côté, 1999). It can be roughly compared with the first half of the "10 years and 10,000 hours of deliberate practice" rule of thumb regarding expertise acquisition (Ericsson, 2016; Simon & Chase, 1973). At this stage, individuals gradually adapt their focus from the initial play and informal learning to mastering their skills. Although some levels of exploration are still present, such as playing two musical instruments (personal experience from the first author) or being involved in many sports (personal experience from the second author; see also Ericsson *et al.*, 2007), more formal types of learning are also experienced, the most common one being deliberate practice (Côté *et al.*, 2003). One successful research neurologist described in Bloom (1985) summarizes the transition from exploration to specialization: "I had left high school winning some sort of award in biology, so I automatically assumed I'd go into biology or medicine" (Bloom, 1985, p. 384). This stage involves a developing identification with the activity. The area of specialization gradually becomes an integral part of the person's life through an increased use of one's free time that is devoted to the activity, of time given to rehearsal and practice, and general involvement in extracurricular activities related to the area of specialization (such as attending professional concerts for musicians or aquiring more specialized equipment; Bloom, 1985b; Coleman & Guo, 2013).

The specialization stage is characterized by an increase in the level of passion for the activity of interest. For instance, in one study that examined the development of passion with teenagers who were specializing in various activities (e.g., dance and ecology), Mageau *et al.* (2009, Study 2) have found that, at the specialization stage of expertise, 92 percent of individuals were passionate. Further, greater differentiation between harmonious and obsessive passions takes place at this second stage, and Mageau *et al.* concluded that autonomy support (or lack of it) from parents plays a key role in such differentiation. Specifically, preferences for what may be too early activity specialization from the teenagers and their parents led to the development of more obsessive types of passion in the teenagers. Presumably, experiencing pressure to specialize too early in a given activity leads to obsessive passion for the activity. In the same vein, Côté, Lidor and Hackford (2009) have suggested that early exploration of various activities can be beneficial to the later stage of expertise developments, but their arguments towards an early activity specialization were mixed. Another study qualitatively examined the links between passion and early activity specialization and reached the same conclusion: The young people interviewed who displayed high levels of specialization seemed to display an almost obsessive passion towards their activity (Fredricks, Alfeld, & Eccles, 2010).

Among other factors contributing to passion and expertise development at this stage, Fredricks and colleagues (2010) also noted that the social context needs to provide an adequate level of challenge, as boredom was seen as an obstructive factor in the development of passion, and the desire to specialize further in an activity. In addition, the more passionate individuals in Fredricks *et al.*'s sample had more opportunities to demonstrate their competence through competitions or other means. Finally, an enduring lack of challenge in the activity may lead people to "fall out" of passion and to stop the activity altogether (Aujla, Nordin-Bates, & Redding, 2015; Fredricks et al., 2010).

To operationalize this second stage, specialization should be accompanied with the following: (a) a choice of one or two activities in which more time is invested; (b) an increasing focus on deliberate practice and decreasing focus on play and informal activities; (c) a strong influence of the social environment seen through autonomy support and control that promote or hinder harmonious or obsessive passion, respectively; and (d) increasing levels of passion towards the activity that is better discriminated between the harmonious and obsessive types. Signs of transition between the specialization and the next stage of development are: the activity that becomes an integral part of the person's identity, higher levels of both harmonious and obsessive passions, and a progression towards an (almost) full-time engagement in the activity.

Passion and the Investment Stage of Expertise Development

The investment stage of expertise development is marked by a full-time involvement in the activity with the explicit desire to excel in the activity (Bloom, 1985; Côté et al., 2003). At this stage, individuals are completely invested in, and passionate about, the activity that they usually love to do more than anything else. Many studies conducted with hundreds of participants concluded that almost, if not 100 percent of individuals who attain the investment phase of expertise are passionate about their activity (e.g., Bonneville-Roussy et al., 2011; Mageau et al., 2009; Vallerand et al., 2007, 2008). This research has shown that passion is the most important psychological drive that allows people to maintain the energy to go through the high demands of the investment stage.

Another important characteristic of the investment stage is the full-time attention to practice and improvement, by the use of sustained deliberate practice (Ericsson et al., 1993; Starkes, Deakin, Allard, Hodges, & Hayes, 1996). It is not surprising to see that the sheer amount of deliberate practice seems to increase dramatically, to reach a weekly number of hours that varies between 10 and as many as 40, depending on the sample and activity at play (Krampe & Ericsson, 1996). Further, the content of such practice moves toward excellence. Indeed, experts-to-be seem to focus their attention on improving precision and control, and to "practice to perfection" (Bloom, 1985). Because such practice is so demanding, passion is the key factor providing the energy to sustain such practice over time.

Further, we see a full integration of the activity into the person's identity: The activity has now become an integral part of who they are (Bloom, 1985; Bonneville-Roussy et al., 2013; Côté et al., 2003). A successful research mathematician in Bloom's research sums up his later years of expertise development as "I'm certainly seduced by mathematics. I couldn't help myself *being a mathematician*" (Bloom, 1985, p. 329). Bonneville-Roussy *et al.* (2013) replicated this finding quantitatively by showing that integration of the activity into the identity was an important predictor of the development of harmonious and obsessive passions. Mageau *et al.* (2009) have shown that as compared with individuals who were still exploring options, individuals in transition between the investment and the expert levels of expertise display higher levels of harmonious and obsessive passion, and the criteria of passion: activity valuation, love for the activity, and time investment.

Coaches or mentors have an increasing role to play in order to provide fine-grained feedback and in preparation for performances and examinations during the investment stage of development (Bloom, 1985; Carpentier & Mageau, 2014). Bonneville-Roussy *et al.* (2013) have found that musicians at the investment stage also benefit from an autonomy-supportive style from their instructor (see also Mageau *et al.*, 2009). In this study, musicians who perceived more autonomy support from their music teachers tended to develop a more harmonious passion later on, and those who perceived more control tended to report having a more obsessive passion. Côté (1999) noted that family and significant others also provide important emotional and material support at this stage.

Since the investment stage of expertise is characterized by an intense involvement in the activity, and since most individuals are passionate, the type of passion individuals hold can greatly influence the quality of outcome derived from investment in the activity. Three main sources of outcomes have been investigated regarding the links between passion and expertise at the investment stage of development: performance, persistence, and well-being.

Harmoniously passionate individuals at the investment stage tend to experience an enhanced well-being when engaging in their activity, as compared with obsessively passionate individuals (Bonneville-Roussy *et al.*, 2011; Vallerand *et al.*, 2007, 2008). This finding can be related to the way passion is manifested when individuals are highly involved in their activity. That is, harmonious passion has been associated with a more flexible approach to engagement in the activity which leaves space for other important activities, such as family and friends gatherings (Vallerand, 2015; Vallerand *et al.*, 2003). On the contrary, obsessively passionate individuals tend to display a rigid involvement in their preferred activity, and other activities are often seen as obstacles that create internal or external conflicts (e.g., feelings of guilt or conflict with others; Vallerand *et al.*, 2003).

In terms of performance, research has shown that passion and deliberate practice were some of the most important predictors of achievement at the investment stage (Bonneville-Roussy & Bouffard, 2014; Hambrick *et al.*, 2013; Vallerand *et al.*, 2007, 2008). Bonneville-Roussy and Bouffard (2014) have found that the sheer amount of musical practice was not enough to predict performance at the investment stage of expertise development, and that deliberate practice was the most important predictor of performance at this level. Deliberate practice usually explains between 18 percent and 34 percent of the variance in expert performance, and although these percentages are lower than was previously claimed, deliberate practice remains a very important predictor of performance (Ericsson et al., 1993; Ericsson, 2016; Hambrick et al., 2013; Macnamara, Hambrick, & Oswald, 2014). Research has shown that being harmoniously or obsessively passionate towards an activity leads to performance through a greater use of deliberate practice and more time spent on the activity (Mageau et al., 2009, Study 1; Vallerand et al., 2008, Study 1).

Research has also indicated that the links between passion and deliberate practice are mediated by achievement goals (Elliot, 1999). That is, when mastery (desire for personal improvement), performance-approach (to perform better than others) and performance-avoidance goals (to avoid performing worse than others) are assessed, both harmonious and obsessive passions are linked to the use of mastery goals that leads to a greater use of deliberate practice. However, only obsessive passion is linked with the use of performance-approach and performance avoidance goals, that are either unrelated or negatively related to deliberate practice (Bonneville-Roussy et al., 2011; Vallerand et al., 2007, 2008).

In sum, if both types of passion are related to deliberate practice and to performance at the investment stage, it seems that individuals who are predominantly harmoniously passionate follow a more adaptive path to performance by their use of mastery goals. Conversely, individuals who are predominantly obsessively passionate for their activity make their lives harder by pursuing both mastery and performance goals.

In terms of persistence, having a harmonious passion has been related to lower levels of dropout and a better quality of engagement in the activity (Aujla et al., 2015; Aujla, Nordin-Bates, Redding, & Jobbins, 2014; Bonneville-Roussy et al., 2013; Vallerand et al., 2003) as well as higher levels of psychological well-being (Bonneville-Roussy et al., 2011; Vallerand et al., 2007, 2008). It may be that, for harmoniously passionate individuals, the activity is almost always seen as enjoyable, and the positives outcomes they experience with their activity outweigh the negative consequences sometimes encountered. This assumption has been supported in dance and music research (Aujla et al., 2015; Bonneville-Roussy et al., 2013).

To operationalize this stage, there is (a) a full-time investment in one activity, (b) an intense focus on deliberate practice to master specific skills, (c) a strong influence of peers (or colleagues) and mentors, coaches or teachers, and (d) a strong passion towards the activity that leads to more adaptive outcomes when the passion is harmonious as compared with obsessive. Transition is seen from this stage to the next when individuals finally reach expertise. According to our definition, expertise would be measured with external and measureable indicators, such as a professional career in the area of expertise, the winning of high stakes competitions, or success in one's area of study (such as obtaining a PhD or another skilled qualification).

Passion and the Refinement Stage of Expertise Development

We define the refinement stage of expertise as the point when someone has gained a considerable amount of experience in their area of expertise and the focus is on maintaining, consolidating, and refining such expertise over time. Individuals at this stage are termed "eminent," "renowned experts," "old experts," "masters," or "elites" (Bonneville-Roussy *et al.*, 2011; Krampe & Ericsson, 1996; Macnamara *et al.*, 2010a, 2010b; Simonton, 2000). Little is known about what happens to experts when they finally reach the highest levels of expertise and need to maintain and continuously refine their skills. It seems that renowned experts need to overcome different challenges, spend less time practicing, and pursue fewer performance-oriented goals than in the earlier stages of expertise development (Bonneville-Roussy *et al.*, 2011; Krampe & Ericsson, 1996; Macnamara *et al.*, 2010a). Macnamara *et al.* (2010a) have found that expertise maintenance in sports was related to the challenges of dealing with occasional failures and sustaining high levels of motivation. Research has also shown that renowned expert musicians required a significantly smaller amount of time doing deliberate practice in order to maintain their skills, but they were significantly better at processing skills-related tasks than younger experts (Krampe & Ericsson, 1996).

In terms of passion, experts seem to display levels of passion that are equivalent to those of individuals at the investment stage of expertise (Bonneville-Roussy *et al.*, 2011). That is, it is expected that most if not all experts retain their passion for the activity over time. However, it is possible that a self-selection process occurs and that only the more harmoniously passionate experts stay in the activity in the long run, since harmonious passion, but not obsessive passion, has been related to a greater long-term persistence in the activity (Aujla *et al.*, 2015; Bonneville-Roussy *et al.*, 2013). This avenue needs to be explored further to draw a clearer picture of the roles of passion in the later stage of expertise development. Research has shown that having a harmonious passion towards an activity generally leads to the experience of more positive emotions, greater life satisfaction, and higher levels of subjective well-being (for reviews, see Curran *et al.*, 2015; Vallerand, 2015). Harmonious passion also buffers the negative effects of stress and negative experiences (Carbonneau, Vallerand, Fernet, & Guay, 2008; Gustafsson, Hassmén, & Hassmén, 2011; Schellenberg, Gaudreau, & Crocker, 2013). On the other hand, obsessive passion generally leads to both positive and negative outcomes (Curran *et al.*, 2015; Vallerand, 2015). In particular, individuals who are obsessively passionate tend to display a form of dependence towards the activity (see Orosz, Vallerand, Bőthe, Tóth-Király, & Paskuj, 2016; Vallerand, 2015). Obsessively passionate individuals also experience a mixture of positive and negative affect, and are more likely to experience burnout and physical injuries (Carbonneau *et al.*, 2008; Curran, Appleton, Hill, & Hall, 2011; Gustafsson *et al.*, 2011; Rip, Fortin, & Vallerand, 2006; Schellenberg *et al.*, 2013; Vallerand *et al.*, 2003).

Taken together, experts at the refinement stage seem to be less focused on acquiring new skills, and more on refining and maintaining those that are already present. Since much less research has been done on this stage of expertise development, the operationalization of the variables is less detailed than in the former stages. Renowned experts may be more harmoniously passionate because the more obsessively passionate individuals may have dropped out of the activity at an earlier stage and/or having achieved high levels of success may lead obsessive passion to subside. Extrapolating from this analysis, renowned experts may also experience more positive outcomes derived from their preferred activity, because they are more harmoniously passionate. These speculations about the role of passion in the later stage of expertise development open many avenues for future research.

Applications and Future Research

We believe that this developmental model may be applied to any area of expertise, from music and sports to higher education and work. Further, we propose that the four stages are not age-specific. Earlier research has described the age-specificity of the development of expertise in the performing arts and sports (Côté *et al.*, 2003; Ericsson *et al.*, 1993). In both domains, exploration starts early in childhood and expertise is attained early. In other areas, such as skilled work (e.g. nursing, medicine, piloting, and research), and to some extent the visual arts, the stages seem to happen much later (see Bloom, 1985).

In establishing how passion drives expertise development, the present model has implications for educational, work, and talent development settings. As our model shows, the development of a passion is conducive to expertise and is facilitated by a positive involvement of significant others. A cost-effective strategy to foster the development of a more harmonious form of passion and a more adaptive path to expertise, that is supported by research on the DMP, is to promote environments that are autonomy supportive. In performance domains such as sports and the performing arts, it is important to increase instructors' awareness of the benefits of an autonomy-supportive style, and the potential thwarting effects of psychological control, on the development of harmonious passion, which in turn leads to more adaptive processes and outcomes, such as deliberate practice, performance, and persistence (Bonneville-Roussy *et al.*, 2011; Mageau *et al.*, 2009). This strategy can also be applied in domains where expertise develops later, such as in the visual arts, the sciences, higher education, and many work domains such as business and entrepreneurship, as the roles of mentors have been shown to be very important for the development of a harmonious passion (e.g., Bonneville-Roussy *et al.*, 2013), well-being, and optimal functioning of adults (see Vallerand, 2015).

Research on passion and expertise is still in its infancy, and the present model sets the stage for future research. First, the role of passion at each stage of expertise needs to be examined thoroughly. For instance, we know little about what triggers passion in the exploration stage of development. Additional research is needed to extend our knowledge of the development of passion that leads to expertise, from the first introduction of a new activity, to the development of a strong interest and eventually passion for this activity. The examination of transitions (for instance, from undergraduate to graduate studies, or from study to work) would be a natural first step to assess how passion and expertise develop in times of change. Although we are starting to get a clearer picture of the exploration and investment stages of development, research is needed on the levels of passion at the specialization and refinement stages. That is, more work is needed to understand the psychological processes that trigger activity specialization, and the evolution of passion at the refinement stage of expertise. In addition, future research should investigate what factors may lead people to "fall out" of passion, and abandon their passionate activity, at any stage of expertise. These questions, and the whole model, would benefit from longitudinal studies that would examine the development of passion and expertise concurrently. Finally, the role of passion in the development of expertise in many domains, such as the arts, education, sport, and work merits further investigation.

Conclusion

In this chapter, we have presented a model in which passion is posited to represent the psychological force that drives individuals to become experts. We have described the exploration, specialization, investment, and refinement stages of expertise development. We linked these stages with passion development, contextual influences, and psychological outcomes. In this model, we operationalize the most important characteristics of the four stages in terms of passion and expertise, and the signs of transitions between an earlier and a later stage. We suggest that this model of passion and expertise is not domain-specific and we have demonstrated how some of its principles can be applied. Research has found strong links between passion and the development of expertise and our proposed model suggests a framework to study those processes. Many aspects affect expertise acquisition. However, the role of passion is crucial at each stage of its development. We are optimistic that future research will shed additional light on the very processes that link passion with expertise.

References

Aujla, I. J., Nordin-Bates, S. M., & Redding, E. (2015). Multidisciplinary predictors of adherence to contemporary dance training: Findings from the UK Centres for Advanced Training. *Journal of Sports Sciences*, *33*, 1564–1573. doi:10.1080/0264041 4.2014.996183

Aujla, I. J., Nordin-Bates, S. M., Redding, E., & Jobbins, V. (2014). Developing talent among young dancers: Findings from the UK Centres for Advanced Training. *Theatre, Dance and Performance Training, 5,* 15–30. doi:10.1080/19443927.2013.877964

Baker, J., Côté, J., & Abernethy, B. (2003). Sport-specific practice and the development of expert decision-making in team ball sports. *Journal of Applied Sport Psychology, 15,* 12–25. doi:10.1080/10413200305400

Baltes, P. B., Staudinger, U. M., & Lindenberger, U. (1999). Lifespan psychology: Theory and application to intellectual functioning. *Annual Review of Psychology, 50,* 471–507. doi:10.1146/annurev.psych.50.1.471

Bloom, B. S. (1985). *Developing talent in young people.* New York: Ballantine Books.

Bonneville-Roussy, A., & Bouffard, T. (2014). When quantity is not enough: Disentangling the roles of practice time, self-regulation and deliberate practice in musical achievement. *Psychology of Music, 39*(1), 123–138. doi:10.1177/0305735614534910

Bonneville-Roussy, A., Lavigne, G. L., & Vallerand, R. J. (2011). When passion leads to excellence: The case of musicians. *Psychology of Music, 39,* 123–138. doi:10.1177/0305735609352441

Bonneville-Roussy, A., Vallerand, R. J., & Bouffard, T. (2013). The roles of autonomy support and harmonious and obsessive passions in educational persistence. *Learning and Individual Differences, 24,* 22–31. doi:10.1016/j.lindif.2012.12.015

Carbonneau, N., Vallerand, R. J., Fernet, C., & Guay, F. (2008). The role of passion for teaching in intrapersonal and interpersonal outcomes. *Journal of Educational Psychology, 100,* 977–987. doi:10.1037/a0012545

Carpentier, J., & Mageau, G. A. (2014). The role of coaches' passion and athletes' motivation in the prediction of change-oriented feedback quality and quantity. *Psychology of Sport and Exercise, 15,* 326–335. doi:10.1016/j.psychsport.2014.02.005

Chi, M. T. H. (2006). Two approaches to the study of experts' characteristics. In K. A. Ericsson, N. Charness, P. J. Feltovich, & R. R. Hoffman (Eds.), *The Cambridge handbook of expertise and expert performance* (pp. 21–30). Cambridge: Cambridge University Press. doi:10.1017/CBO9780511816796.002

Coleman, L. J., & Guo, A. (2013). Exploring children's passion for learning in six domains. *Journal for the Education of the Gifted, 36,* 155–175. doi:10.1177/0162353213480432

Côté, J. (1999). The influence of the family in the development of talent in sport. *The Sport Psychologist, 13,* 395–417. doi:10.1177/1527002502003003001

Côté, J., Baker, J., & Abernethy, B. (2003). From play to practice. A developmental framework for the acquisition of expertise in team sports. In J. Starkes & K. A. Ericsson (Eds.), *Expert Performance in Sports. Advances in Research on Sport Expertise* (pp. 89–110). Champaign, IL: Human Kinetics.

Côté, J., Lidor, R., & Hackfort, D. (2009). ISSP position stand: To sample or to specialize? Seven postulates about youth sport activities that lead to continued participation and elite performance. *International Journal of Sport and Exercise Psychology, 7,* 7–17. doi:10.1080/1612197X.2009.9671889

Curran, T., Appleton, P. R., Hill, A. P., & Hall, H. K. (2011). Passion and burnout in elite junior soccer players: The mediating role of self-determined motivation. *Psychology of Sport and Exercise, 12,* 655–661. doi:10.1016/j.psychsport.2011.06.004

Curran, T., Hill, A. P., Appleton, P. R., Vallerand, R. J., & Standage, M. (2015). The psychology of passion: A meta-analytical review of a decade of research on intrapersonal outcomes. *Motivation and Emotion, 39,* 631–655. doi:10.1007/s11031-015-9503-0

Deci, E. L., Eghrari, H., Patrick, B. C., & Leone, D. R. (1994). Facilitating internalization: The self-determination theory perspective. *Journal of Personality, 62*, 119–142. doi:10.1111/j.1467-6494.1994.tb00797.x

Dreyfus, S. E., & Dreyfus, H. L. (1980). *A five-stage model of the mental activities involved in directed skill acquisition.* Berkeley: University of California.

Eccles, J. S., & Wigfield, A. (2002). Motivational beliefs, values, and goals. *Annual Review of Psychology, 53*, 109–132.

Elliot, A. J. (1999). Approach and avoidance motivation and achievement goals. *Educational Psychologist, 34*, 169–189. doi:10.1207/s15326985ep3403_3

Ericsson, K. A. (2016). Summing up hours of any type of practice versus identifying optimal practice activities: Commentary on Macnamara, Moreau, & Hambrick (2016). *Perspectives on Psychological Science, 11*, 351–354. doi:10.1177/1745691616635600

Ericsson, K. A., & Charness, N. (1994). Expert performance: Its structure and acquisition. *American Psychologist, 49*, 725–747. doi:10.1037/0003-066X.50.9.803

Ericsson, K. A., Côté, J., & Fraser-Thomas, J. (2007). Sport experiences, milestones, and educational activities associated with high-performance coaches' development. *The Sport Psychologist, 21*, 302–316. doi:10.1080/10413200390180035

Ericsson, K. A., Krampe, R. T., & Tesch-Römer, C. (1993). The role of deliberate practice in the acquisition of expert performance. *Psychological Review, 100*, 363–406.

"Expert." (2016). *Oxford English Dictionary.*

Forest, J., Mageau, G. A., Crevier-Braud, L., Bergeron, E., Dubreuil, P., & Lavigne, G. L. (2012). Harmonious passion as an explanation of the relation between signature strengths' use and well-being at work: Test of an intervention program. *Human Relations, 65*, 1233–1252. doi:10.1177/0018726711433134

Fredricks, J. A., Alfeld, C., & Eccles, J. S. (2010). Developing and fostering passion in academic and nonacademic domains. *Gifted Child Quarterly, 54*, 18–30. doi:10.1177/0016986209352683

Gibson, D. E. (2004). Role models in career development: New directions for theory and research. *Journal of Vocational Behavior, 65*, 134–156. doi:10.1016/S0001-8791(03)00051-4

Gustafsson, H., Hassmén, P., & Hassmén, N. (2011). Are athletes burning out with passion? *European Journal of Sport Science, 11*, 387–395. doi:10.1080/17461391.2010.536573

Hambrick, D. Z., Oswald, F. L., Altmann, E. M., Meinz, E. J., Gobet, F., & Campitelli, G. (2013). Deliberate practice: Is that all it takes to become an expert? *Intelligence.* doi:10.1016/j.intell.2013.04.001

Hatfield, E., Walster, G. W., & Reading, M. A. (1978). *A new look at love.* Reading: Addison-Wesley.

Helsen, W. F., Hodges, N. J., Van Winckel, J., & Starkes, J. L. (2000). The roles of talent, physical precocity and practice in the development of soccer expertise. *Journal of Sports Sciences, 18*, 727–736. doi:10.1080/02640410050120104

Ho, V. T., Wong, S.-S., & Lee, C. H. (2011). A tale of passion: Linking job passion and cognitive engagement to employee work performance. *Journal of Management Studies, 48*, 26–47. doi:10.1111/j.1467-6486.2009.00878.x

Houser-Marko, L., & Sheldon, K. M. (2006). Motivating behavioral persistence: The self-as-doer construct. *Personality and Social Psychology Bulletin, 32*, 1037–1049. doi:10.1177/0146167206287974

Krampe, R. T., & Ericsson, K. A. (1996). Maintaining excellence: Deliberate practice and elite performance in young and older pianists. *Journal of Experimental Psychology. General, 125,* 331–59.

Lafrenière, M.-A. K., St-Louis, A. C., Vallerand, R. J., & Donahue, E. G. (2012). On the relation between performance and life satisfaction: The moderating role of passion. *Self and Identity, 11,* 516–530. doi:10.1080/15298868.2011.616000

Macnamara, A., Button, A., & Collins, D. (2010a). The role of psychological characteristics in facilitating the pathway to elite performance-Part 1: Identifying mental skills and behaviors. *Sport Psychologist, 24,* 52–73.

Macnamara, A., Button, A., & Collins, D. (2010b). The role of psychological characteristics in facilitating the pathway to elite performance-Part 2: Examining environmental and stage-related differences in skills and behaviors. *The Sports Psychologist, 24,* 74–96.

Macnamara, B. N., Hambrick, D. Z., & Oswald, F. L. (2014). Deliberate practice and performance in music, games, sports, education, and professions: A meta-analysis. *Psychological Science, 25,* 1608–1618. doi:10.1177/0956797614535810

Mageau, G. A., Carpentier, J., & Vallerand, R. J. (2011). The role of self-esteem contingencies in the distinction between obsessive and harmonious passion. *European Journal of Social Psychology, 41,* 720–729. doi:10.1002/ejsp.798

Mageau, G. A., Vallerand, R. J., Charest, J., Salvy, S.-J., Lacaille, N., Bouffard, T., & Koestner, R. (2009). On the development of harmonious and obsessive passion: The role of autonomy support, activity specialization, and identification with the activity. *Journal of Personality, 77,* 601–646.

Orosz, G., Vallerand, R. J., Böthe, B., Tóth-Király, I., & Paskuj, B. (2016). On the correlates of passion for screen-based behaviors: The case of impulsivity and the problematic and non-problematic Facebook use and TV series watching. *Personality and Individual Differences, 101,* 167–176. doi:10.1016/j.paid.2016.05.368

Parastatidou, I. S., Doganis, G., Theodorakis, Y., & Vlachopoulos, S. P. (2012). Exercising with passion: Initial validation of the passion scale in exercise. *Measurement in Physical Education and Exercise Science, 16,* 119–134. doi:10.1080/1091367X.2012.657561

Philippe, F. L., Vallerand, R. J., & Lavigne, G. L. (2009). Passion does make a difference in people's lives: A look at well-being in passionate and non-passionate individuals. *Applied Psychology: Health and Well-Being, 1,* 3–22. doi: 10.1111/j.1758-0854.2008.01003.x

Rip, B., Fortin, S., & Vallerand, R. J. (2006). The relationship between passion and injury in dance students. *Journal of Dance Medicine and Science, 10,* 14–20.

Ryan, R. M., & Deci, E. L. (2000). Intrinsic and extrinsic motivations: Classic definitions and new directions. *Contemporary Educational Psychology. Special Issue: Motivation and the Educational Process, 25,* 54–67.

Schellenberg, B. J. I., Gaudreau, P., & Crocker, P. R. E. (2013). Passion and coping: relationships with changes in burnout and goal attainment in collegiate volleyball players. *Journal of Sport & Exercise Psychology, 35,* 270–80.

Simon, H. A., & Chase, W. G. (1973). Skill in chess. *American Scientist, 61,* 394–403.

Simonton, D. K. (2000). Creative development as acquired expertise: Theoretical issues and an empirical test. *Developmental Review, 20,* 283–318. doi:10.1006/drev.1999.0504

Starkes, J. L., Deakin, J. M., Allard, F., Hodges, N., & Hayes, A. F. (1996). Deliberate practice in sports: Acquisition, what is it anyway? In K. A. Ericsson (Ed.), *The road to excellence: The acquisition of expert performance in the arts and sciences, sports, and games.* (pp. 81–106). Mahwah, NJ: Erlbaum.

Stenseng, F. (2008). The two faces of leisure activity engagement: Harmonious and obsessive passion in relation to intrapersonal conflict and life domain outcomes. *Leisure Sciences, 30*, 465–481. doi:10.1080/01490400802353224

Trépanier, S.-G., Fernet, C., Austin, S., Forest, J., & Vallerand, R. J. (2014). Linking job demands and resources to burnout and work engagement: Does passion underlie these differential relationships? *Motivation and Emotion, 38*, 353–366. doi:10.1007/s11031-013-9384-z

Vallerand, R. J. (2015). *The psychology of passion: A dualistic model*. New York: Oxford University Press.

Vallerand, R. J., Blanchard, C., Mageau, G. A., Koestner, R., Ratelle, C., Léonard, M., … Marsolais, J. (2003). Les passions de l'âme: On obsessive and harmonious passion. *Journal of Personality and Social Psychology, 85*, 756–767. doi:10.1037/0022-3514.85.4.756

Vallerand, R. J., Mageau, G. A., Elliot, A. J., Dumais, A., Demers, M.-A. A., & Rousseau, F. (2008). Passion and performance attainment in sport. *Psychology of Sport and Exercise, 9*, 373–392. doi:10.1016/j.psychsport.2007.05.003

Vallerand, R. J., Rousseau, F. L., Grouzet, F. M. E., Dumais, A., Grenier, S., & Blanchard, C. (2006). Passion in sport: A look at determinants and affective experiences. *Journal of Sport & Exercise Psychology, 28*, 454–478.

Vallerand, R. J., Salvy, S.-J., Mageau, G. A., Elliot, A. J., Denis, P. L., Grouzet, F. M. E., & Blanchard, C. (2007). On the role of passion in performance. *Journal of Personality, 75*, 505–534. doi:10.1111/j.1467-6494.2007.00447.x

23

PLAY DURING CHILDHOOD AND THE DEVELOPMENT OF EXPERTISE IN SPORT

Karl Erickson, Jean Côté, Jennifer Turnnidge, Veronica Allan, and Matthew Vierimaa

Introduction

The purpose of this chapter is to provide an overview of the literature regarding the contribution of children's play to expert performance in sport. Specifically, this chapter focuses on the outcomes of play (in contrast to structured practice) with respect to the development of sport expertise and the unique determinants of play, culminating in a proposed conceptualization of play behavior in children's sport activities. Based on this review we argue that *deliberate play* is a valuable but neglected form of childhood activity with wide-reaching physical, psychosocial, and developmental implications that contribute to the foundation of expertise development in sport. In order to derive the potential benefits associated with deliberate play, we suggest that youth sport programs should consider less, rather than more organization, with an emphasis on simply creating the necessary psychological, social, and environmental conditions for engagement and experimentation. We posit that, rather than competing with more structured sport activities, deliberate play may represent a crucial contribution to the balance of sport activities necessary for the development of expertise. In particular, deliberate play may be especially important for youth in the early stages of their athletic development, and may provide a foundation for the extensive deliberate practice (Ericsson, Krampe, & Tesch-Römer, 1993) and effortful training required at later stages of expertise development. For the purposes of this chapter, youth are defined as individuals aged 13 years and younger, and the terms youth and children will be used interchangeably to describe this population.

Conceptual Framework

Expertise development in the sport domain does not occur as a single instance; rather, it is a process that takes place over time and in multiple settings. Based on retrospective studies of elite athletes' development and qualitative studies of developing athletes, the Developmental Model of Sport Participation (DMSP; Côté, 1999, Côté, Baker, & Abernethy, 2007), one of the most prominent models of holistic athlete development (Bruner, Erickson, Wilson, & Côté, 2010), proposes that athletes progress through a series of qualitatively different stages within one of three pathways over the course of their sport involvement. The three pathways are (a) recreational participation through sampling, (b) elite performance through sampling, and (c) elite performance through early specialization. Each of these pathways and the stages within them are differentiated by changes in the type of sport activity in which athletes participate and the amount of involvement in these activities.

In particular, the DMSP distinguishes between two types of sport activities: *deliberate play* and *deliberate practice*. Sport activities that encompass deliberate play (Côté, 1999), such as street hockey or pick-up basketball, are designed purely for enjoyment and often involve the modification of standard rules to meet the needs of participants. Deliberate play activities are informal, youth-driven, and relatively free of adult organization and direction. In contrast, activities characterized as deliberate practice (Ericsson *et al.*, 1993)—typical of more organized sport—are explicitly designed to improve performance and develop physical skills. Notably, deliberate practice activities in sport are often directed and monitored by a coach.

The DMSP suggests that both the elite performance and recreational participation through sampling pathways share a common foundation and are posited to produce positive athlete development (Côté, Lidor, & Hackfort, 2009). The *sampling years* (ages 6–12), as this common foundation is known, are characterized by participation in a variety of sports with a heavy emphasis on deliberate play as the primary type of sport activity. Following the sampling years, athletes can choose either to pursue elite performance through the *specializing years* (ages 13–15) and *investment years* (ages 16+), which are characterized by an increasing focus on deliberate practice activities, or to remain involved in sport at a recreational level with more play-type activities. Beginning at initial entry into sport, athletes in the elite performance through the early specialization pathway focus unvaryingly on a single sport with high amounts of deliberate practice. The early specialization pathway is explicitly focused on the development of sport talent and has been associated with a number of negative developmental outcomes (e.g., reduced enjoyment, burnout, dropout, and injuries; Fraser-Thomas, Côté, & Deakin, 2008). Thus, the environment of each stage is defined by the type and nature of the sport activities they entail, differentiated broadly between coach-driven deliberate practice typical of structured sport and youth-driven deliberate sport play.

The Nature of Sport Play

What makes an activity playful? While a universally accepted definition of play has not been settled upon, a number of characteristics are present in most definitions. Typically, play theorists (see reviews by Lester & Russell, 2008; Smith, 2010) have defined activities as playful if they meet three primary criteria: (a) freely chosen, (b) personally directed (youth themselves, rather than adults, control the structure and form of the activity), and (c) intrinsically motivated (engaged in the activity for enjoyment itself, rather than for any purposeful goal). Central to this description is the agency of the participant to decide what to do and how to do it, purely for his/her own ends. Thus, these criteria might be summarized as youth led. Further, it is the enjoyment of the process of playing—the act of doing—which drives the participant to play, rather than any potential outcome of the process. Though youth may sometimes derive developmental outcomes from the play experience, with benefits accrued immediately or deferred until maturity (Pellegrini, Dupuis, & Smith, 2007), these outcomes are not the primary reason for youth's participation.

The specific activities constituting youth-driven play are characterized by two additional criteria: (a) a high degree of novelty and unpredictability, and (b) flexibility in their structure and form (Lester & Russell, 2008). In this context, novelty and unpredictability refer to the notion that even within familiar games that have established rules, youth expose themselves to new physical, social, and emotional situations (e.g., adapting to new team members and opponents as teams are shuffled to keep the game competitive and fair). These physical, social, and emotional experiences are not regulated or predetermined by adults, but rather arise from the unstructured interaction of the youth with his/her environment and peers. While these interactions may not always be immediately positive, they are unmediated by adult intervention and thus fully experienced and dealt with by the young people themselves. With respect to structure and form, the course of a play session and the interactions that occur within it are not fixed as within a typical sport practice. Such flexibility is related to the youth-driven nature of play. With control over structure and form, youth can (and do) invent, adapt, and negotiate activities and rules to suit their own immediate wants and needs and those of other participants. This ownership of control enables youth (both as individuals and as groups) to have the responsibility and agency to decide what they want from their time and to structure their play activities accordingly.

Deliberate sport play is characterized by this same youth-driven negotiability of rules, necessary to provide an equitable game between players of differing abilities and physical competencies (Côté *et al.*, 2007; Jarvis, 2007). For example, the composition of teams is often rearranged if one team is winning too easily. Younger, less-skilled players are also often accommodated or allowed to play by different rules to minimize size and skill advantages, thus exhibiting the key flexibility of play activities. This flexibility also reveals the nature of competition within these activities. The focus of participation is on the act or process of competing (i.e., intrinsically motivated) while also keeping the game going in a fair and fun manner (Jarvis, 2007), rather than on the outcome of winning as in adult-driven structured sport. As such, the participants themselves take ownership over the flexibility and negotiability of rules in order to maintain fun competition between players of differing abilities and often different ages (Côté et al., 2007).

The term deliberate play was chosen for this chapter to reflect those aspects or types of children's play that involve locomotor movement and resemble or are based on a formal sport activity (e.g., soccer, volleyball, basketball). Côté and colleagues (Côté, 1999; Côté & Erickson, 2015; Côté, Erickson, & Abernethy, 2013) define deliberate play as early developmental sport play activities that are intrinsically motivating, provide immediate gratification, and are specifically designed to maximize enjoyment. Deliberate play activities, such as street hockey or backyard soccer, are regulated by rules adapted from standardized sport rules and are set up and monitored by the children or by adults involved in the activity as participants. Deliberate play shares the contextual characteristics of more primitive forms of physical activity play, such as running, climbing, jumping, and rough-and-tumble play (Denzin, 1975; Pellegrini & Smith, 1998), yet displays more organized and unique behavioral patterns.

While a number of terms have been used to define physical activity play, including free play, locomotor play, unstructured/unorganized physical activity, and active play, in different disciplines (e.g., developmental psychology, health promotion, exercise psychology, sport psychology), the term deliberate play has been used in the sport expertise literature to describe a specific activity that is inspired by formal sport games. Deliberate play differs from the non-sport physical play activities of infancy or early childhood (Pellegrini & Smith, 1998), the specific pedagogical games or play designed by adults to improve performance (e.g., teaching games for understanding; Griffin & Butler, 2005), and the structured practice activities typical of organized sport. As previously outlined, the concept of deliberate play also contrasts greatly with the notion of deliberate practice activities (Ericsson et al., 1993)—those activities that have an explicit objective to improve performance. In sum, we consider deliberate play the first type of activity that resembles an organized sport activity that children typically engage in, but that is not led by an adult or does not have the goal of performance improvement. It is *play* because the goal is enjoyment and *deliberate* because the activity is inspired by a structured sport activity. Deliberate play is often one of the first activities that children engage in on a regular basis that contributes to the development of expertise in sport (Côté & Erickson, 2015).

The Nature of Structured Sport Activity

Structured sport activities (e.g., formal training programs or organized sport games) do not fit the description of deliberate play because they are typically adult-led. In these types of sport activities, the degree of unpredictability is reduced as adults plan the range of actions and monitor their implementation (i.e., discipline, mistake correction, etc.). The activities may also be flexible, but adult leaders drive this flexibility; the ownership of control does not rest with the youth participants. Youth participation in adult-led sport activities may be intrinsically motivated, but is not necessarily so as in deliberate play; pure enjoyment of the activity itself is only one of the many possible reasons for participation.

Perhaps most critically, structured sport activities are inherently achievement or performance-oriented contexts (Wang & Biddle, 2007)—that is, the outcome matters. This focus is especially evident in competitive sport where league standings are recorded and selection criteria are used to determine less or more *talented* youth. The emphasis on outcomes also applies to less explicitly results-driven activities such as recreational sport programs. We contend that if an adult has selected the activity (or even range of activity options) and monitors or provides feedback about the activity, the inherent and underlying message (intended or not) is that something about the way the activity is performed matters. This message pervades even in simple comments about effort, learning progress, or degree of participation rather than relative ability.

These characteristics of structured sport activities are not necessarily negative. It may be that these qualities are key to the possible positive outcomes noted for participation in such activities, which are discussed in the following section and in more depth in other chapters in this volume (e.g., Chapter 22, The Role of Passion in the Development of Expertise: A Conceptual Model). These characteristics are highlighted purely to differentiate structured sport activities from deliberate play.

Outcomes of Deliberate Play

A number of studies employing retrospective designs to examine the developmental histories of elite and expert athletes have reported high levels of participation in deliberate play activities during childhood (e.g., Baker, Côté, & Abernethy, 2003a; 2003b; Berry, Abernethy, & Côté, 2008; Soberlak & Côté, 2003). For example, in their retrospective study of expert versus less-skilled tactical decision makers in professional Australian football, Berry and colleagues (2008) found that athletes in both groups had accumulated well over 1,000 hours of deliberate play on average before the initiation of their professional careers. Additionally, expert decision makers accumulated significantly more hours of deliberate play in invasion-type games (e.g., soccer, hockey) during their development than did the less-skilled decision makers. Findings from these studies suggest that participation in high amounts of deliberate play during childhood can facilitate the eventual acquisition of sport expertise (Côté *et al.*, 2009).

Despite the benefits that result from involvement in deliberate play, there is currently no direct empirical evidence that supports its value in the development of expertise, given the difficulty of isolating effects of such necessarily loose and unpredictable activities. However, a growing body of indirect evidence and theoretical work suggests a unique pattern of development resulting from participation in play-like activities such as deliberate play. Youth likely derive both immediate and deferred benefit from these developmental outcomes (Pellegrini *et al.*, 2007; Pellegrini & Smith, 1998); therefore, all discussed outcomes should be considered in light of their immediate impact on youth's daily functioning and learning as well as their ongoing contribution to optimal functioning in maturity.

Despite the comparisons we have drawn, deliberate play does share many characteristics with structured sport activities. As one would expect, several outcomes derived from deliberate play and organized sport are similar. For instance, both deliberate play and structured sport activities have a high degree of active movement, with play-like activities associated with higher levels of physical activity (Brockman, Jago, & Fox, 2010). The increased level of physical activity associated with participation potentially contributes to increased overall physical health, cardiovascular fitness, and muscular strength and endurance (Pellegrini & Smith, 1998; Smith, 2010). It is interesting to note, however, that the same physical health and fitness benefits resulting from structured sport may be accrued from deliberate play activities that are typically simpler and less resource-intensive (Farley, Meriwether, Baker, Watkins, Johnson, & Webber, 2007; Fjørtoft, 2001). For example, though not specific to sport, a study in a Norwegian kindergarten class (Fjørtoft, 2001) demonstrated significant increases in children's general motor ability across a broad range of tasks simply by providing unstructured access to a nearby forested area for 1–2 hours per day. These increases in motor ability, attributed to play experience on rough and diverse natural terrain necessitating a variety of movement styles (i.e., climbing, sliding, crawling), were significant in comparison to a matched control group. Thus, whereas structured activities require considerable adult investment, play can be as simple as providing the space to be active.

In addition to offering a range of movement opportunities, play activities in sport create a unique context for technical, tactical, and strategy learning, particularly suited to the developmental level of children. For example, play contexts expose children to unpredictable situations and their intrinsically motivated objectives provide the freedom from actual or perceived performance pressure constraints to explore, experiment, and occasionally fail within this unpredictability. In fact, Memmert, Baker, and Bertsch (2010) noted that time spent in unstructured play activities was associated with increased creativity in sport. Chow and colleagues (Chow, Davids, Renshaw, & Button, 2013) argued from a nonlinear pedagogy perspective (i.e., a conceptualization of human motor learning as a nonlinear dynamical system, whereby expertise is a dynamic and emergent property of functional relations between the performer, task, and context) that unstructured sport play during childhood provides optimal conditions for the encouragement of variability, flexibility, and adaptability in motor skill performance that is key to successful athletic performance. Further, studies of implicit learning in sport have revealed performance advantages, particularly in conditions of stress or pressure, for motor skills learned without structured instruction from an adult (Masters & Maxwell, 2004). Consistent with this perspective, Masters, van der Kamp, and Capio (2013) argued that implicit approaches to motor skill acquisition, as likely created in deliberate play activities, may be particularly suited to children's level of cognitive maturity. These authors highlight the significant load placed on executive cognitive functions by explicit approaches to learning (i.e., rule-based instruction) and suggest that "given the limitations associated with verbal development and rule use by children, skill acquisition approaches that avoid loading working memory are likely to have greater efficacy for motor performance" (p. 27).

In addition to the role that youth-led activities may play in setting an early foundation for motor skill acquisition, deliberate play also has several social and psychological benefits relevant to sport expertise development. It is these distinct outcomes that reveal the true potential of deliberate play to contribute to overall youth development and, ultimately, sport expertise in adulthood. For example, it can be argued that empirical findings linking play to specific positive psychosocial outcomes such as improved social problem solving ability (Pellegrini, 1988; Smith, 2010), emotional regulation (Smith, 2010), and overall social competence and adjustment (e.g., Pellegrini *et al.*, 2007) might be explained through the development of general capacities for creativity, innovation, and adaptability. All of these outcomes are based on and require these creative, innovative, and adaptable capacities integrated within young people's inter- and intrapersonal behavioral strategies (Pellegrini *et al.*, 2007). Thus, the learning of such capacities through opportunities for behavioral experimentation in stimulating environments may be thought to act as the mechanism by which deliberate play fosters the development of skills critical for the future achievement of expertise in sport.

In addition, the intrinsic motivation inherently guiding improvement and performance in sport through deliberate play is itself associated with a number of positive outcomes, with regard to both psychological aspects (such as enhanced self-esteem and overall well-being) and continued sport participation (Markland & Ingledew, 2007). This early motivation has important implications for future development. Indeed, Fry (2001) notes that an individual's motivational orientation appears to be set by age 12 or 13. In order to promote lifelong intrinsically motivated sport participation and its related positive outcomes (Rhodes, Fiala, & Conner, 2009), as well as the motivation to persist in the sometimes unpleasant training activities that later expertise development requires, the foundation must be set during childhood. High amounts of deliberate play may provide that motivational foundation.

Finally, the youth-led nature of deliberate play is a critical component of social development that is crucial to the long-term achievement of expertise in sport. Without a coach to organize, structure, and regulate both the task and social environment, children in play are exposed to more uncontrolled and diverse social situations (Erickson & Côté, 2016; Lester & Russell, 2008; Smith, 2010) that are unmediated by adult intervention. Inherent in this experience then is the autonomy to negotiate social interactions for both social and functional aims (e.g., keeping the game running, working with teammates; Jarvis, 2007; Erickson & Côté, 2016). Children themselves are thus afforded the opportunity to practice taking responsibility for the nature of their own social participation. For example, Imtiaz, Hancock, and Côté (2016) conducted a quasi-experimental study where the same young children were exposed to both adult-led (i.e., a structured practice) and peer-led (i.e., deliberate play) sport sessions. Based on systematic observation of the children's behavior in each context, these authors found that, when in the peer-led play condition, children engaged in significantly higher rates of prosocial behavior, and both sport-related and general communication with peers than when in the adult-led condition. In an extensive review of peer and group research in youth sport, Bruner, Eys, and Turnnidge (2013) suggested that these early social experiences with peers in sport are particularly influential for the development of interpersonal skills and the achievement of expertise in sport. Later in development these interpersonal skills become critical to expert performance (Gould, Dieffenbach, & Moffett, 2002), with respect to both intra-team processes in team sports and the ability to work with and establish productive relationships with significant others in the performance domain (e.g., coaches).

As with structured sport activities, however, there may be both positive and negative consequences resulting from deliberate play behaviors or contexts. To our knowledge, no research has directly examined any potential negative consequences associated with play-type activities in sport. Despite this lack of evidence, it might be theorized that the relative lack of direct adult involvement necessary for a number of the noted positive outcomes also means a reduced ability to monitor and address bullying or other negative social experiences. One might also argue that the more unsupervised active play settings (often outdoors) represent an increased risk for physical injury. While this certainly may be the case, recent evidence suggests that moderate levels of physical risk are necessary for children's healthy growth and development and that over-control of risk can have negative developmental consequences (see Little & Wyver, 2008). It would seem reasonable that similar processes regarding moderate levels of psychological challenge and risk (i.e., negative social experiences) might influence children's development in a similar manner, provided such challenge or risk is not overly extreme or frequently recurring.

In sum, deliberate play can offer a unique contribution to sport expertise development during childhood and early adolescence, as evidenced by high participation in these activities during the development of many expert athletes. The social and environmental milieus created by the developmental contexts in which deliberate play typically occurs are qualitatively different from more structured practice activities, as are the resultant learning and motivational outcomes. Deliberate play facilitates unique interactions between the developing youth and his/her physical and social environment, which allows young athletes to experience a range of opportunities and sport experiences. While further empirical evidence is still needed, the contribution of deliberate play during early stages of expertise development appears to be functional with respect to (a) facilitating developmentally appropriate skill acquisition contexts, and (b) providing a motivational, psychological, and social foundation for later stages of expertise development. Thus, rather than competing with structured sport as contributors to expertise development, participation in high amounts of deliberate play during childhood may actually facilitate participation in concurrent and subsequent organized training activities—in effect, a temporally sequenced interaction effect whereby early deliberate play may enhance later deliberate practice. Such a view may explain the transition from high play and low practice to low play and high practice seen in the developmental trajectories of a number of elite athletes (e.g., Berry *et al.*, 2008; Soberlak & Côté, 2003). This view is supported by empirical evidence from more general youth development research (e.g., Busseri, Rose-Krasnor, Willoughby, & Chalmers, 2006), which shows that a breadth of experiences and different types of play activities in early development is an indicator of continued involvement in more intense activities later in life and of adaptive development.

Determinants of Play in Youth Sport

Côté and colleagues (Côté & Erickson, 2015; Côté, Turnnidge, & Evans, 2014) recently used some of the features of the Developmental Model of Sport Participation (DMSP; Côté, 1999), previous youth sport research, and principles from developmental systems theories (Lerner, 2006) to propose an integrated system of athlete development: The Personal Assets Framework (PAF). In essence, the PAF is a set of key elements that should be combined to design and deliver quality sport programs that positively contribute to the well-being of a person and the specific development of expertise in sport. In line with developmental system theories, the PAF considers personal factors (i.e., personal engagement in activities), relational factors (i.e., quality relationships), and organizational environments (i.e., appropriate social and physical settings) as the elements necessary to understand the processes through which development occurs in and through sport.

In sum, the PAF is designed to account for the processes that occur over time to facilitate positive developmental outcomes (including expertise), encompassing the interaction of three dynamic elements—personal engagement in activities, quality relationships, and appropriate settings—to generate immediate, short-term, and long-term outcomes in sport (Côté *et al.*, 2014). Despite the relatively well-established findings that more training and practice eventually results in better skills (e.g., Ericsson *et al.*, 1993), studies in sport suggest that different forms of sport activities including deliberate play are an important determinant of sport expertise. The next section will use the determinants of the PAF (personal engagement in activities, quality relationships, and appropriate settings) as the basis to describe play environments in youth sport that are conducive to continued participation and long-term expertise development in sport.

Personal Engagement in Deliberate Play

The PAF suggests that *personal engagement in activities* acts as a proximal process to promote development in sport. Côté, Erickson, and Abernethy (2013) recently reviewed the literature on youth sport activities and provided a taxonomy of activities that could be generally categorized as either practice or play. The fundamental difference between practice and play resides in the general goal that the activity aims to achieve in a specific sporting situation. The goal of practice activities is to improve performance, whereas the goal of play activities is to have fun. The various practice and play activities that constitute sport fulfill different needs in youth and ultimately affect their current and future sport involvement. The intrinsically motivated and self-directed nature of primarily play-oriented activities contrasts with the outcome-oriented and often adult-driven nature of mainly practice-oriented activities. We will discuss below the important role of deliberate play activities as the foundational base of personal engagement in sport and an essential building block to the achievement of expertise.

At the simplest level, a primary individual level determinant of engagement is the fact that children appear to need movement innately (Smith, 2010). The more children like an activity, the more likely they are to participate in it. However, structured sport activities are not always enjoyable. This area is one where the distinction between structured sport activity and deliberate play is most obvious; deliberate play, by definition, is enjoyable and intrinsically motivating. Play activities are not always fun, but deliberate play activities are freely chosen and directed by youth so that if a particular activity is not enjoyable it will be quickly modified by the participants. By exercising this free choice and self-direction, youth ensure that the overall course of a deliberate play session is enjoyable (Lester & Russell, 2008). If they lack ownership of control, as is the case in structured sport, youth are not able to continuously structure and direct their own participation toward intrinsically motivated forms in the same manner.

The other main individual determinant of structured sport activity is self-efficacy or perceived competence. Deliberate play, on the other hand, is not an explicitly achievement-, learning progress-, or performance-oriented context, so no minimal external standards exist and steps are often taken by more competent children to ensure participation of less competent peers simply to allow the activity to happen (Côté *et al.*, 2007). However, this is not to say that exclusion on the basis of ability never occurs and that interactions with mixed-ability peers are always positive. Even when exclusionary behavior may be exhibited, youth in deliberate play retain the agency to freely switch activities, rather than being forced to continue participation in unpleasant social circumstances.

Quality Relationships

Integrated within the different activities of youth sport, the interpersonal relationships (e.g., peers, coaches, parents) that are formed represent a critical element of athlete development. In fact, the study of youth development more generally has highlighted the central role of interpersonal relationships as key drivers of individual development (Lerner, 2004).

In contrast to the instrumental support of significant adults as enabling determinants of structured sport activity, quality relationships that promote deliberate play are related more to the mitigation of the concerns and behaviors of parents and other adults acting as barriers to such play. These determinants are especially prominent in the urbanized, industrialized western societies upon which most of the referenced literature is based. In particular, the inhibitory influence on deliberate play of parental safety fears (e.g., traffic, crime, drugs, injuries) and risk aversion tendencies has been highlighted by a number of studies (Bringolf-Isler, Grize, Mäder, Ruch, Sennhauser, & Braun-Fahrländer, 2010; Lester & Russell, 2008; Veitch, Bagley, Ball, & Salmon, 2006). Parents are often afraid (sometimes justifiably) to let their children play in the relatively unsupervised, mobile manner necessary for true deliberate play.

The heightened supervision of all activities (O'Brien & Smith, 2002) limits children's freedom to make mistakes and truly set their own play agendas. Several studies have demonstrated the beneficial effect of light supervision—just enough to ensure safety—and the disruptive effects of adult interference (Farley *et al*, 2007; Jarvis, 2007). Jarvis (2007) reported such an effect in her detailed account of young boys' (4.5–6.5 years old) schoolyard soccer. The boys' modified version of soccer (no teams, only one goal area) functioned relatively smoothly all year, with the exception of a teacher attempting to show them how to "play properly" (p. 253), resulting in a breakdown of activity for a significant portion of the recess break as most of the modifications (e.g., picking teams) were poorly understood and not adhered to by the boys. Relatedly, this increased scheduling and structuring of children's time, referred to by some as the "institutionalization of childhood" (Lester & Russell, 2008, p. 32), has the simple effect of dramatically reducing time available for deliberate play and increasing adult control of children's activity choices.

As in structured activity, the participation of friends and anticipated opportunities to spend time with them are associated with active play activities such as deliberate play (Spink, Shields, Chad, Odnokon, Muhajarine, & Humbert, 2006).

Unique to deliberate play, however, is the linkage with mixed-age interaction, where children regularly interact with older and younger peers in a shared activity (Balish & Côté, 2014). Bringolf-Isler and colleagues (2010) reported that having younger siblings was associated with increased time spent playing vigorously outdoors, which is consistent with the age-mixing and helping of younger peers that is characteristic of deliberate play (Côté et al., 2007; Jarvis, 2007). The desire for social interaction combined with unstructured availability (i.e., who is allowed outside to play) means that more social forms of deliberate play will often require all available participants—regardless of age, ability, or experience—in order to function satisfactorily. Such mixed-age interactions in play are posited to provide distinct developmental benefits for both the younger and older peers (Balish & Côté, 2014; Gray & Feldman, 2004). Younger children are helped to participate in more complex activities and social interactions than they could on their own, while older children are provided opportunities for leadership and to consolidate their existing skills and knowledge through teaching.

Appropriate Settings

Perhaps the most prominent determinants of children's deliberate play noted in the existing literature are the physical characteristics of the environment in which it takes place. Although the physical setting is closely associated with the social environment and types of relationships that are formed, it is still important to distinguish the unique impact of these two independent elements. Therefore, we will discuss *appropriate settings* as the physical environment in which deliberate play is taking place independent of the *quality relationships* or the *personal engagement in activities* discussed in the previous sections.

In sport research, Carlson (1988) used Bronfenbrenner's ecological approach to conduct an innovative study of elite tennis players in Sweden. He highlighted the importance of the *place of development* (i.e., the community in which the individual athlete develops, with associated athletic, physical, social, and cultural resources) as an important determinant of talent development and opportunities to play sport for fun. More recently, a series of studies has examined the features of larger systems such as communities and cities that are consistently associated with athletes' performance (e.g., Balish & Côté, 2014; Côté, MacDonald, Baker, & Abernethy, 2006; MacDonald, Cheung, Côté, & Abernethy, 2009). In terms of long-term performance, studies that examine the birthplace of professional athletes in various countries and in different sports (e.g., basketball, baseball, ice hockey) show a strong tendency for elite level athletes to be born in smaller cities than in big urban centers (for a review see MacDonald & Baker, 2013). Although discrepancies regarding the optimal city size for development have been found across different sports and different countries (Baker, Schorer, Cobley, Schimmer & Wattie, 2009), the birthplace effect has a significant influence on how athletes will first be exposed to sports and can ultimately limit or benefit sport expertise development.

These findings show that small communities and cities appear to contain a set of unique features related to the physical environment that are conducive to athletes' involvement in deliberate play and the eventual development of expertise in sport. For example, smaller communities provide children with more space for unorganized physical activity behaviors such as cycling, running, skating, and playing sports with peers (Balish & Côté, 2014; Kyttä, 2002). Furthermore, Balish and Côté (2014) recently showed that the intimate nature of a smaller community facilitates access to sport facilities and promotes engagement from youth and their families in deliberate play activities. Finally, the proximity of schools, playing fields, and gymnasiums promote a network of connections between people (i.e., coaches, teachers, parents) that enable the transmission of common adaptive social norms between different activities (e.g., school, sport, and family). Under such circumstances, young athletes appear to be more likely to develop competence and confidence in their ability and acquire the necessary motivation for sustained involvement in sport (Imtiaz, Hancock, Vierimaa, & Côté, 2014; Turnnidge, Hancock, & Côté, 2014).

Integration of the PAF into a Model of Children's Deliberate Play Participation

Based on the discussed determinants and outcomes of deliberate play, a model is proposed to explain children's deliberate play behavior (see Figure 23.1). As a number of authors have argued (e.g., Spink *et al.*, 2006), the unique features of the different types of children's physical activity (i.e., deliberate play vs. structured sport programming) likely influence the strategies most effective in promoting each activity type. Thus, activity promotion efforts would be aided by a comprehensive understanding of the nature of these different activities for children. To this end, we feel that a theoretical model of children's deliberate play, distinct from structured sport activity, is warranted. This tentative model is intended to provide a summary of the existing research and theory on children's deliberate play, as well as offer an initial framework to guide future examination of children's deliberate play.

As we have argued throughout this chapter, it appears that deliberate play behavior will occur if enabled by the appropriate conditions. As such, the proposed model differs from traditional models of structured sport programing and expertise development in that its central premise is based on a conditional threshold for participation. If the necessary dynamic features (determinants) are present and sufficient to reach the threshold, active play will be "allowed" to occur and, in turn, children will be likely to engage in deliberate play activities. These necessary conditions are in the initial boxes on the left side of the model and include both social (i.e., quality relationships) and environmental

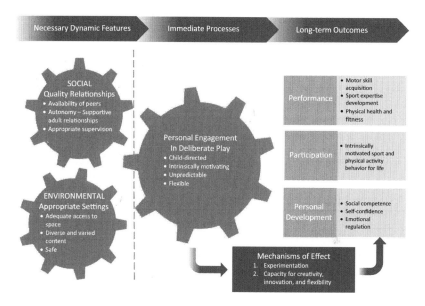

FIGURE 23.1   Model of Children's Deliberate Play Participation

(i.e., appropriate settings) conditions that must be met and must interact. Social conditions relate to availability of peers, as well as to support from adults, especially parents and teachers, both for children's autonomy and freedom and for their safety (as in minimal supervision). Environmental conditions relate to the adequate access to space that is physically safe, but also provides varied and diverse content.

Should the threshold (vertical grey dashed line) be exceeded, the occurrence of deliberate play is described in the central portion of the model. As shown, the intermediate process of deliberate play is composed of two main parts: children's personal engagement in deliberate play and the mechanism of effect. Children's personal engagement reflects the inherent qualities of deliberate play, such that it is child-directed, intrinsically motivated, unpredictable (physically, socially, and emotionally), and flexible in structure and form. These features produce the mechanism of effect, which is broken down into two distinct components. The first component is children's experimentation with novel behaviors, responses, and strategies. The second component is children's increased capacity for creativity, innovation, and flexibility—learning to learn and learning to adapt to new circumstances. Within the mechanism of effect, the first component is proposed to lead causally into the second.

Finally, the end products of the mechanism of effect (located at the extreme right of the model) are the probable physical and psychosocial outcomes associated with deliberate play, which are argued to be facilitated by the capacity for creativity and innovation. These include motor skill acquisition and sport expertise development, physical health and fitness, social competence, emotional regulation, and self-confidence, and continued intrinsically motivated sport and physical activity participation.

Summary

In this chapter, we have presented evidence to suggest that deliberate play constitutes an important developmental activity in the acquisition trajectory of sport expertise. More specifically, we argue that deliberate play is particularly critical for young athletes (i.e., children) in the early stages of expertise development, uniquely suited to young athletes' developmental and maturational needs. This consideration of stage of development situates deliberate play as an initial foundation upon which later deliberate practice activities may be grounded, and perhaps made more effective. Summarizing the processes through which these effects are potentially made manifest, we propose a tentative model of children's development through deliberate play. While the model was developed to explain sport play and expertise development, such a model including similar principles and concepts may have extended applicability in other, non-sport domains of expertise development as well. However, significant further research attention is needed on all aspects of the processes depicted in the model; we finish with a call for more such research, both within sport and across other domains of expertise.

References

Baker, J., Côté, J., & Abernethy, B. (2003a). Learning from the experts: Practice activities of expert decision makers in sport. *Research Quarterly for Exercise and Sport*, *74*, 342–347.

Baker, J., Côté, J., & Abernethy, B. (2003b). Sport-specific practice and the development of expert decision-making in team ball sports. *Journal of Applied Sport Psychology*, *15*, 12–25.

Baker, J., Schorer, J., Cobley, S., Schimmer, G., & Wattie, N. (2009). Circumstantial development and athletic excellence: The role of date of birth and birthplace. *European Journal of Sport Science*, *9*(6), 329–339.

Balish, S., & Côté, J. (2014). The influence of community on athletic development: An integrated case study. *Qualitative Research in Sport, Exercise and Health*, *6*(1), 98–120.

Berry, J., Abernethy, B., & Côté, J. (2008). The contribution of structured activity and deliberate play to the development of expert perceptual and decision-making skill. *Journal of Sport & Exercise Psychology*, *30*, 685–708.

Bringolf-Isler, B., Grize, L., Mäder, U., Ruch, N., Sennhauser, F. H., & Braun-Fahrländer, C. (2010). Built environment, parents' perception, and children's vigorous outdoor play. *Preventative Medicine*, *50*, 251–256.

Brockman, R., Jago, R., & Fox, K. R. (2010). The contribution of active play to the physical activity of primary school children. *Preventive Medicine*, *51*(2), 144–147.

Bruner, M. W., Erickson, K., Wilson, B., & Côté, J. (2010). An appraisal of athlete development models through citation network analysis. *Psychology of Sport and Exercise, 11*(2), 133–139.

Bruner, M. W., Eys, M. A., & Turnnidge, J. (2013). Peer and group influences in youth sport. In J. Côté & R. Lidor (Eds.), *Conditions of children's talent development in sport* (pp. 157–178). Morgantown, WV: Fitness Information Technology.

Busseri, M. A., Rose-Krasnor, L., Willoughby, T., & Chalmers, H. (2006). A longitudinal examination of breadth and intensity of youth activity involvement and successful development. *Developmental Psychology, 42*, 1313–1326.

Carlson, R. (1988). The socialization of elite tennis players in Sweden: An analysis of the players' backgrounds and development. *Sociology of Sport Journal, 5*, 241–256.

Chow, J. Y., Davids, K., Renshaw, I., & Button, C. (2013). The acquisition of movement skill in children through nonlinear pedagogy. In J. Côté & R. Lidor (Eds.), *Conditions of children's talent development in sport* (pp. 41–60). Morgantown, WV: Fitness Information Technology.

Côté, J. (1999). The influence of the family in the development of talent in sport. *The Sport Psychologist, 13*, 395–417.

Côté, J., Baker, J., & Abernethy, B. (2007). Practice and play in the development of sport expertise. In G. Tenenbaum & R. C. Eklund (Eds.), *Handbook of sport psychology* (3rd ed., pp. 184–202), Hoboken, NJ: Wiley.

Côté, J., & Erickson, K. (2015). Diversification and deliberate play during the sampling years. In J. Baker & D. Farrow (Eds.), *The Routledge handbook of sport expertise* (pp. 305–316). New York, NY: Routledge.

Côté, J., Erickson, K., & Abernethy, B. (2013). Play and practice during childhood. In J. Côté & R. Lidor (Eds.), *Conditions of children's talent development in sport* (pp. 9–20). Morgantown, WV: Fitness Information Technology.

Côté, J., Lidor, R., & Hackfort, D. (2009). ISSP position stand: To sample or to specialize? Seven postulates about youth sport activities that lead to continued participation and elite performance. *International Journal of Sport and Exercise Psychology, 7*(1), 7–17.

Côté, J., Macdonald, D. J., Baker, J., & Abernethy, B. (2006). When "where" is more important than "when": Birthplace and birthdate effects on the achievement of sporting expertise. *Journal of Sports Sciences, 24*(10), 1065–1073.

Côté, J., Turnnidge, J., & Evans, M. B. (2014). The dynamic process of development through sport. *Kinesiologia Slovenica, 20*(3), 14.

Denzin, N. K. (1975). Play, games and interaction: The contexts of childhood socialization. *The Sociological Quarterly, 16*(4), 458–478.

Erickson, K., & Côté, J. (2016). An exploratory examination of interpersonal interactions between peers in informal sport play contexts. *PLOS ONE, 1*(5), e0154275.

Ericsson, K. A., Krampe, R. T., & Tesch-Römer, C. (1993). The role of deliberate practice in the acquisition of expert performance. *Psychological Review, 100*(3), 363.

Farley, T. A., Meriwether, R. A., Baker, E. T., Watkins, L. T., Johnson, C. C., & Webber, L. S. (2007). Safe play spaces to promote physical activity in inner-city children: Results from a pilot study of an environmental intervention. *American Journal of Public Health, 97*(9), 1625–1631.

Fjørtoft, I. (2001). The natural environment as a playground for children: The impact of outdoor play activities in pre-primary school children. *Early Childhood Education Journal, 29*, 111–117.

Fraser-Thomas, J., Côté, J., & Deakin, J. (2008). Examining adolescent sport dropout and prolonged engagement from a developmental perspective. *Journal of Applied Sport Psychology, 20*(3), 318–333.

Fry, M. D. (2001). The development of motivation in children. In G. C. Roberts (Ed.), *Advances in motivation in sport and exercise* (pp.51–78). Champaign, IL: Human Kinetics.

Gould, D., Dieffenbach, K., & Moffett, A. (2002) Psychological characteristics and their development in Olympic champions. *Journal of Applied Sport Psychology, 14*, 172–204.

Gray, P., & Feldman, J. (2004). Playing in the zone of proximal development: Qualities of self-directed age mixing between adolescents and young children at a democratic school. *American Journal of Education, 110*, 108–145.

Griffin, L. L., & Butler, J. I. (Eds.). (2005). *Teaching games for understanding: Theory, research, and practice.* Champaign, IL: Human Kinetics.

Imtiaz, F., Hancock, D. J., & Côté, J. (2016). Examining young recreational male soccer players' experience in adult-and peer-led structures. *Research Quarterly for Exercise and Sport*, 87(3), 295–304.

Imtiaz, F., Hancock, D. J., Vierimaa, M., & Côté, J. (2014). Place of development and dropout in youth ice hockey. *International Journal of Sport and Exercise Psychology, 12*(3), 234–244.

Jarvis, P. (2007). Dangerous activities within an invisible playground: A study of emergent male football play and teachers' perspectives of outdoor free play in the early years of primary school. *International Journal of Early Years Education, 15*, 245–259.

Kyttä, M. (2002). Affordances of children's environments in the context of cities, small towns, suburbs and rural villages in Finland and Belarus. *Journal of Environmental Psychology, 22*(1), 109–123.

Lerner, R. M. (2004). *Liberty: Thriving and civic engagement among American youth.* Thousand Oaks, CA: Sage.

Lerner, R. M. (2006). Developmental science, developmental systems, and contemporary theories of human development. In W. Damon & R. M. Lerner (Eds.), *Handbook of child psychology. Vol. 1: Theoretical models of human development* (6th ed., pp. 1–17). New York: Wiley.

Lester, S., & Russell, W. (2008) *Play for a change: Play, policy and practice: A review of contemporary perspectives – Summary report.* Play England, retrieved from http://www.playengland.org.uk/media/120519/play-for-a-change-summary.pdf

Little, H., & Wyver, S. (2008). Outdoor play: Does avoiding the risks reduce the benefits? *Australian Journal of Early Childhood, 33*(2), 33–40.

MacDonald, D., & Baker, J. (2013). Circumstantial development: Birthdate and birthplace effects on athlete development. In J. Côté & R. Lidor (Eds.), *Conditions of children's talent development in sport* (pp. 197–208). Morgantown, WV: Fitness Information Technology.

MacDonald, D. J., Cheung, M., Côté, J., & Abernethy, B. (2009). Place but not date of birth influences the development and emergence of athletic talent in American football. *Journal of Applied Sport Psychology, 21*(1), 80–90.

Markland, D., & Ingledew, D. K. (2007). Exercise participation motives: A self-determination theory perspective. In M. S. Hagger & N. L. D. Chatzisarantis (Eds.) *Intrinsic motivation and self-determination in exercise and sport* (pp.23–34). Champaign, IL: Human Kinetics.

Masters, R. S. W., & Maxwell, J. P. (2004). Implicit motor learning, reinvestment and movement disruption: What you don't know won't hurt you? In A. M. Williams & N. J. Hodges (Eds.), *Skill acquisition in sport: Research, theory and practice* (pp. 207–228). London: Routledge.

Masters, R., van der Kamp, J., & Capio, C. (2013). Implicit motor learning by children. In J. Côté & R. Lidor (Eds.), *Conditions of children's talent development in sport* (pp. 21–40). Morgantown, WV: Fitness Information Technology.

Memmert, D., Baker, J., & Bertsch, C. (2010). Play and practice in the development of sport-specific creativity in team ball sports. *High Ability Studies, 21,* 3–18.

O'Brien, J., and Smith, J. (2002). Childhood transformed? Risk perceptions and the decline of free play. *The British Journal of Occupational Therapy, 65*(3), 123–128.

Pellegrini, A. D. (1988). Elementary-school children's rough-and-tumble play and social competence. *Developmental Psychology, 24*(6), 802.

Pellegrini, A. D., Dupuis, D., & Smith, P. K. (2007). Play in evolution and development. *Developmental Review, 27,* 261–276.

Pellegrini, A. D., & Smith, P. K. (1998). Physical activity play: The nature and function of a neglected aspect of play. *Child Development, 69,* 577–598.

Rhodes, R. E., Fiala, B., & Conner, M. (2009). A review and meta-analysis of affective judgements and physical activity in adult populations. *Annals of Behavioral Medicine, 38,* 180–204.

Smith, P. K. (2010). *Children and play.* Chichester, UK: Wiley-Blackwell.

Soberlak, P., & Côté, J. (2003). The developmental activities of elite ice hockey players. *Journal of Applied Sport Psychology, 15,* 41–49.

Spink, K. S., Shields, C. A., Chad, K., Odnokon, P., Muhajarine, N., & Humbert, L. (2006). Correlates of structured and unstructured activity among sufficiently active youth and adolescents: A new approach to understanding physical activity. *Pediatric Exercise Science, 18,* 203–215.

Turnnidge, J., Hancock, D. J., & Côté, J. (2014). The influence of birth date and place of development on youth sport participation. *Scandinavian Journal of Medicine & Science in Sports, 24*(2), 461–468.

Veitch, J., Bagley, S., Ball, K., & Salmon, J. (2006). Where do children usually play? A qualitative study of parents' perceptions of influences on children's active free-play. *Health & Place, 12*(4), 383–393.

Wang, C. K. J., & Biddle, S. J. H. (2007). Understanding young people's motivation toward exercise: An integration of sport ability beliefs, achievement goal theory, and self-determination theory. In M. S. Hagger & N. L. D. Chatzisarantis (Eds.) *Intrinsic motivation and self-determination in exercise and sport* (pp.193–208). Champaign, IL: Human Kinetics.

PART V
Perspectives

24

FOUR KINDS OF EXPERTISE

Robert J. Sternberg

Introduction

Once upon a time, I made a living pretending to be an expert. In 1975, I was a new assistant professor at Yale, but a few weeks before I had been a third- and final-year graduate student at Stanford. I didn't feel like an expert at all, although, as a faculty member, I was supposed to be one. The mid-1970s, when I started as a pretend expert, were heady times. Chase and Simon (1973a, 1973b) had recently published their classic work on expertise in chess, and people's notions of expertise were being transformed. Formerly, cognitive psychologists, including myself (Miller, Galanter, & Pribram, 1960; Sternberg, 1979, 1981a, 1981b), viewed expertise in terms of particularly adept skills of information processing. Chase and Simon's work suggested a different interpretation—that expertise was a function of tens of thousands of stored patterns that could be accessed as needed. What mattered, therefore, seemed to be two things—that the patterns are stored and that they could be accessed as needed (see essays in Davidson & Sternberg, 2003; Sternberg, 1994).

Reitman (1976) and many others extended Chase and Simon's (1973) results to other domains, such as the game of Go, but the dominant paradigm at the time was Chase and Simon's—namely, showing that experts know more than novices. As it turns out with most extreme positions, neither the knowledge position nor the processing position quite captured the whole of expertise. In this volume, Campitelli (Chapter 3) and Staszewski (Chapter 4) show that one needs both in a complete cognitive model of expertise.

One direction to take this research was to show that, in some ways, experts are not always better than novices. Sometimes they know less, or at least are at a disadvantage, relative to novices. Adelson (1984) and Frensch and Sternberg

(1989) both took a crack at research in this direction. For example, Frensch and Sternberg showed that expert bridge players were readily able to accommodate changes in the basic structure of the game of bridge. When the names of the suits (clubs, diamonds, hearts, spades) were changed to neologisms, the experts were not hurt much at all, but neither were novices. But when the fundamental rules of the game were changed, experts had more trouble adjusting than did novices. One could argue the same thing applies for the game of science. As investigators grow older, they tend to get left behind—the field changes, but they often don't change with it, or at least not fast enough (Lubart & Sternberg, 1995; Sternberg & Lubart, 1995).

The issue of knowledge versus, or in conjunction with, processes was of course never fully resolved. These issues never really are. As Hegel pointed out many years ago, there tends to be a thesis (processes), an antithesis (knowledge), and then some kind of synthesis (both). Once a synthesis is reached, a field moves on to new questions. So the old question isn't really answered; it just becomes irrelevant to the questions scholars later are asking. And a next big question scholars asked was whether expertise was driven largely by deliberate practice, genetic predispositions, or some combination of both.

The question was thrust on the world largely by Ericsson, Krampe, and Tesch-Römer (1993) and by Ericsson and Charness (1994). Ericsson has championed the view that deliberate practice, discussed at length in this volume, is sufficient for the development of expertise (Ericsson & Pool, 2016). It now appears that deliberate practice is more a necessary condition for expertise than a sufficient one (see, e.g., in this volume, Drake & Winner [Chapter 7] and Macnamara *et al.* [Chapter 9]), but in the end, there are always more data to be collected. Today, the genetic versus environmental dichotomy is viewed as being as out of date as, say, the process versus knowledge dichotomy. Virtually everyone in the field of behavioral or molecular genetics agrees that genes and environment work together through gene-environment correlation and probably, as well, gene-environment interaction (in this volume, see chapters by Tucker-Drob [14], Thompson *et al.* [15], Mosing *et al.* [16], and Tan and McPherson [17]). Even deliberate practice, which would seem to be as environmental as possible, can be driven by native talents (Sternberg & Horvath, 1999; Tucker-Drob, this volume). In the end, the deliberate practice-innate talent dichotomy seems quite empty and in need of more synthetic models, as proposed in chapters in this volume by Gagné (18), Simonton (19), and Ullén *et al.* (21). Moreover, as Bonneville-Roussy and Vallerand (this volume, Chapter 22) point out, cognitive expertise is not enough—experts are passionate about what they do.

I believe that a problem in at least some of the work on expertise is assuming that expertise is one construct—that there is a single construct properly called "expertise." The chapters in this volume point out that expertise is, at least in part, domain-specific with respect to professional content (see, e.g., chapters in this volume by Mosing *et al.* [16] and Tan and McPherson [17]). But returning to the process view, one might view expertise as in part also specific with regard to the kinds of information processing it involves.

The Four-Way Model

I have proposed a model of human skill development that I believe is relevant to the current conversation about expertise (Sternberg, 2003a, 2003b). The model (Figure 24.1) suggests that expertise is multi-faceted. People can be experts in the same field, but in four different ways, or in a combination of those ways. These kinds of expertise can be mutually facilitative. But they also potentially can interfere with each other.

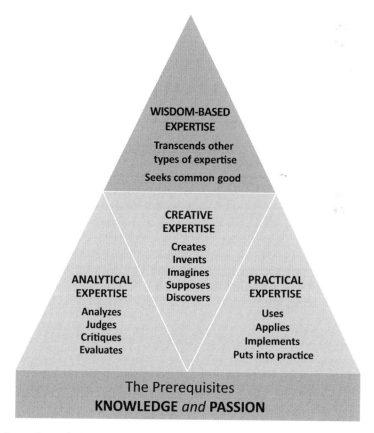

Sternberg's Four-Way Model of Human Skill Development
The *consummate expert* is analytically, creatively, and practically expert, and also is extremely wise.

FIGURE 24.1 Sternberg's Four-Way Model of Human Skill Development.

The Prerequisites: Knowledge and Passion

In the proposed model, knowledge is a prerequisite for all four kinds of expertise. You cannot think in any meaningful way if you lack the knowledge to think with. But knowledge in itself is not sufficient for expertise. Even in the Chase and Simon (1973a & b) work, storage of patterns was not enough. Once an expert retrieved a pattern of chess pieces, he or she still had to know what to do with the pattern. No two games of chess are identical, so one could not get through a game simply by remembering past games. Chess requires knowledge of patterns, but it also requires strategic thinking.

It also is exceedingly difficult to acquire expertise without passion (in this volume, see Bonneville-Roussy & Vallerand, Chapter 22). Although various scientists might argue whether 10,000 hours in particular are necessary for the development of expertise, they probably all would agree that one needs to spend a tremendous amount of time acquiring expertise at anything. Without passion for a special something, it will be difficult to get oneself to engage sufficiently to be an expert.

I believe that past models, including my own, have underestimated the role of passion. Passion is certainly not sufficient: How many potential medical doctors have found that their passion for medicine was not enough to get them through the rigorous curriculum of medical school, or even to get them into medical school in the first place? But passion is what makes the expression of everything else even possible.

Analytical Expertise

Analytical expertise involves analyzing, evaluating, judging, or critiquing a product or process. Analytical expertise is one of the reasons that many child prodigies never become adult experts (see Chapter 6 by Ruthsatz, Stephens, & Matthews, this volume). The prodigies are able to turn out stunning performances but not to analyze the elements that they would have to change to make it to the next step.

In science, analytical expertise is involved in taking an idea and operationalizing it in a scientific investigation, in reviewing articles, in editing articles, and in critiquing one's own ideas. Art, music, and literary critics need to be powerfully analytical in their work, as do athletic coaches in their work, figuring out the strengths of their own teams and finding the weaknesses of opposing teams. A musical conductor needs to figure out why the sound of his or her orchestra is not what it should be, and how to make the sound what it should be. Game players of any kind need to analyze opponents' moves and, more generally, their vulnerabilities (see, e.g., in this volume, Bilalić *et al.* [Chapter 11] and Campitelli [Chapter 3]).

Analytical expertise is important for many kinds of tasks but it often is not sufficient. One needs, for many domains of expertise, not only to analyze, but also to create.

Creative Expertise

Creative expertise is what one uses when one creates, imagines, supposes, discovers, or invents. Creativity involves the production of ideas or products that are novel, surprising, and compelling (Kaufman & Sternberg, 2010). Creative expertise is another reason that many child prodigies do not become adult experts—they do not have the creativity to develop their own distinctive and adult musical, artistic, literary, or other style. Creative expertise is needed to write music or play music in a distinctive and aesthetically pleasing way. It is needed to create original art or literary works, such as poems, short stories, or novels. Creativity is what scientists use to generate new theories or experiments, and, in general, to go beyond where the field has been (Sternberg, 1999). Actors are creative when they put themselves in roles that are novel with respect to their past repertoires, and conductors are creative when they work with their orchestra to offer a new interpretation of a symphonic work. Columnists are creative in their work when they offer something new and compelling to the conversation about current events.

To be truly creative, one needs also to be analytically strong, because creativity involves, in part, analyzing one's own and others' ideas to determine what can be done better (Sternberg, in press; Sternberg & Lubart, 1995). But analytical expertise is not sufficient. There are many scientists, for example, who try to build careers on tearing down other people's work rather than coming up with their own ideas, largely because they don't have so many of their own ideas. The best scientists not only see what is wrong with other people's ideas, but also what they can do better. They also know how to negotiate the practical demands of their field.

Practical Expertise

Whereas analytical and creative expertise are exercised primarily within a domain of inquiry, *practical expertise* is exercised primarily within a field—the social organization of the domain (see Csikszentmihalyi, 2013). Practical expertise is involved when one uses, utilizes, implements, puts into practice, or applies what one knows.

Practically skilled experts understand the tacit (unspoken) knowledge of their field (Sternberg & Horvath, 1999). They are experts at understanding how to get ahead in their chosen occupation. Sometimes professionals whose particular strength is practical expertise seem to others in their field unfairly to have gone beyond where one would have expected based on the actual quality of their work. This feeling of unfairness is understandable, although it does not fully take into account that various aspects of practical expertise—getting one's articles in journals, getting grant proposals funded, getting one's work exhibited in top galleries, achieving rapport with one's audiences during performances—all are part of what makes a well-rounded expert. Politicians tend to gravitate toward their field because of their practical expertise, which often is salutary but sometimes is unfortunate, because it can lead to the election of narcissistic demagogues whose main skill is in manipulating people to vote for and then to follow them. Hitler Germany and Mussolini Italy are prime examples, but the United States has not shown itself over time to be immune—far from it.

Wisdom-based Expertise

Wisdom-based expertise in a sense transcends the other kinds of expertise. The wise expert seeks a common good—for him or herself, but also for others in the field and even outside it. The wise expert is ethical and is able to balance his or her own interests with the interests of others and of larger entities, such as society in general. The wise expert further gives advice that benefits not just an individual, but a field and even the world as a whole. He or she looks at the long term as well as the short term, and realizes that what advances one's interests in the short term sometimes can be prejudicial to those interests in the long term.

The wise expert is able to give advice that can help others achieve or even first to shape their goals. He or she tends to be more advanced in his or her field, but experience in itself is not sufficient for achieving wisdom-based expertise. What matters most is how and how much an individual has learned from his or her experience.

Combinations of Kinds of Expertise

The *consummate expert* is analytically, creatively, and practically expert, as well as being extremely wise. Such experts are rare. Different environments value different kinds of expertise, and so these environments tend to promote some experts at the expense of others. For example, one university might look for the most creative scholars in each field, but another may advance "operators"—scholars who are practical experts but have not necessarily done stellar work in their domain. Still others may advance analytical experts who are good at critiquing others but who have few ideas of their own.

Sometimes, the different kinds of expertise can be in conflict with each other. For example, the practical expert may recognize that in his or her environmental milieu, lip service is paid to creativity but actual creativity is ignored or even punished. Or the creative expert may expend his or her resources doing creative work and ignore the practical considerations that would advance him or her in the field.

Primary and secondary schools tend by far most to value analytical experts—people who can achieve high scores on conventional standardized tests—and so students may learn from an early age to develop analytical expertise at the expense of other kinds of expertise (Sternberg, 1997). Although we would like to believe that the other kinds of expertise might follow, it is just as likely that other skills, such as creative ones, will be drummed out of the students by the time that they actually need to develop broader kinds of expertise.

Moreover, some mentors are creative themselves but seek mentees only who carry on the mentors' creative work—they advance their own careers at the expense of the careers of their students, sacrificing the development of their own wise expertise for the sake of personal advancement. Such experts may be creative but they also are unwise or even foolish (Sternberg, 2002). Thus, developing one kind of expertise does not necessarily lead to the development of other kinds of expertise and in some cases may actually interfere.

Conclusion

When we talk about expertise, we are not talking about a single thing, either across domains of expertise or across kinds of expertise. Experts may excel in analytical, creative, practical, and/or wisdom-based skills. But to be experts, they need as prerequisites a solid knowledge base and passion. The knowledge base continually needs to be updated, because the knowledge that suffices for expertise at one time likely will be insufficient shortly thereafter. It may not only become out of date, but even counterproductive if the questions and answers in a field change over time, as they usually do. Hence, to understand an individual's expertise, we need ask not only if the individual is an expert, but what kind or kinds of expertise the individual possesses.

When I started out in the field, I was a bit of a fake expert. Today, I hope I have developed at least a little bit more. At the very least, I hope I have been able to develop the wisdom-based expertise that will help produce the next generation of scholars who advance our knowledge and our understanding of psychological science.

References

Adelson, B. (1984). When novices surpass experts: The difficulty of a task may increase with expertise. *Journal of Experimental Psychology: Learning, Memory, and Cognition, 10*(3) 483–495.

Chase, W. G., & Simon, H. A. (1973a). Perception in chess. *Cognitive Psychology, 4*, 55–81.

Chase, W. G., & Simon, H. A. (1973b). The mind's eye in chess. In W. G. Chase (Ed.), *Visual information processing.* New York: Academic Press.

Csikszentmihalyi, M. (2013). *Creativity: Flow and the psychology of discovery and invention.* New York: Harper Perennial.

Davidson, J. E., & Sternberg, R. J. (Eds.) (2003). *The psychology of problem solving.* New York: Cambridge University Press.

Ericsson, K. A., & Charness, N. (1994). Expert performance: Its structure and acquisition. *American Psychologist, 69*, 725–747. doi:10.1037/0003-066X.49.8.725

Ericsson, K. A., & Pool, R. (2016). *Peak: Secrets from the new science of expertise.* Boston: Houghton-Mifflin Harcourt.

Ericsson, K. A., Krampe, R. Th., & Tesch-Römer, C. (1993). The role of deliberate practice in the acquisition of expert performance. *Psychological Review, 100*, 363–406. doi:10.1037/0033-295X.100.3.363

Frensch, P. A., & Sternberg, R. J. (1989). Expertise and intelligent thinking: When is it worse to know better? In R. J. Sternberg (Ed.), *Advances in the psychology of human intelligence* (Vol. 5, pp. 157–188). Hillsdale, NJ: Lawrence Erlbaum Associates.

Kaufman, J. C., & Sternberg, R. J. (Eds.) (2010). *Cambridge handbook of creativity*. New York: Cambridge University Press.

Lubart, T. I., & Sternberg, R. J. (1995). An investment approach to creativity: Theory and data. In S. M. Smith, T. B. Ward, & R. A. Finke (Eds.), *The creative cognition approach* (pp. 269–302). Cambridge, MA: MIT Press.

Miller, G. A., Galanter, E., & Pribram, K. H. (1960). *Plans and the structure of behavior*. New York: Henry Holt.

Reitman, Judith S. (1976). Skilled perception in Go: Deducing memory structures from inter-response times. *Cognitive Psychology, 8*(3), 336–356.

Sternberg, R. J. (1979). The nature of mental abilities. *American Psychologist, 34*, 214–230.

Sternberg, R. J. (1981a). A componential theory of intellectual giftedness. *Gifted Child Quarterly, 25*, 86–93.

Sternberg, R. J. (1981b). Testing and cognitive psychology. *American Psychologist, 36*, 1181–1189.

Sternberg, R. J. (1994). Cognitive conceptions of expertise. *International Journal of Expert Systems: Research and Applications, 7*(1), 1–12.

Sternberg, R. J. (1997). What does it mean to be smart? *Educational Leadership, 54*(6), 20–24.

Sternberg, R. J. (1999). A propulsion model of types of creative contributions. *Review of General Psychology, 3*, 83–100.

Sternberg, R. J. (Ed.). (2002). *Why smart people can be so stupid*. New Haven: Yale University Press.

Sternberg, R. J. (2003a). WICS: A model for leadership in organizations. *Academy of Management Learning & Education, 2*, 386–401.

Sternberg, R. J. (2003b). *Wisdom, intelligence, and creativity synthesized*. New York: Cambridge University Press.

Sternberg, R. J. (in press). A triangular theory of creativity. *Psychology of Aesthetics, Creativity, and the Arts*.

Sternberg, R. J., & Horvath, J. A. (Eds.). (1999). *Tacit knowledge in professional practice*. Mahwah, NJ: Lawrence Erlbaum Associates.

Sternberg, R. J., & Lubart, T. I. (1995). *Defying the crowd: Cultivating creativity in a culture of conformity*. New York: Free Press.

25

THE RELATIONSHIP BETWEEN EXPERTISE AND GIFTEDNESS

A Talent Development Perspective

Rena F. Subotnik, Paula Olszewski-Kubilius, and Frank C. Worrell

Introduction

The development of talent is a process that takes place over time. It begins with *potential*, and with the provision of opportunities, study, disciplined practice, and psychosocial factors moves to higher stages of *competency* and *expertise*—and in rare cases, *eminence*. Expertise, in our view, involves recognition by one's peers as an authority on domain-specific tasks and knowledge and having good solutions to important problems generated by others. However, experts may not necessarily break domain boundaries, see in a qualitatively different way, or set the questions for a field. Within this framework, *giftedness in adulthood* is viewed as a stage beyond expertise to eminent performance or creative productivity.

Our commentary is derived from a review of the psychological literature on giftedness and talent that resulted in what we call a mega model for the development of talent across varied and multiple domains (Subotnik, Olszewski-Kubilius, & Worrell, 2011). Some of the basic tenets of the model are as follows: (a) domain-specific abilities are critical to achievement within domains, and these are malleable; (b) different domains of talent have different trajectories including starting points, peaks, and end points, and these have implications for the timing of identification and programming; (c) talent development depends on the provision of appropriate opportunities, and these must also be taken; and (d) psychosocial skills are critical to capitalizing on opportunities, especially progressing to and through the higher stages of talent development. These skills can be taught and acquired. We use this conceptual framework as a lens through which to view chapters within this book. Notably, the experience of reading the chapters left us with questions about our own model that we address in the final section.

Domain-Specific Abilities Over Time

As a way to better identify and nurture potential talent in children, we have advocated for greater understanding of the specific abilities that relate to exceptional performance within domains. Two themes emerged across various chapters with respect to domain-specific abilities. One is the synergy between having high levels of specific skills that dispose an individual towards potential expertise in a domain and developing those abilities through intense engagement. Second, study, practice, and training lead to automaticity in skills, allowing for greater flexibility in cognition, chunking, and schemas to aid memory and retrieval, and space for more complex cognitive processes and creative thinking.

For chess, according to Campitelli (Chapter 3, this volume), pattern recognition would qualify as an ability necessary for a successful chess career. Chamberlain (Chapter 8) suggested that enhanced visual memory is essential in visual arts and is harnessed only when drawing. Macnamara *et al.* (Chapter 9) make a compelling argument for the benefits derived from both general and specific abilities in making efficient and effective use of guided practice. The notion of exploring the importance of various abilities at different points in development is modeled by Campitelli, who shows that for chess players, cognitive abilities are the primary influence in the early stages, whereas deliberate practice makes more of an impact on success in later stages of the domain trajectory. Similarly, Wai and Kell (Chapter 5,) argue for ability and interest as the driving force for trajectories in STEM until after the terminal graduate degree, when a multitude of factors differentiate the paths of elite professionals. According to Drake and Winner (Chapter 7), openness to experience is needed to make the transition from a child art prodigy to an adult professional artist.

Additionally, the Chamberlain and the Bonneville-Roussy and Vallerand chapters (8 and 22) present stages of development for achieving expertise. For example, teachers initially guide visual arts students in identifying strengths and weaknesses and, over time, expect students to take more responsibility for their own improvement, with the goal of optimizing their strengths. Bonneville-Roussy and Vallerand (this volume) model the progression of passion after the stages proposed by Bloom (1985), from (1) "falling in love" with a domain or topic; to (2) acquiring the skills, knowledge, and values of the domain, to (3) capitalizing on stage two to generate a special niche as a creative scholar or artist. In each case, the authors conflate expertise with eminence to describe a person who has a creative, productive influence on a field. We prefer to view the two separately, with expertise a precursor to eminence.

Domains Start, Peak, and End at Different Times

Campitelli's (this volume) description of the trajectory of chess players exemplifies our conception that domains have starting points, peaks, and end points. Chess stars often begin as prodigies, capitalizing on their early start with practice and experience, peak at 35 years, and maintain high levels beyond that, although not with the same level of brilliance. The pattern of trajectories varies by and within subfields of domains (see Figure 25.1) and is affected by physical demands, emotional maturity and psychological strength, opportunities for guided practice, and accumulated knowledge or experience. Although many great performers and producers of creative ideas were, according to biographical data, identified as child prodigies, most prodigious abilities do not carry through to adult creative productivity (see Drake and Winner [this volume] and the model of a boy soprano in Figure 25.1). Finally, although we might be delighted but not entirely surprised to encounter a violin prodigy, we would be much less likely to hear about or even seek out a 14-year-old diplomat, much less a 9-year-old.

Adult giftedness and expertise differentiate from one another in what is defined as the peak of a career. In our view, giftedness in adulthood is manifested in making creative contributions to one's field that leads others in the field to transform or reassess their own work.

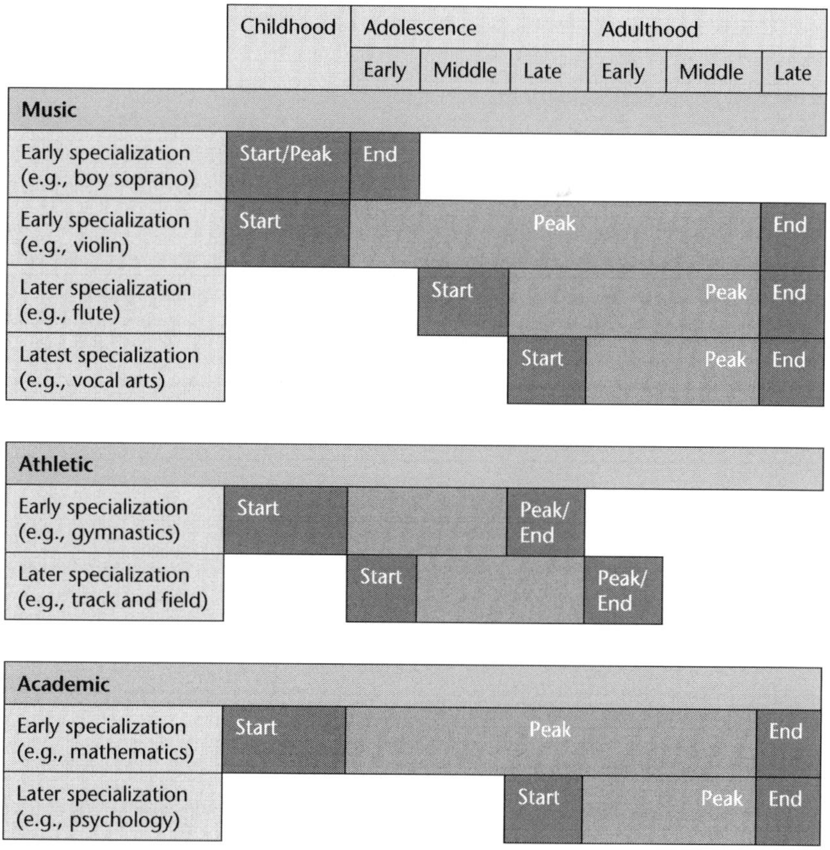

	Childhood	Adolescence			Adulthood		
		Early	Middle	Late	Early	Middle	Late
Music							
Early specialization (e.g., boy soprano)	Start/Peak	End					
Early specialization (e.g., violin)	Start		Peak				End
Later specialization (e.g., flute)			Start			Peak	End
Latest specialization (e.g., vocal arts)				Start		Peak	End
Athletic							
Early specialization (e.g., gymnastics)	Start			Peak/End			
Later specialization (e.g., track and field)		Start			Peak/End		
Academic							
Early specialization (e.g., mathematics)	Start		Peak				End
Later specialization (e.g., psychology)				Start		Peak	End

FIGURE 25.1 Trajectories vary by and with subfields of a domain.

The Role of Opportunity Both Given and Taken

In our mega model, we emphasize that opportunity to engage in a domain is critical to the further development and automatization of domain-specific abilities, and that it fuels motivation. These opportunities can come in the form of school-based programs, outside of school programs, or informal, independent activities at home. Domains differ in the extent to which these opportunities for talent development can be made available either through self-initiated, parent-supported activities, such as in drawing, or through direct parental actions to secure coaches and competitions, such as in chess. These differences account, in part, for why prodigies are found more in some domains than others. Historical accounts of eminent individuals in various domains typically include engagement and exposure via parents or family activities—that is, early access to opportunity. Of course, there has to be a "match" between opportunities and the propensities of the child in order for interest and involvement in the domain to continue.

Even when opportunities are offered, they must also be taken, and they must be of a certain type at each stage of talent development. For example, early experiences that are playful and enjoyable facilitate excitement and engagement. At the next stage of talent development, acquiring technique, basic skills, and competencies further fuels motivation and disciplined, deliberate practice. Opportunities to be immersed in the culture of the domain and to work on authentic problems with practicing professionals become important in developing from competence to the level of expertise in a domain. Many students lack the motivation to engage in deliberate practice or lack the psychosocial skills that gain them opportunities to do authentic work in real-world settings.

Several chapters illustrate the importance of opportunities. Many fields now have a surfeit of coaches and competitions that allow freedom and support to specialize early when passion and abilities meet, such as in drawing and chess. The performing arts (e.g., music) as well as sport fields and chess have well-defined benchmarks that guide talent development, demarcate progress, and indicate one's developmental stage and ranking in a domain. Such benchmarks do not exist in many academic fields, making it difficult to help students continue on talent development trajectories and successfully navigate critical stage transitions.

Psychosocial Skills

Psychosocial skills incorporate both mental skills and social skills. Mental skills are those that must be mastered in order to have optimal control over your emotions, thoughts, and experiences. Social skills are those that involve interactions with others, either directly in the creative process, or in the process of facilitating public awareness of one's work. Individuals vary in their psychosocial strengths, but all can be enhanced to some degree with training and intervention. Particularly at the highest level of creative productivity, these skills and abilities play an essential role. Think of withstanding harsh criticism when breaking with the status quo, or the courage to capitalize on chance opportunity.

The chapter by Bonneville-Roussy and Vallerand was devoted fully to the psychological dimension and, like our model, views psychosocial skills as the driver that supports the transition from one developmental stage to the next by cushioning the psyche from competition, isolation, and setbacks that are inevitable in creative and leadership arenas. The authors distinguish harmonious from obsessive passion. Clearly it is optimal to have a healthy and happy relationship with your work and thoughts, and, according to Csikszentmihalyi (1996), a more harmonious response to one's creative productivity leads to more enjoyment of one's accomplishments. We would argue, however, that the intensity of focus that often accompanies the creative process, at least as recorded biographically, can take a toll on relationships and health, and many great performances and creative products are driven by the rage to prove oneself in response to others' disparagement. (Ochse, 1990).

Expertise Vs. Eminence

Our definition of eminence (see Worrell, Subotnik, & Olszewski-Kubilius, in press) comes out of the mega model and, as noted previously, situates eminence as a stage beyond expertise. We contend that eminent is a label that should be reserved for the *gifted among the gifted* in individuals with fully developed talents. Earning this label requires that the individual has had a substantial domain-altering impact, whether the domain be tennis, music, physics, chess, or psychology. Thus, by definition, eminence is extremely rare. On the other hand, expertise can be acquired by a substantial number, even if a minority, of individuals in a domain.

Chi's (2006) distinction between relative and absolute experts, cited by Bonneville-Roussy and Vallerand (this volume) in their discussion of passion, is useful here. *Absolute* experts are considered authorities in their domains even by other experts and include only a few individuals, whereas *relative* experts take into account a person's ranking along the developmental trajectory from beginner to accomplished. Thus, we would contend that only absolute experts could be considered eminent in a field, although there may be many relative experts. Examples from real-world contexts are useful here. As this chapter is being written, it is the season of awards in the field of acting (i.e., the Golden Globes; the Oscars). Every year, a select group of actors, directors, and other producers and performers associated with television and film are nominated for awards. Some of them are first-time nominees, and some have many nominations and even wins behind them. All are relative experts, but only a select few are absolute experts or eminent. Similarly, tenured full professors in selective institutions are all relative experts but again, only a handful would be considered eminent. And this distinction can be applied to singing, basketball, chemistry, or any other performance or production domain.

Considerations and Questions

The chapters in this book raised many interesting and intriguing points for us to ponder from the perspective of our work in talent development and gifted education. We share below some questions that stand out for us and cut across various perspectives on expertise represented in the book. How much expertise is necessary? Is there a threshold of expertise for eminence or creative productivity and does this vary by domain?

Simonton's chapter (19, this volume) addresses the distinction between expertise and creativity in a domain, making the point that not all creators were the most expert in their fields, and some were far from fully expert. In our model, domain expertise is a necessary stage that precedes creative production in a domain, but that still begs the question of what level of expertise is needed for creative productivity and whether this level varies by domain. It seems, for example, that expertise in academic domains such as STEM fields is needed to generate elegant, creative solutions to problems. However, is the same level of expertise needed to pose the most important and critical questions to investigate? We know that a high proportion of individuals who win Nobel prizes in science were mentored by individuals who also won them (Zuckerman, 1977), but is this finding a result of expert knowledge or due to modeling and guidance towards identifying important questions and the most promising areas of research? New art forms do not appear to be a function of mastering all the previous techniques, which leaves us wondering, what is the nature of expertise in some domains?

In order to better understand what expertise means, more research is needed on what are the "drop dead" abilities and propensities needed to allow for eventual expertise and beyond. How do initially high levels of domain-specific abilities affect the honing and automaticity of skills and ability to capitalize on deliberate practice? Finally, which skills and states of mind play the most important roles at different points in the developmental process toward expertise and beyond?

We have operated under the assumption that psychosocial skills are malleable and, therefore, teachable, at the same time recognizing that people start off with different levels of developed skills in these areas. Two chapters address psychosocial phenomena, that is, *rage to master* and *openness to experience*, as critical to the development of expertise and creativity. These are typically viewed as innate traits, but an important question for researchers is to what extent these can be actively and deliberately cultivated in the service of helping individuals reach higher levels of creative productivity.

What if the source of one's drive is not altruistic but oppositional, or derived from rage—from disappointment, heartbreak, or disillusionment? Can we enhance the likelihood that the children and youth we work with establish a healthy relationship to their creative work? We would like to think that this is a worthy endeavor, but also fear that *privileging* intrinsically motivated or harmonious relationships with work as optimal may stigmatize those who create to assuage their pain or fears. We must acknowledge that unhealthy relationships with work have been conducive to productivity and creativity for some outstanding creators. Perhaps the question is not whether the relationship to one's work is harmonious or not, but to what degree it is motivated by negative rather than positive emotions and at what points in one's talent development trajectory.

Wanting to achieve to prove oneself to others with low expectations or to receive acclaim may not be harmful if coupled with other motives or if they are eventually taken over by enjoyment derived from true engagement with the major issues in the field. The role of teachers and parents may be to recognize the tremendous motivation required to reach expertise and eminence and help children achieve a more balanced motivational set over time. Research has tended to view intrinsic and extrinsic motivation as opposites when, in reality, most individuals are motivated by both types of rewards. Investigating the extreme levels of motivation required in getting to expertise and creativity in a domain would enable us to discern possible pressure points where interventions might be appropriate or not.

Conclusion

Many research questions are addressed in the field of gifted education and talent development. However, most of these are not focused either on expertise or eminence. The majority of research is on identifying individuals for gifted and talented education programs, especially individuals from groups that are underrepresented not just in K-12 settings, but also in undergraduate and graduate programs. Although clearly important, these studies deal with the beginning of the trajectory. The scholars in this book who study—for example, problem solving, deliberate practice, intelligence, creativity, and passion—will be viewed by many in the broader community of scholars in gifted education as fellow travelers, as they deal with moving individuals from potential and achievement to expertise. We also need to study which variables, beyond chance, can facilitate the movement from expertise to eminence.

References

Bloom, B. (Ed.). (1985). *Developing talent in young people.* New York, NY: Ballantine.
Chi, M. T. H. (2006). Two approaches to the study of experts' characteristics. In K. A. Ericsson, N. Charness, P. J. Feltovich, & R. R. Hoffman (Eds.), *The Cambridge*

handbook of expertise and expert performance (pp. 21–30). New York, NY: Cambridge University Press. doi:10.1017/CBO9780511816796.002

Csikszentmihalyi, M. (1996). *Creativity, flow and the psychology of discovery and invention.* NY: HarperCollins.

Ochse, R. (1990). *Before the gates of excellence: The determinants of creative genius.* New York, NY: Cambridge University Press.

Subotnik, R. F., Olszewski-Kubilius, P., & Worrell, F. (2011). Rethinking gifted education: A proposed direction forward based on psychological science. *Psychological Science in the Public Interest, 12,* 3–54. doi:10.1177/1529100611418056

Worrell, F. C., Subotnik, R. F., & Olszewski-Kubilius, P. (in press). Talent development: A path towards eminence. In S. Pfeiffer (Ed.), *APA handbook of giftedness and talent.* Washington, DC: American Psychological Association.

Zuckerman, H. (1977). *Scientific elite: Nobel laureates in the United States.* New York, NY: Free Press.

26

EXPERIENCE, SKILL ACQUISITION, AND DELIBERATE PRACTICE

Robert W. Proctor and Aiping Xiong

Introduction

The entry for *expert* in the *Online Eytomology Dictionary* (etymonline.com) includes:

> late 14c., "having had experience; skillful," from Old French *expert*, *espert* "experienced, practiced, skilled" and directly from Latin expertus (contracted from *experitus*), "tried, proved, known by experience," past participle of *experiri* "to try, test" (see experience).

Thus, at least as far back as the 14th century, *experience*, *practice*, and *skill* have been regarded as essential to expertise, and the meanings provided by the same dictionary for *experience* stress "knowledge gained by repeated trials" (also see Simonton, Chapter 19).

Given the meaning of *expert*, it is not too surprising that the most influential theoretical article on expertise in the past 25 years, "The Role of Deliberate Practice in the Acquisition of Expert Performance," by Ericsson, Krampe, and Tesch-Römer (1993), emphasized experience and skill acquisition. As noted by Macnamara *et al.* (Chapter 9), the tremendous impact of that article is documented by its extremely high citation rate (as of March 17, 2017, it had 2,231 entries in the Web of Science and 6,886 in Google Scholar). According to Macnamara *et al.* (Chapter 9), a likely reason for this popularity is that "it reinforces the idea that through hard work and determination, anyone can accomplish anything they set their mind to—an idea many people embrace" (p. 000). Although this may be the reason why it has been advocated in popular books (e.g., Colvin, 2008), a more fundamental reason for the article's influence in psychology seems to be that it captures the indispensable aspects of acquisition of expertise: Expert performance is a skill that is acquired, and deliberate practice plays a key role in acquiring such skill.

Skill Acquisition

Perhaps the most critical point of Ericsson *et al.*'s (1993) article is that expert performance should be viewed as an acquired skill. This fundamental point, which tends to be overlooked, is made early in the article, where the authors state that recent research has shown that "important characteristics of experts' superior performance are acquired through experience and that the effect of practice on performance is larger than earlier believed possible" (p. 363). In this book, seven of the first 23 chapters include the term *skill acquisition* or *skill development*, and only those by McAbee and Oswald (Chapter 2), Tucker-Drob (Chapter 14), and Erickson *et al.* (Chapter 23), give it significant discussion. Other chapters include treatment of skill acquisition without using the term, but in general there is a relative lack of consideration of it, which is an indication that its implications are not being thoroughly considered.

What are the implications of viewing expert performance as an acquired skill? One is that expertise is relative: There are different levels or stages along the acquisition process. What may be an appropriate level of expertise in one job or level of education may not be in another. In fact, different skill sets may be required at various levels, as witnessed by the numerous college athletes who do not transition effectively into being professional athletes (Wolfson, Addona, & Schmicker, 2011). Also, different levels of expertise are required within a team or group. Our proposition that expertise should be viewed along a continuum of skill is similar to that reached by Baker, Wattie, and Schorer (2015), who argue, "Movement away from these simple [expert-novice] comparisons would be useful for understanding the qualitative and quantitative changes that performers go through in their development from naïveté to expert" (p. 147). Likewise, Swann, Moran, and Piggott (2015) propose a taxonomy of sport expertise that distinguishes semi-elite, competitive elite, successful elite, and world-class elite athletes according to increasing level of accomplishment.

Skills can be trained, so the large literature on factors that influence skill acquisition, including the structure and duration of practice and training, becomes relevant (Healy & Bourne, 2012; Johnson & Proctor, 2017). An associated benefit is that experimental methods can be brought to bear on many issues in skill acquisition (Proctor & Vu, 2006). These include the following:

- How do task instructions influence the learner's "task set," or mental model, and how should they be framed to best promote skill acquisition (Gaschler, Frensch, Cohen, & Wenke, 2012)?
- How should practice sessions be scheduled and structured to support skill acquisition (Lundy, Carlson, & Paquiot, 1995)?

- What is the role of feedback, and when and how should it be provided (Nunes *et al.*, 2014)?
- Should attention be directed to the action goals (Wulf & Lewthwaite, 2016) or bodily movements (Toner & Moran, 2015)?
- What is necessary to retain, or maintain, a given level of skill (Ellington, Surface, Blume, & Wilson, 2015), and what practice conditions lead to transfer of skill (Proctor, Yamaguchi, & Miles, 2012)?
- What do computational models imply about changes in cognitive representations and processes that occur as skill acquisition progresses (Tenison & Anderson, 2016)?

A related issue from the skill acquisition perspective is this: Is there an endpoint to acquisition of expertise across the life span? The emphasis on life-long learning implies that there is always room for someone to become more skilled, or to extend their expertise into domains in which they were not previously experts. Merriam and Kee (2014) make an explicit statement to this effect: "Pre-retirement learning might also prepare retirees for contributing their acquired skills and expertise post retirement through volunteering, mentoring, and intergenerational programs" (p. 141). Learning new applications of one's expertise certainly involves acquisition of new skills. Thus, there are multiple aspects to attain for expertise within a specific domain. Beyond the individual level, describing expertise as acquired skills is also consistent with the changing levels of performance in different historical eras due to improvements in training methods and techniques (e.g., from 1913 to 1999, the world-record time for the men's one-mile race decreased from 4:14.4 min to 3:43.13 min; https://en.wikipedia.org/wiki/Mile_run_world_record_progression).

We end this section by pointing out that we agree with the recommendation of McAbee and Oswald (Chapter 2) with regard to fundamental methodological issues for research on expertise: "Researchers must continue their investigation of skill acquisition broadly, going beyond the experts themselves" (p. 27).

Deliberate Practice

Ericsson *et al.*'s (1993) specific focus was on the central role of *deliberate practice* in acquisition of expert performance. Their abstract makes this point, stating:

> In most domains of expertise, individuals begin in their childhood a regimen of effortful activities (deliberate practice) designed to optimize improvement. Individual differences, even among elite performers, are closely related to assessed amounts of deliberate practice. Many characteristics once believed to reflect innate talent are actually the result of intense practice extended for a minimum of 10 years. (p. 363).

Ericsson and colleagues have conducted systematic research focusing on deliberate practice in the ensuing years, and essentially all authors of chapters in this book—even those who think that other factors are important—acknowledge the crucial role played by deliberate practice.

To evaluate Ericsson *et al.*'s (1993) deliberate practice framework, one needs to be able to identify and accurately measure deliberate practice. Ericsson *et al.* included a page-long section titled "Characteristics of Deliberate Practice," but the term does not appear until the final sentence. In the section, they state:

> When laboratory training is extended over longer time periods, studies show that providing a motivated individual with repeated exposure to a task does not ensure that the highest levels of performance will be attained. Assessment of subjects' methods shows that inadequate strategies often account for the lack of improvement. (p. 367)

This sentence conveys that amount of practice *per se* cannot be equated with amount of deliberate practice. (A similar point was made in an earlier section of their article—titled "Does Practice and Experience Inevitably Lead to Maximal Performance?"—to which the answer was "no.")

Ericsson *et al.* (1993) go on to stress that participants who try out new strategies or methods show great improvements in performance, whereas those who do not make this effort show little improvement. This characterization seems to fit the definition in their abstract of "a regimen of effortful activities." It is also in agreement with Chamberlain's conclusion in Chapter 8: "The uptake of strategies for practice, rather than cumulative time spent practicing, has been shown to be a prominent predicting factor in expertise development in the domains of music . . . and chess . . ., and artistic expertise is no exception" (p. 140). Whereas she views this assessment as counter to the deliberate practice framework, we see it as in agreement with the gist of deliberate practice.

After their relatively clear exposition of deliberate practice described above, Ericsson *et al.* (1993) then say, "To assure effective learning, subjects ideally should be given explicit instructions about the best method and be supervised by a teacher to allow individualized diagnosis of errors, informative feedback, and remedial part training" (p. 367), and the remainder of the section emphasizes instruction. The section ends with this statement:

> The teacher designs practice activities that the individual can engage in between meetings with the teacher. We call these practice activities *deliberate practice* and distinguish them from other activities, such as playful interaction, paid work, and observation of others, that individuals can pursue in the domain. (p. 368)

Thus, although the term seems to entail effortful, active engagement in the learning process, the last sentence implies that deliberate practice can occur only

through activities provided by an instructor. This discrepancy, which is mentioned by Macnamara *et al.* (Chapter 9) in their critique of the deliberate practice
framework, is a source of confusion. From our perspective, the more fundamental
idea is *what* processing the person engages in when practicing and not *who* brought
about that processing. This seems to be Macnamara *et al.*'s understanding as well.

Issues in Assessing Deliberate Practice

Perhaps the most important point to note about deliberate practice is that
it cannot be assessed directly. Consequently, Ericsson *et al.* (1993) made the
"monotonic benefits assumption" for their research, which assumes that "the
amount of time an individual is engaged in deliberate practice activities is
monotonically related to that individual's acquired performance" (p. 368). But
amount of time is only a correlated measure because the quality of the practice
is an essential part of deliberate practice. We know from the extensive research
on practice schedules in the area of motor learning that different schedules can
result in very different amounts of learning (Schmidt & Lee, 2011). If one person is engaging in higher quality deliberate practice than another, this difference
will not be reflected in the amount of practice measure. Thus, a low correlation
of amount of practice with level of expertise cannot be taken as evidence that
deliberate practice is only a minor contributor to expert performance.

Other questions that arise when attempting to assess deliberate practice include
the following: When does deliberate practice begin? Should deliberate play, as
highlighted by Erickson *et al.* (Chapter 23), count? Or should it be considered a
precursor that sets the stage for deliberate practice? Is there a critical period during
which deliberate practice is most beneficial? The violinist Midori Goto, who played
with the New York Philharmonic at age 11 years, emphasized in an interview
that her mother was her best teacher: "Midori's mother, Setsu Goto, was her first
teacher, when she began playing as a toddler in Osaka, Japan" (Niles, 2014). Was
this early training responsible for Midori developing into a world-class violinist?
Does performance in a concert or game count as deliberate practice? Ericsson *et al.*
(1993) seem to exclude that, but, certainly, musicians constantly critique their performances with the goal of improving their playing and increasing their expertise.

What Initiates and Maintains (Motivates) Deliberate Practice?

Ericsson *et al.* (1993) emphasized that deliberate practice is effortful and "not
inherently enjoyable" (p. 368). So what maintains deliberate practice? There has
not been a lot of consideration of this issue. One possibility proposed for child
prodigies is that they have an innate predisposition to engage in a narrow range of
activities (e.g., Ruthsatz, Stephens, and Matthews, Chapter 6). However, for most
persons, the motivation is thought to come about from a drive, which has been
described by several terms that are similar but which have distinct implications.

A theme that appears throughout the book, with particular emphasis in Bonneville-Roussy and Vallerand's Chapter 22, is that of *passion*, which emphasizes emotion. Yet, passion seems to miss the mark. One certainly can be passionate about a topic or area but not engage in the amount of effortful deliberate practice required to become an expert. Alternatively, one may engage in deliberate practice for other reasons. The word "engage" in the prior sentences suggests that *engagement* is a critical factor, as Erickson *et al.* (Chapter 23) stress. This term conveys the emotional aspect of passion, but adds the concepts of *involvement* and *commitment*, both of which seem to be essential components of deliberate practice. Commitment includes a state of being *obligated*, which again seems to capture a key feature of deliberate practice.

Ericsson *et al.* (1993) mentioned that deliberate practice has the goal of improving performance, but goals can play significant other roles in acquisition of expertise. *Meaning in life* is a topic of interest in psychology that seems to fit the goals of experts. Martela (2016) distinguishes three components: *coherence*, or a sense of comprehensibility; *purpose*, or a sense of core goals and direction; and *significance*, a sense of having a life worth living. Meaning often seems to be a goal that drives experts. It is evident in Midori's community outreach activities: These include "Midori and Friends" and "Music Sharing" foundations that bring music education to K-12 students in New York City and Japan, and her "Partners in Performance" and "International Community Engagement" programs that bring music to small towns in the U.S. and schools in Cambodia, Indonesia, and Mongolia. It is also evident in cellist Yo Yo Ma's Silk Road Project, which brings together musicians from several countries with the goal of advancing global understanding through the arts. Thus, bearing the goal of improving performance in mind affords an adaptive acquisition progress which makes the acquired expertise multi-faceted. With regard to *purpose*, the Merriam-Webster dictionary defines it as "something set up as an object or end to be attained: intention." This definition implies an overriding goal or imperative, which links into the role of intention in action control (Hommel, Brown, & Nattkemper, 2016), which is currently a major topic of research in human performance.

Regardless of how one conceives the motivational aspect of deliberate practice, viewing expert performance as a skill allows one to incorporate research on motivational factors in skill acquisition. For example, Wulf and Lewthwaite (2016) presented evidence that skill acquisition is improved when conditions enhance expectancies for future performance success and influence the sense of agency or autonomy, both of which strengthen the combination of goal and actions.

Conclusion

Expert performance is first and foremost a high-level skill that is acquired through extensive experience. This is true regardless of the position that one takes regarding innate abilities, genetic determinants, developmental factors, and so on. One simply does not become an expert without acquiring skill through experience in the particular domain. What is the best way to characterize the experience that is necessary to achieve a high level of skill, or expertise? Deliberate practice in the broad sense of effortful engagement with an intent to improve performance seems to be an intuitively accurate way to describe the type of experience that is needed. The precise definition of deliberate practice is indeed vague, and the lack of specificity for what exactly constitutes deliberate practice and how much of it in which a person has engaged renders the view essentially irrefutable, as Macnamara *et al.* (Chapter 9) argue. Does that make the view of little value in the study of acquisition of expertise? We think that it does not because the view provides a framework for generating and testing hypotheses about specific aspects of expertise and its acquisition, much as the theory of event coding (Hommel, Müsseler, Aschersleben, & Prinz, 2001) is an untestable framework for studying perception-action relations that has been productive as a source of insightful, creative research.

In closing, we note the similarity of Ericsson *et al.*'s (1993) deliberate practice framework for acquisition of expertise to Craik and Lockhart's (1972) highly influential levels-of-processing framework for human memory. Both emphasize a fundamental insight into learning and memory: The processing that is performed when engaged in a task determines what will be learned and retained. Craik noted in 2002, "As I see it now, one of the main contributions of the levels-of-processing (LOP) article was to reinforce the idea of remembering as processing" (p. 306). Craik also points out, "The concept of depth of processing is not hard to grasp — 'deeper' refers to the analysis of meaning, inference, and implication, in contrast to 'shallow' analyses such as surface form, colour, loudness, and brightness" (p. 308). But, he precedes this point with, "One major criticism of the LOP framework is the absence of an objective index of depth of processing. Lacking such an index, it is all too easy to claim that any well-remembered event must therefore have been deeply processed" (p. 308). These quotes apply equally well to the concept of deliberate practice. It intuitively makes sense and seems to capture the crucial aspect of practice and training that underlies acquisition of expertise, but the lack of precise index makes it untestable.

Recently, Craik (2016) reiterated many of the points from his 2002 article in a chapter intended for a more general readership. His chapter was one of a hundred included in *Scientists Making a Difference: One Hundred Eminent Behavioral and Brain Scientists Talk about their Most Important Contributions*, which featured what the editors described as the most eminent psychologists of the modern era. Craik and Lockhart's (1972) article is rightly considered to be a classic, despite the acknowledged limitations of the LOP approach. We think that the contribution of Ericsson *et al.*'s (1993) article is equally meritorious, despite the comparable limitations of the deliberate-practice approach, and that it should be accorded similar respect.

References

Baker, J., Wattie, N., & Schorer, J. (2015). Defining expertise: A taxonomy for researchers in skill acquisition and expertise. In J. Baker & D. Farrow (Eds.), *Routledge handbook of sport expertise* (pp. 145–155). New York: Routledge.

Colvin, G. (2008). *Talent is overrated: What really separates world-class performers from everybody else*. New York: Penguin Group.

Craik, F. M. (2002). Levels of processing: Past, present … and future? *Memory, 10*, 305–318.

Craik, F. I. M. (2016). Levels of processing in human memory. In R. J. Sternberg, S. T. Fiske, D. J. Foss (Eds.), *Scientists making a difference: One hundred eminent behavioral and brain scientists talk about their most important contributions* (pp. 128–131). New York: Cambridge University Press.

Craik, F. I. M., & Lockhart, R. S. (1972). Levels of processing: A framework for memory research. *Journal of Verbal Learning & Verbal Behavior, 11*, 671–684.

Ellington, J. K., Surface, E. A., Blume, B. D., & Wilson, M. A. (2015). Foreign language training transfer: Individual and contextual predictors of skill maintenance and generalization. *Military Psychology, 27*, 36–51.

Ericsson, K. A., Krampe, R. T., & Tesch-Römer, C. (1993). The role of deliberate practice in the acquisition of expert performance. *Psychological Review, 100*, 363–406.

Gaschler, R., Frensch, P. A., Cohen, A., & Wenke, D. (2012). Implicit sequence learning based on instructed task set. *Journal of Experimental Psychology: Learning, Memory, and Cognition, 38*, 1389–1407.

Healy, A. F., &. Bourne, L. E., Jr. (Eds.) (2012). *Training cognition: Optimizing efficiency, durability, and generalizability*. New York: Psychology Press.

Hommel, B., Brown, S. B. R. E., & Nattkemper, D. (2016). *Human action control: From intentions to movements*. Cham, Switzerland: Springer International Publishing.

Hommel, B., Müsseler, J., Aschersleben, G., & Prinz, W. (2001). Codes and their vicissitudes. *Behavioral and Brain Sciences, 24*, 910–926.

Johnson, A., & Proctor, R. W. (2017). *Skill acquisition and training: Achieving expertise in simple and complex tasks*. New York: Routledge.

Lundy, D. H., Carlson, R. A., & Paquiot, J. (1995). Acquisition of rule-application skills: Practice schedules, rule types, and working memory. *American Journal of Psychology, 108*, 471–497.

Martela, F. (2016). The three meanings of meaning in life: Distinguishing coherence, purpose, and significance. *Journal of Positive Psychology, 11*, 531–545.

Merriam, S. B., & Kee, Y. (2014). Promoting community wellbeing: The case for lifelong learning for older adults. *Adult Education Quarterly, 64*, 128–144.

Niles, L. (2014). Violinist.com Interview with Midori, Part 2: Teaching. *Violinist.com.* http://www.violinist.com/blog/laurie/20141/15452/

Nunes, M. S., Souza, M. X., Basso, L., Monteiro, C. M., Corrêa, U. C., & Santos, S. (2014). Frequency of provision of knowledge of performance on skill acquisition in older persons. *Frontiers in Psychology, 5*, 1–7.

Proctor, R. W., & Vu, K.-P. L. (2006). Laboratory studies of training, skill acquisition, and retention of performance. In K. A. Ericsson, N. Charness, P. J. Feltovich, & R. R. Hoffman (Eds.), *Cambridge handbook of expertise and expert performance* (pp. 265–286). Cambridge, UK: Cambridge University Press.

Proctor, R. W., Yamaguchi, M., & Miles, J. D. (2012). Acquisition and transfer of basic skill components. In A. F. Healy & L. J. Bourne, Jr. (Eds.), *Training cognition: Optimizing efficiency, durability, and generalizability* (pp. 89–111). New York: Psychology Press.

Schmidt, R. A., & Lee, T. D. (2011). *Motor control and learning: A behavioral emphasis* (5th ed.). Champaign, IL: Human Kinetics.

Swann, C., Moran, A., & Piggott, D. (2015). Defining elite athletes: Issues in the study of expert performance in sport psychology. *Psychology of Sport and Exercise, 16,* 3–14.

Tenison, C., & Anderson, J. R. (2016). Modeling the distinct phases of skill acquisition. *Journal of Experimental Psychology: Learning, Memory, and Cognition, 42,* 749–767.

Toner, J., & Moran, A. (2015). Enhancing performance proficiency at the expert level: Considering the role of 'somaesthetic awareness'. *Psychology of Sport and Exercise, 16,* 110–117.

Wolfson, J., Addona, V., & Schmicker, R. H. (2011). The quarterback prediction problem: Forecasting the performance of college quarterbacks selected in the NFL draft. *Journal of Quantitative Analysis in Sports, 7*(3), 12. https://doi.org/10.2202/1559-0410.1302

Wulf, G., & Lewthwaite, R. (2016). Optimizing performance through intrinsic motivation and attention for learning: The OPTIMAL theory of motor learning. *Psychonomic Bulletin & Review, 23,* 1382–1414.

27

SCIENTIFIC METHODOLOGY AND EXPERTISE STUDIES

Massaging the Scar Tissue

Robert R. Hoffman

Introduction

I present some comments stimulated by the chapters in this volume and my own observations of the field of expertise studies. While I chastise researchers, I also commend them. My points all involve issues of measurement, both measurement of expertise and measurement of performance.

Defining Expertise

Over the decades since my first work on expertise (Hoffman, 1985), I have seen no reason to depart from or modify definitions that are presented in Table 27.1. The only modification I would be tempted to make is to more explicitly assert that experts are adaptive. Notions of adaptivity and resilience have become common parlance (cf. Hollnagel, Woods, & Leveson, 2006), and the concept of "adaptive expertise" has been discussed (Hatano & Inagaki, 1986). I've always taken it for granted that experts are by definition adaptive, as in the phrase "can effectively deal with rare and tough cases."

My main reason for re-presenting this here is to emphasize the point that expertise cannot be fully understood without also understanding the levels of proficiency that lead to it and wrap it. In the in-depth proficiency scaling I have done, especially in weather forecasting (see Hoffman *et al.*, 2017), I have found it necessary also to distinguish sub-levels: junior apprentice, apprentice, senior apprentice, and so forth up the scale.

The definitions given in Table 27.1 are conceptual. They need to be linked to one or more operational definitions that describe, to whatever level of detail is required, precisely how to go about the act of measurement—determining that an individual can be placed into one or another of the categories.

TABLE 27.1 Definitions of proficiency levels (adapted from Hoffman, 1998).

Naïve	One who is ignorant of a domain.
Novice	One who is new—a probationary member. There has been some ("minimal") exposure to the domain.
Initiate	One who has been through an initiation ceremony—a novice who has begun introductory instruction.
Apprentice	One who is beyond the introductory level. Traditionally, the apprentice is immersed in the domain by living with and assisting someone at a higher level. The length of an apprenticeship depends on the domain, ranging from about 1 to 12 years in the craft guilds.
Journeyman	One who can perform a day's labor unsupervised, although working under orders. An experienced and reliable worker, or one who has achieved a level of competence. It is possible to remain at this level for life.
Expert	The distinguished or brilliant journeyman, highly regarded by peers, whose judgments are uncommonly accurate and reliable, whose performance shows consummate skill and economy of effort, and who can deal effectively with rare or "tough" cases. Also, an expert is one who has special skills or knowledge derived from extensive experience with subdomains.
Master	Traditionally, a master is any journeyman or expert who is also qualified to teach those at a lower level. A master is one of an elite group of experts whose judgments set the regulations, standards, or ideals. Also, a master can be that expert who is regarded by the other experts as being "the" expert, or the "real" expert, especially with regard to subdomain knowledge.

In short, it is crucial that any evidence-based claim or argument made about the qualities of experts be accompanied by convincing empirical evidence that the individuals who are called experts are, in fact, experts. One of the most frustrating things I see in the vast literatures on cognition in which reference is made to studies of experts is that nearly always there is no convincing evidence. Quite the contrary—we are told only that "The participants were experienced at . . ." and all this really means is that they had been on the job for two years. Or we see that the "experts" were graduate students, believed to qualify as experts only because they are compared to freshmen, who are indubitably not experts. Worse still, it is nearly always assumed that the entire population of the planet can be neatly divided into just the two categories, of novice and expert. The so-called novices are typically not really novices. More often they are initiates or junior apprentices. Rarely does the paper cross my desk in which claims made about experts are wrapped in convincing evidence that the individuals referred to are, in fact, experts.

Now, back to the matter of operational definitions. I have always argued for a multi-measure approach. I have referred to "three legs of a tripod": performance analysis, career analysis, and sociometric analysis. For some situations, it is difficult to impossible to obtain evidence of one of the three types. Thus, I advocate for developing proficiency scales based on at least two of the three legs. What are the kinds of situations where one cannot utilize all three scaling approaches? There are domains in which there are only a few "experts." There are domains where it is hard to see how performance could properly be anchored to just one single task. There are domains where the ostensive primary task is not, in fact, the task at which the individuals manifest their expertise. In all such situations it is non-obvious how to form performance baselines, and thereby determine when performance is "superior." Hence, one can rely on career analysis and sociometry. And regarding career analysis, the popularized "ten-year rule" is obviously both superficial and misleading. Career analysis must go into great depth (see Hoffman *et al.*, 2017). Furthermore, when results of one method dovetail with results from another, the convergence of evidence is especially compelling (e.g., individuals having more experience also had more different kinds of experience, and also showed better performance on their primary tasks).

The bottom-line is that the field of Expertise Studies, as a scientific endeavor, is at risk of self-destructing unless researchers gets clear and consistent on these matters of terminology and proficiency scaling.

Issues of Statistics and Data Analysis

Many younger scientists unknowingly suffer from statistics propaganda. The "normal" curve is actually quite rare (Hoffman *et al.*, 2009a, 2009b). (As cases in point, see Figure 4.10 in Chapter 4, An Investigation of Problem-solving Expertise, and see Figure 9.2 in Chapter 9, The Deliberate Practice View: Inconsistent Definitions, Controversial Claims, and Empirical Evidence, which is a good example of what one expects in time or trials to criterion learning curves, that is, an approximate negative binomial.) Means are often not the best measure of central tendency. And since the mean is not a best measure of central tendency, the variance is not a good measure of variability. Hence, standard methods of parametric statistical testing (t-tests, F-ratios, etc.) and methods for determining power and sample size are all suspect. Medians, modes, and ranges are often more informative in the assessment of performance data and learning curves. Yet because grant sponsors expect parametric testing, researchers conduct it. Statistics should be understood as an exploratory toolset. Instead it is treated as an algorithmic substitute for judgment and decision making.

The sample size issue is raised in a number of chapters in this volume. One can scour books on experimental design and statistics and not find many useful discussions of the sample size question. In some statistics texts, the topic of sample size is not directly taken up at all. The reasoning that characterizes parametric statistical testing (rejects a hypothesis about a population based on results from sample) leaves one with no real sense of how many participants, generally, actually should be involved in a given psychological/cognitive experiment. Keppel (1973) put it this way: "The question concerning the number of subjects required is usually unanswerable, for the simple reason that many factors influence the answer and some of these factors are unknown" (p.12). Go figure.

Expertise research aimed at generating knowledge bases and cognitive task analyses have looked at the "diminishing return" as sample size increases (Chao & Salvendy, 1994; Crispen, 2010; Hoffman *et al.*, 2006). A handful of experts will get you most of what you need to know, and with each additional expert you involve, you gain less and less information. Thus, I proposed the "3+2 Rule":

Step 1. Conduct the knowledge elicitation or task decomposition with three individuals who have been empirically demonstrated to qualify as genuine experts.

Step 2. Successively apply a reliable and meaningful measure of the yield. A yield measure might be number of procedural rules, or number of propositions, for example. Judge whether the successive elicitations seem on track to reach a marginal utility of about 10 percent.

Step 3. If the marginal utility for the third participant does not hit the 10 percent mark, conduct the procedure with one more expert.

Step 4. If the marginal utility for the fourth participant does not hit the 10 percent mark, conduct the procedure with one more expert and then STOP.

The 3+2 Rule applies to situations where (1) the group of interest is small to begin with and access to experts is limited by inescapable practical constraints, (2) the goal is to make limited generalizations (i.e., only to experts in some particular specialty area) and not estimate a parameter of some broader population, and (3) the goal is to evaluate *practical* significance and not statistical significance (as this concept is usually understood).

Practical significance is another methodological concept that is mentioned in chapters in this volume. In the study of expertise especially, statistical significance with regard to group averages is intrinsically insufficient: After all, one can obtain a statistically significant improvement in the average performance of a group because of the superior performance of a small number of outliers while a majority of the participants might actually perform worse than they had before the experimental intervention (Hoffman *et al.*, 2009a, 2009b). The conclusions deriving from parametric tests are about aggregations (e.g., group means) and the differences that are obtained do not necessarily generalize to all the individuals. Indeed, in the study of proficiency the "outliers" are not aberrations that would cloud the statistical analysis. The best performances show what is humanly possible, and the worst performers point you to what may be either a selection issue or training issue. You want to find, and then drill-down on the outliers.

The concept of practical significance has actually been around for a while, and pops up in diverse literatures on occasion (e.g., Boring, 1919; Hodges & Lehman, 1954; Kirk, 1996). Unfortunately no one has really pegged it down in any rigorous mathematical way. But this is actually fortunate, since Expertise Studies would be a perfect venue for exploring the concept, refining, and specifying it.

Epistemic Priority

The controlled laboratory is premised on the assumptions that (1) if what are presumed to be the important causal factors, as represented by variables, are manipulated and (2) if all "causal factors" other than the manipulated ones can be prevented from having an influence (i.e., control), that then and only then can one reach conclusions about causal hypotheses. The controlled academic laboratory does not have scientific priority—the "real world" does (Hoffman, 2010; Schraagen, Klein, & Hoffman, 2008). Naturalistic inquiry is what drives the laboratory work. But further than this, we can and often do "bring the lab into the world" by controlling and manipulating variables in research conducted in the field setting (Hoffman & Deffenbacher, 2011; Hoffman et al., 2006). A cognitive task analysis procedure conducted in a conference room at a work-place is not essentially different from doing the same in an academic lab. It is certainly as possible to emphasize ecological validity and representativeness in laboratory research as it is beyond the forbidding walls. Indeed, psychologists have been champions of this notion for decades (e.g., Gibson, 1979).

There is a long tradition of control and manipulation of variables in experiments conducted in work settings and a long tradition of naturalistic approaches as a key contributor to the overall scientific enterprise. The phrases "work setting" and "operational context" are far better than the phrase "real world," which tacitly prioritizes the academic laboratory.

"Objective" Measurement

Epistemic priority is often granted to so-called "objective" measures. The dis-tinction between objective and subjective measures was obliterated in philosophy of science decades ago, yet belief in its Everlasting Validity persists, another con-sequence of how graduate students get propagandized. All measures have both "subjective" and "objective" aspects. Let one example suffice: The hardness of a substance. This is Real physics. There are many ways of measuring it: you can try and stretch it, bend it, drop something on it, and so forth. It is not entirely clear that each of the measurement methods really gets at the same thing. Choice of a measure depends on two things: the purpose for which the material is to be used and the knowledge, skill, and judgment of the metrologist. "All measurement is subjective in that human acts and judgments are involved in every step of the process of measurement" (Muckler, 1977, p. 169; see also Collins, 1992). Conversely, even so-called subjective measures have an objective aspect.

Behavioral methodolatry has persisted since Knight Dunlap, John Watson, and others proposed the "behavioral attitude"—the exclusive reliance on objective measures—as psychology's claim to genuine science. Naïve objectivism devalues the theoretical utility and explanatory value of subjective reports by assuming, for instance, that just because verbal reports are not always valid or reliable, we should therefore throw out both the baby and the bathwater and never bother to ask our participants any questions at all about what they believe or what they experienced while reasoning their way through our experiments.

All too often, rants are offered that one or another measure does not work well, and that must be because it is subjective. So rather than asking people questions, we measure eye movements (for example) on the assumption that what people are gazing at tells us what they are paying attention to (or what they are thinking). Really?

While rejecting verbal reports, introspections, retrospections, or task reflection, researchers rarely say in their Results section that they actually bothered to ask their participants any questions about what they thought during the experiment. The irony is that psychologists themselves almost always explain their results by reference to their own intuitions, reflections, and speculations on the task and what is going on in the heads of the participants. In applied perception research, for example, one is hard pressed to find a single hypothesis or theory about some phenomenon (e.g., attention) that was not derived from the task reflections of the experimenters, couched using metaphors such as mental effort, or the paying of attention, or focused attention, or the attentional bottleneck (Hoffman, Cochran, & Nead, 1990).

Graduate students (in cognitive sciences) are rarely informed about the considerable discussions in the first part of the twentieth century about crucial distinctions among introspection, task reflection, and systematic post-experimental retrospection. Rather, they are indoctrinated in a methodology that devalues human judgment and capacity for insight. Of all the psychological sciences, Expertise Studies should elevate and not devalue these.

The Mind–Body Problem

Attitudes about epistemic priority also manifest in discussions of neuropsychology. In recent times we have witnessed a great many programs of research that have involved neurophysiological measurement intended to link mental events to brain events. Some chapters in this book serve as examples. We absolutely need this research: Some of it is both interesting and informative. What we in Expertise Studies must rail against is the stance, often tacit but often present, that if you can link something to a bunch of neurons then that makes it objective and therefore "real" science. The degree to which today's scientists dance gleefully over the mind–body problem is nothing less than staggering. This epistemic goofiness is another consequence of failure to teach adequately the history and philosophy of science to our graduate students.

I temper my rant about unbridled enthusiasm for neuropsychology with an expression of a long-standing belief that perceptual learning is a "holy grail" of Expertise Studies. The phenomenon in which experts come to "see the invisible" is one of the things that drew me to the study of experts in the first place (see Klein & Hoffman, 1992). Neurophysiological studies have great potential for helping us understand how people can learn to perceive concepts, that is, patterns that exist only across multiple dynamic data types (Hoffman & Fiore, 2007)

The Common Thread

What unites all my comments is this: Avoid methodolatry—the worship of particular methods. All measures are interpretations. A main purpose of making measurements is to improve the measures. All measures have both "subjective" and "objective" aspects. All methods are limited; all of them have strengths. *In Expertise Studies, of all sciences, we must get inside people's heads.* So do not throw the baby out with the bathwater. Do not treat theoretical terms as you would any empty jargon: All of our concepts must be considered mindfully, and none of them is sacred.

We also need to stop making terminological transgressions, such as by using the word "subjects" and the humiliating "SME" designation. I can rant about terminology because I have myself made some glorious errors. To confess just one, I referred to knowledge elicitation as "extraction," as if the knowledge of experts were ore to be mined (Hoffman, 1987). More accurately and honestly, knowledge elicitation is a co-discovery or even a co-creation process.

Opportunity and Obligation

As the field of Expertise Studies matured, it became clear that a significant opportunity and challenge was that of leveraging our scientific knowledge about the nature and development of expertise into methods for accelerating the achievement of high proficiency (Hoffman, Fiore *et al.*, 2009). This is, to be sure, one of the fundamental and long-standing topics for the field of Training and Instructional Design. Researchers in that area always have to grapple with the challenge of having to train more, and do so in less time. How might Expertise Studies contribute? Our understanding of performance and capabilities across the proficiency scale should map to scales developed in the training community. But more than that, ideas about how expertise is achieved should suggest methods for helping individuals achieve higher proficiency in less time. The notion of "case based time-compression," which would leverage methods of cognitive task analysis, has been proposed as one method (Hoffman *et al.*, 2010, 2014). A program to attempt acceleration would itself be costly and time consuming. We would hope that advocates for Expertise Studies would also advocate for funding and research programs that support the study of methods of acceleration.

Another crucial advocacy activity is to counter argue those pundits who question the very concept of expertise. One of the claims is that expertise is an elitist concept with no factual basis. Another is that so-called experts in some domains do not perform very well (e.g., economic forecasting, weather forecasting, etc.). Such claims are typically reductive, parochial, uninformed, and agenda-driven. All those who conduct expertise studies should be ever alert for manifestations of the negativist stance, and be prepared to counter argue, especially when those who take the negative stance lack scientific credibility (see Klein, Hoffman, & Shneiderman, forthcoming).

In reading the chapters of this book, and reflecting on them, I am most pleased that Expertise Studies as a field is rich and exciting, and is itself a co-discovery and co-creation process.

References

Boring, E. G. (1919). Mathematical versus scientific significance. *Psychological Bulletin, 16*, 335–338.

Chao, C. -J., & Salvendy, G. (1994). Percentage of procedural knowledge acquired as a function of the number of experts from whom knowledge is acquired for diagnosis, debugging and interpretation tasks. *International Journal of Human-Computer Interaction, 6*, 221–233.

Collins, H. M. (1992). *Changing order: Replication and induction in scientific practice*. Chicago: University of Chicago Press.

Crispen, P. D. (2010). Identifying the point of diminishing marginal utility for cognitive task analysis surgical subject matter expert interviews. Doctoral Dissertation, Rossier School of Education, University of Southern California.

Gibson, J. J. (1979). *The ecological approach to visual perception*. Boston, MA: Houghton-Mifflin.

Hatano, G., & Inagaki, K. (1986). Two courses of expertise. In H. Stevenson, J. Azuma & K. Hakuta (Eds.) *Child development and education in Japan* (pp. 262–272). New York, NY: W. H. Freeman & Co.

Hodges, J. L., & Lehman. E. L. (1954). Testing the approximate validity of statistical hypotheses. *Journal of the Royal Society, Series B (Methodological), 16*, 261–268.

Hoffman, R. R. (1987, Summer). The problem of extracting the knowledge of experts from the perspective of experimental psychology. *The AI Magazine, 8*, 53–67.

Hoffman, R. R. (Ed.) (1992). *The psychology of expertise: Cognitive research and empirical AI*. Mahwah, NJ: Erlbaum.

Hoffman, R. R. (1998). How can expertise be defined? Implications of research from cognitive psychology. In R. Williams, W. Faulkner, & J. Fleck (Eds.), *Exploring expertise* (pp. 81–100). New York: Macmillan.

Hoffman, R. R. (2010). Some challenges for macrocognitive measurement. In E. Patterson & J. Miller (Eds.), *Macrocognition metrics and scenarios: Design and evaluation for real-world teams* (pp. 11–28). London: Ashgate.

Hoffman, R. R., Andrews, D., Fiore, S. M., Goldberg, A. Andre, T., Freeman, J., & Klein, G. (2010). Accelerated learning: Prospects, issues and applications. In *Proceedings of the 54th Annual Meeting of the Human Factors and Ergonomics Society* (pp. 399–402). Santa Monica, CA: Human Factors and Ergonomics Society.

Hoffman, R. R., Cochran, E. L, & Nead, J. M. (1990). Cognitive metaphors in the history of experimental psychology. In D. Leary (Ed.), *Metaphors in the history of psychology* (pp. 173–209). Cambridge, UK: Cambridge University Press.

Hoffman, R. R., Coffey, J. W., Ford, K. M., & Novak, J. D. (2006). A method for eliciting, preserving, and sharing the knowledge of forecasters. *Weather and Forecasting, 21*, 416–428.

Hoffman, R. R., & Deffenbacher, K. A. (2011). A multidimensional analysis of the relations of basic and applied psychology. *Theoretical Issues in Ergonomic Science. 15*(4), 339–353. DOI: 10.1080/1464536X.2011.573013

Hoffman, R. R., & Fiore, S. M. (2007, May/June). Perceptual (re)learning: A leverage point for human-centered computing. *IEEE Intelligent Systems, 22*(3), pp. 79–83.

Hoffman, R. R., Fiore, S. M., Klein, G., Feltovich, P. J., & Ziebell, D. (2009, March/April). Accelerated learning (?). *IEEE: Intelligent Systems, 24*(2), pp. 18–22.

Hoffman, R. R., LaDue, D., Mogil, H. M., Roebber, P., & Trafton, J. G. (2017). *Minding the Weather: How Expert Forecasters Think*. Cambridge, MA: MIT Press.

Hoffman, R. R., Marx, M., Amin, R., & McDermott, P. L. (2009a). "How good is that new software tool? The mathematical modeling of performance metrics." In P. McDermott & L. Allender (Eds.), *Advanced decision architectures for the warfighter: Foundations and technology* (pp. 107–120). Boulder, CO: Partners of the Army Research Laboratory Advanced Decision Architectures Collaborative Alliance.

Hoffman, R. R., Marx, M., McDermott, P., & Amin, R. (2009b, October). The metrics problem in the study of cognitive work and a proposal for a family of solutions. In *Proceedings of the Annual Meeting of the Human Factors and Ergonomics Society* (pp. 324–328). Santa Monica, CA: Human Factors and Ergonomics Society.

Hoffman, R. R., Ward, P., DiBello, L., Feltovich, P. J., Fiore, S. M., & Andrews, D. (2014). *Accelerated expertise: Training for high proficiency in a complex world*. Boca Raton, FL: Taylor and Francis/CRC Press

Hollnagel, E., Woods, D. D., & Leveson, N. (Eds.) (2006). *Resilience engineering: Concepts and precepts*. Aldershot, UK: Ashgate.

Keppel, B. (1973). *Design and analysis: A researcher's handbook*. Englewood Cliffs, NJ: Prentice Hall.

Kirk, R. E. (1996). Practical significance: A concept whose time has come. *Educational and Psychological Measurement, 56*, 746–759.

Klein, G. A. & Hoffman, R. R. (1992). Seeing the invisible: Perceptual-cognitive aspects of expertise. In M. Rabinowitz (Ed.), *Cognitive science foundations of instruction*. (pp. 203–226). Mahwah, NJ: Erlbaum.

Klein, G., Shneiderman, B., & Hoffman, R. R. (forthcoming). The war on expertise. In P. Ward, J.-M. Schraagen, T. C. Ormerod, & E. Roth (Eds.). *The Oxford handbook of expertise*. Oxford: Oxford University Press.

Muckler, F. A. (1977). Selecting performance measures: "Objective" versus "subjective" measurement. In L.T. Pope & D. Meister (Eds.) *Symposium Proceedings: Productivity enhancement: Personnel performance assessment in Navy systems* (pp. 169–178). San Diego, CA: Navy Personnel Research and Development Center.

Schraagen, J. M., Klein, G., & Hoffman, R. (2008). The macrocognition framework of naturalistic decision making. In J. M. Schraagen, L. G. Militello, T. Ormerod, & R. Lipshitz (Eds.), *Naturalistic decision making and macrocognition* (pp. 3–25). Aldershot, England: Ashgate.

PLATE 1 Rubik's Cube in permuted state (left) and goal state (right). Figure 4.1 shows the structure-transforming operations the cube permits. The solver's task is to restore the cube to its original state. The problem can take 43 quintillion (4.3252×10^{19}) states, contributing to its difficulty; learning and retaining specific sequences of operators is obviously an intractable solution strategy, assuming that the solver can find solutions.

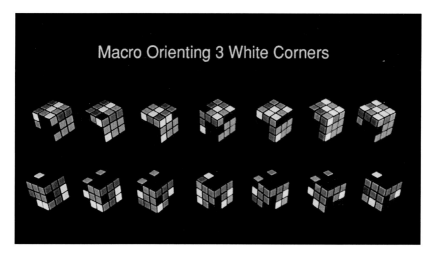

PLATE 2 Problem states produced by application of the expert's macro-operator for orienting three white corners. The top row shows the states seen from the expert's perspective while the operations are applied. The bottom row shows the effects of macro application on previously solved portions of the cube. Notice the temporary displacement of previously properly positioned and oriented cubies of the blue face, which is opposite the white face. Subgoal starting state is shown at the left and problem state upon subgoal completion shown at the right.

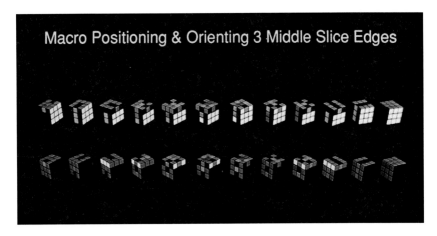

Macro Positioning & Orienting 3 Middle Slice Edges

PLATE 3 Effects of application of one of the macros that the expert uses to simultaneously position and orient three middle slice edge cubies upon the already solved white face (top row) and blue face (bottom row). Subgoal starting state is shown at the left and problem state upon subgoal completion shown at the right. This sequence is another example of how macro-operators temporarily disrupt previously achieved progress toward solution in the course of their application.

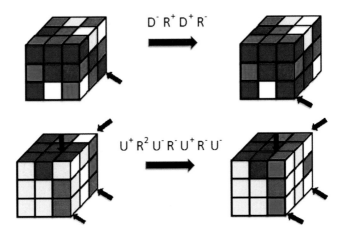

$$D^- R^+ D^+ R^-$$

$$U^+ R^2 U^- R^- U^+ R^- U^-$$

PLATE 4 Exemplars of two macro types. Single-cubie macros position and orient individual cubies. Multi-cubie macros either position or orient (or both) a group of cubies simultaneously. The top pair of cube configurations shows starting problem state (left) and finishing state (right) following application of a single-cubie macro that positions and orients an individual cubie on the blue face. The bottom pair shows the start or trigger state (left) for a multi-cubie macro that simultaneously re-orients four white corners that are already correctly positioned relative to one another, but not correctly oriented. The primitive operators of each macro are shown between the cubes.

Perceptual Chunks for Triggering Macros

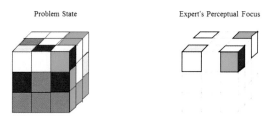

Problem State   Expert's Perceptual Focus

Trigger state for executing macro-operator for orienting White Corners

Trigger state for executing macro-operator for orienting Middle Slice Edges

PLATE 5 Local, abstract perceptual chunks trigger goal-specific macros. Illustrations on the left show the patterns as they appear on the complete cube. Cubies highlighted on the right show the subsets of cubies that define the trigger patterns, which are presumed to be the focus of the expert's attention and determine selection of the macros that will solve the current subgoals.

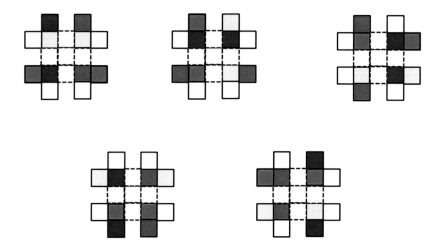

PLATE 6 2D "flattened" views of the cube's white face showing exemplars of abstract "Knight" pattern that triggers a macro that orients four white corner cubies (already in their correct relative positions).

PLATE 7 Non-representational painting by Arrian, age 2 yrs, 3 mths. Reprinted by permission of Rebecca Smith.

PLATE 8 Complex scene drawn on a place mat by Arkin Rai at age 5, and with part of image enlarged. Reprinted by permission of Dinesh Rai.

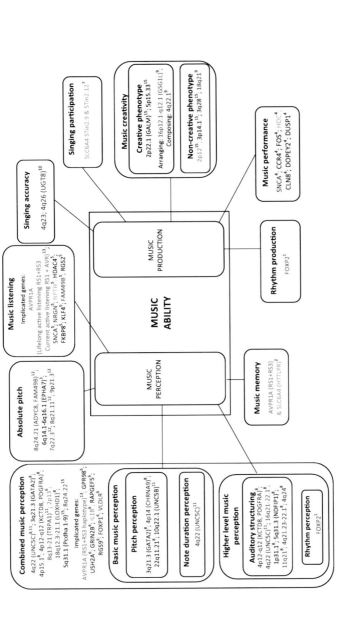

PLATE 9 A summary of possible genetic determinants of music ability and music-related traits. Genes or chromosomal loci that are in the vicinity of one another are represented in the same font colors. Potential candidate genes found at an implicated locus are enclosed in parentheses. [1] Alcock *et al.* (2000); [2] Granot *et al.* (2007); [3] Gregersen *et al.* (2013); [4] Kanduri, Kuusi, *et al.* (2015); [5] Kanduri, Raijas, *et al.* (2015); [6] Liu *et al.* (2016); [7] Morley *et al.* (2012); [8] Oikkonen *et al.* (2015); [9] Oikkonen *et al.* (2016); [10] Park *et al.* (2012); [11] Pulli *et al.* (2008); [12] Theusch *et al.* (2009); [13] Ukkola *et al.* (2009); [14] Ukkola-Vuoti *et al.* (2011); [15] Ukkola-Vuoti *et al.* (2013).

INDEX

ABA *see* Applied Behavioral Analysis
ability 5–6; ability threshold hypothesis 79, 81, 83n4; chess 19–20; Multifactorial Gene-Environment Interaction Model 367, 368; *see also* cognitive ability; natural abilities; talent
ABLE 356
abnormality xv, xvii
absolute expertise 377, 378, 431
absolute pitch (AP) 154–155, 225, 273, 276–278, 283, 284, 286, 290–292
academic expertise 429, 430, 431–432; *see also* educational achievement
achievement 309, 310, 311
Ackerman, P. L. 250, 370
acquired savant syndrome 93–94, 98
ACT-R 356
Action Control Theory 317, 325
action observation 221–222, 223, 226, 228–229, 230, 231
activity internalization 380–381, 382, 388–389
actors 431
adaptive expertise 444
Adelson, B. 419–420
aesthetic evaluation 131, 142–143
African cultures 296
age: chess players 31, 41, 42; mixed-age interactions in deliberate play 409; multifactorial models 5; surgeons 232
agent modeling 360
agreeableness 112, 141, 317

AI *see* artificial intelligence
Alain, C. 352
Allan, Veronica 398–415
AlphaGo 357
amateurs 160
amputees 229
Amunts, K. 224
amusia 273
analytical expertise 421, 422, 423, 424
Angoff, W. H. 310, 324
anxiety 266–267
Anzai, Y. 53, 57, 65
AP *see* absolute pitch
Applied Behavioral Analysis (ABA) 92
appropriate settings 407, 409–412, 412
aptitudes 309, 310, 311, 322
AQ *see* Autism Spectrum Quotient
Arden, R. 111
arginine vasopressin (AVP) 286, 288–289
Aristotle 2, 339
Arnheim, Rudolf 125n1
arousal 289
art 129–150; analytical expertise 422; creativity 423; drawing precocity 101–128; gray matter density 225–226; passion 376; perception and production 130–132, 142–143; practice strategies 438; prodigies 91, 94–96, 97, 98; right hemisphere 113; savants 88, 91, 94, 97, 113–115; *see also* drawing ability
artificial intelligence (AI) 49, 348

Asperger, Hans 88
Asperger's disorder 90
assertiveness 141
association analysis xvi, 277–278, 284–286, 288, 289, 295, 297
Aston, J. A. 176
Atkinson, J. W. 318
attention: attention switching 90; chess 31; double take of expertise 196; drawing expertise 132, 134, 135, 138, 143; flexible 134, 135, 137, 143; Multifactorial Gene-Environment Interaction Model 371; pattern recognition 191; perceptual expertise 208–209
attention to detail 89–90, 97, 109, 115
Au, T. K.-f. 131
Augustin, D. 131
autism: drawing ability 109, 114–115; perceptual expertise 208; prodigies compared with 87, 88, 89–94, 96–98; *see also* savants
Autism Spectrum Quotient (AQ) 90
automaticity 428, 432; neural efficiency 226–227, 230; problem solving 47, 63, 64, 69
autonomous stage 218–219
autonomy 380, 440; deliberate play 405, 412; support for 381–382, 384–386, 387, 388, 389, 392
AVP *see* arginine vasopressin
Awalé 359
awareness 308, 314, 317, 323
Aziz-Zadeh, L. 229

Bach, Johann Sebastian 3, 273
background factors 5–6
Baduk (Go) 182, 195, 357, 359, 419
Bahrami, P. 222
Baker, J. 403, 436
Balish, S. 412
Balser, N. 222, 228
Baluch, B. 159
Barenfeld, M. 353
Barnett, Jacob 92–93
Baron-Cohen, S. 90
basal ganglia 192–193, 220, 227
basketball 21–23, 177, 225, 334
Baylor, G. W. 352
Beamon, Bob 1
Beauchamp, M. H. 176
Beckmann, J. 317
behavioral approach xiv–xv, 6–7

behavioral genetics xv, 241, 262, 268, 420; "equal environments" 251n1; individual differences 254; innateness 321–322; methods 242; Multifactorial Gene-Environment Interaction Model 372; music expertise 283; quantitative genetic methodology 255–257; reading and math ability 253; univariate and multivariate models 266
Behrens, T. E. 177
Beilock, S. L. 267
Belleville, S. 114
Benbow, Camilla P. 74, 75, 76
Bengtsson, S. L. 177, 224–225
Bernardi, G. 225, 227
Bernoulli family 3
Berry, J. 402
Berstein, H. 158
Bertsch, C. 403
Bhaskar, R. 356
Big Five personality factors 141, 317, 343
Bilalić, Merim 7, 40, 182–199, 351
Binet, A. 36, 37
biological factors 308, 319–320, 321, 322, 326
birthplace effect 409–412
blind variation and selective retention (BVSR) 341–342
Block Design Task 109, 114
blood flow 172, 200
Bloom, B. S. 378, 383, 386, 387, 388–389, 428
Boden, M. A. 331
BOLD signal 172, 200, 207
Bon Jovi, Jon 376
Bonneville-Roussy, Arielle 7, 376–397, 420, 428, 431, 440
Boomsma, D. I. 276
Bouffard, T. 389–390
Bradshaw, G. L. 356
brain 171–181; absolute pitch 291; acquired savant syndrome 94; artists 130; functional reorganization 175, 178, 179, 226–230, 231, 367–368; left and right hemispheres 94, 110, 112, 113, 125n2, 189, 205–206, 208; motor expertise 219, 220–233; Multifactorial Gene-Environment Interaction Model 367–368; music ability 297; object recognition 186–189; "pathology of superiority" 113; pattern recognition 189–191; perceptual expertise 200–212; PPP model 41–42; problem

solving 191–195; reading and math ability 267; structural changes 175–178, 179, 195–196, 209–210, 220, 223–226, 231; see also neural approaches; neuro-imaging techniques; neuroplasticity
bridge 420
Bringolf-Isler, B. 409
Bronfenbrenner, U. 409
Brown, S. 297
Bruner, M. W. 405
Burgoyne, Alexander P. 40, 151–168
Burns, B. 35–36
Buschkuehl, M. 177
BVSR see blind variation and selective retention

"cafeteria of experience" 250, 251
Callan, D. E. 222, 226–227, 228–229
Calvo-Merino, B. 228
Cambridge Handbook on Expertise and Expert Performance 4
Campbell, D. T. 341
Campitelli, Guillermo 1–9, 419; chess expertise 7, 19, 31–46, 428; deliberate practice 5, 154; PPP model 351
Canal-Bruland, R. 221
Capio, C. 404
car expertise 202, 203, 204, 208, 211
career analysis 445–446
Carey, G. 275–276
Carlsen, Magnus 1, 31, 162, 372
Carlson, R. 409
Carson, J. A. 163
case based time-compression 450
categorization: levels of expertise 25–26; perceptual expertise 204–205
Cavanagh, P. 134
CEOs see chief executive officers
cerebellum 220, 222, 225–226, 227, 228, 230
Chamberlain, Rebecca 7, 129–150, 226, 428, 438
chance 318, 325, 342, 343
Charness, N.: chess 14–16, 41; chunking theory 354, 357–358; deliberate practice 158, 420; expert performance 160; hard work 107; self-teaching 102
Chase, W. G.: chess 3–4, 33, 36–37, 66, 419, 422; chunking theory 353; retrieval 67, 68; Skilled Memory Theory 66
Chassy, P. 357

chess 1, 3–4, 102, 419, 422; blindfold 36, 39, 44n3, 66; brain structure changes 195–196; chunking theory 353; classifying levels of expertise 26, 335; cognitive processes 31–46, 316; computational models 350, 351–352, 353–354, 356–357, 358–359; deliberate practice 5, 32, 116–117, 154, 162, 372; development of expertise 32; domain-specific abilities 428; emotional control 141–142; expert performance 160, 182–183; hours of study 14–16; intelligence 368, 370; IQ 140; mathematical modeling 351; number of experts 312–313; object recognition 184, 185, 187–188; pattern recognition 189–191, 428; perceptual expertise 205; Practice, Plasticity, and Processes model 40–43; practice strategies 140, 438; precocity 107; range enhancement 23–25; range restriction 18–20, 21; research 129; talent development 428–429, 430; template theory 357; training 369; transfer studies 39, 43
Chi, M. T. H. 49, 65, 377, 431
chief executive officers (CEOs) 73, 77–79, 80
Chiesi, H. L. 68
child development 250, 315, 321
childhood play 398–415
Chinese character writing 131–132
Chow, J. Y. 403
CHREST (Chunk Hierarchy and REtrieval STructures) model 34, 38, 347, 354, 355, 357–360
chromosomes 98, 274, 278, 284–287, 290–292, 294–295
chunking: automaticity 428; chess 33–34, 35, 37, 41–42, 43; CHREST model 358–359; computational models 352–355, 356; mathematical modeling 351; neural efficiency 176; problem solving 49, 53–55, 56, 57–62, 64–65, 68–69; Skilled Memory Theory 50, 66–67; template theory compared to chunking theory 357–358
classification 25–26
cognitive ability: chess 39, 40, 41, 42, 428; drawing 111, 142; genetic and environmental influences 266; giftedness 313; heritability 250, 323; intellectual precocity 321; math

performance 265, 266; Multifactorial Gene-Environment Interaction Model 254, 370; professional expertise 73–74, 75–83; *see also* intelligence
cognitive architectures 348, 356
cognitive disinhibition 343
cognitive processes 316, 347, 428; chess 31–46, 205; CHREST model 358; creativity 336; drawing expertise 130, 143; games 183–186, 196; gray matter density 225; problem solving 64–65, 69; stage theory of motor learning 218; *see also* information processing; memory; perception
Cohen, D. J. 135
Cokely, E. T. 162
Colvin, Geoff 5, 152
combinatorial creativity 336–337
commitment 440
communication 90
competence 380, 407–408, 412
competencies 308, 309, 311, 314, 319
complexity 182
compulsion to draw 106–108, 115
computational models 34, 38, 347–364, 437; chunking networks 352–355; connectionist 348, 350, 356–357; criticisms of 350; definitions 348; heuristic search 351–352; mathematical modeling 350–351; problem solving 55–57, 58–59, 60–62, 65, 68; production systems 355–356; strengths of 348–350
Conci, Anna 182–199
congenital amusia 273
connectionism 186, 348, 350, 356–357
connectivity analyses 231
Connors, M. 35–36
conscientiousness 139–140, 141, 317, 367
consensual creativity 329, 332–333, 338–339, 340–341
consensual expertise 334–335, 338–339, 340–341
consummate experts 424
Coon, H. 275–276
corpus callosum 224–225
correlation: correlation coefficients 14–16, 17, 18, 23, 27n1; genetics 243–244, 246, 265, 277–278; twin studies 275
Côté, Jean 7, 378, 383, 387, 389, 398–415
Craig, I. W. 320

Craik, F. I. M. 441
creative expertise 421, 423, 424, 425
creativity 83n4, 129, 328–346, 423, 432, 433; consensual 329, 332–333, 338–339, 340–341; definitions of 329, 331–332; deliberate play 404, 412–413; individual differences 140; "little-c" and "Big-C" 329; mentors 425; music 284, 289, 293–295; personal 329–332, 336–338, 339, 340–341; sport 403
Csikszentmihalyi, M. 309–310, 431
culture: drawing ability 102–103, 106; music 284, 296–297
Cupchik, G. C. 131, 134

Dagher, A. 176
dance 219, 225, 368, 370, 390
darts 158, 159
Darwin, Charles 3, 342
Davidson, J. W. 154
de Bruin, Anique B. H. 7, 158, 218–237
de Candolle, Alphonse Pyrame 3
de Groot, A. D. 3, 32–33, 34–35, 351, 354, 359
Deaner, R. O. 162
Debarnot, U. 177, 219, 227, 232
decision making: chess 31, 33, 205; computational models 357; games 192–195
default mode network 344n3
DeFries-Fulker (DF) analysis 262–263
DeFries, J. C. 246, 320
deliberate play 398–415, 439
deliberate practice 4, 101, 151–168, 231, 365–366, 420, 437–440, 441; chess 5, 19–20, 24–25, 32, 39–40, 42, 116–117, 428; classifying levels of expertise 26; debate about 360; definitions of 156–160; deliberate play and 398, 399, 401; Developmental Model of Sport Participation 399; drawing ability 107–108, 112; education 319; empirical tests 153–155; incidental range restriction 21–23; investment stage 388, 390; motor expertise 219; Multifactorial Gene-Environment Interaction Model 254, 367, 368, 369, 371; music 116, 274; neuroplasticity 224; passion 382, 390, 392; personality mediated by 141; popularization of the theory 140, 435–436; precocious realists 107; professional expertise

83; self-teaching 102; skew effects 27n2; Skilled Memory Theory 66; specialization stage 386–387, 388; talent development 316, 430; *see also* hard work; practice; training
delusions 132, 133–134
depression 294
D'Esposito, M. 176
Detterman, D. K. 89
development of expertise 377–378, 431; chess 32; deliberate play 407, 413; Developmental Model of Sport Participation 399; passion 383–392, 393, 428; *see also* talent development
Developmental Model for Natural Abilities (DMNA) 307, 308, 320–324, 325–326
Developmental Model of Sport Participation (DMSP) 399, 407
developmental processes 5–6, 308, 314, 316, 319, 324
Di Rienzo, F. 177, 219
Dickinson, Emily 333
Dicks, M. 221
Diedrichsen, J. 227
Diersch, N. 228
Differentiating Model of Giftedness and Talent (DMGT) 307, 308, 309–319, 320–321, 322, 324–325
diffusion tensor imaging (DTI) 173, 177, 267
discoveries 102
discretizing data 26
DLPFC *see* dorsolateral prefrontal cortex
DMGT *see* Differentiating Model of Giftedness and Talent
DMNA *see* Developmental Model for Natural Abilities
DMP *see* Dualistic Model of Passion
DMSP *see* Developmental Model of Sport Participation
DNA xvi–xvii, 163, 242–243, 297, 320; *see also* genetics
domain-specific knowledge 5–6, 131, 183, 184, 186, 189, 196
domain-specific objects 187–188
domain-specific skills 427, 428, 432; Multifactorial Gene-Environment Interaction Model 367; perceptual expertise 211; prodigies 95, 96, 98; Summation Theory 89
domain-specific traits 41, 369

domain specificity 6, 162, 420; memory 66; motor expertise 219, 229; Multifactorial Gene-Environment Interaction Model 372; observational drawing 129; PPP model 41; problem solving 63; visual memory 135
dopamine 285, 287, 289–290, 292, 297–298
dorsolateral prefrontal cortex (DLPFC) 192–195
double take of expertise 189, 196
Doyon, J. 176
Draganski, B. 177
Drake, Jennifer 7, 101–128, 140, 141, 428
drawing ability: cognitive and perceptual correlates of expertise 132–136, 143; domain-specific abilities 428; gray matter density 225–226; observational drawing 129–130, 141, 142; practice strategies 140–141, 144; precocity 101–128; role of practice 139–140; talent development 430; tools and techniques 136–138, 143–144; *see also* art
Drawing Backbone 139
Drayna, D. 276
drive 107, 115, 439
driving 219, 222, 225, 227
DTI *see* diffusion tensor imaging
Dualistic Model of Passion (DMP) 379, 380, 392
Duckworth, A. L. 158
Duffy, L. J. 159
Duke, Annie 13
Dunlap, Knight 449
dyslexia 112–113, 285

Ebbinghaus, H. 244, 245
educational achievement 253, 319; ability threshold hypothesis 81; deliberate practice 154; genetic variance xvi; professional expertise 74–75, 77–79, 82; *see also* academic expertise
Edwards, Betty 133
EEG *see* electroencephalography
effect sizes 16–17, 25, 39
Einstein, Albert 13, 93, 223, 328–329, 330, 332, 333, 339
electroencephalography (EEG) 171–172, 232
Elementary Perceiver and Memorizer (EPAM) 352–353, 354, 360
Elementary Perceiver and Memorizer IV (EPAM-IV) 354–355, 358

elite schools 77–79, 82
Elo, A. E. 18, 26
Elo ratings 18–20, 24–25, 31, 44n2,
    312–313, 335, 370, 372
eminence 427, 428, 431–432, 433
emotions: computational models 360;
    emotional regulation 404, 412, 413;
    emotional stability 317; negative 433;
    passion 440; positive 112, 391
encoding 135, 357
endophenotypes 267, 320, 321
energy expenditure 226–227, 230
environmental factors xv–xvi, 3,
    4, 27, 164, 420; Developmental
    Model for Natural Abilities 323;
    Differentiating Model of Giftedness
    and Talent 314, 317–318, 319,
    325; "equal environments" 251n1;
    Integrative Model of Talent
    Development 308; Multifactorial
    Gene-Environment Interaction
    Model xv, 265–266, 367, 372;
    multifactorial models 6; music
    culture 297; music expertise 279,
    298; professional expertise 83;
    quantitative genetic methodology
    255–257; radical environmentalism
    298; reading and math ability
    253–254, 258–261, 263, 265,
    266–267; shared and nonshared
    environmental effects 242–243,
    255–262, 265, 266, 275; see also
    gene-environment interaction;
    social environment
EPAM see Elementary Perceiver and
    Memorizer
EPDs see experience-producing drives
epigenetics 322
episodic memory 193
epistemic priority 448, 449
Epstein, R. 337
Erickson, Karl 7, 398–415, 436, 440
Ericsson, K. Anders: deliberate practice
    4, 42, 151–155, 156–164, 316, 365,
    420, 435–436, 437–440, 441; expert
    performance 218, 311–312, 313; hard
    work 107; IQ 79; long-term memory
    354; physical traits 21; retrieval 67,
    68; self-teaching 102; Skilled Memory
    Theory 66
Eriksson, H. 276
evolutionary factors 207, 298
exophenotypes 320, 321

experience 162–163, 164; "cafeteria of"
    250, 251; chess 4, 18–19; classifying
    levels of expertise 26; definition of
    435; domain-specific 6; drawing
    expertise 137–138; perceptual expertise
    200, 202, 211
experience-producing drives (EPDs)
    248, 249
expert performance 218, 365–366,
    440–441; brain correlates 219, 223;
    definitions of 160–161, 197n1,
    311–312, 313; deliberate practice
    365–366, 369; games 182–183;
    genetic factors 163; investment stage
    of expertise development 389–390;
    motor expertise 219; multidisciplinary
    nature of 232–233; Multifactorial
    Gene-Environment Interaction Model
    265–266; passion 392
expertise, defining 377, 435, 444–446
exploration stage 383, 384–386, 392, 393
extended cognition approach 37, 38
extended-family studies 242
extraversion 141, 317, 370
extreme groups design 23–25
Eyrolle, H. 357
Eys, M. A. 405

Fabbro, F. 230
face recognition 200–202, 203, 205,
    207–208, 209–210, 211
Faloon, S. 4
familial aggregation 273, 274
familiarity 183, 184, 187, 189
family: Differentiating Model of
    Giftedness and Talent 317; exploration
    stage 384, 386; extended-family
    genetic studies 242; investment stage
    of expertise development 389; music
    expertise 273, 274; opportunity to
    engage 430; prodigies/autism link 91,
    96, 97
feedback 152, 248, 249, 437, 438
Feigenbaum, E. A. 353
Feldman, D. H. 88, 94–95
Feltovich, P. J. 49
FFA see fusiform face area
FFM see Five Factor Model
FIDE see World Chess Federation
Fields, R. D. 177
Fine, R. 36
Fitts, P. M. 218
Five Factor Model (FFM) 141, 317, 343

Fleming, Alexander 342–343
Fleming, E. 136
flexibility: attentional 134, 135, 137, 143; cognitive 428; play 400–401, 403–404, 412; problem solving 53, 63–64, 65, 69; structured sport activity 402
flow 112
fluid intelligence 40
flying 218, 219, 228–229
fMRI *see* functional magnetic resonance imaging
folk music 296–297
forgetting 41–42
four-way model of human skill development 421–425
Frank, David J. 151–168
Fredricks, J. A. 387–388
Frensch, P. A. 419–420
Fry, M. D. 404
functional magnetic resonance imaging (fMRI) 172, 267; drawing blind 136; games 190, 196; motor expertise 219, 221–223, 226, 231–232; perceptual expertise 200, 207, 210; VWFA activation 206; *see also* neuro-imaging techniques
functional reorganization 175, 178, 179, 226–230, 231, 367–368
fusiform face area (FFA) 130, 200–202, 203–205, 206, 207, 208, 209–211

Gagné, Françoys 4–5, 7, 307–327, 420
Galaburda, A. M. 113, 125n2
Galileo Galilei 339, 343
Galton, Francis 3
games 182–199; analytical expertise 422; CHREST model 359; cognitive processes 183–186; cortical thickness 209; deliberate practice 154; neural underpinnings of expertise 186–196; research approaches 182–183; Scrabble 206; *see also* chess
Garavan, H. 176, 177, 178
Garlick, D. 42
Gates, Bill 13, 93
Gauthier, Isabel 7, 200–217
Gaze Shift Strategy 136
GCTA *see* Genome-wide Complex Trait Analysis
gender 91, 97
gene-environment interaction xvi, 241, 243–244, 250–251, 265, 420; Developmental Model for Natural Abilities 323;

gene-environment transactions 246–248; Multifactorial Gene-Environment Interaction Model xv, 254, 265–266, 268, 279, 365–375; music expertise 274, 279; polygenic scores xvii; *see also* environmental factors; genetics
general intelligence (g) 73, 77, 80, 82; Multifactorial Gene-Environment Interaction Model 371; prodigies 94–95, 96, 98; Summation Theory 89; *see also* intelligence
general theory of problem solving (GPS) 49
generalizability 14, 25, 141, 447
Generativity Theory of creativity 337
genetics xiv–xv, xvi, 7, 164, 366, 420; absolute pitch 155; deliberate practice 369; Developmental Model for Natural Abilities 324; Differentiating Model of Giftedness and Talent 310, 320, 321; drawing expertise 142; epigenetics 322; expert performance 163; individual differences 5; innateness 321–322; Multifactorial Gene-Environment Interaction Model xv, 367, 368, 369, 371, 372–373; multifactorial models 6; music expertise 272–282, 283–304; prodigies/autism link 91–92, 97, 98; professional expertise 83; reaction range 244–246; reading and math ability 5, 253–254, 258–268; theoretical concepts 241–252; *see also* gene-environment interaction; heritability
genius 328, 333
genome-wide association studies xvi–xvii, 278, 284–286, 297
Genome-wide Complex Trait Analysis (GCTA) 257
genotypes 245–250; African cultures 296; Developmental Model for Natural Abilities 308, 322; Differentiating Model of Giftedness and Talent 320, 321; Genome-wide Complex Trait Analysis 257; Integrative Model of Talent Development 324
Gervain, J. 291–292
Geschwind, N. 113, 125n2
giftedness: in adulthood 429; definition of 313; Developmental Model for Natural Abilities 320, 324; Differentiating Model of Giftedness and Talent 310–311, 315, 319, 325; eminence 427, 431, 433; Integrative Model of Talent Development 308, 309; *see also* talent

Gilmartin, K. J. 351, 354
Gitschier, J. 276
Gladwell, Malcolm 5, 81, 83n4, 152
Glaser, R. 49
Glazek, K. 136
Glöckner, A. 357
Go 182, 195, 357, 359, 419
goals 390, 440; computational models 352; Differentiating Model of Giftedness and Talent 317, 325; problem solving 51–52, 53–57, 59–65, 68–69
Gobet, Fernand: chess expertise 19, 32, 34–36, 37–38, 40, 42, 43; CHREST model 38, 360; computational models 7, 347–364; deliberate practice 5, 32, 154; retrieval 68; template theory 357; transfer studies 39
golf 152, 160–161, 177, 222, 225, 227, 334
Golomb, Claire 104–105, 125n1
Gordon, A. 106
Gordon's Test of Music Audiation 89
Goto, Midori 439, 440
Gottesman, I. I. 244–245, 320
Gottfredson, L. S. 80
Gould, T. D. 320
Gowen, E. 136
GPS *see* general theory of problem solving
Grabner, R. H. 19, 40
Graf, Mario 182–199
Granot, R. Y. 288
gray matter 173, 177, 209, 224, 225–226, 231
Greeks, ancient 1–2, 376
Gregersen, P. K. 291
grit 141, 158, 367, 368
Gross, Carol A. 253–271
Gross, Susan I. 253–271
Grossmann, Marcel 328–329
groups 26, 27
Gruber, H. 232
Guatto, E. 230
Guida, Alessandro 7, 171–181
Guillot, A. 177, 219

Hackfort, D. 387
Haier, R. J. 175
Hambrick, David Z. 1–9; deliberate practice 32, 39–40, 116, 151–168; heritability of music accomplishment 249–250; Multifactorial

Gene-Environment Interaction Model 7, 365–375; music expertise 276, 277, 370; working memory capacity 5
Hancock, D. J. 405
handedness 102, 109, 110, 113
hard work 101, 107–108, 115–116, 117, 152, 200; *see also* practice
Harlaar, N. 259
harmonious passion 379–380, 381–392, 431
Harvard University 77–79
Hawking, Stephen 93
health 403, 412, 413
Hegel, G. W. F. 376, 420
Helsen, W. F. 159
heritability xv, xvi, 243, 248; cognitive ability 250, 323; concept of 241–242; gene x environment interaction 250–251; increasing over time 249–250; intelligence 3; mathematics ability 260–261, 263, 265; music expertise 273, 275–277, 279, 293, 294; quantitative genetic methodology 255–257; reading ability 260, 263; *see also* genetics
heuristics: computational models 349, 351–352, 356; intelligence 43; PPP model 41–42; problem solving 49, 69
Hildreth, G. 107–108, 125n1
Hirose, S. 227
hloss 41–42
Hodges, N. J. 159
Hoffmann, Robert R. 8, 444–452
Hofstadter, D. 50
Holding, D. H. 34, 35
holistic individuation 203, 204
Holland, John 315–316
Holm, L. 276
hormones 113
Howard, R. W. 43
Howe, M. J. A. 154
Hsiao, J. H.-w. 131
hybrid modeling 348, 356

identity 379, 380–381, 382, 386, 388–389
illusions 132
ILTS *see* International Longitudinal Twin Study
imagery: chess 31, 36–38, 43, 44; motor 222, 223, 226, 229–230, 231; visual imagery ability 108, 111, 112, 139–140
imagination 90
impulsivity 367, 368, 371

IMTD *see* Integrative Model of Talent Development
Imtiaz, F. 405
incidental range restriction 21–23
individual differences 1, 3, 4–5; chess 4, 39–40, 42, 43; classifying levels of expertise 26; creativity 140; deliberate practice 151, 152–155, 160, 164; drawing ability 101; genetics 241, 242, 246, 249, 254, 265; intelligence 73, 209; Inventory for Children's Individual Differences 111; Multifactorial Gene-Environment Interaction Model 368; music expertise 274–279; natural abilities 322; neuroscience 319; passion 382; perceptual expertise 211; range restriction 19; reading and math ability 258, 261, 263, 265; traits 366
individuation 203, 204–205
informal theories 348, 349
information processing 370, 419, 421; artistic perception 131; cerebral resources 175; chunking 354; neural context 178; problem solving 63; Skilled Memory Theory 66; *see also* cognitive processes
innateness 321–322, 325, 344n4
"institutionalization of childhood" 408
Integrative Model of Talent Development (IMTD) 307–309, 324–326
intelligence: chess 40, 43, 370; cortical thickness 209; drawing expertise 111–112, 138, 139–140; genetic variance xvi; heritability 3; Multifactorial Gene-Environment Interaction Model 368, 371; musical auditory discrimination 366, 368; PPP model 41–42, 351; prodigies 94–96, 98; professional expertise 73–86; Summation Theory 89; *see also* cognitive ability; IQ
interests: Developmental Model for Natural Abilities 323; drawing precocity 107; Multifactorial Gene-Environment Interaction Model 254, 367, 368, 370; prodigies/autism link 90, 97; stages of expertise development 378
interference 36, 37–38
International Longitudinal Twin Study (ILTS) 259
intrapersonal catalysts 308, 314, 316–317, 319, 323, 325

intuition 359
Inventory for Children's Individual Differences 111
investment stage 378, 383–384, 385, 388–391, 393, 399
IQ 79, 80, 83n4; drawing expertise 111–112, 138, 139–140; dyslexia 113; Multifactorial Gene-Environment Interaction Model 367; prodigies and autism 89; tests 310; *see also* intelligence

Jaeger, G. J. 329
James, C. E. 177, 225
Järvelä, Irma 283, 284–287, 289, 292
Jarvis, P. 408
Jensen, A. R. 83n4
Johansen-Berg, H. 177
Johnson, N. F. 57–60
Jongman, R. W. 351
Jonin, Pierre-Yves 171–181
Jonsson, B. 230

Kagan, Jerome 323
Kalakoski, V. 37
Kanner, Leo 88
Karjakin, Sergey 31
Karma Music Test (KMT) 285–286
Kasparov, Garry 1
Kauffman Brief Intelligence Test (K-BIT) 111
Kee, Y. 437
Keith, N. 157
Kell, Harrison J. 7, 73–86, 428
Kelly, A. C. 177, 178
Kenin, R. 130
Keppel, B. 447
Kerr, T. 159
Kim, W. 227
kinetic motor imagery 222
King, Michael J. 151–168
Kirby, T. A. 158
Kissin, Evgeny 1
Klein, M. C. 177
Kleine, B. M. 159, 163
KMT *see* Karma Music Test
knowledge: acquired knowledge structures 186; aesthetic evaluation 131; chess 34, 40; chunking networks 352; declarative and procedural 241, 356; domain-specific 5–6, 131, 183, 184, 186, 189, 196; drawing expertise 134; elicitation 450; four-way model

of human skill development 421, 422; functional reorganization 178, 179; perceptual 65; prior expertise 337; problem solving 49; production systems 355–356; Skilled Memory Theory 66; solid knowledge base 425
Köhler, W. 332, 337
Kok, Ellen M. 7, 218–237
Koltanowski, George 36
Korf, R. E. 49, 53, 57
Kornysheva, K. 227
Kozbelt, A. 134, 135–136
Krampe, R. T. 4, 102, 151–152, 156–158, 313, 420, 435–436
Kuhl, J. 317
Kuja-Halkola, R. 277
Kulkarni, D. 356

Laine, T. 355
Landau, S. M. 176
Lane, Peter C. R. 7, 347–364
Lang, Marc 44n3
Langley, P. 356
language 288, 297, 360
Lappi, O. 222
Larkin, J. 49, 65
Larsson, A. 230
learning: CHREST model 358, 360; computational models 355, 357; drawing expertise 102, 138, 139, 141, 144; EPAM theory 353; error-based 220; feedback 152; giftedness 315; individual differences 4–5, 248; informal 308, 323; motor 218–219, 227, 249, 404, 439; music perception 286, 287, 290; music performance 292; perceptual 204–205, 211, 450; reaction range 244–246; skill acquisition 437
learning disability 261–262
Leder, H. 131
Lee, P. 136
Lehmann, A. C. 157, 161–162, 163, 311–312
Leonardo, A. M. 356
Leonardo da Vinci 130
letter recognition 206
levels-of-processing (LOP) framework 441
Lewthwaite, R. 440
Lidor, R. 387
Liew, S.-L. 229
linguistic deficits 102, 109, 112–113

linkage analysis 277–278, 284, 285–286, 290–291, 294, 295
Liu, X. 287
Lloyd-Kelly, Martyn 7, 347–364
Lockhart, R. S. 441
Loehlin, J. C. 246
Logan, J. A. R. 258–259, 260
Lombardo, M. P. 162
London taxi drivers 209
long-term depression (LTD) 294
long-term memory (LTM): CHREST model 358; chunking 33–34, 37, 353, 354; computational models 352, 354, 355; domain-specific knowledge 196; games 185–186; informal theory 349; Multifactorial Gene-Environment Interaction Model 367; problem solving 64–65; retrieval structures 4; Skilled Memory Theory 66–67; template theory 357; see also memory
LTD see long-term depression
LTM see long-term memory
Lubinski, David 74, 75, 76
Lukowski, Sarah 253–271
Lundstrom, P. 228
Luo, J. 229–230
Lyons, I. M. 267

M1 see primary motor cortex
Ma, Yo-Yo 13, 440
Mach, Ernst 343
McAbee, Samuel T. 6–7, 13–30, 436, 437
McCartney, K. 250
McGuffin, P. 320
McGugin, R. W. 209–210
McLaughlin, Dan 152, 153
McManus, I. C. 133, 136
McMillan, A. 261
Macnamara, Brooke N. 1–9, 391, 428; chess and cognitive ability 40; deliberate practice 7, 22, 151–168, 435, 439, 441; variance in expert performance 366
McPherson, Gary E. 7, 283–304
macro-models 348
macros 49, 52, 53–54, 55–63, 64–67
Madison, G. 276, 277
Mageau, G. A. 381, 384, 387, 389
magnetic resonance imaging (MRI) 173, 201, 204, 222, 223, 231–232; see also functional magnetic resonance imaging

magnetoencephalography (MEG)
171–172
Maier, N. R. F. 337, 340–341
Maieron, M. 230
Makel, M. C. 76, 82
Mann, D. 221
MAPP *see* Memory-Aided Pattern
Perceiver
Margetis, J. L. 229
Mariné, C. 357
Martela, F. 440
Masters, R. 404
mastery 115, 390
MATER 352, 353
mathematical models 350–351
mathematics 253–257, 335; chess transfer
studies 39; Einstein 329, 339; genetic
and environmental influences 260–
267; non-computational theories 348;
passion 388–389; prodigies 91, 94–96,
97, 98, 107; right hemisphere 113;
savants 88, 91, 93, 94, 97, 114; Study
of Mathematically Precocious Youth
74–77, 81, 82; training 369; valuing of
mathematical ability 102
Matthew Effect 245, 248
Matthews, Mark 87–100
maturational processes 308, 315,
322–323, 324
Mayr, U. 102
meaning in life 440
MEG *see* magnetoencephalography
Meinz, Elizabeth J. 5, 116, 151–168, 370
Memmert, D. 403
memory: autism 89; automaticity 428;
chess 31, 32–34, 37, 40, 43–44,
205; CHREST model 358, 359;
computational models 349–350,
352, 354–355, 357; double take of
expertise 196; drawing expertise 132,
143; EPAM theory 353; episodic 193;
games 185–186; levels-of-processing
framework 441; motor expertise 218–
219; Multifactorial Gene-Environment
Interaction Model 367, 368; music
memory 278, 284, 288–289, 296, 298;
music perception 286, 287, 290; music
performance 292; problem solving
64–65; prodigies 89, 95; retention and
forgetting 244; retrieval structures 4,
50, 66–68, 355; savants 89, 97; sight-
reading skills 5, 116, 366, 370; Skilled

Memory Theory 47, 49–50, 65–68,
69; twin studies 267; visual 110–112,
114, 129, 135, 139, 142, 428
Memory-Aided Pattern Perceiver
(MAPP) 354, 358
Mencken, H. L. xiv
Mendel, Gregor 333
mental ability 19–21, 24–25; *see also*
cognitive ability
mental calculation 66, 125n2; double take
of expertise 189; savants 114, 115
mental imagery 222, 226, 229–230, 231
mentors 317, 381, 384–386, 389, 390,
392, 425
Menuhin, Yehudi 116
Merriam, S. B. 437
metacognition 371
"methodolatry" 8, 449, 450
metrics: broad and narrow 27; Elo ratings
18–20, 24–25, 31, 44n2, 312–313,
335, 370
MGIM *see* Multifactorial Gene-
Environment Interaction Model
Miall, R. C. 136
micro-models 348
Miksza, P. 371
Milbrath, C. 96, 104
Milton, J. 227
mind-body problem 449–450
mind's eye 35, 43, 44, 194
minimal expertise 312–313
Mireles, D. E. 357
mirror neuron system 228
mixed-age interactions 409
mnemonics 66, 354, 361n1
models *see* computational models
molecular genetics 257, 283–304, 420
Monet, Claude 130
mood 289
Moore, D. G. 154
Moran, A. 436
Moreau, D. 154
Morelock, M. J. 94–95, 313
Morley, A. P. 278, 295
Mosing, Miriam A. 7, 272–282, 365–375
motivation 433, 439; classifying levels of
expertise 26; deliberate play 404, 407,
407, 412; Differentiating Model of
Giftedness and Talent 308, 314, 317,
325; drawing precocity 101, 107,
112; experience-producing drives
248; expertise maintenance 391;

genetics 249; learning strategies 141, 144; math performance 265, 267; Multifactorial Gene-Environment Interaction Model 254, 367, 368, 371; multifactorial models 5; opportunity to engage 430; PPP model 41–42; young athletes 412
motor cortex 220–221, 224, 227
motor expertise 218–237, 316; deliberate play 403–404, 412, 413; experimental paradigms 221–223; functional neuroplasticity 226–230; heritability 249; music performance 292; structural neuroplasticity 176–177, 223–226
motor imagery 222, 223, 226, 229–230, 231
motor processing 132, 136, 143
Mottron, L. 114
Mozart, Wolfgang Amadeus 116
MRI *see* magnetic resonance imaging
Muckler, F. A. 449
multi-voxel pattern analysis (MVPA) 210–211
Multifactorial Gene-Environment Interaction Model (MGIM) xv, 254, 265–266, 268, 279, 365–375
multifactorial models 5–6
music: analytical expertise 422; creativity 284, 289, 293–295, 423; culture 284, 296–297; deliberate practice 4, 116, 151, 154–155, 366; experience 163; expert performance 160; expertise maintenance 391; gene-environment correlation 248; genetic factors 142, 249–250, 272–282, 283–304, 366, 368; intelligence 368; investment stage of expertise development 389–390; IQ 140; listening 278, 284, 289–290, 292, 296, 297–298; mental imagery 230; motor expertise 219, 229, 232; music memory 278, 284, 288–289, 296, 298; music perception 273, 278, 283–292, 294, 296, 297–298; neural efficiency 226, 227; openness to experience 368; passion 376, 381, 390; performance 284, 292–293, 297–298; physical traits 368, 370–371; practice strategies 140, 438; prodigies 87–89, 91, 93, 94–96, 97, 98, 107, 319; right hemisphere 113; savants 88, 91, 94, 97, 114, 115; sight-reading skills 5, 116, 366, 370; singing 284, 295–296; structural brain

changes 176–177, 209, 224–225; talent development 429, 430; training 369; valuing of musical ability 102
MVPA *see* multi-voxel pattern analysis

Nadia (drawing savant) 114
Naito, E. 226–227
Nananidou, A. 159
Nandagopal, K. 161, 163
natural abilities: Developmental Model for Natural Abilities 307, 308, 320–324, 325–326; Differentiating Model of Giftedness and Talent 309, 311, 314, 315–316, 319, 322, 325; Integrative Model of Talent Development 308, 324; *see also* ability
naturalistic inquiry 448
nature, drawing 105–106
nature versus nurture 4, 6, 116, 164, 226, 231, 265; *see also* gene-environment interaction
negative emotions 433
negativism 451
Nettleton, D. 163
networks: chunking 352–355; neural 267, 357
Neubauer, A. C. 19, 40
neural approaches xiv–xv, 7, 171–181, 449–450; chess 32; games 186–196; motor expertise 219, 220–233; music expertise 273; perceptual expertise 200–217; *see also* brain; neuro-imaging techniques; neuroplasticity
neural context 178
neural efficiency 175–176, 225, 226–227, 230, 231, 265
neural networks 267, 357
neuro-imaging techniques 171–181; absolute pitch 291; individual differences 319; perceptual expertise 200, 202, 206–207, 210, 211; *see also* functional magnetic resonance imaging; magnetic resonance imaging
neurobiology 254
neurodegeneration 290, 293
neuronal recycling hypothesis 207–208
neurons 172, 173, 196, 203, 228, 449
neuroplasticity 41–42, 178, 210; motor expertise 223–230; Multifactorial Gene-Environment Interaction Model 367; music perception 287; perceptual expertise 200, 208; synaptic 294

neuroprotection 290, 292
neuropsychology 449–450
neuroticism 139–140, 317, 370
Newell, A. N. 49
Newton, Isaac 339
Niles, L. 439
Noël, Audrey 171–181
non-ability factors 5–6
non-right-handedness 102, 109, 110, 113
nonobviousness 331, 335–336
normal curve 3
novelty 331, 335, 400
NSS chess program 352
nucleus caudatus 192–194, 195, 196
Nyad, Diana 1
Nyberg, L. 230
Nyiregházi, Erwin 87

object recognition: games 183–184, 185, 186–189, 190, 191, 196; perceptual expertise 200–201, 204–205, 208, 209–210, 211
"objective" measurement 448–449, 450
observational drawing 225–226
obsessive passion 379–380, 381, 382–392, 431
Oikkonen, J. 278, 285–286
Oliver, I. 360
Olsson, C. J. 228, 230
Olszewski-Kubilius, Paula 8, 427–434
openness to experience 317, 343, 344n4, 432; artists 111, 112, 141, 428; Multifactorial Gene-Environment Interaction Model 367, 368
opportunities 427, 430
originality 330, 332, 340
Ostrofsky, J. 135–136
Oswald, Frederick L. 6–7, 13–30, 154, 436, 437
oxygen 172, 200

PAF see Personal Assets Framework
Palmisando, Samuel 93
Pamjav, H. 296
parahippocampal gyri (PHG) 190–191, 193, 195, 210, 230
parents 5
Park, H. 295
Parker, A. 38
passion 376–397, 420, 425, 428, 431, 440; definition of 378–379;

Developmental Model for Natural Abilities 323; four-way model of human skill development 421, 422; passionate interests 90, 97
Pasteur, Louis 343
patents 75, 331, 335–336
"pathology of superiority" 113, 114
pattern recognition: chess 31, 33–36, 41–42, 43, 44, 428; games 189–191, 192, 194, 196; perceptual knowledge 65; problem solving 49, 55, 61, 68
PCC see posterior cingulate cortex
Pedersen, N. L. 277
peer review 332, 335
penicillin discovery 342–343
PERCEIVER 353–354, 358
perception: applied research 449; artistic 130–132, 142–143; brain areas 190; computational models 357; delusory 133–134; double take of expertise 189, 196; drawing expertise 132–134, 142, 143, 144; EPAM theory 353; illusory 132–133; motor tasks 219; music 273, 278, 283–292, 294, 296, 297–298; perceptual expertise 108–109, 131–132, 200–217; perceptual knowledge 65; perceptual learning 450
perceptual chunks 53–55, 56, 64–65, 66–67; see also chunking
Perdreau, F. 134
Peretz, Isabelle 7, 272–282
performance analysis 445–446
persistence 379, 382, 385, 389, 390, 392
Personal Assets Framework (PAF) 407–412
personal creativity 329–332, 336–338, 339, 340–341
personal engagement 407, 407–408, 412
personal expertise 333–334, 336–338, 339, 340–341
personality: Differentiating Model of Giftedness and Talent 314, 317; drawing ability 111, 112, 138, 139–140, 141–142; Multifactorial Gene-Environment Interaction Model 254, 367, 368, 370, 371; multifactorial models 5; professional expertise 73, 83
perspective 104–105, 108, 114, 118
PET see positron emission tomography
Petrill, Stephen A. 253–271
phenotypes xv, 241, 243, 245, 250–251, 366; Developmental Model for Natural

Abilities 308, 322; Differentiating Model of Giftedness and Talent 320, 321; Genome-wide Complex Trait Analysis 257; mathematics ability 265–266, 267; Multifactorial Gene-Environment Interaction Model 367, 369, 372; music-related 284, 293, 294, 295, 298; Williams-Beuren syndrome 274; *see also* traits

PHG *see* parahippocampal gyri

physical environment 409–412, 412

physical health 403, 412, 413

physical traits: basketball players 21–23; Differentiating Model of Giftedness and Talent 308, 314, 316–317; Multifactorial Gene-Environment Interaction Model xv, 254, 367, 368, 370–371; *see also* traits

Picasso, Pablo 104, 106, 116

Piggott, D. 436

place of birth 409–412

plasticity 41–42, 178, 210; motor expertise 223–230; Multifactorial Gene-Environment Interaction Model 367; music perception 287; perceptual expertise 200, 208; synaptic 294

Plato 2, 343n1

Platz, F. 366

play 398–415, 439

playfulness 400

Plomin, Robert J. xiv–xvii, 5, 7, 246, 261, 320, 321–322

ploss 41–42

PMC *see* premotor cortex

pMTG *see* posterior middle temporal gyrus

Pokémon card game 202, 205

Poldrack, R. A. 175–176

polygenic scores xvi–xvii, 243

polymorphisms 243, 257, 277, 288–289, 293, 295–296, 298

Pool, R. 79, 156

positive emotions 112, 391

positron emission tomography (PET) 172, 232

Posner, M. I. 218

posterior cingulate cortex (PCC) 193, 194–195

posterior middle temporal gyrus (pMTG) 187–189, 190, 191, 193, 195–196

Posthuma, D. 276

potential 309, 310, 427

power, statistical 14, 23, 446

Poznyanskaya, E. D. 353

PPP *see* Practice, Plasticity, and Processes model

practical expertise 421, 423–424

practical significance 16–17, 25, 447–448

practice 3, 4–5, 101, 151–168; brain scanning paradigms 174–175; chess 4, 5, 19–20, 24–25, 32, 39–42, 372; compulsive 115; deliberate play 407, 407; Differentiating Model of Giftedness and Talent 310; drawing expertise 102, 138, 139–141, 142, 143; genetics 244–246, 249–250, 251, 366; investment stage 388; Multifactorial Gene-Environment Interaction Model xv, 371, 372; music 116, 274, 277, 279, 366; perceptual expertise 204; PPP model 41–42; reading and math ability 261; stages of expertise development 378; strategies for 140–141, 438; structural brain changes 177, 223; Summation Theory 89; talent development 428; *see also* deliberate practice; training

Practice, Plasticity, and Processes (PPP) model 40–43, 224, 351

pre-shot routines 222, 227, 230

precision 14–16

precocity: drawing 101–128; intellectual 321; *see also* prodigies

precuneus 193, 194, 195–196

premotor cortex (PMC) 220–221, 222, 225, 227, 228–229, 230

prevalence of expertise/talent 310–311, 312, 313

Prietula, M. J. 162

primary motor cortex (M1) 220, 221, 222, 227, 230

"problem finding" 334, 337, 338

problem solving 47–72; chess 32–33; computational models 352, 357; creative 336–337; games 191–195; mathematics 266, 267; social 404

processing speed 40

Proctor, Robert W. 8, 435–443

prodigies 1, 5, 87–100, 429, 439; analytical expertise 422; chess 31; creative expertise 423; definition of 88; drawing 135, 144; Multifactorial Gene-Environment Interaction Model 372; music 319; openness to experience 428; opportunity to engage 430; *see also* precocity

production systems 355–356

productivity 432, 433
professional expertise 73–86, 366
proficiency levels 25–26, 436,
    444–446
prosopagnosics 209, 211
psychopathology 129
psychosocial skills 427, 430–431, 432
Pullen, James Henry 88
purpose 440
Putallaz, M. 76

qualitative research 14
quantitative genetic methodology
    255–257
Quetelet, Adolphe 3

rACC *see* rostral anterior cingulate cortex
radical environmentalism 298
"rage to master" 102, 112, 115, 141,
    144, 432
range enhancement 23–25
range restriction 17–23
Raufaste, E. 357
reaction range 244–246
reading 5, 253–257; artists 113; chess
    transfer studies 39; genetic and
    environmental influences 258–260,
    261–267; perceptual expertise
    131–132; precocity 107; reading
    disability 261
realism, artistic 104–107, 109, 111,
    112, 115
Reecy, J. M. 163
refinement stage 383–384, 385,
    391–392, 393
Reingold, E. 158
Reitman, Judith S. 419
relatedness 380
relational processing 131
relationships 405, 407, 408–409, 412–
    412; *see also* social skills/competence
relative expertise 377, 431–432, 436
reliability 17, 207
repeated measurement designs 14
representational decisions 135–136, 143
research 129, 365–366; chess 32;
    laboratory studies and real-world
    settings 448; methodological issues
    437; "objective" measurement
    448–449; observational drawing 142;
    passion 379–380, 392–393; prodigies
    87–88; statistical methods 13–30
restaurant service 66
retrieval 69, 354–355, 428;

domain-specific knowledge 186, 189;
    episodic memory 193; Skilled Memory
    Theory 50, 66–68
retrosplenial cortex (RSC) 190–191,
    193, 195
Révész, G. 87
rhythm 273, 276, 277, 284, 285, 288, 296
Richman, H. B. 355
Rikers, R. M. J. P. 158
risk 405, 408
role models 384
Roring, R. W. 159, 161, 163
rostral anterior cingulate cortex (rACC)
    193, 194–195
RSC *see* retrosplenial cortex
RUBIK model 55–57, 58–59, 60–62,
    65, 67
Rubik's Cube 47–69
Rumiati, R. I. 230
Runco, M. 329
Ruskin, John 132
Ruthsatz, Joanne 5, 7, 87–100, 114–115

Saariluoma, P. 36–37, 355
Sakakibara, A. 154–155
Sala, G. 39, 40
sample size 14–17, 262, 265, 446–447
sampling stage 378, 386, 399
Sarrazin, C. 352
SAT *see* Scholastic Assessment Test
savants: calculation 125n2; drawing ability
    101, 102, 109–110, 113–115; prodigies
    compared with 88–89, 92–94, 96–97;
    see also autism
scaffolding 178
scanning-training-scanning (S-T-S)
    paradigm 174–175
Scarr, S. 250
schemas 130, 143, 357, 428
Schmidt, H. G. 158
Scholastic Assessment Test (SAT) 17, 21,
    74, 76, 77, 113
Scholz, J. 177
Schorer, J. 436
Schumacher, E. H. 176
Schumann, Clara Wieck 93
Schwenkreis, P. 224
science 332, 335, 342, 420, 422, 423, 432
Scrabble 206
search: chess expertise 34–36, 43, 44;
    computational models 356; heuristic
    351–352; neural underpinnings of
    expertise in games 194; problem
    solving 65, 69

SEARCH model 35, 41–42, 351
self-confidence 412, 413
self-determination theory 381
self-efficacy 407
self-teaching 102, 105, 108
semantic processing 131
sensory processing 131
serendipity 342–343
Shakeshaft, N. G. 261
Sheng, T. 229
shogi 191, 192, 193–194, 195
short-term memory (STM): chess
    players 40; chunking 33–34, 353,
    354; computational models 349, 352,
    354, 355; mnemonics 361n1; Skilled
    Memory Theory 66–67, 69; stores 43;
    see also memory; working memory
sight-reading skills 5, 116, 366, 370
Simon, Herbert A.: chess 3–4, 33, 34–37,
    43, 66, 419, 422; computational
    models 351, 352, 353–354, 355, 356;
    EPAM theory 353; problem solving
    49, 53, 57, 65; template theory 357
Simonton, Dean Keith 4, 7, 328–346,
    420, 432
singing 284, 295–296
single nucleotide polymorphism (SNP)
    243, 295
situational factors 6
skill: acquisition 19, 27, 152–153,
    248, 356, 377, 404, 436–437, 440;
    deliberate practice 151–152, 154;
    expert performance approach 183;
    expertise approach 183; four-way
    model of human skill development
    421–425; games 184; genetics
    244–246, 248–249, 251; reading 258;
    relative approach to expertise 377; *see
    also* domain-specific skills; talent
Skilled Memory Theory (SMT) 47,
    49–50, 65–68, 69
Sloane, K. D. 106
Sloboda, J. A. 154
SMA *see* supplementary motor area
Small, S. L. 227
SMG *see* supramarginal gyrus
Smith, J. 218
SMPY *see* Study of Mathematically
    Precocious Youth
SMT *see* Skilled Memory Theory
SNP *see* single nucleotide polymorphism
Soar 356
SOAR IV 55
soccer 218, 227

social cognition 286, 298
social environment 381, 384–386,
    387–388, 404–407, 409, 412
social interaction 409
social problem solving 404
social skills/competence 90, 92, 404,
    405, 412–413, 430–431; *see also*
    psychosocial skills
socioeconomic status 5, 250, 253, 323
sociometric analysis 445–446
Soden, B. 259
Soewito, F. 56
Solodkin, A. 227
Sonnentag, S. 159, 163
Sosniak, L. A. 106
Sowden, P. T. 222
specialization stage 378, 383–384, 385,
    386–388, 393, 399, 429
spelling 113, 158
Sperduti, M. 177, 219
Spilich, G. J. 68
sports 1, 102, 129; analytical expertise
    422; cognitive processes 316;
    computational models 352; deliberate
    play 398–415; deliberate practice
    154, 159, 162; expert performance
    160, 161; expertise maintenance 391;
    exploration stage 392; incidental range
    restriction 21–23; IQ 140; mental
    imagery 229–230; motor expertise 218,
    219, 222, 227, 228–230, 232; passion
    376, 382, 392; physical traits 368,
    370; stages of expertise development
    378; structural brain changes 225–226;
    structured sport activity 401–402, 403,
    407; talent development 429, 430;
    taxonomy of expertise 436
stage theory of motor learning 218–219
stages of expertise development
    377–378, 431; deliberate play 407,
    413; Developmental Model of Sport
    Participation 399; passion 383–392,
    393, 428
Stanford-Binet test 89, 94–96, 260
Stanley, Julian C. 74
Starkes, J. L. 159
Staszewski, James 7, 47–72, 355, 419
statistical methods 13–30, 446–448;
    classifying levels of expertise 25–26;
    extreme groups design 23–25; range
    restriction 17–23; sample size 14–17
statistical significance 16–17, 25, 447
Stephens, Kimberly 87–100
Stern, E. 19, 40

Sternberg, Robert J. 8, 419–426
STM *see* short-term memory
stroop paradigm 184
structural equation modeling 243, 257, 275
Study of Mathematically Precocious Youth (SMPY) 74–77, 81, 82
subjective measures 449, 450
subliminal priming 184
Subotnick, Reba F. 8, 427–434
Summation Theory 89
Sunday, Mackenzie 7, 200–217
supplementary motor area (SMA) 220, 221, 222, 225
supramarginal gyrus (SMG) 187–189, 190, 191, 193, 195–196
surgery 218, 219, 222, 230, 232
surprise 330–331, 332, 340
Swann, C. 436
symbolic modeling 348
synesthesia 291
system production tradition 186

Tabachnek-Schijf, H. J. M. 356
talent xiv; biological underpinnings of 319–320; definitions of 309; Developmental Model for Natural Abilities 325–326; Differentiating Model of Giftedness and Talent 309, 315–316, 317–318, 319, 325; drawing ability 101, 102, 109, 115–116; innate 322, 325, 344n4; Integrative Model of Talent Development 307–309, 324–326; musical 273, 274, 279; prevalence 310–311; "rage to master" 112, 115; *see also* giftedness; skill
talent development 307, 310–311, 313–320, 324–326, 386, 427–434; *see also* development of expertise
Tan, Yi Ting 283–304
task execution 222–223, 230
task factors 6, 164
taxi drivers 177–178, 209
Tchalenko, J. 136
TEDS *see* Twins Early Development Study
temperament 5, 314, 317
template theory 34, 38, 41–42, 43, 351, 357–358
10-year rule 161–162, 386–387, 437
10,000 hours rule 152, 162, 386–387, 422
Tesch-Römer, C. 4, 151–152, 313, 420, 435–436
Tetris 209

thalamus 293
theories, classification of 348
Theusch, E. 276
Thompson, Lee A. 7, 253–271
Thorndike, Edward 3
3+2 Rule 447
Tiessen, Zac 94
Tikhomirov, O. K. 353
Tinio, P. P. L. 130
TMS *see* transcranial magnetic stimulation
Tomasino, B. 230
training xiv, 4, 152–153, 369, 370, 436; brain scanning paradigms 174–175; chess transfer studies 39; drawing ability 142; exploration stage 386; genetics 248–249, 251; individual differences 4–5, 248; mental imagery 230; motor expertise 231; music 154–155, 274, 279; one-size-fits-all xvi; perceptual expertise 204–205, 209; problem solving 193–194; talent development 428; *see also* deliberate practice; practice
training-scanning (T-S) paradigm 174–175
traits: Developmental Model for Natural Abilities 323; Differentiating Model of Giftedness and Talent 314, 316–317; domain-specific 369; genetic variance xvi–xvii; Genome-wide Complex Trait Analysis 257; individual differences 366; Integrative Model of Talent Development 308; Multifactorial Gene-Environment Interaction Model xv, 254, 368, 370, 372–373; music expertise 278–279, 283, 297–298; PPP model 41–42; *see also* phenotypes; physical traits
transcranial magnetic stimulation (TMS) 211–212
transfer 39, 43, 47, 64, 69
Treffert, D. A. 89
Trzaskowski, M. 261
Tso, R. V.-y. 131
Tsukayama, E. 158
Tucker-Drob, Elliot M. 7, 241–252, 276, 277, 436
Tuffiash, M. 158, 159
Turner's Syndrome 262
Turnnidge, Jennifer 398–415
twin modeling 275
twin studies xvi, 242, 366; music expertise 275–277, 279; research design 257; Western Reserve Reading and Math Project 253–268

...ly Development Study (TEDS) ..5, 258, 260–261
typing 177, 225

Ukkola-Vuoti, L. 293–294
Ullén, Fredrik 7, 254, 265, 268, 272–282, 365–375, 420
United States Patent and Trademark Office 331, 335–336
universities 77–79
Urbach, J. 114–115
utility 330, 331–332, 335, 340

Vaci, Nemanja 18–19, 182–199
Vallerand, Robert J. 7, 376–397, 420, 428, 431, 440
valproate 292
van der Kamp, J. 221, 404
van der Maas, H. L. J. 35
van der Sluis, S. 276
van Harreveld, F. 35
van Leeuwenhoek, Antonie 339
Vanderbilt Expertise Test 207
variation: deliberate practice 366; genetic 242, 243, 262; see also individual differences
Vasyukova, E. 158
VBM see voxel-based morphometry
Vierimaa, Matthew 398–415
Vinkhuyzen, A. A. 276
visual imagery ability 108, 111, 112, 139–140
visual memory 110–112, 114, 129, 135, 139, 142, 428
visual-spatial ability: drawing expertise 95, 96, 102, 109, 110–112, 143; dyslexia 113; math performance 265
Visual Word Form Area (VWFA) 205–206, 208
Vogt, S. 229
volition 308, 314, 317, 325
Voss, J. F. 68
voxel-based morphometry (VBM) 173, 177, 222
VWFA see Visual Word Form Area

Wagenmakers, E.-J. 35
Wai, Jonathan 6, 7, 73–86, 428
Wan, X. 191, 192–194

Ward, P. 159
Warhol, Andy 130
Waters, A. J. 35
Watson, John 3, 4, 163, 449
Wattie, N. 436
Wei, G. 229–230
Weir, P. L. 159
well-being: deliberate play 404; passion 383, 385, 389, 390, 391, 392; Personal Assets Framework 407
Western Reserve Reading and Math Project (WRRMP) 253–268
Williams-Beuren syndrome 274
Williams, G. 38
Williams, M. A. 159
Williams, Venus 227–228
Wilson, Sarah J. 283–304
Wimshurst, Z. L. 222, 228
Winner, Ellen 7, 101–128, 141, 428
wisdom-based expertise 421, 424, 425
word recognition 205–206, 208
working memory: chess 205; drawing expertise 143; informal theory 349; motor expertise 218–219, 404; Multifactorial Gene-Environment Interaction Model 367, 368; music expertise 287, 288–289; prodigies 89, 95, 97; savants 89, 97; sight-reading skills 5, 116, 366, 370; Skilled Memory Theory 50; visual 135; see also short-term memory
World Chess Federation (FIDE) 18, 19, 44n1, 44n2, 312
Worrell, Frank C. 8, 427–434
Wright, M. 222
writing 131–132
WRRMP see Western Reserve Reading and Math Project
Wulf, G. 440

Xiong, Aiping 8, 435–443

Yan, Yi Ting 7
Ying, B. T. Z. 136
youth development 404, 407, 408

Zatorre, R. J. 177, 179n1
Zytkow, J. M. 356